# A History of West G

## VOLUME 1

*France and Jessica*

# From Shadow to Substance 1945–1963

Second Edition

## Dennis L. Bark

and

## David R. Gress

BLACKWELL
Oxford UK & Cambridge USA

First published 1989
Second edition 1993
First published in paperback 1993

Blackwell Publishers
238 Main Street, Suite 501
Cambridge, Massachusetts 02142, USA

108 Cowley Road, Oxford, OX4 1JF, UK

*British Library Cataloguing in Publication Data*

A CIP catalogue record for this book is available from the British Library.

*Library of Congress Cataloging in Publication Data*
Bark, Dennis L.
   A history of West Germany/Dennis L. Bark and David R. Gress. – 2nd ed.
      p.   cm.
   Includes bibliographical references and index.
   Contents: v. 1. From shadow to substance, 1945–1963.
   v. 2. Democracy and its discontents, 1963–1991.
   ISBN 1-55786-323-7 (hb: set). – ISBN 1-55786-3210 (pbk. v. 1) – ISBN 1-55786-3229 (pbk. v. 2)
   1. Germany (West) – History.   I. Gress, David, 1953–
II. Title.
DD258.7.B37   1993        92-20997
943 – dc20                CIP

Typeset in 10½ on 12pt Ehrhardt
by Joshua Associates Ltd, Oxford
Printed in Great Britain by
T. J. Press, Padstow

This book is printed on acid-free paper

*Verstandene Geschichte ist nach meinem
Dafürhalten die wahre Philosophie der Geschichte.*
Leopold von Ranke


*Tot nos praeceptoribus, tot exemplis instruxit
antiquitas, ut possit videri nulla sorte nascendi
aetas felicior quam nostra, cui docendae priores
elaborarunt.*
Quintilian, *Inst. Orat.* xii, 11, 22

# Contents

PART III

## The Establishment of the Federal Republic, 1949–1955

PART IV

## Consolidation and Division, 1955–1961

PART V
## The End of the Adenauer Era, 1961–1963

VOLUME 2
# Democracy and its Discontents: 1963–1991

PART VI
## Erhard as Chancellor, 1963–1966

PART VII

# The Grand Coalition, 1966–1969

PART VIII

# The Fourth Chancellor of Germany, Willy Brandt, 1969–1974

PART IX

# The Era of the "Macher," 1974–1982

# Foreword

L ike many Americans and Germans today, I have no personal memory of World War II. By the time I came to Bonn in 1985 as the US Ambassador, the Federal Republic had become the economic powerhouse of Europe, and its citizens enjoyed a degree of political stability and security, and a standard of living, that was unthinkable 40 years ago. Fewer and fewer Germans remember the formidable process of political, social, and economic reconstruction that faced Germany at the end of the war. Nor does the postwar generation of Americans appreciate the remarkable transformation which has taken place in postwar Germany.

Without the prostrate condition of Germany at the end of the war as a reference point, it is easy to slip into comfortable cliches and take for granted the Federal Republic's status as a solid pillar of the Atlantic Alliance. In a changing world, that sort of complacency is dangerous. Therefore, a clearer understanding not only of the chronology of postwar events in Germany, but also of the nuances at the margins of these events is essential if America is to forge a mature partnership with its most important strategic and economic ally. Indeed, a fuller, more precise and profound knowledge of each other is desirable for the continued security of both countries as we confront together the challenges of maintaining peace in Central Europe.

The great analyst of the young United States, Alexis de Tocqueville, once noted that an outsider's perspective is valuable because it is un-impeded by the historical, societal, and cultural prejudices that other-wise cloud the insider's view. While that is not always true, the outsider can often strike the right balance between generalization and detail, between objectivity and subjectivity. In this book, two lively outsiders, both Americans, have collaborated in a successful endeavor to create a fresh perspective from which to view and understand the changes in postwar Germany.

Dennis Bark and David Gress present a penetrating interpretation of

the forces which have molded the complex society that is today the
Federal Republic of Germany. Their view of postwar German history,
aimed both at scholars and the interested layman, comes at a time when
voices on both sides increasingly question aspects of the contemporary
US–German relationship. For example, some Germans have concluded
that America's interest in Europe has waned in recent years, a perception I have assured my German contacts is not correct. Although it is
true that American interest in, for example, Latin America and Asia is
increasing, there is no evidence to suggest that interest in Europe is
decreasing. Indeed, this book, in its clear and compelling style, helps
show that interest in Germany, both scholarly and diplomatic, on the
American side of the Atlantic is in fact strong and healthy.

The public opinion landscape in the Federal Republic is a minefield
of contradictions. Surveys show that most Germans support NATO
membership, but are at odds with NATO doctrine. They concede that
Warsaw pact conventional forces are superior, but they are against
offsetting this imbalance with nuclear deterrence or conventional arms
modernization. Nonetheless, we can console ourselves with the fact that
young Germans are fascinated by America as an innovative and modern
culture. Recent polls consistently indicate that younger Germans (the
successor generation), although often critical of American policy, view
the United States, more than any other country, as a model for the FRG.
Their interest in America is keen. For example, nearly a million
Germans visited the United States in 1988. This fact is significant
because it means the Germans know a good deal about America – not as
much as they think they know, certainly, but more than we Americans
know about Germany. This is fortunate, because that basic knowledge is
the foundation for understanding between the two countries. Americans
need to develop the same level of awareness of the history and culture of
the Federal Republic. The strength of *A History of West Germany* is that it
provides a roadmap of the German postwar experience which the
American successor generation will find essential as a means to understanding today's Federal Republic. This book is a lucid, coherent, and
highly readable interpretive history of the Federal Republic that will
also inform the scholar of German affairs and the concerned observer.
Americans in general, unfamiliar with developments in the Federal
Republic since the war, need the kind of background provided here if
they and the Germans are to come to terms with the dilemmas and
complexities of their shared political future.

Richard Burt
*United States Ambassador*
*to the Federal Republic of*
*Germany, Bonn*
*January 1989*

# Preface

The authors of this book discovered their fascination with Germany separately. One of us (Bark) grew up in the United States and had no particular interest in Germany until one day, in 1962, he witnessed an event in Berlin that turned out to be one of the most symbolic and tragic events of the Cold War, though of course he did not know it at the time. On August 17 of that year, while in Germany for the first time in his life, he had crossed to East Berlin in the company of his brother to visit the museums in that part of the city. He was in the very act of returning through the Berlin Wall at Checkpoint Charlie into West Berlin when he heard shots being fired to his left. An East German policeman aimed his rifle at him and yelled at him in German to stop. And there he and his brother were forced to stand, unable to see or understand what was happening, for more than an hour. What he did not know then was that only a few yards to his left, just on the same side of the Wall, a young man, Peter Fechter, was bleeding to death. Fechter and a young friend had tried to climb the wall and escape. The friend succeeded but Fechter, who helped him across, was a second too late and was hit as the East German guards opened fire. West Berlin policemen threw first-aid materials across the Wall, but Fechter was too weak to use them. East German soldiers came to the Wall and watched Fechter bleed to death for over an hour. Finally, the border guard lowered his rifle and permitted the Americans to move the few feet to the freedom of West Berlin.

Bark emerged from Checkpoint Charlie determined to find out what had happened and why. This interest led him to change his major at Stanford University from theater to history and later to return to Berlin to take his doctorate in history under one of Germany's most famous living historians, Hans Herzfeld.

The other author's introduction to German affairs was much less dramatic. He (Gress) grew up in Denmark, where fear and suspicion of

Germany were part of the national culture. Perhaps for that reason he became fascinated by Germany, first by the Nazi period and later by other, more civilized epochs. In 1966 he saw a German television show that was a sort of science-fiction story about how the two Germanies were going to be reunited in 1976. In the mid-1970s he found himself reading a good deal of German scholarship for his graduate research in medieval European history. This led to an interest in the historic role of Germany in European culture as well as in contemporary German politics.

In the early 1980s, both authors were concerned with the widening disparities of opinion and knowledge among both Germans and Americans concerning the causes and effects of West Germany's postwar development. Many influential people, both in Europe and America, regarded the division of Germany as a guarantee of peace in Europe. Some even argued that the communist regime of East Germany had become legitimate and accepted by its subjects, and that West Germans should therefore stop hoping for unification. In truth, few people anywhere in the early 1980s thought that Germany would ever be united in the foreseeable future, or that unification was an important political issue. On the other hand, many people, especially in the professions of journalism and higher education, were quite critical of West Germany as a society and as a constitutional state. They were quick to point out weaknesses, but less ready to recognize its tremendous achievements.

A typical illustration of these disparities was a colloquium on West Germany held at a leading American university in the spring of 1985. The purpose of the colloquium was to present to a student audience viewpoints on Germany 40 years after the end of World War II. On that occasion we heard what we considered to be a series of one-sided and distorted views of West German politics of the democratic commitment of West German leaders, whether liberal or conservative, and of the true nature and value of the German–American alliance. It was not explained to the audience that these views were merely opinions, and not the truth, or that there existed other opinions of equal if not greater merit. Both of us recognized the views presented as typical of much of academic opinion in both West Germany and the United States. Likewise, both of us agreed that these views had little in common with the political or social reality of life in the Federal Republic.

One participant, for example, asserted that the American president and the German chancellor wanted to strengthen authoritarian control and subservient patterns of behavior in the Federal Republic, because such control would promote an alleged German–American policy of militarization in West Germany in the interests of international capitalism. To bring about this result, the speaker continued, the American and German leaders were trying to indoctrinate the German people into feeling threatened by the Soviet Union, whereas in fact the Soviet threat was a myth.

Another participant claimed that the United States under President Truman was primarily responsible for the division of Germany after 1945, and that only the communist regime of East Germany had carried out a systematic purge of Nazis in the bureaucracy and industry. No one objected that the German communists in the east did not carry out this purge to build democracy, but in order to replace one dictatorship, that of Hitler, with another, namely their own. Nor did anyone explain the fundamental difference between the liberal democracy of West Germany with its institutional guarantees of personal rights and liberties and the totalitarian despotism of East Germany. In the east, under the regime that lasted from 1945 to the end of 1989, the people were servants of the state and were prevented from exercising their rights of free expression and movement by the Berlin Wall and the killing zone that separated them from their compatriots to the west. No one mentioned that the government of the Federal Republic was the only German government freely elected and the only one that could claim to represent the expressed wishes of its citizens. Until 1990, the Federal Republic included only a part of the German people; as a result of the unification that took place that year, the government of the Federal Republic became the authentic representative of all Germans. Likewise, no one mentioned that West Germany in 1985 had been a stable democracy for 35 years, through two major changes of government. No one referred to the extraordinary achievement of creating democratic institutions and practices in a country devastated by war. Finally, no one mentioned that, until 1989, only West Germany accepted the full burden of the past, not only in acknowledging the responsibilities thrust upon it by the Reich, but in granting indemnification to the survivors of those who had lost their lives or their property under National Socialism.

The common denominator of this colloquium was at best a lack of interest in, and at worst outright contempt for, the democratic institutions of West Germany. Perhaps the participants merely took those institutions for granted. If they did, they at least owed it to the student audience, who had no knowledge of how democracy came to Germany, to explain that the (real or imagined) faults they were criticizing must be seen in the context of democracy, and not in a vacuum, as though democracy did not exist. We found it lamentable that a forum pretending to objective scholarship could present such caricatures as though they were the whole picture. West Germany in 1985 was in fact one of the least militaristic and least authoritarian societies in the world. The United Germans of 1990 showed no inclination to change this image. Some West Germans in the 1980s, indeed, condemned military values so fervently that others, especially in France and America, questioned the will, and therefore the ability, of the West German state to defend itself. Further, to blame America for the division of Germany was to ignore completely the role and policies of the Soviet Union and the strategic realities of international relations in Europe in 1945. Third, to state that only in the German Democratic Republic was there a genuine purge of Nazis was to ignore not only the reasons for and circumstances of that purge, but also the fact that many former Nazis, some of them in high positions, played important roles in the GDR.

Those who pick and choose from the past to make polemical points in the present undermine the basis for understanding both Germany's achievements and its problems since 1945. In particular, they make it almost impossible for outside observers to appreciate the developments that led to German reunification. In contrast to most political and economic leaders in Europe and the United States, many academic and literary observers of unification were extremely critical: so critical, in fact, that one might suspect them of hoping that unification would fail, or that it would lead to danger and instability. We did not and do not think that Germany's problems are trivial. We do, however, believe strongly that no one can understand them or the implications of German unity who does not understand the whole picture. Younger Americans and Europeans know little of West Germany's record of maintaining peace and stability in Europe, or of the culture, society, values, and life-styles of post-1945 Germany. Yet the political, economic, and cultural shape of the Europe in which they will live depends in large part on the beliefs, commitments, and institutions of the postwar era.

As colleagues at the Hoover Institution we began to discuss these matters during the Christmas holidays of 1984 and discovered our mutual interest and concern. We both found it extraordinary that the achievements of West Germany were not better understood and appreciated in the United States. We share the conviction that it is of continuing importance to recall those achievements, how they were accomplished and the reasons for them. We thus decided to review the literature on the history of the Federal Republic and discovered, to our surprise, that there did not exist a complete interpretative history of the Federal Republic in English. We recognize that it is not possible to know all the sources or to review all the events that comprise that history. But we also believe it of value to present it as seen by two foreigners who value historical fact and reject historical fiction.

The history of West Germany since 1945 is one of the most fascinating sagas of the modern world, the story of how a morally and materially ruined country – or at least a large part of it – managed, with help, but mainly by dint of its own people's efforts, to achieve a degree of prosperity and democracy undreamed-of in 1945 or indeed at any earlier date in German history. We have written this book to provide, at least, our perspective as well as to convey, we hope, some of the enthusiasm as well as the doubts shared by the protagonists of the drama – and it is a drama. We have our own views and do not hide them. We believe that the history of the Federal Republic – whatever its economic and cultural struggles, its political dilemmas, and its moral burdens – has a great deal to teach about freedom and commitment, and about the value of having the courage of your convictions. Some critics say the Federal Republic is not perfect; that it did not completely root out Nazi or anti-democratic thinking; that it could do better and do more for peace and world progress. We think these critics see shadows where there is substance. The question is not whether West Germany was perfect, or whether United Germany is perfect, but how well has it done, given the alternatives, the point of departure, and the standards of democracy and civility that the West Germans set for themselves when establishing their post-war republic in 1949. We doubt if any country could do more for peace and progress than West Germany did in the four decades of its existence. We even wonder if a single-minded focus on peace may not be counterproductive – but this is a debate for future historians.

In the preface to the first edition of this work, we argued that West Germans could never feel completely confident or safe until the division of Germany was solved, either by unification or by some form of confederation involving open borders and free movement of people and ideas. They had built an impressive political society, we wrote, but they did not know whether they should be loyal to it absolutely or, since it was not complete, only conditionally. Before unification, many people argued that West Germans should by now give up hope of reunification and focus their political loyalties on the Federal Republic within its (pre-1990) borders.

When, in 1989, the Soviet leadership abandoned the German communists to their fate, most Germans soon chose freedom and unity in a single democratic and federal state. That state was not a new creation, but simply the Federal Republic expanded to include the territory of the GDR. Thus the Germans did not, in 1990, have to choose between provisional loyalty to the Federal Republic and permanent loyalty to the dream of a united Germany. They simply combined the two, and did so by the process of free elections.

So much of what both outsiders, and Germans wrote about West Germany during the four decades of its existence focused on doubts and troubles that readers often got the impression of a neurotic, obsessive society whose members did not know how to enjoy life. This generalization contained only limited truth. What struck the visitor to West Germany in the 1980s was its confidence, without which West Germans would never have risen to the challenge posed by the revolution in East Germany and by the chance of unification. We wrote in 1988 that West Germans were far more self-assured and confident as members of a society than as citizens of a political state. They knew what it meant to be German, but found it hard to express it publicly in ways that would not offend or raise troublesome questions.

Unification answered some questions while posing many new ones. Germans in the 1990s faced not only the challenge of integrating the former GDR into the Federal Republic while respecting and accommodating justifiable and normal hopes and uncertainties; they also faced the task of showing that they would become confident citizens of a political state; namely, their own, freely chosen, united, and democratic state. Some observers feared that the expanded Federal Republic would turn from the path of European economic and political integration back to a path of parochial nationalism. Others regretted the passing of the old Federal Republic, and lamented the disappearance of an asserted cultural heritage of the GDR. Precisely because unified Germany did not include the whole nation as it had existed in 1937, some contended that the new Federal Republic would not become a healthy, national state but would evolve into a nation without national pride and national commitment. We do not believe these concerns warrant large amounts of introspection any more than we thought in 1985 that the participants in the American seminar were being honest in their distortion of fact and selective criticism. The future, however, is always open. The best we can do here is set forth a reasonably broad view of the record, and let readers judge for themselves.

One writer on Germany accurately concluded in 1987: "An ingot cast out of the slag of war, West Germany is fated to be a country of contrasts – and of souls which, if they are not always tortured, are at least perennially being searched."[1] We, for our part, do not find it nearly as useful to search souls as to interpret a fascinating story.

The way we have chosen to do that differs from a good deal of mainstream academic history. First of all, we are writing contemporary history and that presents special problems, since conclusive judgements are often not possible. Second, we are not writing only for our academic colleagues, but for those outside academia who want and need to know more about the world they live in. Through this book we hope they will

[1] David Marsh, *Financial Times*, June 20, 1987.

discover that Germany is a fascinating as well as a complex and challenging society, and why this is so. History is the record of what individuals, sometimes in collaboration with others but ultimately alone, have done, achieved, created, and built, as well as what they have failed to do, neglected, or lost. In the end, the history of a nation or of a state consists of the deeds or misdeeds of individuals who, with their fellows, constitute a people.

While we have taken care to study and use the important documents for the constitutional, economic, social, and cultural history of West Germany, we saw an important task of research in talking to individuals, including, of course, historians. We have based our narrative, in part, on what they told us. No single historian, ourselves included, is in sole possession of the truth. Therefore we met with many people, from many walks of life, and used what they told us as the basis for what follows in this book.

We found, after beginning our work, that many Germans and Americans agreed that this book was a necessary undertaking. We were, in the best sense of the word, overwhelmed with the support given us by many of those figures who have played and continue to play roles of all dimensions in the social, cultural, economic, and political life of the Federal Republic. Our interpretation of their historical record and our retelling of their experiences is not their responsibility, but for their kindness, time, and honesty, we owe them all our appreciation.

First, we wish to thank those who gave of their valuable time and effort in reviewing most or all of our unwieldy manuscript. In Germany, Hans-Peter Schwarz, Werner Weidenfeld, and Hans-Joachim Veen, and in the United States, Donald Abenheim, Lewis Gann, and Agnes Peterson between them pointed out numerous lacunae and errors of fact as well as offering much forthright and useful criticism of many of our judgements and opinions. We are deeply grateful for this indispensable assistance; what use we have made of it is our sole responsibility. Since, in our book, we offer many opinions that will inevitably be seen as controversial by different readers, it is more than usually necessary to stress that we alone are responsible for any errors or debatable judgements that remain.

Second, many people offered critical advice and information on specific points or discussed the subject matter with us in a more general way. In the United States, we received help from Martin Anderson, Annelise Anderson, Thea B. Bacon, William C. Bark, Eleanor C. Bark, Jared C. Bark, Gordon Craig, Milton Friedman, Robert Held (deceased), James W. Hodgen, Seymour Martin Lipset, H. Joachim Maitre, and Alvin Rabushka.

If this work does even partial justice to a remarkable story about a remarkable country, it is due in large part to the constructive and critical help we encountered in conversations in Europe with Wolfgang Bergsdorf, Isabella von Bülow, Ernst Cramer, Theodor Eschenburg, Ernst Falz, Wilfried Forstmann, Elsa Gress (deceased), Christian Hacke, Marie Herzfeld, Karin Friedrich Hess, Eberhard and Cornelia Hoene, Hans Horchem, Gerhard Kunze, Werner Kaltefleiter, Albrecht Knaus, Kurt Leube, Heinrich Lummer, Peter Männing, Hisako Matsubara, Detlef and Christiane Merten, Hans Messer, Henrik Nebelong, Dietrich Papenfuss, Friedbert PfLüger, Jean-François Revel, Freiherr von Richthofen, Klaus Riebschläger, Krafft von Rigal, Volker Rittberger, Klaus Ritter, Peter-Carl and Christl Rühland, Alexander and Constantin Rühland, Rolf Sammet, Ulrike Schumacher, Tøger Seidenfaden, Wolf Jobst Siedler, Rüdiger Soltwedel, Ernst Ludwig Graf von Stauffenberg, Klaus Stern, Dietrich Stobbe, Horst Teltschik, Michael Thomas, Peter Trapp, P. Heinz Wanke, Ernst-Godeke von Wedel, and Michael Zöller. All of these friends and critics, on both sides of the Atlantic, have offered useful help. If we have not made proper use of it, reproof belongs with us alone.

Third, a book like this does not appear without the substantive and practical assistance of many individuals and organizations. Both the authors are fellows of the Hoover Institution at Stanford University and deeply appreciate the unstinting support provided for this project from its inception to its conclusion by the former director of the Institution, W. Glenn Campbell. His philosophy of intellectual freedom in research honors the best traditions of scholarship. The leadership that Glenn Campbell has given the Hoover Institution for three decades has many beneficiaries. We are two of them. While we ourselves owe his understanding of academic freedom a tremendous debt of thanks, so, too, do the readers of this history. In 1989 Glenn Campbell retired after leading the Hoover Institution for almost 30 years. His successor, first as acting director, then as director, is John Raisian. To Dr. Raisian we also owe special thanks. He undertook to provide us with generous and continual support, as we began preparation of the second and expanded edition of our history, as well as preparation of a French-language edition – both editions to include the dramatic events of 1989 to 1991 as seen from the perspective of 1992.

We also thank those members of the Hoover Institution staff who stepped in, often at short notice, to help us solve frustrating problems: Bill Bonnett, John Cogan, Helen Corrales, Sandra Biers, Elena Danielson, Thomas Henriksen, Diane McIntosh, Wendy Minkin, Charles Palm, Helen Solanum, and Deborah Ventura.

Various outside organizations also contributed materially to this project. The Konrad Adenauer Foundation and the Alexander von Humboldt Foundation, both in Bonn, helped with travel and research assistance. The staff of the German Information Center in New York, particularly Hannelore Köhler and Uta Hoffmann, took days out of their schedule to help provide illustrations, for which we cordially thank them. The second edition of this history, in both English and French, is richer as a result of a grant we received from the German Marshall Fund of the United States in Washington, DC. The Fund's support, together with that of the Hoover Institution, allowed both authors to make a research trip to united Germany in early 1991. In Germany, the Federal Press and Information Office, the Bundeszentrale für politische Bildung, the Spiegel Verlag, the Federal Statistical Office, the Institut der deutschen Wirtschaft, and the Informationsgemeinschaft zur Feststellung der Verbreitung von Werbeträgern all responded swiftly to our anxious requests for statistical and other information.

We are especially indebted to three individuals in France who have made the French edition possible: Guy Schoeller, Directeur de la collection BOUQUINS; Georges Liebert, our editor and the editor of the collection; and Madame Odile Demange of Strasbourg, our translator. The publication of the French edition has been aided immeasurably by a grant from the Smith Richardson Foundation, Inc., New York, for which we are particularly grateful.

In an undertaking of this magnitude one is, and we were, dependent on excellent research assistance. At an early stage, we had the help of Iris Clarissa Bettina Massion, then a student at Stanford University. Our principal *gute Engel* in this task was Ursula Morris-Carter, who helped us for almost four years as this book wound its way from early draft to final version. Without her interest, knowledge, forbearance, and, most of all, commitment, this book would not have been completed. In the final half year of earnest and, occasionally, intense preparation of the manuscript for the publisher, we were equally fortunate in being able to draw on the professionalism and expertise of Vaiva Semion. Much of what is good, and none of what is bad, is due to their care and vigilance.

When this project was still no more than an idea, someone prepared an outline so we could read it. And from that time onward, from the beginning to the end, that individual especially has suffered and contributed in countless ways with grace, understanding, conviction and efficiency to what occupied a large part of her life, as well as our own, for four years. That this manuscript finally arrived, on time and in good order, in the hands of the publisher, is also thanks to Janet Dutra.

A history like this, which is neither an academic monograph nor a work of popular journalism, requires a publisher that understands both realms, that of scholarship and that of narrative aimed at a broader public. It was our very good fortune to find that publisher in Basil

Blackwell of Oxford and its editorial director, John Davey. His early faith in the project, his acuity and good humor, were indispensable. Were he not convinced of the value of a history full of paradoxes, this story of West Germany would undoubtedly have appeared, if at all, in a very different form.

We also thank the copy-editor Alex McIntosh, and the editorial and production staff at Blackwell: Gillian Bromley, Carol Busia, Jan Chamier, Alison Kelly, Ginny Stroud-Lewis, Sophie Hartley, and Ann McCall.

With such help, the authors have no excuses for those errors and imperfections that remain. Nor have we anyone but ourselves to reproach for those judgements and opinions which we have included, often against the undoubtedly wise advice of many of our friends.

*D.L.B.*
*D.R.G.*
Hoover Institution
Stanford, California
April 1992

# Acknowledgements

The authors and publishers are grateful to the following for permission to reproduce material which originally appeared elsewhere:

Temple University Press for a figure from Peter Katzenstein, *Policy and Politics in West Germany*, © 1987 by Temple University. Jane's Information Group Limited, and the authors David C. Isby and Charles Kamps, Jr, for a map from *Armies of NATO's Central Front*. John Johnson Agency for extracts from Douglas Botting, *From the Ruins of the Reich*. Thames and Hudson Ltd and Bertl Berner for the English translation of the poem "Ich hab' es nicht gewollt" (© by Felix Berner/Heirs, Stuttgart, West Germany, 1989), which appeared in Richard Mayne, *Postwar — The Dawn of Today's Europe*. Faber & Faber Ltd and Harcourt Brace Jovanovich, Inc. for an excerpt from "Burnt Norton" in T. S. Eliot, *Four Quartets*, copyright © 1943 by T. S. Eliot, renewed 1971 by Esme Valerie Eliot. Bertelsmann Lexikon Verlag for a map taken from *Facts about Germany*, sixth revised edition (1988), Verlagsgruppe Bertelsmann GmbH/Bertelsmann Lexikon Verlag GmbH, Gütersloh. *Der Spiegel* for the title page of issue number 48, November 21, 1977. Landesbildstelle Berlin for pictures of Berlin church. Archiv der sozialen Democratie; Bundesgeschäftsstelle der CDU; Bundesgeschäftsstelle der FDP; Bundesarchiv Koblenz; and Hanns-Seidel-Stiftung for four sets of posters taken from *Informationen zur Politischen Bildung*, nos 185 (1980) and 202 (1988). Seewald Verlag for a map taken from Gerhart Binder, *Deutschland seit 1945* (1969). Statistisches Bundesamt, Wiesbaden, for material taken from *Statistisches Jahrbuch für die Bundesrepublik Deutschland, 19XX*. Suhrkamp Verlag and Paragon House for permission to publish the authors' own translation of excerpts from Ruth Andreas-Friedrich, *Schauplatz Berlin*, copyright © 1947 by Ruth Andreas-Friedrich (English translation published by Paragon House as *Berlin Underground 1938–1945*). Bantam Books, a division of Bantam, Doubleday, Dell Publishing Group, Inc., for two lines from Goethe's "Faust," translated by Peter Salm, copyright © 1985 by Peter Salm. Harald Boldt Verlag for a table from Karl Heinz Rothenberger, *Die Hungerjahre nach dem Zweiten Weltkrieg* (1980). Harcourt Brace Jovanovich, Inc. for an excerpt from Martin Anderson, *Revolution*. Ullstein Bilderdienst and the *Berliner Morgenpost* for two prints of the title page of the *Berliner Morgenpost*, "Bundesrepublik heute souverän." Beck'sche Verlagsbuchhandlung for material from two tables from R. Rytlewski and M. Opp de Hipt, *Die Bundesrepublik Deutschland in Zahlen, 1945/49—1980*.

# Abbreviations

| | |
|---|---|
| ABM | Anti-ballistic missile |
| ADN | Allgemeiner Deutscher Nachrichtendienst (official news agency of the GDR) |
| AL | Alternative Liste (Alternative List) |
| Antifa | Antifaschistischer Aktionsausschuss (anti-fascist action committee) |
| APO | Ausserparlamentarische Opposition (Extraparliamentary Opposition) |
| B90 | Bündnis 90 |
| BBC | British Broadcasting Corporation |
| BBU | Bundesverband Bürgerinitiativen Umweltschutz (citizens' environmental group) |
| Benelux | Belgium, Netherlands, Luxembourg |
| BfV | Bundesamt für Verfassungsschutz (internal security agency) |
| BGAG | Beteiligungsgesellschaft für Gemeinwirtschaft |
| BFW | Bund Freiheit der Wissenschaft (Association for the Freedom of Scholarship) |
| BHE | Bund der Heimatvertriebenen und Entrechteten (Bloc of Expellees and Disenfranchised) |
| BLK | Bund/Länder Kommission |
| BMG | British Military Government |
| BND | Bundesnachrichtendienst (Federal Intelligence Service) |
| BP | Bayernpartei (Bavarian Party) |
| CARE | Cooperative for American Remittances to Europe |
| CDU | Christlich Demokratische Union (Christian Democratic Union) |
| CEEC | Committee for European Economic Cooperation |
| CFE | Conventional Forces in Europe |
| CFM | Council of Foreign Ministers |

| | |
|---|---|
| CGB | Christlicher Gewerkschaftsbund (Christian Trade Union Federation) |
| CIA | Central Intelligence Agency |
| CND | [British] Campaign for Nuclear Disarmament |
| CPSU | Communist Party of the Soviet Union |
| CSBM | Confidence and Security Building Measures |
| CSCE | Conference on Security and Cooperation in Europe |
| CSU | Christlich-Soziale Union (Christian Social Union) |
| DA | Demokratischer Aufbruch (Democratic Awakening) |
| DAG | Deutsche Angestelltengewerkschaft (union of white-collar workers) |
| DA/VR | Deutsche Allianz–Vereinigte Rechte (German Alliance–United Right) |
| DBB | Deutscher Beamtenbund (German Civil Servants' Federation) |
| DBD | Demokratische Bauernpartei Deutschlands (Democratic Peasants' Party of Germany) |
| DCV | Deutscher Caritas Verband |
| DDP | Deutsche Demokratische Partei (German Democratic Party) |
| DEKT | Deutscher Evangelischer Kirchentag (German Protestant Assembly) |
| DGB | Deutscher Gewerkschaftsbund (German Trade Union Federation) |
| DIHT | Deutscher Industrie und Handelstag (German Assembly of Industry and Commerce) |
| DJ | Demokratie Jetzt (Democracy Now) |
| DKP | Deutsche Kommunistische Partei (German Communist Party) |
| DP | Deutsche Partei (German Party) |
| DPA | Deutsche Presse-Agentur (official news agency of the FRG) |
| DSU | Deutsche Soziale Union (German Social Union) |
| DVP | Deutsche Volkspartei (German People's Party) |
| EAC | European Advisory Commission |
| EC | European Community |
| ECSC | European Coal and Steel Community |
| ECU | European Currency Unit |
| EDC | European Defense Community |
| EDIP | European Defense Improvement Program |
| EEC | European Economic Community |
| EKD | Evangelische Kirche in Deutschland (Evangelical Church in Germany) [Protestant] |

| | |
|---|---|
| EMS | European Monetary System |
| EPC | European Political Cooperation |
| ERP | European Recovery Program (Marshall Plan) |
| ERW | Enhanced radiation warhead |
| EURATOM | European Atomic Energy Community |
| FBIS | Foreign Broadcast Information Service (US) |
| FCMA | Friendship, Cooperation, and Mutual Assistance [Treaty] |
| FDP | Freie Demokratische Partei (Free Democratic Party) |
| FOTL | Follow-on to Lance [missile] |
| FRG | Federal Republic of Germany |
| GATT | General Agreement on Tariffs and Trade |
| GCND | German Campaign against Nuclear Death |
| GDR | German Democratic Republic |
| GLCM | Ground-launched cruise missile |
| GSFG | Group of Soviet Forces in Germany |
| GVP | Gesamtdeutsche Volkspartei (All-German People's Party) |
| HICOG | [Office of the] High Commissioner for Germany |
| HLG | High Level Group |
| HO | Handelsorganisation (retail trade organization in the GDR) |
| HVA | Hauptverwaltung Aufklärung (Central Espionage Directorate) |
| ICBM | Intercontinental ballistic missile |
| IHK | Industrie- und Handelskammer (Chamber of Industry and Commerce) |
| IFM | Initiative Frieden und Menschenrechte (Initiative Peace and Human Rights) |
| IM | Inoffizielle Mitarbeiter (part-time informers [for Stasi]) |
| IMF | International Monetary Fund |
| INF | Intermediate-range nuclear forces |
| IPPNW | International Physicians for the Prevention of Nuclear War |
| IRBM | Intermediate-range ballistic missile |
| JCS | Joint Chiefs of Staff |
| Jusos | Jungsozialisten (Young Socialists) |
| KPD | Kommunistische Partei Deutschlands (Communist Party of Germany) |
| KVP | Kasernierte Volkspartei (barracked People's Police) |
| LDPD | Liberaldemokratische Partei Deutschlands (Liberal Democratic Party of Germany [in the GDR]) |
| MBFR | Mutual and balanced force reductions |

| | |
|---|---|
| Mifrifi | Mittelfristige Finanzplanung (medium-term fiscal strategy) |
| MLF | Multilateral Force |
| MVD | [Soviet] Ministry of Internal Affairs |
| NATO | North Atlantic Treaty Organization |
| NDPD | National-Demokratische Partei Deutschlands (National Democratic Party of Germany [in the GDR]) |
| NF | Neues Forum (New Forum) |
| NKVD | People's Commissariat of Internal Affairs [Soviet Union] |
| NORAD | North American Aerospace Defense Command |
| NPD | Nationaldemokratische Partei Deutschlands (National Democratic Party of Germany) |
| NPG | Nuclear Planning Group |
| NSDAP | Nationalsozialistische Deutsche Arbeiterpartei (National Socialist German Workers' Party) |
| NRR | Net reproductive rate |
| NVA | Nationale Volksarmee (National People's Army) |
| OECD | Organization for Economic Cooperation and Development |
| OEEC | Organization for European Economic Cooperation |
| OKW | Oberkommando der Wehrmacht (High Command of the Armed Forces) |
| OMGUS | Office of Military Government for Germany, United States |
| OPEC | Organization of Petroleum Exporting Countries |
| OSS | Office of Strategic Services |
| ÖTV | Gewerkschaft Öffentliche Dienste, Transport und Verkehr (Public Services and Transport Workers' Union) |
| PDS | Partei des Demokratischen Sozialismus (Party of Democratic Socialism) |
| PLO | Palestine Liberation Organization |
| RAF | Rote Armee Fraktion (Red Army Faction) |
| REP | Republikaner (Republicans) |
| RIAS | Rundfunk im Amerikanischen Sektor (Radio in the American Sector) |
| RSHA | Reichssicherheitshauptamt (Reich security main office) |
| SACEUR | Supreme Allied Commander Europe |
| SAG | Soviet AG [Soviet Corporations] |
| SALT | Strategic Arms Limitation Talks |
| SA | Sturmabteilung (stormtroopers) |
| SBZ | Sowjetische Besatzungszone (Soviet Occupied Zone) |

| | |
|---|---|
| SD | Sicherheitsdienst (Security Service) |
| SDI | Strategic Defense Initiative |
| SDS | Sozialistischer Deutscher Studentenbund (German Socialist Student Federation) |
| SDP | Sozialdemokratische Partei (Social Democratic Party [in the GDR]) |
| SED | Sozialistische Einheitspartei Deutschlands (Socialist Unity Party of Germany) |
| SHAPE | Supreme Headquarters Allied Powers Europe |
| SI | Socialist International |
| SMAD | Soviet Military Administration in Germany |
| SOFA | Status of Forces Agreement |
| SPD | Sozialdemokratische Partei Deutschlands (Social Democratic Party of Germany) |
| SRP | Sozialistische Reichspartei (Socialist Reich Party) |
| SS | Schutzstaffel (elite squad of the NSDAP) |
| UEM | United Europe Movement |
| UFV | Unabhängiger Frauenverband (Independent Women's Association) |
| UN | United Nations |
| VDS | Verband deutscher Studentenschaften (German Student Body Association) |
| WAV | Wirtschaftliche Aufbau-Vereinigung (Economic Reconstruction Party) |
| WEU | West European Union |

# Introduction

The Federal Republic of Germany, 40 years old in 1989 and informally known until 1990 as West Germany, is the second democratic state on German soil. Unlike the first, the Weimar republic of 1919–1933, it has been, from the outset, a stable and increasingly successful democracy offering more freedom with responsibility and better chances for a satisfying spiritual and material life for its citizens than any other state that has ever existed in Germany. Until 1990, the Federal Republic coexisted in Germany with a communist state, the German Democratic Republic (GDR) or East Germany, which consisted of the territory of the Soviet zone of occupation established in 1945. This history deals primarily with democratic Germany, but looks at East Germany whenever that is necessary to understand the division of Germany or the major events in either of its parts: in particular, when we discuss the unification of 1989–90.

With formal unification on October 3, 1990, the Federal Republic expanded to include East Germany, creating out of that territory five new federal *Länder*: Brandenburg, Mecklenburg-Vorpommern, Saxony, Saxony-Anhalt, and Thuringia. It did not, however, include the old German provinces east of the Oder and Neisse rivers whose inhabitants were forced to flee to West Germany in and after 1945. As a result of this and other population transfers, almost all people who considered themselves German were, in 1990, inhabitants of the united Federal Republic, even though that state covered only about 75 per cent of the territory of the pre-1945 Reich.

Some postwar observers wondered whether the West Germans had purchased stability and democracy at the price of giving up hopes for national unity. Yet when Mikhail Gorbachev made it clear that the Soviet government would not support the communist dictatorship of the GDR militarily, the dictatorship crumbled; and the East Germans asserted their desire for unity precisely because West Germany was free, democratic, stable, and prosperous. As West Germany's first chancellor, Konrad Adenauer, correctly foresaw, a democratic and prosperous West Germany, firmly allied with its neighbors in Western Europe, would become such a powerful attraction to Germans in the east that even harsh communist rule would be unable to prevent them from achieving unity. Unification was thus the result of a process and of a principle called liberty.

Unity posed, in a new form, another question that many observers had asked in the 1950s and again in the 1980s. West Germany, they argued, should be a bridge between east and west, should rediscover Germany's Central European heritage, and should forge new links to the communist autocracies of Poland, Czechoslovakia, Hungary, and the Soviet Union. In this way, they went on, West Germany had a mission to make a unique contribution to peace and stability in Europe. As a result of the revolutions in Central Europe in 1989, Poland, Czechoslovakia, and Hungary began moving toward liberal democracy and free markets. Now, any German special mission to the east was no longer a mission to save detente or to appease an aggressive Soviet Union, but a mission of assistance to bring the formerly communist countries back into democratic Europe where they properly belonged. This theme cannot be understood without reference to the record of the years since the end of World War II.

For 40 years after 1949 the Federal Republic grew in importance within both NATO and the European Community. The West Germans provided the single largest military contingent in NATO, the Western world's mutual defense organization, and were hosts to hundreds of thousands of allied troops and matériel, including hundreds of short-range nuclear weapons. Ironically, NATO's success in deterring Soviet attack led many to question its importance and even its utility in the 1980s in the era of arms control, new detente, and *glasnost* in the Soviet Union. Again, the revolutions in Central Europe and German unification radically changed the terms of the debate. In 1990, NATO and the Soviet Union agreed to large reductions in their armed forces in Europe. United Germany agreed to reduce its armed forces substantially. Yet with European and wider international obligations, Germany was and is unlikely to disarm completely. The theme of German political and military power, and the controversies it generated, is also a major focus of our story.

In the early years, the question of military security dominated the thinking of the leaders of democratic Germany. As peace endured, they turned their attention increasingly to the economic integration of the European democracies in the European Community. Since the Rome Treaty of 1957, which established the first version of the Common

Market, West Germany has contributed more resources and, arguably, more political will and intellectual commitment to the principles and the practice of European integration than any other country. Here, perhaps, we find the most dramatic break of all with the past. The leaders of the Federal Republic embraced the West, offering their economic and human resources in a mutually beneficial arrangement that supported growth in Western Europe while promoting stability and democracy in West Germany. The reconciliation of Germany with France, and subsequently with other West European nations, is the greatest success story of the postwar era and a fourth theme of the work.

So far, these have been themes of high politics, of international relations and grand strategy. They are the most important, because they affect the entire Western world (and part of the Eastern world, too), and because without success in these areas, there would be no German democracy today. Far less known, but at least as fascinating, are the origins and history of democracy within West Germany itself. In a way the domestic themes are as important as the international ones, because the value of West Germany's international engagements, and the trust that West Germany slowly won among its erstwhile enemies, depended completely on what happened inside the country. Could the Western democracies trust the new Germany? How strong was democracy? How were the Germans dealing with the legacy of National Socialism? What were the dangers of resurgence of anti-democratic forces? In this book, we make a special effort to emphasize these themes, which are as engrossing and impressive as they are unknown to the majority of the public in the West.

Even in the 1980s and the 1990s, there were people outside Germany who said that democracy was in danger there, that the Germans have not been truly converted from former evil ways. Some of these people were sincere, but we suspect that others who argued in this way were concerned less with Germany than with promoting an agenda of their own. In the 1980s, this group included both the radical left, spokesmen for East European communist regimes, and some on the right in America and France who saw West Germany drifting toward neutralism and alignment with the interests of the Soviet Union. They drew their evidence from sporadic statements by some Germans or from facile analyses of West Germans as a people without a nation that, while they contained elements of truth, were often overdrawn or implausible.

Unification powerfully stimulated these arguments and created new ones. Critics and polemicists both inside and outside Germany publicly wondered whether unity was the prelude to a resurgence of nationalism. There were no communist spokesmen around any more to rage that the Federal Republic harbored aggressive designs, but in Poland especially voices were heard accusing united Germany of wishing to exploit Poland economically and of presenting a threat to its newly-won independence. On the other hand, the first democratic president of Czechoslovakia since 1948, the playwright Vaclav Havel, welcomed German unity as an asset to Europe and looked forward to peaceful cooperation as a mutual benefit. As for German alignment with Moscow, this was a concern that did not disappear with unity; on the contrary, many in Western Europe, particularly in France, feared that the Germans would see their task as one of maintaining stability in the Soviet Union by economic and political aid, and that this preoccupation with Russia would detract from Germany's commitment to the West.

Before unification, American and French conservatives looked at the map of Europe, at the military power of the Soviet Union and the skillful diplomacy of the Gorbachev regime, and judged the Germans vulnerable to blandishments by the East. According to them, the Germans justifiably feared that the North Atlantic Alliance of Western democracies was coming unraveled, and that the Federal Republic would be forced to seek an accommodation with Moscow even at the cost of its own democratic freedoms. Unification and the beginning of Soviet military withdrawal from Central Europe called this argument into question. What remained was fear in some quarters that Germany might come to see itself as Russia's main friend in the West and might engage in a new form of Rapallo politics, modeled on the Rapallo treaty of 1922 by which Germany became the first European power to offer diplomatic and political support to the communist regime in Russia. Those who argued in this way ignored the fact that while Germans certainly respected and admired Gorbachev and believed that he sincerely wanted to reform and modernize the Soviet Union, no German seriously argued that united Germany should weaken its ties to the West in order to help Russia. On the contrary, both before and after unity German leaders consistently maintained that only thanks to its integration into the West was Germany able to help reform and democratization in the East. Sympathy for the Soviet Union was, for Germany, a matter of diplomatic choice; association with the West a matter of political and economic, and psychological and strategic, necessity. Despite occasional quarrels and worries, we judge this to be the basic lesson of the years since 1949, and it is another central theme of our narrative.

These basic themes of foreign and domestic politics and policies run through our work. In addition, we touch on and, we hope, illuminate the major controversies and turning points of postwar German history. Different observers judge each of these differently; there is no final answer. The best we can do is give reasons for our own judgements. It is a mistake to think that consensus on major events grows as time passes. Sometimes political events and new attitudes cause revisions in judgement of quite remote events. The most obvious example is how Germans view the history of united Germany from 1871 to 1945. For some time after World War II, most Germans wanted reunification and regarded the unified national state as the high point of their history, even if they were sometimes very critical of how that state acted. Since the late 1960s, a growing number of Germans have doubted that national unification would be either particularly valuable or particularly significant. The division of Germany since 1945, a political development, in time produced a questioning of many hitherto hallowed aspects of national history. We as writers and readers see both ancient and recent events through the spectacles of our time, our place, and our outlook. That by no means signifies that interpretation is arbitrary; events are events, and some judgements are clearly more sensible than others. But it does mean that controversy in the writing of history – any history – is inevitable, and particularly so in as contested an area as that of postwar Germany.

Five controversies are so salient and illuminate such fundamental political and cultural aspects of our subject that they deserve to be mentioned at the outset. They are, moreover, parallel: the same people have tended to appear on the same side in all five debates.

First is the question of 1945 itself: was the end of the war and of the Hitler regime a defeat or a liberation for the Germans? Was postwar Germany a genuinely new beginning, or was it a (partial or complete) restoration, and if so, of what? Were the Germans collectively guilty of Nazi crimes, and what did and does it mean to speak of guilt or responsibility in this context? Have the Germans dealt adequately with the complex legacy of Nazism?

Second, the question of national division into communist ruled eastern and democratic western part, with a huge area to the east excised by force. What were the origins of division? Whose fault was it? What were its effects? How did the two German states deal with those effects? Did the Germans remain one nation during the years of division? What was the meaning of nationality and identity in divided Germany, and what is the role of these ideas in united Germany?

Third, the question of cultural and political change in West Germany, especially in the 1960s. Many observers noted that the Federal Republic was in certain important respects a different kind of country in 1970 from what it was in 1960. What were these changes, were they good or bad, and in what ways? Did they bring more democracy, and if so, of what kind, or were they, rather, symptoms of exhaustion and decadence?

Fourth, the question of Ostpolitik, of what policy democratic

Germany should adopt vis-à-vis the communist regimes ruling the territories of Germany's former enemies and victims in the east. The main controversy here centers on the diplomatic initiatives of the Brandt–Scheel government of 1969–74. Were these initiatives signs of strength or of weakness? What did they achieve, and at what price?

Fifth, the question of peace and military security. Ever since 1945, the overriding concern of all democratic German politicians has been to prevent another war. The controversy turned on how best to preserve peace: by a strong defense in NATO, or by reaching out to the Soviet Union? Did the Soviet Union have aggressive intent toward Europe, or was it concerned only with holding what it had? These controversies were particularly acute during the political struggles over NATO doctrine and Germany's place in it that recurred periodically in the 1950s, 1970s, and 1980s. Gorbachev's strategic revolution of the late 1980s, by which the Soviet Union promised to abandon Soviet military occupation of Central Europe ended the old questions; but new ones emerged, concerning Germany's dedication to a peaceful international order, kept alive by problems arising in the Middle East and elsewhere.

Each of these five controversies has its roots in a particular period of West German history, but each has also continued to the present. In some cases, later events refueled the controversy and changed people's views of the past.

First and foremost is the question of 1945, of the end of the war and of Nazism. We referred above to those who fear a resurgence of adventurism and militarism in Germany. They are the intellectual heirs of those who, with much greater justification, in 1945 regarded the Germans as irredeemably vicious. For them, the Nazi death camps, other German atrocities during World War II, and the war itself symbolized the true German character – amoral, chauvinistic, duplicitous, and ruthless. The Allied observers, judges, politicians, and journalists who saw and recorded what the Nazis had done taught a generation in the West to see Germany as the main source of war and genocide in Europe, and to ask whether the Germans of 1945 were either willing or able to reject that heritage.

Their anger and fear was understandable, but their conclusions were nevertheless wrong. The Germans were, if anything, less warlike than their European neighbors before 1939. Prussia, the most important state in Germany before 1871, and the united German Reich of 1871–1945 fought fewer wars than Britain, France, or Russia. The observers of 1945 judged all Germans as if they were fanatical Nazis, and all of German history as though it were a preamble to Nazism.

This was mistaken, but equally mistaken were those Germans who, for whatever motive, pretended that Nazism had nothing to do with normal German history and was a wholly alien element that, once destroyed, could be conveniently placed in a special compartment and ignored. The fact was that millions of Germans had served the regime as soldiers, officials, producers of armaments and poison gas, propaganda experts, and killers. Democratic Germans in 1945 and after faced the agonizing task of constructing democracy, justice, liberty, and the rule of law on the ruins of a regime that had ruled virtually unopposed in Germany for twelve years while bringing death and untold suffering to tens of millions of Europeans.

Friedrich Meinecke (1862–1954), the author of seminal works on the history of political ideas in Germany, had been one of the few prominent historians to support the Weimar democracy. In 1945, he sat down to write his last major work, a meditation on the errors of German history that led to Nazism. In that work he wrote about "the German catastrophe:"

> The German state is crushed, and wide lands are lost to us. Rule by foreigners is our destiny for a long time. Shall we succeed in saving the German spirit? Never in its history has this spirit had to endure such a severe test. Historical examples of success or failure do not help us very much here. The task each time is a new and individual one. Deep faith and anxious care must help us in our attempts to solve it. Then let us look up to the highest spheres of the Eternal and Divine from whence resound for us the words: "We bid you to hope."[1]

The German spirit was indeed stretched to the breaking point. Millions of Germans, including Meinecke himself, had lost their homes. The end of the war brought no relief from shortages; in fact, they became worse. Not only was the country ruined and occupied, but the crimes committed by Germans in the name of the German nation added shame and confusion to the already overwhelming trials of daily existence.

West Germany's first chancellor, Konrad Adenauer, touched on a corner of the dilemma when he said, in 1949, that he was obliged to govern either with very old people or with people who were too young to understand democracy because they did not remember the first German republic, that ended in 1933. "We can't use those in between, because they were in the [Nazi] party," he lamented. He himself was 73 and a victim of the Nazis. Even so, he was soon forced to use many people who had held high rank and authority under Hitler. The best he, and other democratic Germans, could hope for was that the worst offenders had

---

[1] Meinecke, *German Catastrophe*, 121.

already been punished or weeded out. His hope was not unfounded, but inevitably he, and others, made choices that critics both inside and outside Germany leaped on to prove their contention that little had changed, that the old Nazi guard was still in charge.

So, inevitably, the policies of the occupiers as well as of the new German democracy itself posed the question whether 1945 marked a defeat or a liberation, a new beginning or a restoration. For about twenty years after 1945, most Germans answered that 1945 was a defeat, but that precisely for that reason it indeed marked a new beginning. Around the mid-1960s, a number of critical historians and social scientists in Germany and abroad began distinguishing between the Nazi state, which was certainly defeated, and certain negative features of German society which, they claimed, were not. On the contrary, the Federal Republic was a restoration – a restoration of the ruling classes, of inherited patterns of behavior, of authoritarian social relationships. This argument was shared with the propagandists of the East German communist regime, which tended to discredit it in the eyes of most West Germans. Yet these critics could point to a considerable body of evidence for their view. The problem was that this evidence all had to do with peripheral matters, with private beliefs, the internal structure of social groups, and the distribution of economic resources in peacetime. The proponents of the restoration thesis could not deny the overwhelming fact that Germany as a state and as a European power was destroyed in 1945 along with the Hitler regime. This fact weighed heavily on the side of those who argued that 1945 marked both a defeat and a new beginning.

The critics responded by modifying their argument: yes, 1945 had marked the chance of a new beginning, but that chance was quashed by the pro-capitalist policies of the American military government and its German allies. In 1946, Jakob Kaiser, the chief representative of the reformist current known as Christian socialism stated that "the era of the bourgeois order is over" and called for redistribution of wealth as the necessary moral and political foundation of a new democratic Germany. A few days later, Konrad Adenauer stated with equal conviction that "the bourgeois era will never end." Adenauer won the resulting struggle over the agenda for German democracy, not primarily because he had the support of the occupiers, but because a significant number of Germans came to agree with him. These were the so-called neoliberals, who believed that the disaster of Nazism and the war had produced a unique chance for Germans to found their new democracy on economic and political freedom. They called their vision the "social market economy," meaning that free competition and free enterprise protected by a strong state from monopolies and cartels was not merely the best, but the only guarantee of general prosperity, stability, and personal happiness. The free market was in and by itself social, for only it held the potential of universal well-being.

By the late 1970s, the best historians in both camps were finding common ground in the middle and seeing 1945 as *both* a defeat *and* a liberation, *both* a restoration *and* a new beginning or, even better, a "destruction" that was also a "transition," in the words of Gustav Sonnenhol, a diplomat who served both the Third Reich and the regime of democratic Germany. This emerging consensus did not include agreement on the moral value of what was destroyed or restored. Leftists continued to argue that West Germany had failed to undergo a "fundamental democratization" during the occupation, that the Federal Republic therefore was an imperfect democracy, because it was not a truly social and economic democracy. Liberals agreed, but pointed out that the "fundamental democratization" that in fact occurred in East Germany was simply the replacement of one despotism by another. They admitted that industry and the bureaucracy were not purged of all who had held positions of responsibility in the Third Reich. This, they argued, was not the point. The point was that the majority of Germans in 1945 and after felt liberated from ideology and henceforth rejected both versions, Nazi as well as Marxist. Even those who perhaps were not convinced democrats in the beginning soon learned to act like democrats. Neo-Nazism and communism were never serious threats to democracy in West Germany. At the same time, many Germans who felt liberated in 1945 also acknowledged that 1945 was a terrifying, total defeat.

How one answers the question whether the effect of 1945 was defeat or liberation, destruction or transition, new beginning or restoration, has direct implications also for the question of Nazism itself, and of the moral burden that Nazism imposed on the defeated Germans in 1945. Some critics of the Federal Republic, like the political philosopher Karl Jaspers, argued that all Germans were collectively guilty of Nazi crimes, not in the sense that all had committed evil acts, but that all were tainted and therefore that all owed the world, and particularly the Jews, a dramatic demonstration of shame, atonement, and spiritual renewal. Others, particularly on the left, demanded that their compatriots accept moral guilt while dissociating themselves from the Germany that had committed the crimes and lost the war.

The responsible leaders of postwar Germany took a third position which was, we judge, the only morally and politically possible one. They held that the Federal Republic was, for better or worse, the continuation of the German Reich that had launched and lost the war and had come close to killing all the Jews of Europe. They therefore accepted the justice of the Allied trials of war criminals as well as their own responsibility to seek out and prosecute surviving Nazis. Most important, they accepted the obligation to indemnify the victims of Nazism as much as possible, knowing that material compensation could never outweigh the murder, torture, and humiliation of millions of innocents. The communist rulers of East Germany, by contrast, rejected any continuity with the Germany of 1945 and before and, until 1988, rejected any obligation to help victims of Nazism. The policy of indemnification put critics of the Federal Republic in an awkward position. They argued, inconsistently, that despite that policy the Federal Republic had not rejected the bad German past thoroughly enough.

At various periods throughout West German history, socialists, liberals, and conservatives, critics and defenders of West German democracy, have conducted stormy political and intellectual debates on the causes and effects of Nazism and its place in German history. In the early 1960s, they debated whether the united Germany of 1871 to 1918 was an aggressive state. In the early 1970s, they debated whether the Federal Republic had been diligent enough in prosecuting Nazi crimes. In the mid-1980s, they debated furiously whether Nazism and the Holocaust were unique events in German and European history. Was Nazism so evil that it bore no comparison with other atrocities and placed a unique moral burden on Germans, or was it a part, however objectionable, of the history of the modern world which it was the responsibility of the historian to understand? These debates were both academic and political. Despite acrimony and confusion, each of them did help to clarify contested aspects of history. In each of them, likewise, the contestants were attempting to impose not only a specific view of the past, but a political agenda in the present. In our view, these debates on the great controversy of the meaning of Nazism and of what happened in 1945 are important less for the specific conclusions that emerged than as evidence of how solid West German democracy has become.

The controversy over the division of Germany – how it began and how it ended – was a continual source of discussion, and sometimes of heated debate, after 1945. In fact, the patience of Germans in the face of the cruel division of their country, which affected millions of families, was truly extraordinary. One can imagine, for example, what it would have meant for a Frenchman if the city of Paris had been divided in half by a wall, impassable to those living on one side of it; or for an American, if the United States had been divided by mines and barbed wire along the Mississippi river. With unification in 1990, the argument over how and why division happened became less of a political debate and more of a historical argument. On the other hand, Germans began to debate, as well as argue, the causes, the course, the costs, and the effects of unity. The two issues – the causes of division and the meaning of unity – are of course intimately related and play a dominant part in our narrative.

Some people foresaw as early as 1945 that Germany would be divided; among them were Konrad Adenauer in Germany and George F. Kennan in the United States. They believed, correctly as it turned out, that the Western interest in a democratic and capitalist reorganization of Germany was incompatible with the Soviet interest in a communist reorganization of Germany. There was no way to satisfy both interests; the only compromise was to let the Soviet Union and the Western Allies hold on to those parts of Germany they had occupied. Although numerous German democratic politicians in the occupation period fought against this conclusion and believed that a neutral Germany could be a "bridge between East and West," the option of neutrality was never realistic. Neither the West nor the Soviet Union could permit Germany and its resources to fall entirely within the other side's sphere of influence.

Few have contested this part of the story. German historians, politicians, and journalists have, however, disagreed vehemently about what Germans call *Deutschlandpolitik*, that is, policies regarding division and unification. Controversy centers on three periods and issues. The first is the early years, 1949–55, when Adenauer promoted West Germany's integration into the emerging Western economic and security network at the expense, some say, of unification. The second is 1969–72, when the Federal Republic reversed its previous *Deutschlandpolitik*, entered into relations with the communist regime in East Germany and accepted the existence of two states on German soil. This new *Deutschlandpolitik* coincided with the new Ostpolitik, which generated its own debates, which we discuss below. Some approved this new policy, saying it was long overdue, others denounced it as a form of useless appeasement of an illegitimate communist regime whose leaders would offer nothing of value in return. The third is the era of Gorbachev, of strategic change, of upheaval in Eastern Europe, and finally of German unity.

During the first period, Adenauer successfully tied West Germany to its Western neighbors and allies partly because he feared that the Germans would seek an accommodation with the Soviet Union if they were not restrained from doing so by firm agreements with the West. Starting in the early 1950s, leftists and progressive liberals in Germany have argued that this policy was hasty and mistaken, since it angered the Soviet Union and foreclosed the option of establishing a neutral, demilitarized zone in Central Europe that would include a united Germany. These critics of Adenauer included many of the people who, in the debate on 1945, argued that the Federal Republic was a restoration and not a new beginning. For them, the new beginning should have meant a foreign policy of neutrality as well as socialist economic policies at home.

We agree rather with those liberal and conservative observers who, at the time and later, pointed out that Adenauer was not opposed to reunification, only to reunification under a communist dictatorship. More important, they have proved, so we believe, that Adenauer in 1949–55 had no choice but to engage West Germany firmly and decisively on a western path. Any other policy would have provoked fears and doubts in the United States, Britain, and France, would have delayed West German economic and political recovery, and would have given the Soviet Union and the German communists in the GDR a chance to disrupt and possibly take control of the democratic part of Germany.

Not all critics of Adenauer came from the left, however. A curious feature of the West German political landscape from the late 1940s to the late 1980s was that the right was divided into a pro-Western and an anti-Western faction. Until the early 1960s, Adenauer was the founder and undisputed leader of the dominant pro-Western faction, which espoused alignment with the United States and put liberty above reunification. After he retired, the pro-Western conservatives lacked an obvious leading figure until Helmut Kohl emerged in the 1970s. Members of the weak, but noisy anti-Western (or, more correctly, pro-Eastern) faction of the German right wanted West Germany to liberate itself from American influence and to seek an independent political accommodation with the Soviet Union, to pursue a path independent of both superpowers.

Both the neutralist left and the pro-Eastern right pointed to the so-called Stalin Note of 1952, in which the Soviet dictator proposed a united, neutral, and democratic Germany with its own armed forces, as the major "lost opportunity" for reunification. At the time, Adenauer and the Western allies denounced the proposal as a transparent attempt to entice the West Germans away from NATO and to expose them to a communist takeover. They did not believe that Stalin seriously intended to give up communist rule in East Germany or that he or the German communists would allow a united Germany to remain democratic or neutral for long.

On several occasions since then, and most vehemently during 1985–6, critics argued that Adenauer and the allied leaders acted in bad faith. The offer, they said, was genuine, or at least worth pursuing. We judge that, in this debate, Adenauer's defenders were right. Nevertheless, we also observe that Adenauer's critics had the support of some distinguished non-German historians who had no stake in internal German arguments. As with many other matters concerning Soviet politics, we may never know the truth, even if all Soviet archives are some day opened. Given what we know of communist practice, there is no reason to assume that even the Soviet foreign ministry's or the communist party archives contain the complete truth about Stalin's intentions.

Foreigners may find it peculiar that it was social democratic politicians and left-leaning historians who denounced Adenauer for not being nationalistic enough. This was another peculiarity of the West German political landscape: the democratic German left always had a considerable nationalistic element. In 1969, the left came to power and thus won the chance to put into practice its own *Deutschlandpolitik*. This provoked the second controversy over division and how to alleviate it. Now the left argued for diminishing the effects of division by dealing directly with the communist rulers of East Germany in the hope that they would respond by permitting more freedom at home and more contacts between the two parts of Germany. This, according to Chancellor Willy Brandt, was a truly national *Deutschlandpolitik*, an attempt to save national identity at the price of recognizing the political division of the nation. The right objected that it was nothing of the kind, because granting legitimacy and prestige to the communist rulers of the GDR, would deepen division rather than alleviate it. Thus, by the early 1970s, the left, in the view of the right, had become anti-national, because it was consorting with the nation's enemies. The left responded that it was carrying out the only possible national policy, since the right's refusal in earlier years to recognize the GDR had clearly not brought about unification.

The controversy over the new *Deutschlandpolitik* concerned three distinct questions. First, would recognizing the GDR harm or help the cause of national unity? Second, what was the best way to preserve the hope of unity – to deal with the communist rulers of the GDR, or to try to subvert them by encouraging dissidents and oppositional groups inside communist Germany? Third, was the division of Germany itself a source of tension and instability in Europe, as most Western political leaders had earlier maintained, or had it, on the contrary, become an element of peace and order that must not be challenged? If division was a source of tension, then a consistent *Deutschlandpolitik* was logically also a policy of reducing tension by reestablishing German unity. If, however, German division was an element of order, as a growing number of political leaders and observers thought, then a serious policy of overcoming division was by definition a policy of disturbing the peace of Europe. Most West German leaders fudged the issues by maintaining that the new policy sought to overcome the effects of division in the hope that sometime, in the far distant future, the communist regime in the GDR would cooperate in building a "European peace order" in which Germans would have freedom of expression and movement, even if they did not achieve political unity. By 1989, when the East Germans started the last steps of the process that led to unification, the new *Deutschland-politik* of 1969 was not new any longer. The Kohl–Genscher government of the 1980s had continued it without radical change, but with greater emphasis on a future "peace order" that would make unity unnecessary, and with less emphasis on granting prestige and favors to the communists in the vain hope that they would in turn recognize a common German national identity. The controversy over the unification process turned on somewhat different questions than did the controversies over the Stalin Note or over the Brandt-Scheel *Deutsch-landpolitik*. In those earlier cases, critics had asked whether the government was sincerely seeking to overcome national division, and what a policy of unification should look like. In 1989–90, they began asking whether unification, now that it seemed possible or even imminent, was in fact a good thing. Not "how can we restore unity?" but "should we want it?" was the key question in the new controversy. Few questioned that substantial majorities in both parts of Germany wanted unity, so the critics of unity were in the difficult position of arguing that these majorities were mistaken, that they did not know what they were doing, or that they had entirely unreasonable expectations about the benefits that unity would bring. The critics pointed to the earlier unification of 1871 and its result, the nationalistic and authoritarian German empire that brought war to Europe in 1914, and to the so-called national revival of 1933, when Adolf Hitler and the National Socialists took power, and argued that Germans had a special political, moral, and psychological obligation to reject notions of national identity and unity and to move beyond nationality to a broader and therefore neutral European role. In 1990 some East Germans who had been intimately involved in the democratic movement in the GDR regretted that their original hopes for a reformed, but independent GDR had been overtaken by what they regarded as unfair pressure for unity stemming from West Germany and from Helmut Kohl in particular. In West Germany, especially socialist political leaders argued that unity would put an end to the West German experiment in creating a "civil society" that transcended the national state. They saw unity as an abandonment of a democratic, anti-nationalist Federal Republic in favor of a less benevolent Germany, one more colored by its historical past.

All of these controversies over nationality, unity, and the right policy to pursue during and after the division of Germany, recur again and again in our narrative. The national theme is, in our view, the single most important theme in postwar German history, even though it was by no means always prominent in public policy debates.

If nation, unity, and identity constituted the most important theme in the history of Germany as a whole, we can say with equal emphasis that the most important theme, the pivot even, of *West* German history was the great cultural change of the 1960s, the period when West Germany became finally and irrevocably part of the Western community socially and psychologically as well as economically and politically. The two themes relate to each other in ways that became clearer in retrospect, after 1989–90. The relationship between them lies in this: neither the Soviet Union nor the Western allies would have permitted German unification had West Germany not become an integral part of Western Europe – both stable and dependable – and not a rebel nation seeking power for itself at others' expense. Only a progressive and European Germany, one that had undergone the cultural changes of the 1960s, could be given the chance of unification. This conclusion implies yet another of the many massive paradoxes of the unification era. At the time of the Stalin Note and for many years after, indeed as late as early 1990, the Soviet Union insisted that only a neutral and disarmed Germany could be unified. During 1990, Soviet leaders came to the conclusion that, on the contrary, only a Germany integrated into the West would be allowed to unite. The reasons for this *volte-face* are logical and clear. Given the upheavals in Central Europe and the crisis within the Soviet Union itself, the last desire the Soviet leaders had, was a powerful, united Germany, unrestrained by NATO or the European Community, fishing in the troubled waters to the east. Much better, from the Soviet perspective, to have a predictable, stable, and un-adventurous Germany integrated in the West and prepared, as a member of the Western networks, to supply aid, investments, and diplomatic help to the Soviet Union.

West Germany's road to full integration in the West is, therefore, the most important aspect of the Federal Republic's history. Without it unity would have been impossible. Our argument in this book is that West German democracy was a slow and often frustrating process, but a successful one that underwent in the 1960s the final stage of a revolution in personal, public, and political attitudes and expectations, in personal morality, and in cultural preferences that brought about the fundamental democratization demanded by the left. We agree with those who see the years after 1945 as both a liberation and a transition, both a new beginning and a restoration.

The phrase cultural revolution may be misleading. By it we do not mean only that, in the 1960s, German writers, directors, and artists produced new kinds of art, wrote new plays, or praised the permissive society. Rather we mean something much broader, of which changes in high culture were only a part. We mean that the fundamental outlook of most Germans and their inherited patterns of behavior and expectations changed.

Perhaps the most important symptom of this set of changes was the growth of central government and of the welfare state. This was a phenomenon that recurred in precisely analogous forms throughout the industrialized world. The mid-1960s saw sharp increases in the rate of growth of government in the United States (the "Great Society"), in Britain, in France, in Scandinavia, and in Italy as well as in the Federal Republic. These increases occurred under socialist, liberal, and conservative governments. West Germany was from the outset a society of organizations. The unions, employer federations, professional interest groups, and other associations devoted to collective action for the benefit of special segments of society had traditionally been strong in Germany. The war and the occupation reduced their importance, and during the early years they worked together in the common interest of reconstruction. By the 1960s, their leaders felt, recovery was achieved, and the time had now come to redistribute the gains. Early anticipations of this trend were the laws on co-determination in the mining and steel industries of 1951, the law on factory councils of 1952, and above all the social security reform act of 1957. By the latter act, the legislators guaranteed to every pensioner a sum the size of which was tied to the cost of living index and confirmed that the pension should in principle "replace the wage" at retirement. These three acts, passed during the heyday of the social market economy, presaged the mixed economy, increased state power, and social collectivism of the 1960s and after.

The relentless and systematic growth of government formed the economic and intellectual backdrop to the cultural revolution in the era of ideas, public debate, journalism, and the universities. Much of this cultural revolution took the form of a long string of victories for the left: the *Spiegel* affair, which removed Franz Josef Strauss, a leader of the pro-Western right, from high office; the play *The Deputy*, which blamed the Catholic Church for complicity in the Holocaust and thus opened a new stage of the controversy on Nazism; the so-called Auschwitz trials of Nazi criminals that contributed to the same wave of debate; the student uprising of 1965–8 that changed forever the face of the German universities; and the political shift that brought the social democrats to power in 1969. Though we are critical of many of the results of these events, we still regard them, in the end, as examples of progress. The cultural and intellectual left finally had its chance to set the agenda of German politics; it succeeded for a while, but the balancing forces of a true democracy asserted themselves, for the first time in German history. We applaud the left's victories while deploring the left's program, because we believe that alternation in power is a fundamental element of democracy, and because we judge that the 1960s showed that Germans, despite some confusion and violence, had truly learned that lesson.

We find in the arguments of the 1960s and in the subsequent debate on that decade the same alignment of forces as in the previous controversies. Leftists and some liberals celebrate the changes as symptoms of a delayed "new beginning;" other liberals, and most conservatives, condemn them as symptoms of weakness and loss of nerve. Both sides agree that the changes had paradoxical effects, the most important of which was the tremendous growth in the size and resources of central government at the expense of regional and institutional autonomy. This was not the left's hope, though foresighted analysts predicted it at the time. Our sympathy lies with those liberals and conservatives who see in large government a danger both to personal liberties and to economic prosperity, though we have few illusions that this tendency, common to all industrial societies, can be dramatically reversed.

The Ostpolitik of the Brandt–Scheel government, and the arguments over that policy, realigned the forces in play in slightly different ways. Both the nationalist and the pro-Western left agreed that West Germany should abandon old claims and positions and reach out to the communist regimes in the East. This, they believed, would not only contribute to liberalizing those regimes, but would give the Federal Republic a better image and contribute to peace and stability. The pro-Western right at first objected by pointing out that abandoning long-held claims simply because they are unenforceable is not a sign of strength, but of weakness, and merely invites the contempt of communist dictatorships. However, even the pro-Western right was forced to accept the fact that West Germany's allies favored the new Ostpolitik. The nationalist left thus found itself, for the first time, aligned with West Germany's allies, who had temporarily abandoned the pro-Western right, their most loyal German friends.

By the 1980s the pro-Western right had succeeded in restricting Ostpolitik to a series of specific and well-directed policies while rejecting the broad aspirations of the left for a general reordering of European politics that would lead to a dissolution of both of the postwar alliance systems. The return to government of the moderate right in 1982 therefore meant little change in Ostpolitik.

Controversy focused, rather, on what to do next. Throughout the 1980s, the pro-Western forces wanted to continue detente and arms control, but within the European framework and the NATO alliance, while some on the left returned to ideas of neutralizing all of Germany and of a demilitarized or at least nuclear-weapon-free Central Europe, in which Germany might be permitted some degree of unity, perhaps in a confederation of both German states.

This muted revival of the leftist national neutralism of the 1950s was overtaken by events in 1989. Both the advocates of the revival and their liberal and conservative opponents were stunned by the speed of revolution in Central Europe in 1989. The liberals and conservatives, in our view, had the advantage of credibility and the better cards to play in the resulting dramatic situation. They had warned, earlier in the 1980s, that the left's hopes for a neutral Europe "beyond the blocs" might, if put into practice, mean the end of democracy in West Germany without any benefit to the victims of communist rule in the East. The revolutions in Central Europe meant that Western governments, including the Federal Republic, no longer had to deal with communist rulers. No one could claim with any credibility that supporting the Poles, Czechs, and Hungarians against their rulers was dangerous or destabilizing, or that supporting the Polish, Czech, or Hungarian governments was to disregard cynically the real wishes and needs of the people. Prudence, justice, and morality coincided. West Germany, and since 1990 united Germany, faced a new and bigger challenge: how to re-Europeanize the nations of Central Europe, how to establish, on the ruins of communist rule, the basis of a greater European Community.

The reader will not be surprised to find the advocates of the restoration thesis and the critics of Adenauer allied once again in criticizing the NATO strategy of peace through deterrence and in advocating policies of non-nuclear defense. During the occupation, the nationalist left under the social democratic leader Kurt Schumacher allied with elements of the moderate right to oppose Adenauer's strategy of building democracy in the Western zones. After independence in 1949, Schumacher and Adenauer agreed that West Germany needed armed forces to defend itself. They split in 1952, after Adenauer rejected the Stalin Note. Ever since that time, a faction of varying strength on the left has suspected that NATO's policy of peace through deterrence was in reality a policy of capitalist restoration. As socialists, these leftists believed that a socialist Germany would be a factor for peace. During the 1950s, they pursued this policy at increasing cost to the party in terms of electoral strength. One reason that German social democrats in the 1950s supported neutralization and opposed NATO's nuclear strategy was that they wanted to atone for what their predecessors had done in 1914. When World War I broke out, the majority of German social democratic deputies in the Reichstag voted for war credits for the Kaiser's government, thus violating the fundamental belief of Marxism, namely that the workers would never support war. After 1945, the German social democrats were torn between the need to prove that they were no longer chauvinistic on the one hand, and the need to prove that they were German patriots on the other. The solution they found was to support neutralism and reunification at the same time, and to argue that this was a policy of peace.

During the 1960s and 1970s most social democrats supported NATO and agreed that peace was maintained by deterring the Soviet Union. Starting in the mid-1970s, groups on the left outside the SPD (Social Democratic Party) grew again in strength, deriving much of their support from the veterans of the student movement of the 1960s and from the intellectual class. In 1978, these groups coalesced to form the Green movement, the first successful new political organization in West Germany since the late 1950s. Against the reigning consensus on how peace was kept, the Greens argued that Western weapons were in themselves a threat of war, and that the road to peace lay through unilateral disarmament. The Greens, who won many sympathizers inside the SPD and among liberals, thus revived the controversy of the 1950s over how to preserve peace. For them, the Soviet Union did not represent a threat, and therefore the road to peace was not through deterrence.

Many who were neither Green nor leftist accepted some or all of this view. Many Germans, perhaps a majority, in the 1980s felt uncomfortable with the NATO strategy of peace through nuclear deterrence and the accompanying threat of first use of nuclear weapons in response to a Soviet attack. The Reagan administration perceived policy of moving away from the theory of assured destruction and toward anti-missile defenses further alarmed many in Germany, both on the left and on the right. Since the early 1960s, an influential group of American military strategists had argued that the best guarantee against nuclear war between the US and the Soviet Union was that each of the two states should have enough weapons to threaten the assured destruction of the other as a viable political, social, and economic entity. Given such a stalemate, neither side would launch a nuclear strike, since to do so would automatically lead to "mutual assured destruction" (MAD). In fact, the notion of deterrence through MAD was never the only or even the main element of actual American strategic doctrine, though the public, both in America and Western Europe, came to believe that it was. In the late 1970s, the media learned that the US president had issued a directive on nuclear strategy that implied that nuclear weapons could be used in war short of MAD. Journalists and scholars critical of the US, of nuclear weapons, or both, used this directive, and other semi-official pronouncements and articles, to foment an atmosphere of fear and alarm concerning American military doctrine, as though American leaders were departing from a stable system of deterrence and developing plans to destroy the Soviet Union with nuclear bombs. This was, of course, not true; what was true was that many American policy-makers were unhappy with the notion of MAD, whether or not it was official strategy, and wished to move away from a situation in which MAD was possible. One of the directions they chose was research into a defense against nuclear weapons, the so-called Strategic Defense Initiative (SDI), formally announced by President Ronald Reagan in March 1983. In West Germany, one result of these American debates and initiatives was that the anti-American left and the old pro-Eastern right joined forces in calling for an accommodation with the Soviet Union and a farewell to NATO and US nuclear arms.

Between 1987 and 1990 the United States, NATO, and the Soviet Union signed a series of far-reaching arms control agreements that, if properly carried out, would dramatically reduce the number and density of forces of all kinds, conventional as well as nuclear, in Europe. In 1990 Germans argued less whether NATO's policy of peace through deterrence was inadequate or too aggressive. Rather, they embarked on what was probably a far more important debate, on the role of united Germany in maintaining peace and freedom in Europe, and its legitimate status as a European power.

These five controversies mark the stages of West German history. Its 45 years from 1945 to 1989 fell into three roughly equal periods. The transitions between the periods are fluid; they are not exactly the same for foreign policy and diplomacy as for domestic policy, culture, or personal beliefs. Nor is the starting date completely correct, despite the cataclysm of defeat and moral shame brought by the destruction of the Nazi Reich. The devastation of 1945 was so complete that many Germans then and later referred to that year as "Zero Hour." However, there is no such thing as a literal "Zero Hour" in the history of any people. The end of the war in May 1945 did not represent a pristine, new beginning, but rather the opportunity for most Germans to continue their lives in peace. Moreover, Germany's defeat in 1945 was inevitable long before, probably from the day Hitler launched his attack on the Soviet Union on June 22, 1941.

The history of West Germany properly speaking begins before 1945 in at least two respects. In the immediate sense, it begins at the moment that the wartime Allies decided the zonal division of Germany and laid down the demarcation line between East and West that existed until 1989. They did this in 1944. It also begins at the point where the

Western Allies started formulating their policies of democratization and denazification, because in doing so they were implicitly making plans for Germans that could only be carried out with Germans.

In the more distant sense, the history of democratic Germany after 1945 is the continuation of the history of German democrats before 1945, because the Federal Republic is, to a very large degree, the heir of the movement for liberal democracy in Germany that began in the 1820s and 1830s. The victories of Prussia in the 1860s and the Prussian chancellor Bismarck's unification of Germany into an authoritarian state in 1866–71 were defeats for the democratic movement, but it did not die. It failed to establish a durable democracy in 1919–33, but when Hitler disappeared the democrats were still there, few in number perhaps, but determined that this time the experiment was going to succeed.

Leftists may be surprised at our judgment that 1945 was no "Zero Hour," since it resembles their thesis that what happened after 1945 was a restoration. The difference is that they consider the restoration bad, whereas we argue that, insofar as there was a restoration, it was largely beneficial and was in any case swept away by the cultural revolution of the 1960s.

The cultural revolution began shortly after the communist regime in East Germany built the Wall around Berlin in August 1961. The Wall symbolized and expressed the permanent division of Germany, the communist regime's will to suppress its people by terror and force, and the impotence of the West in the face of this terror. It put a final end to the era of plans for neutralization and reunification and to fond hopes for a third way for Germany between East and West. The Wall was thus the last act of the postwar era and the opening signal of the cultural revolution. For, as many observers have commented, the closing of the border to the East turned the energies of West Germans inward. Instead of focusing on national division and reunification, Germans turned to domestic renewal and change.

The second period of West German history was the period of the cultural revolution and the Brandt–Scheel Ostpolitik. It runs from the *Spiegel* affair in late 1962 through the other events of the 1960s and through the diplomatic revolution of 1969–74, when the Federal Republic rejected its previous foreign policies. In fact that rejection antedated Brandt's appointment as chancellor. It began in 1966, when the social democrats entered federal government for the first time. The same year marked the first high point of the student movement and the publication of one of the most important books in West German history, namely *The Future of Germany* by the political philosopher Karl Jaspers. In that book, Jaspers repeated his old argument that the Germans were collectively guilty of Nazism and called for repentance and atonement in the form of concessions to Germany's former victims. When Brandt and Scheel launched their Ostpolitik in 1969, they seemed to many to be acting out the moral prescriptions in Jaspers' book.

The third period began with the energy crisis of 1973–4 and with the appointment of Helmut Schmidt as chancellor. It ended with German unification in 1989–90. The background scenery of the first period was the Cold War, and that of the second the cultural revolution. The background scenery of the third was the sense of caution brought about by the energy crisis and its economic repercussions. The period that followed, and which has barely begun as we write, was not just a fourth stage of West German history, but a new stage of German history as a whole, following the stages that began in 1945, 1933, 1918, and 1871.

The new Federal Republic of the 1990s faces the immense challenge of integrating its eastern part and bringing its 16 million new citizens up to the social, cultural, and economic level enjoyed by their 59 million compatriots in former West Germany. It has the best possible foundations for carrying out that task successfully. At the time of unification, West Germany was a prosperous, solid society with little to fear from domestic upheaval or foreign invasion. Still, the task is enormous and contains many psychological, cultural, and spiritual challenges that go far beyond mere material or economic needs and calculations. It will be the dominant task for Germans through the 1990s. A second challenge to the future of Germany is the aging and declining population. An intangible, but definite effect of a birth rate that is below replacement is an ever-decreasing number of young workers in their most inventive, productive, and dynamic years. Increasingly, Germany risks becoming what the French demographer Alfred Sauvy called "a nation of old and tired people sitting in old and tired houses thinking old and tired thoughts."

A third challenge is to combine integration of East Germany into a united Germany with integration of that united Germany into a broader and stronger European Community. Germany's neighbors and allies hope, and expect, that the Germans will not become so obsessed with unity that they forget Europe, and that they will not turn unity into arrogance and claims to special status or special rights within the community. The history of West Germany gives many grounds for this hope and few reasons to fear united Germany. Throughout the year of unification, German leaders across the political spectrum emphasized repeatedly that they wanted a "European Germany" and not a "German Europe," in the words of Thomas Mann from 1945. Yet the geopolitical and economic weight of united Germany, as the major center of economic and political power in Europe, cannot help but have effects on the shape of Europe and on Germany's place in it.

A fourth challenge is the problem of the environment. West Germany is one of the most densely populated and most heavily industrialized regions of the world. The Germans have a strong tradition of love and respect for nature, and many have been pained to see the harm done by acid rain, chemical effluents, and automobile exhaust to once-flourishing forests and rivers. East Germany, though much less densely populated, was an ecological disaster area after 40 years of communist rule. The Elbe river was a sewer of industrial, agricultural, and human effluents for much of its course in the former GDR. East German industry had neither the means nor the incentives to regulate pollution, and was moreover of a primitive standard, producing far more pollution for each unit produced than any Western industry. Most Germans clearly agree that protection of the environment must rank close to the top of the policy agenda for the future. They have yet to confront the dilemma of nuclear power, which promises cleaner energy at less risk than fossil fuels, but which many, mostly but by no means exclusively on the left, view with apocalyptic fears of radioactive disaster. These fears grew explosively after the Soviet reactor catastrophe at Chernobyl in 1986, despite the fact that the Soviet reactor was of a completely different and far more primitive type than those in use in Western Europe. Instead of drawing the lesson that Soviet civilian nuclear technology is backward, many Germans drew the lesson that all nuclear energy is dangerous. Will they choose to abandon nuclear energy, thus dooming their land to pollution by coal and oil? Or will they follow the agenda of the Greens, who insist that Germans must reduce their living standards dramatically in order to reduce the use of fossil fuels to a minimum while simultaneously rejecting nuclear energy? And what about nuclear energy in the former GDR? The East German nuclear reactors, which resemble Chernobyl more than they resemble the safe and efficient plants of Brokdorf and Wyhl in the Federal Republic, were temporarily closed down in 1990 for fear of a possible nuclear disaster.

If the reader of this book can examine, critically, postwar German history, perhaps it will bring light and life to a period of time which is rich in commitment to belief in a nation that was in ashes just more than four decades ago. In fact, while the Germany of the classical age of the great poets, Goethe and Schiller, is no more, there is nonetheless, in West Germany, a Germany of imagination, industriousness, creativity, and of spirit. Its men and women have recorded incredible achievements in what, in the history of Europe, is a short period of time. They have not only survived and prospered, but they have earned respect as a consequence of a commitment to freedom and peace.

Shadows no longer haunt Germany – though some claim to see them still, and in them the forms of ghosts of Germany past. These shadows occasionally take on more substance, as in the furious debate over Nazism's place in German and European history and on German national identity that took place in the mid-1980s or in the even more furious debate about unity and its consequences that broke out in 1990. Still, we believe that the united Federal Republic of 1990, almost two full generations after 1945, is not a land of shadows but, more than ever, a land full of vibrant and vital substance. Certainly, Germans face frustrations as well as successes, not least in the task of finding each other again after 45 years of division, but we would not have written this book if we believed that the Germans could not overcome their challenges, or if others could not appreciate and learn from their history. As we have explained in this overview, not all Germans are enthralled with West Germany's achievements or with the German unity that, to such a large extent, flows from and builds on those achievements. That is their privilege, granted to them by the very democratic society which they criticize. Since 1945, Germans of all democratic persuasions have striven successfully to secure that privilege for all. Not until 1990 were they entirely successful.

If there is one poignant note in the celebrations of unity in freedom, it is that so many who hoped and dreamed for it could not live to see it come about. Yet that striving for freedom, unity, and peace is the one thing that ties together such radically different personalities as Konrad Adenauer, Kurt Schumacher, Ernst Reuter, Theodor Heuss, Franz Josef Strauss, Ludwig Erhard, Kurt Georg Kiesinger, Gustav Heinemann, Willy Brandt, Walter Scheel, Helmut Schmidt, Hans-Dietrich Genscher, Richard von Weizsäcker, Helmut Kohl, Lothar de Maizière, Otto Graf Lambsdorff, Rita Süssmuth, Alfred Herrhausen, Edzard Reuter, Heinz Ruhnau and the dozens of other political and economic leaders who will appear in these pages. Beside and behind them stand the many millions who, since 1945, created the conditions of their own liberty.

Throughout the years since 1945, Germans and others asked whether the Germans would continue to make the choice of liberty and democracy in the future as well as in the past. The events of 1989–90 answered that question with a resounding yes. Yet the future is always uncertain. History can tell us only that the question is vital. What it does not tell us is what the choice will be.

# PART I

# The Beginning and the End

*... it's a hell of a mess any way it's taken.*

Harry Truman, Potsdam, July 20, 1945

*Adolf Hitler was nothing if not thorough. ... Because his work of demolition was so complete, he left the German people nothing that could be repaired or built upon. They had to begin all over again, a hard task perhaps, but a challenging one, in the facing of which they were not entirely bereft of guidance. For Hitler had not only restored to them the options that they had had a century earlier but had also bequeathed to them the memory of horror to help them with their choice.*

Gordon A. Craig, *Germany 1866–1945*

# Introduction

When the guns fell silent at 11:01 p. m. Central European time on May 8, 1945, few in Europe, or indeed in the world, doubted that an epoch of world history had come to an end. Germany, which for four centuries had been the pivot of the Continent and the scene of repeated attempts to dominate its neighbors, was no more. Moreover, as the victorious Allies had already discovered, they had defeated not only an enemy nation in battle, but an inhuman regime that had committed against those it defined as its enemies atrocities on a scale hardly paralleled in all the annals of Western history. On that day, the Germans, whether they realized it or not, whether they, as individuals, were guilty or not, received a double burden, a burden of moral as well as material devastation. Thanks to their own energies and stamina and, later, to the help they received from the West, they were able to deal with the material devastation far more effectively than anyone could have foreseen on that day. The moral burden, on the other hand, proved far more difficult, even impossible, to cancel. It grew in significance and prominence, even as the material problems diminished, and there was no sign, more than 40 years later, that it would or could ever disappear.

The regime of the National Socialist German Workers' Party (NSDAP), the Nazi regime, was not the only thing that ended on May 8, 1945. The war that ended on that day was also, and perhaps primarily, the last act of a great struggle between two totalitarian ideologies and the states they controlled – a struggle between the National Socialism of Germany and the communism of the Soviet Union. Those two ideologies were themselves fruits of the political, social, and economic conflicts that had plagued Europe since the middle of the nineteenth century. Both existed, in some form, throughout Europe, within each country, albeit in extreme form in Germany and Russia. For this reason one can call World War II the last act of a European civil war, a battle for power and mastery over territory and over the minds and energies of men that had now ended.

The battle's end marked also the end of Europe as the center of world power. Henceforth, two outside powers decided the fate of the old continent. One of these powers, the United States, was largely European in culture, but not in geography. The other, the Soviet Union, was partly European in geography but remained an ideological state committed to overturning the world order. It rejected the positive heritage of European culture in international relations, and the principle that the use of force must be restrained by justice and the search for freedom and peace. What role the Germans could possibly play in this wholly and frighteningly new setting was, at first, not for them to say. That they managed, in time, to take some measure of control of their own destiny, albeit on a far more modest and realistic level than before, is an astonishing achievement, and is the main theme of this story.

# 1

# The Stage

A graffito appeared on a Berlin wall in March 1945: "Enjoy the war –
the peace is going to be terrible."[1] The graffito was gratuitous, but
the truth was not. What descended on Germany was horrible.

The celebration of VE Day occurred on Tuesday, May 8. But victory
in Europe did not mean an end to human tragedy and suffering. For the
Anglo-American-French alliance with the Soviet Union it signaled the
end of a war in which fathers and mothers, brothers and sisters, nieces
and nephews, cousins and friends had been maimed, tortured, and
killed. But for Europe – and especially for the Germans – it was also the
beginning of a new tragedy whose face was defined by food lines, thirst,
no money, a black market, millions of homeless, the horrors of concentration camps, sickness, looting, plunder, rape, revenge, the separation
of Germans from Germans by zones of occupation, and ultimately by
minefields dividing East from West and a wall dividing Berlin.

Thirteen days before surrender, south-east of Hamburg, on Wednesday, April 25,

the church bells of the town of Salzwedel began to ring the alarm and the
air-raid sirens howled ceaselessly over the town as a motorized column of the
American 84th Division drew near. The shops were locked and shuttered, the
windows of the houses were shut, the doors bolted. The only people who
dared to come out in the streets that morning were the erstwhile prisoners of
the place – some two thousand slave-laborers of various nationalities, a
transport of Allied prisoners-of-war, several hundred women from a nearby
concentration camp, and a group of Jewish women who had emerged from
hiding. They heard the crump of artillery fire, saw columns of dust and smoke
rising everywhere, watched the jeeps racing down the road into the town and
the squadrons of planes roaring over on their way to distant targets in the east
– and knew that the longed-for moment of liberation was at hand. At noon the

[1] Botting, *From the Ruins of the Reich*, x.

clouds rolled away, the sun came out and the day promised to be a glorious one. But it did not proceed as they had imagined, and there were those among them who, having survived their many years of captivity, did not outlive their first day of freedom.

Appropriately the first liberating American to reach the tattered emalion [*sic*] assembly of ex-slaves and prisoners outside the Rathaus was himself a descendant of slaves, a well-built black soldier in steel helmet and shiny brown boots, who drew up in a jeep to an effusive welcome. Frenchmen broke into song. Italians blew kisses, Poles and Ukrainians bowed low and wept, and Hungarian women kissed his hands. The soldier pushed them aside without a word, forcing his way through the crowd. He saw little significance in the occasion or his own role in it. He had a simple task to do and he did it. Walking up to the nearest traffic pole, he nailed up a traffic sign which read: SLOW. Then he took off his helmet to fan himself, paddled his way back through the crowd to his jeep, jumped in, blew his horn and drove off. Thus were the prisoners of Salzwedel delivered out of Nazi hands – and the first dreadful hours of liberty began.

More American liberators followed, rumbling down the streets of the captured town in trucks and tanks. Broad-shouldered young men gazed blankly at the cheering crowd of prisoners, casually returned their greetings by raising their leather gloves to their helmets, and tossed packs of Chesterfield cigarettes from their armored cars. The Nazis had gone. Though the Stars and Stripes had been hoisted on the Rathaus, the Americans had not taken full charge of the town. The ex-prisoners and slaves seized the opportunity of this short inter-regnum to give full rein to their pent-up passions, the overriding one of which was a thirst for vengeance against the Germans. Gangs of women smashed windows with their bare fists. Barefoot Rumanians hurled buckets of marma-lade out of a smashed shop front. A wild Russian peasant grabbed handfuls of herrings out of a barrel. A wounded SS man was dragged out of his hiding place under a car in a garage and trampled, torn and bitten to death by the mob of ex-prisoners that fell upon him. Mobs poured into houses and threw radios, clocks, mirrors and portraits of German soldiers out of windows. Even the sick dragged themselves from their deathbeds, crawling on hands and knees along the pavement behind the main body of the mob, driven on by an irresistible urge to participate in this ritual act of hatred and revenge.

In the Protestant cemetery the Nazi mayor and his wife and young daughter had been smoked out of their hiding place in the family vault by a rampaging mob of Russians. The mob tied the mayor to a tombstone, then stripped his wife and daughter almost naked and pulled them by their hair across the grass, while the mayor bucked and screamed like a cock crowing. An elderly, well-mannered Russian in a pilot's jacket and a looted derby hat directed the proceedings. He made the mayor's wife crouch on her hands and knees like an animal and formed the younger Russians into a queue in front of the mayor's huddled daughter. Then he shouted to the mayor in broken German that his own wife had suffered a similar fate in Kharkov during the German advance. There was a moment's silence, then the first man in the queue, a squat Mongolian from Siberia, went down on the young girl and forced his way into her. The mayor uttered a last cry, then tore the tombstone to which he was bound clean out of the ground, and fell dead. His body, still lashed to the tombstone, was thrown into the family vault, the next in line took their turn with his screaming wife and daughter, as the elderly Russian in the derby walked impassively out of the cemetery and left them to their fate.[2]

The Russian in this story was no doubt one of the several million forced laborers that the German occupation forces in Russia and elsewhere in Eastern Europe sent back to toil in the factories and on the farms of the Reich. Hundreds of thousands of them had been worked to death or died of malnutrition. When they were liberated, the survivors were seized by an understandable rage for revenge.

Many Soviet soldiers in the advancing Red Army behaved in a similar way, though not all. Most Germans then and later believed that the Red Army soldier was inherently more likely to rape, loot, and pillage than his Western comrade in the American or British armies. What evidence there is indicates that this belief was correct, even though many Germans, who had never seen a Russian before 1945, derived their ideas about Russians from Nazi propaganda that depicted Jews, East Europeans, and Russians as vicious subhumans.

If the Soviet soldiers raped and killed more than others, and treated the civilian population more harshly, they certainly had what they considered good reasons for such behavior. Warfare on both sides in the East was brutal and extreme in many ways unknown or rarely seen in other theaters of combat. The propaganda of both sides depicted the other as intrinsically evil, not merely as an enemy to be defeated and restrained but as a foe to be exterminated to the last man, woman, and child. Moreover, the Germans had started the war and, during their advance into Russia in 1941–2, had carried out mass killings and other atrocities that provided the Russians with plentiful motivation for revenge. Millions of the Soviet soldiers who poured over the frontiers and into the heart of Germany in 1944–5 mourned comrades, wives, friends, or other relatives who had died at German hands. Many more died in captivity, since the Germans deliberately starved the millions of prisoners they took from the Red Army, mostly in 1941–2. Finally, the Red Army did not know the concept of leave: many of its soldiers had fought without letup since June 22, 1941. Frustration is surely a mild word to describe the emotional state of many of these men.

Despite this record there were Russian soldiers and officers who treated the defeated Germans well and earned their respect. Sometimes the first wave of Red Army soldiers were non-Russians, half-trained, under-equipped and underfed, let loose to do their worst. Those

[2] Ibid., 18–20.

Germans who survived that first wave occasionally found to their surprise that the Russian officers who then appeared were men of civilized bearing, many of them with a knowledge of German. Some Soviet administrators even impressed the Germans with a certain cynical brand of humor.

An example is the following conversation, which is reported to have actually occurred. The Soviet commandant of a small town nominated a respectable citizen to be mayor, but the man was neither a worker nor a communist; he felt uncertain of his own abilities, as he had neither political nor administrative experience. The commandant gently guided the German to a window and pointed to a tree in the courtyard. "Do you see that tree, my dear fellow?" "Yes, sir." "Would you like to hang from that tree?" "No, sir." "In that case, my dear mayor, let me be the first to congratulate you on your new office."[3]

It was a nightmare when normal people could not live civilized lives. The Germans themselves, however, also participated in the chaos that followed surrender. Mothers who had never stolen anything and who had raised their children to be honest and forthright, suddenly faced the dilemma of how to obtain food when there was little food, of how to obtain wood and coal for heat when there was not enough for everyone. To survive they smoked cigarettes to lessen the pangs of hunger, and drank schnapps and wine, if they could find it, to keep warm. And they stole. There emerged, as a consequence, a black market that was necessary for survival:

> A pound of butter was offered to a hungry friend for 350 Reichsmarks. As he did not have enough money on him he bought it on credit. He would pay the next day. Half the pound went to his wife. With the remaining half he went out to "compensate." At a tobacconist we got 50 cigarettes for the half pound. Ten cigarettes we kept for ourselves. With the remainder we went into a bar. For 40 cigarettes we received a bottle of wine and a bottle of Schnapps. We took the wine back to the house, but the Schnapps we took into the country. Before long we found a farmer who would exchange the Schnapps for us for two pounds of butter. Next morning my friend took back the pound of butter he had been offered originally on the grounds that it was too expensive. Our "compensating" had brought us in one and a half pounds of butter, a bottle of wine, 10 cigarettes and the pleasure of a tax-free bit of business.[4]

During the next four years, following the euphoria of Victory in Europe, the meaning of victory changed for both the vanquished and the victors. The territory and people of Germany were ruled by those who had won, the United States, the Soviet Union, Great Britain, and France. During that time the common alliance, forged by war, between the Western

---

[3] Private communication by Lewis H. Gann.
[4] Botting, *From the Ruins of the Reich*, 235.

democracies and the Soviet Union, against Germany, fell apart. Its *raison d'être* had disappeared. Alliance was replaced by political and strategic struggle. The peace that reigned in Europe was an undeclared conflict.

In 1948, the struggle between East and West reached its critical point. The Soviet government blockaded access to Berlin. At the same time the Western powers transferred their authority in the parts of Germany they controlled to a national German government. This government was constituted by a Basic Law written and approved by the Germans voting in the Western zones of occupation, and ratified by the occupying powers. The result, in September 1949, was that three-quarters of the prewar German population were divided from the other quarter. They lived on just over half of the prewar territory of the German Reich, but they had a government of their own. Their government was fully aware that it existed by sanction of the three Western occupying powers, that it had been freely elected, but not by all Germans, and that its jurisdiction did not extend to all of Germany. Nevertheless, it was for 40 years the political system chosen democratically by the majority of those Germans who enjoyed the liberty to express their political views. It therefore regarded itself as representing those Germans in the Soviet zone of occupation who had not been able to vote for it. From 1949 to 1969 the paradox of a German government claiming to represent all the German people, emerging from elections in which not all Germans could take part and exercising control over only part of Germany, was a reality of German life. In 1969, the government stopped claiming to represent Germans east of the dividing line. The facts of division, however, remained the same.

The first two parts of this book follow the uncertain and twisting road that led from the surrender of Germany in May 1945 to the establishment of a free West German state in May 1949. It is not a single road, but roads which intersect and criss-cross. In 1945 no one could legitimately claim to foresee where they would lead. In 1985, when this book was begun 40 years later, few argued that all the roads taken were perfect. One can, however, with the advantage of hindsight, fall prey to the temptation to judge events in the light of one's own knowledge of how things turned out. This can easily lead to a distorted perspective in which the reader overestimates the significance of various facts and trends that anticipated, or led to, the final result, and ignores others. In the case of Germany between 1945 and 1949 this danger is especially marked. The roads were many and the problems to overcome were enormous.

The hostility between the former Allies was, to a large extent, caused by their disagreements on how to handle the question of Germany's political future. To this question, therefore, are related all others. The most important of these questions, which faced both Germans and occupiers, and which led to conflict between the occupiers, were the questions of reparations, of what to do about Nazi war crimes, of economic reconstruction, of the rebirth of education, culture, and religion, and of East–West relations generally which overshadowed them all.

The end of World War II and the history of Germany in the first years thereafter still, 40 years later, affected the political shape of Europe and the fate and interests of many millions of people both on the continent and elsewhere. Through the 1980s, the political map of Europe remained determined by what happened in and around Germany between 1945 and 1949, though the Central European revolutions of 1989 and the German unification of 1990 removed the most inhuman aspects of that legacy.

To return to 1945 from the late 1980s was to go back to a world that seemed infinitely remote to a generation habituated to affluence and peace. It was also painful for many of the now aging survivors to revisit the depths of night – those who were the occupiers and those who were the occupied. Even more than 40 years later many of them, when interviewed on television, for example, still burst into tears – so profound were the memories of the time, the ambivalence of the time, as they were remembered, and perhaps, too, distorted in memory.

Sometimes the disputes were scholarly, as for example concerning the actual history of Western Allied planning for occupied Germany. Almost always, however, the scholarly disputes had a political dimension as well. The debate over Soviet war aims and Soviet plans for Germany was perhaps the most important example of a political dispute which could not be solved by scholarly investigation, because the evidence needed was inaccessible and was likely to remain so.

# 2

# Defeat or Liberation?

W ere the Germans defeated or liberated on May 8, 1945? Certainly most Germans at the time considered themselves defeated, whereas few Germans a generation later disputed the contrary view that the Allies had, on that day, liberated them from Nazism. What it meant to be a German, a member of the German nation, changed over time. Just as obviously, thoughtful Germans posed the question of defeat or liberation to themselves throughout their postwar history. It was a theme they never abandoned. The most important reason for this was that no German could answer the question of what it meant to be German without confronting May 8, 1945, and its implications: defeat or liberation – or what? A closely related reason was that to answer that question was also to answer the question of who was responsible, not only for the war and for Nazism, but for how Germany was reconstructed after 1945, socially, economically, and politically. The German who admitted that May 8 was indeed the day his country was catastrophically, decisively defeated, was also the German who took responsibility (whatever his degree of personal involvement or guilt) for German history in the dark years of 1933–45, but who, in taking that responsibility, also could take credit for reconstruction. On the other hand, the German who saw May 8 as a day of liberation, and thus rejected what went before as not pertaining to him, as not being a true part of German history, had also, arguably, less claim to being part of the German nation that so heroically reconstructed itself, as far as conditions permitted, in the years thereafter.

On the fortieth anniversary of the surrender, the president of the Federal Republic, Richard von Weizsäcker, who had been a decorated lieutenant in the famous Ninth Infantry Regiment of Potsdam and belonged to a distinguished family of south-west German Protestant nobility, declared unambiguously: "May 8, 1945, was a day of liberation!"

He was referring to the liberation of all Europeans and indeed all mankind from the threat or reality of Nazi tyranny.

Understanding the day of surrender in this very general, utopian sense became common in certain circles in West Germany after the mid-1960s. To understand what the feelings were in 1945, however, we turned to those scholars and thinkers who lived through that day, either in Germany or in exile, and who reflected on its meaning. Ernst Nolte, a controversial historian of modern ideology, examined the question in 1985 and concluded:

And even if the Germans of 1945 had been inclined to consider themselves "liberated," the Allied thesis of collective guilt would have quickly taught them a different lesson. Even Wilhelm Pieck [1876–1960, co-chairman of the East German communist party, the Socialist Unity Party, and later president of East Germany, the German Democratic Republic] spoke at that time, with heavy emphasis, of the "shared blame of the German working class." And when ever in history had the liberator taken away from the liberated people one quarter of their nation's territory and expelled the population? And how could one possibly expect the Russians or the Poles to "liberate" the Germans, a people who had brought them close to physical destruction?[1]

In 1949 the publicist and later political scientist at the University of Heidelberg, Dolf Sternberger, expressed the combination of liberation and defeat in these words:

We did not free ourselves from the tyranny of the Third Reich by ourselves. Nor were we, in the proper sense, liberated by others. The tyranny was destroyed, but, at the same time, the German people as a whole were defeated and the German territory totally occupied. This was unavoidable, yet highly disastrous. We did not liberate ourselves, nor were we liberated; however, certain defined "liberations" were imposed on us.[2]

Sternberger enumerates these "liberations:" from militarism – this was complete and very much welcomed, except by a few – and from National Socialism. He concluded that liberation from National Socialism was a misnomer.

Nobody can free himself from his past, except through repentance. There is free repentance and forced repentance. . . . To force repentance you need a court of inquisition. . . . Denazification courts, however, are not courts of

---

[1] Nolte, "Zusammenbruch und Neubeginn." *Zeitschrift für Politik* 32 (1985): 297–8.

[2] Sternberger, "Die deutsche Frage," in *Bundesrepublikanisches Lesebuch*, ed. Glaser, 278.

inquisition. They lack the dogmatic power. They cannot force repentance, they can merely elicit pathetic self-accusations, or counter-evidence, or hurt feelings, or all of the above. Or mockery.[3]

The only way for defeat and denazification to work as liberation would have been if it had led to repentance. For some it did; but for many others it did not. Ernst von Salomon, a writer who had belonged to a radical right-wing group in the 1920s, published *Der Fragebogen* (The questionnaire) in 1952, in which he questioned the whole process. The novel ridiculed the questionnaires concerning Nazi affiliation which the Germans were required to complete after the war and illustrated the bitterness that some Germans felt for the policies of their occupiers, or liberators.

The view that denazification, and therefore liberation, failed because it did not lead to moral repentance, was widespread in Germany. But, in fact, Germany was both defeated and liberated, and the question quickly arose whether defeat applied to "bad" Germans and liberation to "good" Germans. This was a questionable distinction, and if it could be made at all it implied that responsibility for the German tragedy could be clearly assigned. Curiously, both the right and the left agreed throughout postwar German history that there were indeed good Germans and bad Germans – it was just that they attached their labels to different people. Only those in the moderate center (in later years, on the center-right) accepted that all Germans, whatever their personal guilt or that of their ancestors, shared responsibility for the consequences of the past, but by the same token could also take pride in what was good in that past.

The great writer and exile, Thomas Mann, presented an early version of this argument in a talk he gave at the Library of Congress in Washington, DC, in May 1945, a few weeks after the surrender. He began by admitting that it was both impossible to avoid talking about Germany and impossible to do so fairly:

Germany's horrible fate, the tremendous catastrophe in which her modern history now culminates, compels our interest, even if this interest is devoid of sympathy. Any attempt to arouse sympathy, to defend and to excuse Germany, would certainly be an inappropriate undertaking for one of German birth today. To play the part of the judge, to curse and damn his own people in compliant agreement with the incalculable hatred that they have kindled, to commend himself smugly as "the good Germany" in contrast to the wicked, guilty Germany over there with which he has nothing in common, – that too would hardly befit one of German origin. . . . There are *not* two Germanys [*sic*], a good one and a bad one, but only one, whose best turned into evil through devilish

---

[3] Ibid., 279.

cunning. Wicked Germany is merely good Germany gone astray, good Germany in misfortune, in guilt, and ruin.[4]

Defeat, liberation, or both? And in what ways? How Germans came to answer these questions after 1945 significantly affected their political, social, economic, and ideological choices.

[4]  *Thomas Mann's Addresses*, 48, 64.

# 3

# The Fate

The political factors that determined Germany's fate in 1945 were primarily the character, aims and policies of the Soviet Union, the United States, Great Britain, and, to a lesser extent, France, and the other countries of Europe. During the early phases of the war, until the German attack on the Soviet Union in June 1941, the aim of Germany's main adversary, Great Britain, was the restoration of the status quo in central Europe. Adolf Hitler would have to be removed from power in Germany; but the British had no plans for dismembering Germany, for unconditional surrender, or for the destruction of German power. The British prime minister, Winston Churchill, and many other British leaders, had a healthy fear of what might happen if Germany should cease to be an independent, viable power in Central Europe. According to his biographer, Martin Gilbert, Churchill asked in 1943: "Will it be said of me that I was so obsessed with the destruction of Hitlerism that I neglected to see the enemy rising in the East?"[1] The result, they suspected, could be that the Soviet Union with its communist ideology would become the predominant power on the European continent. In 1939, the Soviet Union had signed a pact with Nazi Germany that gave it carte blanche to extend its control over large parts of east central Europe. Until Hitler turned on his ally in 1941, therefore, the British were inclined to regard the Soviet Union under its ruler, Joseph Stalin, as only slightly less hostile to British interests than Nazi Germany itself.

The German attack on the Soviet Union radically altered these terms, for it thus became a co-belligerent and an ally of Great Britain and, after December 1941, of the United States. By early 1943, the US and British war aims were unequivocally the destruction of German power, the dismemberment of Germany, and the assumption of full political authority on German territory by the Soviet Union, the United States,

---

[1] Cited in Charlton, *Eagle and the Small Birds*, 33.

and Britain. Increasingly, the British, and to a lesser extent the Americans, came to regard Germany as a threat to European and world peace that must be destroyed once and for all. The way to do this was to occupy the entire country and to ensure that the Germans would never again be able to reconstitute a unified and potentially aggressive state.

The position and aims of the Soviet Union were never fully known. The undisputed fact is, however, that the Soviets concluded the war, after immense suffering, in a position of greater potential power than ever before. The Red Army controlled central Europe and looked across the threshold of western Europe. Regimes loyal to Moscow were, in 1945, in the process of being installed in Poland, Czechoslovakia, Hungary, Romania, Yugoslavia, Bulgaria, and Albania. The Baltic states of Lithuania, Latvia, and Estonia, and parts of Poland, Romania, and Finland, obtained by Stalin under the pact with Hitler, remained in Soviet control. Prussia (and its successors, the united German Reich from 1871 to 1918, and following World War I, the Weimar Republic from 1919 to 1933 and Nazi Germany from 1933 to 1945), which, from the early eighteenth century, had been the primary rival of Russia for control in central Europe, was no more. The fate of Europe would henceforth be determined not from its center, but from its periphery: by Moscow in the East, by the principal European powers in the West, and by the United States across the Atlantic Ocean.

Most historians, given their own and the source materials' limitations, concentrated on the origins of the Cold War rather than on Soviet policies as such. This was possibly a mistake; for it led logically to a narrowing of perspective by Western scholars that largely excluded the foreign policy of the Soviet Union. The great debate on the origins of the Cold War concerned the question whether it was provoked by the West, or by Stalin, or whether it was simply inevitable and the question of responsibility irrelevant. The interpretation of Stalin's motives was always part of that larger debate. There were, generally speaking, three views. The first saw him mainly as a victim of Nazi aggression; the second as a skilful strategist committed to the expansion of communist power, but still acting in situations determined primarily by Nazi and, later, Western actions. The third saw Stalin as controller, rather than victim, throughout. The choice between these interpretations must be made on the basis of circumstantial evidence, including the reader's general, informed conception of the character and policies of the Soviet Union.

The second general interpretation was that of many well-informed diplomats and historians at the time and probably the most widely accepted in the West in the 1980s (e.g., Ulam, *Expansion and Coexistence: Soviet Foreign Policy, 1917–73*). Its adherents shared the first view's assessment of Stalin's prewar foreign policy. He sought to control Western communist parties, but was at the same time genuinely afraid of Nazi Germany and made sincere efforts to rally the Western democracies against Hitler. The pact in 1939 was both a necessary means to gain time and a cynical exercise of power politics by which Stalin obtained important territorial gains in Eastern Europe. He seriously did not expect Hitler to break the pact when he did, nor did he have a long-term strategy for Soviet policy in Europe between 1939 and 1941. It was the German attack on June 22, 1941, that was the ultimate cause of the expansion of Soviet power. This idea – that Soviet control of central Europe and the destruction of Germany was provoked by the German attack on the Soviet Union – was the crucial element of this interpretation. The leading proponent of this view wrote in 1979:

Not only did Hitler's gratuitous aggression open the door through which the Soviet Union eventually stepped out to become the world's mightiest and perhaps last imperial power; it also provided the dubious justification for Stalin's imperialism. The humiliation of his life, the Nazi treachery imbued Stalin with an extraordinary drive to justify in retrospect the wisdom of the expansionistic policies he had initiated during his abortive association with the German dictator.[2]

It also followed from this view that the postwar conflict between the Soviet Union and the Western democracies, the Cold War, was neither the necessary result of Western hostility to a basically peace-loving Soviet Union, as the first view had it, nor of a long-standing Soviet drive for power in Europe. Mastny presented the argument as follows:

In bringing the war against Nazi Germany to a victorious end, Stalin created the Soviet empire as a by-product. He had not originally sought a military conquest of the whole area he had won. .... Apt at both exploiting the existing opportunities and creating new ones, he let his aspirations grow until he realized that he had misjudged the complacency of his Anglo-American partners – as they had misjudged his moderation. So he plunged his country into a confrontation with the West that he had neither desired nor thought inevitable.[3]

The Soviet position at the end of the war, according to this view, was basically opportunistic. Central Europe was under Soviet control, and it was in the Soviet interest that it should remain so. The future of Germany, therefore, would be the object of contention with the West.

[2] Mastny, *Russia's Road to the Cold War*, 307.
[3] Ibid., 308–9.

The revisionist view, that is to say the first view, was more an expression of radical dissatisfaction with American society and politics in the 1960s than of genuine historical judgement. The truth probably lay in a blend of the second and third views, which were not necessarily incompatible, but rather expressed different perspectives. So the Australian journalist Michael Charlton believed that "it was in collusion with Hitler that Stalin formulated his design for Eastern Europe and forged the means of achieving it."[4] Adam Ulam, one of the most authoritative American historians on the Soviet Union, concluded similarly that Stalin in 1939 hoped that there would be a prolonged European war like that of 1914–18, which would "leave all the capitalist powers weakened and create new opportunities for communism."[5] Whether Stalin had a truly grand design for European hegemony in the 1930s or whether the war gave him opportunities he would not otherwise have seized for himself, was something we are unlikely ever to know. But the results for the victims were in any case clear enough.

By 1943 the Western Allies had decided for themselves that the destruction of Germany and the assumption of control over that country by the victors, including the Soviet Union, were necessary preconditions for postwar peace. The decision to defeat Germany was therefore not made on the basis of knowledge of the atrocities of the Nazi Reich, particularly the organized murder of at least six million Jews. These atrocities were in fact questioned by Western Allied leaders, who repeatedly refused to plan their operations in ways that might prevent or delay the massacres. One of the great paradoxes of World War II is that Germany was not destroyed as a penalty for its crimes. The two processes – the Nazi atrocities and the planning and execution of the defeat of Germany – proceeded in parallel. The one did not determine the other.

In Western Allied thinking, both British and American, Germany deserved to be defeated and occupied not because of the ideology of Nazism, but because Germany had for a second time in twenty-five years made a violent bid for power in Europe; it was therefore necessary to prevent this from happening again by suppressing Germany for good. In the minds of Allied leaders, National Socialism as an ideology was inextricably linked to Prussian militarism and expansionism. The defeat of Germany must therefore include not only the destruction of the Nazi Party and its organizations, but also the end of the German Reich as a state and the dissolution of all institutions and traditions that, in the eyes

---

[4] Charlton, *Eagle and the Small Birds*, 19.
[5] Ulam, *History of Soviet Russia*, 141.

of Germany's enemies, were the sources of German aggression both in 1914 and 1939. Allied planning for Germany's defeat operated wholly within the assumption that Germany, not just Nazism, was the enemy, and that Germany must not be allowed to survive as an independent state. The treatment of Germany, therefore, was not to be affected by the principles of the Atlantic Charter formulated by President Franklin Roosevelt and Prime Minister Winston Churchill during a meeting "somewhere in the Atlantic" in August 1941. The declaration incorporated the "common principles" which both countries were committed to defend; namely, the self-determination of peoples, a rejection of territorial aggrandizement, and "the final destruction of Nazi tyranny" with magnanimity in victory.

During 1942 and 1943, following the Japanese attack on Pearl Harbor in December 1941, the US position, advocated above all by the president and his immediate associates, developed further along these lines. Germany would be occupied and the Soviet Union included in the system of collective security and peace that would emerge from the wartime alliance of the "United Nations." That system would be based on the principles of state sovereignty and non-intervention, on the restoration of democracy in Europe and on the gradual expansion of democracy elsewhere. The Americans believed that peace and democracy were largely synonymous, and that the Soviet Union, by being included in the proposed collective security system as a "world policeman" along with the United States, Britain, and China, would itself eventually develop in the direction of internal democracy. In the meantime, the Soviets would pose no threat to the rest of Europe. Many Americans believed not only that Stalin had no imperialistic designs, but also that even if he did, British power, which would predominate in Western Europe after the defeat of Germany, would frustrate them.

During the Teheran summit between Stalin, Roosevelt, and Churchill in November 1943, the three leaders expressed their "determination that our nations shall work together in war and in the peace that will follow," and that they would "seek the cooperation and active participation of all nations, large and small, whose peoples in heart and mind are dedicated, as are our own peoples, to the elimination of tyranny and slavery, oppression and intolerance."[6] It became clear soon thereafter, however, that the British would not be in a position after the war to secure, with their own resources, the peace and development of Western Europe. At the same time, Soviet actions began to sow doubt in the minds of some, such as the young US diplomat George F. Kennan, that Stalin would in fact be content with the defeat of Germany.

[6] Münch, ed., *Dokumente*, 1: 4–5.

In January 1945, while deputy chief of mission at the US embassy in Moscow under Ambassador Averell Harriman, Kennan wrote a letter to Charles Bohlen, a close aide of Roosevelt's, in which he took a very pessimistic view of the chances of postwar US–Soviet cooperation. The Soviet Union, he believed, was driven by ideology and by Russian historical tradition to expand westward into Europe as far as it could. The end of the war would give it an unprecedented opportunity to do so, and this would inevitably lead to conflict with independent European states. If the Western powers, the United States and Britain, did not have the will to contest Soviet rule in Central and Eastern Europe, as they clearly did not, Kennan went on, then the only solution was to determine a demarcation line in Europe that the Soviets could not cross without risking open war. This was tantamount to the division of Europe into spheres of interest, a type of thinking alien to most Americans, but familiar to European diplomats and to a few well-educated Americans like Kennan. As far as Germany was concerned, Kennan argued, it was already clear that the eastern half of the country would be occupied by the Soviet Union, and the United States would therefore have to "accept as an accomplished fact the complete partition of Germany."[7] To prevent further Soviet encroachments, Kennan concluded, the US should immediately open discussions with the British and the French with a view to establishing a West European political, economic, and military union which would also come to include the political entities that might be established in that part of Germany occupied by Western troops.

Since Kennan's evaluation of January 1945 almost exactly reflects what in fact happened, one may well ask why it took so long for his colleagues and superiors in Western governments to come to the same realization. The main reason that the political leaders were slow to see what Kennan saw was that most of them, and particularly the Americans, believed that Stalin shared their hopes for a peaceful world order and that the Soviet Union was moving, albeit slowly, toward a more liberal and democratic form of government. Even Winston Churchill, the most skeptical of the Western leaders, believed that one could make deals with Stalin and expect them to be honored, though he had no illusions about the character of the Soviet communist regime. The overwhelming consensus of Western policymakers in the spring of 1945, in any event, was that Stalin's policies and aspirations were compatible with Western interests.[8] It was not until the winter of 1946–7 that the majority of US and British political leaders finally adopted the realistic view presented by Kennan two years earlier.

[7] Bohlen, *Witness to History*, 176.
[8] Sherwood, *Roosevelt and Hopkins*, 870.

# 4

# Planning for Occupation

In October 1943, the US, Soviet, and British foreign ministers met in Moscow to discuss concrete plans for postwar Europe. The meeting marked an intensification of the wartime cooperation between the "Big Three" which continued until the Potsdam Conference of July 1945. The meeting was also the first of a series of foreign ministers' conferences which the Americans, and to a lesser extent the British, hoped would be a useful tool for administering the postwar world and especially Europe.

At the Moscow meeting, Cordell Hull, the US secretary of state, Anthony Eden, the British foreign secretary, and Vyacheslav Molotov, the Soviet people's commissar for foreign affairs, decided to establish a European Advisory Commission (EAC) consisting of permanent representatives of the Big Three. The EAC, based in London, would work out detailed proposals for the Allied governments concerning all matters – administrative, logistical, diplomatic, and military – arising from the conclusion of the war. The most important such matter was the planning for postwar Germany, which had two main parts: the division of Germany into zones of occupation for purposes of demilitarization and reparations, and the punishment of German war criminals.

The agreements on the administrative control of occupied Germany were issued by the EAC on September 12 and November 14, 1944. During the phase of actual surrender, supreme authority would rest with the commanders-in-chief of the armed forces of the Big Three. As soon as that phase had ended, the commanders-in-chief collectively would establish an Allied Control Council. This agency would govern Germany under the immediate authority of the Allied governments and would, in turn, "control the German central administration, which will operate under the direction of the Control Council and will be responsible to it for ensuring compliance with its demands."[1] The Council would meet once every ten days, while the practical execution of its orders and the direct supervision of the German administration was to rest with a Coordinating Committee. As for the administration of Berlin, the capital of Germany, the EAC agreement envisaged an "Inter-Allied Governing Authority," or Kommandatura, under the general direction of the Control Council.

The EAC worked out the actual plans for the division of Germany into zones of occupation during 1944 and presented them in a protocol dated September 12 of that year. Under this agreement, just under half of the prewar Reich territory, comprising the provinces of East Prussia, Pomerania, East Brandenburg, Silesia, as well as the territory known today as East Germany, became the Soviet zone of occupation. In later negotiations during the winter of 1944–5, the Americans and the British agreed to let the Soviet Union annex outright the northern part of East Prussia with the city of Königsberg. The rest of German territory east of the Oder and western Neisse rivers went to Poland in compensation, or so Stalin insisted, for the Eastern part of that country seized by the Soviets in 1939 under the Hitler-Stalin Pact. In this as in other matters, Stalin insisted on keeping his gains under that pact. The Western Allies accepted the argument that Poland, which was after all the country on whose behalf Britain declared war on Germany in 1939, deserved this compensation. The German population of these German provinces, some ten million people in 1939, would be expelled.

The Big Three approved the revised zonal division at their meeting in Yalta, in the Crimea, in February 1945, but maintained the previous demarcation line between the Soviet, the British, and the US zones. This decision left the Soviets with almost half of the remaining German territory, the rest being divided between Britain and the US. Subsequently, France obtained a zone of occupation made up of parts of the original US and British zones. The capital, Berlin, was not included in the zonal division and was ultimately divided, for purposes of occupation, into four sectors in much the same proportions as the country in general.

Despite the intensive planning of 1944–5, the decision on how to treat the German population and all the principles guiding the conduct of occupation government, had not been finally determined by the Western Allied governments when the war ended. The Soviets, for their part, initially de-emphasized their insistence on completely separate zonal occupation policies, in favor of an equally strong insistence on the need for a unified postwar administration. Having a say in the conduct

[1] Dept of State, *Documents on Germany*, 7.

of affairs in the other zones would not only allow the Soviets to claim reparations from zones other than their own, but might also be a basis from which to build up pro-Soviet political forces throughout the country.[2]

Allied leaders wavered between two opposed concepts of how to treat Germany. One view, going back to the earlier British war goals of restoring the status quo and refraining from the total destruction of Germany, regained some popularity in 1944–5 as it became clear to some that Soviet policies in Eastern Europe were not compatible with Western interests; and, moreover, that the West could not rely purely on Stalin's goodwill for postwar peace in Europe but would need to exercise some military and political power of its own to balance Soviet power.[3] Those who held this view thought that the Germans should be helped and encouraged to constitute a democratic and economically self-sufficient Germany as a necessary element of a peaceful European order. The other view, whose most conspicuous proponent was the US treasury secretary, Henry J. Morgenthau, was that the Germans were ineradicably evil and aggressive, and that they deserved the most stringent punishment for their aggression.

"Desire for war has been as firmly planted in the German as desire for freedom in the American," wrote Morgenthau in 1945.[4] Thus, punishment should take the form of a permanent partition of Germany into several pieces, initially the end of all higher education, and the destruction and future prohibition of all heavy industry. The extreme version of this view, the Morgenthau Plan, was official US and British policy from September 1944 to the spring of 1945. Although it was never put into practice, the idea of revenge and punishment as the principle of occupation was more widespread than the hope for reconciliation and reconstruction as the war in Europe drew to a close.

Harold Zink, an American who was chief historian of the US High Commissioner for Germany and wrote the first authoritative history of the American occupation, described the Morgenthau Plan as a result of domestic American political pressures. "It seems almost unbelievable," he wrote,

that such large numbers of Americans could have been gullible enough to subscribe to the unrealistic proposal to de-industrialize one of the most highly industrialized countries of the world. But emotions are blinding and the dastardly conduct of the Nazis involving the Jews, those advocating world peace, many of the clergy, American airmen, and others stirred up resentment

[2] See Mastny, *Russia's Road to the Cold War*, 150, 233–7.
[3] Graml, *Die Alliierten und die Teilung Deutschlands*, 36–9.
[4] Morgenthau, *Germany Is Our Problem*, 114.

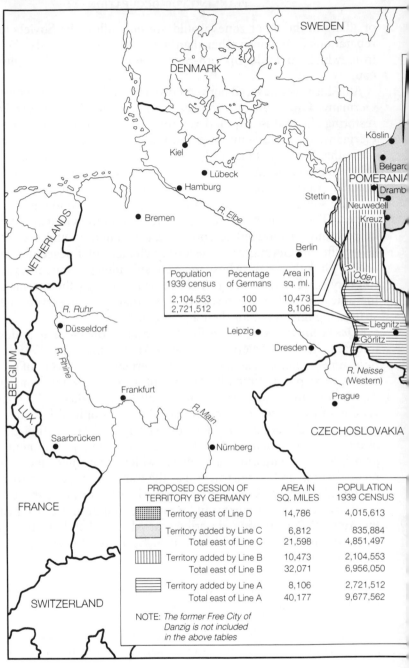

| Population 1939 census | Pecentage of Germans | Area in sq. ml. |
|---|---|---|
| 2,104,553 | 100 | 10,473 |
| 2,721,512 | 100 | 8,106 |

| PROPOSED CESSION OF TERRITORY BY GERMANY | | AREA IN SQ. MILES | POPULATION 1939 CENSUS |
|---|---|---|---|
| | Territory east of Line D | 14,786 | 4,015,613 |
| | Territory added by Line C | 6,812 | 835,884 |
| | Total east of Line C | 21,598 | 4,851,497 |
| | Territory added by Line B | 10,473 | 2,104,553 |
| | Total east of Line B | 32,071 | 6,956,050 |
| | Territory added by Line A | 8,106 | 2,721,512 |
| | Total east of Line A | 40,177 | 9,677,562 |

NOTE: *The former Free City of Danzig is not included in the above tables*

Map 1.1   The genesis of the Oder–Neisse line: proposed territorial changes in Germany and Poland.
*Source*:  De Zayas, *Nemesis at Potsdam*, 54–5

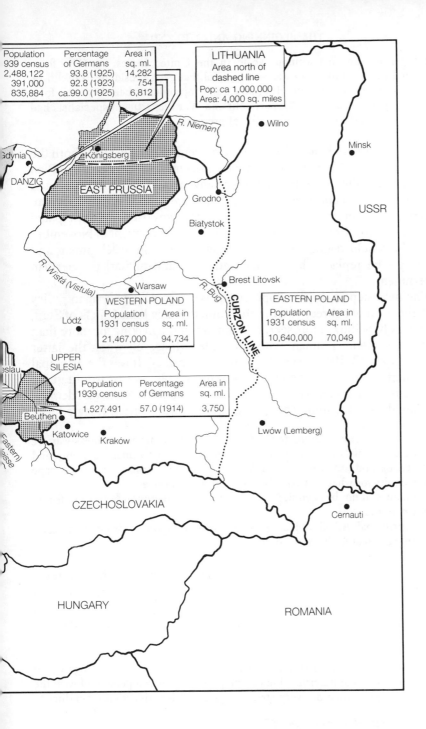

| Population 939 census | Percentage of Germans | Area in sq. ml. |
|---|---|---|
| 2,488,122 | 93.8 (1925) | 14,282 |
| 391,000 | 92.8 (1923) | 754 |
| 835,884 | ca.99.0 (1925) | 6,812 |

**LITHUANIA**
Area north of dashed line
Pop: ca 1,000,000
Area: 4,000 sq. miles

Wilno

Minsk

R. Niemen

Gdynia

Königsberg

DANZIG

EAST PRUSSIA

Grodno

USSR

Biatystok

R. Wisła (Vistula)

Warsaw

Brest Litovsk

R. Bug

CURZON LINE

**WESTERN POLAND**

| Population 1931 census | Area in sq. ml. |
|---|---|
| 21,467,000 | 94,734 |

**EASTERN POLAND**

| Population 1931 census | Area in sq. ml. |
|---|---|
| 10,640,000 | 70,049 |

Łódź

UPPER
SILESIA

eslau

| Population 1939 census | Percentage of Germans | Area in sq. ml. |
|---|---|---|
| 1,527,491 | 57.0 (1914) | 3,750 |

Beuthen

Katowice

Kraków

Lwów (Lemberg)

(Eastern)
isse

CZECHOSLOVAKIA

Cernauti

HUNGARY

ROMANIA

and bitterness on an enormous scale in the United States. ... The force generated by this movement was so powerful that even President Franklin D. Roosevelt, Secretary of State Hull, and other top officials bent before it for a time. The plans of the State Department and War Department specialists had to be shelved in the face of such political pressure. ...[5]

In the last weeks before the German surrender in May 1945, both the US and the British governments moved away from the Morgenthau Plan and adopted the position that Germany should be politically and economically decentralized in order to prevent a future German government from preparing another war. Both governments anticipated that the Control Council envisaged by the EAC agreement of November 14, 1944, would regulate the broad lines of German development and ultimately be replaced by a democratic and anti-militaristic German government.

The next step in the development of Western Allied German policy took the form of a directive from the United States Joint Chiefs of Staff, known as JCS 1067, a top-secret document in the making for more than a year. President Truman, who succeeded Roosevelt when the latter died on April 12, 1945, issued JCS 1067 on April 26. It was the principal document setting forth the purposes and the policies that would guide US occupation of Germany, and dealt with economic controls, denazification, demilitarization, education, and political activity. It stated:

It should be brought home to the Germans that Germany's ruthless warfare and the fanatical Nazi resistance have destroyed the German economy and made chaos and suffering inevitable and that the Germans cannot escape responsibility for what they have brought upon themselves.

Germany will not be occupied for the purpose of liberation but as a defeated enemy nation. ...

The principal Allied objective is to prevent Germany from ever again becoming a threat to the peace of the world.[6]

It was addressed to General Dwight D. Eisenhower, the Supreme Commander of the American Forces, and, therefore, was binding only in the US zone, but it nevertheless expressed the most widely held Western Allied view at the time of surrender. Harold Zink summed up its content and implications as follows:

In general, it was a harsh and stern set of instructions largely negative in character. It forbade fraternization on the part of American personnel with the German people, ordered a very strict program of denazification extending to

[5] Zink, *United States in Germany*, 87.
[6] Dept of State, *Documents on Germany*, 17–18.

both public life and business, emphasized agricultural reconstruction, and prohibited American aid in the rebuilding of German industry. Under this directive the German people were definitely considered a menace to humanity and guilty of crimes against other people. . . . Punishment was to be meted out by reducing their standard of living drastically and by preventing them from regaining economic strength . . . This directive showed the United States as a short-sighted country, motivated largely by revenge, and with little appreciation of the fundamental problems of an occupation. It constituted what may be called without undue exaggeration a heavy millstone around the neck of the American military government.[7]

JCS 1067 remained in force from April 1945 to July 1947, although American administrators soon found ways to ignore or bypass its harsher provisions. The document reflected the political mood in America in the winter of 1944–5 and the influence of the Morgenthau Plan. When President Truman published it in April 1945, he and other high American officials had, as Zink notes, "seen the folly of their earlier position and no longer supported the unrealistic policy of de-industrializing a highly industrialized country such as Germany."[8] The Joint Chiefs of Staff nevertheless issued the directive, partly because it reflected their earlier views, partly because they had received the authority to direct policy in Germany, and partly because there was no time in the spring of 1945 to produce new guidelines. Moreover, there were still many influential politicians and advisors in the Allied governments who were determined to uphold a punitive policy.

Some, like Treasury Secretary Morgenthau and the British politician Lord Vansittart, were obsessed with vengeance and subscribed to a primitive anti-German fanaticism that found public expression in the then common opinion that Nazism was not a new phenomenon but one with deep roots in German history. Morgenthau and Vansittart advocated the destruction of German industry and the fragmentation of the country, which would necessarily have led to mass starvation and death.[9]

The men who were to govern their respective zones of occupation were all distinguished military officers participating in the defeat of Germany. The first Soviet military governor, commander-in-chief of the Soviet occupying forces, Marshal Zhukov (1896–1974), remained in Germany until 1946, when Marshal Vasiliy Sokolovsky (1897–1968), who had entered Germany with his troops in the winter of 1945, succeeded him. The French military governor, General Marie Pierre

[7] Zink, *United States in Germany*, 94.

[8] Ibid., 92.

[9] Morgenthau, *Germany Is Our Problem*, 16–29, 155–63; see also quote by Lord Vansittart in Eschenburg, *Jahre der Besatzung*, 111.

Koenig (1898–1970), had, during 1944–5 served as military governor of Paris, and he remained as military governor in Germany from 1945 to 1949. Sir Bernard L. Montgomery, later Viscount Alamein (1887–1976), the first military governor in charge of the British zone, was followed by his deputy, Sir Brian Robertson (1896–1974), who became military governor in 1947. Robertson had, during the war, from 1943 to 1945, served in the Italian campaign. However, the most famous postwar Allied figure in Germany was the American general, Lucius D. Clay (1897–1978), who, from April 1945 to January 1947 acted as deputy military governor, first under General Eisenhower, then under General Joseph T. McNarney, and became military governor in 1947.

Clay's role, as that of his counterparts, was a peculiar one, since it was in theory strictly military and apolitical, but in fact, of course, highly political, because he had to deal not only with the Soviet Union and the other Western Allies, but increasingly with the Germans themselves. Though he was only deputy governor until 1947, he quickly took charge of the OMGUS administration and was, in practice, its head from the middle of 1945 onward. Writing in the mid-1950s, Harold Zink summarized Clay's virtues and the challenges he faced as follows:

> With almost no background in political matters, even in the United States, General Clay undertook as difficult a politico-military assignment in Germany as could be imagined. ... A clean-cut, slender-built man, General Clay had little of the physical front sometimes associated with top brass, but his piercing eye and self-confidence suggested decisiveness and force. Very few human beings in any walk of life worked as hard as General Clay: he frequently arrived at his office well before anyone else and not uncommonly remained after the normal closing hour far into the night. Sundays and holidays meant little to him. He was more informal than most men who bear his responsibilities and had little liking for red tape. Rather quiet and on the surface mild, he developed what some regarded as imperious mannerisms as the years passed by in Germany. ...
>
> General Clay was rarely at a loss and, rather than delay action until he could consult his experts, he often made an immediate decision. ... Fortunately General Clay possessed a shrewdness, and at times it almost seemed a sort of uncanny sixth sense, which made this way of proceeding less hazardous than might first appear to be the case.[10]

Observers then and later pointed out that Clay owed his freedom of action to the fact that Washington left Germany largely to itself in 1945–8. The president was absorbed in domestic politics, and the State Department was too weak to challenge Clay's procedures and policies. Thus, as the American journalist Edwin Hartrich pointed out, Clay

---

[10] Zink, *United States in Germany*, 68–70.

"almost single-handedly reversed the punitive and unrealistic American policy toward defeated Germany and then forced the US government to follow in his turbulent wake. . . . Clay was the founding father of the Bundesrepublik Deutschland."[11]

Lewis Douglas, an advisor to Clay, called JCS 1067 the work of "economic idiots." Clay himself also doubted the wisdom of seeking to punish while simultaneously supporting the freedom necessary to rebuild the German economy if a minimal standard of living was to be maintained. In hindsight it seemed clear that the wording of the directive was less important than the imagination of the men asked to carry it out, like Clay. John J. McCloy, the assistant secretary of war in 1945 who later played a great role in German-American relations, wrote in 1981 that "I think he [Clay] several times said he thought that this was a document under which he could very well progress. The emphasis upon JCS 1067, if you look at it, was that it was temporary. The word *temporary* was used in the introduction to it . . . I do not think it really interfered with the development of Germany. It certainly did not bring about any drastic or Draconian applications."[12] Not all would agree, but certainly Clay's interpretation of it was enlightened. It was also practical, and it was a view shared by other Americans who were staggered by the extent of destruction in Germany. In 1946, when the food shortage became acute, President Truman asked former President Herbert Hoover to review the efforts to feed Germany's postwar population. Hoover reported: "You can have vengeance, or peace, but you can't have both."[13]

[11] Hartrich, *Fourth and Richest Reich*, 105.

[12] McCloy, "From Military Government to Self-Government," in *Americans as Proconsuls*, ed. Wolfe, 120.

[13] Hartrich, *Fourth and Richest Reich*, 108–9; see also Eschenburg, *Jahre der Besatzung*, 336.

# 5

# The Hour at Zero

In late April 1945 American forces occupied Garmisch-Partenkirchen in the Bavarian Alps. The following day the local newspaper published its last issue, in which its editor wrote:

> This is no time for complaining. After all, every one of us is guilty and we must all admit it. Why have we always lain down like dogs and taken everything our gangster bosses expected of us?[1]

Ruth Andreas-Friedrich wrote in her diary in Berlin on May 1, 1945: "There is no water. There is also no gas, no electricity, and no telephone. There is only chaos. Indescribable, impenetrable chaos."[2] The war caused the destruction of millions of homes, the breakdown of communications, serious shortages of food and other necessary goods, and physical and psychological dislocations unparalleled in modern history. The American and British bomber offensive had left untouched no city with a population over 50,000 as far east as Berlin, which had itself suffered a population decline since 1939 of over 30 per cent to barely 3 million in 1945. In the final winter of the war the British Royal Air Force conducted "Baedeker raids" (the name is that of a famous series of travel guidebooks) against cities of importance to German communications and the German war effort, and which were also of particular architectural and artistic value. The effect of these raids was to destroy much of the medieval city centers and to cause great loss of life. Although the cities were rebuilt, no one could restore the historical charm and atmosphere that had made them famous.

After surrender, survivors calculated that the removal of rubble in Berlin, where only 25 per cent of all buildings had remained untouched, would require 16 years, with ten trains of 50 cars each operating daily. In

---

[1] Thayer, *Unquiet Germans*, 22.
[2] Andreas-Friedrich, *Schauplatz Berlin*, 19.

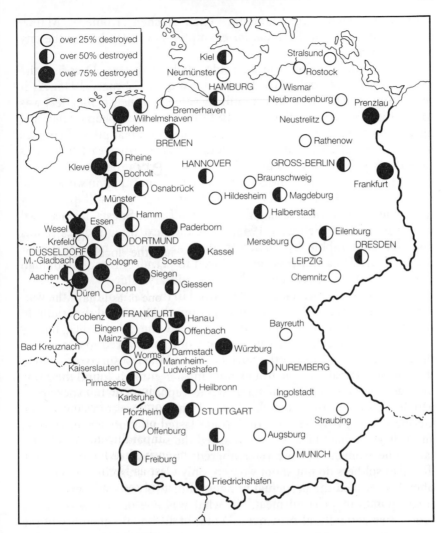

Map 1.2   The destruction of German cities in the war. The extent of
destruction in Germany in 1945 is difficult to comprehend, even with
the assistance of maps like this one.
*Source*: G. Binder, *Deutschland seit 1945*

Cologne 72 per cent of its buildings were destroyed, and of the city's
former population of 770,000 only 40,000 remained living in the ruins.
In Düsseldorf 90 per cent of the city was uninhabitable and in Frankfurt
80,000 of 180,000 buildings were damaged, while in Hannover less than
1 per cent of the entire city had suffered no damage.[3] In Stuttgart,

[3]   Steininger, *Deutsche Geschichte*, 1: 87.

Würzburg, Magdeburg, Hamburg, Kiel, Aachen, Koblenz, Mainz, Kassel, Münster, and Bremen, for example, more than half of the city was destroyed.

Some of the most terrible air raids, such as that on Dresden, the capital of Saxony, took place late in the war in February 1945. As it turned out they had little direct military value and their main effect was to terrorize the civilian population. In Dresden too few people remained alive to bury the dead, and for days after the raid great piles of corpses were still being set alight with flamethrowers. Further east there was little damage from air raids until the Soviet front approached in the fall of 1944, but the effects of the Soviet advance and occupation were all the more severe. The last major German city that was still physically untouched by war was Breslau, the capital of Lower Silesia. Its medieval core was intact in February 1945. Over the next three months it was pounded into rubble by Soviet artillery and bombs because Hitler declared Breslau a "fortress" and refused to permit surrender although the city could not be relieved and had no military value.

Königsberg, like Breslau, was destroyed in the last months of the war. It fell in early April 1945. After occupation, the Soviets did nothing to restore the functions of the city or to feed the inhabitants, mostly women, children and elderly men. Many of them starved to death over the next two years. In 1947 the Soviets allowed the last survivors to go to the Soviet occupation zone from which most eventually found their way to West Germany. Some of them wrote reports of their experiences which are among the most shocking of any to have come out of the German east, partly because the ordeal lasted so long. Rape, looting, and pillage defined life: "We often asked the soldiers to shoot us" after rape, one woman survivor remembered, "but they always answered: 'Russian soldiers do not shoot women, only German soldiers do that.'" She also recalled the perpetual hunger: "For two years we never saw a single potato or piece of meat," in what was one of Germany's most productive agricultural provinces. Worst of all was the memory of the children.

Many children were a terrifying sight, gray and swollen . . . and completely apathetic. I shall never forget the whimpering of the children, who were too weak to cry properly. Once, in the wintertime, as I was turning the corner, I heard, about five doors down the road, a child whimpering terribly. I didn't want to look because I couldn't do anything to help. A Russian sentry standing guard at the corner in front of a general's house called to me and pointed to the child. I explained in Russian that the child had nothing to eat, nor did I. He shook his head eagerly and told me that they had given the child a loaf of bread and potatoes. Well, even though my shoes were full of holes, I had to wade through high snow to get to the child. It did not answer my questions, just whimpered insanely, grasping an empty bottle. I realized what might have happened and finally learned that the child had only managed to move past five houses with his treasures. Passing neighbors had seen an officer take the bread and potatoes from the poor wretch.[4]

One of the many terrible ironies of 1945 was that the vengeance of the Soviets fell mainly on civilians rather than on those responsible for the war or for the atrocities committed by Germans in Russia. Yet many Germans after the war had to face the uncomfortable truth that, before 1945, they had considered humanitarian scruples to be an affliction of weak minds and had jeered at what they called *westliche Humanitätsduselei* (Western bleeding-heart humanitarianism). A majority of Germans believed in 1941 that the war with the Soviet Union was a war of annihilation and that it was their rightful destiny to defeat the peoples of the East and destroy Bolshevism. Soviet troops in eastern Germany in 1944 and thereafter were enacting the scenario that the Nazi leadership had proposed for Russia. That does not make the individual suffering any less dreadful, it merely puts it in historical context.

This fate occurred in eastern provinces which, unbeknownst to their inhabitants, had been granted to the Soviet Union and Poland. The Russian author Aleksandr Solzhenitsyn, at the time an artillery captain in the Red Army, described the attitude of the Soviet soldiers during the January offensive in 1945. It was the first time significant parts of German territory were occupied. "For three weeks the war had been going on inside Germany, and all of us knew very well that if the girls were German they could be raped and then shot. This was almost a combat distinction."[5] One of Solzhenitsyn's fellow-officers in the Red Army units that invaded East Prussia was Lev Kopelev. Not only was Kopelev a Soviet officer, but he was also a Jew, who risked his life to protect German civilians. For his pains he was condemned to 25 years in the Gulag (the Soviet concentration camp system). Many years after his release, he wrote the story of his wartime acts and his trial. He tells of an argument he had with his commanding officer, a Colonel Zabashtansky, a fanatical communist. Kopelev provides the following example of Zabashtansky's view of the Germans: "'So what's needed now? First, for the soldier to go on hating, so he'll want his revenge. And second, for the soldier to have a personal interest in going on fighting. . . . So . . . everything is his – goods, women, do what you want! Hammer away! So their grandchildren and great-grandchildren will remember and be afraid!'"

Kopelev asked Zabashtansky whether he thought the soldiers should deliberately murder women and children. The colonel replied: "'Don't

---

[4] Mühlfenzl, ed., *Geflohen und vertrieben*, 167, 170, 172.
[5] Solzhenitsyn, *Gulag Archipelago*, 1: 21.

be silly. Why bring in children? . . . if there are any who will do it, let them kill the little Fritzes in the heat of the moment, until they get sick of it themselves. . . . That's war, buddy – not your philosophy and literature. . . . First let's send Germany up in smoke, then we'll go back to writing good, theoretically correct books on humanism and internationalism.'[6]

Those who could not flee faced a terrible ordeal. Depending on the Soviet order of battle in any particular area, some of the first troops encountered by Germans might be disciplined troops who did not rape or loot and who treated the native population correctly. Inevitably, however, sooner or later the others arrived. These were the vast majority, soldiers drafted and thrown into battle from all corners of the Soviet Union, few of whom had ever seen cities with paved streets, electric lighting, and toilets with running water, and who had moreover been taught for four years that the only good Germans were dead German men and raped German women. A typical story, one of many thousands, from Danzig:

It was about eight a.m. on that tragic day, March 27, 1945. We were just beginning to breathe more easily when the first Russian trucks stopped in our street. Before we even understood what was happening, ten, twenty, thirty plundering Russians were thrashing through our house and cellar. All inhabitants fled from their apartments and returned to the cellars. What happened before our eyes was unbelievable. Hordes of Russians swarmed robbing, looting, and singing through the cellars, all of them drunk, throwing bottled fruit off shelves, cutting up linens, clothes, cases, and cupboards. Whatever they wanted, they took, all the rest was trampled and torn to bits. . . .

And then began the most terrible time for the girls and women. I myself was nineteen and a half at the time. . . . When I saw that all the women, screaming and crying, were pulled into the cellar, I fled into our courtyard. . . .

My mother had meanwhile found me. . . . She hid me under old blankets and boxes and stood in front of me to protect me. A terrifying night followed. From the basement I heard, hour after hour, the women and girls and the "grey nuns" [who ran an old people's home next door] screaming for help. Uninterruptedly the Russians moved along the basement passageway, always looking for new victims. My mother did not move one inch away from me, even though she was shoved and beaten. Only thanks to her I wasn't found.[7]

George Kennan summarized the fate of East Germany as follows:

[6] Kopelev, *To Be Preserved Forever*, 52–3.
[7] Bundesministerium für Vertriebene, *Die Vertreibung der Deutschen Bevölkerung*, 302–3.

The disaster that befell this area with the entry of the Soviet forces has no parallel in modern European experience. There were considerable sections of it where, to judge by all existing evidence, scarcely a man, woman, or child of the indigenous population was left alive after the initial passage of Soviet forces. . . . The Russians . . . swept the native population clean in a manner that had no parallel since the days of the Asiatic hordes.[8]

Out of ten million Germans at the end of 1944 inhabiting Germany's eastern provinces and parts of western Poland, almost six million fled behind the retreating German lines, and of this number over a million perished in flight. Civilian "treks" – lines of horse-drawn or even man-hauled carts on which people had piled a few belongings – crept westward, often only a few hours ahead of the Red Army. They were regarded as fair game by the Red Air Force, and those unfortunate enough to be overtaken by the enemy found no mercy; indeed, many chose suicide.[9]

In those eastern areas of Germany given to Poland by the Soviet Union in 1945 the remaining Germans, including a goodly number who returned from their refuges in the West after hostilities ended, were pressured, more or less brutally, to leave. First they were put in camps that were no better than Nazi concentration camps at their worst – little or no food and drink for days on end, brutal warders and no medical care.

People died constantly. The little children lay dead in their beds in the morning. There was no milk. They fell asleep and died from exhaustion.

One of the guards was called Wyborski. He had an assistant who was just as brutal as he was. When they were drunk they tortured us especially much. They made people fetch sand with their bare hands to put out an imaginary fire. When the people got to the "fire" they were shot with submachine guns. I had to join in but they missed me. In the meantime my parents also died. But I don't know how.[10]

Starting in the summer of 1945, the Poles shipped trainloads full of Germans from their homes to points in the Soviet zone of occupation. The transports had little or no food, and often took many days or even weeks to arrive in Berlin, which for most was the necessary entry point to the West. Moreover, Poles along the way plundered what few belongings the refugees might have managed to save. Many thousands died of starvation or illness (primarily of typhoid fever) during the expulsions. After 1946 the expulsions became less brutal in execution,

[8] Kennan, *Memoirs*, 265.
[9] de Zayas, *Nemesis at Potsdam*, 70–2.
[10] Mühlfenzl, ed., *Geflohen und vertrieben*, 192–3.

but their inhumanity remained unchanged. By 1950, when the expulsions largely ceased, leaving less than a million Germans still living on their former lands, over seven million lived in what remained of Germany and somewhat over two million had perished.[11]

In the early 1950s, the German ministry for expellees, refugees and war victims published a massive collection of eyewitness reports and other information about the flight and expulsions, but after that silence fell on the subject. It was not until foreign scholars like the American lawyer Alfred de Zayas began taking an interest in Allied war crimes against Germans and published a study of the expulsions in 1977 that interest began to revive. Largely thanks to de Zayas, the expulsions became a permitted subject for debate in West Germany – but never in communist-ruled East Germany, where they are referred to as "resettlements." In 1980, for the first time, the expulsions became the subject of a documentary program on West German TV which led to more audience reaction than any other program in the history of West German broadcasting. The producers also published an illustrated volume of reports, and this and other publications of the 1980s indicated that the taboo on discussion of the expulsions might have been broken.

Very few people in western Europe or in the United States knew or wanted to know about the expulsions. Public attention was focused, instead, on what the Germans had done to the Jews and other victims. Of all the tragedies that were to emerge, or were yet to occur, the realities of the concentration camps were the most grotesque. In the camp of Belsen, south-west of Hamburg, what Germans had done to their prisoners, "who had once been Polish officers, land workers in the Ukraine, Budapest doctors, and students in France," as well as Germans, was discovered by the British Eighth Corps:

Under the birch trees in distant corners of the camp lay tangled heaps of naked corpses. The SS had made great efforts to dispose of the bodies of the 17,000 inmates who had died before the British arrived. They had burned many of them in [a] gigantic, stinking funeral pyre, and tossed others into a mass grave. But the prisoners died more quickly than they could be buried and when the British arrived there were 10,000 corpses still lying unburied. From some of the corpses the brains, heart and livers had been cut out and eaten by the starving survivors. The SS staff were formed into a burial party to collect the bodies and bury them. The inmates greeted their former guards with howls of execration wherever they went. Some were so tired that they fell exhausted among the corpses. If any of them tried to run away the British soldiers, filled with an implacable anger, shot them to death. . . . The ghastly job of stripping

[11] See de Zayas, *Nemesis at Potsdam*, 85–130.

the inmates and moving them out of the huts fell on the soldiers of No. 11 Light Field Ambulance. The sights and smells inside the huts were so awful that the men could only work in them for ten minutes at a time, and though they wore protective clothing twenty of them went down with typhus. The uninfected were sent in batches to the bathhouse, dusted with delousing powder, and taken by lorries, a thousand or so a day, to new accommodations in the large Panzer Training Barracks at Bergen a mile down the road. But with the best will in the world it took time to treat and evacuate 40,000 people caught up in a human calamity beyond anyone's experience. Even the simple logistics were daunting – 750 new beds had to be found from somewhere every day, for example, to keep pace with hospital admissions. . . .

On April 24 the German mayor[s] of Celle and other towns round about were summoned, as representatives of the German people, to view the horrors of Belsen. They were led to the edge of the burial pit, which was half full of corpses and skeletons, and the SS men and women were paraded on the other side of the grave. The Military Government officer in charge of nonmedical work in the camp, Colonel Spottiswoode, then read a statement in German which was broadcast across the whole camp through Derrick Sington's loud-speaker car: "What you will see here is the final and utter condemnation of the Nazi Party. It justifies every measure which the United Nations will take to exterminate that Party. What you will see here is such a disgrace to the German people that their name must be erased from the list of civilized nations. You stand here judged by what you will see in this camp. It is your lot to begin the hard task of restoring the name of the German people to the list of civilized nations. But this cannot be done until you have reared a new generation amongst whom it is impossible to find people prepared to commit such crimes. We will now begin our tour." One German mayor covered his face with his hand and wept as the Colonel spoke; another was sick.[12]

In Berlin, which in May 1945 was not yet occupied by American, British or French troops, but only by Soviet forces, Ruth Andreas-Friedrich wrote in her diary on Sunday, May 6:

In uncontrollable lust the [Soviet] army of our conquerers has fallen on the women of Berlin. We visit Hannelore Thiele, a friend and classmate of Heike. Cowering she squats on her couch. She barely looks up as we enter the room. "I should kill myself," she cried pitifully. "I cannot live like this." . . . It's terrible to look at her swollen eyes, terrible to look at her distorted face. "Was it really so bad?" I ask. She looks at me pitifully. "Seven," she says and shakes with disgust. "Seven in a row. Like animals."

Inge Zaum lives in Klein-Machnow. She is eighteen years and knew nothing of love. Now she knows everything. Sixty times repeated. "How is one to defend oneself?" she says apathetically, almost dully. "When they hammer on the door

12  Botting, *From the Ruins of the Reich*, 43, 45–6.

TABLE 1.1   POPULATION OF THE EASTERN TERRITORIES: THE GERMAN POPULATION IN THE AREAS OF EXPULSION

| *Before expulsion* | | *After expulsion (1945–50)* | |
| --- | --- | --- | --- |
| German population in 1939 | | Survived the flight and expulsion | |
| Eastern areas of Germany | 9,575,000 | from the Eastern areas of Germany | 6,944,000 |
| East Prussia | 2,473,000 | from Czechoslovakia | 2,921,000 |
| Eastern Pomerania | 1,884,000 | from other countries | 1,865,000 |
| Eastern Brandenburg | 642,000 | | 11,730,000 |
| Silesia | 4,577,000 | | |
| Czechoslovakia | 3,477,000 | Remained in the home area | |
| Baltic States and District of Memel | 250,000 | | |
| Danzig | 380,000 | in the Eastern areas of Germany | 1,101,000 |
| Poland | 1,371,000 | in Czechoslovakia | 250,000 |
| Hungary | 623,000 | in other countries | 1,294,000 |
| Yugoslavia | 537,000 | | 2,645,000 |
| Romania | 786,000 | Presumed still alive as prisoners | 72,000 |
| Total* | 16,999,000 | Total | 14,447,000 |

*In addition in the Soviet Union $1\frac{1}{2}$–2 million

| | | Dead and missing during the flight and expulsion | |
|---|---|---|---|
| Excess of births over deaths 1939–45 | +659,000 | in the Eastern areas of Germany | 1,225,000 |
| | 17,658,000 | in Czechoslovakia | 267,000 |
| | | in other countries | 619,000 |
| War losses 1939–45 | −1,100,000 | | 2,111,000 |
| German population at the end of the war | 16,588,000 | Total | 16,558,000 |
| | | | |
| War losses | 1,100,000 | Total number of German expellees in 1966 (estimated): | |
| Expulsion losses | 2,111,000 | in the Federal Republic of Germany | 10.6 million |
| Total losses | 3,211,000 | in the German Democratic Republic | 3.5 million |
| | | in Austria and other Western countries | 0.5 million |

*Note:* Figures given in this chart and those that appear elsewhere concerning the number of refugees and expellees differ depending on the source. It is, however, reasonable to conclude that the number was approximately 10 million, allowing for a margin of error of 10 per cent.

*Source:* De Zayas, *Nemesis at Potsdam*, xxv

and shoot mindlessly in all directions. New ones every night, different ones every night. When they took me the first time and forced my father to watch, I thought I was going to die."[13]

And Andreas-Friedrich continued her entries into her diary on the same day:

"Honor lost, everything lost," says a distraught father who presses a cord into the hand of his daughter who has been violated twelve times. Obediently she goes and hangs herself at the next window transom. "If one violates you, there remains nothing but death," explains a teacher to her girls' class two days before capitulation. More than half of the students draw the required inference and drown themselves in the nearest body of water. Honor lost, everything lost. Poison or bullet, cord or knife. They kill themselves by the hundreds. "Frank," I ask, "Do you understand all that?" He shakes his head. "But we must understand it. If we don't understand it, our future will have stopped before it even begins."[14]

Compared to what occurred under the Red Army, the fate of Germans in the Western zones though serious, was mild in contrast, as for example, in the British zone of occupation:

Clearly the military units of an invading army could not be expected to share their billets with enemy subjects. But there were times when it seemed exceptionally harsh to push an obviously harmless German family on to the streets with nowhere to go. On such occasions the regulations were ignored and everyone was happy – the German family was safe from DP's [displaced persons] for as long as the soldiers stayed, and the soldiers had someone to do their cooking and their washing for them. For Leonard Mosley, guest of the military governor of the city of Hanover, there could be no such compromise. If he was going to stay in the city it would have to be in a whole house from which the occupants had been evicted. With heavy heart he accompanied the requisitioning officer, a Canadian Captain, to his new quarters – a small modern dwelling in a miraculously undamaged street of modest working-class houses. The Canadian rang the door bell and an attractive teenage girl answered it. "You speak English?" asked the Captain.

"A little," the girl replied. "Please?"

"It is now two o'clock. You will leave your home by three o'clock, for this officer."

"Please?" the girl said again. "*Ach Gott, was ist? — Mama! Mama!*" She ran back into the house.

The captain turned to the war reporter. "Can't give them more than an hour," he said. "Gives them too much time. They take everything. You got a radio?"

[13] Andreas-Friedrich, *Schauplatz Berlin*, 22.
[14] Ibid., 23.

Mosley nodded.

"Guess we'll let them take their radio, then. Sheets? Okay, let them take their sheets. But nothing else. Wonder if they've got any wine?"

By 3:15 the German family had moved out and Mosley and his friend had moved in.[15]

At "Zero Hour" the greatest obstacles and sufferings in the Western zones were not caused as much by the acts of the occupying forces, as by the mere destruction and disorganization. For example, normal social relationships were disrupted or changed in unforeseen ways. One million soldiers were prisoners of war, and another million were missing. By October 1946 approximately eight million requests to locate missing persons were in the hands of the Red Cross. By 1980, 35 years later, the Red Cross had solved almost all the cases; but 30,000 people were still unaccounted for, their fate unknown.

In the summer and fall of 1945, thousands of refugees were arriving in Berlin each day. By October 1.3 million had arrived, and before they continued their journey they received one bowl of soup and about three ounces of bread. These terrible circumstances gave real meaning to the phrase, "necessity is the mother of invention;" for example, sawdust was mixed with food to increase the quantity and, for the sake of make-believe, potatoes were served in the shape of a fish. Entire trains were plundered and rows of trees lining streets were completely cut down for fuel.

While only about a quarter of industrial capacity was destroyed, physical destruction was everywhere. An equally grave problem was a lack of supplies and capital for renewed production and housing. Not only was over half the housing in many major cities destroyed, but the pressure on the remainder was vastly increased by the arrival, mostly in 1945–7, of approximately 9.5 million refugees from the East.[16] These problems could not begin to be seriously addressed until a political and trans-regional structure of reconstruction had been created.

[15] Botting, *From the Ruins of the Reich*, 33–4.

[16] In the *10th Quarterly Report on Germany* (Jan. 1 to Mar. 31, 1952) issued by HICOG in the spring of 1952, the number of refugees living in West Germany is given as 9.8 million: "About 9.8 million people who now reside in the Federal Republic lived outside the Federal Republic's boundaries at the outbreak of World War II. The bulk of these people, some 8 million strong, consists of Germans who came from German areas east of the Oder–Neisse Line or from countries such as Czechoslovakia, Poland, Hungary, and Romania. In addition there are some 1,700,000 persons from the Soviet Zone or from East Berlin who have sought refuge in the Federal Republic for political or other reasons. One of the chief causes of the present plight of these new citizens is their uneven distribution over the eleven states of the Federal Republic" (pp. 56–7).

A second, even more important aspect of the destruction wreaked by Soviet and Western forces before and during their invasion of Germany was the loss of life. Postwar calculations, never precisely determined, yielded a figure of 6.5 million German lives lost as a consequence of the war. Of this figure, 3.2 million or about half were soldiers, that is, men mainly in their physically most active years. Another two million men were severely disabled. One result of these casualties was, clearly, a surplus of women over men in 1945 in the age group from 18 to 35. The cohort of 1918 – which included the later chancellor Helmut Schmidt – was especially badly affected; about two-thirds of all German males born in 1918 did not survive the war.[17]

The surplus of women (or shortage of men) in the years when, under normal circumstances, people choose careers, marry, have children, and settle down, had momentous long-term social, psychological, and economic consequences. In 1945, at Zero Hour, the immediate effect was both physical and psychological. The lack of men meant, first, that a great deal of the initial labor of clearing ruins and starting industries and services fell on women, thus continuing and accelerating the incorporation of women into the labor force that had begun during the war. Many women were obliged to fend for themselves as they never had before, although of course many were already used to long absences of their menfolk on military duty. As hundreds of thousands of young women went through the ordeal of surviving on their own, most learned that they could do so; doing hard labor with very little food, and in many cases, with little hope or expectation of a family, and in others, with children to support. They achieved a resigned self-confidence that later played a great part in promoting movements for sexual equality in the workplace and in society in general, even though these movements did not become serious factors until long after the war.

In one of the most impressive and vivid accounts of the "treks", but even more importantly, of the role that women played in 1945 and thereafter, Christian Graf von Krockow recounts the story of his family – his stepfather, his mother, and his sister – who lived near Stolp, west of Danzig (renamed Gdansk after the war), in Pomerania. The story was told to Krockow by his sister, Libussa Fritz-Krockow, but was not published until 1988. In her early twenties in 1945 and 1946, Libussa Fritz-Krockow saved her family with extraordinary courage. She was, in her own words, not a heroine, but simply had no choice:

[17] 179,000 males born in 1918 survived World War II, compared to 316,686 females, according to Ausschuss der deutschen Statistiker, *Volks- und Berufszählung vom 29. Oktober 1946*, 1: 50. Total births in Germany in 1918 were 495,953 males and 460,298 females (figures exclude Alsace-Lorraine), according to Statistisches Reichsamt, *Statistisches Jahrbuch 1921/1922*, 23.

Because the circumstances demanded it, I have increasingly assumed the initiative that Father Jesko has lost. It confuses and humiliates him; it destroys his view of the world and wounds his self-confidence. And suddenly I also sense how wrong I am. Father is not afraid for himself, but for us women, for mother and me. What he has lost, that is above all his pride, his male role as protector.[18]

And so Libussa Fritz-Krockow stole food, and dealt on the black market, and bribed Russian soldiers and Polish officers, in order to feed her child, born on March 23, 1945, and her mother and stepfather and relatives; despite the fact that her stepfather accused her of being a thief, of bringing shame to the family, and of losing her honor. But it was not a question of bringing dishonor to the family. It was simply the only way to survive. The Russian soldiers sent all of the farming equipment to the Soviet Union, and forced the German women to drive all of the farm animals in herds to the Soviet Union as well; so that by the winter of 1945–6 there was almost nothing left to eat.

After the Russian soldiers had stolen and raped, came the Poles to whom the Russians had given the administrative authority over the areas east of the Oder and western Neisse rivers, including Pomerania, that were now to become Polish. The cities were renamed with Polish names, and the Poles began their turn at pillage and rape. And, as the Germans in the autumn and winter of 1945–6 were forced to leave, to go to the Soviet zone of occupation and further west, the trains they rode in – in sealed box cars – were again pillaged, and the women again raped, this time by the Poles. And since these Germans could carry very little with them, they had taken only their valuables – money and jewels – and they arrived in what was left of Germany with nothing. Those German men from these provinces who had not been killed or who were not in prison camps, fell back on their honor, which was of little help.

Oh these Prussians, these German men! They are so strong, simply fabulous, one can conquer half the world with them: The dignity of the office and the task, the obligation and the honor, victory or catastrophe! But in catastrophe they are suddenly of no use at all anymore, not even to steal spinach, and we, the women, have to be responsible for figuring out how to feed our children. ... I even understand these men. One educated them this way, from generation to generation. Only one thing: to stoop to steal spinach and to crawl on your stomach just to survive, entirely without honor and office, for that they are worthless. That remains for us to do. ... What I learned and found in those gloomy years that lie behind me, concerning self-confidence and independence: God knows, it was an expensive purchase that I will not throw away, for any price.[19]

[18] Krockow, *Die Stunde der Frauen*, 106–7.
[19] Ibid., 123, 250.

Not only had the war taken the lives of millions of young men, it had also destroyed, seemingly for good, the devotion to masculine and martial values so characteristic of Germany in earlier years. As the war ended, the sense that many Germans already had in 1939, namely that it was a pointless war that could lead to no good end, returned with a vengeance after the years when the sheer need for survival and solidarity in the face of enemy air attacks overrode earlier skepticism. German men, so many of whom had claimed to see the realization of their innermost being in battle and combat and in heroic devotion to duty, however irrational, had not only lost the war, but also the respect of many of their fellow-citizens. Military values and skills were less than irrelevant to the task of survival or reconstruction; moreover, they were seen as dangerous and provocative. Edwin Hartrich commented at the time:

There was a widespread revulsion to the war and all things associated with it which had sunk deep into the German psyche. The militarists had become disillusioned and converted to pacifism. . . . When it was all over there was no hero's welcome as there had been after World War I for the 2.5 million soldier survivors of this war. The German soldier's combat record was degraded for having served at the command of the Nazi war criminals.[20]

When Soviet troops arrived and began to rape the women, the men, the self-styled defenders of German honor, including the honor of German women, were conspicuously unable to prevent the worst from happening. Many were simply not there or already dead. Those others who were present, cut an even worse figure. If they tried to protect their women, they would be killed. So, apart from a few foolhardy heroes, most looked aside, solving the cruel dilemma by telling themselves that they owed it to their families, including the very women who were being raped, to survive. And they were right, but it was a terrible choice to make. Although in most cases the argument was sound enough, it was hardly consoling, and it perfectly illustrated what many came to feel was the irrelevance of traditional notions of male duty or sex roles. Only gradually, as the economy improved enough to give most of them jobs, were German men able to recover their self-esteem and to channel their energies into the task of reconstruction.

Even so, life never returned to the old pattern. Patriarchal and masculine values were forever changed, and, in the view of many, were made ridiculous by the war. In 1948, a young director, Helmut Käutner, presented a dilemma of masculinity and the failure of masculine virtues in a film entitled *Der Apfel ist ab* (The Apple is Fallen). It elicited strong

[20] Hartrich, *Fourth and Richest Reich*, 61.

protest from Michael Cardinal Faulhaber, the archbishop of Munich, who criticized the way the film dealt with the issue of original sin. Yet, no society in the West has been quite as loud or consistent in its satirization of masculine pride, devotion to military duty, or patriotism, as West Germany, and no society has been as fearful of allowing its own military efforts to set values for society in general.[21]

The skepticism or even cynicism regarding military and patriarchal values in the Germany of 1945 was part of the general "basic emotion" of Zero Hour. This "basic emotion" or, rather, combination of emotions and feelings which was so widespread that survivors forty years later again and again referred to it, included two other related aspects: a contempt for the older generation, those really or allegedly responsible for the war and all that went with it, and a widespread collapse of interest in or commitment to political ideology. National Socialism itself did not disappear overnight, but professed loyalty to its ideology did. It took perhaps 15 years for vestigial Nazi ideas to become genuinely marginal, but even in 1945, those Nazis who thought Hitler was right remained silent. At most, they may have constituted one-quarter of the adult population.

The combined effect of the three aspects of the "basic emotion" – skepticism regarding masculine and military values, loss of faith and interest in ideology, and distrust of the older generation – was an overwhelming wish: "Never again!" In fact, this prevailing condemnation of the war had, in addition, other practical explanations. So-called "anti-fascist groups" sprang into existence in 1945 as the end of the war approached. And once it ended there were many who claimed to be "anti-fascists," but who had joined these groups only as the war was ending in order to protect themselves. One way to exonerate oneself was to denounce others; another was to change one's name.[22]

Postwar German history was also influenced by how Germans dealt with the inevitable feelings of guilt in 1945, of who was responsible, and for what. It is difficult, almost half a century later, to understand why the crime, violence and injustice of the Nazi regime – that was not laid bare to the world until Zero Hour – did not result in permanent resentment and recrimination in Germany, whether the victims bore their torment and suffering in concentration camps, or whether they were brutally expelled from their homelands.

Perhaps one explanation lies with the nature of the human spirit and how it deals with tragedy of almost incomprehensible magnitude. For

[21] Glaser, *Kulturgeschichte der BRD*, 1: 59–65; Vogel, "Familie," in *Die BRD*, ed. Benz, 2: 98–9, 116–17.

[22] Andreas-Friedrich, *Schauplatz Berlin*, 34; Steininger, *Deutsche Geschichte*, 1: 101–2; and Klessmann, *Die doppelte Staatsgründung*, 396–400.

the human spirit to survive it needs hope; without it, it will wither and die. In Germany, in 1945, there was certainly denunciation, resentment, and recrimination, but the Germans also turned to the expectation of a rebirth of civilized life that hope could give. To dwell on the past would solve little, and perhaps this is one reason why most Germans – after the process of denazification and judicial punishment – focused on hope for the future, rather than on incessant condemnation of each other. In the course of making restitution, they avoided the psychological burden of having to explain to themselves why they formerly accepted the inhumane treatment of Germans by Germans. A few accepted the burden of responsibility for torture and death. Most merely acknowledged the Holocaust as an act committed by a political regime against a certain people, and not by a German government against German citizens.

# 6

# The Potsdam Conference:
# Unworkable Compromises

In the last weeks before his death on April 12, 1945 President Roosevelt had begun to change his mind about the chances of collaboration with Stalin after the war. He had begun, in fact, to accept Churchill's view that once the Nazis were gone, the Soviets would constitute at least as great a threat to the democracies of Europe. Truman instinctively shared these views, but from the time of his succession to the presidency until early 1946 he was influenced at different times by advisors who believed that Stalin was not really hostile to the West; in fact, that the real troublemaker after the war was likely to be Britain. The British government, they argued, was resentful that the US was now the chief power in the West and would use any trick to sow discord between the US and Stalin in order to preserve its own power. Moreover, they insisted, the British would want to keep their empire and their colonies to justify their world role, and America should not let itself be drawn into protecting imperialism of this nature.

Churchill, at various times during the war, and especially at Yalta, had been at least as friendly toward Stalin as any American figure. But he later declared that, on the very day of the German surrender on May 8, he realized fully that "the Soviet menace . . . had already replaced the Nazi foe."[1] Thus, from that day onward, it was Churchill, not Truman, who insisted on the Soviet danger and who tried to convince the American president to join him in resisting it. Only a few days after the German surrender, on May 11, Churchill cabled Truman proposing a meeting of the Big Three "at some agreed unshattered town in Germany." The British prime minister thought it was important that they not meet in any place under direct Soviet control. "*Meanwhile,*" he added, "*I earnestly hope that the American front will not recede from the now*

---

[1] Churchill, *Second World War*, 6: 569.

*agreed tactical lines*" (Churchill's italics).[2] By this Churchill meant that he wanted the American forces to stay where they were when the war ended, and not move back to the line of demarcation between the occupation zones as agreed by the EAC and confirmed at Yalta. In fact, US forces were on the line of the river Elbe and thus occupied the entire south-west corner of the Soviet zone. Churchill was clearly already thinking in terms of pressure and counter-pressure; he distrusted Stalin and thought that by occupying some of the Soviet zone he and Truman might force Stalin to cooperate with the Western Allies in the occupation of Germany.

The most important issue concerned Poland. Churchill was furious that Stalin had, first of all, installed a communist group to run the Polish government, thus depriving the Polish people once again of their liberty, for which Britain had gone to war in 1939. He was angry because Stalin had kept the eastern part of Poland acquired from Adolf Hitler, thereby maintaining the terms of the iniquitous Nazi-Soviet Pact of 1939, and had compensated the Polish government, now under communist control, by the gratuitous gift of the German territories east of the Oder and western Neisse rivers. Not only did Germany need the coal as well as the industrial and food products of these provinces, but it was a cruel irony that they should be given as a gift to a Polish government that was a dictatorship.

The next day, Churchill sent another cable to Truman, which became famous in history as the "Iron Curtain" telegram. In it, he repeated his view that Stalin was hostile to the West and that Soviet power posed a new and terrible threat to a war-weakened Europe.

I have always worked for friendship with Russia, but, like you, I feel deep anxiety because of their misinterpretation of the Yalta decisions, their attitude towards Poland, ... the combination of Russian power and the territories under their control or occupied, combined with the Communist technique in so many other countries, and above all their power to maintain very large armies in the field for a long time. What will be the position in a year or two, when the British and American Armies have melted and the French has not yet been formed on any major scale, when we may have a handful of divisions, mostly French, and when Russia may choose to keep two or three hundred on active service?

An iron curtain is drawn down upon their front. We do not know what is going on behind. .... Meanwhile the attention of our peoples will be occupied in inflicting severities upon Germany, which is ruined and prostrate, and it would be open to the Russians in a very short time to advance if they chose to the waters of the North Sea and the Atlantic.[3]

[2] Ibid., 571.
[3] Ibid., 573.

Churchill's anxiety at first availed him little. On June 5, 1945, the commanders-in-chief of the Allied forces issued, in Berlin, a "Declaration Regarding the Defeat of Germany and the Assumption of Supreme Authority by the Allied Powers." In it they stated that the four Allied governments "hereby assume supreme authority with respect to Germany," but this "does not affect [*sic*] the annexation of Germany." Furthermore, these four governments "will hereafter determine the boundaries of Germany," and "will take such steps, including the complete disarmament and demilitarization of Germany, as they deem requisite for future peace and security. . . . All German authorities and the German people shall carry out unconditionally the requirements of the Allied Representatives."[4]

On the same day the Allies issued a "Statement on Control Machinery in Germany," in which they confirmed the EAC agreements of September and November 1944 concerning the Control Council, the Coordinating Committee, and the Kommandatura. The Control Council held supreme authority over the entire country, and was composed of the military leaders from each of the four zones, at first, General Marie Pierre Koenig (France), Field Marshal Sir Bernard Montgomery (Great Britain), Marshal Georgi Zhukov (Soviet Union) and General Eisenhower (US). They did not specify a starting date for the operation of the Control Council, nor the conditions under which its work would be terminated. This failure was a first sign of the fundamental incompatibility of conflicting aims in Germany which soon after emerged at the Potsdam Conference.

The headquarters of the Control Council was a

546–room German court building known as the Kammergericht (Appellate Court) and located . . . in the borough of Schöneberg [Berlin].

Each day . . . the four national colors were raised high on four identical flag-staffs in front of the building, the colors on the right being those of the nation which was in the chair at the moment. The conference room itself had been the scene of the notorious People's Court in which the fiendish Nazi judge, Dr Roland Freissler, had sentenced to death after a travesty of a trial the leaders in the July 20, 1944, effort to kill Hitler.[5]

The Control Council's purpose was to coordinate allied policy throughout Germany, and it began operations in July 1945. But, in fact, each of the four zones was administered separately, with economic, cultural and political policies and programs designed and implemented by the respective occupying power. The result was that the Soviet and Western

[4] Dept of State, *Documents on Germany*, 33, 37–8.
[5] Clay, *Decision in Germany*, 35.

zones became, almost immediately, estranged from each other, and increasingly so with the passage of time, as they conformed to the ideals of their occupying powers.

Truman, and indeed most Americans apart from Kennan and a few others, still wanted, in the summer of 1945, to trust Stalin and believed that if he were not provoked the wartime alliance could yet be saved. There was, therefore, no question of maintaining the American occupation of part of the Soviet zone to put pressure on the Russians; US forces withdrew as agreed in the first days of July, at precisely the same time that the Soviets permitted the Americans, the British, and the French to enter their respective sectors of Berlin, almost two months after the end of the war. The Soviets, indeed, had insisted that they would not allow the Western Allies to enter the German capital until the Americans had begun withdrawal from the Soviet zone. Truman and Eisenhower were not prepared to test the proposition.

If the Americans still wanted to trust Stalin, not so Konrad Adenauer, the newly appointed mayor of the city of Cologne. He too, just as Churchill had done before him, worried about the "iron curtain" that had come down on the Russian front. On July 5, 1945, in a personal letter to Hans Rörig (editor of the *Kölnische Zeitung* until the end of the war), Adenauer, asking for strictest confidentiality, wrote:

> I am looking at the developments in Germany with [growing] concern. Russia is lowering an iron curtain. I do not believe that it [Russia] will let itself be influenced by the Central Control Commission when it comes to the administration of the one half of Germany under its responsibility.[6]

His conclusion, as Churchill's, proved prophetic.

Ten weeks after the war the leaders of the Big Three, Truman, Stalin, and Churchill, met together for the last time at Potsdam near Berlin from July 17 to August 2, 1945. All three heads of state were accompanied by their foreign ministers, James Byrnes (USA), Vyacheslav Molotov (USSR) and Anthony Eden (Great Britain), and large delegations of advisors. Since Potsdam was located in the Soviet zone of occupation, it had fallen to the Russians to prepare for the accommodations and meetings. Truman, who arrived two days early, used this time for a private meeting with Churchill, and, on the day before the start of the conference, was visited by Stalin in the "Little White House," as Truman's residence in a manor house on the shores of Lake Griebnitz, had quickly been baptized. The meetings themselves took place in the

---

[6] *Konrad Adenauer: Briefe*, 16.

Cecilienhof Palace, in whose garden the Russians "had planted a twenty-four-foot star of red geraniums."[7]

The idea for the meeting came from Churchill and Truman, who recognized that it would be preferable to achieve President Roosevelt's hope that the wartime alliance with the Soviet Union could continue as the foundation of world peace. The conference concerned primarily the administration of Germany and the question of Germany's borders. The boundaries of the German territory to be given to Poland were, so Stalin asserted at Potsdam, agreed upon by the British as early as 1941, before the United States entered the war, and reaffirmed by the British and the US at Yalta in February 1945. The British and the Americans apparently believed that they had secured Soviet agreement that Poland's border with the Soviet Union would be the so-called Curzon Line, which was virtually the same as the demarcation line agreed upon by Hitler and Stalin when they divided Poland in 1939, and that Poland's border with Germany would be defined by the Oder and *eastern* Neisse rivers. This German-Polish border would have left the central and western parts of Silesia, an agricultural and industrial area with three million inhabitants and including the city of Breslau, as a part of Germany, and therefore a part of the Soviet zone of occupation.

At Potsdam, however, the British and the United States attempted to introduce changes to the boundary agreement of Yalta, as they now understood it,[8] because the Soviet Union had already given the communist regime in Poland the administrative authority for all of the German territory east of the Oder and *western* Neisse rivers. In effect, this meant that the Soviet government had violated the agreement that Churchill and Truman thought they had concluded with Stalin at Yalta, namely, that the boundary dividing Poland and Germany would be the Oder and *eastern* Neisse rivers. Churchill and Truman maintained "that we had agreed to divide Germany into four zones of occupation, based on her 1937 frontiers. . . . I [Churchill] did object to Silesia being treated as though it were already part of Poland. Stalin persisted that it was impossible to upset the present state of affairs." The "present state of affairs" meant that all of the Germans living east of the Oder and *western* Neisse rivers, namely eight and one half million people, were subject to expulsion into what remained of Germany by the Polish regime. Therefore, between July 17 and 25, Churchill urged that the forcible transfer of eight and a half million Germans was "wrong," and that the food and fuel supplies from the Oder–Neisse provinces were essential if the

[7] Bohlen, *Witness to History*, 226–7.
[8] Graml, *Die Alliierten und die Teilung Deutschlands*, 17–19.

German population in the Western zones was to survive.[9] He wrote later:

> I intended, if I were returned by the electorate, as was generally expected, to come to grips with the Soviet Government ... neither I nor Mr Eden would ever have agreed to the Western Neisse being the frontier line. The line of the Oder and the Eastern Neisse had already been recognized as the Polish compensation for retiring to the Curzon Line, but the overrunning by the Russian armies of the territory up to and even beyond the Western Neisse was never and would never have been agreed to by any Government of which I was the head. Here was no point of principle only, but rather an enormous matter of fact affecting about three additional millions of displaced people. ... All this negotiation was cut in twain and brought to an untimely conclusion by the result of the General Election ... but the destruction of the British National Government and my removal from the scene at the time when I still had much influence and power rendered it impossible for satisfactory solutions to be reached.[10]

British elections had been held on July 5, but because so many voters were spread across the world in the armed forces, the outcome was not available until July 26, which fell in the middle of the Potsdam Conference. Churchill flew home to hear the results, and when he saw that the Labour party under Clement Attlee had won an overwhelming victory he immediately tendered his resignation to King George VI, who called on Attlee to form the new government. Attlee, who had not really expected to win, was not well versed in foreign policy, yet he was obliged to travel immediately to Potsdam to lead the British delegation in Churchill's place. He took over as an instinctive opponent of Churchill's hard line; as a socialist, Attlee wanted to believe in postwar collaboration with Stalin as well as in welfare reform at home.

Even if Churchill had won the election, however, it is doubtful that his continued presence at Potsdam would have produced any changes in Poland's borders and those of the Oder–Neisse territories. The Polish communist regime, in control of Poland in 1945, was an instrument of the Soviet Union and the creation of Stalin. It was unrealistic for any Western statesman to believe that Stalin's generous gifts of German territory to Poland could be modified ex post facto. Stalin and the Polish regime not only wanted the territory, but considered it a symbol of victory. Indeed, in later years they propagated the idea – absurd to anyone familiar with West German politics – that the West German government wanted to recapture these former German provinces by

[9]  Churchill, *Second World War*, 6: 654, 657, 658.
[10]  Ibid., 672–4.

force, and thereby sought to generate solidarity among the Polish people with a communist regime they resented.

Stalin's annexation of the eastern provinces was just as unusual and legally dubious. Annexation, as distinct from military occupation in time of war, requires the sanction of the government whose territory is annexed. Only a German government could legally give away German territory. In 1970, West Germany declared that it had no claims on the Oder-Neisse territories. In 1990, before unification, both German governments issued similar declarations. Since unification was not accompanied by a full peace treaty, the question remained legally open, but the declarations of 1990 closed it for all practical purposes.

Quite apart from the lack of a legal sanction for the annexations themselves, merely the expulsions of the native population against its will, and the gross atrocities and violations of international law under which those expulsions took place, destroyed the validity of the Allied dispositions. The principles set forth in the Atlantic Charter, for which the Allied governments fought – Britain and the US unambiguously, and Stalin ostensibly – were political freedom and the self-determination of peoples. To signal the war's end with annexation and expulsions violated these principles in the most flagrant fashion. This development did not bode well either for the seriousness of the Western democracies' commitment to their own principles or for the chances of agreement on the postwar peace order for which those democracies hoped.

At the Potsdam Conference, the British leaders and Truman sought to obtain Stalin's agreement to specific procedures for governing Germany and to general measures for postwar cooperation. The official Protocol of the Conference indicated a far greater measure of agreement than in fact existed. This was partly achieved by dwelling at length on the evils of Nazism, the responsibility of Germany for the war and the need to eradicate Nazism and militarism. These may have been worthy thoughts and understandable at the time, but they had little relevance to the task at hand, which was to establish practical principles of administration. The Big Three were able to agree, at least verbally, on the need for what became known as the "four d's:" denazification, demilitarization, decartelization (breaking up large industrial conglomerates), and democratization. But they were not able to agree on Germany's boundaries with Poland, nor on how to put into practice the "four d's."

Germany was to be regarded as a single economic unit, and the German economy was to be regulated by the Allies jointly; their authority was to be exercised through a unified German administration. However, these statements of purpose, which had no force per se, were vitiated by the simultaneous failure of the Conference to reach agreement on the most important economic issue from the Allied perspective, which was reparations to be paid by Germany to the victims of German aggression, in addition to dismantling all German industry that could be used to support military purposes.

Initially, the US and Britain proposed that the entire Reich territory as of 1937 – that is, including the eastern provinces – should be the basis for calculating reparations and should be treated as one entity. The Soviet government refused, since it regarded the eastern provinces as no longer part of Germany. The US secretary of state, James F. Byrnes, then proposed that the four zones be treated as wholly separate for reparations purposes. The Soviets would extract their reparations from their own zone and the Western Allies likewise. In return for Soviet agreement to this, Byrnes said, the US and Britain would accept Polish and Soviet control of Germany east of the Oder and western Neisse rivers – that is to say, control of the eastern provinces – subject to final settlement of Germany's borders in a peace treaty.

The result was a fateful compromise. The failure to agree on a common reparations policy was in effect also a failure to agree on treating Germany as an economic unit. The decision to allow the Soviets to extract their full claim in reparations from only their own zone, was an act, deliberate or not, of devastating consequences. The reparations that followed deprived the surviving Germans in that zone of their remaining means of livelihood.

In fact, the Soviet Union not only dismantled and removed entire industrial plants from their zone, but received machinery and industrial supplies from the western zones as well. This decision was made in principle at Yalta, when the Big Three decided that Germany's total reparation obligation would be $20 billion, of which the Soviet Union would receive one-half. At Potsdam this agreement was refined so that the Soviet government would take its reparations from its zone, but would also receive 10 per cent of reparations taken by the Western Allies from their zones in exchange for the supply of certain raw materials from the Soviet zone, such as food, wool, and coal. The Soviet government did not honor this agreement, however, and therefore General Clay halted reparation shipments to the Soviet zone in May 1946.

The compromise in Potsdam, in effect, violated the Western Allies' own principles and promises by imposing unnecessary hardship on millions of Germans and failed to achieve the realistic purpose of a unified administration of Germany to secure its development in an approved direction. In view of the balance of military power the Western Allies were unable to oppose successfully the methods of resettlement, plunder, expulsion, and annexation by which Stalin and the Polish,

Czech, Hungarian, and German communists were imposing their rule in what used to be Central Europe, and which would come to be known in the future as Eastern Europe. Although it was not their intention, at Potsdam the Western Allies appeared to be telling the victims of those methods – the peoples of Germany and Central Europe – that the victory over fascism and Nazi Germany was not a victory for freedom and democracy in all of Germany or in all of Europe. Instead, the conference demonstrated that the Soviet Union and the Western powers had contradictory and incompatible interests in Germany and Europe, and, equally important, very different methods of trying to attain them. Within a year Stalin, by his actions, had persuaded both Attlee and Truman to resist and oppose the policies of the Soviet Union, a decision that led directly to the Marshall Plan of 1947, the formation of the North Atlantic Alliance in 1947–9, and the establishment of the Federal Republic of Germany in the latter year.

The Big Three did agree on a framework for future consultation to secure world peace. They formed the Council of Foreign Ministers (CFM), consisting of the United States, Britain, the Soviet Union, and France. It was the western hope that the CFM would become the vehicle to continue the wartime alliance and to maintain the special responsibility of the Big Three for world peace or, as the Soviets phrased it, "common security." The pessimists, among them Churchill, who was no longer in power, recognized that if the CFM was to fulfill its purpose, there had to exist a common definition of what peace and common security might mean, but the Soviet behavior in Germany and in Poland prior to the meeting in Potsdam did not suggest such a common definition was possible.

As an instrument of European order, however, the CFM proved to have little significance. As an institution, it was based on the notion that the wartime Allies, leaders of the so-called United Nations, agreed on all important and vital issues of world peace. Since this was not the case, it became, in fact, a forum for acrimonious conflict which was sometimes glossed over by meaningless communiques. That the CFM was contemplated and created, but then developed a history very different from the intention, perfectly illustrates the change from what seemed to be wartime unity to Cold War.

Looking back in 1957, twelve years after Potsdam, former President Truman wrote a letter to his last secretary of state, Dean Acheson; a letter dated March 13, 1957, and found in his presidential papers, but which Truman never actually sent:

I hardly ever look back for the purpose of contemplating "what might have been:" Potsdam brings to mind "what might have been." ... Certainly ...

Russia had no program except to take over the free part of Europe, kill as many Germans as possible, and fool the Western Alliance. Britain only wanted to control the Eastern Mediterranean, keep India, oil in Persia, the Suez Canal, and whatever else was floating loose.

There was an innocent idealist [Truman] at one corner of that Round Table who wanted free waterways, Danube-Rhine-Kiel Canal, Suez, Black Sea Straits, Panama all free, a restoration of Germany, France, Italy, Poland, Czechoslovakia, Rumania, and the Balkans, and a proper treatment of Latvia, Lithuania, Finland, free Philippines, Indonesia, Indo-China, a Chinese Republic, and a free Japan.

What a show that was! But a large number of agreements were reached in spite of the setup – only to be broken as soon as the unconscionable Russian Dictator returned to Moscow! And I liked the little son of a bitch. . . .[11]

There was a curious and ironic postscript to the conference in Potsdam, a fact that was made public by the Soviet news organization Tass in May 1990. A trusted British intelligence officer who defected to the Soviet Union in 1963, Kim Philby, had provided Stalin the strategy of the Big Three. According to Tass, "Philby's reports were responsible for Stalin's cunning smile at the conference, which was noted by a number of journalists in attendance."[12]

[11] Ferrell, ed., "Truman at Potsdam." *American Heritage* 31, no. 4 (June/July 1980): 47.
[12] *San Francisco Chronicle*, May 10, 1990.

# 7

# Germany: Post Potsdam

The German military leaders who signed the unconditional surrender on May 8, 1945, had been authorized to do so by Grand Admiral Karl Dönitz, who had been appointed president of the Reich by Adolf Hitler the day the latter committed suicide in his bunker on April 30, under the Reich Chancellery in Berlin. Dönitz had constituted a government in the picturesque town of Flensburg on the Danish border in the British zone of occupation. The Allies recognized this government de facto when they obtained the unconditional surrender of German forces on May 8, 1945. Further, the Allies did not demand that the government surrender political authority and accept the dismemberment of Germany, only that it order its armed forces to surrender. Having initially recognized the Dönitz government de facto, however, the Allies then formally arrested its members on May 23. The arrest and dispersal of the last Reich government – since it had not been asked or compelled to surrender political authority – was a clear violation of the principles of international law, which the Allies had presumably fought to uphold.

The Allies argued at the time that Hitler's Reich government, by unleashing war in 1939, had already put itself so far beyond the bounds of international law that there could be no question of applying its principles to that government or its successor. They certainly had a point. Karl Dönitz, for his part, was a convinced Nazi trusted by Hitler and by no means among those officers who secretly conspired against the regime or who took part in the failed coup of July 20, 1944. During his two weeks of freedom in Flensburg as head of the German state Dönitz did nothing to distance himself from Hitler's criminal regime. For example, he could have formally abrogated the so-called Nuremberg race laws of 1935 that officially sanctioned discrimination against and exploitation of Jews. Even though such an action would have had no real effect, since Dönitz' government controlled no territory and no institutions, it would have signaled his intent to make a new start. Having made this argument, however, it must also be acknowledged that the very point of international law is that civilized nations apply it even in dealing with their enemies. If civilized nations only apply it among themselves and thereby observe a double standard, it has little moral or political value.

Although there has been no government of the German Reich since that day in 1945, the Reich did not, in international or constitutional law, cease to exist. The Reich merely became incapable of acting since on that day it lost all its power, organs, and institutions. All the Allied measures regarding Germany, from the wartime plans for zonal occupation, reparations, dismantling of industry, and denazification, to the actual policies as carried out in occupied Germany were, as the historian H. W. Koch points out, "*res inter alios acta* – the Latin expression in international law for a procedure in which alien powers deal with a third power which has not offered its agreement, and therefore is not compelled to accept what has happened, however long ago."[1] This legal dilemma was one important part of the postwar German question.

In their joint declaration of June 5, 1945, the Allies declared that they had no intention of annexing German territory or abolishing it as a state. Therefore, legal scholars later concluded that they intended Germany to continue to exist in some form. This was confirmed by the Allied expectation, expressed during the war and again in the Potsdam Protocol, that at some future date the Allied powers would sign a peace treaty with a responsible and legally constituted German government. What happened, however, was that the Allies could not agree on the constitution of a German government, so they each terminated their occupation in different ways, transferring authority to German governments which they had authorized, and so ended the state of war de facto, but not de jure.

The ensuing development of postwar German government created a paradox. For the war to be terminated and a European peace established, there had to be a peace treaty with Germany defining Germany's place in Europe and its obligations. But the Allies could make no such peace treaty with Germany because there was no German government to make peace with. There was no German government because the only realistic way for a German government to come into being after May 23, 1945, was by Allied permission, since the Allies had occupied Germany and were the sole source of political and administrative authority. They had, by their own will and acts, put the German state into abeyance, but had not abolished it. However, they could not agree on the logical next

---

[1]  Koch, *Constitutional History of Germany*, 316.

step, which would have been for them to return authority to a German government they could accept. Stalin would not tolerate any German government acceptable to the Western Allies and vice versa. The Germans themselves could have attempted to reconstitute a government, but Allied political differences made that impossible, given Allied control. In addition, the Allies could have prevented any such attempt even if enough Germans could have agreed to make it.

The united state of Germany, therefore, went into legal and political limbo on May 23, 1945. Neither the democratic Federal Republic nor the communist German Democratic Republic – both established in 1949 – was a government of a united Germany, though the Federal Republic asserted until 1969 that it had the right to speak for all Germans, since it was the only democratically elected German government. In several important rulings following its formation in 1951, the Federal Constitutional Court stated that the Reich continued to exist and that the Federal Republic was not its successor, but rather represented a political reorganization of part of Germany. The Reich continued to exist, the court argued, because the only way for a state to be abolished was for its territory to be annexed by foreign powers. Neither in 1945 nor at any other time had the Allies declared any intention to annex all of Germany. Nor had the German authorities themselves voluntarily dissolved the Reich. It therefore lived on, but in limbo, since it had no executive, legislative, or other administrative agencies.

During the first years of the occupation most Germans hoped and assumed that eventually the four Allies together would withdraw and allow the Germans to reconstitute a united Reich administration. The new or reformed political parties held "Reich conventions" in 1945–6. When the Germans recognized, in 1947–8, that a Reich government would not be restored, at least not unless they accepted Soviet control, those living in the Western occupation zones agreed to establish a federal republic as a provisional measure. The paradox of an emerging provisional government that was credible and real, versus an imaginary, but authentic and permanent government that was unobtainable, remained to trouble Germans and their leaders for decades after 1945.

From the Potsdam Conference onward, the history of Germany became the history of Germans in the different zones. From this point forward, therefore, the development of the three Western zones became the history of the Federal Republic. This book treats events in the Soviet zone, later to become the German Democratic Republic, mainly in view of their effect on events and people in the Western part of Germany.

The period from the Conference to the establishment of the Federal Republic fell into three phases. The first phase ran from the Conference

Map 1.3    This map shows Germany in its borders of 1937 and the division of the country at the end of World War II in 1945.
*Source*: Department of State

to the winter of 1946–7. During 1946 there occurred a shift of opinion in leading Western circles that finally ended the illusion of common ground with the Soviet government and the associated illusion that the task of policy in Germany was to punish the Germans and not to introduce political pluralism and democracy. Even during the first phase, there were many people in the Allied (henceforth, this word will mean *Western* Allied) occupation forces who were more interested in reeducation than in punishment. But the main thrust of official Allied policy and practice remained one of punishment, vengeance, and future deterrence, although the ground was slowly shifting at the same time.

Map 1.4   The partition of Germany as applied to Great Britain and the United States.
*Source*:  De Zayas, *Nemesis at Potsdam*, 186

The second phase ran from the amalgamation of the US and British zones and the constitution of the Bizonal Economic Council, the embryo of a West German government, through the abolition of rationing and the currency reform carried out by that Council and approved by the Allies in June 1948. These events provoked the Soviet blockade of West Berlin. The Berlin blockade and the simultaneous preparation of a Federal West German constitution and government by German politicians and statesmen in 1948–9 were the main events of the third phase, which ended in the promulgation of the Basic Law in 1949, four years after the unconditional surrender.

# 8

# The Trials

The principal event of the first phase was the war crimes trial which began on November 20, 1945, in the Palace of Justice in the medieval city of Nuremberg. The Columbia Broadcasting System (CBS) reporter, William L. Shirer, visited the city on November 18, 1945, and later described what he found in his memoirs:

The old town, the Nuremberg of Dürer and Hans Sachs and the Meistersingers and the venerable churches of St. Lorenz and St. Sebald and Our Lady and the old Rathaus and my favorite inn, the *Bratwurstglöcklein*, was "99 per cent dead." Half of the wonderful old frame dwellings along the river Pegnitz had caved into the stream.[1]

The ruins of the magnificent city of Nuremberg were a tombstone of the rich civilization of Germany, and the city was an awesome symbol of the nightmare that the Reich had become. The trial took place in the city in which the Nazi party had held its annual party meetings, the *Nürnberger Parteitage*, a frightening spectacle filmed by Leni Riefenstahl in her famous movie of 1934, entitled *Triumph of the Will* (*Triumph des Willens*).

The Nuremberg trial system as a whole – procedures, principles, and charges – was part of the American occupation program as it had emerged since the late summer of 1944. As early as 1942, the US and British governments took the position that some form of retribution against Hitler and the other Nazi leaders was necessary, but they had made no concrete plans. Stalin for his part proposed simply to execute large numbers of top administrators.

Basically, the victorious Allies could choose either to make a "political disposition" of the leading Nazis, or to put them on trial. A political disposition meant summary execution or imprisonment

[1] Shirer, *20th Century Journey,* 2: 631.

without trial. The Soviet government and the British for various reasons favored the political disposition method, whereas the Americans tended to believe not only that a trial was a morally superior way of dealing with the problem, but that it was very important that the victorious powers demonstrate that the Nazis were criminals according to prevailing and accepted standards of justice.

American officials began discussing the question of a trial and of the charges to be brought in August 1944. In November 1944 and again in January 1945, the secretary of war, Henry L. Stimson, and his aides produced memoranda proposing to define the Nazi regime and all its institutions as "criminal organizations" and suggested that an international tribunal charge a list of named Nazi leaders with membership in those organizations and with "conspiracy" to wage aggressive war and to murder vast numbers of innocent noncombatants. Both the British and Soviet governments rejected this plan. Not only did they still favor political disposition, but the very notion of political "conspiracy" as a chargeable offense was unknown in continental, including German, law. To charge the top Nazis with conspiracy would therefore appear to many in Europe as nothing more than a legal cover for what was in reality a political act of vengeance. Therefore, the critics said, it was better simply to execute these Nazis and declare it was a political act designed to destroy the enemy leadership.

By the war's end the British, the French, and the Soviet Union approved the concept of a tribunal and accepted "conspiracy" and "membership of criminal organizations" as legitimate charges. At the London conference of the four victorious powers in June 1945, their representatives accepted the final draft of a plan for the trial system, a draft which, like the earlier memoranda, emanated almost entirely from the US government and its legal advisors. This draft became the London Charter, the basic constituting document of the International Military Tribunal and the whole Nuremberg trial system.[2]

The Charter by no means, however, solved the ambiguities inherent in trying the leaders of defeated Germany. On the one hand, they were clearly responsible for war and for the death and suffering of millions of innocents. On the other, the very notion of a trial implied rules of evidence, a defense, and at least the theoretical possibility of acquittal. Conducting the trials, therefore, confronted the Allied powers with a dilemma which Bradley Smith, the leading American historian of the Nuremberg process, described as follows:

the conspiracy/criminal-organization proposal was created as an alternative to the Morgenthau plan. It was developed by a government leery of long-term,

[2] See Smith, B., *Road to Nuremberg*.

expensive commitments in postwar Europe, and therefore it sought to purge Nazi Germany through a judicial operation that would move swiftly through the Third Reich from top to bottom. Sensitive to any criticism implying the plan deviated from due process, the fathers of the Nuremberg system were nonetheless anxious to make the prosecution so comprehensive that all malefactors would be punished and Germany would be made safe for democracy. Since they lacked hard, accurate information on how Hitler's system actually operated, they stretched the bounds of legal propriety so that the prosecution would be able to advance any charges against the Nazi leaders and organizations that the evidence might ultimately warrant. . . .

For the system to work as intended, the prosecution had to convince a court, which was trying to appear legally respectable, that it should overlook shaky evidence, as well as its scruples, and condemn millions of organization members on the basis of collective guilt.[3]

That among the accusers was the Soviet government, which itself was guilty of atrocities at least as terrifying against its own population, created another dilemma. For representatives of such a regime to sit in judgement over others appeared to those aware of Stalin's crimes, a travesty of justice. Even had the character of Stalin's regime been better known in the West, however, the commitment to united action by the wartime Allies and sympathy for the Soviet Union were so great that the trials would have proceeded without much debate.

There were four kinds of war crimes trials after the war: the trial of "main war criminals," the trials held by individual military governments in the occupation zones, the trials held during and after the occupation by German courts, and trials held in countries occupied by Germany during the war for crimes committed on their territory.

The best known was the trial of "main war criminals;" namely, of the top leaders of the Third Reich and the Nazi Party, held by the International Military Tribunal, consisting of representatives from the United States, the Soviet Union, the United Kingdom, and France. Among the judges was Robert H. Jackson, a justice of the United States Supreme Court, who defined the purpose of the trial: "We propose to punish acts which have been regarded as criminal since the time of Cain and have been so written in every civilized code."[4] The indictment resulted in the trial of 22 prisoners for conspiracy against peace, crimes against peace, violations of the laws of war, and crimes against humanity. The proceedings were broadcast twice daily by German radio, and the judgement was reached on October 1, 1946.

Of the 22 accused at least three were born Austrians (Kaltenbrunner, Schirach, and Seyss-Inquart), excluding Hitler, also Austrian by birth.

[3] Ibid., 249.
[4] Shirer, *20th Century Journey,* 2: 633.

The *Frankfurter Rundschau*, in a special edition of Wednesday, October 2, 1946, almost one year after the start of the trial, wrote: "At 14 hours 55 minutes [2:55 p. m.] the International Tribunal began to conclude the last chapter of National Socialism ... The accused entered the courtroom in the order of their seating. The time required to bring them in, to read the verdict and to take them out again amounted to four minutes exactly. The unbelievable tension that hung over the courtroom was underlined by the characteristically sober atmosphere which had prevailed during the trial." The judgements reached and executed were as follows:

Hermann Göring, Luftwaffe chief, Reich marshal, and president of the Reichstag; death by hanging. (He poisoned himself on the evening of October 15, 1946.)

Joachim von Ribbentrop, foreign minister; death by hanging.

Wilhelm Keitel, field marshal, chief of staff of the High Command of the German armed forces; death by hanging.

Ernst Kaltenbrunner, head of the Reich Security Main Office, which included the Gestapo (secret state police) and the organizations responsible for the mass murder of Jews; death by hanging.

Alfred Rosenberg, Reich minister for the eastern occupied territories and chief Nazi ideologist; death by hanging.

Wilhelm Frick, minister of the interior 1933–43 and Reich protector of Bohemia and Moravia 1943–5; death by hanging.

Hans Frank, Hitler's attorney, minister of justice, and governor-general of occupied Poland; death by hanging.

Julius Streicher, Gauleiter of Franconia and the chief "Jew-baiter;" death by hanging.

Fritz Sauckel, plenipotentiary for the allocation of labor, i.e. slave labor; death by hanging.

Alfred Jodl, chief of the operations staff of the High Command of the German armed forces; death by hanging.

Arthur Seyss-Inquart, deputy governor of Poland, Reich commissar of Holland; death by hanging.

Rudolf Hess, Hitler's deputy until he flew to Britain in 1941 ostensibly to offer a separate peace; life imprisonment.

Walther Funk, economics minister before the war and president of the Reichsbank during the war; life imprisonment.

Erich Raeder, commander-in-chief of the German navy; life imprisonment.

Baldur von Schirach, Hitler Youth leader and Gauleiter of Vienna; 20 years imprisonment.

Albert Speer, minister of arms and munitions; 20 years imprisonment.

Konstantin Freiherr von Neurath, foreign minister 1932–8, and Reich protector of Bohemia and Moravia 1939–43; 15 years imprisonment.

Karl Dönitz, Raeder's successor and Hitler's successor, commander of the navy; 10 years imprisonment.

Hjalmar Schacht, before the war president of the Reichsbank and economics minister; acquitted.

Franz von Papen, chancellor in 1932 and ambassador to Austria and Turkey during the Third Reich; acquitted.

Hans Fritzsche, head of German radio propaganda; acquitted.

Martin Bormann, Hess' replacement as Hitler's deputy, and chief of the Party chancellery of the NSDAP; condemned to death in absentia (it was not known at the time that Bormann had been killed while trying to escape from Hitler's bunker on May 1, 1945).

These were the men whom the tribunal found directly responsible, after Hitler himself and those already dead, such as propaganda minister Joseph Goebbels, for the atrocities, the mass murders, the innumerable violations of the most elementary morality, which had cost the lives of approximately six million Jews and several million others whom these Nazi leaders, and the regime they served, had defined as unworthy to live. According to the London Charter, they were charged as individuals with conspiracy to wage aggressive war and as members of one or more of six criminal organizations: the Reich cabinet, the SS (Elite Squad), the SA (Storm Troopers), Gestapo-SD (Secret State Police and Security Service), the OKW (High Command of the Armed Forces), and the Leadership Corps of the Nazi Party. The conspiracy charges held up, whereas the criminal organization charges did not. As Bradley Smith wrote, "To prove such an accusation exceeded the facts, the evidence, and the ability of the Nuremberg prosecutors. In consequence, the tribunal quashed the criminality charges against three organizations. . . ." Further, the tribunal ruled that "in any secondary hearing the prosecution would be required to show that the individual was a voluntary member who had known of the criminal purposes of the organization at the time he joined." So, the "great dream of sweeping thousands, perhaps millions, of hard-core Nazis to the gallows or into labor or internment camps through administrative hearings was thereby rendered impossible. . . . A systematic campaign to identify and apportion blame to all those responsible for the evils of Nazism was never carried out."[5]

These decisions did not avail the twelve whom the tribunal condemned to death in the fall of 1946. Those to be executed were hanged

[5] Smith, B., *Road to Nuremberg*, 249, 250.

between 1 and 3 a.m. in the morning of October 16, 1945, in the gymnasium of the Nuremberg prison, in the presence of approximately 30 persons, including four representatives of the Allied Control Council and two German officials, Wilhelm Hoegner, the minister-president of Bavaria, and Jakob Leistner, the state prosecutor for the district of Nuremberg. As a consequence of Göring's suicide with cyanide at 10:45 p. m. on October 15, the prisoners were all handcuffed as they were led to the three gallows, only two of which were used. Ribbentrop was first, and died at 1:29 a.m., followed by Keitel, who died at 1:31 a.m. Each of the guilty was given the opportunity of a last word. Alfred Rosenberg chose to say nothing, but Julius Streicher, who had contributed to sending so many Jews to their death, yelled, in a shrill voice, "This is my celebration of Purim 1946, I am now going to God. The Bolshevists will hang you all one day! Adele, my dear wife. . . ." But it was Ribbentrop's final words that were perhaps most prophetic: "My last wish is that Germany will again find her unity, that an understanding between East and West may be achieved and that peace in the world may govern." And it was Seyss-Inquart who was the last to be hanged: "I hope that this execution will be a lesson and the final act of the tragedy of the Second World War, so that peace and understanding will rule among people. I believe in Germany!"[6]

The second kind of trial, those held by the individual military governments of the Western Allies, subsequently resulted in conviction of 5,006 individuals of war crimes, of whom 794 were sentenced to death and 486 executed.[7] Almost all the remaining accused and imprisoned were released before 1956.

Trials in German courts began only after the Allies had at least partially purged and reestablished the judicial system in late 1945. Allied Control Council directive no. 10 of December 20, 1945, defined the terms "war crime" and "crime against humanity" and specified a range of punishments ranging from death to loss of civil liberties. With this directive, the Control Council intended in the first instance to regulate trials by Allied tribunals, but it also permitted the military governments to authorize German courts to try crimes committed by Germans against other Germans. Such German courts, however, had to use the criminal definitions in directive no. 10, and not the provisions of the German criminal code, whenever possible. This created a problem even for honest and anti-Nazi judges, because it meant that they were

[6] *Frankfurter Rundschau*, October 17, 1946. Streicher's reference to Purim was a particularly macabre reference to a Jewish holiday of celebration; a joyous holiday in commemoration of the deliverance of the Jews from the massacre plotted by Haman, an enemy of the Jews hanged for plotting their destruction.

[7] Steininger, *Deutsche Geschichte*, 1: 127.

ordered to apply a law that did not exist when the crimes were committed. In doing so, they were violating not only the general legal norm forbidding retroactive legislation, but a specific provision of Allied Control Council directive no. 1, which threatened German judges with the death penalty if they applied laws retroactively![8]

In fact the German criminal code was fully adequate to deal with crimes by Germans against Germans in the Third Reich. By the end of 1950, German courts had convicted 5,228 persons, mostly on the basis of evidence from victims. However, most of the crimes were minor; only 100 sentences were for murder.[9] Investigators found it difficult to assemble evidence and find suspects. The main reason was that most Germans were so concerned with immediate worries about food and housing that they had little time for what they considered politics, and investigating Nazi crimes appeared to most as a political, not a legal or a moral matter. The military government trials and the denazification effort also appeared to many Germans as examples of victors' justice, of political activity by one side against another, defeated side. As a result, they became cynical about the whole idea of punishing people for what they did under Hitler. These and other factors permitted many guilty parties to lie low and survive unmolested.

In 1950, the Allied High Commissioners (who succeeded the military governors in 1949) transferred authority to German courts to try all Nazi crimes under German criminal law. Between 1951 and 1955 German courts convicted 628 additional suspects, many of them former guards in some of the major concentration and extermination camps.[10] The low number reflected a growing reluctance, not so much of the investigators and prosecutors, but rather of the public, to see Nazi criminals found out and put on trial. At the end of 1955 the statute of limitations on any crime punishable by ten years' imprisonment or less ran out. From that time on, only premeditated murder could still be prosecuted.

One might have expected public concern to disappear completely after that, especially as many public figures in the mid-1950s called for "drawing a final line under" and "putting a stop to" the discussion about war crimes, war guilt, and the whole moral and legal issue of Nazism. However, thanks largely to the effort of a few diligent lawyers and politicians, prosecution of some of the worst mass murderers by German courts took place in the late 1950s and 1960s. Though far fewer in number than the trials of the 1940s, they had much greater public impact.

[8] See Rückerl, *NS-Verbrechen vor Gericht*, 107–9.
[9] Ibid., 121 and table, 329.
[10] Ibid., 136 and table, 329.

In 1955 the occupation ended and occupation law was suspended. Henceforth German tribunals were fully competent to try all crimes without exception, as they saw fit, except in the case where a suspect had already been tried by an Allied authority. As a result of this last provision, "high Nazi functionaries who had been investigated by British, French, or American prosecuting authorities on suspicion of specific crimes, but whose cases had been dropped for lack of sufficient evidence, could not be put on trial again, even if the evidence of their guilt had meanwhile become available."[11] This had the ironic and, to many, upsetting result that high-ranking commanders of death squads walked the streets of Germany, immune from prosecution, while many of their subordinates, who had carried out their orders, went on trial and thence to prison.

The crucial step that made the prosecutions of 1956 and after possible was the establishment of the Central Office of *Land* Justice Departments in Ludwigsburg near Stuttgart in 1958. Its first head was Erwin Schüle, who had led the investigation leading to the so-called Ulm death squad trial of 1958. The facts of the Ulm case spurred the German authorities to establish the Central Office. An SS commander who was responsible for the mass murder of Jews in Lithuania in 1941 had, amazingly, been declared a "non-offender" in the denazification procedure. In 1956 this man, who in civilian life had been chief of police in the city of Memel and was now living in Ulm, applied for reinstatement in the civil service. Since the rank of police chief was an important one, the man's application was reported in the local press. By pure accident a newspaper reader recognized the name and reported him to the authorities as a mass murderer.

The Ulm case demonstrated that many Nazi atrocities, especially ones committed in the east, had never been examined in court, nor had any effort to trace the guilty parties been made. To remedy this, the ministers of justice of the West German *Länder* authorized the Central Office to collect evidence of crimes committed against civilians outside the jurisdiction of existing German courts. This was a complex and difficult task, partly because most of the crimes had occurred in the east, and the communist regimes now in control of those territories were not often helpful in providing documentation or other evidence. The Central Office established task forces for each of the major geographical areas, such as Danzig, the *Generalgouvernement* (including most of occupied Poland, where the main extermination camps were located), and the northern, central, and southern regions of occupied Russia. The lawyer in charge of each area gradually became familiar with the Nazi

11 Ibid., 139.

administrative system, with the main types of persecution and murder, and even in some cases with the names and details of individuals. The Central Office then passed on this information to state prosecutors for action.

A special case was the leading personnel of the former Reich Security Main Office (*Reichssicherheitshauptamt*, RSHA), who were directly responsible for the extermination camps. The RSHA was located in Berlin, though its actions affected millions of people in thousands of square miles of mostly Polish and Soviet territory. As the scene of the crime – planning mass murder – was Berlin, the responsible authority was the state prosecutor in Berlin. However, that office did nothing to investigate any crimes or locate any suspects for a full 18 years, from 1945 to late 1963, when the ministers of justice of the Federal Republic finally ordered it to initiate proceedings based on information from the Central Office, Allied governments, and other sources.

Schüle's successor as head of the Central Office, Adalbert Rückerl, commented later that to carry out its task, the Central Office had "to reverse the procedure hitherto adopted in prosecuting Nazi crimes. Investigations no longer took place only after a report was received against an individual suspect; rather any information whatever about any legally punishable act triggers an investigation of those responsible, even if they or their whereabouts are unknown."[12] By the end of 1964, the Central Office had begun 701 investigations. Thanks largely to this effort, major trials took place in the early 1960s of concentration and extermination camp guards and officers, and of the officers and men of SS and other death squads active in eastern territories during the war. At that time few expected that the German government would extend the statute of limitations for murder, which was 20 years. Accordingly, this final and most serious category of Nazi crimes would cease to become subject to prosecution 20 years after the end of the war, in May 1965. In fact the German government did extend the statute, leading to a new flood of activity for the Central Office as well as to a huge public debate on the Third Reich. We shall return to this subject later in this work.

The fourth kind of trial served, in a manner of speaking, as the original model, since the wartime Allies had agreed in Teheran and Yalta that Nazi and German atrocities should be prosecuted by states whose citizens were victims of those atrocities. Only the very senior Nazi leaders, whose actions affected many countries, were tried by the International Tribunal. Others were extradited and tried under laws in force in the jurisdictions where they had allegedly committed atrocities. Notable trials were those of Rudolf Hoess (not to be confused with

---

[12] Ibid., 145.

Hess), who was commandant of Auschwitz during the height of the massacres there, and of Erich Koch, Gauleiter (Nazi party chief) in East Prussia. Both were tried in Poland, as Auschwitz is situated within Poland's 1939 borders. Koch, for his part, was tried not for his acts as party chief in German territory, but for his war crimes committed after the occupation of Poland on territory that was Polish before the war. These trials took place in the late 1940s, and both Hoess and Koch were hanged.

As might be expected, Soviet courts were severe and often punished on the basis of trivial, irrelevant, or invented evidence. Rückerl estimated that the number of prisoners and sentences in Soviet courts far exceeded the total of those of all other governments involved in prosecuting Nazi crimes. On this issue, the federal minister of justice reported in 1950:

After the occupation of eastern and central Germany [the Oder–Neisse territories and the Soviet zone] there began an indiscriminate wave of arrests and internments of all Germans regarded by the Soviets as dangerous. Tens of thousands filled the prisons, jails, and concentration camps, e.g. Buchenwald, Sachsenhausen, Neubrandenburg, Mühlberg, and Bautzen. Through hunger and in part through torture "confessions" were obtained which were then used as the basis of trials in Soviet military courts in the cases where the prisoners had not already died as a result of privations, disease, and ill-treatment. . . .

Likewise, thousands of German soldiers captured by the Soviets were put before military courts and in speedy trials sentenced – mostly on the basis of forced confessions or merely for belonging to particular units – to a standard punishment of 25 years in prison, or in many cases to death. For example, a sapper was sentenced because he had used wood "belonging to the people" to build a bridge, and a medic because he had tended soldiers wounded by partisans. There were, however, also persons among the condemned who had committed serious crimes, for example the concentration camp guards Hempel, Höhn, Schubert, and Sorge, and the concentration camp doctor, Baumkötter, all of whom have been again prosecuted in the Federal Republic. The condemned were in many cases transported to penal service in the Soviet Union. Their number cannot be precisely determined; Soviet sources state that in May 1950 there were still 13,532 persons convicted of war crimes in Soviet camps.

Of the persons condemned by Soviet military courts, 10,513 were handed over to [German] authorities of the Soviet occupation zone "to serve their sentences," according to a letter of January 1950 from the Soviet general, Chuikov, to Ulbricht.[13]

---

[13]  Cited ibid., 100.

In the 1980s trials were still being conducted in Israel and Germany, and Klaus Barbie, the "Butcher of Lyon," was sentenced to life imprisonment in France in July 1987. Deportations to Israel of accused war criminals continued in 1986,[14] and resulted in conviction in 1988. John Demjanjuk was sentenced to death by an Israeli court in Jerusalem on April 25, 1988, for crimes committed as "Ivan The Terrible," at the Treblinka extermination camp in German-occupied Poland.[15] In January 1987 the Simon Wiesenthal Center for Holocaust Studies, in Vienna, announced that a list of 44 suspected Nazi war criminals was being sent to the West German chancellor, Helmut Kohl, with the request "that they be investigated, tracked down and brought to justice."[16]

Actively prosecuting and punishing persons for committing outright atrocities and violations of the laws of war, as well as punishment for "crimes against peace," which did not exist in international law, was one consequence of the measures agreed upon by the wartime Allies at Teheran, Yalta, and Potsdam. A second consequence was the eradication of the Nazi party and any institutions of the defunct German government and administration deemed by the victors to have played an active part in permitting or carrying out these crimes. Another was the concept of reparations and the policy of dismantlement. And yet another was denazification, and the first stirrings of political activity, that dominated public life in occupied Germany through 1946. By 1947, denazification in the Western zones was eclipsed by the economic and political activity which, in an interplay of Allied and German initiatives, moved with increasing speed toward the constitution of a West German state.

[14] *New York Times*, March 1, 1986.
[15] *San Francisco Chronicle*, April 25, 1988.
[16] Ibid., January 6, 1987.

# 9

# Denazification

Although the term denazification originated in Eisenhower's staff, the idea was by no means purely an Allied invention.[1] German exile groups, notably the Union of German Socialist Organizations in London, as well as resistance groups in Germany itself, had called for the arrest of all top and middle-ranking NSDAP cadres and for their removal from office pending trial of all leading officials, civil servants, and professionals who had aided the Nazi seizure of power and the preparation of war. There was no question in anyone's mind that leading Nazis and those industrialists and civil servants whose cooperation had been essential to the regime should either be put on trial for war crimes or purged. But there was debate concerning the means and the extent of denazification. Opposed to the ideas of Morgenthau and Vansittart, there stood the view that the best alternative was a rapid purification to be followed by a consistent policy of economic and political reconstruction.

JCS 1067 divided Nazis and sympathizers into two groups, active and nominal. The active category again included two subsets. The first included all leading administrative officials down to the level of village mayors, Nazi party cadres down to the level of *Ortsgruppenleiter* (local group leader), as well as all members of the SS and military general staff officers. All of these were subject to removal from office and internment pending trial. The second was an even broader category of persons provisionally subject to removal following an investigation. When OMGUS enforced this decree, the result, by late 1945, was the wholesale depopulation of all administrative offices and an impossible burden of work for US military personnel, who were in addition being demobilized and reduced in numbers. Most internees in the US zone were middle-class professionals, local officials and minor civil servants.

---

[1] Eschenburg, *Jahre der Besatzung,* 112.

Anyone removed and interned lost employment and pension rights. In Bavaria, by the beginning of August, 100,000 Nazi officials had been fired from their jobs in the municipal administrations, in other public service positions, and in the postal and telephone service.[2]

The threatening chaos led in late 1945 to a change of procedure. Thereafter judgement depended on investigation of individual cases, and the criterion for removal and punishment was to be how the individual had actually behaved, and not simply the fact that he had held a certain office or was a member of certain organizations. All persons having any business with the occupation authorities were required to answer a questionnaire of 131 questions, known as the *Fragebogen*. By early March 1946, 1.4 million of these had been filled out and about half processed.

An OMGUS committee in January recommended new rules and transfer of responsibility for denazification to German hands. On March 5, 1946, accordingly, the *Länderrat* at the urging of OMGUS passed a law for the emancipation of Germany from National Socialism and militarism, which came to be known as the Law for Liberation, repeated for all four zones in Allied Control Council directive no. 38 of October 12. This was the most important law passed in Germany during the occupation. In accordance with the Potsdam decision to eradicate militarism and promote democratic self-government in Germany, it regulated the arrest and punishment of war criminals (i.e., those not already tried at Nuremberg or under indictment for trial by the Allied military governments or German courts under directive no. 10), Nazis, and militarists. All Germans would fall into one of five categories: (I) major offenders, (II) offenders, (III) lesser offenders, (IV) followers, and (V) non-offenders. Membership in the NSDAP or in any Nazi professional organization was, per se, grounds for classification at least as a follower. Thirteen million questionnaires were filled out under these new rules. Of this number, three million contained responses requiring that the individual be tried by special German denazification courts. Finding persons able and willing to sit on the courts was difficult, and many of the more serious cases were never tried. However, all persons heavily compromised were interned for periods of several weeks up to several months. Though not all were tried, this imprisonment and the obvious need to adapt to new ways and attitudes had a profound effect.[3]

Rolf Lahr, diplomat and state secretary in the foreign ministry from the 1950s to 1973, described in detail his denazification in one of his many enlightening letters to his family:

[2] *Frankfurter Rundschau*, August 11, 1945.
[3] See Plischke, "Denazification in Germany," in *Americans as Proconsuls*, ed. Wolfe, 198–225.

Three denazifications are behind me, more may follow – *peu importe*. I do not believe that what the Australian sergeant or the Canadian lieutenant . . . think about my behavior after 1933 must be decisive for me personally. However, of extreme importance is what I have to reproach myself with . . .

Denazification is not set up to find the criminals and punish them – they are known ad nauseam – no, it is aimed at punishing fundamental beliefs, punishing formation of a "wrong" political opinion, "wrong" voting, and to prevent joining the "wrong" party. Freedom of opinion and the execution of the right to vote have always been the basis of democracy, which, according to the will of the Allies, we are to learn again. But it seems that, also in this respect, the Allies have taken their cues from Hitler.[4]

The problem with the procedure adopted in the US zone was its excessive formalism, a combined result of the American belief in questionnaires and statistical methods and a perceived need for absolute equality of treatment. But treatment was far from equal. First, the courts required affidavits attesting good character for persons in all but the non-offender category, from all Germans seeking government employment; but this procedure was an open invitation to falsification, corruption and other forms of procedural deformation. Second, since many persons in the lightly affected categories, many of whom were minor officials, had much-needed skills, their cases were entered for processing in the courts while more serious cases were held up. The effect was that proportionately far more of the "smaller fry," most of whom would not have been re-employed in public service anyway, were fined, while categories I and II escaped more lightly because OMGUS abandoned the whole enterprise before their cases could be processed.

In focusing primarily on Nazi party membership, and not on other evidence of a person's political ethics, the denazification courts committed obvious injustices and errors that only served to discredit the enterprise further. Many Nazis had managed to conceal their membership when the war ended, and although the Allies found some membership lists which they could use to test what people told them, they were by no means a guarantee. The following anecdote illustrates what was probably not an unusual pattern of behavior at the war's end:

When we heard that the French had crossed the Rhine, my grandfather said, "Now, Winnie, we have to take off these Party badges. If anyone asks, we are social democrats and always have been." My mother turned to him and said, "Dad, with all due respect, that's outrageous." "No," said my grandfather, "it isn't outrageous. New times are coming and we must adapt to them."[5]

[4] Lahr, *Zeuge von Fall und Aufstieg*, 105, 113.
[5] Niethammer and Plato, eds, *Lebensgeschichte*, 3: 277.

Gustav Sonnenhol was a foreign service officer who had joined the SS in 1939. In 1946 the lawyer for state secretary Ernst von Weizsäcker (1882–1951), permanent political head of the foreign ministry from 1938 to 1943, who was accused of active support of the regime, asked Sonnenhol and some other colleagues to testify that Weizsäcker was not a "real" Nazi.[6] The other colleagues made excuses and did not appear; Sonnenhol did, to help Weizsäcker, who was a friend. The prosecutor asked Sonnenhol if he regarded joining the SS as an honor, expecting him to say that he had done it "to try to prevent the worst from happening" – this was the standard excuse. To everyone's amazement Sonnenhol answered: "Yes sir, at that time, I regarded it as an honor!" Sonnenhol later believed that he was penalized in various ways throughout his later career for having been honest when others were hypocritical.

In his memoirs, published in 1984, Sonnenhol described life in the foreign ministry during the war and argued that most foreign service professionals were anti-Nazi and protected each other from investigation or arrest as long as possible. He also strongly criticized the denazification procedures of 1945–8:

Belonging to National Socialist organizations or holding party positions was no criterion of guilt, just as having a "spotless vest" was no guarantee of innocence. What happened was too complex, many-layered, and opaque for such simple judgments. So it was that military judges like Filbinger, who was passing senseless death sentences in the last weeks of the war, rose to the highest honors and positions, and that a war reporter like Nannen could set himself up as a moral teacher of Germany . . . just because neither of them was formally compromised. Generals who followed the orders to resist to the last man were acquitted, while a young Waffen-SS volunteer might face a lifelong prohibition against public employment. An abyss of lies, *Persilscheine* and weathervanes opened, which has poisoned the political atmosphere to this day.[7]

Sonnenhol's point was that formal criteria, like being a member of the Nazi party or one of its auxiliary organizations, were not in themselves evidence of criminal behavior. Henri Nannen worked as a war reporter in one of the hundreds of "propaganda companies" in the armed forces whose job it was to paint a rosy picture of the war to boost morale at home and rally popular support for the regime. After the war, Nannen

---

[6] Weizsäcker's two sons, Richard von Weizsäcker and Carl Friedrich von Weizsäcker, were to play prominent roles in the life of postwar Germany.

[7] Sonnenhol, *Untergang oder Übergang?*, 119. *Persilscheine* refers to "Persil," a brand of detergent. Thus, whoever had a *Persilschein* had an affidavit of good and clean character. The reference to "weathervanes" suggests that there were many whose political attitudes were shaped by how they perceived the political winds to be blowing.

began a phenomenal career as head of a publishing empire centered on the weekly *Stern*, where he proved himself adept at guiding and pleasing public opinion in postwar Germany. In the 1950s, *Stern* supported Adenauer and especially Ludwig Erhard, whose economic policies were successful and popular. In the 1960s, the magazine began supporting radical causes favored by the leaders of the student movement and became increasingly pro-leftist and anti-American, a stance it maintained throughout the 1980s.

The case of Hans Filbinger was very different, and Sonnenhol was mistaken in accusing him of "passing senseless death sentences in the last weeks of the war." Filbinger, a commercial lawyer in civilian life, was an assistant military judge with the German Navy in Norway from 1943–5. During that time he took great personal risks on several occasions to delay or mitigate punishment of navy personnel accused of the crime of *Wehrkraftzersetzung*, literally, "corruption of the defense effort." This crime specifically included having opinions critical of the Nazi regime. In fact, Filbinger was himself an anti-Nazi and had tried to avoid service on the court precisely so he would not have to prosecute people for having opinions that he himself shared. The myth that he passed "senseless death sentences" was invented in 1978 out of whole cloth by the leftist playwright Rolf Hochhuth and eagerly repeated by several leading journals of opinion. The successful defamation of Filbinger, however, belongs to the history of the later 1970s and will be described in due course.

In early 1947 opinion in the United States was running strongly against the whole idea of massive denazification. The lengthy process of character testing via the questionnaire, or "character washing," as a cynical critic, Schrenck-Notzing, later called it,[8] was gradually abandoned. One reason was the new hostility to the Soviet Union.[9] Because the Soviets had used draconian denazification methods to achieve a political revolution in their zone, the Americans now did not want to be seen doing anything similar in their zone. Furthermore, the basic priority of US policy in West Germany was shifting from punishment of Nazis to economic reconstruction in the general interest of West European security against the Soviet threat. Thus, the new secretary of defense, James Forrestal, in August 1947 ordered Clay to cease denazification procedures. Then the German authorities objected. The easy cases – almost 600,000 – had been processed, whereas 30,000 cases of categories I and II remained. Nevertheless, the US decision stood, and on March 31, 1948, denazification in the US zone was officially

8  See Schrenck-Notzing, *Charakterwäsche*.
9  Eschenburg, *Jahre der Besatzung*, 116–17.

terminated. Accordingly there was a widespread and not unjustified feeling both in West Germany and abroad that the big fish had escaped and the small fry had served as scapegoats. This feeling was an important motive in the leftist agitation of the later 1960s, which pilloried West Germany as a restored state of crypto-Nazis and reactionaries that had never really been purified.

Was denazification a failure? Many thought so at the time, including General Clay, who, when Reinhold Maier, a political leader of the liberal party, asked him about it in 1955, said, "Please have mercy and don't remind me of the biggest mistake."[10] In the late 1940s a number of American political scientists published studies of the program; a representative verdict was that of John H. Herz who concluded, "That denazification has not been a success in Germany is today admitted by the serious students of the problem."[11] Left-wing Americans, of course, went much further. Paul Sweezy, a radical economist of some note, wrote in 1949 that "the policy ... of denazifying the personnel of government and business has ironically turned into removing the Nazi stigma from former stalwarts of the Hitler regime."[12]

This latter conclusion was at the core of the criticism. What began as a grandiose plan to purge all Nazis from leading roles in public life and to punish severely persons who had held responsible positions in the Third Reich was, in practice, transformed into a procedure by which major offenders were slapped on the wrist and minor offenders exonerated. Left-wing critics like the historian Lutz Niethammer, who published an exhaustive study of denazification in Bavaria, argued that the idea of a purge was impossible. If the Allies really wanted to change Germany they should have introduced fundamental "anti-fascist reforms," presumably similar to those in the Soviet zone, such as expropriation of private property and nationalization of industry. Since they did not do so, and since a complete purge of party members was impossible, because it would denude administration and make organized life impossible, the whole procedure, according to Niethammer, was a failure. The result of the exercise was simply to convince the broad mass of former Nazis that the new order of parliamentary democracy and pluralism was "a more effective guarantee of their interests" – meaning their class interests – than the Third Reich had been.[13]

Niethammer was able to point out that there were more former NSDAP members in the civil service of the Länder of the US zone in 1949 than under Hitler, and in industry and the professions the

[10] Cited in Niethammer, *Die Mitläuferfabrik*, 15–16n.
[11] Cited ibid., 15n.
[12] Cited ibid., 13.
[13] Ibid., 666.

numbers were even higher. On the other hand, the critics, like Niethammer, who argued that those who joined the Nazi party in the Third Reich simply changed their tactics and after 1945 supported democracy in the service of similar – undefined but presumably suspect – interests, did not seem to regard the democratic transformation of Germany as important. If denazification had been a failure, one would have expected to see Nazi ideas enduring in West Germany and causing a failure of the democratic experiment. Unpunished and unrepentant Nazis would have infiltrated and controlled the new institutions, depriving them of the desired effect.

They did not do so, partly because it was dangerous since they were forbidden to do so, and partly because their numbers had decreased by 1945. In fact, as evidence from wartime Germany indicates, the number of committed Nazis began shrinking rapidly as the fortunes of war changed in 1942–3, as a consequence of disillusionment and opportunism. Throughout the Nazi era, the internal security police conducted surveys of opinion in Germany to determine the state of mind and attitudes of the population. The British historian Ian Kershaw examined these reports exhaustively and concluded that what he called "the Hitler myth" began to evaporate long before the war ended.

By the phrase "the Hitler myth" Kershaw meant the belief that Hitler was supremely wise and right, and the resultant implicit faith that the leadership of Germany was in good hands. Even though the risk of speaking out critically grew dramatically towards the end of the war, the secret police reports noted not only a continuing stream of critical utterances, but a steadily growing "silent majority" disgusted with the Nazi regime. Though they continued to fulfil their duties and showed little inclination to open rebellion, Germans worried increasingly about the consequences of defeat. In April 1944, a woman in an air raid shelter in Schweinfurt was overheard saying: "It's easy for the Führer, he has no family to take care of. When the war really goes bad, he'll leave us stuck in the garbage and put a bullet through his head." In early 1945, Goebbels, the propaganda minister, published a last exhortation to heroic resistance and called on all Germans to "fight to the last in order to enter into history." A secret police report on reactions to this article noted that "The mass of people couldn't care less what the Europe of the future looks like. One can deduce from all conversations that comrades of every political shade wish for the prewar standard of living back as soon as possible and place no value whatever on entering into history." Kershaw concluded that the Third Reich depended for its power not on a strong ideology that could survive the death of Hitler, but on the myth of the man himself. Once the myth was gone, "the effect of this person disappeared without a trace, just as the ashes of his physical remains."[14]

It is true that as late as 1952 polls found a hard core of 10 per cent of the respondents in West Germany who thought that Hitler was the greatest statesman of the century, and in 1953, 13 per cent would have welcomed a return to power of the NSDAP.[15] From a democratic viewpoint, these are certainly alarming facts. What is astonishing, however, is that these beliefs failed to manifest themselves in political action.

What did occur was adaptation. As long as democracy was not yet a way of life in Germany, adaptation was not the worst possible effect of occupation. Outright sabotage and resistance would have been worse, and they were scarcely found at all. The most important example of a failed reform was the case of the German bureaucracy. The military governments wanted to put an end to the special status of German civil servants, since they regarded them as especially infected with a mentality of excessive respect for state power. They were largely right, although few Americans fully appreciated either the complex history of the German civil service, its traditional relationship to political authority, or the rigid distinctions in pre-1945 Germany between civil servants (*Beamte*), white-collar salaried employees (*Angestellte*), and blue-collar workers (*Arbeiter*). *Arbeiter* and *Angestellte* regarded themselves as belonging to two radically different social and cultural worlds, divided by what a historian of German social development called the "collar line."[16] This line was far more rigid than the corresponding distinction in America between wage-laborers and salaried employees. Thus, one of the reasons for the support given Hitler was the fear of many *Angestellte* during the Depression that they were losing status and sinking to the economic and – far worse – the social level of *Arbeiter*.

In 1945 most *Angestellte*, like most *Arbeiter*, worked in private industry and business. Before 1933, they had belonged to separate unions and pursued distinct interests. The *Angestellte* wanted to resemble true civil servants as much as possible; they wanted their salaries to reflect seniority and authority rather than merit, and they wanted security of tenure in their jobs. However, both *Arbeiter* and *Angestellte* retained the right to strike, which fundamentally distinguished both groups from the *Beamte*.

The German bureaucracy proper in its modern form, the *Berufsbeamtentum* (vocational civil service), arose in the western parts of Germany during the Napoleonic era. Inspired by Napoleon's reforms of French administration, German rulers established corps of officials to operate

[14] Kershaw, *Der Hitler-Mythos*, 176, 193, 194.
[15] Noelle and Neumann, eds, *Jahrbuch 1947–1955*, 137, 276.
[16] Kocka, *Die Angestellten in der deutschen Geschichte*, 171, 226–8.

the government, distinguished from other public employees by security of tenure, by oaths of office or similar solemn engagements, and by a special relationship between each individual *Beamter* and his political master. The *Beamter* received a personal commission from the ruler, promising in turn to serve that ruler to the best of his ability. By the late nineteenth century, the *Beamtentum* included the senior staff of all Reich, Land, and local government departments, but also judges, professors, tax collectors, and official inspectors of all kinds. One important category for the *Beamter*'s own self-image were the *Staats-rechtler*, that is, academic lawyers engaged in interpreting and defending state authority. The *Staatsrechtler* developed the image of the apolitical *Beamte* and explained the higher ethos which in theory animated them.

The *Beamter*, by applying for and accepting the ruler's commission, abjured the right to strike or withhold his service, in return for security and protection against involuntary dismissal or demotion. In complete contrast to the Anglo-American traditions of civil service, the German *Beamter* was eligible for election to the Reichstag or other political assemblies without having to surrender his commission. Curiously, the *Staatsrechtler* did not argue that election as a representative of a political party vitiated the *Beamter*'s apolitical ethos. Further, the bureaucrats received their stipend in strict accordance with seniority and rank, regardless of individual competence. They held this principle to be a fundamental element of corps cohesion; without it, each *Beamter* would be competing with his colleagues for the ruler's attention and would be looking out for his own advantage and advancement – an idea wholly alien to the entire concept and world-view of the *Beamte* class.

Many *Beamte* came to feel an emotional attachment to the monarchy and therefore regretted its replacement with the Weimar Republic. Some, including judges, used the right of free political expression granted by the Weimar constitution to conduct blatantly political activity directed against the democracy. "The administration of the Republic's business," one historian wrote, "was left in the hands of professional civil servants who were perhaps not overtly anti-republican but shared a basically anti-democratic approach to government . . . the great majority of the bureaucrats were more intent upon preserving the administrative methods of the Wilhelmine period than they were on adjusting to the requirements of a pluralistic society with a parlia-mentary government."[17] Few of them became fanatical Nazis, but even fewer resigned their commissions when the Nazi regime ordered them to violate hallowed principles of justice or civilized norms of decency. Most of them continued to believe that they alone of all groups in

[17] Craig, *Germany 1866–1945*, 420.

Germany were selfless servants of the state. In fact, the Hitler regime politicized the civil service to enforce its criminal policies and – in violation of the traditional principles of the civil service – removed from office any *Beamter* who was either of Jewish descent or who refused to carry out orders, whatever their content.

Nazism demonstrated that the notion of "service to the state as an ethically superior and especially valuable activity was invalidated by the course of German history."[18] Nothing illustrated the discrepancy between the *Beamter*'s self-image and the reality better than the pathetic statement of a leading *Staatsrechtler*, Carl Heyland, in 1949: "By adhering to the idea of the state, which stands above the parties, the German civil servant received the ability to serve with exemplary devotion to duty and selflessness within whatever political system ruled in Germany, in the absolute and the constitutional monarchy, in the democratic and parliamentary republic as well as in the national socialist Führer state."[19] Heyland, like many of his colleagues, assumed that this vision of apolitical service was still viable and that life would therefore soon resume as before. Quite innocently or deliberately, he entitled his book *The Vocational Civil Service in the new Democratic State*.

Between 1945 and 1952 the Allies tried and failed to reform the civil service. They regarded the destruction of the *Beamte* class, with its special ethos and social position, as an essential part of German democratization. Some 58,000 *Beamte* out of a total of about one million lost their jobs through denazification.[20] In 1946 the Allied military governments, with OMGUS in the lead, introduced laws designed to purge the civil service, replacing the existing structure with one based on merit and commitment to democratic values. They further abolished the bureaucracy's historical status as a special group under public law and transformed the *Beamter*'s relationship with his employing institution into a simple contract like that between any employee and his employer. For example, one of the terms of the reform was that a *Beamter* could be dismissed for cause, something that the Germans regarded as a gross violation of inherited privilege. In short, the reform implied that *Beamte* would henceforth work on the same terms as *Angestellte*. The new civil servants would have the right to strike, and would not be allowed to accept election to political assemblies without leaving public service.

Had these reforms taken hold, the *Beamtentum* would have lost its special status and the *Beamte* would have turned into *Angestellte*. Initially, this effort met with some success. In 1947 *Beamte* in the British

---

[18] Wunder, *Geschichte der Bürokratie in Deutschland*, 210.
[19] Cited ibid.
[20] Ibid., 167.

zone formed a union which the British military government recognized. However, the German authorities, including the SPD which in the Weimar years had insisted on a thorough democratization of the civil service, resisted the Allied measures, at first by delaying tactics, and later by open rejection of the reforms. In 1949, very few *Beamte* joined the Trade Union Federation. By 1951, the inherited rights, privileges, and status of the *Beamtentum* were fully restored.

As in the case of denazification, liberal and radical critics of the occupation era pointed to the continuity of the *Beamtentum* as evidence that the Federal Republic was a fundamentally flawed democracy, because inherited anti-democratic and authoritarian social structures and cultural attitudes persisted. Next to education, the survival of the *Beamte* was indeed an egregious example of successful German resistance to a policy that the Allies repeatedly declared as both essential and desirable. The fact remained that German *Beamte* did, by and large, become loyal servants of the democratic state. For reasons having nothing to do with deliberate policy and everything to do with the social and economic transformations of postwar Europe and Germany, the traditional vocational bureaucracy changed beyond all recognition in the first thirty years after 1945. A generation after the war, German *Beamte* resembled their counterparts in Britain and America far more than they resembled their direct predecessors in Germany. Thus, the case of the *Beamte* provided an illustration that what made Germany democratic was not so much grand Allied policy as a combination of many individual decisions and broad social and economic developments that affected the victors as much as the defeated.

Gustav Sonnenhol summed it up well. As a foreign service officer he knew the best traditions of the German civil service from the inside. German civil servants had great pride in their "calling" (*Beruf*) which they understood as service for the public good, regardless of who was political master. They had been taught that resistance to political authority was not their business no matter how morally justified it might be, an attitude that was both a weakness and a strength. After 1945, Sonnenhol wrote in 1983, "many of them thought this through in the internment and prison camps. They became a 'skeptical generation'. If they were to serve any state in the future they wanted it to be a better state."[21]

Sonnenhol's view of the civil service was overly optimistic. During the Weimar Republic, many leading judges, professors, and other senior civil servants had only reluctantly served the democratic regime. Many in lower ranks openly declared that they would prefer to see the

[21] Sonnenhol, *Untergang oder Übergang?*, 121.

monarchy restored, even though such opinions violated the laws governing the civil service. The historian Friedrich Meinecke, who as professor of history in Berlin was himself a senior civil servant, coined the phrase *Vernunftrepublikaner* (republicans out of common sense) to describe those, like him, who felt emotionally bound to the old order but who realized intellectually that democracy promised greater human freedom. Unfortunately, many of his colleagues either never achieved or quickly forgot that intellectual conviction when the Nazis took power in 1933 and declared that civil servants must henceforth "support the national state without reservation."[22] Most enforced the Nazi laws and served the Nazi state as they had served previous regimes; a smaller number, who were anti-Nazis, remained in their posts to oppose Nazi repression; yet others became convinced followers of Hitler.

One case that became famous because of its implications for postwar Germany was that of Hans Globke, a civil servant in the ministry of justice who wrote the commentary on the Nuremberg race laws. The official commentary contained the guidelines on interpretation of the laws that judges, lawyers, and administrators were supposed to follow in enforcing them. Globke and his defenders later claimed, with some justification, that he had written the commentary in such a way that it mitigated the effect of the laws. This, of course, did not satisfy his critics who argued that a truly apolitical and honorable civil servant should not have dealt with any laws that violated civilized legal norms and established civil rights. The very fact that Globke dealt with the laws as a non-Nazi gave them a spurious legitimacy. The case became a prime political affair in the young Federal Republic when the first chancellor, Konrad Adenauer, appointed Globke as his personal assistant.

The case of Globke and others, as well as analogous cases in industry and the professions, led Niethammer and other critics to reject Sonnenhol's defense as blatant apologia. To Niethammer the failure of neo-Nazi agitation, the "skepticism" of the ruling elite of the new state, and the lack of overt anti-democratic activity in the Federal Republic, simply confirmed his thesis that most former Nazis regarded their interests as better served by adhering to democracy. But, one may be allowed to ask, if they acted like democrats as long as they lived and quite clearly did not try to indoctrinate their children or colleagues in Nazism, what was the significance of their "real" interests? Niethammer was probably right that the result of denazification was not an "anti-fascist transformation" of society, but simply the indoctrination of the

---

[22] From the Nazi law for the restoration of the civil service, in Hattenhauer, *Geschichte des Beamtentums*, 379.

mass of old Nazis with the notion that they had no viable alternative. So they behaved like democrats. And if that was realistic only as much as one might expect, it was also more than enough, for the time being. The cultural and social changes of the 1950s and 1960s continued to fulfill the task of democratic transformation. While the critics of denazification had much to support their arguments, much of their criticism was also misplaced.

The question, moreover, was whether a full-scale purge of persons who happened to have been members of the Nazi party, whatever their actual behavior or attitude, was ever a realistic and useful idea. Nazi ideology, by the sheer force of occupation, was virtually extinguished in 1945, and even committed Nazis could not repeat its dogma if they wanted any sort of position of dignity or influence in the society that emerged after the war. Critics, especially on the West German and international left, argued that the problem was not so much the survival of Nazi ideas as the survival of a much broader range of authoritarian views and types of behavior. The continued service of many judges and lawyers who had been Nazis, they held, contributed to prolonging a certain authoritarianism and paternalism in West German society, and a travesty of political beliefs that was inconsistent with West Germany's claim to be a fully democratic society. In the view of these critics, democracy in Germany could never be achieved unless this broader and vaguer legacy from the authoritarian past could be destroyed.

They were right in the narrow sense that denazification did not fulfil the hopes of its early proponents, but wrong in the broader sense that the vast majority of Germans were, in fact, denazified – not by the tribunals, but by the war and by changes in society and in their own beliefs. Harold Zink, the chief historian of the US High Commissioner (who replaced OMGUS in 1949), pointed out in his authoritative study of the American occupation that "denazification was intimately tied to personal emotions on the part of many Americans and that it became a political issue of considerable strength in the domestic scene in the United States."[23] Leading American officials during and immediately after the war believed fervently that fascism in Germany must be thoroughly and ruthlessly uprooted. The system of denazification created to achieve that end was not perfect; indeed, it punished many who had done little and ignored many who had done much. Despite its faults, however, and along with occupation initiatives in education, the media, and public administration, it put on record that to have been a devoted follower of Hitler was to have supported crime and violence on

[23] Zink, *United States in Germany,* 167.

a massive scale. In doing so, it was a success. In political terms it turned Nazis from being the accusers to being the accused. The concept worked.

The critics, furthermore, vastly overestimated not only the influence of conservative and authoritarian values in West Germany, but also the very possibility of the sort of radical purge and transformation of political opinions and instincts that would have been called for under the denazification process. A good deal of old-fashioned authoritarian conservatism did exist in the early years of West German history, but it was probably a positive factor in the environment of destruction and destitution that prevailed at least until the early 1950s. This legacy of conservatism was a vital counterforce to the moral collapse of the early occupation years, when the currency was no good, the black market governed economic relations, and the combination of dire need and the shortage of working-age men drove many women to prostitution and other highly unorthodox activities. Moreover, when it had served its purpose, the legacy was used up and disappeared. Beginning in the early to mid-1960s, West Germany found itself in a process of sustained and profound social and cultural change that was only gradually reflected in elections, political life, and personal views, but which marked the true transition to civic democracy.

That transition owed as much to the Western Allies and their occupation policies as to the Germans themselves. Some younger German scholars, particularly but by no means exclusively on the left, argued, in the 1980s, that the Allied occupation of Western Germany was much less laudable than heretofore asserted. This might in some instances have been true, but that was not the point. The purpose of occupation policy was to ensure three things: that Germany should never again become a military threat, that the Germans should accept and admit the criminal nature of the Nazi regime, and that Germany – or as much of it as possible – should become democratic. Together, the Allies and the Germans achieved that purpose. In doing so, the Germans received better treatment than many thought they deserved in 1945. Nazism died, not to rise again as a serious threat to the democratic order. By 1947, moreover, Allied officials and German workers were busy repairing the worst war damage and had restored most essential services. They also managed to avoid mass starvation, though there was certainly widespread suffering, malnutrition, disease, and high infant mortality.

The Allies did their job without the benefit of a large and trained administration. By late 1945, with most conscripted troops already home, the Allied military governments were grotesquely understaffed in relation to the job they had set themselves. Furthermore, they suffered from rapid turnover of personnel and lack of consistent policy guidance from the top. The British and French especially suffered from lack of material resources. Given these problems and especially the shifts in policy that emanated from Washington, London, and Paris, the accomplishments were all the more remarkable.

The famous study of Gabriel Almond and Sidney Verba, *The Civic Culture*, done in 1960, purported to show that West Germany was formally, but not instinctively or psychologically, democratic. It was cited as evidence for the endurance of anti-democratic authoritarianism long after 1945, but in fact the attitudes measured were already on the verge of disappearance. This shift of the 1960s owed very little, if anything, to the moralism of the denazification procedures and every-thing to the Christian ethic in Germany, to the broader processes of development of Western industrial societies, and to the prosperity that allowed Germans to loosen some of the inner bonds of behavior that were so necessary in the phase of reconstruction and the establishment of provisional security, both foreign and domestic.

Although the US zone only contained about one-third of the German population, the experience of the questionnaires, the elaborate denazification apparatus that seemed to fail in the very cases where it should have succeeded, the arbitrary application of rules without proper regard to individual case histories, and the corruption and dishonesty engendered by the procedures involved – especially the affidavits of good character – became, in German popular memory, the typical experience of Allied occupation policy. Denazification was and remained a hopelessly ambiguous procedure. Not only could OMGUS not decide whether it wanted to punish people for their past opinions or for actual misdeeds, but it left the Germans themselves in the extremely uncomfortable position of being obliged to purify them-selves, but without either full responsibility or full recognition for doing so. Despite this, the proceeding marked the high point of Allied occupation policy. When OMGUS began winding it down in late 1947, the Germans themselves were already well on their way to self-government and, what was more important for the ordinary German and his family, on their way to economic recovery. As they proceeded along this path, there remained the memory and the experience of absolute physical and moral devastation, the "Zero Hour" of May 8, 1945, which Konrad Adenauer, the later chancellor, recalled ten years later in these words:

The National Socialist dictatorship, the collapse of which on May 8, 1945, freed innumerable human beings throughout the world and in Germany from a nightmare, left in its wake unimaginable devastation. The very basis of existence seemed to have been destroyed, and the millions of dead and crippled made even the biological survival of the German people look doubtful. What weighed equally heavily was the fact that Germany had lost the confidence of the world.[24]

[24] Press and Information Office, *Germany Reports*, preface.

# PART II

# Reconstruction and Division

*Sunday, September 16, 1945*

*The clock has been turned back an hour, which gives me fourteen hours' sleep. I am catching up on the many short nights of the past months. In church today, the local priest — a pocket Savonarola — uttered a fiery sermon with much ranting against the Nazis. Now!*

*Drove back to Johannisberg via Bad Schwalbach through the beautiful forests of the Taunus. The silence is total, the sense of quiet and peace pervasive. . . .*

Marie Vassiltchikov, *Berlin Diaries, 1940–1945*

*But May 8, 1945, will also be recorded by history as the day when the division of Germany began. This division has created a source of disquietude in the heart of Europe. The obliteration of the unnatural boundary between West and Central [sic] Germany will be the primary concern of every German government. Reunification can only be achieved by peaceful means. Until it is accomplished the German people will have no domestic peace and no means of livelihood, nor will the population of the Soviet occupation zone attain freedom from want and liberty of thought.*

Konrad Adenauer, 1955

# 1

# Politics and Leadership

The first free election in Germany since 1932 occurred on August 10, 1945, in Wohlmutschüll, a village of 480 inhabitants, none of whom had ever belonged to the Nazi party. This fortunate circumstance was the reason that the occupation authorities permitted this special election. The village, which had been under the administrative authority of the neighboring town of Ebermannstadt in Bavaria during the war, elected Johann Sponzel, a 44-year-old farmer, as mayor.[1]

In 1945 anti-Nazi Germans were able to begin political activity in two distinct ways: by organizing national political parties, and by reorganizing local, regional, and *Land* governments. Both activities required military government approval, but this was usually quick in coming. The Americans in particular were anxious to reconstruct a federal system of government in their zone, starting with villages and towns and moving via counties and districts to the level of the *Land* (equivalent to a state). Thus, the occupation period saw two separate but equally important dimensions of political authority in Germany: the dimension of party politics and organization, and the dimension of regional government. Given the absence of a central government, German regional leaders probably had more authority and influence than at any time since Bismarck established the united Reich in 1866–71.

The Wohlmutschüll election was not the first step in reorganizing German government. As soon as the Allies had occupied a town, they were faced with the task of finding reliable, anti-Nazi Germans to take over the administration, maintain law and order, repair water, electricity, and gas works, organize transport, and secure a supply of food. Harold Zink, the chief historian of the US High Commissioner, described the process as follows:

---

[1] *Frankfurter Rundschau*, August 11, 1945.

American military government detachments began the process of constructing German local governments within a few days of their arrival, and very shortly after the German surrender new local government structures were to be seen throughout the American Zone. . . . There was a mayor (*Bürgermeister*) and a handful of other officials in the cities, a county manager (*Landrat*) in the counties, and some progress had usually also been made to get new officials in the many villages (*Gemeinde*). . . . Records had to be dug out, carted from some remote place, or started anew. The tax machinery had to be modified. It was not then for many months or even several years that local governments in anything like the normal sense existed in Germany.[2]

Administration under any conceivable circumstances would have been difficult in an occupied land. In May 1945 the mayors of the major cities and the heads of the old *Länder* and provinces either resigned or were instantly removed. On October 1, 1945, General Clay established OMGUS, the Office of Military Government (US) in Frankfurt. But "the word 'military' in the title was meant to be purely vestigial. . . . The object was to convert military government to a civilian operation and separate it from the military structure as soon as possible."[3] The wide gap between fragmentary local governments at one end and the military governments at the other provided a broad arena for permissible political activity. The Nazi regime had suppressed the autonomy of the *Länder* in 1933, but many of the former regional leaders had survived in

---

Map 1.5 (opposite)   *Landesfürsten* ("Regional Princes") of the Federal Republic. The minister-presidents of the *Länder* of the Federal Republic, known as *Landesfürsten* ("regional princes"), all played decisive roles in the early development of democracy in West Germany. This map shows the names of the most important in their respective *Länder*. Four of them, Altmeier in the Rhineland-Palatinate, Kaisen in Bremen, Zinn in Hesse, and Röder in the Saar, each led his *Land* government for two decades or more without interruption. All those listed governed for at least eight years, with two exceptions: Hoegner of Bavaria, included because of his powerful role vis-à-vis the US military government in 1945–9, and Reuter of Berlin, included because of his role during the Berlin blockade and airlift. Though the autonomy and national importance of the "regional princes" was greatest in the early years, figures like Strauss of Bavaria, Späth of Baden-Württemberg, Rau of North Rhine-Westphalia, and Vogel of the Palatinate have demonstrated the continuing force of federalism in postwar Germany.
*Source*: Adapted from Federal Statistical Office, *Statistical Compass 1987*, 3

[2] Zink, *United States in Germany*, 173.
[3] Ziemke, "Improvising Stability and Change in Postwar Germany," in *Americans as Proconsuls*, ed. Wolfe, 64.

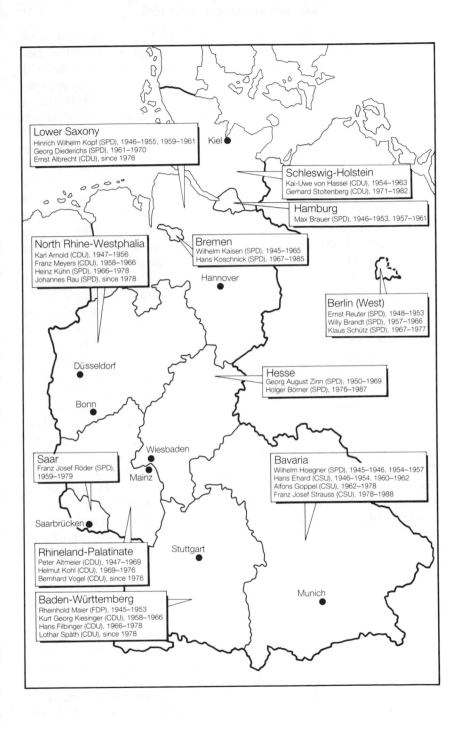

**Lower Saxony**
Hinrich Wilhelm Kopf (SPD), 1946–1955, 1959–1961
Georg Diederichs (SPD), 1961–1970
Ernst Albrecht (CDU), since 1976

Kiel ●

**Schleswig-Holstein**
Kai-Uwe von Hassel (CDU), 1954–1963
Gerhard Stoltenberg (CDU), 1971–1982

**Hamburg**
Max Brauer (SPD), 1946–1953, 1957–1961

**North Rhine-Westphalia**
Karl Arnold (CDU), 1947–1956
Franz Meyers (CDU), 1958–1966
Heinz Kühn (SPD), 1966–1978
Johannes Rau (SPD), since 1978

**Bremen**
Wilhelm Kaisen (SPD), 1945–1965
Hans Koschnick (SPD), 1967–1985

Hannover ●

**Berlin (West)**
Ernst Reuter (SPD), 1948–1953
Willy Brandt (SPD), 1957–1966
Klaus Schütz (SPD), 1967–1977

Düsseldorf ●

Bonn ●

**Hesse**
Georg August Zinn (SPD), 1950–1969
Holger Börner (SPD), 1976–1987

**Saar**
Franz Josef Röder (SPD),
1959–1979

Wiesbaden ●

Mainz ●

**Bavaria**
Wilhelm Hoegner (SPD), 1945–1946, 1954–1957
Hans Ehard (CSU), 1946–1954, 1960–1962
Alfons Goppel (CSU), 1962–1978
Franz Josef Strauss (CSU), 1978–1988

Saarbrücken ●

**Rhineland-Palatinate**
Peter Altmeier (CDU), 1947–1969
Helmut Kohl (CDU), 1969–1976
Bernhard Vogel (CDU), since 1976

Stuttgart ●

**Baden-Württemberg**
Rheinhold Maier (FDP), 1945–1953
Kurt Georg Kiesinger (CDU), 1958–1966
Hans Filbinger (CDU), 1966–1978
Lothar Späth (CDU), since 1978

Munich ●

obscurity or semi-retirement. After the Third Reich, moreover, most anti-Nazi Germans with political ambitions agreed that the new Germany should be a federal system made up of constituent states with real powers of their own. A remarkably effective set of strong regional leaders emerged after 1945: Reinhold Maier and Gebhard Müller in the south-west, Wilhelm Hoegner and Hans Ehard in Bavaria, Karl Arnold and Fritz Steinhoff in the industrial Rhineland, Max Brauer and Wilhelm Kaisen in Hamburg and Bremen, Peter Altmeier in the Palatinate. So powerful did they become that observers began to refer to them as *Landesfürsten* (regional princes). This was the name given to the territorial princes of the late medieval German empire, who from the thirteenth century onward became so strong that their authority in their own territories completely eclipsed that of the Holy Roman Empire. By the seventeenth century, the *Landesfürsten* had reduced the imperial government to a mere shell with no power to tax, no jurisdiction, and virtually no authority to set policy. The war produced an analogous situation, since there was no central government in 1945.

The new *Landesfürsten* in the western zones of occupation led the reemergence of historically important regions of Germany that had been eclipsed by Prussia since the early nineteenth century. Prussia controlled almost two-thirds of the territory and population of the old Reich in a wide swath from the Rhineland in the west across the north German plain to Prussia proper in the east. Prussia's breakthrough to power in western Germany occurred in 1814, when it annexed the lower Rhineland including its capital, Cologne, and the future industrial heartland of Germany, the Ruhr valley. Many non-Prussian Germans resented the fact that the united Reich of 1871–1945 was to a large extent a Prussian Reich, governed according to Prussian methods and traditions and conducting policies in the Prussian interest. Thus, in 1945 they had the opportunity to remedy what many of them considered a historical injustice. In doing so they were able to draw on a wide range of expertise provided by many scholars and civil servants who likewise applauded the disappearance of Prussia and the chance to build a federal government in Germany. Two such experts, Theodor Eschenburg and Herbert Blankenhorn, each played a material role, the former in shaping West German constitutional government, the second in designing its foreign policy.

Postwar West Germany eventually consisted of eleven *Länder*, including the western sectors of Berlin and the Saar which joined in 1955. The other nine fell into five regional groups: Bavaria, Swabia (the south-west), the Frankfurt region, the industrial Rhineland, and the north. Bavaria was entirely within the US zone; Swabia, the Frankfurt region, and the Rhineland were split among all three Western Allies; and the north belonged to the British zone. The Rhineland and the north had been part of Prussia before 1945.

Bavaria was the only ancient *Land* to emerge from the war virtually unscathed in territorial extent. Bavarian regionalists thus had little difficulty in building on the population's sense of emotional and cultural continuity with more than 800 years of history of Bavaria as a distinct political and cultural entity. Bavarians took great satisfaction in the fact that their domineering rival within Germany, Prussia, was defunct. The leaders of the restored *Freistaat Bayern* (Free State of Bavaria), as they called it, succeeded in carving a unique space for themselves in the political system of postwar Germany.

Swabia consisted of the territory of the former *Länder* of Württemberg and Baden. In 1945, the US and France split this territory across the middle, creating three temporary *Länder*, two in the French and one in the American zone. Politically and culturally the Swabians had much in common. Baden and Württemberg were the home of German liberalism in the nineteenth century and had looked always to France and the west for trade and ideas rather than to Prussia, which was to the Swabians more of a foreign country than was France. Württemberg-Baden, in the US zone, was an artificial combination of the northern halves of the two old *Länder*, torn from their southern halves south of the line of the autobahn that ran from Karlsruhe on the Rhine southeastward toward Munich. The parts south of the autobahn from Karlsruhe to Ulm, where the autobahn crossed the Danube into Bavaria, became the main part of the French zone of occupation. The temporary consolidation of the northern halves was the work of William Dawson (1892–1947), a professor of law at the University of Cleveland, who became the senior US official of the *Land* from 1945 to 1947. He knew that the southwestern parts of Germany – the old kingdom of Württemberg and adjacent areas – although never politically united as an independent *Land*, nevertheless shared common cultural and political traditions. The most important of these were an independent, spiritual form of Protestantism and political liberalism. The liberals of the German south-west had in the nineteenth century been strong opponents of the authoritarian Prussians. Now, after 1945, their philosophical and political descendants saw their chance to create a *Südweststaat*, a southwest state which would once and for all provide a vigorous counterweight to those northern and eastern traditions they saw as dangerous. From 1945 the Swabian leaders worked with determination and ultimate success to establish such a united south-western *Land* as a counterweight to Bavaria and to the industrial Rhineland, and to ensure that a new German government would reflect their own interests in strong federalism and in reconciliation with France.

The Frankfurt region included the pre-1933 *Land* of Hesse and the Prussian province of Hesse-Nassau on the right and the Palatinate on the left banks of the Rhine, and part of the former Prussian Rhine province. The Palatinate was part of Bavaria until 1945. The largest city of Hesse was Frankfurt, where OMGUS was located, though its own capital was Darmstadt. Hesse was consolidated into a *Land* on the advice of Professor Walter L. Dorn, an advisor to OMGUS, who was a specialist in German constitutional history and familiar with German regional traditions. The Palatinate and the southern tip of the Rhine province fell to the French, who combined the two areas into one new *Land*, the Rhineland-Palatinate, in May 1947. Unlike most of the other new *Länder*, this had no historical or organic unity. Like Lower Saxony in the north, it was a largely rural region of villages and small or middle-sized cities. Even in the 1980s, after three decades of rapid urban growth throughout West Germany, most of the inhabitants lived in communities with a population of 10,000 or less.

The industrial Rhineland, centered in the Ruhr district where most of prewar Germany's heavy industry was located, included the Prussian Rhine province and the province of Westphalia. Here, in August 1946, the British military government established the new *Land* of North Rhine-Westphalia which became the largest, most densely populated, and most heavily industrialized *Land* of the Federal Republic. Demographically, politically, and culturally, the area was a mosaic. It included some rural districts as well as the huge conurbations of Düsseldorf, Dortmund, Wuppertal, and Cologne. Along with Berlin and the area of Chemnitz and Plauen now in the Soviet zone, the Ruhr was one of the three bastions of the German working class and hence of the SPD (Social Democratic Party). The districts around Cologne and Münster, however, were heavily Catholic, which counterbalanced socialist dominance. These districts provided the future voters of the Christian Democratic Union, the CDU. The rest of the middle class and much of the business community became staunch supporters of the postwar liberal party, the FDP (Free Democratic Party).

The north yielded two new *Länder*, Lower Saxony and Schleswig-Holstein, and two independent cities, Hamburg and Bremen. Most of the territory had been Prussian before 1945, except for Hamburg and Bremen and a few independent enclaves that had escaped annexation by Prussia because they were too insignificant or too poor. Lower Saxony was all that remained in the western zones of the great north German plain. Both it and Schleswig-Holstein became the temporary or permanent home of millions of refugees from the east after 1945. The refugees exhausted the capacity of these regions to provide food for

Map 1.6   Occupied areas of Germany divided into zones and *Länder*.
*Source*: Office of Military Governor for Germany (US), *Monthly Report*,
April 1949, No. 46

export. This also contributed to the development of Schleswig-Holstein as one of the poorest *Länder*, as well as one of the smallest.

Hamburg and Bremen were special cases. Both were ancient republics of the Hanseatic League of the late Middle Ages, which was a confederation of towns in northern Germany devoted to trade and mutual political assistance. Throughout the centuries they had retained their independent government. Nazism was never very strong in either place, and the Allies quickly found able and eager leaders to participate in government. The Americans included Bremen in their zone, since they needed the city and its port of Bremerhaven on the North Sea as the port of entry for goods and personnel arriving in Germany by sea.

The provisional *Länder* of the American zone were established by the end of 1945. The others came into existence in 1946–7. The most important of them, the south-western *Land* of Baden-Württemberg, did not formally exist until 1952, when three *Länder* of the US and French zones were combined. Yet even in their embryonic form, the new *Länder* were an arena of political activity for democratic Germans that was indispensable for the future success of the Federal Republic.

The next step was to certify German governments in these *Länder* that would carry out in a responsible fashion the decisions of OMGUS and to secure a denazified administration on the local level. Only by conferring limited autonomy on German administrations could the basis for democratic re-education be laid. In Bavaria, where strong regional political traditions re-emerged with the fall of the Third Reich, a provisional government was installed by the US authorities under Fritz Schäffer, a conservative Catholic supported by the Catholic Church under Cardinal Faulhaber, the archbishop of Munich, and by the Bavarian civil service. A left-leaning group in the US military administration in Munich accused the Schäffer administration of opposition to denazification measures, and on September 28, 1945, it was dismissed by Eisenhower and replaced by a government of broader political views under a social democrat, Wilhelm Hoegner. In Württemberg-Baden the military governor appointed Reinhold Maier, in the Weimar Republic a leading member of the pro-business German Democratic Party (DDP), as minister-president. Hesse was given a bipartisan government under Karl Geiler, a lawyer, who had no party affiliation of any kind.

The governments of all three *Länder* formed the Council of States (*Länderrat*) of the US zone, established by General Clay in October 1945 and organized by James K. Pollock, a Michigan political scientist. Immediately after the first local elections throughout the American zone in 1946, Clay assigned to the *Länderrat* responsibility for food, agriculture, industry, transportation, and prices, so that, as the leading authority on US occupation policy noted, "it soon took on the character of a central government of the American zone."[4] The Council of States met in Stuttgart and consisted of the minister-presidents of the three *Länder*, Wilhelm Hoegner (SPD) of Bavaria, succeeded by Hans Ehard (CSU, Christian Social Union), Reinhold Maier (FDP) of Baden-Württemberg, and Karl Geiler, succeeded by Christian Stock (SPD) of Hesse, joined in 1947 by the Senate president of the city state of Bremen, Wilhelm Kaisen (SPD). The *Länderrat* proved very effective, and became an influential precursor of the administrative bodies created prior to the founding of the Federal Republic in 1949.

The British zone was the most populous and most heavily industrial-ized of all the zones, and also the one with the smallest amount of arable land. In accordance with wartime policy and the Potsdam agreements, the British focused on controlling industrial concerns and eliminating the Nazi party; but given their own political traditions, were unprepared to take in hand the organization of a federal system. The process of building a German network of civil administration was therefore slower and less smooth than in the US zone. The British insisted on the reduction to four *Länder* of the confused administrative structure of their zone, which consisted of several small *Länder*, various Prussian provinces, and the Free City of Hamburg, but refused to allow German elements to play a major role in this process. It was not complete until late in 1946, just before the administrative unification of the British and US zones. In early 1946, the *Länder* of the British zone, as they then existed, were given provisional parliaments to advise the military government, which appointed their members.

The greatest difference was in attitudes to inter-regional initiatives. The Americans considered the *Länderrat* a necessary stage in develop-ing a new German administration responsible for most of the daily tasks of government. The British remained, for a much longer time, deter-mined to keep close control of regional and interregional administra-tion, but allowed an increasing measure of informal consultation among the German administrative organs themselves. An example of this was the private discussions, discovered by Michael Thomas, a British liaison officer to German administrators and political leaders, between the mayor of Hamburg, Rudolf Petersen, and the heads of other *Land* governments in the British zone. As it turned out his discovery of these German liaison activities in the British zone was extremely fortunate. It led to semi-official permission for their continuance and, in due course, to the formation of the Zonal Council in February 1946, the British counterpart to the *Länderrat*.

[4] Gimbel, "Governing the American Zone of Germany," in *Americans as Proconsuls*, ed. Wolfe, 94.

The French had very direct annexationist concerns in their zone. Their political and economic rule was strict and ·they were less interested in promoting German self-government. The French appointed an academic of half-French descent, Carlo Schmid, as state councillor (*Staatsrat*), a sort of extraordinary minister-president, of the southern halves of Württemberg and Baden, a temporary *Land* called Württemberg-Hohenzollern. Schmid, a colorful and powerful member of the SPD, succeeded in gaining access to Stuttgart in the US zone, where the northern halves of Württemberg and Baden were being governed, and had himself appointed state councillor of Württemberg-Baden by Maier. He was the only man under the occupation regime to have been a member of two different *Land* governments in two different zones. An equally important German figure in the French zone, however, was the lawyer Gebhard Müller, who became head of the CDU in the state and subsequently played a very important role in the Federal Republic as chief justice of the Federal Constitutional Court from 1958 to 1971.

The biggest problem of the French zone was the territory on the French border called the Saarland, which France fully intended to annex. It was, therefore, separated officially from the French zone in July 1945 and administered by the French government in Paris. In June 1946, the Council of Foreign Ministers approved French annexation of the Saar as compensation for the formation, in the British zone, of the *Land* North Rhine-Westphalia. The creation of this new *Land* encompassed all of the industrialized Ruhr district, which meant that France had to abandon its hopes for an internationalization of the principal components of German industry in the west. Therefore, since France no longer had the opportunity to control the resources of the Ruhr district, the French insisted on direct control of the resources of the Saar which included coal.

The other great arena of activity, the establishment of national political parties, was slower to start because of the very difficulties that gave the *Landesfürsten* such great scope of action, namely the zonal divisions and the problems of interzonal and interregional communication. Under JCS 1067 and the Berlin Declaration of June 5, 1945, no political activity of any kind was permitted without special permission of the occupation authorities. Nevertheless, in the final weeks of the war, as Ruth Andreas-Friedrich describes in her diary, groups had appeared spontaneously in a number of German cities, most of which called themselves "Anti-Fascist Action Committees," known as "Antifa." Their main goal was to remove the remnants of Nazi rule, but some went much further. In Stuttgart, the Antifa organization announced, in a proclamation of May 7, 1945, that capitalism was discredited by history and demanded "planned socialist reconstruction." In Bremen, two communists led one of the largest Antifa organizations in the Western zones; during most of the occupation period, they were members of the city senate. Communists and syndicalists – people who believed that the trade unions should bring about the revolutionary transformation of society by means of strikes and other direct action – dominated the more active Antifas.

By late summer 1945, however, the occupation authorities had banned most of this kind of activity, while simultaneously permitting the formation of regular political parties. The newly emerging parties had a broader agenda than mere denazification; they were concerned with introducing democratic practice and with economic and psychological recovery. A license was required under Allied military government for all organized activity, whether political, cultural, or commercial. Without a license, no political entity could legally function, register members, collect dues, take public positions or participate in elections. In 1945, the four Allies agreed on licensing parties of four types in each zone or *Land:* communist, social democratic, Christian democratic and liberal. These Allied decisions largely determined the structure of West German party life for the future. The outlines of this structure were clear within a few months of surrender, but a stable framework did not emerge until the mid-1950s.

The first zone to allow formation of political parties was, ironically, the Soviet zone, in June, 1945. The establishment of political parties in the Western zones occurred thereafter, primarily at the local level. The Center Party (Zentrum), KPD (Communist Party of Germany) and the SPD (Social Democratic Party of Germany) had existed before the Third Reich. All other parties were new creations. The most remarkable, as well as the most successful, was the Christian Democratic Union (CDU) and its Bavarian adjunct, the Christian Social Union (CSU). In retrospect it might seem logical that there should be one single large non-socialist party, but from the perspective of German party history this was not logical at all. Until 1933, the non-socialist vote had been split between a half-dozen or more parties, each appealing to a particular social, cultural, or religious interest. The founders of the CDU wanted to establish something entirely new in German politics, a large, national people's party based on Christian principles that would appeal to *both* Catholics and Protestants who shared a commitment to democracy and freedom. Initially, the CDU was not what Europeans would call a liberal party, that is, a party of the free market, though it became so later. Partly for that reason, liberals in the occupation era formed their own party, which later became the Free Democratic Party (FDP). The FDP also became the home of voters who, while non-socialist, could not support the overtly pro-Christian orientation of the CDU. From the beginning, this Liberal Party – liberal primarily in the European economic sense of laissez-faire, not the American sense of the political liberal – was split between social liberals with a tolerant view of cultural change and personal behavior, and national liberals who were essentially conservative but who rejected the strongly Catholic flavor of the CDU. The FDP, politically progressive and economically conservative, came to play a pivotal role in German politics, because – though small by comparison – it served as the principal coalition partner with the CDU or the SPD.

The parties of the old system that ended in 1933 were very different in structure and social position and composition from those of 1945. In the old system, every political party belonged to and represented the particular interests, feelings, mentality, and behavior of part or all of a specific "social milieu." There were four such milieus in Germany: the socialist or working-class, the Catholic, the liberal, and the conservative. These milieus were not the same as social classes or the mere expression of economic interests, but reflected the historical cleavages of German society as these had developed in the era of industrialization and national unification during the nineteenth century.

These inherited social milieus were not wholly destroyed by Nazism and the war. They continued to play a role in the shadows of West German social and cultural life for at least two decades after 1945. By the 1960s they lost much of their remaining significance, as West Germany completed the transition to a society stratified according to function and economic status in which middle-class attitudes, behavior, and expectations were dominant. Though differences in social milieu later re-emerged at the margins, notably in the so-called "new social movements" of the 1970s and 1980s, these developments could not reverse the broad trend toward functional stratification and uniformity. The political parties reflected this trend in their tendency to present themselves as "people's parties." The modern party, in West Germany as in the USA and elsewhere, increasingly presented itself as a party for the entire people and no longer the political expression of a specific social stratum. Such a party had mass membership and a strong apparatus that formulated electoral strategy, distributed patronage, and rewarded supporters by giving each special interest its due.

Initially the parties were torn between the inherited influence of social milieus and the clearly felt need for a dramatic change from the old system, to a new system of universal mass parties. Important regional and sectional interests fell victim to the dislocations of the war and disappeared. They were replaced by a new and different concern, which cut across the old boundaries, namely the struggle to remain alive, and survive. Many of the leaders, moreover, shared a common background in the resistance to Hitler, notably Konrad Adenauer, Eugen Gerstenmaier, Jakob Kaiser, Ernst Lemmer, and Gebhard Müller of the CDU, Josef "Sepp" Müller of its Bavarian counterpart, the CSU, and Kurt Schumacher, Erich Ollenhauer, Ernst Reuter and Carlo Schmid of the SPD. These figures all shared a commitment to freedom and peace, as well as to restoring respect for Germany and the Germans. It was the courage of their convictions that, in many cases, enabled them to survive Nazi Germany, and that gave them the fortitude they needed to rebuild Germany's political life.

The parties were not allowed to communicate and operate between the zones, though they did so informally; in fact, civilian telephone use was not permitted between the Western zones until 1946. The division between the Soviet and the Western zones increased the difficulties in this important area, as it did concerning other issues. The parties in the Soviet zone were reduced, between 1946 and 1949, to mere tools of the real holder of power, the KPD. Even after interzonal party cooperation began to take place in late 1945, the parties were only allowed to deal with local and regional problems, primarily concerning denazification and reconstruction.

Even in the Western zones many Germans regarded the new parties with suspicion, and many more were uninterested. Politics was not the first priority, when merely surviving from day to day was hard enough. Yet a large minority from all walks of life took an immediate and intense interest in establishing democratic parties, and yet others engaged themselves just as intensely in building up the administration of local areas and of the *Länder*. These politically interested Germans intended to prove to the Allies that they were worthy of trust and capable of democracy. They also hoped that the military governments would soon allow free elections in order to gain a first impression of the balance of democratic forces.

Fortunately, the military governments agreed with this interest. Eisenhower and Clay announced future elections in the US zone in September 1945, four months after the end of the war. Newspapers gave reality to the hope. So the *Münchener Zeitung* carried the headline on September 22, 1945, "Elections in the USA-Zone – Election regulations must be presented by October 15 – First political meetings." There was, indeed, a tremendous hunger for information, since Germans had been cut off from the outside world for so long.

Clay's main reason for elections was to have democratically elected German representatives to whom he could transfer more responsibility, given the rapidly declining numbers of US personnel and the intention of the US government to reduce the size of OMGUS, and ultimately to transfer the administration of the occupation from the Army to the State Department. Elections in communities of less than 20,000 inhabitants were scheduled for January 1946, and in larger communities for March and May. When the elections were called in the American zone, political parties were still being licensed, while in the British and the Soviet zone political parties were already officially in existence.[5] In all three US *Länder* legislative elections followed in November-December 1946. The city state of Bremen, which formed a US enclave in the British zone because it was the entry point for shipments from the US, was allowed elections in October.

The elections provided legitimate governing authorities in the *Länder* of the US zone and allowed work to begin on devising democratic constitutions for them. Germans were still not permitted to take steps toward formation of a national government, but by late 1946 the groundwork was being laid more quickly than many observers realized.

The conditions common to all political parties in 1945 were shaped by two main factors, one ideological and one geopolitical. The ideological factor was a universal skepticism of the role of political parties, because their leadership, or lack of it, had contributed to Hitler's rise to power. Any program or system that bore any resemblance to Nazism, or that might conceivably lead to Nazism, was suspect. This rejection was expressed in programs and statements appealing to all the values and principles that had been despised and suppressed under Hitler: individual rights, republican democracy, social and political decentralization, respect for religion, judicial independence, and the will to remain at peace with Germany's neighbors and other European states.

The geopolitical factor was the division of Germany into occupation zones. Although parties were intended to operate on a national basis and immediately made national appeals for support, zonal division, the personal qualities of the political leaders present in each of the zones, and the variations in Allied policy on political activity meant that party organizations first arose regionally. Three areas, aside from the Soviet zone, were particularly active; Berlin (all four sectors), the Rhineland, and Munich. Leaders of the new parties eagerly debated what kind of social and economic structures should emerge in postwar Germany. The winners of this debate had a decisive impact on what Germany would become. In tone the party leaders were all decidedly "antifascist," although the communists enjoyed little support anywhere in Germany. This characteristic dominated political discussions throughout the Western zones to such an extent that there was little difference, if any, between the CDU and the SPD on this issue.

[5] Ziemke, "Improvising Stability and Change in Postwar Germany," in *Americans as Proconsuls*, ed. Wolfe, 63–4.

At the first public meeting of the SPD in Frankfurt, the Frankfurt party chairman, Wilhelm Knothe, declared that "all Nazis are responsible for the fact that Germany, and with it all of Europe, has become a poorhouse. For this reason we must insist that even the last Nazi is mercilessly removed from the city administration and from all important economic posts."[6] Andreas Hermes, a leader of the CDU in Berlin, spoke with equal conviction when he emphasized that his party "will not be outdone by any German party in the seriousness of its demand for punishment of the guilty. . . ."[7]

[6] *Münchener Zeitung,* September 22, 1945.
[7] Ibid., October 6, 1945.

# 2

# Adenauer and Schumacher

The leading initiatives in the Western zones came from two exceptional men who were based in the British zone: Konrad Adenauer in
Cologne, who became the leader of the Christian democrats, and Kurt
Schumacher in Wennigsen near Hannover, a social democrat. Both
were political geniuses, though completely different in character and
outlook. Adenauer, the conservative, turned out to be the foremost
internationalist of postwar Germany, advancing policies of growth,
progress, and prosperity. Schumacher, whose tradition was that of
proletarian internationalism, became a fierce nationalist suspicious of
foreign entanglements.

Adenauer, born in 1876, was a Rhinelander who felt superior to
Prussian traditions and the ideals of the Prussian state, which was overwhelmingly the largest in the old Reich. He became mayor of Cologne in
1917 and in the 1920s was one of the leading political figures of the
Center. Following World War I, Adenauer proposed the separation of
the Rhineland and other western provinces from Prussia. He was an
ambitious and popular mayor with an incredible capacity for work and
for concentration on the business at hand. His work is still evident today
in Cologne, in the city's stadium, in the huge park surrounding the
Rhineland metropolis, and in the first autobahn ever built, that between
Cologne and Bonn.

Hans-Peter Schwarz, author of the most authoritative biography of
Adenauer and a leading political scientist, asked the question:

What kind of a person was he, anyway? In English, this question is
occasionally phrased as "What makes him tick?"
The physical and spiritual reserves which Adenauer, even at an advanced
age, mustered to cope with his workload, are more than remarkable. His vigor,
his patience in fulfilling his duty, his tempo, his inexhaustible thirst for
information, his intellectual presence, his temperament and the wide variety of
finely shaded emotions, encompassing everything from captivating charm and

The Römer, the central square of Frankfurt, in 1945. The city was the birthplace of Johann Wolfgang von Goethe, the greatest poet in the German language. It was also the site of election of the kings of Germany since the ninth century and of the National Assembly of 1848−9, one of the most important events in the history of democracy in Germany, held in St Paul's Church (upper right). [*Source*: German Information Center (GIC), New York]

The same view thirty years later. The skyscrapers in the background, headquarters of German and international banks, mark the city's role as the financial capital of West Germany and of continental Europe. The restored Römer and St Paul's Church stand as reminders of a past that seems distant. [*Source*: GIC]

Bonn, later the capital of the Federal Republic, as it looked immediately after being occupied by American troops in March 1945. [*Source*: Bundesbildstelle Bonn]

Nuremberg, the capital of northern Bavaria on the river Pegnitz, in 1945. Superstitious Nazis, like Adolf Hitler himself, regarded the city with awe because it had formerly sheltered the sacred insignia of the Holy Roman Empire. He therefore chose it as the site of the annual Nazi party rallies. In Allied eyes, it became a symbol of the Nazi regime. [*Source*: GIC]

The central landmark of Berlin, the Brandenburg Gate, in 1945. The Gate, completed in 1797, marks the approach to the old city of Berlin from the west. East of it lies the old central government district (*Mitte*), west of it the Tiergarten park and the western districts of Charlottenburg and Schöneberg. Today it stands just a few yards within the Soviet sector of Berlin, which is divided from the American, British and French sectors by the Berlin Wall. [*Source*: GIC]

*Right* Returning German prisoners of war in Frankfurt, 1946. [*Source*: GIC]

*Trümmerfrauen* (literally, rubble-women) were a familiar sight in occupied Germany. Since most able-bodied, working-age men were either in prison camps or in the remaining factories, the task of clearing the mountains of rubble in the streets of virtually all German cities fell to women. This photo shows *Trümmerfrauen* clearing streets in Berlin. [*Source*: Bundes- bildstelle Bonn]

DOENITZ
C.-in-C. of the German Navy

RAEDER
Inspector of the German Navy

SCHIRACH
Nazi Youth Leader

SAUCKEL
Gauleiter of Thuringia

ROSENBERG
Minister for Eastern Occupied Territories

GOERING
Successor Designate to Hitler

HESS
Deputy to Hitler

RIBBENTROP
Nazi Foreign Minister

KEITEL
Chief of the High Command

KALTENBRUNNER
Chief of Security Police

Sector border in occupied Berlin, 1948. [*Source*: German Pictorial Collection, Hoover Institution Archives]

*Below* The defendants in the trial of "main war criminals" at the International Military Tribunal in Nuremberg, 1945–6. [*Source*: BBC Hulton Picture Library]

Konrad Adenauer, first chancellor of the Federal Republic and CDU chairman 1946–66, was lord mayor of Cologne 1917–33. After the Nazis fired him from that post, he had time for his hobby, which was cultivating roses. As Kaiser's victorious rival, Adenauer was the leading proponent of the view that the only chance for democracy in Germany was for the western part to associate itself intimately with the West. For him, dreams of neutrality and "Christian socialism" were dangerous illusions. In postwar Germany he continued to pursue his life-long interest in cultivating roses. [*Source*: GIC]

*Above left* General Sir Brian H. Robertson, the military governor of the British zone of occupation, in which the city of Bonn, that became the capital of the Federal Republic, was located. [*Source*: German Pictorial Collection, Hoover Institution Archives]

*Above right* General Lucius D. Clay, the military governor of the US zone of occupation, was the most powerful man in Western Germany during the occupation. Understanding both the need for order and for democratic political recovery he laid a strong basis for the limited independence granted to West Germany in 1949. [*Source*: German Pictorial Collection, Hoover Institution Archives]

*Above left* Jakob Kaiser, leader of the CDU in the Soviet zone and Berlin from 1945 to 1947, addressing an electoral rally in West Berlin during the blockade in 1948. He was the leading proponent of the view that a neutral postwar Germany, constructed on the principles of "Christian socialism," could become a "bridge between East and West." [*Source*: GIC]

*Above right* Despite severe disability due to imprisonment in concentration camps, the SPD leader Kurt Schumacher fought for his belief that only the German working class and its party, the SPD, had the moral right to govern after 1945, and that only a neutral and socialist Germany could guarantee peace in Europe and security against communist encroachment. He was a leader of principle who had the courage of his convictions. [*Source*: GIC]

Berlin children at Tempelhof airfield watching an American transport landing, 1948–9. They dubbed these planes *Rosinenbomber* (raisin bombers), because many of the pilots had the habit of scattering raisins or candy from the cockpit. [*Source*: GIC]

The monument to the Berlin airlift erected by the city of Berlin, known colloquially as the *Harke* (harrow). [*Source*: GIC]

*Inset* Ernst Reuter, the German hero of the airlift as governing mayor of (West) Berlin, wearing his beloved beret. His death in 1953, following that of Kurt Schumacher in 1952, was a great loss for the SPD. [*Source*: GIC]

*Right* The original of the Basic Law was signed by all 65 members of the Council on May 23, 1949. The picture shows the first of these signatures, namely those of Adenauer (CDU, president of the Council), Adolph Schönfelder (SPD, first vice-president), and Hermann Schäfer (FDP, second vice-president). [*Source*: GIC]

Der Parlamentarische Rat hat das vorstehende Grundgesetz für die Bundesrepublik Deutschland in öffentlicher Sitzung am 8. Mai des Jahres Eintausendneunhundertneunundvierzig mit dreiundfünfzig gegen zwölf Stimmen beschlossen. Zu Urkunde dessen haben sämtliche Mitglieder des Parlamentarischen Rates die vorliegende Urschrift des Grundgesetzes eigenhändig unterzeichnet.

BONN AM RHEIN, den 23. Mai des Jahres Eintausendneunhundertneunundvierzig.

PRÄSIDENT DES PARLAMENTARISCHEN RATES

I. VIZEPRÄSIDENT DES PARLAMENTARISCHEN RATES

II. VIZEPRÄSIDENT DES PARLAMENTARISCHEN RATES

The Parliamentary Council voting by 53 to 12 to accept the Basic Law in Bonn on May 8, 1949. Max Reimann, the communist leader, is seen not voting (front row, left). For him, the democratic Basic Law was the denial of the totalitarian dictatorship he sought to install. To the right of him are Walter Menzel (CDU), Carlo Schmid (SPD), Theodor Heuss (FDP). Note also the representative of the British Military Government on the extreme left. [*Source*: GIC]

Adenauer presenting his first cabinet to the Allied High Commissioners on September 21, 1949. He deliberately strode on to the carpet where the High Commissioners were standing to claim equality, rather than waiting in a subservient position in front of it, as he was expected to do. From left to right: Fritz Schäffer (CSU, finance), Thomas Dehler (FDP, justice), Kaiser (CDU, all-German affairs), Adenauer, Franz Blücher (FDP, vice-chancellor and economic cooperation). [*Source*: GIC]

In the above photograph, taken in 1949, Adenauer meets with SPD leader Kurt Schumacher (left) and Carlo Schmid, who served as a member of the Parliamentary Council. [*Source*: Bundesbildstelle Bonn]

*Below* The funeral of SPD leader Kurt Schumacher in 1952. Hundreds of thousands lined the streets as the hearse passed by. His death marked the passing of an era in West German politics. [*Source*: Bundesbildstelle Bonn]

As director of the Economic Council of the Bizone and later as economics minister under Adenauer, Ludwig Erhard was responsible for the extraordinarily successful economic system of postwar West Germany in the 1950s and 1960s, the social market economy. Under his guidance, West Germans achieved prosperity and international economic power that was unimaginable in 1945 or even 1948. In this photograph, he is holding his famous book *Prosperity through Competition*, published in German in 1957. [*Source*: GIC]

Erich Ollenhauer, the chairman of the SPD from 1952 to 1964, was the last social democratic leader of the Weimar generation. He courageously defended ideological purity, often without political success. [*Source*: GIC]

Adenauer with Theodor Blank (CDU), the head of the "Blank Office," the forerunner of the ministry of defense, in the early 1950s. [*Source*: GIC]

Hans Globke, *right* Adenauer's chief aide in the chancellery from 1950 to 1963. His enormous labors in establishing and running the West German government and its foreign policy were overshadowed in the public mind by the fact that he had served in a high position during the Third Reich. He thus became the focus of an intense and emotional debate on the morality of public service and West Germany's relation to its Nazi past. [*Source*: GIC]

Adenauer was a faithful son of the Catholic Church but, unlike Christian socialists such as Kaiser, he did not believe in mixing religion and politics. Here he is shown during his first US visit with the archbishops of New York and Los Angeles, Francis Cardinal Spellman (left) and Francis Cardinal McIntyre (right), under a portrait of the then-reigning pope, Pius XII, who was a strong supporter of Adenauer. [*Source*: GIC]

Friedrich Meinecke (1862–1954), the dean of German historians, was one of the few of his profession who supported the Weimar democracy. In his eighties when the war ended, he wrote one of the most stirring philosophical accounts of Nazism in *The German Catastrophe* (1946). His humanistic, cosmopolitan outlook had few direct heirs, but nevertheless inspired a generation of scholars both in Germany and abroad. [*Source*: GIC]

Hans Herzfeld (1892–1982) *below* in the garden of his Berlin home in 1976. He was called to succeed Friedrich Meinecke, at his request, as professor of modern history at the Free University of Berlin in 1950. [*Source*: Dennis L. Bark]

joyous relaxation down to cutting outbursts – all that is forever surprising, particularly because he manages, once more, to unfold the full range of his capabilities in the eighth and ninth decades of his life. . . .

The characteristics which for me are the most remarkable are his indefatigable energy and a life-long determination to assert himself, fighting opponents and opposition. In addition, a concentrated inner sovereignty, which nobody who closely knew or worked with him could completely escape from. Not to be forgotten, an unbreakable pride, which manifested itself most impressively after the collapse of 1945, when Adenauer represented the case of his defeated and guilt-ridden nation to the Occupying Powers. However, it is Adenauer the fighter who most impressed me and who receives my full sympathy, notwithstanding some reservations towards him as a person. I don't mean a fight in the sense of sterile confrontation, rather his tough determination to win support, mobilize majorities, convince adherents, and outwit opponents in the often insoluble daily tasks and in his decisive pursuit of large initiatives. Starting with the time as mayor of Cologne up to the protests against the nuclear non-proliferation treaty during the last months before his death, Adenauer's life is a drama, a continuous fight, and he himself a worker who is never satisfied with the world the way it presents itself.[1]

Other, and to some, less attractive characteristics, were also evident: Adenauer possessed the invaluable political gift of being able to say exactly the right words when he wished and to whom he wished, in order to achieve his purpose. His enemies called it Machiavellian manipulation and deceitfulness. He was also the archetypal political man in his total lack of interest in the complex maze of political ideology. His language was simple and direct (some called it primitive), and he was not a great stylist. However, in Germany after 1945 he became a practical statesman of the first rank. His patience and control were qualities vitally necessary in 1945. Don Cook's assignment with the *New York Herald Tribune* took him to Bonn in 1949, and his remembrance of Adenauer centers on "his great dignity and old-fashioned courtesy and composure. Dignity was rare in Germany in those days, when attitudes often varied from sullen arrogance to insufferable obsequiousness. With Adenauer it was much more than just dignity of age. It was a dignity of character and intellect as well."[2]

During the Third Reich he was arrested on several occasions and spent much of his time in hiding and moving from place to place. He was put in prison for the last time following the abortive assassination attempt on Hitler's life in July 1944. His son Max, who was a lieutenant in the German army, interceded on his father's behalf at Gestapo headquarters in Berlin, which resulted in Adenauer's release. He returned to

[1] Schwarz, *Adenauer*, 970–1.
[2] Cook, *Ten Men and History*, 55.

his home in Rhöndorf, near Bonn, "without shoelaces, belt, tie, or suspenders"[3] at the end of November 1944 and remained there until the war ended in that part of Germany in mid-March 1945. On April 10, 1945, he wrote to an old friend and colleague, Hertha Kraus, who in 1933 had emigrated to the United States, where she taught economics at Bryn Mawr College:

Very difficult times lie behind us. My wife was imprisoned for some time in September 1944, [and] I was, for more than three months, up to the end of November, in a concentration camp, and then in the Gestapo prison in Brauweiler [near Cologne]. If the advance of the American army had not taken place so surprisingly near us here, I probably would have been taken away and killed by the Gestapo. Unfortunately, our three sons have not yet returned, and we are very concerned about them.[4]

Adenauer's wife Gussie, whom he had married in 1919, died in March 1948, as a result of her imprisonment in the Gestapo prison in Cologne-Brauweiler in 1944.[5]

Cologne, although in the British zone, was initially occupied by US forces and it was the Americans who found Adenauer at home. They reinstated him in his office of mayor, from which the Nazis had expelled him in 1933 following his refusal to allow Nazi flags to fly from Cologne's public buildings. Although persecuted by the Nazis, he showed little interest in joining any organized resistance group. One reason for this was his lack of faith in the ability of any such group to achieve success. He used to tell the story of how he had been invited to come to a meeting of an anti-Nazi group that included a number of military officers. Upon seeing the officers' caps in the foyer, he left – since he believed German officers incapable of overthrowing the government.

Adenauer's main political role was not to come until later, partly because of what seemed an unfortunate blunder on the part of the British military authorities. He had been working quietly for the new CDU during the summer and officially joined in August, but his work in Cologne prevented wider activities. Then in October the British commander, Brigadier Barraclough, who resented Adenauer's outspoken criticism of the British for seeking to cut down the trees in Cologne's parks for use as fuel as well as his views on the future of Germany, dismissed him from his post. Adenauer used his enforced leisure – he had now been fired twice from the same job, once by the

[3]  Ibid., 66.
[4]  *Konrad Adenauer: Briefe über Deutschland,* 13.
[5]  Ibid., 106.

Nazis and once by the British – to think more deeply about the prospects for Germany. One result of his reflections was confirmation of his conviction that the division of Germany and Europe was already an accomplished fact, in view of the drastic political and economic policies introduced in the Soviet zone. He therefore concluded that the only hope for self-determination and progress in "the free part" of Germany (Adenauer used this term as early as October 1945) was for Germans to organize themselves politically into a decentralized, federal state with close ties to France, Belgium, the Netherlands, and Britain. This belief became, in fact, a goal toward which he worked for the remainder of his life, until he died in 1967.

Between May and October 1945, while Adenauer was still mayor of Cologne and facing the hopeless-looking task of clearing the rubble from the city's streets and trying to organize food and supplies for its inhabitants, the party he was to join, the Christian democratic party, was in its initial stages of creation.

The new party resulted from a variety of independent actions in 1945 to establish an interdenominational Christian political party. This was a new idea in German politics. Before 1933, few Germans believed that Catholics and Protestants could or should agree on a common position on politics and social development. The two denominations were sharply divided socially, politically, and culturally. Most liberal and democratic Protestants supported the German Democratic Party (DDP) or the DVP, whereas the Catholics supported the Center Party (Zentrum). Although both parties supported the Weimar democracy, their broader agendas and the attitudes of their supporters were entirely different. The Catholic Center party grew out of the struggles of Catholics in the nineteenth century to preserve their religious and cultural independence in a Germany that was largely Protestant. During the 1870s and early 1880s, the Prussian and Reich governments under Bismarck attempted to take control of clerical appointments and thereby to make the Catholic church in Germany subordinate to the state. Although they largely won the resulting *Kulturkampf* (cultural battle), many Catholics came to believe that the best chance of keeping their identity was to form a political party drawn from a broad variety of associations more or less closely tied to the church. The result was the Center party. The party's political program was designed exclusively to protect the Catholic religion and in particular Catholic control of education in the Catholic regions – Bavaria, Upper Silesia, parts of Westphalia, the Rhineland, and parts of Swabia. Behind the religious facade, the Center included people of all shades of opinion, from republicans and liberals at one end to monarchists and nationalists at the other. It also included many workers, especially in the coal-producing areas of Silesia and the Rhineland.

During the Weimar Republic, the Center and the SPD formed a close alliance as the two parties that most loyally supported the republican constitution and system of government. The Wilhelmine Reich had discriminated against both workers and Catholics, giving those groups a common stake in preserving the republic. The Center, moreover, included an important working-class and socialist component and supported a system of Catholic trade unions, as well as numerous other associations dedicated to advancing Catholic interests and educational policies. During the Weimar Republic, the Catholic trade unions included about a million members and were second only in size among workers' organizations to the SPD-controlled so-called free unions.[6] The Center provided the chancellor for eight out of the 13 years of the Weimar regime and was both the pivot and the binding glue of the coalition of parties that supported the constitution. Its own policies remained resolutely focused on cultural and educational issues. As the social and cultural authority of the church began to wane in the face of social change, however, the incompatible views of the groups within the Center became more difficult to reconcile. Toward the end of the Weimar period a growing number of Center party leaders, among them Adenauer, became increasingly convinced that to uphold Christian ethical principles in politics would require an interdenominational party including democrats from both the major religious groups.

This was the situation when the Nazis abolished all other political parties in June 1933. The dictatorship brought about an entirely new situation for Christian politicians and public figures. The Nazis shut down the entire broad range of Catholic associations, which had hitherto provided opportunities for cultural, social, and political activity, and restricted religious activity to the parishes. As a result, many Catholics questioned whether religious forms of political activism were still credible. Moreover, during the twelve years of the Third Reich anti-Nazi Catholics and Protestants discovered they had a great deal in common. Many worked together in the resistance and agreed that postwar Germany would need a powerful infusion of Christian ethical principles in economic, social and political life. Former members of the Catholic youth and liturgical movements were particularly committed to the interdenominational idea, which found support also among the important German Catholic thinkers of the time, such as Romano Guardini, Reinhold Schneider, and Hans Urs von Balthasar, all of whom called on the church to be more active in the world's affairs and to cooperate with all democratic and liberal forces in a spirit of tolerance. Accordingly, "in 1945 Catholic and Protestant Christians who had

[6] Schulze, *Weimar*, 60.

found each other either in resistance circles opposed to National Socialism or in individual isolation from all political activity out of opposition to the National Socialist regime, and who had struggled to establish a sufficiently sturdy common foundation of future political action, seized the initiative to found Christian union parties, at first on a regional basis."[7]

Christian socialism was a prominent feature of the West European political landscape in the years immediately following World War II. Starting in the 1880s, the Church had taken a great interest in the workers' movement, hoping to develop a theological doctrine of the dignity of labor that would be a counterweight to Marxist socialism. Its adherents in the 1930s and 1940s rejected both capitalism and Soviet communism in favor of an often ill-defined "third way" to social and economic justice. Its German variant derived from two streams of thought and action. On the one hand, it drew on Catholic trade unionism inspired by the so-called social encyclicals of popes Leo XIII and Pius XI, and the belief in a Catholic form of social and economic organization, a "genuinely Christian socialism," developed by the Jesuit thinkers Gustav Gundlach and Oswald von Nell-Breuning on the basis of the papal documents. On the other hand, it derived from what the writer and publicist Walter Dirks called the "second Catholicism." Members of this tendency were primarily urban intellectuals like Dirks himself, estranged from the established church but unable to commit themselves to Marxism or any other purely political form of radicalism. They called for "socialism blended with Christian responsibility" and for a socially active, politicized theology. The spokesmen of the "second Catholicism" soon found themselves without much of a voice in the emerging Christian democratic party. This in no way hindered many of them from becoming powerful figures in the West German cultural and media milieus.

Jakob Kaiser (1888–1961) represented, after Adenauer and Schumacher, the third great party-political current of the occupation era. In the first years after 1945, Kaiser's Christian socialism was no less viable a political choice than Adenauer's Christian democratic capitalism or Schumacher's socialism. His vision of Germany was no less complete than that of his rivals and included both a comprehensive foreign and a domestic policy agenda.

Kaiser's career began in the Christian trade union movement of the Weimar Republic. During the Third Reich he became first a dissident, and then an active conspirator. He was closely involved with the

[7] Forster, "Der deutsche Katholizismus in der Bundesrepublik Deutschland," in *Der soziale und politische Katholizismus*, ed. Rauscher, 1: 219.

participants in the plot of July 20, 1944, and only chance saved him from arrest and execution. The end of the war found him in Berlin, where he seized the opportunity to found his new party.

Kaiser's domestic economic policy called for nationalization of heavy industry and worker co-determination in operating business enterprises. He shared the Catholic socialist view that because workers were indispensable to production and had definite interests of their own as a social class, they had a right to exercise those interests in setting the terms of their employment and in enjoying a direct share in the profits resulting from their work. Concerning Germany's position in central Europe, Kaiser saw the new Germany as a bridge between east and west. He believed that a neutral, socialist German government based on Christian principles could mediate between the Soviet Union and the West and help to maintain peace in Europe by reassuring both sides that they had nothing to fear from each other or from Germany.

In Berlin Jakob Kaiser and Andreas Hermes, both associated with the Catholic trade unions of the Weimar period, led the call in June 1945 for an alliance of all Christian and democratic forces in a Christian Democratic Union. The Soviet Military Administration (SMAD) approved the party, but only in order to bring it under control. Although he fought heroically, Kaiser was unable to prevent the German communist party in the Soviet zone, the SED, from gradually taking away his party's independence. Finally, in 1948, he abandoned the Soviet zone CDU to its inevitable fate and gave his efforts to the democratic CDU in the Western zones. He remained, however, committed to Christian socialist ideas and to a neutral, reunited Germany, which put him permanently at odds with his party leader, Konrad Adenauer.

Although Kaiser's Berlin group came first, lasting success belonged to those who established the Christian democratic party in the Western zones. It was Adenauer and the other former Center leaders in the Rhineland who decided in the summer of 1945 that they did not wish to reconstitute the Center, but to extend the new party to include both liberal and conservative Protestants. Unlike Kaiser, they were not all strongly committed to Christian socialism. Adenauer in particular did not believe in expropriating industry or in establishing a workers' party in competition with the SPD, though he certainly hoped that many workers would see their best interests served by Christian rather than social democrats. He believed that the only way to rally a majority of Protestants and liberals to the new party was to support the free market and democratic capitalism. However, until 1948 he was not the absolutely dominant figure in the party, and for the first few years after 1945 its policy positions were largely Christian socialist in inspiration.

The Rhineland groups constituted themselves as the Christian Democratic Party in Cologne in July 1945 and issued a first program statement. In these "Cologne principles," the founders of the new party argued for an egalitarian wage policy and redistribution of industrial resources. The principles also suggested that the owners of heavy industry were largely to blame for helping Hitler to power and for the war. In educational policy, the one area that had held the old Center party together, the Christian democrats did not insist on restoring the pre-1933 denominational school, in which the Catholic church controlled public education in Catholic regions. Instead, as part of the opening to the Protestants, the document called for the option of religious education in either denomination to be offered in every school.

The new party held to its Christian socialist principles for almost three years after 1945, although in fact the Christian socialists like Kaiser soon lost influence on party policy and strategy. A group of leaders of the new party formally constituted it as the Christian Democratic Union (CDU) at a "Reich conference" in Bad Godesberg in December 1945. Resolution no. 1 of the conference stated:

In all parts of Germany, without mutual approach and contact, a new political movement has developed with the goal of building a new democratic Germany deploying stronger Christian ideas and values in the political, economic and cultural life of our people. It emerged during the discussion in Bad Godesberg, which was attended by participants from all zones and parts of the country, that there is agreement on the spiritual basis and the political goals. In order to stress this unity, a uniform name, valid for all parts of the country, has been spontaneously requested. Specifically in order to show solidarity with our political friends in the East, we decided to adopt the joint name: "CHRISTIAN DEMOCRATIC UNION OF GERMANY."[8]

The original organizers of the CDU did come overwhelmingly from the Catholic social milieu of the old Center. Yet within a short time, Protestants and Catholics, small businessmen, civil servants, and industrialists, farmers and city-dwellers, joined together in a single democratic mass movement. The attempt at uniting Catholics and Protestants in a common political party was risky and seen by many as doomed to failure. Given their experience of isolation and discrimination, the Catholics in particular had no tradition of broad cooperation with other social groups. Nevertheless the experiment succeeded beyond all expectation, perhaps in part because the proportion of Catholics in the western zones of Germany was higher than in the old Reich so that Protestant domination was less of an issue. Also, and very

[8] Deuerlein, *CDU/CSU 1945–57*, 61–2.

important, even if the Protestant electorate had been more sensitive to Nazism than the Catholic electorate, the reaction in religious circles to Nazism had cut across the old denominational boundaries and created a strong sense of inter-Christian solidarity.

If Adenauer mistrusted Prussia and feared the political hegemony of a strong central government, Kurt Schumacher demonstrated the opposite traits, usually regarded as conservative, of an abiding respect for Prussia and an unyielding belief in the need for a strong government of a unified Germany. Schumacher, born 1895 in Culm on the Vistula river in West Prussia, a region that became part of Poland in 1920, was severely wounded in World War I, and after being discharged from the army in 1915 he studied law and economics while becoming active in the SPD, first in Berlin and later in Württemberg.

The SPD of the Weimar Republic was a tragic case of a great political force with enough inherent strength to protect German democracy, but without the strategic leadership or the inner unity to do so. Since before World War I the SPD had been the strongest party in the Reichstag, despite electoral rules that, until 1919, severely penalized the SPD and favored the conservative parties with their voters mainly in rural districts. It remained the strongest party, with about a quarter of the total vote, until 1932. Nevertheless the SPD leaders, despite the insistent voices of realistic younger members like Schumacher, remained fundamentally ambivalent about the Weimar Republic: was it a truly democratic state worth supporting, or a merely "bourgeois" democracy to which socialists owed only ambivalent allegiance? They were ambivalent because they could not decide whether the SPD should be a party of revolutionary Marxism dedicated to the complete transformation of society, or a party protecting society and the democratic republic order, including capitalism, in order to make socialist policy. This ambivalence reflected in part the inherent logic of the various ideological strands, in part the makeup of the SPD voting body. Only about two-thirds of its members were actual blue-collar workers, the rest were middle-class liberals and radicals, including a fair number of white-collar *Angestellte* (salaried employees), the fastest-growing social group in the Weimar years. Nor did all workers support the SPD; Catholic workers supported the Center party almost to a man.

In 1914 the SPD split on the issue of support for the war. Against the hopes of many socialists throughout Europe, the SPD, the party that supposedly followed most faithfully the internationalist teachings of Karl Marx, voted overwhelmingly for war credits for the Kaiser's government. The minority opposed to the war formed a splinter party that survived until 1924. In 1918–19, more socialists left both the main party and the splinter group to form the German Communist Party (KPD), which remained unremittingly hostile both to the SPD and to the Weimar democracy.

Schumacher included in himself many of these contradictions: he was a socialist and a nationalist, committed, perhaps inconsistently, to both radical reform of the economy and to democratic rights. During the Weimar years he fought vigorously to give the national leadership the courage to take power and wield it to protect the democratic constitution. He failed. Too many social democrats thought that the purpose of party activity was to uphold the truth, as they saw it, rather than to seek power and use it. Ironically, the SPD leaders could not agree on the definition of the truth in socialist ideology. The result was a party that neither sought power aggressively nor had a clear vision of what to do with power when it had it.

In the terms of the 1920s Schumacher was a realist. He feared, correctly, that the radicals of the right and left would destroy German democracy if the largest party, the SPD, did not commit itself consistently and effectively to protecting the republic. In 1926 he completed his dissertation on attitudes to state power in the SPD of the 1890s. He was a member of the Reichstag from 1930 to 1933 and chairman of the SPD in Württemberg from 1932 until the party was banned one year later. Not believing that Hitler's rule would last, he refused to emigrate and spent ten of the twelve Nazi years in concentration camps, eight of them in Dachau outside Munich. He survived the starvation, illness, and tortures of the camps by virtue of his determination to outlive the tyrants and to gain and use political power to build a new Germany.

Believing him almost dead, and harmless, the Nazi authorities released him from Dachau in March 1943. He was ordered to live in Hannover, where he began to seek out other social democrats and sympathizers to plan the future after Hitler. In May 1945 he had already established the headquarters of the resurrected SPD in Hannover, and was very soon in contact with old party members throughout the Western zones. By the time the British military government and OMGUS licenced political activity later in the year, the SPD was operational throughout much of the Western zones. In complete contrast to its history of weak if well-meaning leadership and regional decentralization, the cadres and members of the revived party showed Schumacher unquestioning obedience and loyalty. Schumacher was both a German nationalist and an unrelenting convert to German socialism. While Adenauer's first priority as chancellor was to end the occupation of his country as quickly as possible, Schumacher often appeared to be querulous; "it did Adenauer no political harm to have Schumacher as the 'democratic alternative' in unbridled opposition."[9]

Schumacher was, without doubt, one of the most unusual and complex personalities of postwar Germany. The British liaison officer, Michael Thomas, met him for the first time at the end of November 1945, when he called on him in his office. He was received by his secretary, Annemarie Renger, who was elected to the Bundestag in 1953 and served as its president from 1972 to 1976. Thomas' description of his impression of Schumacher painted one of the most telling portraits of a man whose political commitment to Germany was without peer:

There he sat, with one arm, a haggard face, high forehead, with penetrating, glowing eyes, flickering a little, tense, nervous, poised to spring, watchful as to who might enter, prepared to attack or to defend his convictions. I understood the fire that was burning inside this man. I understood his ardent nationalism. I understood the obsession of this man, who had spent ten years in concentration camps, to gain the power to guide the destiny of the country according to his ideas. With all due respect and regard for Adenauer's sober approach, and regardless of the fact that I was politically closer to Adenauer's way of thinking, I felt, already at the first meeting with Schumacher, a personal warmth towards him that I was never able to feel towards Adenauer. In addition, Schumacher's humanity and his sense of humor really opened my heart towards him. On the other hand, the almost hysterical tone of his speeches was not particularly appealing, and the dislike by many British [officers] of this kind of rhetoric, which they compared to Hitler's speeches, was quite understandable.

Schumacher wanted a strong, centralist state, and intensely disliked the federalistic tendencies of the regional barons: the *Länder* [as far as he was concerned] were nothing more than building blocs for a future Germany. To him communism was a deadly threat . . . Germany should orient itself toward the West. In the long term, the SPD should carefully move away from Marxism.[10]

[9] Cook, *Ten Men and History*, 93.
[10] Thomas, *Deutschland, England über alles*, 149.

# 3

# Berlin

Nowhere was the political conflict among Germans, or between the wartime Allies, more evident than in Berlin. The Wehrmacht's final surrender took place in Berlin; it was in Berlin that the Allied commanders-in-chief, acting on the orders of their political masters, established the Control Council and the Kommandatura and declared the complete subjection of all Germans to their will. It was near Berlin, at Potsdam, that the Big Three met for the last time in what the optimists saw as an attempt to give shape to the postwar world. But Berlin was not only the first and, for many years, the primary stage of the conflict which, despite the optimists' best wishes, soon engulfed the world. It was also the stage of a fierce confrontation between the German allies of the Soviet Union and those Germans who put their hope and trust in democracy. In Berlin, determined men and women continued, on a small but vital scale, the great European struggle between democracy and totalitarianism which many hoped had ended with the destruction of National Socialism. Though this is a history of West Germany and therefore not, in the first instance, of the struggle of East and West on German soil, nevertheless in Berlin that struggle is so bound up with the formation of West Germany and of the contemporary German spirit that it demands attention.

The great German capital, which in 1930 was the largest city on the European continent with about five million inhabitants, was but a shadow of its former self in 1945. At the surrender, the population of the city was just under three million. Of this total, 500,000 inhabitants were public charges of one sort or another. In 1945–6, moreover, 1.5 million refugees passed through the city, many of whom stayed for many months. Available housing, at 800,000 units in 68,000 buildings, was just over half the amount of 1939. There was little or no electricity, gas, water, or public transportation. Keeping time was not an easy matter either, when the Russians first occupied the city. In May 1945 the Soviet occupation authorities ordered the Berliners to set their clocks to Moscow time – that is to say those clocks that had not been taken by Russian soldiers. What this meant was that "not only the clock, but also the spirit begins to gradually become easternized."[1]

Map 1.7    Berlin with sector borders. Berlin was divided into four sectors of occupation. The population of prewar Berlin was approximately 4.3 million. In August 1945 it was about 2.8 million, a decline of about 35 per cent. By January 1949 the population of Berlin had risen to approximately 3.25 million, which represented about 75 per cent of the city's prewar population.
*Source*:  Office of Military Government, *Four Year Report*, 62

The Soviet sector of the city was the largest, with 45 per cent of the area and 37 per cent of the population. Most important, it included the central government district, *Mitte,* which contained the main city administrative offices, the surviving archives, libraries, and bureaux of the Prussian and Reich governments, the University of Berlin and the famous main street, *Unter den Linden.* The city's institutions were therefore exposed to Soviet exploitation and intimidation. Soviet occupation

[1] Andreas-Friedrich, *Schauplatz Berlin*, 42.

of Berlin-Mitte also deprived the Western sectors of the city's traditional focal point and eventually provoked the development of new "downtowns" in the borough of Schöneberg and along the Kurfürstendamm, formerly on the margins of the old central city. The US sector included 23 per cent of the area, but 30 per cent of the population; the British, 19 per cent of the area and 19 per cent of the population, and the French, 13 per cent of the area and 14 per cent of the population.[2]

Lucius D. Clay, who attended the second working session of the Control Council on July 7, 1945, as deputy military governor, announced after the meeting that he did not believe that the Soviet Control Council member, General Zhukov, would lie to him and that he trusted Soviet assurances that Soviet power would not be used to promote the victory of communism in Germany. He was unaware of the extent to which German communists had already pre-empted crucial political choices in the Soviet zone, and that they had started doing the same in all of Berlin ever since their occupation began in early May. In retrospect it seems clear that the Soviet government and Walter Ulbricht, the head of the communist party in the Soviet zone, believed that it would be possible to drive the Western Allies from Berlin by intimidation and harrassment, supported if possible by political victories among the population. Had this occurred sometime during 1945 to 1948, a new Reich government under communist control could very possibly have been proclaimed in a united Berlin. Such an event would have posed a severe challenge to the legitimacy of any West German state, because of the symbolic importance of Berlin as the old German capital.

The first postwar German administration of Berlin was called into being by the Soviets on May 12, 1945. Its most important figure was the deputy mayor Karl Maron, a communist, and a member of the "Ulbricht Group" which returned to Germany from the Soviet Union on April 30, 1945. That group, which was in effect the core of what later became the communist government of East Germany, had no official status, but was nevertheless the most powerful political force in the Soviet zone after the SMAD itself.

Its leader, Walter Ulbricht, was a Stalinist apparatchik of the purest type. Unlike many older communists, particularly those who had suffered imprisonment in the Third Reich, his reputation was of a man devoid of human sentiment or feeling other than a burning desire to achieve power by serving the Soviet Union. Wolfgang Leonhard, the son of German communist parents who had been raised in the Soviet Union, had worked with the German communist leadership in Moscow since

---

[2] Hauptamt für Statistik, *Berlin in Zahlen 1947,* 29; Mehnert and Schulte, eds, *Deutschland-Jahrbuch 1949,* 8.

1943 and was a member of the group. He defected in 1949 and later wrote an autobiography, *Child of the Revolution,* which is also a profound portrayal of Stalinism, the Soviet Union before and during the war, and the early years of communist rule in the Soviet zone. He described how the Ulbricht Group arrived in Berlin and began taking control over the heads of the surviving local communists. Leonhard particularly noticed the contrast between the genuine camaraderie and human feelings that existed among the local population and the cold arrogance of Ulbricht.

The Soviet military administration ordered the so-called "anti-fascist transformation" with the help of local anti-Nazi politicians and administrators at the same time that they brought in the Ulbricht Group to ensure communist control of this "transformation." However, as Ulbricht told his associates with the grim humor that was his main human characteristic: "It's quite clear – it's got to look democratic, but we must have everything in our control."[3]

Order no. 2 of the SMAD, dated June 10, 1945, permitted the formation or reorganization of democratic political parties. This looked very promising, but the SMAD retained the absolute right to abolish pluralism and to define democracy as it chose. The first party to be constituted under the SMAD order was the German Communist Party (KPD), which established itself in the Soviet zone one day later, and was followed by the SPD, the CDU and the LDPD (later called the FDP). The KPD's opening manifesto declared that Germany must pass through a phase of bourgeois democracy before the time was ripe for socialist transformation, and accordingly called for free competition in the economy and free political activity. When an old Berlin communist asked Ulbricht in surprise how this program differed from the program of a social democratic party, Ulbricht grinned at him: "You'll soon see, comrade! Just wait a bit!"[4]

The difference was that in a democratic party, such a program would reflect a real commitment on the part of the party leadership. SMAD, Ulbricht, and the Central Committee of the KPD had no intention of allowing free political activity or pluralism, but they announced these principles to lure other parties, especially the SPD, into collaboration with them instead of opposing KPD control of important administrative functions. During 1945–6, the most important instrument of the SMAD-KPD strategy was the United Front of Anti-fascist and Democratic Parties, known as the Antifa bloc, established July 15, 1945. The strategy was to force all parties into the bloc, which would then become the only legitimate political forum in the zone. Decisions of the bloc

[3] Leonhard, *Child of the Revolution*, 303. See also Weber, *Geschichte der DDR*, 54–9.
[4] Leonhard, ibid.

leadership had to be unanimous, thus preventing the genuinely democratic parties from ever taking control away from the KPD.[5]

The Ulbricht Group's activities in the spring and summer of 1945 were carried out in absolute conformity with the wishes of Stalin as transmitted by SMAD. Technically, however, SMAD's responsibilities took place at a level different from the activities of the Ulbricht Group which, formally speaking, were to be regarded as anti-fascist political activities by Germans. Both the SMAD and the Ulbricht Group, however, served the same purpose. One of the most important measures of SMAD was to abolish the traditional tenure of city officials, replacing it with ordinary employment contracts revocable at any time. These *faits accomplis* of the SMAD and the Ulbricht Group were accepted by the Western Allies in the joint Kommandatura that began work on July 10, following the arrival of the Western Allies in their sectors. Consequently, the West burdened itself with the liability of respecting, in the name of democratic principles, the measures taken by the Soviets for what later appeared as the clear purpose of seizing all of Berlin. It was not until 1948 that the joint efforts of the Western Allies and the democratic elements within the city's government and political parties succeeded in rescuing the Western sectors from the threats posed by these communist measures.

Knowing that they would be abandoning the Western sectors of the city, the Soviets from early May to early July, when the Western Allies arrived in Berlin, removed from them 85 per cent of the industrial capacity remaining at the time of surrender, leaving West Berlin with only 6 per cent of its 1936 capacity. Furthermore, the continued influence of the Soviets in the Western sectors granted by the Western Allies was unmatched by any corresponding concessions by the Soviets. Until the early 1950s Soviet agents carried out numerous kidnappings in the Western sectors and, between 1945 and 1948, used the Berlin police to organize mass transportation of East Berlin workers to forced labor in the Soviet zone.[6]

The Berlin police was, from 1945 to 1948, the most important Soviet and KPD tool in the struggle against the Western Allies and the democratic government of the city. At the surrender, the police force was the only executive authority intact in any locality of Germany. Control of it was, therefore, a uniquely valuable prize that, in Berlin, fell uncontested to the Soviets since they were in sole command of the capital for two months. In June, SMAD appointed Colonel Markgraf police chief of Berlin and, through him, appointed loyal communists to

[5]  See Weber, *Geschichte der DDR*, 69–85.
[6]  Herzfeld, *Berlin in der Weltpolitik*, 67–8.

control most of the precincts and, in particular, the criminal division. Colonel Markgraf was a member of the National Committee for a Free Germany, a group founded in 1943, whose members included high-ranking German POWs who agreed to collaborate with the Soviets and which gradually became a tool of communist control. All attempts by non-communist elements of the city government to compel the police to exercise impartial justice failed, and the crisis was ultimately only solved by the establishment of a separate West Berlin police force in 1948.

The defeat of Germany was the opportunity for Stalin and Ulbricht to include at least part of Germany in the communist system and to restructure it in their interests. This restructuring was carried out primarily not by the Soviet occupation authorities, but by German communists, and was largely complete by late 1946. It was publicly presented as part of the necessary "anti-fascist and democratic transformation" of Germany, in which the KPD would work with other parties. In reality it was a process of eliminating all non-communist civil servants, landowners, industrialists, labor and religious leaders, and political figures of all kinds. The enemy of the communists in this operation was not so much former Nazis, as all who might resist communist domination.

What took place in the Soviet zone in 1946 was, in fact, a process of *Gleichschaltung*, a phrase originally used by the Nazis to describe the reordering of all public administrative and political activity to the purposes of the new regime. During that year, the leaders of the other parties in the Soviet zone increasingly came to realize that there was not going to be genuine democracy and that the non-communist parties were largely propaganda devices, hollow shells designed to serve the purposes of the SMAD-KPD regime, and to give it an appearance of pluralism. The KPD, aided by the SMAD, granted itself privileged powers in organization and resources and, largely thanks to the absorption of the SPD in March 1946, became the largest party in the zone in terms of membership, calling itself the Socialist Unity Party of Germany (SED, *Sozialistische Einheitspartei Deutschlands*). The process of *Gleichschaltung*, the hollowing-out of the non-communist parties and their gradual forced subservience to SMAD-SED control, meant that the local and regional elections which were held in the zone in 1946 were rigged, and were meaningless. In all *Länder* of the Soviet zone the SED, thanks to the strength of the now defunct SPD, emerged victorious.[7] By late 1946 the SMAD-SED regime was taking the Germans in the Soviet zone back into totalitarian rule and away from the democratic road of choices that was still open to their compatriots in the West.

[7] Weber, *Geschichte der DDR*, 142.

# 4

# Challenges of Occupation

Denazification and the permission and promotion of democratic political activity went hand in hand with the measures taken by the military governments to organize the administration of their zones. This process, by necessity, was carried out largely by Germans, and more intensely after the initial postwar demobilization of Allied troops during 1945 and 1946. The way in which these activities were handled directly reflected the different Allied attitudes toward Germany and how to deal with it.

General Clay believed that German industrial capacity and skills should be restored and used to support the growth of a modern democratic society in Germany. If correctly managed, this combination of industrial reconstruction and political democratization could elicit the support and generate the enthusiasm of the German people. Such a development would, by its very nature, contradict the values of militarism and expansionism, completely discredit Nazi ideas, and lead to the rise of a new Germany allied to Western democracy.

The most prevalent attitude among US and British officers and administrators in Germany was that expressed by the poet and journalist Stephen Spender. In response to complaints by a German professor and his wife about the hardships they faced and the behavior of Allied troops, he said:

[T]heir complaints were groundless, because the Germany of Hitler had called down upon itself, not an army of liberating angels, but simply the Occupying Forces, the Red Army, the GIs, the Tommies and the Poilus, with all the defects of the individual soldiers of whom these were composed. The Occupiers of Germany did not wish to be there, I insisted, it was the Germans who had invoked them.[1]

---

[1] Mayne, *Postwar*, 53.

This was the basic sentiment of 1945 among Allied personnel and politicians, just as the basic emotion of the Germans was "Never again!" In hindsight, Allied resentment at the Germans for having started a war and causing untold misery, ruin, and death, disappeared remarkably swiftly. The spectacle of millions of desperate, starving men, women, and children in Germany, the spectre of a highly literate, bureaucratic, and complex modern society reduced in many cases to less than subsistence level, evoked pity rather than contempt, even though their predicament was directly caused by their own leaders. Sometimes, pity at German misery led to outrage at the apparent follies of Allied occupation policy, as described by Victor Gollancz in *In Darkest Germany*, first published in London in 1946. Gollancz (1893–1967), a British Socialist and a Jew, writer and publisher, was "one of the first to attack the barbaric policy of the victors:"

I have been living for six weeks in a madhouse. I don't mean this metaphorically; I mean it literally. The world, unfortunately, has grown so used to being mad that it no longer notices its own condition. But as I drove through ruined Cologne at late dusk, with terror of the world and of men and of myself in my heart, for a moment I just couldn't believe that we were deliberately, 18 months after the end of the war, adding further ruin to this unspeakable desolation. But that, and nothing else, is just what we are doing.[2]

What Gollancz described was the consequence of reparations; namely the willful and arbitrary closure and dismantling of industrial plants that produced goods the Germans needed to survive. The closure of the firm Mathes and Weber of Duisburg, one of only two firms in the British zone manufacturing soda, was a case in point. One needs soda to produce washing powder, and the Germans needed soap desperately. Then there was the blanket-making firm which was allocated coal, but no power to run the machines; or worse yet, the destruction of the three ship-building firms in Hamburg, Bloehm & Voss, Howaldt, and Deutsche Werft, which, as Gollancz describes it, were "dynamited into a mass of shapeless metal that oppresses the mind with a sense of darker obscenity. . . ."[3] Filled with frustration and desperation he asked in an article written for the *Daily Herald* on November 23, 1946:

What sort of re-education is this that we are doing, with our mania for destruction ? Is that the way to make men democrats?. . . .
I hate fascism from the bottom of my heart. From the day Hitler came to

[2] Gollancz, *In Darkest Germany,* 8, 175.
[3] Ibid., 180, 182.

power I thought of nothing from morning till night but how to prevent him and his accomplices and dupes from having their evil way. But I say that if now we choose the path of destruction rather than of reconstruction: if we fill the German people with despair rather than with hope: if we make them hate and despise us, when they are ready for emotions of a very different kind – then the Nazis, in spite of everything, have won, and tomorrow's world will be of their pattern and not of ours.[4]

His was an illustrated report that probably did more to promote in public opinion the change that had already occurred in government circles, namely, that the rescue of what was left of Germany was both a civilized duty and in the common political interest, because only the Soviet Union would gain from a prolongation of poverty, starvation, and despair. Gollancz's observations illustrated vividly that dismantling, for the purposes of reparation and demilitarization, was having harsh and unintended effects. It was causing resentment and was making it much more difficult for both the occupation authorities and the Germans to introduce democracy in Germany. It meant administering a state in torment, and cities full of economic contradictions; even though dismantling by no means completely paralyzed German industry. In short, it made little sense, and General Clay had in fact recognized this in May 1946, when he halted all major dismantling in the US zone, but it continued in the British and French zones, and to a minimal degree in the American zone.

[4] Ibid., 178.

# 5

# Food and Labor

Both the Allied military governments and the local German administrative authorities and political parties that continued or developed
in the zones after 1945, had to contend with overwhelming economic
and physical problems left by the war and its continuing effects. These
problems concerned primarily matters which needed urgent attention:
housing, food supplies, and industrial production. In this area, the
Germans also had to contend with two of the "four d's:" decartelization
and dismantling. Dismantling was the demand, codified at Potsdam,
that each zone of occupation not only should bear the costs of occupation but should also provide its occupying power and others with
reparations in kind. Decartelization expressed the Allied insistence that
the German economy as a whole be reconstructed so as to take power
away from the cartels – the interlocking groups of industrial leaders
whom many regarded as heavily responsible for Hitler's rise to power
and his ability to wage war. Some argued that this reconstruction had to
involve the socialization of industry, that is, an end to private capitalism;
others – those who eventually prevailed – that it should not.

In the *Länder* and in the zonal institutions of the *Länderrat* in the US
zone and the Zonal Council (*Zonenbeirat*) in the British, German
officials dealt with their problems as best they could. Given the
tremendous obstacles they faced, both material and bureaucratic, what
they accomplished was impressive. Interzonal transport was strictly
controlled and in effect made shipment of ordinary industrial goods
impossible. By the terms of JCS 1067, producers were not allowed to
supply retailers across zonal borders. Retail trade was thus severely
curtailed, which did not increase the ability of or the incentive for
ordinary workers to perform. Goods could be exported from the zones
to non-German areas, but only on payment in dollars, which the rest of
Western Europe did not have.

In 1945–6 the Western Allies, primarily the US, contributed $700 million to their zones in Germany, whereas the Soviet Union plundered material from its zone in the value of $500 million, not counting the value of the labor of those forcibly deported to the USSR. The French remained concerned with the prospect of German economic revival just as they opposed the resurrection of German political power. The French government took longer to admit that a revived West Germany would not represent a threat, but rather an essential ally. Among the few Frenchmen to recognize this in 1945 was Jean Monnet (1888–1979), the "father of Europe," who conceived the idea of the Coal and Steel Community, became its first president, and played a leading role in the effort to unify Western European economic, political and military policies.

The greatest obstacle, and one that never disappeared, was the destruction of the economic unity of Germany, and hence, of the economic balance between different regions and sectors of the national economy. Before the war, the principal food-producing areas of Germany were in the North, the center and especially the East (Prussia, Pomerania, East Brandenburg, Silesia). However, even in 1939, Germany had been only 75 per cent self-sufficient in food production. When the Soviets gave Poland the Oder–Neisse areas and established their zone of occupation in 1945, the most important food-producing areas of Germany were in effect amputated, and the Western part of the country became less than 60 per cent self-sufficient in food. The Morgenthau Plan foresaw transformation of this rump Germany into an agricultural country, elements of which survived in JCS 1067 and the Potsdam Protocol; but it was impossible to implement because 10 to 15 million Germans would have starved, since it was not possible to produce enough food for the entire population in the remaining area. Such a development was not desired by even the most fanatically anti-German Allied leaders, because it would have caused catastrophic personal suffering and because such a process would undoubtedly have created tremendous anti-American, British and French feelings.

The industries of central Germany (Saxony, Thuringia, Berlin and Brandenburg), which had provided the heavy industries of the West (the areas of the Ruhr, Frankfurt-Mainz, Mannheim-Ludwigshafen, and Hamburg) with manufactured goods, parts, and tools in exchange for coal, were located in the Soviet zone. These industrial products were unavailable after surrender because at Potsdam the US had agreed to the economic fragmentation of Germany and because the Soviets plundered their zone at the expense of aiding the Germans in Germany. The most important traffic artery of prewar Germany, the old Reichsstrasse 1 that ran from Aachen on the Belgian frontier via Berlin to

Königsberg in Prussia, was broken and now led nowhere. West Germany had to develop, across the zonal borders, a new north- south artery connecting the remaining points of concentration in Hamburg, the Ruhr, Frankfurt, Mannheim, and Stuttgart. The types of industry had to change also. The West had to generate electric and tool industries to make up for the loss of those in Saxony and Thuringia and increase coal output to make up for the loss of Upper Silesia. The latter was absolutely essential as long as the main source of energy in Europe was coal and not oil or nuclear power.

In 1945 OMGUS and the British Military Government (BMG) adopted the existing wartime rationing system, introduced in August 1939. Every calendar month constituted a new distribution period, for which the particular amounts available of any particular product to each individual were specified. The system included all goods without exception, including clothing, and the ration book became the most important and most essential document in daily life. In fact, rationing broke down quickly after the war ended, forcing the Germans to turn to the ever-present black market.

Deliveries of agricultural goods to the cities were sporadic. Though food production in the Western zones was inadequate to feed the population, which in 1946 was 46 million compared to 40 million for the same area in 1939, the rural population did reasonably well, as did those urban dwellers with the resources to trade on the black market or to obtain food outside official channels.

The food shortage in the Western zones was the greatest single source of misery during 1945–9. It was alleviated extremely slowly and with great difficulty, partly because of Allied policy but also because a critical food shortage was caused in Europe by the drought of 1946–7. Bread rationing, unknown in Britain during the war, was introduced there in 1947. Whereas in 1936 the League of Nations had formally established the guideline for daily calorie intake at 3,000 calories, the British set the daily intake in their zone of occupation at 1,150. In July 1945 every adult in the city of Essen received 700–800 calories per day, and if one was fortunate one received two pieces of bread, a spoonful of milk soup, and two small potatoes. In the middle of 1946 the average weight for men in the American zone of occupation – where food was the most plentiful – was 112 pounds. In March of 1946, in Hamburg, the ration of bread for the entire month was eaten in two weeks. The food rations in the Western zones, which in the last months of the war averaged 2,000 calories per day, ranged from 1,200 calories per day for ordinary workers to 4,000 for mineworkers in the Ruhr in 1946–7. At its lowest, the calorie intake dropped again to 700–800 calories per day for normal consumers (persons not receiving special allocations, e.g. for heavy labor) in the Ruhr district in early 1947, approximating that of inmates in Soviet or Nazi concentration camps.

On such a diet, death from starvation is ultimately inevitable, but long before that the emaciated body falls victim not only to common diseases one might otherwise overcome, but to specific effects of malnutrition. Even the British zone average of 1,400 calories per day was less than half that available in Britain and was rightly considered as barely above starvation for individuals performing no labor. The infant mortality rate in Berlin in the summer of 1945 was about 60 per 1,000, whereas the norm in industrial countries four decades later was 9–12 per 1,000. Of 31,928 births in Berlin in 1945, 11,474 infants died. In 1946 2,806 of 22,894 infants died, and in 1947, 3,744 of 30,878 infants died.[1] More than two million Germans died during or because of the effects of expulsion from eastern provinces, the Sudetenland in Czechoslovakia, and Poland. Deaths from starvation and/or cold in the winters of 1946 and 1947 reached the hundreds of thousands and included victims found frozen to death in their beds.

Since all able-bodied Germans were needed for labor of various kinds, it was not surprising that serious labor shortages soon appeared as a consequence of diseases that the undernourished bodies could not resist. Between 1945 and 1947 most Germans lived in a constant state of emaciated exhaustion, which made thought and planning difficult, and heavy, sustained labor almost impossible. Few outside Germany were aware of the magnitude of the problem, and when Victor Gollancz wrote his two books, *In Darkest Germany* and *Our Threatened Values*, about it in 1946, he was vilified as a traitor to his people (the Jews) and "soft on the Germans."

I have just returned from visiting a "bunker" – a huge air-raid shelter, without daylight or air, where 800 children get their schooling. In one class of 41 children, 23 had had no breakfast, and nothing whatever to eat until half-past two, when they had the school meal of half a litre of soup, without bread . . . Seven of these children had the ugly skin-blemishes that are mixed up in some way with malnutrition; all were white and pasty. Their gaping "shoes" . . . mean the end of what little health they have when the wet weather comes. . . .

Bits of dirty rag: a thin strap over a stocking full of holes: soles – innumerable soles – completely broken away from the uppers – these were common form. Then there were the children hobbling painfully in shoes borrowed from a younger brother: and children slopping about in their mother's or father's shoes . . . The teachers estimated that when the really wet weather started, "shoe absenteeism" might amount to 50 per cent. . . .

On arriving in the Ruhr (October 27, [1945]) I visited homes and schools, and was horrified by what I found. Many were living, the day I visited them, on a

---

[1] Hauptamt für Statistik, *Berlin in Zahlen 1947*, 128, 152.

cup of milkless "coffee" for breakfast, potatoes with cabbage for lunch, and the same in the evening, bread being entirely absent.[2]

Still, what appeared to him as barbaric callousness, permitted or ordered by the governments of countries that had just fought a great war and shed much blood to defeat barbarity, was less the effect of deliberate policy, as advocated by Vansittart and Morgenthau, than the result of poor planning and opposing political interests in the Soviet zone on the one hand and in the Western zones on the other. The Allied military governments employed many thousands of secretaries, drivers, and other support personnel, who often fainted from hunger on the job; however, many German employees of the Allies enjoyed access to supplies of food and cigarettes. Many workers had to take many hours off a week to scavenge for food. The long-term damage to children born in these years for whom adequate nourishment, especially fats, was essential, would never be precisely calculated.

The shortages of food, housing, and capital, and the destruction of the transportation and economic networks of the country make the accomplishments that did take place seem all the more miraculous.

I am almost frightened by the vitality these Germans show after what they've undergone. I believe, once they've been given the word GO, they'll have a bridge over the Rhine in three months, and that in a short time their output of steel will be huge.[3]

By June 1946, the 1,000 kilometers of usable rail track (out of 13,000 kilometers) in the British zone had increased to 12,000, and 800 bridges, including two over the Rhine, were again functional. It was the result of the combined efforts of the occupation authorities and German civilians. The Reichsbahn train system, supported in this instance by OMGUS and BMG, performed miracles, only to suffer renewed serious setbacks in the disastrous winter of 1946-7.[4]

At the end of the war, the industrial capacity in the Western zones was in theory not markedly less than that of the same territories in 1936. According to some calculations the total value of fixed assets in the Western zones was actually greater, despite the effects of war, in 1945 than it had been in 1936. Those same calculations also show that the total value of all dismantling – the much-feared "fourth d" – was a mere 4.4 per cent of the value of fixed assets of 1936.[5] Still, there were great

[2] Gollancz, *In Darkest Germany,* 26, 74, 35.
[3] British colonel, the Ruhr, May 2, 1945, cited in Barnett, *Pride and the Fall,* 9.
[4] Eschenburg, *Jahre der Besatzung,* 267.
[5] Berghahn, *Americanisation of West German Industry,* 77.

differences between industrial sectors. The coal, iron, and steel industries were relatively lightly damaged, whereas most manufacturing was much more seriously impaired. The average total production index for the US-British zones in September 1945 was only approximately 14 per cent of that of the same areas in 1936, and subsequently rose to an average of 34 per cent for 1946, 40 per cent for 1947, and 60 per cent for 1948. Coal production in the Ruhr, which was 384,000 tons/day in 1936, was at 173,000 in the second half of 1945, 178,000 in 1946, and 235,000 in 1947.[6]

If it is true that there was much less physical destruction or subsequent dismantling than many people thought at the time, then it is even more clear that what mattered in 1945–9 was less the physical condition of factories than the motivation of the Germans who worked in them. This is obvious in hindsight if we compare the postwar economic fate of the Soviet and Western zones. In the West, rapid reconstruction led to widespread affluence by the 1960s, whereas much of East Germany in 1990 was in no better a physical condition than in 1950.

Motivation depended, in both East and West, on the amount and above all, the kind of freedom the occupation authorities conceded. In the East, the Soviet occupiers and their German communist allies wanted to, and did, put an end to private capitalism. The result was poverty for all, except for a narrow ruling class. In the West, after two years of argument and uncertainty, the British and American authorities made a fundamental choice in favor of a capitalist, free-market economy in which industry would be privately owned but with constitutionally specified public responsibilities. The result, within a very few years, was outstanding material success. That some critics later asserted that this material success took away attention from the moral burden of guilt was not, and could not be, an argument that the material success was, in some way, inappropriate.

The immediate task in 1945 for German industrialists and labor leaders, as well as for the occupiers, was to mobilize the work force while complying with occupation regulations. This was not easy since each group, and subgroups within each group, had radically different preferences and ambitions. Many industrialists wanted to retain a capitalist economy, but were willing to abandon the inherited structure of German industry based on cartels in favor of an internationally open market. From 1945 to 1947, most labor leaders not only hoped for, but expected socialization and a permanent end to privately owned large-scale industry. Their reasons were both moral and practical: they

[6] Eschenburg, *Jahre der Besatzung*, 265–6.

believed that German capitalism bore a heavy burden of responsibility for Nazism, that German capitalists had profited greatly from the crimes of the Third Reich. In practical terms they also believed that the interwar depression, and the war itself, had shown that capitalism was inefficient as well as unjust, and that it therefore had no future. On the occupation side, the Americans in general, influenced by Roosevelt's "New Deal," believed that the German economy should be reconstructed along the lines of a modified free-enterprise model, whereas the British, at least until early 1947, were more sympathetic to the demands of the labor leaders.

The early attitudes and expectations of workers in the Western zones were captured in the observations of a member of the British military government:

After a few words of thanks for their liberation (we were still liberators in those days) the speakers launched a tirade against their former bosses, many of whom had been Nazis and had by then disappeared. They were not, however, after their blood, nor did they even want to see them sent to prison. They merely wanted to see them take their coats and collars off and do some real work, by which they apparently meant manual labour. I always knew when a speech was veering round to an attack on the bosses, as the passage invariably started with the words: "Let them take a pick and shovel ..." and the rest was usually drowned in applause.[7]

In the Western zones, the Anti-Fascist Committees, and later the SPD, demanded that heavy industry, particularly coal and steel, utilities, oil refineries, most manufacturing, transportation, insurance, and banking all be nationalized. In 1945, this was by no means only a demand of the extreme left. For several years after the war, many who later became Christian democrats, or free democrats, shared the idea that capitalism had failed, that morality, social justice, and the need for recovery, all called for some degree of nationalization and workers' control. Jakob Kaiser, the first head of the CDU in Berlin, who believed that the new Germany should be a bridge between East and West, had worked in the resistance to Hitler and strongly urged a "Christian socialism" as the principle of the new social order. Kaiser and his allies succeeded in making Christian socialism the basis of the first CDU program, the Ahlen principles, of early 1947, although by that time occupation policy was clearly against it. The idea behind Christian socialism was that morality called for workers' and employees' control of their workplace and of economic decisions in general. Kaiser hoped that Christian socialism would take some of the wind out of the sails of the SPD, which

[7] Mayne, *Postwar*, 13.

was calling for nationalization in the name of efficiency as well as morality. The economic history of the Western zones from 1945 to 1948, is in large part the history of how both Christian socialism and the SPD hopes for socialist planning failed, partly because the people who made the decisions – mainly Allied officials – opposed those ideas, and partly because many who supported them initially, later changed their minds.

# 6
# Unions

A llied policy on trade unions and other collective organizations between 1945 and 1947 set the pattern for the structure of these institutions in the future. Historically, collective organizations had played a very important role in German society and politics. Until 1933, when the Nazis suppressed all independent union activity, German workers and employees belonged to one of three national union groups divided along religious-political lines. The largest was the socialist or social democratic group, the heart of the old German labor movement first organized by Ferdinand Lassalle and his allies in 1864. The second was the Christian labor movement, which in fact included primarily Catholic workers and was allied politically with the Catholic or Center Party. The third, and smallest, was a group of unions with ties to the centrist or liberal parties.

Trade unionists from all three groups played a part in the anti-Nazi resistance, and several of them were arrested and executed in the purges following the attempt to assassinate Hitler on July 20, 1944. As soon as the war was over, union leaders re-emerged and some of them were active in the early *Antifa* organizations. One of their leaders was Hans Böckler (1875–1951), a social democratic member of the Reichstag in 1928–33 and a district secretary of the social democratic union organization. Many union leaders remembered him, and his influence on how to proceed was therefore important. In fact, both he and Kaiser, along with others, had decided during the resistance years that it was absolutely essential after the fall of Nazism that German unions be consolidated into a single organization in order to overcome the old ideological and cultural division into socialist, Catholic, and liberal groups. Böckler and Kaiser agreed that this division had fragmented the power of German workers and employees in the 1920s, and had thus helped pave the way for the Nazi takeover. They regarded a single national union as essential if democracy were to take root and survive, a second time.

Thus, German unionists had four basic goals for the labor movement and the economy in 1945: (1) a single national union organization to replace the three ideologically divided groups which had existed until 1933, (2) nationalization of large and intermediate industry, (3) workers' co-determination in individual factories, and (4) national economic planning. In their eyes, the four goals were interdependent; all were equally necessary for social democracy in the new Germany. The salient point is that in 1945 these were not just socialist or even communist ideas; they were shared by many across the re-emerging political spectrum.

When the Allied forces arrived in Germany, representatives of pre-1933 unions were often ready to begin reorganizing the workers. The occupation authorities at first tolerated these informal workers' councils. Eisenhower had announced in late 1944 that "German workers will be allowed ... to form democratic labor unions,"[1] but when German labor leaders started organizing workers in individual factories and cities and approached the occupation authorities with the request that the new unions be allowed to merge across a wider area or even across zonal borders, they were turned down. From May to August 1945 both blue- and white-collar organizers continued to form local unions illegally, but increasingly both the British and the American authorities cracked down on organizations which might become the foci of discontent or resistance.

In the summer of 1945, Böckler established a Committee of Seven in the North-Rhine area (the Ruhr), where he lived. This committee recommended moving quickly toward a centralized national union organization. Within this overarching union organization the committee proposed industry-wide unions. Such broad unions could be organized in two ways. One, familiar in Britain and the US, was the craft principle, which meant that all workers doing a certain kind of job belonged to one union, no matter where they worked. For example, all waiters everywhere would be members of a union for waiters. The Germans rejected the craft principle, which had operated within each of three pre-Nazi union groups, because in their view it weakened the labor movement as a whole. On the individual plant level it gave management the opportunity to play each union against the other, and on the national level it made coordinated opposition to threatening political movements, such as Nazism, much more difficult. Therefore, labor leaders wanted unions that would include or represent all employees in a given industry, regardless of what jobs they did. So, for example, all employees of all breweries would belong – or, at least, would have their working

---

[1] Eschenburg, *Jahre der Besatzung,* 211.

conditions negotiated by – a single union, regardless of whether they hauled bottles, typed letters, filed invoices, or served food in the canteen.

While sympathetic to Böckler, the BMG, in late 1945, turned down his request to form a centralized union as too ambitious. For the occupation authorities the purpose of the unions was to help denazification and decartelization in industry, not to lead a revival of the German labor movement. Faced with this decision, Böckler turned to a plan to organize workers and employees locally in autonomous unions under an umbrella federation. This appealed to the BMG, because it served the purpose of mobilizing workers to defuse discontent. Accordingly, BMG approved the statutes of such an umbrella organization in 1946. By April 1947 two million workers in the British zone had joined local unions, each using a variant of the statutes. This was far more than the total membership of the political parties in the British zone, and it had an explanation. Many workers remembered the weakness of the political parties in the Weimar Republic and expected the unions to be able to do far more for them in terms of living conditions and organizing social life than the new parties which, to many, promised little more than a repetition of the useless squabbles of the 1920s.

The BMG took the lead in designing policy towards workers' organizations because what was left of German heavy industry – the largest plants with the largest numbers of politically active employees – was located mainly in the British zone, specifically in the coal and steel district around the Ruhr river. OMGUS, therefore, largely took its cue from BMG on union policy, permitting workers and employees to form unions in Württemberg-Baden and in Hesse in January 1946, but not until 1947 in Bavaria.

Starting in December 1946, representatives of the union groups of all four zones of occupation met every other month until August 1948. Although these meetings did little to prevent the deepening division of Germany, they were nevertheless one of the few occasions for politically active Germans from all four zones to meet. They met primarily to discuss plans for consolidating the four zonal unions into one national union. In August 1948, after the beginning of the Berlin blockade, representatives of the unions in the three Western zones finally presented a draft plan for a national union. By this time, the SED had thoroughly purged the Soviet zone union of any democratic elements, so it was not surprising that the Eastern representatives rejected the Western proposal. That was the end of official contacts between the emerging Western trizonal union and the Soviet zone organization, which the SED, with cruel irony, had named the *Freie Deutsche Gewerkschaftsbund* (Free German Trade Union Federation).

The unions of the US and British zone joined forces in August 1947 and admitted the union of the French zone in December 1948. Finally, after the formation of the Federal Republic, the German Trade Union Federation (*Deutscher Gewerkschaftsbund,* DGB) came into being in October 1949. It included 16 individual industry unions, each with its own full powers of negotiation and control of finances, with a total membership of five million, of whom 4.2 million were blue-collar workers, 530,000 white-collar employees and 270,000 *Beamte.*

The same mistrust with which the Allies regarded the German bureaucracy, they felt, probably to a greater degree, toward the economic sector. Germany's businesses had, after all, produced the means of war and mass murder of the Third Reich. Reconstructing private industry involved three of the four d's: decartelization meant breaking up the industrial combines that had provided the interlocking directorates of control of the prewar German economic system; democratization meant elimination of pro-Nazi bosses; and dismantling meant removing as much industrial production or plant as the Allies might desire.

Decartelization actually accorded with the interests of many German business leaders, who realized in 1945 that if German industry was to have any place in the postwar world it would have to adapt to foreign, especially American methods, and that meant open markets and a rejection of cartels. Such businessmen worked with the Allies and through the Chambers of Industry and Commerce (IHK, *Industrie- und Handelskammer),* some of which had remained intact, in an effort to direct the reorganization of German business. In the British and French zones the chambers functioned as semi-public bodies, as they had in the Weimar Republic. In the American zone, however, the chambers were run privately until 1957. Leadership and direction of the chambers differed widely and was mainly dependent on the industry and commerce prevailing in the district of location. Not until 1949 did the chambers manage to become a supraregional organization, under the name of German Assembly of Industry and Commerce (*Deutscher Industrie- und Handelstag,* DIHT), with headquarters first in Frankfurt and after 1949 in Cologne.[2]

The chambers rapidly assumed significant influence, since they had to take over and run many businesses whose directors were interned or in prison charged with war crimes. Some union leaders feared that the Allies, in order to get German industry moving and increase output, treated the old bosses too leniently, and did not allow the employees the opportunity for genuine socialist reconstruction of the economy. As in

[2] Berghahn, *Americanisation of West German Industry,* 66–7.

the case of denazification, there is much truth to these charges, which, however, beg the question of whether socialization was a good idea in the Germany of 1945. Given that very few in the occupation government thought so, the chambers were of greater importance to the Allies than unions. This gave the Allies a common interest with the vast majority of German factory owners and businessmen, who were more concerned with reviving the economy than with ideology.[3]

Agriculture organizations *(Landesbauernschaften)* maintained contact between the four zones until January 1949, when the effects of growing division divided them as well. They operated via the regional Chambers of Agriculture *(Landwirtschaftskammern)*. As a co-founder with Jakob Kaiser of the CDU in Berlin and in the Soviet zone, Andreas Hermes, who was minister of agriculture during the Weimar Republic, made every effort to preserve the unity of the agricultural organizations, but he recognized also the conflicting political goals of Soviet and Western allied occupation policy. Thus, in the summer of 1946 Hermes founded the Work Association of Expelled Farmers *(Arbeitsgemeinschaft Heimatvertriebener Landwirte)*, out of which came the Farmers' Corporation *(Bauernsiedlung GmbH)*, the largest agricultural finance corporation in West Germany in the early years. In the British zone, in the autumn of 1946, he established the Work Association of German Farmers *(Arbeitsgemeinschaft deutscher Bauernverbände)* out of which grew in 1948 the German Farmers' Association *(Deutscher Bauernverband)*, which became in the 1960s the only professional agricultural organization.

[3] Eschenburg, *Jahre der Besatzung,* 217.

# 7

# The Life of the Mind and Spirit

Cultural renewal was even more a native German effort than the organizational revival, and took place with a minimum of resources. In Berlin there were no concert halls in May 1945, no transportation, no posters, and no announcements. Yet the first rehearsal of the Berlin Philharmonic Orchestra, under the direction of Leo Borchard, was held at almost the same time as the publication of the first newspaper in Berlin since the end of the war. Announcements were made by word of mouth, and musicians walked or rode bicycles throughout the city to gather instruments and to find rehearsal rooms. As Ruth Andreas-Friedrich described it in her diary, she and her four friends had only three bicycles, so they took turns letting one have the honor of riding alone, while the other four doubled up to pedal to concerts or to theater performances, held in the afternoon, to make it possible for people to reach home before the curfew of 11:00 p. m.

At the first concert on May 26, 1945, over a thousand people came by foot or by bicycle. Andreas-Friedrich wrote:

"That such a thing is still possible," stammers a man next to me . . . We do not see the ruins. We have forgotten that there are Nazis, a lost war and occupation troops. Suddenly everything has become unimportant. Important is only what the violins are singing: Tchaikovsky, Mozart and Mendelssohn. Late in the evening I stand with Andrik on the balcony. . . . "That we may live," he says quietly, "that we survive. . . ." A gust of wind blows over us. He shudders and forgets to finish the sentence.[1]

The fate of Leo Borchard, referred to as Andrik in the diary of Andreas-Friedrich so as to protect his identity should her diary have been found, was one of the tragedies and paradoxes of the peace which followed war. Throughout the summer of 1945 the concerts drew increasingly large

[1] Andreas-Friedrich, *Schauplatz Berlin,* 42.

audiences, including officers from the occupation forces. Following a concert on August 24 a British colonel was driving Borchard and Andreas-Friedrich back to their apartment, when his car was fired upon by American soldiers since the driver misunderstood the signal of a lantern signaling his car to stop. Apparently the evening before a shooting had taken place between Russians and Americans in the middle of the city, an almost daily occurrence. Because the British colonel did not stop in time, and the American soldiers apparently did not notice the British license plate, they opened fire on the automobile. Shooting with careful aim because the Russian soldiers often did not react to warning shots, they fired six rounds. One of them killed Leo Borchard.[2]

Following Borchard's death, a black American war reporter, musician, and old friend of Borchard's, Rudolf Dunbar, born in British Guayana, took over as guest conductor. He led the Berlin Philharmonic in the first European performance of the Afro-American symphony by William Still and Tchaikovsky's Sixth Symphony, an event that "would have been impossible until very recently," and that earned him a standing ovation by the 20,000 listeners.[3]

But not only the symphony was important: the Berlin Hebbel Theater opened with the *Three-Penny Opera*, *The Barber of Seville* was performed in the Städtische Friedenauer Oper – "even though not all the required costumes were available and the orchestra could have been larger" and *Fidelio* played in the German Opera House. In Frankfurt, at the same time, a first comedy, "Ingeborg" by Kurt Goetz, was performed with "five actors and no scenery – a piece that was practicable." In Munich the occupation forces gave permission for the first literary cabaret, *Die Schaubude,* to open its doors to the mostly satirical and humorous poems by Ringelnatz, Tucholsky and Kaestner,[4] and the Regensburger Domspatzen (a famous choir) began with a performance of "Hänsel and Gretel."[5]

The Germans found even cultural activity to be full of political traps and ironies. Some considered those Germans who participated in hunts for Nazis in the name of some new ideology, such as democracy of an American flavor, to be either servile toward the occupying power or useless demagogues. Flight from politics in the name of culture combined with personal convenience – who knew where denazification might strike next? Many Germans changed their names. This led to an attitude toward the world that was more immediately practical, less

[2] Ibid., 101.
[3] *Frankfurter Rundschau,* Sept. 8, 1945.
[4] Ibid.
[5] *Münchener Zeitung,* Oct. 6, 1945.

emotional, and at the same time more culturally sophisticated than evident to those who made simplistic judgements in the 1960s about the evolution of German life after 1945.

Hans Wallenberg, Berlin correspondent of the *Münchener Zeitung*, commented:

If one could describe the present situation in Berlin in one sentence, one probably would have to say that this city, formerly so generous and now so poor, is caught up in a fever of normalization. Everywhere attempts are made to reconstruct, to found, to remodel, to open and to plan. Often these attempts appear to be a flight from reality: one is left with the impression that many of the planners want to go back in time, into a period that is irretrievably lost for Berlin. It dawns only slowly on the Berliners that their city is no longer a metropolis such as London and Paris. . . .[6]

The devaluation of politics and the search for renewal of the values provided by moral, ethical, or religious principles were found not only in Germany, but throughout Western Europe. The political systems, procedures, and parties of the interwar years seemed bankrupt to many who had lived under German occupation because they had failed to prevent the war. Likewise, the antidemocratic ideologies were bankrupt because they had resulted in the war. Their promises of a new and glorious future were seen to be not only empty, but a disguise for a violently regressive attack on modern civilization. Soviet communism was not rejected outright or as easily; in France especially, those who saw the Soviet Union as a potential threat to peace faced strong pro-communist opposition. Yet many of the Western Europeans who in 1945 saw the Soviet Union in a very positive light changed their minds between 1945 and 1948, partly as a result of what they learned about communist repression of democracy in East Germany and Eastern Europe. By the early 1950s, ideological skepticism had taken hold in most Western European political parties and milieus.

Among the most intensely anti-ideological people in the first postwar years were the returning soldiers themselves, the *Heimkehrer*. They were more pitied than despised, though their ragged uniforms reminded their civilian compatriots of an immediate past that most wanted to forget as quickly as possible, a picture vividly drawn by Wolfgang Borchert in *Draussen vor der Tür*. It was the story of a German soldier returning from the war, and was first presented as a drama on Radio Hamburg in 1947 and later as a play. It presented two conflicting worlds of the past and the present prompting the central figure to ask, "Does no one have an answer?"

The *Heimkehrer* themselves, however, and others of their generation,

[6] Ibid., Sept. 22, 1945.

did not feel responsible for the politics of Hitler's government, nor did they consider themselves guilty of the crimes of the Nazis. They were soldiers and not members of the dreaded Gestapo. A young poet, Felix Berner, who was born in 1918 and served in the German Army for the entire duration of the war, gave vent to this mix of contradictory feelings in this poem, written just after the war.

> When I bit into the earth,
> wet earth, kneaded with blood,
> when the ground split open,
> I expect I prayed.
> I no longer know, no longer clearly,
> except this: the sky was blue.
>
> And if you ask me:
> How did it begin?
> I didn't want it
> But I went along.
>
> When I was hunted through the wood
> with running, fallen, kneeling,
> with dead and tattered men,
> I expect I screamed.
> I no longer know, no longer for certain,
> except this: that darkness reigned.
>
> And if you ask me:
> How did it begin?
> I didn't want it
> But I went along.
>
> When I went through the streets,
> from balconies, windows, stairways
> hung the bodies of Jews,
> and I said nothing.
> This I know still, this I am sure of,
> no one can take it from me.
>
> And if you ask me:
> How did it begin?
> I didn't want it
> and passed by on the other side.[7]

[7] Cited in Mayne, *Postwar*, 53–4.

Berner's poem reflected an inner *sense* of liberation, in which the desire for return to older, better values suppressed by Nazism and the desire for revolutionary change and wholesale absorption of foreign, especially American values and procedures, were often inextricably intertwined. By their concrete actions, Allied authorities and Germans gave life to these desires. Their actions laid a new basis of cultural and intellectual life, political morality, responsible media, and a new respect for religion and the law. In this process, which was nothing less than the attempt to reconstitute the political culture and symbolic universe of an entire nation, German exiles returning as Allied officers, or on their own, played a particular and often poignant role.

One of the most important fruits of the American encounter with Germany in 1945, and after, was the formation of a transatlantic community of German and American officials, journalists, publicists, and academics that, for at least a political generation (until the 1970s), formed the vital core that gave life and meaning to the US-West German relationship. It is ironic that many of the German members of this community made their first contacts with America as prisoners of war interned in the United States. The gradual disappearance of this group presented a challenge to new political generations on both sides of the Atlantic which, by the later 1980s, had yet to be successfully met. In the late 1940s, however, this group had its focus defined for it. The country needed to be rebuilt, the political, educational, social and economic system needed to be reconstructed, and religious life, journalism, music and the theater, and literature needed to be reborn. In these areas similar attitudes emerged, similar patterns of reaction to defeat and destruction, and parallel hopes for renewal. These tendencies and hopes took varied forms in different institutional and cultural settings and differed also according to Allied occupation policy and the characters of the leading personalities involved.

In 1945 and the years immediately following many people looked to the churches, both Catholic and Protestant, for moral, intellectual, and even to some extent political leadership. One reason was that, unlike the German state which came to an end, at least temporarily, in 1945, the churches continued to function. Both the Catholic and Protestant churches enjoyed, as organizations, a unique status in German constitutional law. Traditionally, each *Land* had one established church financed by taxes levied by the *Land* government on all inhabitants and used to pay priests or ministers and maintain church buildings. During the eighteenth century the rulers of Protestant territories gradually permitted Catholic activities and vice versa, but it was not until the Weimar constitution of 1919 that church government, administration, and finances throughout Germany were fully regulated.

The constitution permitted each of the two major denominations to operate nationally, but designated one of them as *the* established church in each *Land,* entitled to special protection by the state. During the Third Reich this autonomous status permitted a few courageous leaders in each of the churches to form opposition groups. Though these groups were not large, they did give the churches considerable prestige after the war ended, which, combined with their reassertion of their inherited autonomous status, put them in a strong position to claim moral and even to some extent, political leadership in 1945.

In addition, most Germans who thought about politics in the aftermath of war and disgrace, and who were not communist, assumed that Christian ethics and ideas must play a fundamental role in any new political order. The very name "Christian Democrat," as the label of the most influential new party established in 1945, indicates the general feeling that, somehow, Christianity had to be brought back into politics to counteract the atheism and indifference to moral standards that many saw as the root causes of totalitarianism.

The churches in 1945–9 thus played a greater role in forming popular ideas about politics than at any time since the late nineteenth century. On the other hand, they also played a directly political role as institutions by virtue of their exalted position in German society. The Nazis had reduced this position, but it was entrenched in pre-existing constitutional law and custom and, once the Nazi regime was gone, the churches reasserted that position forcefully, precisely because their leaders felt an obligation and a chance to play a part in shaping the new democratic Germany.

This double role of the churches created difficulties in the three-cornered relationship between the ecclesiastical institutions, lay Germans who wanted to bring religion into politics, and the Allied occupation authorities. First of all, the institutional position of the churches in the German state was unlike that of either the established Church of England or the independent religious associations of the United States. In Germany before 1933, the churches were self-governing, but partially supported by public funds. Most *Länder,* including what was then the largest, Prussia, had established Protestant churches, composed of members of the three historical doctrinal divisions in German Protestantism, namely the Lutherans, the Calvinists, and the Unionists. The Catholic church, represented primarily in Bavaria, the Rhineland, and certain parts of south-west Germany, was weaker in numbers and cultural influence, but had greater resources to withstand state power by virtue of its supranational organization. Above the Protestant leaders stood the political authorities, whom church leaders were taught by tradition to respect; above the Catholic hierarchy stood the Pope.

This difference might have encouraged the Catholic leadership to stronger opposition to National Socialism than in fact occurred. That it did not was due to many factors: an inherent sympathy on the part of many Catholics to some elements of Nazism, notably the anti-democratic insistence on a natural hierarchy in society; the pro-German feelings of the Papal Nuncio in Germany, Eugenio Cardinal Pacelli, who reigned as Pope Pius XII from 1939 to 1958; fear of communism and of socialism. One very important factor was the Reich Concordat of 1933, by which the Catholic church, after over a hundred years of struggle against the modern, secular state, obtained legal guarantees for its self-government and its control of education and marriage for its members. The quid pro quo was that the church did not publicly take political positions. According to people who worked with him, Pope Pius XI, who died in 1939, was planning an encyclical denouncing Nazism. It was, however, never published, although the Pope had issued a document in 1937 denouncing Nazi violations of human rights, entitled "Mit brennender Sorge" (Of burning concern). Catholics were therefore given no clear signal by the hierarchy which was itself divided. Some, like Michael Cardinal Faulhaber (1869–1952), the archbishop of Munich and Freising, or Graf von Galen, the bishop of Münster, denounced Nazi actions, including the killings of retarded people or the deportation of Jews, but most others were silent. Because the bishops were unable to save many of those who were persecuted, their authority was slowly undermined.

During the war Pope Pius XII had cooperated with the US Office of Strategic Services (OSS, the predecessor of the CIA) under General William "Wild Bill" Donovan in Washington, DC. Thus, after the war the OSS made arrangements to provide a papal envoy with a special tour of southern Germany, a procedure which was highly irregular since the envoy was dressed in an American uniform so that he would avoid being arrested (German priests were not permitted to travel unaccompanied and at will even within the occupation zone). The purpose of the trip, which continued for some days, was "to reestablish papal authority in southern Germany, as a bulwark against Communist and Soviet intelligence and political machinations in the region."[8] To accomplish this, the envoy met with Catholic leaders, notably Cardinal Faulhaber, the leading Catholic prelate in the Third Reich and one known for his outspoken defense of Judaism.

The Catholic church, as the most important surviving large-scale

[8] Brown, *The Last Hero*, 703–4.

public organization in Germany in 1945, faced an immense challenge. In the words of a later writer, "the beginnings of 1945 and after brought the Church tremendous problems and tasks, the most important of which are indicated by the phrases integration of expellees, adaptation of pastoral structures to considerable societal changes, subsidiary help in guaranteeing a minimum subsistence to large parts of the population, temporary assumption of tasks of social and political representation, pastoral efforts to overcome the anti-Christian effects of Nazi education and propaganda, moral initiatives against the insecurity of ethical norms caused by the war."[9]

The bulk of the physical task fell to the *Deutscher Caritas Verband* (DCV), the umbrella organization of Catholic charities in Germany, comprising hospitals and organized help to the poor. The DCV was the only Catholic public association that the Nazis had not suppressed, and from 1945 to the mid-1950s it had its hands full. One writer estimated that the DCV, through its contacts with international Catholic charities, helped raise and distribute one-quarter of all the aid given to Germany between 1945 and 1962, or about 150,000 tons of food, medical supplies, and other goods. In addition, the DCV played a vital role in resettling the expellees and refugees and in re-establishing in West Germany the 400 or so hospitals and other charitable institutions once located in the Oder–Neisse territories.[10] (On the churches' educational policy and practice, see the chapter on education below).

After Faulhaber, the best-known Catholic leader in late 1940s Germany was undoubtedly Joseph Frings (1887–1978), since 1942 archbishop of Cologne and from 1945 to 1965 chairman of the Episcopal Conference, the umbrella organization of the German Catholic hierarchy. Cologne was the mother see of Germany, with roots going back to Roman times, and with a long and distinguished history as a center of Catholic opposition to hostile political authority. Frings used this immense prestige to the fullest in opposing what he considered harsh and unreasonable occupation policies. Significantly, he had the strong support of Pope Pius XII, who made him a cardinal in 1946. He became popular throughout Germany when, in his Christmas sermon of 1946, broadcast on radio, he declared that stealing food for one's family, and pieces of coal to put in one's grate, were not mortal sins. This gave rise to one of the many slang-words of the occupation regime: *fringsen*, meaning, roughly, to steal innocently for a good purpose.[11]

[9] Forster, "Der deutsche Katholizismus," in *Der soziale und politische Katholizismus,* ed. Rauscher, 1: 212.
[10] Gatz, "Caritas und soziale Dienste," in *Der soziale und politische Katholizismus,* ed. Rauscher, 2: 344–5.
[11] Steininger, *Deutsche Geschichte,* 1: 90.

A vital part of German Catholic life before 1933 was the activity of associations. Some were charitable, and others more political in nature like the Catholic trade unions and professional groups or, on the *Land* and national political level, the Center party. The Nazis had suppressed most such activities, and in 1945 most Catholics found it preferable, as well as more convenient, to let the individual parishes take over many of the tasks of public education and assistance that had formerly belonged to the associations. In 1945 there were only 25,000 surviving members of the Catholic unions, many of their leaders were dead, and from 1945 to 1949 the hierarchy, led by Frings, as well as by lay Catholic politicians like Adenauer, strongly supported the unitary trade union organization.

The most important surviving lay institution of German Catholicism was the *Katholikentag*, or Catholic Assembly. Founded in 1848, the Assembly was an occasion for religious and lay leaders and representatives of various interest groups to meet to discuss political and other issues, or, as a Catholic writer put it, "a place of religious, social, and political education and a point of departure for ecclesiastical, social, and political action."[12] The Nazis forbade the Assemblies, which resumed in 1948 and thereafter were held biennially in rotation with their Protestant counterpart, the *Deutscher Evangelischer Kirchentag* (DEKT). The Assemblies were managed by a Central Committee, renamed in 1952 the Central Committee of German Catholics, an organization that came to play a large part in West German religious, social, and cultural life. On the party level, Catholics and Protestants together decided strongly against sectarian parties and together created the Christian democratic party.

The territorial division of the Catholic church in Germany remained formally unchanged until 1970, which meant the ecclesiastical provinces (archdioceses) of Paderborn and Bamberg continued to include parts of what was now the Soviet zone of occupation. The dioceses of Dresden and Berlin were "exempt;" that is, they were not part of a larger province, but directly subordinated organizationally to the Vatican. In addition, a small area of the Soviet zone around Görlitz, on the Neisse river, belonged to the province of Breslau (the capital of Silesia, controlled by Poland after 1945), which continued to exist on paper until 1970.

The central administrative organization of the church hierarchy in postwar Germany was the Episcopal Conference with headquarters close to the zonal boundary in Hesse at Fulda, a city, like Cologne, with ancient Catholic traditions. It was not until 1978 that the Polish pope

---

[12] Friedrich Kronenberg, "Deutscher Katolikentag," in *Staatslexikon*, 2: 14.

John Paul II declared that the Fulda Conference could no longer speak for the Catholic hierarchy in East Germany.

German Catholic theology and social thought had flourished in the 1920s and early 1930s; many of its proponents had survived the Nazi years in semi-retirement or exile in Rome (an option not open to Protestants); after 1945, these thinkers – Romano Guardini, Oswald von Nell-Breuning, Gustav Gundlach, Josef Pieper – enjoyed belated recognition and influence. Nell-Breuning and Gundlach took opposite sides in the argument over workers' co-determination: Nell-Breuning, who fervently believed in the justice of socialism, argued that modern man could find fulfilment in life only if he shared in the control of his place of work, which meant not merely co-determination but eventual control of private industry by the unions. Gundlach, on the other hand, who had worked with Pope Pius XI in the 1930s, argued that private ownership of the means of production and private enterprise could be justified ethically and theologically and rejected socialism on the grounds that it led to a far worse kind of despotism over the workers than any seen under liberal capitalism. He also took a strong stand in the late 1950s in favor of nuclear deterrence, even going so far as to argue that the destruction of the world in a nuclear war was a lesser moral evil than communist domination.

Catholic laymen, such as Adenauer, Heinrich von Brentano, and Theodor Blank, who later were to become cabinet members of the West German government, likewise took more prominent roles. Adenauer's religion was inextricably bound up with his cultural conception of the historic unity of Western Europe and with his sense of the vital importance of promoting that unity as the only way to preserve the independence of the region from domination by the Soviet Union. He shared this political-religious sense of the role of West European civilization, Catholicism, and civil law with two other important Continental leaders of the time, Robert Schuman of France and Alcide de Gasperi of Italy. This common concern was of vital importance in providing mutual sympathy and thus laying the foundation of the West European community which these three helped create. An interesting circumstance about the meetings between Adenauer, Schuman, and de Gasperi was that they spoke German, since Schuman was from the German-speaking part of France and de Gasperi was born in northern Italy as a subject of the German-dominated Habsburg Empire. Thus, in the construction of the European Community, the old hegemony of the German language across the central zone of Europe played a last and not inglorious role.

During the Third Reich, the Protestant state churches, the *Landeskirchen*, adopted a neutral stance vis-à-vis Hitler's regime and its policies. A small minority of Protestants in the so-called Faith Movement of German Christians actively supported Nazism and anti-semitism under the slogan "the swastika on our breasts, the cross in our hearts."[13] In response to the German Christians and their agitation, a Berlin pastor and World War I submarine veteran, Martin Niemöller (1892–1985), organized a group of anti-Nazi clergymen. It formed the core of what later became the Confessing Church, which was the main Protestant organization opposed to the regime. Most of its leaders, including Niemöller himself, spent time in prison or concentration camps, and some, like Dietrich Bonhoeffer, were executed. Many persons associated with the Confessing Church played important roles in postwar Germany. The most important, apart from Niemöller himself, was Gustav Heinemann, the leading opponent of arming the Federal Republic and later minister of justice and federal president.

After surrender, the *Landesbischof* (chief prelate of the established Protestant church) of Württemberg, Theophil Wurm, summoned representatives of other *Land* churches to a conference at Treysa in Hesse, in August 1945, to discuss the future of the Protestant church in Germany. Wurm had led a semi-clandestine group of leaders of the Lutheran and Reformed (Calvinist) *Land* churches since 1941 and now wished for this group to form the nucleus of a new national organization. In October, the Protestant leaders met again in Stuttgart, where they issued the Stuttgart Confession of Guilt. The authors of this document, which was of fundamental importance for the subsequent history of German Protestantism and political theology, declared that the church shared the guilt of the German people because it "had not confessed more courageously, prayed more faithfully, believed more joyfully, and loved more fervently." Commenting on the confession in a letter to his brother, Niemöller wrote:

> The crimes of Hitler and his helpers are now being blamed on our nation as a whole, and, in fact, we are all to blame, but not in the sense that we are murderers, robbers or sadists, but in the sense that we let all these things happen, without doing our utmost for the victims and against the crimes, as we should have done.[14]

Many Germans resented the Stuttgart Confession because of the implication that all Germans were collectively guilty of mass murder and aggression. An American scholar, Frederic Spotts, quoted the following reaction from the Catholic archbishop of Paderborn to Wurm and the Confession:

---

[13] Cited in Kershaw, *Popular Opinion and Political Dissent in the Third Reich,* 159.
[14] Eschenburg, *Jahre der Besatzung,* 221.

"I respect the spirit of Bishop Wurm's declaration on the subject of War Guilt, but such statements should not be made in open form in the hearing of youth. In order to influence a man you must acknowledge what was right and straight in him." Less explicitly but more frankly, Cardinal Frings in his 1946 New Year's Eve sermon condemned those "who cannot do enough to proclaim the guilt of their own people to the world and to confess repeatedly before mankind."[15]

On the other hand, the Stuttgart Confession earned respect for its authors abroad. Representatives of Protestant churches in the US, Britain, and France attended the Stuttgart meeting, and recommended that the delegates adopt Bishop Wurm's proposal for an umbrella organization which was duly formed under the name Provisional Council of the Evangelical Church in Germany. It became the *Evangelische Kirche in Deutschland* (EKD, Evangelical Church in Germany) in 1948, and Wurm served as its head until 1949. The members of the EKD were the Protestant (Lutheran, Calvinist, and Unionist) *Land* churches as established under the Weimar constitution of 1919, in accordance with the *Land* borders established by the Congress of Vienna in 1815. This meant, in many areas, and especially to the East, that the EKD's ecclesiastical borders did not reflect the political reality of postwar Germany. The EKD leaders, nevertheless, saw a symbolic value in maintaining the old borders until they should be superseded by a peace treaty.

The Stuttgart Confession began a period of political Protestantism based on a new view that the old separation of church and state must now be overcome by ecclesiastical and theological involvement in political and social issues. The EKD and its leadership, the Synod, provided an authoritative moral voice in the discussion of politics and social issues, and many important public figures, notably Gustav Heinemann (president of the Synod from 1949 to 1955), emerged from this group until the 1960s, when the situation of all the churches in divided Germany changed dramatically; the Protestant church was separated completely by the German Democratic Republic (GDR) in 1969 from its counterpart in the Federal Republic. By 1969 a peace treaty had still not been signed; therefore, the EKD decided to cease claiming to represent the Protestant churches in the former Soviet zone. Until 1969, however, although it was always difficult and often impossible, delegates from the churches in the Soviet zone (or GDR) did take part in the EKD's activities.

A forum for regular consultation between religious and lay leaders, that influenced public and political affairs, was the *Deutscher Evangel-*

---

[15] Spotts, *Churches and Politics in Germany*, 92.

*ischer Kirchentag* (DEKT, Protestant Assembly). Unlike its Catholic counterpart, the DEKT had no previous history when lay leaders organized it in 1948–9 as an institution "to gather Protestant Christians in Germany, strengthen them in the faith, arm them for responsibility in their church, encourage them to bear witness in the world, and remain with them in the world-wide community of Christendom."[16]

Behind the prestige enjoyed by certain individual churchmen in 1945 lay a much broader phenomenon, the expression of a widely felt need for religion and the return of religious values. Almost all politically active persons who were not communists or committed social democrats shared the belief that Christianity must return to politics, and that Nazism was the fruit, above all, of materialism and of a denial of the spiritual side of life. Hence the reason why the major new postwar party took the name Christian Democratic Union and the tremendous interest shown in the idea of Christian socialism – Christian responsibility for the social policy of the nation – as propagated in the *Frankfurter Hefte* and elsewhere. The editors of the *Frankfurter Hefte* were two left-wing lay Catholics, Walter Dirks and Eugen Kogon, who established the journal under license from OMGUS in early 1946. It was one of the few journals of intellectual culture and political debate that survived the currency reform of 1948. It maintained an independent existence until the mid-1980s when it merged with *Neue Gesellschaft*, an official publication of the SPD.

Dirks and Kogon, who published one of the first postwar books in Germany about Nazi terror in 1946, came out of the leftist political Catholicism of the 1920s. While the Allies recognized the use of the principles of Christianity as a positive influence in the process of re-education, some Germans saw the church as a political tool that had not been seriously compromised. Dirks and Kogon, for example, hoped to influence the Christian democratic movement in a socialist direction, by emphasizing what they saw as the obligation of Catholics to work for a socialist form of economic and political organization. They felt deceived and frustrated when Adenauer, although a Catholic, decided to work with the largely Protestant business circles and free-market economists in designing the economic platform of the CDU. This connection between the religious and the political was inevitable in postwar Germany. But it also tended to diminish the significance of another point. By joining or returning to organized religion and to interest in the political importance of religious values, many Germans were also avoiding the question of May 1945; namely, whether the surrender of the Wehrmacht and the defeat of the Reich was the defeat

[16] Preamble to the "Statutes of the DEKT," in *Staatslexikon*, 2: 5.

of an evil Germany, or the liberation of a truer, better Germany from Nazi domination. It was a question of great importance, and, at least as far as Adenauer was concerned, it found an answer in the leadership he provided.

# 8

# The Media and Literature

Journalism and literature were greatly helped by what at first sight seemed a surprising fact: an excess of money. At the end of the war, the obligations of the Reich – the public debt – stood at almost 400 billion Reichsmark. Because the regime had financed the war effort primarily by borrowing and printing money, and not by taxation, most citizens found themselves in 1945 with a surplus of useless cash. Many necessities were unavailable at the prices established under wartime rationing, which was continued and considerably tightened by the Allied occupation authorities. The black market flourished, but was to a large extent a barter economy, in which the hardest currency was American cigarettes, but which also included coffee, canned food and other items of small size. One of the few items not rationed and almost always sold at the stated price, was printed matter; that is to say, whenever newsprint was available. Once a publisher had a license from the Information Control Division of OMGUS, or its British equivalent, and once he had paper on which to print, publication and distribution were as free as the primitive conditions of transportation allowed. Newspapers, journals, and books were a seller's market, even though newsprint was rationed.

Before the war ended approximately 1,500 Nazi newspapers were published. They were initially replaced with Allied army publications, and then gradually with German newspapers. The first license was granted to the *Aachener Nachrichten* on June 27, 1945, followed by the *Frankfurter Rundschau*, whose first issue appeared on Wednesday, August 1, 1945. It was published twice weekly (Wednesday and Saturday), was initially four pages long, and sold for 20 pfennig. By the end of 1945 all army publications had been discontinued, with the exception of *Die Neue Zeitung*, published in Munich and in Berlin. By the end of 1948, 56 newspapers were being published in the American zone of occupation with a circulation of 4.2 million, whose owners jointly operated the *Deutsche Nachrichten Agentur* (DNA, German Wire Services).[1]

Radio, and above all newspapers, were seen by the Allies, especially the Americans, as the primary tools of re-education (a word coined by a leftist German emigré, the publicist Leopold Schwarzschild). In the first four years of occupation, the Western Allies granted more than 150 newspaper licenses and authorized the establishment of independent, publicly financed radio stations. Direct censorship was abolished fairly early (in September 1945 in the US zone), but open criticism of the occupying powers was forbidden. Licenses were usually given to groups of three persons, and initially the group often included a communist. During 1946–7 this policy changed and journalists too friendly to the Soviets were frequently not granted licenses. The last communist licenses in the Western zones were revoked in 1948.[2]

The first stage of Allied news policy was represented by Allied military newspapers, the majority of which were organized by an exceptional man, Hans Habe, a Hungarian emigré from Vienna who returned to Europe as a US officer in the psychological warfare division. One of the most successful of these newspapers put out by the Allied military governments was the *Allgemeine Zeitung* of Berlin. It only existed from August to November 1945, but for that brief time provided a revival of the best pre-Nazi Berlin journalism. General Clay closed it down in accordance with a revision in policy, which was to emphasize the German role in re-education by licensing Germans to publish their own newspapers. There were two exceptions to this, *Die Neue Zeitung* of Munich, established by OMGUS under Habe's direction as "an American newspaper for the German public," and *Die Welt* in the British zone. Habe's great strength was that he was native to the German world yet completely committed to the principles of re-education. He set out to make *Die Neue Zeitung* the focal point of West German journalism and succeeded. Habe himself, however, had to leave in 1946; he had been accused of being too pro-German in what was, after all, an official American publication.

*Die Welt*, the official newspaper of the British military government, was designed to be a German version of the London *Times*, and was given access to the *Times* World Service. Its first editor was to have been Hans Zehrer, an influential representative of the so-called conservative revolution of the Weimar years, an ideology of corporatism, nationalism, and state socialism, both anti-democratic and anti-Nazi. The social

---

[1] OMGUS, *The German Press*, 1–2.
[2] See Frei, "Presse" and "Hörfunk und Fernsehen," in *Die BRD*, ed. Benz, 3: 275–357.

democrats of Hamburg intervened with the British Labour government to prevent Zehrer's appointment in 1945, and he was replaced by Rudolf Küstermeier, whose opinions tended toward a religious socialism and who, as a Jew, had spent the entire Nazi period in a concentration camp.

The political pluralism on each editorial board required under the licensing system survived the transfer of press jurisdiction to the *Länder* in 1949, and was perhaps the most important legacy of the occupation in the media. Most West German newspapers were born centrist, as it were, and many remained so, although the political center shifted leftward over time. Another legacy was the separation of news reportage from editorial advocacy, which was central to Anglo-Saxon journalism. On the Continent, by contrast, newspapers had always been the organs of particular political milieus, and their readers expected the news to be presented according to a specific world-view. This largely remained the case in France and Italy, but in West Germany, because of occupation, newspapers, unlike political parties, were no longer allowed to belong to sharply defined camps. Neutral reporting and advocacy of the goals of re-education formed the limits of what was permitted.

Among the successful organs in the licensed press were the weeklies *Die Zeit*, *Der Spiegel*, *Christ und Welt*, and the national dailies *Süddeutsche Zeitung* and *Frankfurter Rundschau*. Each reflected and continued to reflect a specific and vital element of postwar German culture and political life. The most prestigious newspaper in West Germany, the *Frankfurter Allgemeine Zeitung*, did not begin as a licensed paper, however. It was founded in 1949 to carry on the European liberal traditions of the pre-Nazi *Frankfurter Zeitung*.

The most successful of all was *Der Spiegel* (The Mirror). It was founded in January 1947 by a 23–year-old war veteran named Rudolf Augstein, who came from a traditional Catholic environment in Thuringia. Intelligent, and often described as irreverent and unscrupulous, he used his license from the British authorities to start an experiment unheard-of in Germany: a weekly newsmagazine specifically geared toward puncturing reputations, denouncing real or, sometimes, alleged scandals, and reducing political and other news to its most unsavory interpretation. All of this was done in a rude, brash style hitherto unknown in German journalism. It had certain precedents in leftist writings of the Weimar period, but was largely created by Augstein himself, who structured it from the beginning as a deliberate and unmistakable house style, a sort of trademark. The experiment was successful. *Der Spiegel* struck a tremendously responsive chord in the German public, so much so that alone among publications it was often traded at fifteen times its nominal price of 1 mark, because *Der Spiegel* was allowed newsprint for only 15,000 copies. The demand proved

durable. When the currency reform ended paper rationing, Augstein
was in the enviable position of being able to increase circulation (to
65,000 instead of the 15,000 authorized by the British). By the early
1980s it was close to the million mark.

*Der Spiegel* was, in one sense, perhaps the most typical product of left-
liberal West German culture. It was a culture that saw itself as progressive and enlightened by comparison with the old German virtues of
seriousness in public and private business, rigid honesty, predictability,
a strong work ethic, and heroism in war and adversity. Spokesmen for
this culture either ridiculed these values, denied that they were ever
really honored, or denounced them as Nazism in disguise. *Der Spiegel*
played a great part in shaping this set of attitudes, and was thus always
something more than a mere newsmagazine, as its outer resemblance to
*Time* magazine in the United States might otherwise indicate. The
purpose of *Spiegel* journalism was never simply reporting, but, as
Augstein admitted, advocacy of a set of cultural and political attitudes
and sensibilities.[3] *Der Spiegel* thus violated the premises of Allied policy,
which reflected the conviction that a separation of news reportage and
editorial advocacy was healthy in a liberal-democratic society. In the
licensing years, however, this tendency was not usually strong enough to
cause difficulties. Most of the slanted stories concerned German politics
and were of little concern to the British military government. Later, the
attitudes fostered by *Der Spiegel* helped to shape a strong liberal-
progressive pole of West German opinion. So influential were these
attitudes that even when conservative forces held political power, as
they did until 1969, cultural legitimacy lay increasingly with the liberal
left. This by no means meant sympathy for the Soviet Union or even
radical socialism, although it often meant criticism of the US; Augstein
promoted a variety of anti-American leftist nationalism in his pages.
Still, over the years, the influence of *Der Spiegel* and other, less important
organs of opinion contributed to a widespread criticism among the
literate public of the US role in Europe and West Germany and of West
German security policies as well. In his anti-Americanism Augstein
followed a well established intellectual view dating from the German
poet, Heinrich Heine, in the nineteenth century.

The other intellectually important weekly, *Die Zeit*, was the result of
an accident. Gerd Bucerius, a Hamburg lawyer and minister for housing
in the first Hamburg government of 1945, was invited by a British press
officer to plan a daily newspaper. The plan was so good that the British
appropriated it and used it as a basis for *Die Welt*, which Axel Springer
purchased in 1952. In compensation they offered Bucerius a license for

---

[3] Glaser, *Kulturgeschichte der BRD*, 204–7.

a weekly, *Die Zeit*, which he accepted "with curses." Publication began on February 21, 1946. The first edition carried an article entitled "Our Task:"

As a wall of darkness and despair the future stands before us. We can only hope to ignite a small light, in order to illuminate the paths on which we must carefully step in the weeks and months to come. We are speaking to a German readership, who, in this paper, should find reflected its worries, its wishes and hopes, and also see them clarified. We shall not say just what the public wants to hear; and that it is impossible to please everyone, is an old wisdom. But even an opinion that may be strange to us, will definitely be respected by us.[4]

By 1990 its circulation had reached approximately 470,000 copies and its annual income over DM 100 million. Under Bucerius' leadership it became a highly respected weekly, liberal rather than conservative in orientation. Its first editor-in-chief, however, (from 1946 to 1956), Richard Tüngel gave it a distinctly conservative image which it kept until his departure. Bucerius himself was elected to the Bundestag in 1949 and remained a CDU member until 1962, when he left the party. *Die Zeit* survived severe financial losses during the 1950s, primarily because Bucerius had purchased 50 per cent ownership of *Stern* in 1949. This magazine was extremely profitable, whereas *Die Zeit* did not begin to make a profit until 1975. In the 1980s Bucerius turned its management over to the former chancellor, Helmut Schmidt.[5]

One of the original members of the staff, still active in the 1990s, was Marion Gräfin Dönhoff, descended from eighteen generations of East Prussian nobility. She was in charge of political reporting from 1951 to 1968, editor-in-chief from 1968 to 1973, and since then co-publisher. In the 1930s she had taken a doctorate in economics at Basel, using the intact archives at her family seat of Friedrichstein near Königsberg, to give a complete account of the social and economic history and culture of a great Prussian landed estate, only a few years before that form of life disappeared forever. Unlike many of her fellow-refugees from East Prussia, she showed no rancor toward the Soviets, regarding the loss of the east, and her family estate, as revenge for German aggression. Politically she supported a "socially ordered – that is, a corrected capitalism."[6] As she grew older, her foreign policy views tended increasingly toward heavy criticism of the US and sympathy for

[4] *Die Zeit*, February 28, 1986.
[5] Gerd Bucerius, "Vierzig Jahre Die Zeit," *Die Zeit*, February 28, 1986; Theo Sommer, "Ein Mann schwimmt gegen den Strom," *Die Zeit*, May 23, 1986.
[6] Eschenburg, *Jahre der Besatzung*, 167.

Soviet goals and interests. In the 1980s Bucerius occasionally expressed public disapproval of the political line of *Die Zeit*, but he never tried to interfere. It remained an influential weekly, covering domestic and foreign policy issues.

The cultural renaissance of 1945–8 was based not merely on radio, newspapers, and weeklies, but on more than 200 literary and political journals. These publications were the great beneficiaries of the cash surplus of 1945–8; by the same token, most of them disappeared when the currency reform made discretionary spending on cultural goods a luxury for most people. They also benefited from the fact that few books were published and distributed in Germany between mid-1944 and 1947.[7]

To the artificial surplus of cash, with little relation to the real value of goods and objects, corresponded an analogous surplus of philosophical, moral, social, and political ideas with little purchase on the reality of the day. Almost all the contributors to the new journals were attempting to define a new social, moral, and political order, but without the experience or the freedom of action and decision necessary for realistic planning. In the words of a practical scholar, the constitutional lawyer Theodor Eschenburg, the proposals were like cooking recipes without a "stove, fire or ingredients."[8] Their common denominator was a rejection of political hierarchy, authority, power, militarism, nationalism, and capitalism, but also of Soviet state socialism. The politicians, on the other hand, who were trying to organize government and administration in the midst of ruin and destruction, had little time for these intellectual schemes. The resulting discrepancy caused critical observers, like the literary historian Klaus Ziegler, to repeat an old complaint of German intellectuals, that Germany's problem was the divorce of "power and the spirit," that the political leadership of the country was unenlightened (and therefore dangerous), while the critical intelligentsia was without power. This argument was repeated at frequent intervals throughout the subsequent history of West Germany, even though it was far from true.

Two of the most important journals were the *Frankfurter Hefte*, founded as a forum for Christian-Marxist dialogue by two left-leaning Catholics, Walter Dirks and Eugen Kogon, and *Das goldene Tor*, founded by Alfred Döblin, author of *Berlin Alexanderplatz*, who returned in French uniform and organized literary and cultural life in the French zone. One important area of concern for these and other organs was the encounter of Germans in Germany with the writings and outlook of those who had gone into exile. This encounter was often unhappy.

---

[7] See Glaser, *Kulturgeschichte der BRD*, 1: 281–8.
[8] Eschenburg, *Jahre der Besatzung*, 159.

Exiles, like Thomas Mann, were quick to argue that any book published in Germany between 1933 and 1945 was by definition bad, whereas anti-Nazis who remained in Germany were well aware that this was not so, and that there were publishers and writers who had overcome tremendous obstacles of censorship and fear to publish the truth, albeit indirectly. Many exiles, however, had little patience with the peculiar requirements of how to tell the truth under totalitarian conditions, and too often failed to distinguish between the subterfuge and discretion necessary to slip truth past the censors without landing the author in a concentration camp, and simple collaboration with the regime.

The renewal of contacts between former friends and colleagues was often fatal to friendship and trust. Peter Suhrkamp, who in 1933 was a talented junior member of the S. Fischer Verlag, publishers of, among others, Thomas Mann and Hermann Hesse, bought the Fischer title in 1934 in order to prevent it being taken over by a Nazi supporter, after the Jewish owners had been forced by the regime to sell. Under Suhrkamp's direction the Fischer Verlag continued to publish Mann in Germany until forbidden to do so in 1936. The exiled Fischer family, however, continued to operate emigré publishing houses abroad under the Fischer name in cities such as Vienna (from 1934 until 1938), Stockholm, New York (until 1945), and Amsterdam (in the postwar years). In 1942 the Nazi propaganda ministry forced Suhrkamp to stop using the Fischer name, but he continued to regard his role as that of a trustee, hoping some day to restore the firm to its morally, if no longer formally entitled owners. He spent the last months of the war ill with pleurisy and emaciated from a stay in a concentration camp. In 1945 he was the first publisher to obtain a license from the Allied Kommandatura in Berlin and he resumed contact with the Fischer family as a preliminary to restoring ownership. This was difficult because the Fischer family, who were now US citizens, were forbidden to undertake any commercial activity in Germany. In 1947 Gottfried Bermann Fischer, the owner of the exiled Fischer Verlag, Suhrkamp, and the US authorities reached an agreement by which Bermann Fischer granted German publication rights for books published by Fischer in Amsterdam to OMGUS, which then in turn granted them to Suhrkamp. However, the relationship between Suhrkamp and the previous owners could not be restored. Petty disagreements concealed a profound alienation of temperaments and outlook, and in 1949 an open breach was imminent. Eugen Kogon succeeded in mediating an out-of-court settlement releasing Suhrkamp from any connection to the Fischer Verlag, which was re-established under another director in Frankfurt. Suhrkamp continued his independent publishing activities; Hermann Hesse and several other notable Fischer authors moved with him, and the new Suhrkamp Verlag became an enterprise as important in West German culture, and in many ways as characteristic, as *Der Spiegel* was in the area of journalism and popular opinion.

By refusing to return to Germany, Thomas Mann also rejected the role of a cultural and moral leader of a people he felt he no longer knew (or wanted to know). And he was filled with doubts about their future:

How will it feel to belong to a people whose history carries with it this ghastly failure, a people who are confused about themselves, who are spiritually burnt out, a people who, admittedly, despair of governing themselves, and who believe that the best solution is to become a colony of foreign powers?[9]

Of all intellectual figures in 1945, the one who came closest to holding the role of a cultural and moral leader, for a time, was the philosopher Karl Jaspers (1883–1969), who had been forbidden to teach by the Nazis. Though ill and tired, Jaspers resumed his lectures to packed, if icy, halls in Heidelberg, until 1948, when he accepted an offer from the University of Basel (Switzerland). He published his first and most important postwar lectures, given in 1945–6, as *Die Schuldfrage* (The question of guilt) in 1946.[10] The lectures themselves bore the title "Concerning the Spiritual Situation in Germany," which was a deliberate echo of the title of his best-known earlier work, a little pamphlet critical of democracy entitled *Die geistige Situation der Zeit* of 1931. In 1945 he wanted to clarify the meaning of guilt and defeat and to advise his countrymen against escaping their guilt by looking only at their immediate, disastrous situation and pointing to Allied severity. He rejected the idea that all Germans were tainted with guilt just by being German. To use this argumentation was to think like the Nazis, who said that all Jews were tainted just by being Jews. On the other hand, all Germans must reflect seriously on their behavior during the Third Reich. Did they take an active part in the regime? Did they hope to survive by adapting? This type of behavior, argued Jaspers, was culpable and demanded repentance and reflection. He concluded that all Germans felt, and ought to feel, a collective moral responsibility, as distinguished from being individually guilty, because only the recognition of this collective responsibility would permit genuine renewal. "The way of purification" from the "depths of awareness of guilt" was the only way to truth.[11]

Many Germans, however, disagreed vehemently with Jaspers' thesis

[9] Cited in Reinfried and Schulte, *Die Sicherheit der BRD*, 25.
[10] Included in Jaspers, *Hoffnung und Sorge*, 65–149.
[11] Ibid., 140.

of collective guilt. But to him, this suggested they had not understood his argument. He was not arguing that all Germans were guilty in a specific legal sense, but that all subjects of the Hitler regime were morally responsible for its crimes. If the Germans did not "cleanse" themselves, they could not be decent citizens of the future world, nor could they honestly join in the continuing struggle against Soviet totalitarianism, which Jaspers saw as a danger to civilization at least as great as Nazism. He concluded that few signs of such self-cleansing were present in postwar Germany, which was the main reason he moved to Basel. Another reason was undoubtedly that his wife was Jewish, and he felt uncomfortable in a country where many did not yet fully admit to the atrocities of the concentration camps, or simply were not interested in discussing it: "What basically had happened to us and by us, the Germans did not register. One did not distance oneself from the totally criminal state which we had become."[12] Even after his move to Switzerland, where he found the quiet and freedom he sought, Jaspers continued to play a great part in West German cultural life, culminating in the debate provoked by his critical dissection of West German politics in his last book *Wohin treibt die Bundesrepublik?*, published in 1966.

One of the more dramatic episodes of the whole re-education period was the case of *Der Ruf*, an "independent journal for the young generation." The title originally belonged to a journal for German POWs published in 1945 by the US War Department and edited by two ex-communists, Hans Werner Richter and Alfred Andersch. They obtained a license in 1946 and in August published the first issue of the new journal. Its raison d'être was advocacy of "socialist humanism," inspired by a rejection of the idea of collective guilt and a critical attitude to OMGUS, and the whole notion of re-education and denazification generally. Although claiming to be hostile to the totalitarian socialism of the Soviet Union, Richter was above all anti-American, and wrote in rosy terms of events and conditions in the Soviet zone. Speaking for the 20–40–year-olds, who felt cheated out of their best years by their elders in responsible positions who had given Hitler credibility and status and who had supported the Nazi system that led to war, Richter and Andersch called on all young Europeans to work together for peace, freedom, and social justice. *Der Ruf* enjoyed enormous resonance, particularly among returning war veterans, and reached a circulation of 100,000 in all three Western zones. Among those associated with *Der Ruf*, who later became prominent writers, were Wolfdietrich Schnurre, Nicolaus Sombart, and Heinz-Dietrich Ortlieb,

[12] *Der Spiegel*, no. 41, 1967.

all representing a humanitarian, anti-authoritarian socialism. However, the increasing criticism of US occupation policy and a pronounced lack of respect led to the withdrawal of the license in April 1947. Richter called the act "a victory of opportunism, the beginning of the second defeat of the Germans and probably the European working class."[13] His and Andersch' professed anti-communism was, however, already beginning to subside in favor of a radical-leftist stance of opposition to the social, political, and cultural order emerging under Allied tutelage in West Germany.

The US closure of *Der Ruf* had an unforeseen and momentous consequence. In the fall of 1947 Richter invited his erstwhile collaborators and others to a meeting at his country house in Lower Bavaria. The meeting became legendary in the annals of German literature; it was the occasion of the founding of what came to be known as the "Gruppe 47" (Group 47). Virtually every single name of consequence in West German literary culture through the 1980s passed through the loose nexus of the Group, which existed from 1947 until 1968: Heinrich Böll, Günter Grass, Martin Walser, Peter Handke, Joachim Kaiser, Hans Magnus Enzensberger, Hans Mayer, Fritz J. Raddatz, Hans Schwab-Felisch, as well as publishers like Reinhard Piper and Siegfried Unseld of Suhrkamp Verlag (publisher of most "Gruppe 47" authors).

Richter defined the Group's governing mentality as vaguely leftist, but it was not a democratic leftism willing to grant legitimacy to the views of the other side, in a mutual respect for the rules of the game. In the "dreamy democratic socialism," as Werner Ross characterized the Group's ideology, "the CDU was not a democratic partner, but a stronghold of reaction. Adenauer's state was simply an enemy to be replaced and eliminated, because it was 'post-Fascist'."[14] Claiming to despise commercialism and the alleged spiritlessness pervading the reconstruction era in West Germany, the Group was in fact a highly efficient instrument of market control, in which "a leftist sensibility and a commercial capitalism entered into an ideal marriage." Its members in the media, like Ernst Schnabel of the Nordwestdeutsche Rundfunk, brought the Group's ideology to constant prominence and helped make it "the most powerful opponent of the CDU-governed state" of the 1950s and early 1960s.

[13] Eschenburg, *Jahre der Besatzung*, 164.
[14] Ross, *Mit der linken Hand geschrieben*, 41.

# 9

# Education

Perhaps the single most important task for the Allied occupiers in 1945 was that of restructuring the educational system at all levels, primary, secondary, and university. Without clearly defined educational policies, principles, and practices, no recently implanted democratic framework would last. Indeed, the conditions of the educational system presented the same problems as the country itself: material and moral destruction and confusion. For twelve years, German schoolchildren had been taught the Nazi ideology of the *Volksgemeinschaft* (national community), which it was the destiny of each individual to serve. Nazi control of teaching was not complete, however. Not only did the churches maintain a certain amount of independence, but even in the secular schools students still read the German classics and, especially in secondary schools, many students developed a cynical and critical view of the politics of the NSDAP, which came to the fore in 1945.

By 1944 most women and children had been evacuated from the major cities, which meant that schools there closed. Normal schooling continued longest in the medium-size and smaller towns or in the countryside. As the war went on, more and more teachers, most of whom were male, were called to military service, leaving teaching increasingly to older men recalled from retirement or to women. In September 1944 Hitler ordered the draft of all males between the ages of 16 and 60. Thus, both teachers and older students were inducted into military service, and the universities had been without most male students since early in the war. At the same time more and more university buildings were being destroyed, since unlike schools, which were to be found everywhere, they were located in larger cities. Teaching on the high school level (*Oberschule* or *Gymnasium*) ground to a halt in many cities and towns by early 1945.

No sooner had the victors arrived than they shut down all remaining school activity. The Potsdam Protocol prescribed that "German education shall be so controlled as completely to eliminate [*sic*] Nazi and militarist doctrines and to make possible the successful development of democratic ideas."[1] This vague mandate to the Control Council implied a problem far deeper than the mere effects of Nazi propaganda. In fact many on the Allied side, as well as on the German left, saw the whole traditional system of education in Germany, established by a series of compromises between the secular middle class and the churches in the nineteenth century, as in need of radical reform if democracy was to take root. In the eyes of the reformers, that system, which strongly resembled the traditional system in many other European countries, had two fundamental flaws. First, it was based on the principle of "streaming" at age ten, after four years of *Volksschule*, that is, on dividing students, according to their performance, into "streams" focusing either on practical training in the *Realschule* or on intellectual preparation in the *Mittelschule, Oberschule* or *Gymnasium* for higher education and the professions. Second, the system gave religion a very large role in the establishment of educational priorities.

The argument against "streaming" was that it denied all students an equal opportunity to pursue a higher education, by arbitrarily separating those judged to be capable of only vocational pursuits, from those judged capable of more intellectual accomplishment. This was unfair, the opponents held, because only graduates of the *Mittelschule* could go on to professional schools. In turn, only graduates of the *Gymnasium* could attend university, and those who graduated with academic degrees enjoyed the most respected and best-paid careers. The system was discriminatory, they argued, because it favored overwhelmingly the children of the upper and middle classes, of fathers who themselves had attended *Gymnasium* and university. In other words, the associated three-tier system of *Volksschule, Real-* or *Mittelschule* according to "stream," and *Gymnasium* for the elite maintained the class structure and kept outsiders out.

The proper place of religion, as part of the educational process, imposed another tripartite division on the German school system which cut across the vertical three-tier system just described. Despite acrimonious battles during the Weimar Republic, no solution had been found for the problem of how to satisfy militant Catholic (and, to a lesser extent, Protestant) demands that religious instruction be guaranteed a place in the public schools while respecting the rights of non-religious families. In postwar Germany religious leaders of both denominations wanted to enforce the traditional conviction that the state, as the public authority, had the obligation of moral and religious as well as practical

[1] Dept of State, *Documents on Germany*, 57.

and substantive instruction. The question, in their view, was not, there-fore, whether the state should assure religious instruction, because there was little dispute on this point except from the socialists, but how the state should do so. The problem was made more complex because traditionally public education was not the responsibility of the national government, but of the regional governments, many of which had been fully sovereign principalities as late as 1867.

As a result, the pattern that prevailed at the time of the Nazi seizure of power in 1933 consisted of three kinds of state-supported, public schools: (1) The Catholic "confessional" schools run by clergy, similar to parochial schools in the US. They offered not merely religious instruction, but a curriculum permeated by Catholic principles, in particular the conviction that the purpose of education was to streng-then the faith of Catholics so that others might be converted. These schools predominated in the Catholic areas of Bavaria, the Rhineland (part of Prussia until 1945), and the south-west. (2) *Gemeinschaftsschulen*, or combination schools without a particular religious mission of their own, in which, for religious instruction, classes were divided into Catholic and Protestant groups. This alternative prevailed prior to 1933 throughout most of Germany, which was two-thirds Protestant. In postwar Germany these schools were found primarily in the south-west, as well as in Hesse, Bremen and the north. (3) A small number of secular schools without religious instruction of any kind.

The Nazis had severely restricted or completely eliminated the autonomy of provincial governments to define educational structure; but had also in the *Reichskonkordat* of 1933, permitted Catholics to continue denominational instruction where it prevailed and, in some cases, to extend it. In 1945 the Catholic church was in the awkward position of wanting to maintain the *Konkordat*, even while repudiating the regime that had defined its educational prerogatives. At the same time, the occupation authorities, the social democrats, as well as liberal Catholics and Protestants, wanted to decentralize education responsi-bility again and return it to the *Länder*, even at the risk that individual *Länder* might choose to end formal religious instruction and state subsidies for it. The result was a struggle:

Recognizing that Protestant *Länder*, whatever political party governed, would establish non-confessional schools, Catholic church officials worked unceasingly after 1945 for a national school settlement. During the occupation period the three Western military governments adamantly refused either to make zonewide regulations or to accede to the requests of Catholic bishops and impose confessional schools upon *Länder* as they were drawing up their consti-tutions in 1947. As a consequence, only in three Catholic *Länder* – Bavaria, Rhineland-Palatinate, and North Rhine-Westphalia – did confessional schools become the norm. Baden and all the Protestant *Länder* decided in favor of non-confessional schools including religious instruction as part of the curriculum. Catholic officials then made their equally unsuccessful attempt to retrieve the situation by securing a guarantee in the Basic Law for confessional schools throughout the Federal Republic. Subsequent negotiations with the *Länder* as school legislation was revised in the early 1950s achieved liberal financial support in some cases for private Catholic schools but no fundamental revision in the system. With all its political ammunition exhausted, the Catholic church had only one other weapon in trying to force the recalcitrant *Länder* to establish confessional schools – the Reichskonkordat.[2]

The concern of the SPD was directed against the German tradition of parochial secondary school education, either Catholic or Protestant, supported by public funds. The CDU wished to maintain this tradition as a bulwark against state power. The resolution of the many arguments over educational policy was a slow process, however, and did not receive national attention until the 1960s and 1970s.

In the period immediately following the war, the occupation authorities insisted that textbooks as well as the background of teachers be thoroughly reviewed before instruction could resume; and basically agreed that purging the educational system was the most important task in the process of denazification and democratization. A difficult problem, however, in this as in other areas of administration and public service, was that a thorough denazification would mean very few teachers and very little instruction for possibly several years. This was unacceptable for two obvious reasons. First, teaching had to continue, at least in non-political, practical subjects; the Allies did not want their policies to produce a cohort of illiterates. Second, in view of the social disruptions – particularly the arrival of millions of destitute expellees from the East, the presence of evacuees from destroyed cities throughout the Western zones, and the number of orphans and other homeless – the schools provided an essential service in keeping children productively occupied for their own safety and welfare.

Accordingly, the military governments ordered the schools reopened for the fall term of 1945. In the American zone elementary schools began instruction on October 1, 1945, almost five months after the end of the war, and high schools reopened in November. There were 1,200,174 elementary school students, taught by 14,176 teachers in 6,477 schools; a student-teacher ratio of 85 to 1. This number excluded more than 510,000 students who were not in school at all, because there were no buildings. Many school buidings had been converted to other uses, such as field hospitals, and others were destroyed, so that the conditions were

[2] Spotts, *Churches and Politics in Germany*, 212–13.

often desperate. One teacher in Lower Saxony, in the British zone, reported 229 students in his elementary school class, whereas classes of 80 or more were still the norm in the countryside in late 1946.[3] It was the responsibility of the Allied education officers to review teacher qualifications and textbooks. Teachers with Nazi backgrounds were dismissed, and by the autumn of 1945 more than five million textbooks were available to replace Nazi books. OMGUS, in particular, tried every method to break the three-tier system and introduce an American-style six-year elementary school followed by middle and high school. The Germans resisted both passively and actively and, finally, successfully. Like the bureaucracy – of which it was a part – the educational sector was an area where Allied occupation policy had little long-term effect. Even the victors had limited power without the enthusiastic collaboration of the Germans.[4]

One reason for stubborn opposition to educational reform was that the German system of education generally enjoyed wide respect in Europe and in the United States. The Germans were justifiably proud of it, and, in the desolation of 1945, it was to them a positive symbol of identity and hope. They were unwilling to see that, too, disappear, and become something foreign and unrecognizable. A typical expression of this attitude was the response of the archbishop of Mainz in October 1946 to French attempts to abolish the denominational school. France had not had state-supported religious schools since 1905, except in Alsace-Lorraine, and the French military government tried quickly to abolish the German system of state support of the churches in its zone. The archbishop of Mainz argued that to do so was to threaten the educational traditions and would resemble measures taken in the Soviet zone.

In the Soviet zone, unlike western Germany, the defenders of the traditional system had little influence, since the communists realized that control of education, and the introduction of political indoctrination and propaganda, was as essential as the confiscation of landed estates or of industry, if they were to install their political system successfully. Accordingly not only were Nazi party members, as in the West, removed from teaching, but the SMAD quickly trained 40,000 people of guaranteed working-class origins to take their place. By June 1946 they were at work, when the *Land* governments of the Soviet zone unanimously passed the Law for the Democratization of German Schools, introducing an eight-year single basic school, followed by a four-year high school or three-year vocational school. With the major difference that offspring of working-class parents had special rights of

[3]  Benz, *Potsdam 1945*, 184.
[4]  Office of US High Commissioner, *West German Educational System*, 10–17.

access to high school, it was a system that retained the concept of "streaming," thereby dividing the future ruling class from the workers, while giving the state and the SED eight years in which to inculcate student obedience and political conformity. As the world saw in 1989–90, the communists failed in their larger purpose of creating a loyal and obedient population.

In the western zones it was abundantly clear, by late 1946, that the Germans were distinctly uninterested in major reform, and saw little merit in tampering with the one area of German culture of which they were proud. Even some social democrats shared this pride and associated resentment at Allied interference, despite their conviction that the old system with its confessional schools, needed change. Adolf Grimme, the last social democratic minister of culture in Prussia in 1932 and the first postwar minister of culture in Lower Saxony, complained often that it was disgraceful to hear foreigners say "do such and such, it has worked well for us," when in fact some of the best ideas for reform were of German origin.[5]

In late 1946 OMGUS appointed a commission under George F. Zook, chairman of the American Council on Education, to evaluate the progress of reform in the US zone. Zook supported the need for a six-year unitary and coeducational grade school, with books and materials supplied at taxpayers' expense (which was not always the case, even in German public schools), to be followed by a high school in which pupils should not be divided according to skill and interests. Instead of having different schools for pupils of the same age, depending on whether they were aiming for a vocational degree or higher education, he argued that Germany should have a single high school bringing students of all backgrounds and talents together, as part and parcel of a democratic educational process.

The Zook report influenced the Control Council's directive no. 54 of June 25, 1947, prescribing reform of the school system, but it was by now too late to enforce change where the Germans did not want it. The directive called for a "comprehensive school system," consisting of primary and secondary schools, to replace the three-tier system with its coexisting vocational and university-bound "streams," with their differing social and intellectual implications.[6] In the *Länder* of Württemberg-Baden, Bremen, and Hesse the German authorities cooperated to some extent, but in Bavaria they resisted so openly that in 1948 OMGUS finally stepped in with a direct order that the Bavarian minister of culture – the conservative Catholic Alois Hundhammer – produce a

[5]  Benz, *Potsdam 1945*, 190.
[6]  Ibid., 184–5.

plan to replace the Catholic confessional school with a six-year basic school. Hundhammer never had to comply; by spring 1948 the Allies judged that the need to resolve broader political issues in Germany and Europe took precedence over efforts to reform the educational system.

Reform at the university level received much less attention than primary and secondary education, primarily because educational structure at the latter level was of basic and fundamental importance; it laid the foundations upon which university education was designed to build. The Allies, therefore, focused reform efforts almost exclusively on the school system, whereas at the university level they concentrated on removing former Nazis and monitoring the behavior of professors and students to see that anti-democratic and nationalistic doctrines were not taught.

The universities were the mothers of German scholarship, science, and industry, and the *fons et origo* of that German world leadership in many humanistic and scientific disciplines that was undisputed from the mid-nineteenth century to 1933. Many Germans in 1945 looked to the university as a source of comfort and a promise of continuity and of standards in a ruined world. For the universities to fulfill this promise it was necessary that they change as little as possible – just as the schools – because their cultural value would be lost, if their identity as German institutions were destroyed. Fortunately for the German academics who saw stability in the university structure, the Allies interfered little with academic governance. Reform, as in the schools, was postponed to the 1960s, and, in the words of a German historian, the universities were, next to the legal profession, the area of German culture and society least affected by denazification and re-education.[7]

It is true that university chairs of dismissed Nazis were not filled with anti-Nazi academics who were readily available from Vienna, Berlin, or the no longer extant universities of Breslau and Königsberg, but were reserved for their former occupants in case the latter should survive the denazification court. For a professor, as for any other *Beamter*, the required affidavit was easily obtainable from friends or colleagues, or for a price. An American official, Walter Dorn, emphasized a concern that did warrant attention:

I know that anti-Nazi professors from Breslau, Berlin, Königsberg, and Vienna have applied at Munich. The invariable reply was that it was necessary to see whether certain professors would be "cleared," a reply that is contrary to the spirit of Article 58 of the Law for Liberation, which speaks of "removal and exclusion," not suspension of ousted officials. The various faculties should be

---

[7] Steininger, *Deutsche Geschichte*, 1: 132.

instructed to make replacements at once, like any other agency of the *Land* Government. If, as reported, the wrong kind of appointments are being made, the source of this should be investigated and corrected.[8]

Dorn's justified criticism to the contrary, the universities during 1945–9 were important, not because they were the object of Allied attention, but because they were a stage where a great deal of the argument over German culture, its value and purpose, and German political beliefs and hopes for the future, was played out. This took very concrete forms, as in the University of Berlin. It was located in the Soviet sector, and educational problems there illustrated the frustrations which the division of Germany was producing. Between 1945 and 1948 SMAD, in cooperation with communist professors and collaborators, changed the curriculum of the university to introduce courses which taught the ideas and concepts of Marx and Lenin; and in so doing eliminated courses such as history, economics, political science, philosophy and law, which were taught based on the idea of academic freedom. The authorities in East Berlin thus did to the University of Berlin exactly what had occurred at Germany's universities during the Third Reich. Out of the University of Berlin the East German government was creating a political weapon which was opposed by those students and professors who rejected totalitarianism in all its forms. Therefore, a small group fled to West Berlin and, with the support of the American occupation government, established the "Free University of Berlin" in a group of old houses and buildings in a residential suburb, Dahlem, in the American sector of the city. They asked the aged historian Friedrich Meinecke (1862–1954), who had been one of the few prominent and non-Jewish German scholars to reject Nazism, to be the first president. It opened in November 1948, during the Soviet blockade of the Western sectors, with 100 professors and teaching assistants, and with an enrollment of 2,200 students, 40 per cent of whom came from the Eastern zone and the Soviet sector. The dedication ceremonies, held in December 1948, made the distinction between the freedom of West Germany and the oppression of East Germany clear. Ernst Reuter, the elected mayor of Berlin, made this point in an eloquent fashion:

Universities must be places in which there exists the freedom to work, to create, and to think, and not places in which policy . . . is made. But a precondition for the freedom to create, to think and to work is that the world in which we live and breathe is itself a free world. . . .[9]

[8]  Cited in Tent, *Mission on the Rhine,* 94.
[9]  Brandt and Lowenthal, *Ernst Reuter,* 466–7.

Student life was austere, but a positive beginning had been made. Women constituted about one-fifth of the students in West German universities. There were only 108,000 university students in 1950/51. The largest university was the University of Munich with 10,997 students. Twelve years later, in 1962/63, 213,000 students studied at West Germany's universities; by 1971 585,000, by 1984 1,314,000 and by 1988 1,410,700 students were receiving higher education.

The only Allied power to establish wholly new universities were the French, who established two, at Mainz and in the Saarland. Of these the university of Mainz was the more important. It owed its founding not only to the French military government, but to a German Jew, Michael Oppenheim, who had been a civil servant before 1933 and had survived the Third Reich with the help of his non-Jewish wife.

The French hoped that these new universities would become centers of French cultural influence and that students from the surrounding regions would be discouraged from attending the old universities in the rest of Germany. Throughout European history victorious or ambitious powers had founded or reorganized universities in recently conquered areas to control elite education and hence the opinions of the leading social groups. From 1871 to 1918, the Germans had used the university in Strasbourg in an effort to influence the Alsatians in a similar way, although without much success. With the foundation of the universities of Mainz and the Saar in 1947, the French in turn were repeating an earlier attempt in 1801–14 to gallicize the left bank of the Rhine. In the 1940s, the French again failed to persuade the Rhinelanders that they were in fact French, but nevertheless the effort helped accomplish something more important. By the late 1940s, the new universities were centers of the burgeoning student movement for a united Europe. Indirectly, the French policy thus helped produce a generation of young German leaders who believed strongly in European integration and cooperation with France.

The lack of fundamental reform in the university system and the rest of the bureaucracy irritated the German left then, as later, since they saw it as part of a conspiracy of the middle and upper classes to prevent basic social change and preserve an unegalitarian social structure. They also argued, as for example did the historian Falk Pingel, that the lack of change in the universities allowed German scholars, and by extension Germans at large, to refuse to come to grips with the Nazi past and learn the right lessons from it. Of course, by the right lessons the left meant the lesson that Germany should become a more socialist society. Pingel added that the preservation of old habits of professorial governance and traditional kinds of scholarship in the universities "prepared the legitimation of a social order which did not take on a clear outline until the end of the occupation period."[10] He meant the social order of the Adenauer period, an order based on faith in stability, hierarchy, and peaceful resolution of problems, domestic and foreign; and the German left regarded that order as fraudulent. But, as in the case of denazification, it may be that the supposedly tragic failure of reform was really a straw man. For the fact was that Nazi agitation in German universities was absent after 1945; German students were overwhelmingly democratic in their attitudes and behavior, and German scholars and students contributed honorably to building a more decent society in the years after 1945.

[10] Steininger, *Deutsche Geschichte*, 1: 133. See also Stat. Bundesamt, *Statistisches Jahrbuch 1988*, 359.

# 10

# The Engine of Recovery:
# Economic Structure and Reality

As cultural life underwent revival, economic life was undergoing reconstruction. The international context that shaped Allied occupation policy led to the decision in 1947 to form the Bizone – the amalgamation of the American and British zones of occupation – a step which made planning for production easier in the Western zones as well as giving German producers and politicians greater autonomy.

For almost a year after surrender, OMGUS under General Lucius Clay and the BMG, led by various officers the most important of whom was Sir Brian Robertson, did not follow a clear economic policy in Germany, because their governments provided no consistent guidance. The governing statutes were the Berlin Declaration of June 5, 1945, and the Potsdam Protocol, in combination with JCS 1067. Looking back in 1977, members of OMGUS said that in their opinion the government, while bound officially by JCS 1067, in fact worked flexibly within it from late 1945 onward.[1] The basic point of JCS 1067 was that the Germans were defeated enemies and deserved no help. The Potsdam Protocol already began moving away from that position, to say that the Germans should be encouraged eventually to form a democratic government. Instead of seeing the "four d's" as measures of revenge, the military governments started to interpret them – denazification, decartelization, dismantling, and democratization – in ways to help the Germans rebuild and, in the eyes of some, such as Churchill, become political allies against the Soviet Union. This process of reinterpretation began in a small way as soon as the war ended. By September 1946, it was more or less official policy.

The original intent of JCS 1067 contradicted the promises of the Atlantic Charter of 1941 that the US and British governments would "further the enjoyment by all States, great or small, victor or vanquished,

[1] See articles by Ziemke and others in *Americans as Proconsuls,* ed. Wolfe.

of access, on equal terms, to the trade and to the raw materials of the world which are needed for their economic prosperity." While OMGUS and BMG followed fairly enlightened policies in the areas of political organization, the press, radio, and cultural activity, policies governing industry and commerce seemed more severe. During the first months after the war, there was no question of giving German industry access to trade and raw materials.

This situation began to change in 1946. On April 1 the Economic Directorate (*Wirtschaftsdirektorium*) of the Control Council published a list of 415 factories (iron and steel factories, shipyards, airplane and defense concerns, electrical, optical, and chemical companies) which were to be dismantled (130 in the US zone, 262 in the British zone, 23 in the French zone). In the same month a shipyard in Bremen, that had been dismantled, was sent to the Soviet Union on a Soviet freighter. A quid pro quo from the Soviets, agreed upon at Potsdam, never appeared. As a consequence, Clay and the British stopped dismantling industrial plants in their zones, because the Soviets were not providing an accounting of their reparations and thus were in breach of the Potsdam Protocol.[2]

By early 1946, Clay had recognized that the Potsdam agreement on four-power administration of Germany, pending formation of a unified democratic German government with which a peace treaty could be concluded, had already become a fiction. He also recognized that a starving, unemployed, chaotic West Germany was not only a drain on US and British resources and susceptible to Soviet propaganda, but that a restored and functioning West German economy was essential to West European recovery in general.[3]

Meanwhile, in Washington and London, the prevailing atmosphere of sympathy for the Soviet Union and widespread trust in Stalin was giving way to fear, suspicion, and the consequent desire to contain the Soviets. The acts that provoked this change were the imposition of communist-controlled governments in Eastern Europe, especially in Poland, and Soviet behavior in Germany, particularly on the question of reparations. In February 1946, George Kennan sent a long cable from the US Embassy in Moscow warning of the implacable and ruthless nature of the Soviet Union and its foreign policy.[4] This cable played a great part in convincing US policymakers that a new policy was needed which would have to include also a new policy in

[2] Klessmann, *Die doppelte Staatsgründung,* 102–3.

[3] Clay, *Papers,* 1: 7–9; see also Clay, "Proconsul of a People, by Another People, for Both Peoples," in *Americans as Proconsuls,* ed. Wolfe, 103–13. See also Thomas, *Armed Truce.*

[4] Kennan, *Memoirs 1925–1950,* 547–59.

Germany, designed to support and encourage reconstruction and democratization. Military and economic aid to Germany and Europe would help to contain the Soviet Union by strengthening the European countries and depriving the communist parties of the support they always obtained from misery and destitution.

The first major signal of a new economic and political approach was a speech given by Secretary of State James F. Byrnes in Stuttgart, in September 1946. It was cautious and far from anti-Soviet; the Secretary insisted that a common policy in Germany was still the US goal. What was important to the Germans, however, was the following statement, which represented an entirely new American approach to Germany:

Freedom from militarism will give the German people the opportunity, if they will but seize it, to apply their great energies and abilities to the works of peace. It will give them the opportunity to show themselves worthy of the respect and friendship of peaceloving nations, and in time, to take an honorable place among the members of the United Nations. . . .

[I]t never was the intention of the American Government to deny to the German people the right to manage their own internal affairs as soon as they were able to do so in a democratic way with genuine respect for human rights and fundamental freedoms. . . .

[T]he purpose of the occupation did not contemplate a prolonged foreign dictatorship of Germany's peacetime economy or a prolonged foreign dictatorship of Germany's internal political life. The Potsdam Agreement expressly bound the occupying powers to start building a political democracy from the ground up. . . .

It is the view of the American Government that the German people throughout Germany, under proper safeguards, should now be given the primary responsibility for the running of their own affairs.

More than a year has passed since hostilities ceased. The millions of German people should not be forced to live in doubt as to their fate. . . .

The United States favors the early establishment of a provisional German government for Germany. . . .

[T]he provisional government should not be handpicked by other governments. It should be a German national council . . . charged with the preparation of a draft of a federal constitution for Germany. . . .

[W]e do not want Germany to become a satellite of any power or powers or to live under a dictatorship, foreign or domestic. The American people hope to see peaceful democratic Germans become and remain free and independent. . . .

The American people who fought for freedom have no desire to enslave the German people. The freedom Americans believe in and fought for is a freedom which must be shared with all willing to respect the freedom of others. . . .

The American people want to return the government of Germany to the German people. The American people want to help the German people to win their way back to an honorable place among the free and peace-loving nations of the world.[5]

The audience noted Byrnes' references to Soviet occupation policy, which he spelled out in his remarks on reparations: "The German people were not denied . . . the possibility of improving their lot by hard work over the years," he said, but then added that Soviet insistence on reparations from current production, which were "wholly incompatible" with the Potsdam Protocol, were inflicting excessive hardship on Germany. The audience, and with them all Europeans, also noted another part of the speech, in which the Secretary publicly reversed earlier US plans to withdraw the bulk of US troops from Europe. For the first time, the US government promised to retain its occupation forces in Germany indefinitely and – by implication – to offer other forms of support to Western Europe: "Security forces will probably have to remain in Germany for a long period. I want no misunderstanding. We will not shirk our duty. We are not withdrawing. We are staying here."

An intelligent listener was bound to conclude from Byrnes' criticism that the Soviet government was preventing the establishment of a unified German administration, and, more importantly, that the US government was moving toward the idea of supporting establishment of a German government in the Western zones only. And that listener would have been correct, although it was still a long way to the Federal Republic. A reconstructed and democratic Germany was indeed the American purpose, although it was not yet clear to all that the price of this reconstruction would necessarily be a final division of what remained of the country, after the loss of German territory to Poland.

The months following Byrnes' speech marked the transition to a new phase of Allied policy in Germany: the goal had become economic and political reconstruction with the strategic purpose of containing Soviet expansion. The exact means to achieve this goal remained to be discovered, and increasingly the Germans themselves were called upon for help.

[5] Dept of State, *Documents on Germany*, 91–9.

# 11

# The Reorientation of US Policy

The logical consequence of Byrnes' speech was clear: US policy now looked forward to German self-government, if necessary in the Western zones only, and not backward to the burden of war and retribution. Nevertheless, if the new American outlook was to become effective, it required a major change of attitude at the very top of the United States government and congress; a change toward commitment to global security and a final rejection of isolationism. In the 1930s, criticizing the isolationists of the time for their illusions, the American political columnist Walter Lippmann had written: "The great question is whether a nation placed as we are, and desiring above all else to live and let live, can preserve its isolation if there is no power in the world which preserves the order of the world."[1] Lippmann's answer, in 1937, was no, but much of the American public did not agree until the Japanese attack on Pearl Harbor in 1941.

Ten years later, in mid-1946, a growing number of influential Americans had rejected isolationism and concluded that the US now had the responsibility for world order, as Lippmann had urged in 1937. The result of these reflections, at the highest level of government, was the doctrine that President Truman announced on March 12, 1947. Prior to the public announcement, Dean Acheson, at that time under-secretary of state (he became secretary in the second Truman administration 1949–53), expressed the doctrine's underlying assumptions at a confidential meeting with Congressional leaders on February 27. "It was clear," he argued, "that the Soviet Union, employing the instruments of communist infiltration and subversion, was trying to complete the encirclement of Germany. In France, the Russians could pull the plug anytime they chose. In Italy a similar if less immediately dangerous

[1] Lippmann, "Rough-hew Them How We Will," *Foreign Affairs* 15 (July 1937): 594.

situation existed, but it was growing worse. In Hungary and Austria the communists were tightening the noose."[2] That is to say, not only was communist subversion threatening the freedom of Greece, the ostensible reason for the doctrine, but all of Europe and particularly Germany.

Truman made his statement while his new secretary of state, George C. Marshall, was meeting in Moscow with his Soviet, British and French counterparts at the Council of Foreign Ministers (CFM). Marshall's intention was to achieve common ground on establishing a provisional central German government, and to agree on a joint policy for future reparations from Germany. It was the fourth meeting of the Council since Potsdam and the last in which the US participated with the hope for an agreement on the shape of Germany's future. The meeting did not fulfill this hope, and US policy henceforth was symbolized by a word that soon became common currency through usage: "containment."

The word, and the idea behind it, were the work of George Kennan who was at that time director of the Policy Planning Staff in the State Department. A few months after Truman's speech and the failed CFM meeting, Kennan published an article entitled "The Sources of Soviet Conduct" in *Foreign Affairs*.[3] Because of his sensitive government position, Kennan signed the article as "Mr X," though his authorship was an open secret in Washington. He argued, much as he had done in his letter to Charles Bohlen in January 1945, that the Soviet government was inherently expansionist and that there might well be war or communist domination in Europe unless the US took clear action to contain the Soviet Union. In his article, he repeated his view that the Soviet Union was unappeasably hostile to the democratic West, but also that it was essentially a fragile system that might break down if faced with determined opposition. To describe the strategy he recommended, he used the term "containment:"

In these circumstances it is clear that the main element of any United States policy toward the Soviet Union must be that of a long-term, patient but firm and vigilant containment of Russian expansive tendencies. It is important to note, however, that such a policy has nothing to do with outward histrionics: with threats of blustering or superfluous gestures of outward "toughness". . . . Soviet pressure against the free institutions of the Western world is something that can be contained by the adroit and vigilant application of counterforce at a series of constantly shifting geographical and political points.[4]

[2] Cited in Lukacs, "The Soviet State at 65," *Foreign Affairs* 65 (Fall 1986): 36.
[3] Reprinted in *Foreign Affairs* 65 (Spring 1987): 852–68.
[4] Ibid., 861–2.

Kennan's recommendations – both political and economic in consequence – became official US policy when President Truman announced the Truman Doctrine – the doctrine that the US would and could help foreign countries threatened by Soviet or communist subversion or attack.

The weakest part of Kennan's argument was that "Soviet power ... bears within it the seeds of its own decay" and that it might well collapse when Stalin died, because the system had no mechanism for the transfer of power. Containment, therefore, and with it a strong US military presence in Europe, should only last ten or 15 years. This was a best-case scenario, and it included no contingency plan in the event that the Soviet Union did not decay or withdraw from Central Europe in the foreseeable future. But Kennan also used the concept of containment in a wider context: the "application of counterforce" could and should occur in China, in southwest Asia, in the Middle East – anywhere that the US might detect Soviet attempts to expand its influence. This loose and, in the view of Walter Lippmann, overambitious view of American capabilities led Lippmann in 1947, ten years after his earlier critique of isolationism, to point out in a response to Kennan's article that the best case might not occur; indeed, that the Soviet Union might remain strong, and that the will of a democratic people, like the Americans, to maintain a long-term overseas military commitment with no clear criterion for determining final success, could not be expected to be permanent. Moreover, the Europeans could have no such confidence. "The real aim of every European nation" would, therefore, be "to extricate itself from the Russian-American conflict." In Lippmann's view, "the policy of containment, in the hope that the Soviet power will collapse by frustration, cannot be enforced and cannot be administered successfully ... it must fail."[5]

Lippmann argued that the US should not seek to contain the Soviet Union in all corners of the world, but focus on reconstructing Europe. In fact, the US and the Europeans were already moving in this direction. The year 1946–7 marked the high point of enthusiasm for European federation and for the belief that the "United States of Europe" was a realistic possibility.

The European federalists were organized in the United Europe Movement (UEM) which was founded in January 1947 at the instigation of Winston Churchill. The idea of the UEM was a result of the war. It reflected the widespread conviction, held by many leading Europeans, that it was absolutely necessary, if war or tyranny were not to recur, for the democratic states in Europe to form a close and active organization

[5] Lippmann, "The Cold War," *Foreign Affairs* 65 (Spring 1987): 877.

with the clear purpose of achieving economic and political integration, and with the ability to move forcefully toward that purpose. After the UEM was founded both conservative and socialist parties of Western Europe formed their own transnational organizations, and they endorsed the concept of a "United States of Europe". Amid the destruction of Europe, this ambition did not generate the broad support they sought, but the basic impetus for a less ambitious goal of West European integration in the interests of peace and prosperity did not disappear.

Ernest Bevin, the British foreign secretary, took the leading role in the effort to unite the West European democracies. During 1946–7 he initiated talks with the French. The first result, and the forerunner of the Western alliance system that came into being in 1948–9, was the Dunkirk Treaty of March 4, 1947, a 50-year treaty of mutual assistance between France and the United Kingdom. In March 1947, moreover, representatives of the Christian democratic parties of France, Italy, the Benelux countries (Belgium, Netherlands, Luxembourg), Switzerland, and Austria met and undertook to cooperate in the construction of a united Europe. In June representatives of the democratic socialist parties, this time including the British, founded the Socialist Movement for the United States of Europe.

In Europe, therefore, the political basis for international cooperation was already laid when Secretary of State Marshall, in a speech at Harvard University in June 1947, drew specific conclusions for US policy from the failure of the Council of Foreign Ministers to agree on a German policy at their meeting in Moscow. The US government had concluded from that failure that the Soviet Union was unlikely to be a partner in European reconstruction. Accordingly, the US should and would aid Europe, if the Europeans wished assistance. This aid would be in the mutual interest of Europeans and Americans, and would combat social and political conditions that might offer opportunities for Soviet expansion.

In his speech Marshall did not allude directly to the failure of the CFM, nor did he focus criticism on the Soviet Union. Instead, he stressed that America could help Europe to recover, and that such assistance would contribute to preserving peace and democracy. Although the American initiative was clearly spurred by the perceived threat of Soviet expansion further into Europe, Marshall's offer, unlike the Truman Doctrine, was not directed overtly against the Soviet government. In fact, Marshall invited the USSR and its satellites to join in the proposed program, which became known officially as the European Recovery Program (ERP), and informally as the Marshall Plan. At first, indeed, Stalin sent Molotov to Paris to discuss Soviet participation, but then abruptly withdrew from negotiations on July 2. In the following months the communist parties of Eastern Europe intensified their purge of all democratic elements and other political, religious, or cultural resistance to the imposition of dictatorship. It is likely that this intensification of communist activity was due to a fear that the success of the Marshall Plan in the West would exert a strong attraction to the inhabitants of Central Europe, unless what little political power they still had was ruthlessly suppressed.

The West European response to Marshall's proposals was positive and came quickly, inspired by the enthusiasm for European federation. On July 12, Ernest Bevin opened the Committee for European Economic Cooperation (CEEC) in Paris. But since the American government had not decided exactly what kind or how much Marshall aid it could provide, the CEEC was not in a position to make definite recommendations, nor did the CEEC members entirely agree with each other. As one scholar has observed: "In spite of the large number of countries which participated in it . . . the CEEC . . . proved an indecisive event. It had done more to reveal the economic and political differences of opinion between Western Europe and the United States and between the Western European countries themselves than to create the strategic bloc which Marshall Aid was intended to produce."[6]

During 1947–8, the American administration campaigned in Congress, and throughout the US, for funding of the Marshall Plan. The first ERP funds began to flow to Europe in early 1948. In April 1948, 16 European governments established the OEEC (Organization for European Economic Cooperation) in Paris, known since 1960 as the OECD (Organization for Economic Cooperation and Development). Also, on October 30 the General Agreement on Tariffs and Trade (GATT) was inaugurated. The purpose of GATT was to coordinate the removal of tariffs and other trade barriers as part of the construction of the OEEC.

The US government intended that the OEEC should be the European administrative organ of the ERP and, as such, "the first stage in the political and economic integration of Western Europe, the embryonic hope for a Western European government . . . a new form of institutional expression of economic interdependence."[7] The differing views of individual European governments, however, effectively prevented the OEEC from becoming anything more than a bureaucratic organization which simply monitored the economic policies of the national governments. One important reason the OEEC failed in the role foreseen for it by the US was that the Europeans could not agree on a policy toward Germany, and specifically on the future administration of the coal and steel industries of the Ruhr district.

[6] Milward, *Reconstruction of Western Europe*, 89.
[7] Ibid.

The Marshall Plan, far from being merely an example of containment, like the aid to Greece given under the Truman Doctrine, was in reality the basis of a distinct, if parallel, conception; one that looked forward to a strong and independent Western Europe. Such a Europe would be able to defend itself and to promote, directly and indirectly, change in communist-ruled Central Europe, and ultimately the withdrawal of both Soviet and American troops from the continent. Only by making Western Europe economically stronger could the US hope to prevent the West European countries from falling under communist influence.

Marshall aid did not produce a West European "strategic bloc." It did, however, help the West European governments bridge their difficulties between 1948 and 1952, at a time when without that aid they would have suffered from a permanent and disabling shortage of dollars. The Marshall Plan as a broad conception, as well as the actual transfers under the aid program, also made a large if immeasurable psychological difference. West Europeans from 1948 onward could assume that the Americans were not going to abandon them; the US was not going to retreat into isolationism, as many feared in 1945. Marshall aid and the associated American diplomatic moves during 1947, 1948 and 1949 were a remarkable departure from traditional practice, whereby victors had always sought to subjugate the defeated rather than helping them to recover.

Under the European Recovery Program, twelve West European countries received about $12.5 billion in grants and favorable loans between mid-1948 and mid-1951, when the ERP was merged with the US defense budget under the label of foreign security assistance. The aid allowed Western Europe "to maintain a high level of investment and imports . . . and in particular it permitted them to maintain a flow of dollar imports." In West Germany about two-thirds of all imports were already financed by American aid in 1945–8, whereas in 1949 the proportion was 39 per cent. Milward adds: "So low was the level of food supply in West Germany . . . that it is obvious that the main contribution of Marshall Aid in this case was in helping the other aid programmes to provide the necessary imports to keep the population alive and able to work." Although this is true, Marshall aid was of far more than merely economic significance. It was hard evidence that the United States were not going to abandon Europe. That restoring European prosperity was also very much in the interests of American business and industry is self-evident; indeed, the point that a less impoverished Europe would be a better market for America was one that Marshall himself made when he first unveiled his proposal. But the program's lasting and long-term goal was, "through furthering the process of economic recovery . . . to develop a bloc of states which would share similar political, social, economic and cultural values to those which the United States itself publicly valued and claimed to uphold."[8]

In the years since the Truman Doctrine and the Marshall Plan, many Europeans and Americans argued that the former, in particular, was ill-conceived because the underlying notion that the Soviet Union was an imperialist and expansive power was incorrect. They maintained that Stalin was interested merely in securing the territory occupied by his armies in 1944–5, but not in going beyond the limits then reached.[9] Thus, while there was very much a threat to the lives and happiness of the peoples under communist rule in 1948, there was in reality no great threat to the rest of Europe. Even in the early 1990s, when Soviet historians were permitted to write more openly about their history, it appeared unlikely that the West would ever learn the complete truth about Stalin's intentions. In fact, neither he nor his successors ever attacked Western Europe, but no Western analyst could assert that they would have been equally restrained in the absence of containment and a will to resist in Western Europe. Containment, and its associated policies, may have seemed unnecessary to posterity simply because it worked, to the limited degree for which it was designed.

[8] Ibid., 98, 99, 123.
[9] Lukacs, "The Soviet State at 65." *Foreign Affairs* 65 (1986–7): 21–36.

# 12

# 1947: The Year of Decision

While American policymakers were debating the future course of US policy in Europe in general, OMGUS and the BMG had already begun to implement the economic policy that Byrnes announced in Stuttgart in the autumn of 1946. The first step toward economic recovery was to unite the US and British zones in a United Economic Area, known as the Bizone. This decision became effective on January 1, 1947, and marked the first measure taken toward West German independence.

The Bizone administration combined the two dimensions of political activity permitted to Germans after 1945: regional organization in the new or reconstituted *Länder*, and party political activity. Hitherto, German regional administrators had rejected intense party politics in the face of the overwhelming challenge of reconstruction. Though they all belonged to one party or another, the party label was less important to them and to the people under their authority than their competence as administrators and organizers in the devastating aftermath of the war. The parties had meanwhile developed their distinct visions of the future of German democracy. The central organization of the Bizone, however, forced German administrators to deal simultaneously with the common requirements of regional reconstruction and the problems posed by competing political interests. The result of this interaction was the blend of federalism and national political mobilization into a limited number of cross-regional parties that formed the basic political landscape of the early Federal Republic.

Initially, the Bizone was controlled entirely by the Allies. This was one reason its beneficial effects for economic and political reconstruction were slow to appear. Another reason was the terrible winter that lasted until late April 1947, and brought some of the lowest temperatures in Europe for over a century. The weather had disastrous effects and reduced the level of life in many parts of Germany to its lowest point. Rail transportation broke down even more completely than during the war. The transportation crisis was the main reason that the recovery of production in the Western zones, which had been impressive from 1945 through 1946, came to a complete halt. The production index of 100 in 1936 fell for the Bizone area to 32 in March. The winter, moreover, was followed by a long dry summer, prolonging the drought of 1945–6. All of Western Europe, not only Germany, was running out of food and clothing, and of dollars with which to pay for US food and industrial supplies.[1]

One of the answers provided was the CARE program, which had vital importance for Germans living in the darkness of cold and hunger in 1947. The word was the acronym for the Cooperative for American Remittances to Europe. What it meant was that millions of Americans, "from the Quakers to the trade unions ... called in the name of humanity for aid to be rushed to Europe in general and to America's erstwhile enemies in particular." It was a remarkable effort, not only in terms of the help it provided, but especially in view of the tremendous anti-German sentiments that understandably existed in the United States such a short time after the war. The first shipment contained 2.8 million US Army ration packets of cheese, coffee, flour, sugar, cocoa, chocolate and powdered milk. The parcels cost the donor between $10 and $15 each, and their shipment costs were paid by the West German *Länder* governments. The packets later contained clothing, medicine, tools, agricultural and scientific equipment, and continued to arrive in Germany until the mid 1960s; by that time packets amounting to more than 80 million dollars had been sent to West Germany, "in an unprecedented gesture of humanity and readiness to lend a helping hand." In April 1953, Adenauer recognized the psychological significance and the material importance of this help: "CARE saved the lives of millions of Germans and gave them back their true belief in humanity."[2]

In Germany the failure of the CFM meeting in Moscow was a blow to those who hoped for a reunification of the four zones. It prompted the Bavarian minister-president, Hans Ehard, to decide that the time had come for a symbolic effort to demonstrate the will of the German authorities, at least for economic if not political unity, as proposed by Byrnes in Stuttgart. Accordingly, he invited the minister-presidents of the *Länder* of all four zones to meet in Munich on June 6, to discuss economic planning. This was the first meeting of regional heads of German government since the war, and in effect since 1933, when the

---

[1] Eschenburg, *Jahre der Besatzung,* 267.
[2] Ronald Rothenburger, *Nürnberger Nachrichten,* June 10, 1986, as reprinted in the *German Tribune,* no. 1233, July 6, 1986.

Nazi regime suppressed the autonomy of the *Land* governments. Ehard and his Western zone colleagues regarded themselves as standing in the place of a united Reich government. They hoped that, by inviting their Soviet zone counterparts, they would be able to prove to the military governments that the Germans were willing to talk together and plan for the future; and thereby to provide a German initiative for unity that would counteract the sinister implications of the failure of the Moscow conference and what they saw as the deepening division of Europe.

The Western minister-presidents had no authority from the military governments to discuss political matters. Furthermore, the SPD leader, Schumacher, had forbidden the minister-presidents of his own party to discuss political matters with representatives of the SED, which he regarded as the enemy of democracy in Germany. Ehard, of course, knew this, but hoped nevertheless that the Soviet zone participants would agree to discuss economic issues, and thereby reaffirm their commitment to economic unity. Unfortunately, the Soviet zone representatives insisted on discussing political issues. When their counterparts from the British, American and French zones stated that they had no competence to discuss the question of a united German government, the German leaders from the Soviet zone left a few hours after arriving, before the conference had even formally begun. Ehard's attempt thus failed, symbolizing on the domestic German level the end of efforts to unify Germany, that was already evident on the international level at the Moscow CFM meeting in April.[3]

The American and British military governments, in their turn, responded to failure in Moscow by reorganizing the Bizone. On his return from Moscow in April Marshall stopped in Berlin to request that Clay and his British counterpart take measures to make the Bizone a functional administrative and economically self-sufficient unit. The military governments then prepared the regulations which represented the most far-reaching measures yet taken to organize a government in Germany. It was all the more ironic that the Germans themselves knew nothing of these plans until they were ready for signature. This reorganization was extremely important for the future political system in Germany, because, for the first time, it gave German authorities real competence and responsibility above the local level.

The significance of the political character of the reform was concealed by its focus on the economic health of the zones, but the reform represented the first real step toward creation of a West German state. The chief feature of the reform was the establishment of an Economic Council (in effect, a provisional government) of 52 members chosen by

[3] Gradl, *Anfang unter dem Sowjetstern*, 88–108.

the parliaments of the *Länder* of the two zones, sitting in Frankfurt. The division of power in the Council was prophetic for the early history of the Federal Republic. In accordance with their strength in the *Land* governments, the SPD and the CDU/CSU each had 20 seats, the KPD had three, the Center (the Catholic Rhineland party that soon merged with the CDU) two, the liberal group (not yet consolidated into one party) had four, the DP (German Party) had two (who voted with the CDU/CSU), and the Bavarian WAV (*Wirtschaftliche Aufbau-Vereinigung; Economic Reconstruction Party*) had one representative. The WAV was founded in 1945 in Munich by a lawyer, Alfred Loritz, who opposed Bavarian separatism and supported a federal structure of government.[4] At the time of the 1946 elections it had grown into the third strongest party in Bavaria. Party members were farmers, workers and members of the middle class as well as refugees.[5]

In July, when the Economic Council chose its Directorate (in effect, the proto-cabinet), the SPD caucus under Erwin Schoettle made the crucial decision to reject a proposed grand coalition with the CDU/CSU and play the role of opposition. This decision gave control of the Economic Council to the Christian democrats, and presaged the role of national opposition party played by the SPD until 1966.

Two events symbolized the impending rebirth of partial German sovereignty. On June 25, 1947, when the Economic Council met for the first time in Frankfurt, the black-red-gold colors of the German Republic were raised in public for the first time in over 14 years. Since the early nineteenth century these colors had been associated with democratic forces in Germany, and they were also the colors of the first German Republic, the Weimar Republic. The American authorities ordered the flags taken down, primarily to avoid the impression that a German state was being created in the Western zones. The other event was the Transition Law passed by the Economic Council on July 23, the first postwar German legislative act conveying authority beyond an individual *Land* or zonal level. The law provided the legal basis for the work of the Economic Council, including passage of subsequent legislation. While all measures of the Council remained subject to OMGUS and BMG approval, the Transition Law nevertheless represented a milestone on the road to independence.

The first director of the Economic Council was Johannes Semler of the CSU, who was dismissed by Clay in January 1948 after he made a speech to a CSU gathering in Bavaria in which he openly gave vent to all the minor and major resentments of German democrats toward Allied

---

[4] Clay, *Decision in Germany*, 93.
[5] Lampugnani, "Architektur und Stadtplanung," in *Die BRD*, ed. Benz, 1: 147.

occupation strictures. Semler attacked the command economy maintained by the military governments and called for its immediate abolition in favor of a free market system, demanded German influence concerning the foreign trade of the Bizone, and expressed fury at what he, and many others, felt to be the patronizing attitude of the Americans. Semler became particularly incensed by an American offer of corn, which in German is *Mais*. *Mais* had been, in prewar Germany, primarily chicken feed. Thus, when Semler learned that the Germans were expected to pay for the corn, he considered this adding insult to injury, and expressed his displeasure in a way which was equally insulting to the military occupation authorities: "It is about time that German politicians refrain from offering public thanks for these food subsidies."[6]

The Semler affair occurred at a time when movement toward West German sovereignty and European reconstruction was accelerating. This issue was discussed at the fifth meeting of the Council of Foreign Ministers which was held in London in November-December 1947. Just as at their previous conference in Moscow in March and April, the Soviet and Western ministers could not agree on the question of the administration and eventual unity of Germany. They adjourned the conference without a conclusion, an act that marked the effective end of the CFM as an institution of practical value. Thus, by the end of 1947, the work of the Economic Council, the development of the Marshall Plan, and British and French efforts to combine the Western European states in a political and military alliance, were developments that indicated to many Germans that the division of their country into East and West was fast becoming a foregone conclusion.

[6] Eschenburg, *Jahre der Besatzung,* 404.

# 13

# Capitalism and the Free Market

The third phase of the Allied occupation began with the collapse of the Control Council, which occurred in March 1948 when the Soviet representative, Marshal Sokolovsky, walked out over a disagreement on Berlin. This phase was marked by open hostility between the Soviet Union and the West, as opposed to the more latent opposition of interests and policies that characterized the first three years of occupation. The dominating event of the third phase was the blockade of the American, British and French sectors of Berlin by the Soviet Union and the East German government. For the history of West Germany, however, the two other events, namely the end of rationing and the currency reform in June 1948, as well as the work of the parliamentary council during the winter of 1948–9, were equally decisive.

In February the communists seized power in Czechoslovakia, and during the first half of 1948 the USSR signed treaties of "friendship, cooperation, and mutual assistance" (so-called FCMA treaties) with all East Central European states, and with Finland. These developments intensified the Cold War, and made the threat of Soviet advance sharply felt in Western Europe. The Western Allies were left with little choice but to acknowledge that four-power rule of a united Germany was a fiction and to concentrate, without excuses or prevarication, on the construction of a West German state. They implemented this decision by giving German leaders in the Western zones increasingly greater voice and authority in structuring economic policy and developing the political institutions which had already been erected.

Semler's replacement as economic director of the Economic Council of the Bizone was Ludwig Erhard, a Bavarian economist who had spent the final years of Nazi rule under the protection of anti-Nazi industrialists, as chairman of an institute for the study of economic problems in Nuremberg. In that position he had written a lengthy paper on the problems of war debt and of fiscal and monetary policy in a defeated

Germany. Had this paper come to the attention of the Nazi authorities, Erhard's life would have been at serious risk. It did not, however, and in April 1945 he was recognized by the US authorities as an academic with clean credentials, and installed in the provisional Bavarian government of Wilhelm Hoegner in September. He was forced out of office in January 1947, through the combined efforts of the SPD and the conservative-agrarian wing of the CSU, partly because he devoted a great deal of time to speculating on the reconstruction of the German economy as a whole and on the chances of a free market system in particular. In September 1946 he had formulated his economic philosophy in an article published in *Die Neue Zeitung* as follows:

> If in the future it will be the state that ensures that neither social privileges nor artificial monopolies prevent the natural equilibrium of economic forces, but that there is room for the interplay of supply and demand, then the market will regulate the deployment of all economic forces in the best way possible and correct any error. . . . Our people will be truly fortunate if we can realize an economic order that makes room for free economic activity that is cognizant of its social responsibility instead of the prevailing and universally detested bureaucratic formalism.[1]

Erhard was not connected with any political party and had never before participated in political life. His astonishing political success, which, as for many of his generation, came late in life because his abilities were not sought after in the Third Reich, was therefore all the more paradoxical. After his removal from the Bavarian government, he became professor of economics at the University of Munich. In October 1947, however, he was appointed to lead the Special Bureau for Money and Credit under the Bizone Economic Council. He was supported for this post by OMGUS, where his philosophical position was better understood than by many of his compatriots, and by the chairman of the CSU, Josef Müller (known as Ochsensepp or Joe the Ox), whose liberal and free-market views were at variance with the Catholic conservatism of most of the party.

In his wartime treatise on debt and finance, Erhard had boldly written that only a free market system could solve the problems of physical devastation and worthless money that were easily foreseeable in 1943–4. Given the experience of post-World War I, Erhard wrote, it was logical to think of a centrally planned economy as the only way to provide capital and purchasing power, especially since there would be enormous public tasks of reconstruction to undertake:

[1] Benz, *Von der Besatzungsherrschaft zur Bundesrepublik*, 122.

But in this situation even the state will not possess either the capital or the purchasing power; and with respect to the creation of credit its hands are tied following the ... financial restructuring. ... There will be narrow limits to economic power and initiative, and it is essentially the task of the economy itself to find ways and means in order to give the German people a new material basis for life by creating a new national product.[2]

This attitude was especially difficult to encourage because belief in the values of capitalism was almost completely dead in 1945, in Germany, and indeed in Western Europe generally. Initially, the luxury of extolling the merits of capitalism, of a free enterprise economy, was overshadowed by the need to focus on rebuilding the means to produce food and to work. With little to eat and with production of basic commodities and foodstuffs hampered by shortages and transportation problems, the primary concern of the German population was to ensure its own immediate livelihood. Ironically, arguments for free enterprise were not welcomed by those who were preoccupied with how to survive in a devastated country – even though it was the operation of the free market that eventually produced a healthy economy.

From the beginning the three Allies differed in their view of how to control the German economy. The basic difference was between the Europeans – the British and the French – who were fearful of German economic power both as a competitive threat to their own heavy industries and as the backbone of a restored German military machine. Most Europeans in 1945 regarded socialism, or at least some form of extensive state control of the economy, as so obviously necessary as to be beyond argument. Socialists argued that it would lead both to greater social justice and to much greater efficiency, and took up also the point disputed by Erhard, that only under state control could the industrial economies possibly handle the overwhelming national and international problems of the postwar period.

The British historian A. J. P. Taylor, who exemplified the dominant thinking of the British liberal establishment as illustrated by the British weekly *New Statesman*, smugly prophesied that "nobody in Europe believes in the American way of life – that is, in private enterprise; or rather those who believe in it are a defeated party and a party which seems to have no more future than the Jacobites in England after 1688."[3] Taylor regarded capitalism as morally objectionable and responsible for unjust social and economic inequalities. Many liberals and leftists, both communists and ex-communists, considered capitalism as partly responsible for the war.

[2] Cited ibid., 120–1.
[3] Maier, "The Two Post-war Eras." *American Historical Review* 86 (1981): 327.

The Americans on the other hand, who in 1945 represented the overwhelmingly most powerful economy in the world, were not fearful of
German economic competition; in fact, they looked forward to it
because most of them believed that free markets and competition – the
"open door" approach – was the best guarantee both of domestic
stability and of international peace. Their main concern in Germany,
therefore, was to redesign the domestic German industrial structure and
open it to international competition by decartelization – breaking down
the networks of interlocking control which had made the prewar
German economy a very closed one.

The British saw the solution to the problem in nationalization. They
believed that socialism in Germany was the best guarantee that
Germany would never again be a threat, and assumed that the SPD
would become the dominant force if given the opportunity. Nationalization of heavy industry was therefore both a means to give the SPD a
boost in its domestic struggle for power, and also, primarily, a means to
keep heavy industry under political control, which the British regarded
as essential if it were not to be used for nefarious purposes in the future.
The British military government reflected the policies of the Labour
government in Britain, which in 1945 began a grandiose program of
expansion of social services combined with nationalization of heavy
industry and transportation. Its leaders were sympathetic to those
Germans, mostly but by no means exclusively in the SPD, who wanted
to nationalize the big industries which were concentrated in the British
zone, in the Ruhr district. The French, for their part, did not endorse
nationalization, because they saw no reason why a nationalized German
coal and steel industry would not be at least as great a threat as a
privately owned one. They did not agree that if German socialist
politicians, and not private industrialists, controlled economic power
the results would be more beneficial to Germany's neighbors. Consequently they saw the solution in international control of heavy
industry, which meant of the Ruhr. This approach, however, was
basically the same policy that the victorious Allies took in 1919, and
which caused tremendous resentment in Germany. The French idea
was to let the Ruhr industries operate under the close control of international authorities, who would have the power to ensure that no
military goods were produced and that the products were not competitive with French ones.

Many Germans in 1945 – Christian democrats and social democrats alike – agreed that socialism was necessary. The SPD's leader,
Kurt Schumacher, thought that Germany would only become democratic if its economy was socialist: "Either we will succeed in making
Germany socialist in its economy and democratic in its politics or we

will cease to be a German people."[4] Yet the military governments, and the Germans who increasingly took over responsibility for their own affairs between 1946 and 1949 did not, in the end, introduce socialism; in fact, by 1947 the majority of those responsible for policy in Germany were turning against it. Left-wing German historians have subsequently deplored this "lost chance:"

> In West Germany socialization did not take place. This fact rightly counts as one of the most important demarcations in the history of the origins of the Federal Republic, since the social structure of the country was thereby decisively "pre-judged" at an early stage. The relevant authors agree that the Western occupation authorities, led by the US, vetoed concrete measures of socialization and thereby also prevented a comprehensive socio-economic restructuring, "enforced" the imposition of capitalism, and introduced a turn toward restoration [of past structures] with less democracy.
> They blame the SPD for having neglected to "start mass struggles" and to offer "decisive resistance."[5]

The closest the Germans themselves came to establishing a socialist economy in the Western zones was in Hesse, where the SPD, the KPD and the majority of the CDU, in the democratically elected constitutional *Land* assembly, introduced, over liberal opposition, an article into the draft of the Hesse constitution calling for public, i.e. government, control of banks and insurance companies, and public ownership of all heavy industry and transportation. Clay was unable to convince the assembly to remove the article and insisted on a popular referendum which was held on December 1, 1946. 72 per cent of the population supported socialization and 77 per cent supported the draft constitution as a whole. Clay then decided to let the article stand, but to postpone putting it into effect, while arguing that socialization was too important a matter for regional governments and would be best decided by a future German parliament.[6]

The SPD had made its position clear at its party congress in Hannover in May 1946, that

> today's Germany is no longer in the position to carry a private, capitalistic profit-economy, and to pay profits from exploitation, capital dividends and bond income. . . . Just as socialism without democracy is not possible, so is, on the contrary, democracy in a capitalistic state in continuous danger. On the basis of these special historical circumstances and the characteristics of the intellectual development in Germany, German democracy needs socialism.

[4] Cited in Steininger, *Deutsche Geschichte*, 2: 317.
[5] Ibid., 318.
[6] Ibid., 323; Thränhardt, *Geschichte der BRD*, 18.

German democracy must be socialist, or the counter-revolutionary forces will destroy it once again.[7]

The CDU, too, could not escape the ramifications of the catastrophic consequences of the war. Meeting in Neheim-Hüsten, in the British zone, in March 1946, the zonal committee of the CDU, which included Adenauer and Anton Storch (who became minister of labor in 1949), agreed upon a party program which emphasized commitment to the "Christian belief and the high ideal of true democracy as the basis of renewal." Adenauer considered this meeting to be "decisive" for the CDU: "we overcame the forces that supported a strong socialist [policy], and we prevented therewith the dissolution of the party."[8] The program was introduced with an accurate description of Germany:

A fate without example has broken over the German people. After two terrible wars within one generation we stand before a field of rubble of boundless dimensions: The most valuable energy of youth has bled to death on battlefields, countless human beings are maimed and imprisoned, the Reich has been overthrown, our cities and villages are destroyed. Our economy and finances are ruined, millions of Germans are without a country, without homes, clothing and bread. Enormous circles of our people are disappointed, embittered, without any spiritual support and without a guiding light, that could show them the way into the future.[9]

Almost one year later, however, in February 1947, at a meeting in the town of Ahlen in North Rhine-Westphalia, the CDU approved a far-reaching statement that supported socialization of heavy industry and certain financial institutions: "The capitalist economic system had not done justice to the national and social interests of the German people."[10] The Ahlen Program's conclusion was the result of the struggle between what many perceived as the evil of capitalism and their recognition that socialization also had its dangers:

The new structure of the German economy must proceed from the assumption that the time of unlimited power of private capitalism is over. But we must also avoid replacing private capitalism with state capitalism, which would be even more dangerous for the political and economic freedom of the individual. A new economic structure must be sought which avoids the mistakes of the past and which allows the possibility of technical progress and creative initiative of the individual.[11]

---

[7] Flechtheim, ed., *Dokumente zur parteipolitischen Entwicklung*, 3: 18–20.
[8] Berhard Woerdehoff, "Die Adenauersche Mumie." *Die Zeit*, February 6, 1987.
[9] Flechtheim, ed., *Dokumente zur parteipolitischen Entwicklung*, 2: 48.
[10] Ibid., 53.
[11] Ibid., 55.

The Ahlen Program was significant because what appeared to be Adenauer's compromise with leftist elements within his own party, was actually a very clever tactical ploy. Unlike Kaiser, Adenauer believed that "with the word socialism we win five people and 20 run away."[12] The Ahlen Program was binding on the party, but was soon superseded thanks to Adenauer's intense efforts, in collaboration with private industry, to move the CDU leaders away from their infatuation with Christian socialism. As far as Adenauer was concerned, the real significance of the program's more liberal economic elements lay in the function they served within the CDU itself. They set clear limits on how far the CDU would go in matters of economic policy vis-à-vis the SPD.[13]

The reason for the program's adoption – it had been six months in preparation – was to provide the party with an economic program which, as a compromise, would minimize internal party argument, and allow the CDU under Adenauer's direction, to continue to concentrate on developing its political program as a whole. Adenauer recognized that at some point in the future West Germans would have to make a choice at the ballot box between a planned economy and a market economy. In 1947, however, the time for this choice had not yet come, and Adenauer and Erhard were still laying the foundation on which it would be made.

In 1947 many Germans still saw capitalism as largely responsible for the soulless materialism of the modern age and for the alienation of man from his spiritual beliefs and from true religious values. This materialism and this alienation were, according to this view, the main reasons for the success of National Socialism. From different starting-points, then, both the main parties of West Germany in 1947–8 saw a free market system as an impossibility. The longer the rationing system and the command economy lasted, moreover, the more difficult it seemed to end them. To dismantle them now, many felt, could not possibly make matters better, and would very likely make them much worse. Those who had little now would have nothing, and those who had some would have less. The command economy, unfair, inadequate, and regrettable though it might be, was the last bulwark against total chaos. To end it was unthinkable.

[12] Berhard Woerdehoff, "Die Adenauersche Mumie." *Die Zeit,* February 6, 1987.
[13] Ibid.

# 14

# The Currency Reform

It was the merit and good fortune of Erhard not only to have the impressive vision to see beyond the immediate circumstances but also to have been in a position to do something about it. For him, the command economy was actively making things worse the longer it endured. The disappearing value of the old Reichsmark currency encouraged the black market and spawned corruption. In the words of an OMGUS report:

Currency reform in Germany was necessary in order to withdraw excess money from circulation, to eliminate the black market, and to create an incentive to produce.

The unstable currency situation in Germany was the result of Nazi methods of finance during the war, which created in Germany an inflated financial structure. At the same time, potentialities for production were drastically reduced by wartime destruction. This disproportion between the money in circulation and the actual output had undermined the economy to such an extent that, except for the purchase of basic food rations, the Reichsmark [RM] was almost valueless, resulting in large-scale barter transactions and in the payment of a part of the wages in kind.

Between 1935 and 1945 the currency in actual circulation increased from about RM five billion to over 50 billion, and bank deposits grew from about RM 30 billion to over 150 billion. During the same period the Reich debt expanded from RM 15 billion to 400 billion, excluding war damage and other war-connected claims of RM 300 to 400 billion. In contrast, the real wealth of Germany decreased by one-third . . . her capacity to produce had been reduced to about one-half the prewar level.[1]

The abundance of money, the report noted, did not provide an incentive to work, "as people have been reluctant to work merely in order to obtain more money with which nothing could be bought." Instead,

[1] OMGUS, *Monthly Report* no. 37 (June 1948), 6.

TABLE 1.2 OFFICIAL PRICES AND BLACK MARKET PRICES 1946/7

| Item<br>(1 kg = 2.2 lbs) | Official price 1947<br>in Reichsmarks (RM) | Black market price 1946/7<br>in Reichsmarks (RM) |
|---|---|---|
| 1 kg meat | 2.20 | 60–80 |
| 1 kg bread | 0.37 | 20–30 |
| 1 kg potatoes | 0.12 | 4–12 |
| 1 kg sugar | 1.07 | 120–180 |
| 1 kg butter | 4.00 | 350–550 |
| 1 kg milk powder | not available | 140–160 |
| 1 liter cooking oil | 2.50 | 150–180 (1946) |
| | 2.50 | 230–360 (1947–8) |
| 20 cigarettes | 2.80 | 70–100 (US cigs) |
| | 2.80 | 50 (French cigs) |
| 1 bottle of wine | 2.00 | 30–40 |
| 1 piece of soap | 0.35 | 30–50 |

*Note*: The average wage of a blue-collar worker in the period from 1945 to 1948 amounted to approximately 150 to 200 RM per month. If one had access to cigarettes, one was fortunate, because the value of tobacco far exceeded the value of currency. This explains why cigarette butts were collected for their tobacco content.

*Source*: Rothenberger, *Die Hungerjahre*, 140

people devoted tremendous energy to finding and hoarding anything of value in order to trade on the black market. This of course included diverting products from factories to the black market. The report estimated that, before currency reform and the abolition of the command economy, 50 to 60 per cent of the total production in the Western zones passed through the black market.

Starting in late 1947, Erhard, as economic director, worked closely with OMGUS to plan the introduction of a new currency, to be known as the Deutsche Mark (German mark). Between October 1947 and April 1948 the new currency was printed in the United States and brought in great secrecy to Frankfurt as part of an operation codenamed "Bird Dog." When the decision was announced on Friday, June 18, 1948, 500 tons of the new banknotes were ready for circulation in Germany.

The currency reform was the triumph, not only of Erhard's vision, but also of the competing forces seeking to influence the design of West Germany's economic system. Erhard's conclusion, written on December 1, 1947, presaged what would develop:

The preservation of social order will, especially in connection with a currency reform, essentially depend on whether, in spite of high burdens [in a financial sense], the disposable incomes will, in the shortest possible time, find goods to purchase. . . . Only through the rational combination of all production factors, which can only be achieved through the toughest competition, will the German people be offered the possibility to achieve a certain life style and the real chance of a gradual economic and social recuperation.[2]

These effects of the command economy were obvious at the time, but Erhard's solution was nevertheless breathtaking in its radicalism, especially given the European-wide view of socialism as a panacea. As economic director he proposed three currency reform laws to be promulgated on June 18, 1948, whereas the abolition of rationing and of all artificial restrictions on consumption within the Bizone followed three days later. The first law established the new currency, the Deutsche Mark, and invalidated the Reichsmark. Every inhabitant was allowed to exchange a per capita quota of RM 60 for DM 60, at a 1:1 ratio, but these quotas were to be deducted from the person's total credit balances which were converted at a 10:1 ratio. Of this sum the individual would receive DM 40 at once and another DM 20 within 60 days. The second law appointed the Bank Deutscher Länder as the exclusive issuing agency for DM. The third law fixed the rates and conditions for the exchange of all the remaining old money, and prescribed changes in the status of old debts, contracts, insurance policies, and other financial rights and obligations. All credit balances as well as outstanding debts were to be converted at a ratio of DM 1 for RM 10 or, in the case of large accounts, of DM 0.65 for RM 10. If you were fortunate enough to have a savings account in RM, your account of RM 10,000 was now worth DM 650. Other liquid obligations were exchanged in the ratio of 1 DM to 10 RM, and were also simultaneously frozen. All wages, rents and pensions, however, would be paid on a 1:1 ratio.

Thus, on June 21, long lines of Germans stood in cities and towns in the French, British and American zones to exchange their old money. A total of 93.5 per cent of all Reichsmark were removed from circulation and replaced with the new Deutsche Mark with a value of 5.7 billion marks. It is estimated that black market dealers burnt or otherwise destroyed about 2.8 billion Reichsmark illegally acquired. The shipment of the banknotes themselves, and their distribution to the various exchange offices, was called the "greatest logistical accomplishment of the American Army since the landing in Normandy."[3]

[2]  Schickling, *Entscheidung in Frankfurt*, 42.
[3]  Abelshauser, *Wirtschaftsgeschichte der BRD*, 49.

June 18, 1948, the day of the announcement of the currency reform, was a Friday. Ruth Andreas-Friedrich noted in her diary:

Two hours of reprieve. We are glued to the radio. In the streets people are running. Hardly any store is still open. Fifteen minutes, ten minutes ... silence! After the storm – or before the storm. – Who knows! Here it comes! The announcer clears his throat. We can hear him breathe and a paper is rustling. "The first law for the reform of the currency, enacted by the Military Governments of the United States, Great Britain, and France, will be effective starting June 20. Devaluation 10:1. The new currency is called Deutsche Mark. The old money will be removed from circulation on June 21. Coins and notes with a value of maximum one mark as well as stamps will remain temporarily valid at one-tenth of their value." And then: "For the moment the currency reform does not apply to Berlin. Berlin, the four-power-city will, for the time being, keep its old currency. No economic barrier between Berlin and the Western zones." The storm blows eleven knots. Blowing across the zonal borders, the sector borders and through the newspaper printing plants of Berlin.[4]

The currency reform was described in *Auf dem Bauche sollst Du kriechen* ..., by Richard Tüngel, editor-in-chief of *Die Zeit*, and Hans Berndorff:

For a journalist like me it [the currency reform] approached like a steamroller. It made me tremble with fear, and I was convinced that it would crush me. In reality the currency reform ... approached like a wave, carrying singing dolphins. The wave took us in and carried us absolutely gently forward.[5]

The day following "Day X," as it was known, euphoria engulfed most Germans at the sight of goods and food items they could only dream about in the past. Bakeries miraculously produced and displayed delicious cakes; vegetables, butter and eggs appeared in abundance. Goods that had obviously been hoarded secretly and had been available on the black market only, suddenly appeared in display windows: a stove for DM 70, a bicycle for DM 80, stockings, a much desired item, for DM 4. Even a Volkswagen could be had within a week for the price of DM 5,300! But most people who crowded the stores were "orientals," people orienting themselves,[6] since the initial amount of DM 40 could not buy major items. It became quickly apparent that many prices were too high. An iron on display on Monday, June 21, for DM 25 could be bought for DM 14 on Thursday, June 24. Trading began rather

---

[4] Andreas-Friedrich, *Schauplatz Berlin*, 235.
[5] Tüngel and Berndorff, *Auf dem Bauche sollst Du kriechen*, 371.
[6] So described by Glaser, *Kulturgeschichte der BRD*, 1: 329.

hesitantly. Uncertainty was in the air. Nobody knew as yet when regular income would normalize life again.

Erhard, however, knew that a currency reform within the centrally planned economy would have little or no beneficial effect, without additional measures. He therefore recommended an end to virtually all rationing and price controls at the same time as the reform. On June 24 the Economic Council gave Erhard the authority to "take the required measures in the area of rationing," and he thus abolished price controls, without seeking advance approval of the military governments. When Erhard's plan was announced, Generals Clay and Robertson were initially appalled because they had not been consulted, and because there was, without question, risk involved. But Clay, sympathetic to the idea of a free market, concurred and convinced Robertson as well; primarily because Erhard himself was convincing. In the course of their meeting in Frankfurt Clay and Erhard had a short, but clear conversation:

"Herr Erhard, my advisors tell me that what you have done is a terrible mistake. What do you say to that?"

The German reply came swiftly and without hesitation: "Herr General, pay no attention to them! My own advisors tell me the same thing."[7]

This meeting, in the view of many, was the "most fateful" event in the history of postwar Germany. The decision resulted in the actual beginning of the "economic miracle," and the "social market economy" thus became the hallmark of the economic and social development of the Federal Republic.[8] The end of rationing was the end of the command economy:

The task of the government was not constant intervention into the economy but to introduce ... a framework [for individual enterprise] and to see to it subsequently that the market was not put out of action by a dense network of cartels and monopolies. It was only on this basis, he [Erhard] believed, that an economic system which was orientated towards civilian production and civilian consumption could flourish.[9]

The effects of the reforms were immediate. The OMGUS report from July 1948 stated:

No event since the capitulation of the German armies has had such an impact on every sector of German life as did the currency reform. ... Overnight the

[7] Hartrich, *The Fourth and Richest Reich*, 4.
[8] Klessmann, *Die doppelte Staatsgründung*, 188–91.
[9] Berghahn, *Americanisation of West German Industry*, 158.

financial and commercial life of tens of millions of persons was transformed. The foundation, upon which normal ways of life could be reestablished, had been erected. . . .

The new money has brought out of hiding a relatively large and well assorted supply of goods. Wages and salaries have again acquired genuine purchasing power. Job efficiency has risen and there are indications of increased output in almost all fields of manufacturing. . . .

The currency reform has created a psychological as well as a material revolution in German life. Psychologically it has introduced the hope of better times and of improved conditions. Cheer and optimism are taking the place of the skepticism and pessimism which previously prevailed. A certain sense of the importance of the individual has also been recaptured. Today the customer has resumed his importance in the majority of business houses. . . . Politeness to the public has returned in shops, restaurants, hotels, railway stations, and in other places, where the customer's money is once again respected.[10]

The reforms – both the new currency and the abolition of rationing and price controls – gave back to people a sense of responsibility, and they accordingly grew less inclined to look for collectivist, socialist solutions to their problems; solutions that are popular when people feel out of control and threatened by dark, amorphous forces. The report noted that not only did the abolition of controls bring goods out of hoards in vast numbers, but that people suddenly became very conscious of cost and quality, a natural reaction when their money was suddenly worth something again. Ersatz goods could not be sold at any price, whereas before reform they were often the only things displayed in shop windows. Shopkeepers became suddenly willing to stay open late, and to forgo their hitherto sacrosanct midday meal and weekly half-day off. With people no longer afraid that stocks of goods were limited, the formerly ubiquitous queues disappeared.

In the 1960s sharp criticism arose from the political left that asserted an "inequality of the income and property distribution,"[11] since the reform did not touch the holders of real property such as land or houses. Nor could it reasonably do so. In fact, the military government required that the German authorities pass measures by the end of 1948 to impose special levies on the holders of real property or other assets that were not reduced in value by the reform. This act was designed to help not only the people who lost their savings in 1948, but to offer some compensation to the expellees from the Oder–Neisse territories or the Soviet zone for the loss of their farms, businesses, or household property. The proposed law soon showed itself to be a staggeringly

[10] OMGUS, *Monthly Report* No. 37 (July 1948), 1–2.
[11] Abelshauser, *Wirtschaftsgeschichte der BRD*, 50–1.

complex matter. It took until the fall of 1949 just for the three Western Allies to reach a policy agreement, then several years of proposals and debates in parliamentary commissions and the Bundestag, before the Equalization of Burdens Act was passed in August 1952. In the words of a member of parliament:

With the Equalization of Burdens Act the Upper House is given a task that has no parallel in economic history. Because of the scope of the resources to be raised and distributed, the Act is one of the largest economic and financial transactions in history.[12]

The act came too late to help many of the people who lost their savings in 1948, and it is true that what has been termed "social injustice" was advantageous for the owners of real property. They were, in a manner of speaking, better off. But it is also true that it would have been socially unjust to confiscate real property, and thus the later decision to tax its value represented, under the circumstances of economic chaos and financial dislocation, a necessary compromise as a consequence of the war. The currency reform itself was designed to solve the problem of illiquidity and to stimulate production, and, therefore, the economy and reconstruction of Germany as a whole.

The success of the currency reform has been called a "myth" when it is cited as the beginning of the economic recovery. It is probably true that levels of production, and of production capacity, before June 20, 1948, were consistently underestimated, because many of these statistics were not recorded during 1946 and 1947.[13] But it is impossible to prove that the dramatic increase in economic production following the reform was misleading, because prior to the reform there were no constant and stable economic indicators against which to draw accurate comparisons. The introduction of a stable currency was absolutely imperative, for the alternative would have been an inflationary disaster similar to the one that befell the Weimar Republic and helped to pave the way for Nazi Germany. The psychological effect was all-important, and the immediate results indicated why.

The reforms did not, by any means, bring instant solutions to financial problems for everyone. The OMGUS report noted that manufacturing productivity was still only about half what it was in 1936. The reasons were that so many men in their best working years had been lost in the war, that the survivors suffered from inadequate training, that they were less able to do heavy labor because of the food shortages of 1945–7, and because much of the machinery was obsolete and replace-

---

[12] Bundesministerium für Arbeit, *Der Lastenausgleich*, 14.
[13] Abelshauser, *Wirtschaftsgeschichte der BRD*, 51.

ments were hard to obtain. The SPD, in particular, pointed to these problems and argued that the ordinary working-man and his family were the great losers in Erhard's game. Indeed, it was not until early 1951 that the economic upswing was permanently under way and those doubting Erhard's vision became convinced of his foresight.

For the majority, however, both the immediate and the long-term effects were of incalculable importance. For factories and businesses it meant that they could begin to do business with a currency that was dependable, and that meant, in turn, that they could make educated estimates for their future economic, financial, and production planning – something that had been virtually impossible prior to June 20. Productivity, indeed, developed well. Available statistics show that the production level increased during the third quarter of 1948 by about 30 per cent, as compared to the previous year, when increases of only 5 per cent were registered.[14] On the other hand, many small companies were hampered by lack of liquidity, and payment of wages became a nightmare – even though a freeze on wage increases was in effect until November 1948 – and led to the closure of numerous businesses toward the end of the year. In addition the literary and theatrical world suffered from the reform, because people no longer had otherwise worthless money to spend on tickets and publications. In Bavaria alone, 300 theaters, orchestras and related undertakings were closed for lack of audiences who could not afford to spend their new money on the price of the tickets. The press in Munich wrote of a "cultural dismantling."[15] Ludwig Vaubel, a major German industrialist in the textile industry, noted:

Too many are now without means, after the initial money has been used and savings disappeared. There are too many who cannot work any more or do not find work. . . . Apart from this, most people still have not yet understood that the lost war, in the long run, will demand sacrifices and doing without certain things, doing without the pleasure of a carefree life and without some of the smaller or bigger conveniences which, in the past, were a matter of course. . . .

Nobody seems to remember that during the last three years one couldn't buy any eggs. . . . When no eggs at all were available in the stores, hardly anyone took offense. But an uproar develops, when eggs are displayed everywhere, however costing as much as 60 or 70 pfennig per egg, and, therefore, cannot be bought in the desired quantity. . . .

If one wants freedom . . . one has to be able to take the consequences. Moreover, we have to learn to "cut our coats according to our cloth." The consequences of the war have to be paid off. But no one wants to admit it. All of

14  Ibid.
15  Glaser, *Kulturgeschichte der BRD*, 1: 262.

that is just beginning. There will be difficult and restless years ahead of us until the people of Germany will have learned to adjust their wishes to their possibilities.[16]

Unemployment doubled, from 442,000 in June 1948 to 937,000 in January 1949 as employers laid off workers they could no longer afford to pay now that money was scarce and worth something. In turn, this development contributed to a strong SPD campaign against Erhard, but by late 1949 this trend was already reversed. Total industrial employment, in fact, rose from 14.2 million to 14.9 million in 1948.[17]

In a manner of speaking, the after-effects of the currency reform were similar to those experienced by someone starving who is suddenly given something to eat. The natural inclination is to eat too much. In some respects this happened in Germany. It was an understandable reaction – short term in nature – but one which, if it had not occurred, would have been very unusual. People focused on what they had been denied, but it was what they had been denied that, once made available to them, allowed them to move forward.

In the 1948–9 period the flood of journals and books subsided, and many saw in this a symbol of a general turning away by West Germans from the serious philosophical and ideological reorientation and debates of 1945–8, to a completely materialistic outlook. Hellmut Jaesrich, co-editor of *Der Monat* and by no means a socialist or romantic utopian, deplored in 1968 "the speed with which the Germans of the West changed from collectors of cigarette butts to Mercedes drivers and which left little time for reflection."[18] There was certainly some relief involved in being able to pay less attention to painful subjects, and to concentrate exclusively on making a living; but much less than the New Left of the 1960s liked to assert. This shift in interest and orientation was a natural consequence of the passage of time, rather than a deliberate renunciation of treasured values, or a calculated attempt to escape from the past. The *Wirtschaftswunder* – economic miracle – made possible by a sound currency and the end of the command economy, was not a repudiation of guilt or a replacement for bad memories, but a necessary and vital element in West European reconstruction. It was an attempt to move forward, out of devastation.

Erhard owed his triumph, in part, to the support of a small but active group of free marketeers among the liberals, whose candidate he had been for the post of economic director after Semler. They were inspired by the thought and writings of the so-called neoliberal

[16] Vaubel, *Zusammenbruch und Wiederaufbau*, 175.
[17] Eschenburg, *Jahre der Besatzung*, 435.
[18] Glaser, *Kulturgeschichte der BRD*, 1: 196.

economic thinkers, the most important of whom were Alfred Müller-Armack, Wilhelm Röpke, Walter Eucken, Alexander Rüstow, and Franz Böhm. During the war Röpke and Rüstow had both emigrated to Istanbul, but the former soon went to Geneva where he remained until his death in 1966. Rüstow returned to Heidelberg in 1949. Eucken and Müller-Armack remained in Germany, where they and other neoliberal economists developed what became the famous concept of the social market economy and began to communicate their ideas in public. The key idea of neoliberalism was the "conscious formation and development of a fundamentally free, but also socially responsible, social and economic order, secured by a strong state."[19] With this idea they were at odds with the consensus of educated European (but not American) opinion in 1945.

They rejected the concept of a completely free market because of the danger of monopolies and the possibilities it offered for small groups to place a stranglehold on society and thus defeat the purposes of the free market itself. The most valuable and important feature of the free market, the root of all its other qualities, was perfect competition. In the dynamic real world, the lack of a strong state gives monopolies and collective organizations, like unions or trade associations, the chance to distort free competition in their own interests. As Rüstow put it, a strong state was necessary to protect capitalism from the capitalists.

This emphasis on the state, and especially on formal legal guarantees, distinguished the German neoliberals from Anglo-Saxon free market liberals, and may also express a certain conviction found on the Continent that societies unprotected by state power are vulnerable. Also very unlike American free enterprise ideas – normally called conservative in America, although they have little or nothing in common with European conservatism – was the insistence by German neoliberals on a strong positive social morality; the word "order" recurred often in their writings, and in 1948 Eucken founded a yearbook, entitled *Ordo*, to publish and discuss neoliberal ideas. Capitalism for them was not incompatible with a certain hierarchy or "natural form" of society, whereas the defenders of American capitalism have usually rejected any such idea as metaphysical nonsense – dangerous, because it might lead to government interference in the private behavior of American capitalism and, therefore, infringe on personal freedom and individual liberty. For the neoliberals, the social market economy rested on principles and ideas which were political and not economic. Wilhelm Röpke expressed this as follows:

---

[19] Lampert, *Wirtschafts- und Sozialordnung*, 84; "BRD: Wirtschaft," in *Staatslexikon*, 1: 971.

We want no restriction of the market economy, of competition and of the freely floating price mechanism. Nor do we want a mixed economy (i.e. a mixture of market, monopoly, and command sectors). We also well know that if we seek a pure free market economy based on competition, it cannot float freely in a social, political, and moral vacuum, but must be maintained and protected by a strong social, political, and moral framework. Justice, the state, traditions and morals, firm standards and values . . . are part of this framework as are the economic, social, and fiscal policies which, outside the market sphere, balance interests, protect the weak, restrain the immoderate, cut down excesses, limit power, set the rules of the game and guard their observance. . . . The free market is a necessary, but not a sufficient condition for a free, happy, wealthy, just, and ordered society. A free market in an atomized, uniform, proletarian society, with economic power concentrated in the hands of a few, is something quite different from a free market in a society with broad distribution of property, solid existence and genuine communities, which, starting with the family, supports and offsets competition and the price mechanism, with individuals who are stable and whose existence has not been detached from the natural foundations of life. In other words: the final destiny of the market economy with its admirable and wholly irreplaceable mechanism of supply and demand is determined outside the sphere of supply and demand itself.[20]

At the same time Röpke and his colleagues legitimately viewed the free market as the best means by which to allow and encourage the reconstruction of Germany and of Europe. The importance they attached to the values of the free market were reflected in the decision taken by Europe's leading liberal economists in 1947, a group which later included Ludwig Erhard, Günter Schmoelders, and Müller-Armack. Friedrich von Hayek (born in Vienna, and who was to receive the Nobel Prize in economics in 1974 jointly with Gunnar Myrdal of Sweden) invited almost three dozen scholars, mostly economists, but also some historians and philosophers, to meet in early 1947 above Vevey, Switzerland, in the small village of Mont Pèlerin. The assembled scholars formed what became in the following decades one of the most distinguished societies of the twentieth century, dedicated to free enterprise. The original group included two younger American economists, Milton Friedman and George J. Stigler, who were to become winners of the Nobel Prize in economics in 1976 and 1981, respectively.

The meeting focused on discussion of the state and the possible fate of liberalism in thinking and practice. The word "liberal" was used in the traditional European sense, "broadly epitomised by a preference for minimal and dispersed government, rather than in its American sense which indicates the opposite preference for an extension and concentration of governmental powers." The Society's founding principles were

[20] Cited in Lampert, *Wirtschafts- und Sozialordnung*, 92–3.

agreed upon on April 10, 1947. In them the founders reiterated their concern with economic freedom and individual liberty:

The position of the individual and the voluntary group is progressively undermined by extensions of arbitrary power. .... The group holds that these developments have been fostered by the growth of a view of history which denies all absolute moral standards and by the growth of theories which question the desirability of the rule of law . . . that they have been fostered by a decline of belief in private property and the competitive market.[21]

[21] Mont Pelerin Society Records, "Summary of History and Aims," 1974. Hoover Institution Archives.

# 15

# The Berlin Blockade and the Emergence of a West German State

Quite apart from its effects on political and economic life within West Germany, the currency reform was also a crucial event in the Cold War between East and West. If 1947 was the year of decision, in the sense that the most important Western Allied leaders decided that the Soviet Union was unappeasably hostile to peaceful, democratic development in Europe, and that the West therefore must carry out its own reconstruction and reorganization in order to remain both free and at peace, the events of 1948 were the logical consequence of those decisions in the East–West arena itself. It was in this latter year that the Western decisions to move ahead in rebuilding Europe had their inevitable effect in terms of the final breakdown of four-power rule in Germany and in the establishment of the Western economic and security system in which the West still lived more than 40 years later.

Following the announcement of the Marshall Plan in 1947, the US and its Western European partners took the further steps necessary to establish international trade. By the spring of 1948 this process was well under way.

The defense and peacekeeping elements of the developing system were slower in emerging. In January 1948 Britain and France suggested to the Benelux countries that they join the Franco-British mutual assistance treaty (the Dunkirk Treaty) of March 1947. This initiative and talks between the British and the Americans led to the London Six-Power Conference held from February 23 to June 2, 1948, whose participants were representatives from the US, Great Britain, France, Belgium, the Netherlands, and Luxembourg. The London Conference reviewed the developments of the preceding year and a half in economic, political, and military security matters affecting US-European relations, and led to decisions that set the course of European history for decades to come. The conference was the most important event in the history of West European economic and political reconstruction between the German surrender and the establishment of NATO in 1949, and the European Coal and Steel Community (ECSC), (the first step toward the Common Market) in 1951. It was more important than the Dunkirk Treaty, the speeches of Byrnes and Marshall, the formation of the Bizone, or the establishment of the OEEC, because it went beyond these individual initiatives to lay the groundwork for a grand Western strategy to meet the military and political threat from the Soviet Union, to direct the economic recovery of Europe, and to define future policy toward Germany.

In March 1948 the conference issued its first recommendation, that the US, Britain, and France should authorize the West German authorities to form a provisional government. The Soviet Union therefore withdrew from the Allied Control Council in Berlin, justifying its unilateral action by claiming that this recommendation violated the occupation agreement of December 1944 and the Potsdam Protocol which, the Soviets argued, forbade creation of any German government above the zonal level, unless such a government were a united government for all of Germany (west of the Oder–Neisse). The Soviet government was to refer to this alleged violation of the Potsdam Protocol on dozens of occasions during the next 20 years. Whenever it did so, it was in order to sow discord among Western governments and, in particular, to drive a wedge between the West Germans and the main Western powers; the Soviet government, however, had never abided by the Potsdam Protocol and had refused to allow the Germans in its zone to form a freely elected government together with their countrymen in the West.

At the first session of the London Conference, the French insisted that a proposed West German state should have no central authority and should be effectively subject to the control of the other European powers, particularly concerning its industrial policy. The French idea was that West Germany should be a source of cheap raw materials, especially coal, but should not be allowed to recover sufficiently to become an economic competitor or a military threat. As Alan Milward pointed out in his exhaustive study of European economic reconstruction, France insisted on close control of the Ruhr district, where German coal and steel production was concentrated. The more it appeared that a West German government was inevitable, the more the French insisted that the Ruhr must be internationalized.

The British and the Americans, on the other hand, regarded a West German state as an essential building-block of the West European economic and security system that was emerging as a result of the Cold War and the Marshall Plan. They considered that the ERP would have little meaning or effect without a West German state.

The United States also believed that German output of coal and steel should not be artificially restrained to protect France. Rather than being a threat, they saw a productive German manufacturing industry as an essential European asset. German industry was primarily a source of investment goods that the rest of Europe could use in its own reconstruction and growth. German supplies would relieve the industries of other countries of serious burdens and help to provide an overall surplus of goods for export. The Europeans vitally needed exports and hard currency revenues if they were to pay for American supplies and equipment. The Americans also considered that the German steel industry in particular was a vital element in European defense. For similar reasons the Americans favored a halt to the dismantling of German capital equipment which both the British and the French wanted to continue.

The temporary solution of the problem was the Ruhr Authority, the immediate forerunner of the ECSC, established on December 28, 1948. The Authority had the power to control and direct production, distribution, and prices of products of the major coal and iron plants in the area. However, largely through American pressure, the French, led by their foreign minister, Robert Schuman, supported cooperation with the Germans, and not suppression, as the only way to secure viable and durable reconstruction and avoid the squabbles and ultimate disasters of the 1920s. The lessons of the post-World War I period were very much in the minds of the members of the London Conference as they planned the organization of Europe.[1]

While the London Conference was taking place European and American diplomats continued discussions on the security of Western Europe. The Truman Doctrine and the Marshall Plan gave political and economic form to postwar Europe, but there was as yet no framework for the integrated military planning necessary for European security. Thus, on March 17, 1948, the foreign ministers of Belgium, France, Britain, Luxembourg and the Netherlands signed two treaties. The first provided for economic, social, and cultural cooperation between the signatories. The second, the Brussels Pact, established a defensive alliance of the European member states, the Western Union. In April, the Brussels Pact members began negotiating with Secretary of State Marshall, and Senators Vandenberg and Connally, on the security and defense of the North Atlantic region, defined as the area of the US and Canada, Europe west of the Iron Curtain, and the Atlantic north of the Tropic of Cancer. Thereafter events moved rapidly. On May 4, Bevin, the British foreign minister, publicly recommended that the Brussels Pact

[1] Milward, *Reconstruction of Western Europe*, 145–64.

alliance therefore include the US and Canada, and thus become a genuine Atlantic community. On June 11, the US Senate passed the historic Vandenberg Resolution which allowed the US government to enter into an Atlantic alliance and to provide military aid to the West Europeans.

The Soviet government attempted, in various ways, to obstruct the progress toward Western unity, urged by the London Conference. Some observers have argued that the Soviets' last real chance to break up the incipient Western community of interest was at the Moscow foreign ministers' conference in March and April of 1947. At that time, when the British and the French were concerned with what might happen if Germany recovered, with the possibility of US withdrawal from Europe, and with their own dire economic problems, Stalin might have been able to forestall, if not ultimately prevent creation of a Western alliance by supporting creation of a unified Germany via free elections. But he adopted, instead, a policy that established, by coercion, communist regimes in all the countries of Central Europe, including the Soviet zone of occupation in Germany; and thus lost for 20 years an opportunity to create divisive interests among the Western countries.

In his effort to consolidate his gains in Central Europe, and in Germany, Stalin chose to put pressure on Berlin as well. The city's Western sectors formed an island in a sea of Soviet power, and were a perfect target. The symbolic and psychological effect of driving the Western Allies from Berlin would have had incalculable repercussions. It is entirely conceivable that the Germans of the Western zones of occupation would have lost confidence in the US and Western allied will to resist communism, and turned to the Soviet Union for security; perhaps the Western Europeans would have done the same.

The Soviet government, therefore, used the currency reform as an excuse to blockade Berlin. When General Clay told Marshal Sokolovsky, the Soviet military governor, of the impending reform, the latter partially closed the overland transit routes from the Bizone to the old capital city. Ruth Andreas-Friedrich, in her diary on June 19, 1948, quoted her daughter: "If they are smart they will close the border. Otherwise," she observed, "they will have a Reichsmark flood on their hands." Since the old Reichsmark would no longer be valid in the Western zones starting Sunday, June 20, anyone holding them would be tempted to smuggle them into the Soviet zone, where they were still legal tender. Ruth Andreas-Friedrich continued:

Protest of the Soviet military government. Protest of the SED. . . . Marshal Sokolovsky calls on the citizens of Germany: "The separate West currency is illegal. Berlin is a part of the Eastern zone. The notes given out in the Western zones are not valid in the Soviet-occupied area nor in the area of Greater Berlin which is part of the Soviet zone. . . ."

The border is already closed. The Iron Curtain fell between Helmstedt and Marienborn last night at midnight with a tremendous roar. . . .

"Pedestrians are no longer permitted to pass control points from the Western zones into the Soviet-occupied zone." There we have the mess! Snap, said the mouse and was caught in the trap! Poor us, poor Berlin mice![2]

When the Western Allies introduced the Deutsche Mark in the Western sectors of Berlin, after all, on June 23, the Soviet military forces closed off all land communications from the Western sectors of Berlin, both to West Germany and to the surrounding Soviet zone. Travel between the Western and Soviet sectors of the city was still possible in some cases, and indeed thousands of so-called "border crossers," who lived in West Berlin, were still able to go to their jobs in East Berlin. But food, electricity, and all other supplies from the countryside around Berlin were cut off. Thus began the blockade. Certainly the pretext for blockading the city was to prevent introduction of the new currency in the Soviet zone of Germany. The real reasons, however, were to force the Allies out of West Berlin, thereby isolating the Soviet sphere of influence from contact with freedom in the Western sectors, and to control and move forward with the political, economic, and social transformation of part of Hitler's Germany into a communist dictatorship.

Maintaining the Western presence in the city became a symbol of Western will to guarantee democracy in West Germany. West Berlin remained independent thanks to the remarkable Allied effort known as the airlift. The decision to run the blockade by air, taken by General Clay, was a highly risky one. No one knew if enough airplanes could be found and maintained, or, even more importantly, if they could transport the basic materials to Berlin that the city's population needed to survive. Clay was very conscious of this when he telephoned the head of the American air force, General Curtis Lemay, in Frankfurt on June 24, 1948:

*Clay*: "Do you have planes that can transport coal?"

*Lemay*: "Transport what?"

*Clay*: "Coal."

*Lemay*: "I cannot hear you very well. It sounds as if you are asking for planes that can transport coal?"

*Clay*: "Exactly, that's what I mean."

*Lemay*: "The Air Force transports anything."[3]

[2] Andreas-Friedrich, *Schauplatz Berlin*, 235–6.
[3] Overesch, *Das besetzte Deutschland*, 535.

The planes of the US and British air forces formed an "air bridge," as it was called, and brought into Berlin virtually everything that was consumed on a daily basis, including milk, meat, fruits and vegetables, medical supplies as well as fuels, such as coal, and raw materials. In November 1948 the calorie ration for the German population was 1,882 per day. Stocks of newsprint were sufficient to meet requirements for five days in advance. The airplanes themselves were known as "candy bombers" since the pilots often dropped candies out their windows for the children watching the planes come and go. At the end of the blockade the Allies had flown 200,000 CARE packets, 782,000 metric tons of coal, 374,000 metric tons of food, 27,000 tons of fuels, and 8,000 tons of newsprint into Berlin. But it had not been an easy task transporting more than 2,325,000 tons of goods to Berlin in more than 275,000 flights. Forty-eight men, most of them pilots, lost their lives, and in commemoration the square in front of Tempelhof Airport still bears today the name "Airlift Square."

At first, the plan to supply West Berlin from the air was a promise that seemed impossible to carry out, and was regarded as a bluff by the Soviet government. The daily requirement for mere subsistence in West Berlin was 8,000 tons of supplies daily, and for the first few months this figure was not reached. The crisis of the airlift came in the fall, when many Allied and German officials feared that the onset of winter and the consequent need of coal for fuel would force a surrender, especially since the Soviet military government and their German communist agents in East Berlin cut off the electricity supply to the Western sectors. However, by November the daily total of necessary supplies was being reached and exceeded. Later in the winter, some days saw 11–12,000 tons arrive at Tempelhof airfield in the US sector.

The airlift's psychological significance was clear to the Berliners themselves:

Every two minutes a plane arrives from West Germany, loaded with food for West Berlin! The sound of the engines can be heard constantly in the air, and is the most beautiful music to our ears. One could stand for hours on the Tempelhof elevated station platform and watch the silver birds landing and taking off. And at night the brightly illuminated airfield with its countless little colored lights is like something out of a phantasy. It is a wonderful sight, which I shall never forget! . . .

In spite of all these vitally important flights, the Americans remembered, as they had many times before, to make the children happy. On a beautiful, clear, sunny weekday, a large crowd of children had been allowed to leave school earlier than usual, because the airfield had been thrown open to visitors. In droves the children threw themselves upon the planes, each according to his own interest, or got friendly "Amis" to explain other things to them. In the afternoon came the surprise. A transport machine landed and a living camel got out. . . .

Suddenly outside the windows and above the roofs, there is paralyzing silence. It lurks there like a mysterious black animal, which one can sense but not see. It is uncannily threatening, this silence. It weighs on one like the silence of a corpse. All at once a whole city is listening to this stillness, and in the breasts of hundreds of thousands terrible uncertainty begins to arise. The airlift has stopped. What has happened? Are they going to abandon us? Will we have to submit? It seems as if all life is suspended for several minutes. Then – after an eternity – the roar can be heard again, and there are a hundred thousand sighs of relief.[4]

In the words of an American air force officer, the Berliners expressed their feelings and emotion in other ways as well:

Seems to me I've met every German in Berlin. They come down here, clutching extremely valuable heirlooms against their breasts, and want to make a little ceremony of giving the stuff to the pilots. Or some child will show up with flowers or a valued picture book. It's no act, either. An old man so thin you could see through him showed up a few days ago with a watch that would have fed him for months on the black market. He insisted on giving it to an American. He called it "a little token from an old and grateful heart."[5]

But in the last analysis it was the Berliners themselves who forced the Soviets to end the blockade. They worked twenty-four hours a day, including their holidays. They walked long distances to work and were seldom late. The Western sector's newspapers, labor unions and political parties all cooperated with each other. They developed a spirit that their city was special, that their city could survive. And they saved it, under the leadership of their remarkable mayor, Ernst Reuter of the SPD. Reuter's thanks, extended to Clay in a special meeting of the city assembly, was an extraordinary commentary for "a military governor from an elected representative of a conquered people":

In our great demonstration in the summer of the past year, we called on the world for help. The world heard our cry. We are happy to have here in our midst as a guest the man who, together with his two colleagues, took the initiative in organizing the airlift in the summer of last year. The memory of General Clay will never fade in Berlin. We know for what we have to thank this man [prolonged stormy applause], and we take advantage of this hour in which he bids farewell to Berliners to say that we will never forget what he has done for us.[6]

[4] Davison, *Berlin Blockade*, 356, 361, 364.
[5] Ibid, 360.
[6] Ibid., 273.

Today, one of the most famous of Berlin's broad and beautiful boulevards is named "Clayallee" in his honor. And the airlift had achieved the reconciliation of German and American people.

In Berlin itself the city government could once again devote its attention to rebuilding. It had first been elected in October 1946 in the only free elections that included a Soviet-occupied territory (namely the Soviet sector of Berlin), and had been dominated by the SPD. During the blockade it was forced out of the "Red City Hall" in the Soviet sector, so named because it was built of red brick, by organized demonstrators and by the city police directed by members and sympathizers of the SED. Since the government offices were located in the Soviet sector the non-communist majority of the legally elected city government emigrated to the district city hall of the borough of Schöneberg in the American sector in November 1948 under the leadership of Reuter, who became the local symbol of resistance to the blockade. Reuter and his aides, including the young Willy Brandt who had returned from exile in Sweden and Norway in 1947, constituted the core of a strongly pro-Western, especially pro-American, group in the SPD. This group was at odds with the party majority in West Germany that did not fully accept the Western orientation of the Federal Republic until 1960.

Concurrent with preparations for the currency reform in the spring of 1948, the members of the London Conference recommended that the three Western Allies authorize the West German minister-presidents of the *Länder* to prepare establishment of a democratic German government for West Germany. When this recommendation became public, the Soviet government condemned it as one more step toward the division of Germany. But from the viewpoint of the Allies there was little alternative. The Soviet government had systematically undermined and violated quadripartite principles and decisions on German unity, as well as the specific principle of self-determination by ignoring the political and economic preferences of the Germans and installing a German-communist-dominated regime in East Germany. The USSR, therefore, had no legal basis for condemning the Western powers and the London decisions, and exacting a "price" for creation of a West German state. The Soviets in 1948 gave a good example of their diplomatic style: they violated the four-power agreements governing occupation and administration of postwar Germany, thereby forcing the Allies to take decisions, such as the currency reform, that technically seemed to be violations of the same agreements. They therefore exacted a price for these violations by blockading Berlin.

The blockade lasted from June 1948 to May 1949 and provided a sinister background to the process leading to formation of the Federal

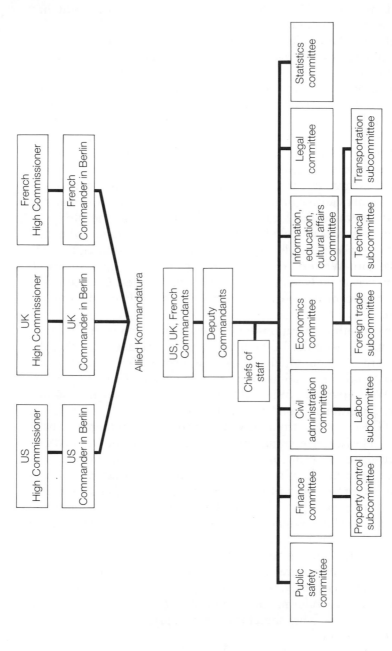

Figure 1.1   Organization for Allied control of Western Berlin. After Soviet representatives left the Allied Kommandatura in 1948, the British, French and US representatives continued to carry out their responsibilities for the administration of the western sectors of Berlin, and do so to the present time. Forty years later, the Soviet Union still has not returned to the Kommandatura.
*Source:* Office of the US High Commissioner, *2nd Quarterly Report,* 1950

Republic. In a meeting on July 1, 1948, at 11: 30 a.m. at OMGUS head-quarters in the former IG Farben building in Frankfurt, the Western military governors, Clay, Koenig, and Robertson, each read one of the three documents, comprising the London Recommendations, to the eleven West German minister-presidents of the *Länder* of the three zones. The Frankfurt Documents, as they were subsequently called, charged the German leaders with calling a constitutional convention for the purpose of establishing a federal republic and reorganizing the *Länder*. In addition, the Allies signaled their intention of promulgating an occupation statute to provide the basis for relations between the prospective West German government and the occupying powers.

The eleven minister-presidents then discussed the Frankfurt Documents and decided that the members of the constitutional convention should be elected indirectly by the *Länder* parliaments. The German leaders also stipulated that the foundation of a West German state must not adversely prejudice the unity of the Reich and could only be a provisional stage on the road to reconstituting a unified German govern-ment. As Carlo Schmid put it at the time, the Federal Republic would not be a new West German state, but the reorganization of part of Germany. It would be, in effect, the sole democratic representative of the German Reich until such time as the other parts of the Reich could participate in a free electoral process to determine their own role in a unified Germany, whose government in turn would sign a peace treaty with the Allies.[7]

For two weeks in August, a committee of senior political, legal, and constitutional experts met on an island in the Herrenchiemsee between Munich and Salzburg, to prepare a draft constitution for the prospective Federal Republic. In order to affirm that the new government of the western part of Germany was a provisional one, pending the formation of a national government of the whole country, the committee avoided the word *Verfassung* (constitution) and chose instead to call the docu-ment they were planning a *Grundgesetz* (Basic Law). The last valid constitution for the whole Reich, which was never formally abrogated or superseded, was the constitution of the German Republic of August 1919, the Weimar constitution.

On September 1, 1948, the constitutional convention called for in the Frankfurt Documents assembled in Bonn. Its 65 members were elected by the *Land* parliaments according to special legislation passed in August by the eleven *Länder* of the Western zones. There was one member for every 750,000 inhabitants, and at least one per *Land*, and five from West Berlin who had observer status. The convention was

[7] Münch, *Dokumente des geteilten Deutschland*, 2: 368.

called the Parliamentary Council and was composed of 27 SPD and 27 CDU/CSU members, five liberals, and two for each of the following: the DP (a regional Lower Saxony grouping), the KPD, and the Center. At its first session on September 1, the convention elected Konrad Adenauer as its president.

The role of the communist members was solely disruptive. At the first session they moved that the Council cease its work because it prejudiced German unity. Apart from the KPD members, the Council proceeded with remarkable consistency of purpose, considering the very different ideas held in the SPD and in the CDU concerning the character and functions of the new Federal Republic. By mid-September work had been divided among six committees meeting in closed sessions and one Principal Committee of 21 members chaired by Carlo Schmid (SPD) which, in 59 public sessions, discussed the various clauses of the proposed Basic Law. The six special committees dealt, respectively, with basic rights, competences, finance, federal organization, constitutional jurisdiction, and legal procedure. An eighth committee prepared the final wording of the Basic Law and ensured the best fit possible with existing prewar legislation (insofar as it had not been annulled by the Allied Military Governments or by acts of the *Länder* since surrender), and with the proposed Occupation Statute that, from the date of birth of the Federal Republic, would govern relations between the new federal government and the Allied authorities.

The main points of contention between the left and the center-right in the Council emerged during the first reading of the final draft in the Principal Committee in November-December of 1948. These points concerned the following questions: the powers of the head of state and of the second chamber of the federal parliament, the distribution of taxes and taxing powers between the federal and *Land* governments, fiscal organization, education policy, family law, and church-state relations. The SPD argued for federal control of education and family issues and for a specific commitment to a socialist economy in the text of the Basic Law, but failed to gain enough support.

The decision reached was a compromise and the Law included a clause in its opening section on basic rights permitting the establishment of private schools, provided the quality of instruction was not inferior to that in public schools. The founding fathers gave the *Länder* responsibility for educational policy, and preserved the traditional right of religious denominations to have religious instruction given in the public schools. The churches remained "corporations in public law," with the right to levy taxes on their members on the basis of the state tax rolls. The Law permitted socialization of the means of production by acts of parliament, but included no general commitment to socialism. It placed marriage and the family under the protection of the state and guaranteed the equality of the sexes but did not touch the older family law, which was gradually superseded by later legislation. Unlike most democratic constitutions, but understandably in view of the abuse of law in the Third Reich, the Basic Law also included a detailed section on legal procedure, forbidding special or emergency courts, establishing a Constitutional Court with the competence to hear cases concerning the constitutionality of public acts, and abolishing the death penalty.

The structure of the parliament was the focus of a debate centering on how much power should be given its representatives by direct election versus appointment by the individual states. All parties endorsed a first chamber elected by popular vote, but the CDU also supported a second chamber of deputies elected in the same manner, as for example, the House of Representatives and the Senate in the United States are elected. The SPD and the Bavarian CSU, however, wanted a second chamber appointed by the *Länder* governments, which would give greater voice to the *Länder* in the federal parliament. The debate was resolved, somewhat surprisingly, against the wishes of Adenauer and the majority of the CDU by an agreement between the SPD and the Bavarian CSU.

There were to be two chambers, a general assembly (*Bundestag* or Federal Diet) elected by direct, secret and proportional balloting, and an upper chamber (*Bundesrat* or Federal Council) of 45 members, including four from Berlin, chosen by the *Land* governments. The number of seats in the *Bundestag* would be determined at each election depending on the number of votes cast according to a complicated formula, designed to guarantee full proportional representation to all parties obtaining either 5 per cent of the vote throughout the Federal Republic or winning at least three seats in any one region.

The *Bundesrat* was to be "the body through which the states of the Federal Republic [would] share in the nation's legislative process." It could delay or change legislation from the Bundestag, but could not initiate legislation. "Its membership is not elected by direct national vote, but delegated by the state governments, whose representation in it is in proportion to their population. The Bundesrat's consent is required for constitutional amendments and for federal legislation ... The president of the Bundesrat, [elected each year by that body], acts as the federal president's deputy."

"The *Federal President* [would be] elected by a majority of the Federal Convention (*Bundesversammlung*), an assembly of all Bundestag members and an equal number of delegates elected by the state legislatures according to the principle of proportional representation. The Federal Convention is convened especially for the occasion by the Bundestag

President, who also presides over the session. If no candidate receives a majority on either of the first two ballots, the plurality candidate is chosen on a third ballot ... The president is elected for five years and can be re-elected only once." As head of state the federal president exercised largely ceremonial functions, and "the political system of the Federal Republic assigns the President a non-partisan role."[8]

The Parliamentary Council worked under the continuing shadow of the Berlin blockade, and to the accompaniment of Western diplomatic movement toward conclusion of the defensive alliance foreshadowed by the Brussels Pact and, indirectly, by Marshall's speech of June 1947. In September 1948, the ministers of defense of the Brussels Pact states – Belgium, Britain, France, Luxembourg, and the Netherlands – agreed to establish a common organization for all military forces of their respective countries, a genuine European defense community. In October representatives of these same five governments discussed defense issues with the representatives of the US and Canada, and reached agreement on the need for a North Atlantic defense union. In December, their representatives began drafting the North Atlantic Treaty in Washington, and shortly thereafter other European states expressed a desire to join. The most important of these new applicants was Italy. In the Scandinavian area Denmark, Norway, and Sweden discussed a purely Scandinavian pact, but these negotiations broke down when the US stated that it could not undertake to sell arms to such an alliance. At that point Denmark and Norway asked to join the North Atlantic Treaty, while Sweden remained neutral. The pact members also invited Iceland and Portugal to become members. That made twelve nations whose representatives signed the North Atlantic Treaty in Washington on April 4, 1949, and thereby established the North Atlantic Treaty Organization (NATO).

At its birth NATO had no structure. It was simply a mutual commitment, made by all member states, to come to each other's assistance in case of armed attack. But the Treaty did include provisions designed to coordinate economic policy and produce cultural collaboration, and it mandated regular consultations. The main significance of NATO at this moment, however, was that it was a declaration to the Soviet Union and to anyone else, that the West proposed to defend itself and to do so in solidarity; and it laid the basis for rapid improvements in West European security. It was not, however, until the Korean War in June 1950 created the fear of imminent Soviet attack in Europe, that defense planning really got under way, and that the other Europeans began considering what role the new German state could play in that defense.

[8] Federal Republic of Germany, *Elections, Parliament and Political Parties*, 9–10.

The Parliamentary Council presented the final draft of the Basic Law to the military governments for their review in March 1949. It reflected the social, cultural, and economic policies and ideas of the Christian democrats, and to some extent of the liberals, whose leader, Theodor Heuss, a constitutional lawyer and member of the Reichstag for the liberal DDP in the 1920s, enjoyed the status and influence of a valued elder statesman second only to Adenauer. Although the draft did not reflect the principles of the SPD political, economic and social program, the party nevertheless voted for the Law to ensure unanimity (the communist party voted against the Law). The SPD faced the dilemma of a party in opposition. Its leaders, especially Schumacher, wanted it to play as positive a role as possible in the construction of the new state. Many of them, notably Carlo Schmid, made essential and positive contributions to the debate that resulted in the Basic Law.

Some social democrats asserted that the Basic Law was promulgated against their wishes. They did not regard it as "their" constitution, and they argued that it was primarily a reflection of conservative views which had the effect of stopping the work of social and economic change that had been begun in 1945. They wished to see that change continue according to their political, economic, and social values. These critics referred to the Federal Republic as "the CDU state," and thus contributed to a division in its culture and body politic that led in turn to unnecessary polarization and eventually, to what many considered the unwise haste and excessive reformism of the first SPD government of 1969–72.

During the work of the Parliamentary Council the SPD often accused its president, Adenauer, who was obliged to respect the Frankfurt Documents if the law were to be approved by the Allies, of acting as an Allied agent seeking to contravene German interests. It was a charge that anticipated a later accusation by Kurt Schumacher that Adenauer was "the chancellor of the Allies." In a sense the charge was true, since Adenauer clearly believed that the world, and especially Europe, was divided between a Western democratic and an Eastern totalitarian sphere, and that the only chance for democracy in Germany was inclusion of the Western zones in the Western sphere. Schumacher, however, also wanted Germany to be democratic and Western, but he wanted the West itself to be socialist. Therefore he opposed Adenauer's policy of *Westintegration*. As he wrote, "The struggle over our future foreign policy is also a struggle over domestic policy and over the social content of our political order. . . . Foreign policy sets the limits of our economic and social policy."[9] The SPD was afraid, from its viewpoint

9 Cited in Hanrieder, *West German Foreign Policy*, 5.

justifiably, that the Western European system emerging under the tutelage of Adenauer, the French foreign minister, Robert Schuman, the Italian premier, Alcide de Gasperi, and with the active encouragement and participation of Winston Churchill, would not be a socialist Europe, but a free-market Europe of private ownership and conservative social and cultural standards.

Yet the SPD was unable, within the Council itself, to convince a majority of the Council members that its ideas for domestic social and economic change should be included in the wording of the Basic Law. The result was a tendency in the SPD, and among its sympathizers in West Germany, to accuse their opponents of blocking progressive reform when in fact there was not, neither in the democratically representative Parliamentary Council nor in the West German electorate at large, a majority in favor of SPD ideas. The irony of this belief was that, while the SPD respected democratic principles, it claimed that the result was inconsistent with democratic practice.

The conflicts in the Council, and the broader question of Allied acceptance of the draft, were resolved in early April 1949. When the foreign ministers of the United States (Dean Acheson), Britain (Ernest Bevin), and France (Robert Schuman) met in Washington to establish NATO, they also discussed future policy in Germany. Clay, the US military governor, favored granting the *Land* governments as much authority as possible, because he feared that a later SPD administration might use a strong central government to institute socialism. However, he was now isolated. Both the British and the French were more sympathetic to the arguments for a strong central government, and in Washington authority over German affairs had been moved from the Department of the Army to the Department of State where social democratic ideas were more popular. Clay was therefore instructed, along with his British and French colleagues, to accept the draft of the Basic Law. This cleared the way for final passage by the Parliamentary Council on May 8, 1949, four years to the day since the surrender of Germany. On May 12, 1949, the military governors Robertson, Koenig and Clay wrote as follows to Adenauer:

The Basic Law passed on 8 May by the Parliamentary Council has received our careful and interested attention. In our opinion it happily combines German democratic tradition with the concepts of representative government and a rule of law which the world has come to recognize as requisite to the life of a free people. . . .

On the completion of the final task . . . the Parliamentary Council will be dissolved. We wish to take this occasion to compliment the members of the Parliamentary Council on their successful completion of a difficult task performed under trying circumstances ... and on their devotion to the democratic ideals toward the achievement of which we are all striving.[10]

The military governors officially approved the Basic Law on the same day, May 12, that the Soviets lifted the blockade of West Berlin. The end of the first Berlin crisis and the official publication of the Basic Law on page 1 of the new *Federal Gazette* on May 23, 1949, marked the end of the first stage of West German history. The basic decisions had been made. A West German state had been established with limited sovereignty, but with the prospect of becoming a full partner in the emerging West European community of democratic nations. Berlin remained a divided city and an enclave in Soviet-held territory, and its Western sectors would be governed democratically as a part of the Federal Republic; although this would never be officially recognized by either the Western Allies or the Soviet Union. The society and economy of the new West German republic would be democratic and capitalist, with a distinct orientation toward social welfare, but nothing like the socialist society that the SPD had sought.

The Basic Law included a detailed catalogue of civil rights, *Grundrechte* (basic rights). For the first time in German history, a constitution not only listed the rights of the citizen, but obliged the government to protect those rights and prevent their subversion. The list of protected basic rights constituted the first chapter of the Law, immediately after the preamble. The list included full personal liberty under the law, equality, freedom of thought and religion, freedom of expression, protection of the family and of marriage, freedom of educational choice, freedom of assembly and association, the privacy of the mails and other forms of communication, freedom of movement, freedom of vocation (career), the security of one's home, and private property.

The catalogue of rights was not in itself new. The Weimar constitution included a very similar catalogue, but it appeared, not at the beginning, but at the end of the constitution. Moreover, constitutional lawyers before 1933 did not consider basic rights enforceable or binding. Their expression in the Weimar constitution reflected the moral beliefs and aspirations of the authors rather than claims that the citizen could make against the state. They were not part of the law that it was the government's duty to enforce.[11]

In recognizing basic rights in the constitution and in making them the foundation of government rather than a list of nonbinding accessories to it, the authors of the Basic Law drew on the traditions of the

[10] OMGUS, *Monthly Report* no. 46 (April 1949), 140–1.
[11] Weber-Fas, *Das Grundgesetz*, 167–212.

nineteenth-century German democratic reformers. Although few people outside Germany would have admitted it in the aftermath of Nazism and war, the draft constitution of the German Reich prepared by the parliamentary assembly in Frankfurt in 1849 (which never came into force) was the most progressive of its time in Europe. Like the Basic Law, it had a list of rights which included equality before the law, freedom of the person, freedom of expression and belief, freedom of petition and assembly, security of property, and privacy. It was therefore not surprising that the German kings and princes of that era had little interest in joining a federation under a constitution that would severely restrict their authority.

The Basic Law reflected not a reactionary effort to return to an authoritarian past, but the deep-seated wish of the majority for stability and peace. The catalogue of civil rights and the protection of federalism and the power of the *Länder* laid a strong foundation for democratic development. The Law did not and could not solve the vexing questions of economic policy or make the choice between socialism and liberalism. It provided a framework, but not a solution. Therefore all parties found it possible to approve the Law in the hope that they would each have their opportunity to give the framework substance according to their own programs.

The expectation of future unification with the Germans of the Soviet zone, and for a final peace treaty that would deal with the traumatic question of the Eastern borders and the expulsions, was still strong. That this hope was not fulfilled during the 1950s, and most dramatically dashed at the time of the Berlin Wall in 1961, goes far to explain the basic tensions between the representatives of differing views on the proper conduct and priorities of foreign and defense policy for the new state. As feelings of impotence and frustration increased with the passage of time, so also opinions changed concerning the importance of German unity. In the late 1960s the inability to help the East Germans determine their own future, by means of the free electoral process, contributed to continually growing frustration, and, eventually, to the victory in 1970, of the view that one must accept the status quo imposed by the Soviet Union in Central Europe, unjust though it might be.

For domestic order, security, prosperity, and opportunity the Basic Law provided a good framework. The vast majority of German and foreign observers rightly claimed that "the German Basic law is a legal high point in the history of the constitutional state. It is the rock on which the state [governmental and political] edifice of the Federal Republic rests ... It is an outstanding constitution of freedom which deserves confidence and the courage of its defenders." Thanks in large part to that law, and the attitudes that inspired it, the Federal Republic might well be called "the most benevolent state that has existed on this territory since the time of Arminius the Cheruscan."[12] Arminius was the tribal leader who defeated the Romans in AD 9. The best German state in almost two thousand years? That was perhaps a presumptuous claim, but there was some truth in it, as events following 1949 suggested.

[12] Ibid., preface.

# PART III

# The Establishment of the Federal Republic, 1949–1955

*[Our policy] demands only that the German people and their government put their great energies and capacities into the making of a liberal, tolerant community, in which all men can walk with dignity and freedom.*

John J. McCloy, US High Commissioner for Germany, April 25, 1951

# 1
# The Basic Law, Sovereignty, and First Federal Elections

American cultural objectives are . . . to encourage and promote those positive forces in Germany which should furnish a democratic bulwark against the resurgence of dangerous movements. . . . The chief obstacle to the accomplishment of such aims is the German authoritarian tradition. Among the elements involved are the disinclination and inability of the German man in the street to seek an active voice in community affairs, his generally patterned acceptance of ready-made concepts, and the psychological consequences of living in a society in which there is so little upward mobility.[1]

The Basic Law was only an initial step to democratic government. The new state needed a capital and parliamentary elections, and special procedures governing relations with the occupation powers.

The Basic Law was approved by ten of the eleven *Länder* of the Western zones in the middle of May 1949. The Bavarian legislature voted against it, led by the CSU, which objected to what it considered an undue emphasis on central government at the expense of states' rights (but also voted to recognize the law as legally binding if approved by two-thirds of the other legislatures). But the Federal Republic did not formally exist as a new state until the middle of September, when the Allied Occupation Statute entered into force regulating relations between the new government and the American, British, and French occupation authorities. In the intervening period the highest German authority was the Conference of Minister-Presidents of the eleven West German *Länder* (as they existed in 1949), plus the governing mayor of Berlin, Ernst Reuter. The conference had been meeting in Bonn since the Parliamentary Council began drafting the Basic Law in September 1948.

After approving the Basic Law in May, the military governors (Clay,

[1] Office of US High Commissioner, *1st Quarterly Report* (September–December 1949), 15.

Robertson, and Koenig) surrendered their functions to their respective governments, and their offices, in the course of the summer, were moved to Bonn, the provisional seat of the German government. The occupation of West Germany was not ended, but occupation authority was now vested in the Allied High Commissioners for Germany. The responsibility for selecting the location of the Commission's offices rested with General Robertson, since Bonn was located in his zone. He chose the Hotel Petersberg, a magnificent resort hotel built in 1886, which sat on a hilltop across the Rhine River from Bad Godesberg, a town next to Bonn. Reception rooms and the ballroom of the Hotel Petersberg were converted into conference rooms and its suites and bedrooms became the offices of the commissioners and their staffs.

The new American High Commissioner was John J. McCloy (1895–1989), a man with broad experience in government, business, politics, and management. During the war he had been assistant secretary of war for civil affairs and military government in liberated and occupied territories. In 1944 President Roosevelt asked McCloy to lead a civilian High Commission in Germany immediately following surrender. According to McCloy, Roosevelt was very much concerned how to introduce democracy in Germany, and he did not support the brutal Morgenthau Plan except temporarily in late 1944. McCloy told the president that he did not think a civilian administration was appropriate for the first period after the end of hostilities and recommended Clay as military governor. Thus, it was Clay's ultimate successor who originally recommended him for his position.[2] In 1948, President Truman, who did not know of Roosevelt's earlier request, asked McCloy, then at the World Bank, to lead the High Commission under State Department authority. McCloy agreed and arrived at US headquarters in the former IG Farben building in Frankfurt in early June 1949, to take over from General Clay in July. *Die Zeit* commented at the time, "since the beginning of the month [June] one might see at OMGUS ... one of those inconspicuously dressed civil servants, who ... on special mission, travels within the American-controlled territory. It is one of the secrets of the success of the 54-year-old High Commissioner: he does not believe in the new broom that must necessarily sweep well. He guides the start of the engine from afar, in order to take over the controls himself when the time is right."[3]

Sir Brian Robertson, the British military governor, continued as civilian High Commissioner under the Foreign Office. General Koenig

[2] McCloy, "From Military to Self-Government," in *Americans as Proconsuls*, ed. Wolfe, 116–18.
[3] *Die Zeit*, June 30, 1949.

retired from Germany with fanfares and parades in July. The French government replaced him with André François-Poncet, who arrived in August 1949. This was a remarkably fortunate choice. François-Poncet had been French ambassador in Berlin from 1931 to 1938 and was to become ambassador to the government in Bonn from 1953 to 1955. After the strict French occupation regime it was fortunate that the chief French authority in Germany was a man who understood the country and genuinely believed that a new and different era of Franco-German relations was beginning. He did much to reduce the great distrust of the new Germany in France, and along with Adenauer, McCloy, and two other Frenchmen, Jean Monnet and Robert Schuman, was one of the architects of the West European revival.

The Bundestag voted to select Bonn as West Germany's new capital city in November 1949, but this choice had been preceded by a major public debate, and resentment concerning the sleepy little town on the West side of the Rhine remained for many years. In the eyes of many "all objective arguments" spoke against Bonn, and for Frankfurt, and many concluded that the arguments favoring Frankfurt should be "decisive in a democracy."[4] Bonn was criticized and condemned for a variety of reasons, including the assertion that it was boring and provincial, and for a certain period of time in German history had been the seat of separatist efforts. Indeed, it could never compare favorably with cities such as Paris, London, Rome, or Vienna. Its size meant that it had no buildings suitable for the government, and it had only one main street. But, undoubtedly, at least some of these considerations influenced Adenauer's support for it. He pointed out that it was located in the largest and most populous *Land*, North Rhine-Westphalia. Located on the left bank, that is on the western side of the Rhine, it had long-standing ties to France and the West. Adenauer also favored Bonn because, indeed, Bonn looked very "temporary." Psychologically, this was an important consideration, since many people in the Western zones still hoped that Berlin would, in the near future, become the capital again. By selecting a major city like Frankfurt, the new government would present the appearance of permanence and, therefore, contribute, albeit only in a symbolic way, to the division of Germany.

But those who favored Frankfurt argued that it was the city in which German kings had been crowned for 1,000 years, in which Goethe was born, and that it was the city of the first democratic German parliament of 1848–9. In addition, it was the business capital of Germany, an influential economic and cultural center, the seat of the Economic Council of the Bizone, and of the most important

---

[4] Lahr, *Zeuge von Fall und Aufstieg,* 142.

stock market in Germany; indeed, "in every way the opposite of Bonn."[5]

The proponents of Frankfurt pointed out that it possessed "an entirely different symbolic power" for the unity of Germany, than did Bonn. The SPD preferred Frankfurt because it had a history of democratic political traditions, and it was also a city governed by their party in 1949, in comparison to Bonn, which had a city government headed by the CDU. Indeed, in 1949 a joke ran: "What's new in Bonn?", the answer being, "Nothing, it is raining, the [railroad crossing] gates are down, we are tired, and the church bells are chiming."[6]

Many of Bonn's critics were right that it was quiet, and charmingly nestled next to the Rhine. For Adenauer it was convenient, since his own home was in Rhöndorf, a village nearby, on the opposite bank of the Rhine. Bonn had few public buildings suitable for the new German government; the German Bundestag took up residence in the building of the local teacher training college. But there was also something stable about it. Bonn was known mainly as the town of a distinguished university, and one of its most famous sons was Ludwig van Beethoven, who was born there. For long it remained, in a manner of speaking, a "provisorium." In time it became a widely respected seat of government throughout Europe, and, because of its special nature, an invitation to those concerned with Germany's future as a unified country, to continue to focus on the tragic consequences of division.

The question of how the new state would present itself was of major importance. One concern was that the new government should not adopt a mantle of symbolic pomp and circumstance, because it would make it appear permanent in a divided country. This conviction manifested itself in many different ways.

The national anthem of the German state of 1871 was "Deutschland über alles" (Germany above everything), written in 1841 by a nationalist democratic poet, Hoffmann von Fallersleben, who looked to German unity as fulfilling progressive democratic ideals. The inspiration of the poem was not nationalistic in the sense of despising other peoples. "Deutschland über alles," as originally conceived, was simply a reflection of a patriotic commitment to one's country, much as "Britannia rules the waves;" but its use during the Hitler Reich had deprived it of legitimate patriotic credibility.

In 1949, most Germans as well as the Western Allies considered the wording of Fallersleben's poem to be unfortunate and provocative. The first federal president, Theodor Heuss, was opposed to the *Deutsch-*

---

[5] Ibid., 143.
[6] Ibid.

*landlied*, as it was called, and wanted to find a completely new poem with a different musical setting to provide yet another symbolic indication that the new Germany was different from the old. Both Kurt Schumacher and Allied spokesmen criticized Adenauer, when in Berlin in 1950 he led a crowd in singing the third verse of the *Deutschlandlied*. In fact the third verse was the most innocuous, since it spoke of "unity and justice and freedom" as the principles embraced by Germans. The final compromise, reached in 1952, therefore was that the *Deutschlandlied* would indeed remain the national anthem, but that only the third verse would ever actually be sung. Haydn's famous music, which was 60 years older than Fallersleben's poem, would continue to symbolize Germany on official occasions throughout the world.

Another issue of symbolic importance was what kind of flag would be appropriate. The colors of the German national democrats in the nineteenth century were black, red and gold in a tricolor of horizontal bars, but they were not used for the national flag of the unified German state of 1871. This state, the second German Reich, was not the state of nationalist democrats, but of the Prussians and conservative interests whose colors were black, white and red. The Weimar Republic of 1919 regarded itself as the heir to those national democrats of pre-1871 and thus its flag became a tricolor of black, red and gold. In 1949, following an intensive and emotional public debate, during which only 25 per cent of the population opted for this flag and an equal number preferred the black, white and red colors of the past, and 35 per cent had no opinion,[7] the new Federal Republic adopted the black, red and gold tricolor.

Following approval of the Basic Law and selection of Bonn as provisional capital of the new republic by the Parliamentary Council in May 1949, the Council began work on drafting a federal election law, so that the people of Western Germany could vote in free, national elections for the first time since 1932. The party structure that had emerged by 1949 – three major national parties and some smaller, primarily regional parties – suggested that the fragmentation and resulting parliamentary stalemates of the Weimar period were unlikely to recur. After lengthy debate and revision, the minister-presidents were able, on June 15, 1949, to approve the law prescribing election to the first Bundestag.

The law on federal elections was revised on several occasions, most extensively in 1953 and 1956. The main purpose of the revisions was to secure more accurate proportional representation. The first election law already included the most characteristic feature of the German voting system, namely the double vote. Half the deputies to the Bundestag (the lower house of the West German parliament) were (and still are) elected

---

[7]  *Die Zeit*, August 11, 1949.

by direct vote in their constituencies; the other half were chosen, according to each party's national vote, from so-called "party *Land* lists" of candidates. A voter might, for example, give his first vote to the candidates of one party and his second to another party's *Land* list. This practice of splitting votes saved the FDP on several occasions. A leading analyst of the German system of government described the double vote, as arranged by the 1956 law on elections, as follows:

In the Federal Republic one decided after 1945 without great debate on an "improved" system of proportional voting. . . . In that system a significant part of the future deputies are elected "directly" in their constituency. . . . In elections to the Bundestag and to the Bavarian Landtag two ballots are to be marked, one containing the names of the direct candidates in the local constituency and one containing the parties' *Land* lists. The second vote, for the party list, determines the relative strength of the parties in the parliament; the first vote provides an initial selection of parliamentary deputies, of whom in this manner about half are chosen directly and so are particularly closely tied to the local constituency. . . .

The voter has two votes. The second vote is cast for a *Land* list; later [vote counters] tally the total number of second votes for each party for the entire federal territory and . . . distribute the seats first to the federal parties and then to the parties' *Land* lists. From this total [they] deduct the seats won by direct election. The number of deputies chosen by direct election is fixed, since constituency boundaries within each *Land* are permanent. The number of other deputies varies. The total number of deputies from each *Land* may depend on the voter turnout. The first vote determines the direct election of deputies. Each party nominates a candidate for each constituency; whoever obtains the most votes wins the seat. In distributing the seats according to the *Land* lists those candidates who have already won a seat by direct election are ignored. Parties which have not obtained at least 5 per cent of the votes cast throughout the federal territory or have not won three direct seats do not participate in the distribution. If in any *Land* a party obtains more direct seats than that party has a right to according to its share of second votes, the total number of deputies to the Bundestag is increased by these "overhang seats."[8]

Thus, about half of the Bundestag consisted of deputies elected directly, and about half consisted of representatives previously chosen by their parties to be part of a *Land* list. The total number of seats in the Bundestag depended on the number of voters. In 1949, it was 402, of which half were elected directly in single member districts and half chosen at large from *Land*-wide lists of the parties.

The first parliamentary election took place on August 14, 1949. The campaign and the subsequent parliamentary negotiations leading to

[8] Ellwein, *Das Regierungssystem der BRD*, 208–11.

the formation of the first government overshadowed, in the public mind, the many and complicated activities which the military governments and the Bizonal authorities had to complete. Adenauer, as president of the Parliamentary Council, formed a preparatory Committee on Measures for Establishing the Federal Organs. It was composed of the eleven minister-presidents (excluding the governing mayor of Berlin), 18 members of the Parliamentary Council (whose work was formally completed when the Basic Law was accepted by the *Länder*), six members of the Frankfurt Economic Council, and four delegates from the French zone. This committee laid detailed plans for the organization, the legislative and judicial functions, and the finances of the future federation. It determined the operating rules and areas of competence of the future federal ministries, decided what occupation, zonal, and bizonal laws should be kept in force, made a list of "immediately required" and "urgent" legislation for the new government, and prepared the first federal budget. The first fiscal year of the Federal Republic was to begin on April 1, 1950; until that date the government used the inherited funds and revenues of the Economic Council.

Sixteen parties and a number of independent candidates campaigned in the first federal elections to the Bundestag. Apart from the CDU/CSU, SPD, and FDP, the parties represented a variety of regional, group, or ideological special interests, including those of the refugees. The days of the ideological mass party, like the Nazi party, the communist party of the Weimar period, or the SPD of the Wilhelmine era, were over. There remained, however, splinter groups, especially on the extreme left and right, who continued to organize and seek a following. On the left, the communists maintained their hopes for a Sovietization of West Germany, but suffered from the widespread distrust and fear of Soviet intentions. They also were discredited by the sad record of the Soviet zone of occupation, Soviet atrocities during the initial occupation of Germany, the impact of the experiences recounted by millions of refugees from the east, and the experiences of German prisoners of war in the USSR. This fear was nourished by memories of communist behavior in the 1920s, by the delayed effects of a combination of Nazi propaganda and the experience of Soviet occupation, by the continuing regimentation of life in the Soviet zone, and by the Berlin blockade (nevertheless, the KPD collected 15 seats and 1.3 million votes). On the right, the German Conservative Party/German Right Party represented the first of a series of attempts to rally former Nazis, disillusioned professional soldiers, purged officials and other dissatisfied and déclassé elements (it obtained only five seats in 1949).

Radical anti-democrats, whether of the right or left, faced a dilemma between fulfilling their ideological mission to combat the democratic system of the Federal Republic on the one hand, and the risk of suppression on the other. Article 21, clause 1 of the Basic Law stated that political parties "shall participate in the forming of the political will of the people," but that their "internal constitution must conform to democratic principles." A party organized internally in a totalitarian fashion, like the KPD, violated this provision. More important was the next clause, which stated that "parties which, in virtue of their aims or the behavior of their adherents, seek to impair or destroy the free democratic basic order or to endanger the existence of the Federal Republic of Germany are unconstitutional. The Federal Constitutional Court shall decide on the question of unconstitutionality." Neither the government nor the Bundestag could by itself order a party or an organization dissolved, but had to apply to the Constitutional Court for a judgement that the party in question was in fact illegal under article 21. Since the Court did not exist until 1951, the radical parties enjoyed an initial grace period. Until 1955, however, Germany was still occupied territory, and under occupation law any party that was, or appeared to be, a successor organization to the NSDAP was forbidden. This deterred most remaining Nazi sympathizers from overt action. In fact, following 1949, the Allies were reluctant to use their reserve powers to intervene in German politics and preferred to let the Germans themselves deal with what could be construed to represent domestic threats to democracy.

Competition was intense and the different interests championed by the numerous parties were well reflected in the election slogans. For example, in Bavaria the CSU was especially concerned with stopping educational reform and saving the tax-supported parochial school system. The party, therefore, distributed election posters depicting an elementary school boy saying: "Father and Mother choose for me – CSU." During the campaign Kurt Schumacher, as head of the SPD, ridiculed the CDU as "a mob haphazardly thrown together" and criticized the party as "clerical, conservative and capitalistic."[9]

Bavaria, already represented within the Christian democratic camp by the CSU, boasted two regional parties which made a fairly good showing in the Bundestag elections but which were absorbed by the CSU within a few years. The Bavarian Party opposed the Basic Law and employed the slogan "Bavaria for the Bavarians." It propagated a mixture of folkloric particularism and monarchism (and obtained 17 seats). The WAV (Economic Reconstruction Party), which won twelve seats, owed its continued existence to the personality of its leader, Alfred Loritz, rather than to any incompatibility of its program with that of the

⁹ Eschenburg, *Jahre der Besatzung*, 525–6.

CSU. Lower Saxony in particular was hospitable to rightist factions; before 1933, the Nazis had been especially popular among the many middle-size farmers, shopkeepers, and small-scale independent businessmen who formed the demographic backbone of the region, and during the Third Reich it had been the bastion of Hitler's agrarian association. Some of these former Nazi elements belonged to the Socialist Reich Party until its dissolution in 1952. Lower Saxony, which had been the kingdom of Hannover until it was absorbed by Prussia in 1866, also had strong regional traditions quite independent of Nazism.

After the war, with the Prussian state defunct, spokesmen for these regional interests saw their chance and founded, in 1947, the German Party (Deutsche Partei, DP), highly conservative but not neo-Nazi, which opposed socialization in general and the SPD in particular, criticized denazification and received 17 seats on a program appealing both to nationalists and regionalists. The area had been ruled in the Middle Ages by the Welf family (in English, this became Guelph), who for a time were the most powerful rivals of the German emperors. They thus came to symbolize regional resistance to centralized authority. In modern times, long after the last Welfs had died out, people continued to refer to Lower Saxony colloquially as *Welfenland* and to Lower Saxon regionalism as "Guelph." In the Rhineland, the CDU had not succeeded in preventing the re-formation of the Center party which, in this strongly Catholic area, received ten seats. Within five years the Center supporters were wholly absorbed by the CDU.

One major constituency was not separately represented, however; namely, the refugees from the eastern provinces and Eastern Europe who comprised about 17 per cent of the population. They were without representation because refugee political parties could not be formed according to military government law (this law was repealed in November 1949). The major parties, however, did include refugee candidates and 61 of them were elected, amounting to 15 per cent of Bundestag membership.

The major issue in the election was the economic system of the new state: socialist or free market? The decisions of Erhard and the Economic Council in 1948–9, the support of Adenauer over the opposition of the Christian socialists in the CDU, the philosophical vigor of the ordo-liberals (i.e. Röpke, Rüstow, Hayek), and the backing of Clay may seem, in hindsight, to have created irresistible momentum for the socially responsible market system that in fact came into being. At the time it was not clear exactly what forces would prevail. The Basic Law called the Federal Republic a "social state," and Schumacher and the SPD hoped for an election victory which would allow them to introduce economic planning, socialization, and an equalization of burdens far more comprehensive than that envisaged by the CDU. Unlike Adenauer, they also believed that the way toward German self-assertion should involve the categorical rejection of the remaining stringent controls on German heavy industry, notably the continuing dismantling and foreign control of the Ruhr district.

They could point in two respects to what had been happening in France. In 1946, Jean Monnet, a merchant banker with excellent American connections who was to become the architect of the European Economic Community, became high commissioner of the French plan for modernization and re-equipment, known in its early years as the Monnet Plan. He was born in Cognac in 1888 to a family that had established a cognac business in the 1830s. He left school when he was 16 years old and entered his father's business. He never attended a university, but was sent abroad by his family to England, Canada, the United States, Sweden, Russia, and Egypt. His common sense and business acumen led him to play a major role during World War I in coordinating shipping and transport between England and France. Following the war he became involved in banking, and his abilities eventually led private banks as well as governments to seek his advice on questions of international finance and economic issues. At the end of World War II de Gaulle (head of the provisional government of France 1944–6) asked him to prepare a memorandum on French economic priorities which became the blueprint for the rebirth of the French economy and served as the step leading to his vision of a united Europe.

Among the men who have molded the history of Western Europe since World War II, Jean Monnet is unique. He never exercised high political power, and he was never a cabinet minister or even a member of a legislature . . . he never belonged to a political party, never ran for public office. . . . He was not a civil servant; he was not a career diplomat. . . . Yet he had a personal impact and left his particular stamp of success everywhere he went and on practically everything he did, and his influence on history at key times and in key places across nearly three-quarters of this century was remarkable. . . . To picture Jean Monnet or to think of him simply as the Western world's most successful *éminence grise* is to miss completely the quality of the man: his personality, his intellect, his vision, his mind, his conversation, his forcefulness with its mixture of assertiveness and selflessness, his human understanding, his integrity, his strength, his greatness.[10]

Basic to the Monnet Plan was the expansion of French steel production with the help of German coal from the Ruhr, and at the ultimate expense

[10]  Cook, *Ten Men and History,* 98–9.

of German steel production. The result, Monnet and the French politicians hoped, would be French political as well as economic dominance on the Continent: German recovery would be hostage to French control. The Plan thus served both economic and perceived security interests, since the French were still far more obsessed with an imaginary revival of German power than with the existing Soviet threat.[11] At the same time, however, Monnet's view was a much broader one. He sought to build a federated Europe in which economic relations of interdependence would not only supersede the parochial national interests that had contributed to two world wars, but which would make Europe itself an economic and political power in its own right.

Schumacher and the SPD rejected the idea of using the products of hard German labor – the coal and coke of the Ruhr – for French purposes, but they also saw the Monnet Plan as just the kind of socialized capitalism they wished for the Federal Republic. On the one hand, they argued that West Germany should reject foreign control of its industry and indirectly of its political and economic system and denounced Adenauer's willingness to tolerate such controls. On the other hand, they called for similar economic planning in non-Soviet Germany.

In the 1949 elections, both the SPD and the CDU/CSU obtained about 30 per cent of the vote. The FDP as well as most other smaller parties were sympathetic to the CDU and did not wish to see the SPD in power. Nevertheless the SPD leaders saw the contest largely as one between themselves and Adenauer's party and were shocked that they had failed to defeat the CDU. Schumacher and the SPD thought it wrong that a bare plurality, as he saw it, should determine the future of the West German economy. The voter's rejection of a planned economy meant not only that West Germany would be rebuilt and reconstructed according to the rules of a free market, but that the SPD would not play the decisive political, economic, and social role of leadership that its members believed their opposition to Hitler entitled them to hold.

Some in Adenauer's own party also accused him of making excessive concessions. Adenauer's plan was to accept the fact of foreign control and to gain Western trust within the constraints imposed by that control. He correctly judged that recalcitrant resistance would lead to stricter controls and to a longer period of occupation. On the other hand, he believed that a combination of modesty and firmness might earn the West German state recognition and equality with the rest of Western Europe much faster than most people predicted in 1949. He realized that the Soviet threat and the resulting defense needs of the West, as

[11] Milward, *Reconstruction of Western Europe*, 129.

well as the need for economic reconstruction, absolutely required West German resources, and he was prepared to demand a price for those resources in terms of greater political independence. He also saw Franco-German reconciliation and economic and political integration as a precondition for West European peace and security, which he regarded as an essential basis for meeting the Soviet threat, and, for earning and maintaining the trust and respect of the British and the Americans. Last, but by no means least, Adenauer thought that only firm integration of West Germany in a broader West European political and economic network, in which major decisions could not be made unilaterally, would save the Germans from themselves and make it impossible for adventurist or anti-democratic ideologues ever again to seize power.

Between 1951 and 1955 there occurred notable incidents illustrating Adenauer's fundamental distrust of the political wisdom of his own people. Among these was the following occurrence. Lothar Ruehl, a correspondent for *Der Spiegel*, in 1954 reported that he had, while hidden behind a column, overheard Adenauer, in conversation with the foreign ministers of Luxembourg and Belgium at Claridge's Hotel in London, insist on the need for firm treaties binding West Germany. Adenauer repeatedly said, "What will become of Germany when I am gone?"[12]

The SPD case for economic planning was supported by the unemployment and inflation figures, which were not encouraging in the summer of 1949. At the end of 1949 unemployment was 10.3 per cent and by March 1950 it had increased to 12.2 per cent, and unemployment among refugees was approximately three times as high. Erhard's currency reform had forced industry to lay off a number of workers, whereas exports and domestic consumption were slow to increase. But Schumacher harmed the SPD's case by his intemperate and *ad hominem* attacks on Adenauer, the capitalists, and the Catholic church, which he at one point called "a fifth occupying power,"[13] and thus contributed to an atmosphere of negativism.

Erhard's view, however, was more hopeful: "Optimism, derided at first, proved nevertheless to be well founded. In the first half of 1950 retail prices fell 10.6 per cent below the level of the first six months of 1949."[14] He campaigned with great optimism on behalf of the CDU for the social market economy, which, in the Düsseldorf Principles (*Düsseldorfer Leitsätze*) of July 1949, became the basis of CDU policy. Gone was

[12] *Der Spiegel*, Oct. 6, 1954. See also Gerd Bucerius, "xxx", *Die Zeit*, April 4, 1986.
[13] Benz, *Gründung der BRD*, 133; and Abelshauser, *Wirtschaftsgeschichte*, 64.
[14] Erhard, *Prosperity through Competition*, 21.

the Christian socialism of the Ahlen Program of 1947, shared notably by the CDU leaders Gradl, Hermes, Kaiser, and Lemmer from Berlin and the Soviet zone, now all in the West. (Hermes had been a member of the Economic Council and all of these four served in later federal governments.)

The importance of the Düsseldorf Principles was that they provided the guidelines for the realization of the social market economy, of which Erhard remarked at that time:

The pressure of falling prices led to a state of affairs which the German public could barely remember. The customer became king again; a buyers' market began. . . . The most thorough increase in efficiency took place in the sectors where pressure of competition was especially strong.[15]

The election was a disappointment for the SPD, yet the social democrats came closer to matching the CDU vote than in any other federal election before 1972, when they surpassed the Christian democrats. The difference was less than two percentage points. Of 31.2 million eligible voters on August 14, 24.5 million cast ballots (78.5 per cent), which gave the CDU/CSU 31 per cent, the SPD 29.2 per cent, the FDP 11.9 per cent and the twelve other parties and the independents 27.9 per cent. Many people feared that the fragmentation and ideological confrontations of the Weimar Reichstag would return, after all. It was partly thanks to economic success and the resulting political stabilization, but also to a conscious effort of both Adenauer and the SPD leaders, that the vast majority of that one-third of the voters who, in 1949, gave their votes to splinter parties were integrated into the three main parties during the 1950s. Never again were the many smaller parties as strong as in the first Bundestag. In 1953, the smaller parties received only 16.5 per cent altogether. In 1957, it was only 10.3, and from 1961 to 1983 there were only three groupings in the Bundestag: the CDU/CSU, the SPD, and the FDP. In 1983 the party of the Greens entered, thus adding a fourth party for the first time in 22 years.

The election results of 1949 made possible a non-socialist coalition. Yet many powerful figures in the CDU, including four minister-presidents, recommended a grand coalition with the SPD, since the country, in their view, needed as broadly based a government as possible in this initial phase in order to win the people's confidence and to lead a credible government. Adenauer was firmly against this, as he had been since 1947. On August 20 he made an agreement with the CSU leader and minister-president of Bavaria, Hans Ehard, that Ehard would

---

[15] Ibid., 29.

become chairman of the Bundesrat, the upper house composed of representatives of the *Land* governments. In return, Ehard supported Adenauer's proposal for a non-socialist coalition. With both the leaders of the Union parties of the same opinion, the final agreement was reached over Sunday afternoon coffee in Adenauer's house in Rhöndorf on August 21. The 73–year-old CDU chief stated his readiness and intention to serve as chancellor: "My doctor tells me that I would be able to carry out this office for at least a year, perhaps for two."[16] In fact Konrad Adenauer led the government for 14 years, a period as long as the entire history of the Weimar Republic.

In the FDP as well as in the CDU and CSU there remained some opposition to a small coalition of those three parties. Free-marketeers in the FDP had supported Erhard and feared the strongly Catholic and Christian socialist wings of the CDU. The latter, on the other hand, were not reconciled to capitalism and still hoped for a grand coalition with the SPD. Three factors undermined the resistance. First, Schumacher himself, outraged at the election results, confirmed the SPD's intention to carry out a complete socialization of natural resources and heavy industry, and declared that a bourgeois government would not last very long, thereby clearly implying that he wanted the SPD to be in opposition and not in government. Second, Adenauer, himself convinced of the merits of the social market economy and highly skeptical of Christian socialist ideas, wanted a small coalition to continue economic reconstruction as it had begun, but also because he thought that a significant parliamentary opposition was essential to teach the Germans democracy. A broad coalition would simply provoke a nationalist, extra-parliamentary opposition which could jeopardize all that was achieved and invite Western intervention. Third, cultural and educational policies, in which religious orientation played a major role, were a state and not a federal matter. Thus both strong Catholics and strong free-market liberals could put their differences on these issues aside as far as forming a federal government was concerned.

A further step toward the small coalition was the election of the liberal leader, Theodor Heuss, as first federal president on September 12. Heuss (1884–1963) was one of the last and best representatives of the German tradition of political humanism, which was particularly strong in his native south-west. He was born in Württemberg and had studied economics and political philosophy. During and after World War I he edited newspapers and journals and in the Weimar period he taught history and political science in Berlin while serving in the Reichstag for the progressive liberal party of the day, the DDP. In 1933 the Nazis

[16] Schwarz, *Die Ära Adenauer, 1949–1957,* 27.

revoked his mandate over his protest and forbade him to write. He continued to publish under a pseudonym and completed several exhaustive biographies of democratic political figures. In 1945 he was one of the licensees for the *Rhein-Neckar-Zeitung* and in September was made minister for culture in Württemberg-Baden and ultimately served in the Parliamentary Council for that state.

Heuss was known for his good sense of humor. His niece, Hanna Frielinghaus-Heuss collected, recounted, and published some of his characteristic anecdotes in a small volume entitled *Heuss-Anekdoten*. In the summer of 1945 Heuss was living near Heidelberg. Several American officers had visited him and asked advice concerning future cabinet appointments. One day, an American officer appeared unannounced and asked Heuss, without any introduction, to take over the position as minister of culture in the *Land* Württemberg-Baden. Heuss happened to be outside his house, beating a carpet, which was hanging over a clothesline. Heuss thought about the offer for a moment, beat the carpet several more times and answered: "Yes, I'll come, just as long as you'll provide me with a cleaning woman."[17]

After his election to the presidency in 1949, Heuss moved into provisional quarters, located high on a hill above the Rhine river with a beautiful view, but very little space. The staff, despite or because of the tight rooming situation, became something of a family. When the time came in 1950 to move down to the new presidential quarters, the Villa Hammerschmidt, everybody was sad to leave the small hill-top house. But Heuss comforted his staff: "It's better to be nearer to Adenauer than to our dear Lord."[18]

The election of Heuss, the liberal candidate, over Schumacher, who made himself the SPD candidate to prevent the nomination of a moderate social democrat acceptable to the supporters of a grand coalition in the CDU/CSU, was the final condition for FDP approval of the small coalition with the CDU/CSU and DP. The cabinet list was ready when the first Bundestag met to elect the chancellor on September 15. The most important posts were occupied by Ludwig Erhard, CDU (economy), Fritz Schäffer, CSU (finance), Jakob Kaiser, CDU (all-German affairs), Franz Blücher, FDP (vice-chancellor and minister for economic cooperation), Gustav Heinemann, CDU (interior), Thomas Dehler, FDP (justice), and Hans-Christoph Seebohm, DP (transport, from 1949 to 1966).

There was no foreign minister for the time being because the Federal Republic was still occupied territory and had no foreign relations other

---

[17] Frielinghaus-Heuss, *Heuss-Anekdoten*, 9.
[18] Ibid., 20.

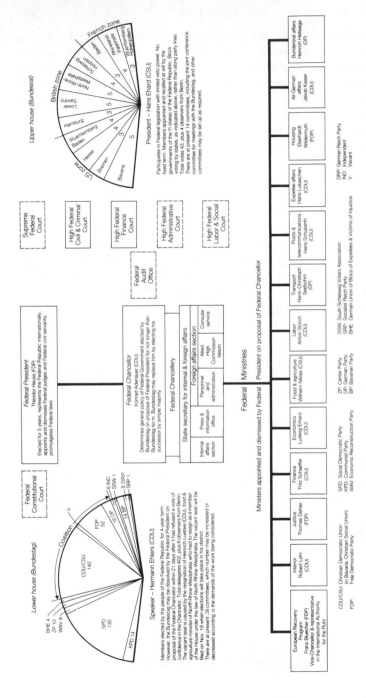

Figure 1.2   Organization of the Federal Republic of Germany, 1949. This detailed figure of the political organization of the Federal Republic shows the administrative foundations of the first German government on German soil in over four years.
*Source:* Office of the US High Commissioner, *4th Quarterly Report*, 1950

than through the Allied High Commission. This at least was the theory. In practice, the new government, from the very beginning, had a very definite foreign policy, namely Adenauer's. For the first 18 months he conducted it through a special section of his own bureau, the Federal Chancellor's Office (*Bundeskanzleramt*), or chancellery, an institution which he turned into a central and indispensable feature of the political and governmental system of the Federal Republic. Adenauer's chief aide in laying the foundations of a West German foreign policy was Herbert Blankenhorn. Like Adenauer, Blankenhorn was a native of western Germany critical of the Prussian role in German history and relieved that, after 1945, Prussia was defunct. He was, however, not a Rhinelander but a native of Baden, the south-westernmost part of Germany. He was congenial to the chancellor, whose views on foreign policy and on domestic reconstruction, especially federalism, he shared completely. Blankenhorn (born 1904) was a career foreign service officer who had been closely involved with the anti-Nazi conspirators against Hitler in 1941–4. In 1950 he became head of the special department of foreign affairs in the chancellery (the forerunner of the foreign ministry established in March 1951) and later enjoyed a distinguished career as German ambassador to NATO, to Great Britain, and to France.

Adenauer's most important aide in the chancellery and, indeed, in the entire government apparatus during his tenure, was Hans Globke (1898–1973), a former official of the Reich interior ministry. Globke was an administrative genius and quickly became the *éminence grise* of the Adenauer era. He was aware of everything that was done and how it was done, and no one, who wanted anything from the Adenauer government, could avoid dealing with the quiet, but extremely forceful, Globke. It could be said of him, as it had been said about the secret councillor for war, Eichel, in the government of Frederick the Great of Prussia (ruled 1740–86): "Seen by no mortal eye, he lives in complete isolation, yet he knows all; strictly guarded like a condemned prisoner, he is on duty the entire year round, without so much as half an hour's vacation; wherever the king goes, he goes too; his chancellery is the true seat of government; every effort to speak to him is vain."[19] Many considered Globke the prime example of how far the Federal Republic was a government of restoration, and not of new beginning, since Globke had worked for the Nazi government and was the principal author of the official commentary to the Nuremberg Laws of 1935, which codified Nazi anti-Semitism. Adenauer, however, believed that Globke had done his best to give the laws the mildest possible interpretation and that Globke, by

[19] Heinrich, *Geschichte Preussens*, 197.

remaining in government, had acted correctly. Adenauer steadfastly supported him throughout the 14 years he was chancellor.[20]

The case of Globke was the most prominent case of a high official of the government of the Third Reich being not merely reinstated but actually promoted to a position of trust and authority in the new democratic Germany. Globke's presence in the government forced the issue of continuity – in personnel, in style of government, in foreign and strategic policy, and in anti-communist ideology – between Nazi Germany and the Federal Republic into the open and provided liberal and radical critics with powerful ammunition. In the narrower sense, Globke was proof positive that the kind of civil service reform demanded by the military governments had not taken place, and critics were quick to argue that continuity in the bureaucracy was equivalent to continuity in authoritarian domestic and aggressive foreign policies. In the wider and more important sense, Globke's career illustrated the entire range of questions concerning power and politics in Germany and the place of the Third Reich in German history. His defenders, including Adenauer and Jakob Kaiser, argued that Globke displayed the best traits of the *Beamter* who was sincerely devoted to the common weal. He had done this, they argued, by remaining in place in a responsible position of influence which might otherwise have been filled by a Nazi party ideologue. By remaining in place, to his defenders, Globke had been able to formulate his commentary to the Nuremberg laws in ways that mitigated their effects and directed judges, administrators, and lawyers to apply them as humanely as possible. This argument did not appease critics who maintained that since the Nuremberg laws in themselves violated basic constitutional norms, any *Beamter* who enforced them in any way was himself guilty of complicity in a criminal perversion of responsible government. These critics, however, could not provide a satisfactory answer to those who pointed to the thousands or perhaps tens of thousands of German Jews who were able to leave Germany thanks to the interpretation of the Nuremberg laws that Globke provided. A fanatical Nazi in Globke's position undoubtedly would have controlled enforcement stringently and prevented any leniency, and according to his defenders would thereby have caused many more deaths.[21]

Adenauer was determined to provide direction in foreign affairs and focused immediately on what was to become a major goal:

to establish a close relationship with our neighbors in the Western world, especially with the United States. We will devote all our energies to having

[20] See Gotto, ed., *Der Staatssekretär Adenauers*.
[21] Ibid., 230–82.

Germany accepted as a member with equal rights and obligations in the European federation as soon as possible. In carrying out these purposes we will collaborate especially closely with the Christian-Democratic forces which are evolving ever more strongly in the Western European nations.[22]

As Adenauer wrote in his memoirs, ". . . to make us trusted was the first commandment. . . . The faster and more firmly confidence in us grew, the sooner the goal of partnership would be reached."[23]

The Protestant and north German wings of the CDU and FDP were not completely satisfied with the cabinet; nine of 14 ministers were Catholic, and the CDU provided only two of the five Protestants. In 1949 the West German population was 51.2 per cent Protestant, and 45.2 per cent Catholic. This meant that they were more evenly distributed than before 1945, but it only increased the resentment of leading Protestants, that the Catholics dominated both the CDU and the government.

[22] Schwarz, *Die Ära Adenauer, 1949–1957*, 55.
[23] Adenauer, *Memoirs 1945–1953*, 193.

# 2

# Chancellor Adenauer

According to the Basic Law, the head of government, the federal chancellor, having been elected by a majority of his fellow Bundestag members, was the chief executive and the political leader of the majority party or coalition in the Bundestag. He had the ultimate responsibility for formulating government policy, in consultation with the cabinet, and for guiding it through the legislative process. Once the elections determined how many Bundestag seats each party has won, the federal president consulted with party leaders and proposed a candidate for federal chancellor to be elected by the Bundestag without debate.

To win, the candidate for chancellor must obtain the vote of more than half the Bundestag. If he did not, the Bundestag, in a second ballot, must choose a majority candidate put up by its own members within 14 days. The winner was appointed to office by the federal president.

This method, unusual in parliamentary democracies, was adopted to ensure that the head of government in fact had the support of a majority of deputies before his formal appointment and thus to make parliamentary challenges unlikely. Another measure designed to make changes of government between elections very difficult was the "constructive vote of no-confidence," a device unique to the West German system. The Basic Law did not permit the dismissal of a chancellor in a "vote of no-confidence" without the simultaneous election of a successor. This "constructive vote of no-confidence" was designed to prevent the country being without a government.

A new chancellor could be elected before expiration of the four-year legislative term: (a) if the incumbent resigned, in which case the Bundestag followed the procedures prescribed for electing a chancellor; or (b) if an absolute majority of Bundestag members passed a "constructive vote of no-confidence," electing a new chancellor. In this event, the federal president was required to abide by the majority decision, dismiss the incumbent and appoint the elected successor. This device was used twice between 1949 and 1988, once in 1972, when it failed, and once in 1982, when it succeeded.

The constructive vote of no-confidence by itself did not trigger an election. The only way for federal elections to occur outside the normal interval of four years (strictly speaking, not less than 46 and not more than 48 months), was if the chancellor himself requested the confidence of the Bundestag, and the Bundestag rejected the motion. The chancellor then might request the president to dissolve the Bundestag. He was not obliged to do so. In practice, if the chancellor failed to obtain the confidence of a majority of the deputies on a direct motion, further government was impossible.

Adenauer was elected chancellor with 202 votes out of 402, with 142 opposed, 44 abstentions, and the remaining members not taking part. That was a majority of one vote, his own; as Adenauer later said, it would have been "hypocrisy" to vote any other way.[1] It was never completely clear how the different parties voted; however, some parliamentarians did not vote at all, and some, mainly from the CSU, did not give Adenauer their vote or abstained.[2]

The outcome of the vote was critical, and much more important than might appear in retrospect almost 40 years later. Adenauer's election could have just as easily gone the other way, and if it had, the postwar history of Germany – at least West Germany – might have been very different. Hindsight gives the historian that great luxury to speculate about what might have been, and it gave Schumacher and the SPD that luxury too in later years. The fact, however, was that the SPD lost the election for chancellor. It was Adenauer who won and not someone else; and in Germany in 1949, as everywhere, it was victory that mattered, for it gave the victor the power of decision. Adenauer himself emphasized how important his victory was in his first speech to the German Bundestag on September 20, 1949, as he explained why a grand coalition with the SPD was not possible:

The question "planned economy" or "social market economy" played an overwhelming role in the election campaign. The German people decided against the planned economy with a large majority. A coalition between the parties who rejected the planned economy and those who supported it would have been directly opposed to the will of the majority of the voters.[3]

Thus began the Adenauer era, if only by one vote. But solid foundations did come later, and their construction was guided in many respects by

[1] Adenauer, *Memoirs 1945–1953*, 182; and Benz, *Gründung*, 136.
[2] Schwarz, *Die Ära Adenauer, 1949–1957*, 34.
[3] Beyme, ed., *Die grossen Regierungserklärungen*, 54.

the members of Adenauer's first cabinet, many of whom played vital roles in the growth of the Federal Republic. Gustav Heinemann, minister of the interior, later was elected the third president of the Federal Republic in 1969; Thomas Dehler, minister of justice, remained a leading figure in the FDP for many years; and the minister of economic affairs, Ludwig Erhard, was elected chancellor to succeed Adenauer in 1963. Ironically, both Heinemann and Dehler became, within a few years, bitter opponents of Adenauer's foreign policy of integration with the West and of arming the Federal Republic. But it was the vision and personality of Adenauer – "der Alte" – that played the overwhelming role in the Federal Republic. He provided what Germany desperately needed – clear, firm, imaginative, and realistic leadership.

The strong position of the chancellor was grounded in the Basic Law, but also very much affirmed by Adenauer. Without the precedent of his 14–year tenure the position of his successors would very likely not have been as influential. One expression of this strength was the "statement of government policy" (*Regierungserklärung*) which each chancellor (or his representative) reads to the Bundestag after the formation of a new cabinet. They also made statements of government policy at other times when issues of special importance were debated, but the one given by the new (or returning) chancellor was and remains the focus of particular attention. In it, the chancellor described the policies he proposed to undertake and the goals he sought.

Adenauer's first statement, on September 20, announced the formation of the government and the entry into force of the Occupation Statute, originally published on April 8, 1949, by the military government. According to its provisions the Allies retained supreme authority, as well as direct control in a number of areas. The most important concerned Allied occupation forces and their needs, foreign affairs, demilitarization, controls on industry and communications, control of the Ruhr, compensation and reparations, foreign trade, and internal security. Other areas of direct control either lapsed or were returned to German authority by 1955, or, in the case of the coal and steel industry of the Ruhr, became subject to the collective authority of the European Coal and Steel Community of 1951 (ECSC), forerunner of the Common Market (European Economic Community, EEC), of which the Federal Republic was a member. During the early 1950s the West German government also gradually took over responsibility for most aspects of the internal security of the state. The Federal Border Patrol (*Bundesgrenzschutz*), established by the military governments in 1949, was not only a border guard but in the early 1950s became a federal security force responsible for assuring the security of government operations, including the physical safety of government personnel. In 1956, the Americans transferred the intelligence service known as the Gehlen Organization to Bonn's control. This service grew out of General Reinhard Gehlen's wartime military intelligence operation on the Eastern front. In 1945, Gehlen secured his records, including lists of agents and invaluable information on Soviet military forces and policies, in a safe place and later turned them over to US authorities. From 1946 to 1956, Gehlen served the Americans. Starting in June 1950, he consulted regularly with Globke and Adenauer, both of whom understood that the Federal Republic needed an intelligence service, especially for counter-espionage. When the Bonn government took over his operation, which became the Federal Intelligence Service (*Bundesnachrichtendienst*), it gained not only a valuable resource of information on Soviet plans and potential, but also a weapon in the domestic struggle against Soviet bloc espionage and infiltration.[4]

One area of domestic security remained under Allied jurisdiction until 1968. This was the power to declare a state of emergency and to mobilize civilian assets in times of crisis or war. A famous definition of political sovereignty is that the sovereign is he who has the power to declare that a state of emergency exists (and to take measures accordingly). According to this definition, then, West Germany was not fully sovereign until 1968. When the debate on the final emergency powers took place in the 1960s, it revived great fears among many liberals and radicals that West Germany was preparing to embark on the road leading to a resurrection of authoritarianism.

On the German question, Adenauer believed that since the German people of the Soviet zone could not exercise their right of national self-determination, the government which the communists were establishing there was illegitimate. Despite the nominal existence of several parties, the SED allowed no deviation from its policies and commands. The People's Congress which passed a "constitution for the German Democratic Republic" in March 1949 was a rubber-stamp for the wishes of the Soviet Union and the German communists. The government of the Federal Republic, on the other hand, resulted from the will of a majority of 23 million voters. "The Federal Republic was therefore," declared Adenauer, "the only legitimate political organization of the German people until German unity was achieved."[5] This position was staunchly maintained and defended by all Bonn governments until November 1969.

On September 21, 1949, the High Commissioners summoned

---

[4] Gotto, ed., *Der Staatssekretär Adenauers*, 184–93.
[5] Adenauer, *Memoirs 1945—1953*, 189.

Adenauer to a meeting at their headquarters on the Petersberg for the official ceremony terminating the institutions of military government and replacing them with civilian government. Adenauer and his party – including the minister of finance, Schäffer, the minister of justice, Dehler, the minister for all-German affairs, Kaiser, the vice-chancellor, Blücher, and five officials from the chancellery – arrived at 10:00 in the morning. For the first time since the war military honors were rendered to German officials as they were saluted by an honor guard of 30 American, British and French military police. Adenauer was not, however, summoned as an equal, but as a petitioner. To symbolize this point the three High Commissioners were waiting on an oriental rug, and Adenauer was to introduce his cabinet ministers from a position just in front of the rug. Adenauer, however, took one step onto the rug, and delivered his prepared statement with both feet on the carpet, thereby implying that he regarded himself as a legitimate equal of the High Commissioners. Following the formal response by the chairman of the High Commission, the entire group adjourned to the veranda for champagne and informal conversation. By 11:00 a.m. the German guests had departed, and the High Commission officially began its work at the same hour.

The primary purpose of this meeting was to give Adenauer the formal copy of the Occupation Statute. The Statute made it clear that the Allies could reassume direct authority if they felt that the democratic system in West Germany was threatened or their own security was in jeopardy. It also required that all measures taken by the federal government and the *Länder* be submitted to the Commission for its approval. At the same time, however, it was also a document which allowed Adenauer considerable flexibility. As Adenauer was congratulated by François-Poncet, the French High Commissioner described its significance as follows:

Western Germany – we regret that we cannot say all of Germany – today possesses the means which should allow her to take the direction of her destiny into her own hands. . . . The principles which must govern our relationship with you and your government, our rights and reciprocal duties, are known to you. They have been carefully defined in an act which takes effect today, at this very moment. This act could be, as you have indicated, the object of a future revision. The more scrupulously this statute is adhered to, the more prompt and broad the revision will be.[6]

[6] Haute Commissariat, "Naissance de la Republique Federale d'Allemagne." *Realités Allemandes* 9–10 (September–October 1949): 38.

François-Poncet's sympathy with the new German state was evident, and he, as did his counterparts, fervently hoped that the Federal Republic of Germany would thrive and flourish.

The disposition of the Statute was not recorded. Adenauer insisted that no one actually handed the original of the Occupation Statute to him, since he regarded that as a gesture of a superior to a subordinate. Instead, an Allied High Commission representative gave an unsigned copy to Adenauer's chief foreign policy aide, Herbert Blankenhorn. When Adenauer asked him in 1962 where the Occupation Statute had been deposited, Blankenhorn produced the copy, but the location of the original remained a mystery.

One of Adenauer's first priorities – an "immediately required" law – concerned the civil service. As part of the democratization and denazification process, the military governments, and at their behest the *Länder*, had undertaken a reform of the civil service, the chief element of which was a purge of all former members of Nazi organizations. The whole system was to be reformed to make it easier for members of hitherto excluded groups to become civil servants as well as for the democratically elected governments to prevent the civil service from becoming a powerful special interest group within the state. OMGUS had sought to abolish the distinction between *Beamte*, officials with tenure for life and other special privileges, and *Angestellte*, ordinary employees of public or private enterprises with normal contracts, the general outlines of which were renegotiated at intervals by representatives of unions and employers' organizations. The Soviets had done exactly this in their zone, in order to destroy the civil service as an independent center of power and possible opposition. For the Western Allies, the purpose was to make sure that an isolated and privileged caste of officials, removed from normal controls and responsibilities, did not arise, since the Allies rightly believed that the existence of such a caste in prewar Germany helped the Nazis construct their regime and execute their policies. Nevertheless the Soviet precedent and German opposition caused the Allies to drop the wider-ranging plan. Yet in 1949, the status of civil servants was still unclear. (See the extensive discussion of this subject in part I, chapter 9, Denazification.)

The Parliamentary Council had included a clause in the Basic Law (no. 131) affecting all those whose civil service careers had been involuntarily interrupted since May 8, 1945. This affected mainly two groups: first, civil servants who were unable to claim their wages because the appropriate bureau no longer existed, e.g. expellees; and second, persons purged under the denazification rules. 58,000 former *Beamte* had been purged and were without their former jobs, as were 110,000 *Beamte* from the Oder–Neisse territories and the Soviet zone.

The first Bundestag passed legislation assisting these groups, while reserving the right to prosecute any purged officials who might be guilty of actual crimes, other than membership in the Nazi party. Two years later, in 1951, the Bundestag passed a law reinstating all former civil servants in their former ranks and pay grades, with seniority added for the intervening years. After the establishment of the Federal Constitutional Court in 1951, the case of the civil servants became an occasion for the Court to specify that the Federal Republic was legally a continuation of the pre-1945 Reich in this area.

Other "immediately required" legislation concerned the welfare of expellees from the Oder–Neisse territories and the general problem of distributing the economic burdens of war and occupation, the legal framework of the social market economy, and the question of the debt and obligations of the pre-1945 Reich, including obligations to the victims of persecution during the Third Reich. The matters of war burdens, government and foreign debt, and reparations to surviving Jewish and other victims of the Hitler government, were all examples of matters where the new government consciously asserted both legal and moral continuity with the old Reich. The Bonn government emphasized continuity because it saw itself as the only legitimate German government, speaking for all Germans, and as the temporary warden of national identity, until a freely elected government of all Germans could conclude a peace treaty with Germany's former enemies. The claim of legitimacy made no sense if the Federal Republic were merely a newly-created government of part of Germany with no connection to the past. Adenauer and his ministers also recognized, however, that if they claimed the Federal Republic was the only true legal representative of the united German government which disappeared in 1945, they must also assume the moral burden of the consequences of the crimes committed under Hitler, and do what they could – and more – to make up for them.

All of these areas were extensively dealt with in the first legislative period of the new republic, which, highly atypical for a modern government, produced more laws and ordinances than any later period. In most cases, the Allied High Commission allowed the new government a great deal of flexibility. But in other areas, the influence of the Commission was more apparent – in foreign trade, the future of the Ruhr industrial area, political settlements with the new state's Western neighbors, and last but not least, the increasingly urgent but very sensitive issue of a West German contribution to the defense and security of Western Europe. Serious problems in any of these areas could have dramatically affected the delicate growth of German democracy. Instead, those problems that did emerge, were resolved between 1949 and 1955 in ways that strengthened that democracy and served the common interests of all Western Europeans.

The common denominator of the solutions was Adenauer's insistence that West Germany become an integral part of a political and economic alliance of the Western European democracies. With the help of his counterparts abroad, Adenauer's policies focused on achieving that integration, by adapting West German domestic policies to emerging European political, economic, and security concerns. In all three areas, but especially the first two, the military governments and the German authorities had done a great amount of preparatory work between 1947 and 1949. Decisions and the initiatives of the Bonn government were based on these preparations. In the areas of economic and political integration, the main decisions fell between 1949 and 1952, and in security and defense, between 1950 and 1954. The processes were mutually dependent: for West Germany to be secure against invasion the Germans had to convince their neighbors to let them contribute to the common defense; on the other hand they could only make that contribution if their economy was strong enough to permit it; and the freedom to develop that strength, in turn, depended on the conviction of Germany's allies that the Germans would not use their economic strength irresponsibly. Domestically, Adenauer needed the confidence of the German electorate, especially among those factions whose cooperation was necessary for growth and stability: labor unions, industrial leaders, and a myriad of other professional and interest groups, among which the churches and the expellees were the most important in the early years. The history of the first Adenauer government, from 1949 to 1953, is in large part the history of how, by great effort, the Germans, led by "der Alte," restored confidence in themselves, and earned, step by step, the respect of their neighbors.

# 3

# The Petersberg Agreement

The first step on the way was the Petersberg Agreement concluded between West Germany and the occupying powers on November 22, 1949. It set the terms for Germany's relationship with her allies far more precisely than the Occupation Statute had done. The Agreement was a legal agreement specifying the rights and prerogatives of the occupying powers; it was also, in a sense, the first international treaty signed with and by the new German government. It marked the first recognition of Germany's independence by her former enemies and set the framework for further progress on the road to sovereignty. It was the basic charter of West German foreign policy in its opening phase. It also inaugurated the close alignment of Bonn with Washington which became a permanent fixture of the emerging Western political, economic, and security system. Finally, by giving West German economic and business leaders clear signals that Germany would be welcome in the community of Europe, it permitted development of a consistent and coherent domestic economic policy which was essential if the new democracy were to survive.

Barely a week after the federal government had formally approved Bonn as the provisional seat of government, the foreign ministers of the three Western Allies met in Paris on November 9–10, 1949, to review the basic course of future Allied policy toward the new German state. In January 1949 Dean Acheson had replaced George C. Marshall as US Secretary of State, a post he held throughout the second Truman administration from 1949 to 1953; Ernest Bevin, although already suffering from the disease that killed him in April 1951, was still His Majesty's Foreign Secretary, and Robert Schuman continued to represent France.

On November 14–15, Acheson visited Bonn, the first foreign minister of any of the victorious powers to visit the new republic. He got along extremely well with Adenauer, who impressed him greatly and who explained his goals for Germany in detail. The goals, as Adenauer stated them, were to integrate Germany in Western Europe and to bury the old enmity between France and Germany. Acheson replied that these were American goals also. He left Bonn convinced that Adenauer deserved unconditional support and that the SPD, led by Schumacher, was not providing constructive opposition.

In the preamble to the Agreement, the signatories stated that its "primary objective is the incorporation of the Federal Republic as a peaceful member of the European community and to this end German association with the countries of Western Europe in all fields should be diligently pursued by means of her entry into the appropriate inter-national bodies and the exchange of commercial and consular represen-tation with other countries."[1] The main "international bodies" in question were the OEEC, in which the Federal Republic continued the Bizone's membership, and the Council of Europe. The latter was an assembly of representatives of governments of democratic European countries (ten at first, increasing to 21 by the 1980s), established in London on May 5, 1949, as an outgrowth of the United Europe Move-ment that developed between 1946 and 1948. The core members were the six signatories of the Brussels Pact, the European forerunner of the Atlantic Alliance, and the administrative offices of the Pact did the preparatory work for the conference at which the Council was founded. Its purpose was to promote peace, freedom, and economic and social progress in accordance with the ideals of the common European heritage. Winston Churchill, who played a great part in the United Europe Movement, had already stated publicly that he thought West Germany should be a member, and in fact the Council invited the Bonn government to discuss membership in March 1950.

Formally, the Petersberg Agreement was a response to letters Adenauer had written to the three Western foreign ministers, insisting on an end to dismantling, which was continuing and which was a source of irritation to the Germans. They could not understand why the Western Allies were encouraging economic reconstruction, while at the same time destroying jobs by dismantling factories. In fact, it was primarily the French who continued to advocate dismantling, since many in the French government were more skeptical than Schuman or Monnet, that new arrangements would prevent German economic power from becoming a threat in the future. In Paris Acheson told both Bevin and Schuman that, as far as the US was concerned, West Germany was now an ally against the Soviet Union – a statement that had far-reaching implications for eventual German contributions to

[1] Dept of State, *Documents on Germany*, 310.

Western defense, though this was an issue no one had yet dared to address in public. The conference recommended the establishment of quotas to limit German steel production and drastically reduced the number of plants still to be dismantled; in effect, dismantling of major plants came to an end, although minor dismantling continued into 1951. The limits on the number and size of ships that German shipyards could build were raised; a matter of great concern to the unions as well as to shipyard owners, all of whom were eager to see this vital pillar of German industry restored. The Agreement further specified that "the Federal Government affirms its resolve as a freely elected democratic body to pursue unreservedly the principles of freedom, tolerance and humanity which unite the nations of Western Europe."

West Germany was also to have its own consular service, the first step toward restoring its foreign ministry. More importantly, the Federal Republic would be required to cooperate with the newly established Military Security Board of the Allied High Commission, to plan for its own domestic security, and would be asked to participate in the Ruhr Authority. This last requirement so infuriated Schumacher, who saw in it an open example of collaboration with international capitalists who wanted to control German industry and ultimately remove it from German control, that, during a marathon night session of the Bundestag on November 24–25, he uttered his notorious denunciation of Adenauer as "the chancellor of the Allies."

The Agreement's position on security was ambiguous, as well it might be, since this question was already taking on a separate life of its own in the broader context of East–West relations in Europe. On the one hand, the Agreement stated that "the Federal Government ... declares its earnest determination to maintain the demilitarization of the Federal territory and to endeavour by all means ... to prevent the re-creation of armed forces of any kind;" but, on the other hand, it also noted that progress towards the objective of integrating Germany into the West depended "upon the re-establishment of a true sense of security in Western Europe."[2] Few outside the inner circles of power recognized as yet that these two principles – demilitarization of West Germany and Western security – were not complementary, but contradictory. One of these principles, therefore, would ultimately have to accommodate the other, and both Adenauer and his Western counterparts knew which one it would be.

[2] Ibid., 310–11.

# 4

# Economic Problems, the Schuman Plan, Co-Determination

The first great challenge was to balance the limited capacity of the population to pay for government expenditures, with the immense claims on the government's budget – for housing, for reconstruction aid, for administration, eventually for security and military forces as well. In 1950 total government expenditures amounted to 11.6 billion marks,[1] of which approximately 4.2 billion marks had to be paid as occupation costs – costs which were borne by the Germans – and which amounted to 36 per cent of the total federal budget. Thus, it was imperative that Adenauer's government undertake measures to stimulate economic growth and reduce unemployment. The method used was the one for which the majority of the Germans had voted, namely the social market economy, that Erhard hoped would work miracles. At the outset, in the autumn of 1949, the government devalued the German mark by 20 per cent to a level of 4.2 marks to the dollar. This followed a devaluation of 30 per cent of the British pound sterling, as well as other devaluations against the dollar. Had the federal government failed to follow suit, German business would have been much less competitive on the export markets during this critical phase of rebuilding, since German exports would have been relatively too expensive. Although necessary in the long term, the devaluation did not produce positive results immediately. In part this was because Germany was adversely effected by the general international recession in 1950. The recession led to a stagnation and a slow-down in West German reconstruction that coincided with the last wave of dismantling which took place at Allied order in 1950.

In addition, the effects of war and the expulsions from the Oder–Neisse territories placed demands on government services and aid that Adenauer's government had difficulty meeting, considering the limited

---

[1] Mitchell, ed., *European Historical Statistics*, 739.

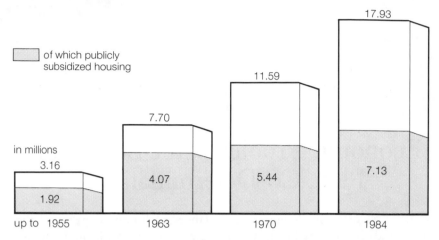

Figure 1.3    Housing unit construction, 1949–1984. In postwar Germany, one of the government's first priorities was to deal with the critical housing shortage. As these figures show, this problem took many years to solve.
*Source*: Press and Information Office, *Housing and Town Planning*

available financial resources. The most glaring such need, and the most complicated to meet quickly, was housing. In 1950, approximately 16 million households in the Federal Republic had 10.1 million housing units to share between them. In 1939 the territories that later became West Germany included 10.8 million housing units, of which 2.3 million were destroyed in the war; between 1945 and 1949 1.6 million had been constructed or minimally restored.

This was only half the problem. Many of those who did have housing in 1950 lived in squalid circumstances, under appalling conditions, frequently with no sanitation or running water and little or no light and heat. Over half of all units did have a gas range, but one-fifth had only coal stoves, and 15 per cent had no kitchen at all. Over two-thirds of all homeowners and "main renters" – persons who were not subleasing parts of a unit from someone else – had no living room, and in one of every ten households parents and children slept in one room. As for heating and plumbing, over 80 per cent of units had coal or, in some cases, kerosene stoves; but less than half had access to a bath, and 11 per cent had no indoor toilet. The young writer Heinrich Böll of Cologne, who published his first works around 1950, described the "living-kitchen stench" as a permanent component of German life in those years.[2]

[2]   Schwarz, *Die Ära Adenauer, 1949–1957*, 384.

The government acted as quickly as it could. On March 28, 1950, the Bundestag passed the Law on Public Housing Construction, which in 1950–7 stimulated the construction of over one million units. Even more important were generous tax incentives favoring investment and construction – rules that often irritated the SPD, whose leaders called them gifts to the capitalists. Ironically, it was thanks to this liberal investment climate that the unions themselves were able to establish, in 1951, a construction company, suitably named *Neue Heimat* or "New Home." Over the decades to come *Neue Heimat* became the largest construction company in Europe, employing over 200,000 people and responsible for over half of all housing in West Germany. The efforts of *Neue Heimat* and others produced 3.9 million housing units between 1950 and 1957, a rate of over half a million units a year, of which 25 per cent was public housing. Mainly because West Germany was now a very densely populated region and because individual home ownership had always been a luxury, most housing took the form of rental apartments in and around the major cities. Thus, the average German was a renter rather than a homeowner, which led to much greater political and legal emphasis on rent control and tenants' rights than in some other countries.

An equally serious problem, in addition to housing, was care of the unemployed and of war invalids or others who might want to work but could not. The bulk of the unemployed and destitute consisted of expellees. A German historian has estimated the total number of the needy in 1950 at close to 17 million;[3] the employed workforce was about 21.5 million. Although those employed were now being paid in sound currency, most wages were still extremely modest and many workers resented the sudden reappearance of obvious wealth and luxury which was also a consequence of the currency reform. Adenauer, Erhard, and their advisors knew that the social market economy in 1949 was engaged in a race with time. The system was not designed to produce immediate results in terms of rising wages. It was a medium-term strategy which, Erhard believed, promised far greater wealth and well-being for all, but not at once. It was his very good fortune, and it may have saved the system, that international conditions, in particular the Korean War, unleashed the full power of the West German economy much more rapidly than anyone was able to anticipate in 1949.

Economic uncertainty, rising unemployment, and continuing dismantling initially made Adenauer's government extremely unpopular. The percentage of those satisfied with the government was at its lowest ebb at any time before or after 1950; and fell by almost half from about

[3] Ibid., 83.

40 to 23 per cent. Had an election been held in 1950, it undoubtedly would have produced a large victory for the SPD. Direct unemployment was over two million in early 1950. At this early date, therefore, it appeared unlikely that economic recovery would take place soon, and few could imagine that it would happen at all.

It later appeared as a minor miracle that the German Trade Union Federation (DGB), successfully restrained its members in 1949–50 from wage demands that would have severely impaired the ability of business to invest its own resources, rather than relying on deficit spending by the government and state control of investment – a condition that was crucial for the success of the social market economy. As the unemployment figures grew, many even in the CDU began to question Adenauer's and Erhard's strategy. In North Rhine-Westphalia the CDU, under Karl Arnold as minister-president, had governed since 1947 in a "grand coalition" with the SPD. After the *Land* elections of February 1950, the CDU governed the *Land* alone, but Arnold had not forgotten the Christian socialism of the Ahlen Program. In June 1950 the CDU-dominated government drafted and approved a new constitution for the *Land* which called for state ownership of heavy industry and of any business "holding a monopoly position in the market."[4]

The federal government's efforts to develop the German economy coincided with the goals of the United Europe Movement, that aimed at political and economic integration. The Movement's advocates represented a broad political spectrum, but its concept and approach were much closer to the views of Adenauer, Dehler, Heuss and Erhard, than to those of Schumacher and leading social democrats, although they were shared by younger SPD members, such as Helmut Schmidt. The movement was strongest in Germany and in Italy, and also in smaller countries such as the Netherlands and Belgium, but was weak in Britain and especially in France.

At the time of the Petersberg Agreement, the majority of the French political elite still operated on the premise that Germany should not be allowed to regain economic strength. Only a minority, including Robert Schuman, the foreign minister, saw the value of a strong democratic Germany and recognized that Western Europe could not survive without it. Schuman was from Lorraine and had been a German citizen until that territory returned to France in 1919. Like Adenauer, therefore, he was raised in that geographical area of German-French interaction that has been so important in European history.

In mid-1948, when the London Conference approved the formation of a West German state, the French government revised its earlier

---

[4] Ibid., 85.

insistence on permanent partition of Germany and French control of the Ruhr industries. The London Conference, therefore, established an International Ruhr Authority, which existed from 1948 through 1951. Schuman believed, however, that there was a better alternative, which did not entail the risk of provoking the type of nationalistic and protectionistic reaction in Germany, of which Schumacher's attack on Adenauer was an example. His concept was to develop a mechanism for Franco-German economic cooperation in production and allocation of coal and steel. In March 1949, he told Clay that "France was no longer interested in elaborate controls and control boards over the German economy ... which the London Conference had laboured so long to include in the preliminary versions of the Occupation Statute. French interest was now, Schuman indicated, more in the general principles by which French and German economic recovery might be harmonized."[5]

Schuman had learned to take this positive view of reconciliation with Germany from Jean Monnet, the true architect of postwar European political and economic integration. As early as the end of World War I Monnet had worked to bring about a European political and economic system based on giving each member state a stake in cooperation rather than confrontation. He failed in the 1920s to overcome the French politicians' inherited fears of Germany; fears that provoked resentment in Germany and thus helped Hitler to power. After World War II, in a much more difficult geopolitical and strategic situation, with the Red Army in control of Central Europe including half of Germany, Monnet tried once again to rally the forces of common sense in the West. This time, he succeeded; so well, indeed, that 40 years later Europe remained at peace.

During 1949–50, Monnet and Schuman developed their plan to accomplish the first steps toward integration. Monnet was a modest man, and another plan, namely the domestic French economic and industrial policy plan, already bore his name. Therefore the new design for international cooperation came to be called the Schuman Plan. Schuman himself announced it in Paris, in a very low-key manner, on May 9, 1950. The Schuman Plan foresaw "that the entire French-German production of coal and steel be placed under a joint High Authority, within an organization open to the participation of other European nations ... this proposal will create the first concrete foundation for a European federation which is so indispensable for the preservation of peace."[6] It was a brilliant and simple concept that Adenauer recognized would contribute, in a fundamental way, toward

[5] Milward, *Reconstruction of Western Europe*, 381.
[6] Ibid., 397.

making West Germany a partner instead of a pariah. In his *Memoirs* Adenauer recalled a personal letter from Schuman hand-delivered to him on May 8. Adenauer recognized

> that the purpose of his [Schuman's] proposal was not economic, but eminently political. In France there was a fear that once Germany had recovered, she would attack France. He could imagine that the corresponding fears might be present in Germany. Rearmament always showed first in an increased production of coal, iron and steel. If any organization such as he was proposing were to be set up it would enable each country to detect the first signs of rearmament, and would have an extraordinarily calming effect in France.
>
> Schuman's plan corresponded entirely with the ideas I had been advocating for a long time concerning the integration of the key industries of Europe. I informed Robert Schuman at once that I accepted his proposal whole-heartedly.[7]

This was a long way from the high ambitions of the United Europe Movement of 1946–8. On the other hand, no one had been able or willing to transform those ambitions into real policy. Here, for the first time, a leading European statesman was prepared to surrender national autonomy over a vital sector of industry to an international authority. It was an unprecedented step, particularly coming from France, which had a long tradition of protection of its heavy industry. Moreover, "after the disillusionment of the return of familiar national governmental figures and systems, after the worse disillusionments of 1947 with the division of Europe and the Cold War, after the failure once more to produce any real promise of a settlement acceptable to Germany, after the failure of pressure groups for European unity, Schuman specifically linked the settlement with Germany to the hope of a united Europe."[8]

The countries that became known as "The Six" – France, West Germany, Italy, and the Benelux countries – discussed the Plan in 1950–1, against the background of growing worries about West Germany's economy. Apart from the problems of housing and help for the destitute, Adenauer's government faced the problem of paying for the imports West Germany needed for reconstruction. Related to this was the problem of West German responsibility for public and private German foreign debt incurred prior to 1945. Since 1947, but especially since the London Conference and the official start of the ERP in early 1948, the US had been pushing for a European Payments Union (EPU), a multilateral clearing agency for trade within Western Europe and between Europe and the US funded by a combination of US support and contributions from those European countries who enjoyed sur-

[7] Adenauer, *Memoirs 1945–1953*, 257.
[8] Milward, *Reconstruction of Western Europe*, 397–8.

pluses on their foreign trade balances. In turn, the EPU would advance short-term credit to countries with deficits, as it did to West Germany for the first and last time in 1950–1. The United States hoped that the EPU, along with the OEEC, would not only supervise and encourage trade, but would be a forerunner of full European political integration. Within that overarching program, the task of the EPU, in the American view, was to integrate the British-dominated trade area with the emerging continental trade area. Once this was done, the EPU would bring about a currency union, abolishing national currencies and creating a genuine common market.

Few Europeans were excited by this grand scheme, and talks about the EPU dragged on desultorily until Schuman proposed his plan in May 1950. Once it was clear that the future of the continental economies would be based on a Franco-German common market in coal and steel, the British became willing to join the EPU if the latter were strictly limited to being a multilateral clearing agency, but without any authority to bring about a currency union, much less to act as a vehicle for political unification. With these restrictions the OEEC countries formally established the EPU on September 19, 1950.

The autumn of 1950 was a moment of crisis for the West German economy. Almost as soon as the EPU officially came into being, Erhard had to acknowledge that West Germany had already spent all of its allotted credit on imports, mainly for food and supplies for industry, and he was forced to ask the International Monetary Fund (IMF), created at the Bretton Woods Conference toward the end of the war, for a special loan. Many critics of Erhard's economic ideas saw the crisis of 1949–50 as proof that free enterprise capitalism was unworkable. The early years of the Federal Republic saw a lively economic debate between believers in the social market economy, and spokesmen for various Christian socialist ideas, but within a parliamentary framework which did not bring the enemies of the social market economy to power. Erhard himself writes about this period:

The CDU meeting in Goslar on October 22, 1950, at the height of the Korean boom, offered me a welcome opportunity to speak openly about the problems of the day. It was at a time when opinion seemed resigned to the ruin of West Germany ... Opposition at home joined with international criticism ... With prices rising day by day, and the foreign trade balance becoming ever more unfavourable, to speak of such things was only possible through a deep conviction that the market economy was right. It still took months before the change became apparent, but this turn towards salvation was, as a result, all the more positive and lasting.[9]

[9] Erhard, *Prosperity through Competition*, 45–6.

During the fall and early winter of 1950–1 many West Germans were discouraged by the apparently insurmountable problem of trade deficits that effectively stopped economic growth at home by diverting output that was essential not only for future exports, but for acutely needed domestic reconstruction. The turnaround, however, was at hand, aided by the Korean War that had begun when the communist regime of North Korea attacked South Korea on June 25, 1950.

The Korean War decisively affected West Germany's economic and political future. It indicated to Western leaders that communist regimes might go to war to achieve their aims. What the communists had done in Korea, many reasoned, was also conceivable in Germany, especially if West Germany were undefended. Therefore, the Korean War led directly to the initial planning for a West German contribution to Western European defense. It also saved the West German economy by generating an insatiable demand throughout the Western world for precisely the kind of industrial products that West Germany was permitted and encouraged to produce under agreements in force and under discussion: the Ruhr Statute, the ERP agreements, the Petersberg Agreement, and the Schuman Plan. When the governments of the United States and Western Europe began an intense program of re-armament, great demands were placed on their industrial capacity. They needed not only steel, including German steel, but also many products, including machinery and chemicals, that only Germany, because it was forbidden to produce armaments, could deliver in large quantities. From the fall of 1950 onward, the world market price of steel and other commodities shot up, which directly benefited Germany. Beginning in February 1951, foreign currency began flowing into, instead of out of, West Germany. By May the IMF loan and the EPU credit were repaid; by mid-year West German employers and the unions within the DGB arrived at wage agreements that, for the first time since 1948, offered workers substantial pay increases. (It should be noted that the DGB itself was not empowered to negotiate wage agreements; these were concluded by the individual labor unions.)

The workers in the coal and steel industries had another reason to look to the future with confidence in early 1951, and that was the agreement on co-determination in the iron and steel industry reached by Adenauer and the head of the DGB, Hans Böckler, in January of that year. It was Böckler's last public triumph (he died at age 76, in February). During the formative phase of the Federal Republic in 1947–9, the DGB had downplayed demands for complete socialization of assets, demands that were nearly universal among unionists from 1945 to 1947, but had continued to insist on universal co-determination by labor and employers, in the management of German business. The unions held fast to the social democratic argument that economic progress required a large measure of union influence in economic planning. The unions demanded that Adenauer establish, with them, a Federal Economic Council, to influence policy in all important social and economic areas. They also demanded parity of representation with employers in the IHKs (the Chambers of Industry and Commerce), as well as co-determination on the boards of individual firms above a certain size. And the unions had considerable public support, which included some CDU leaders like Karl Arnold, Gustav Heinemann, or Jakob Kaiser. The Katholikentag of 1949, held in Bochum, and the Evangelischer Kirchentag of 1950, held in Essen, also issued statements in support of universal co-determination.

The economic problems of 1950 fueled the fire of the union demands, and in the fall many expected a dramatic confrontation between the unions and the government over the issue. On January 3, 1951, the *Betriebsräte* (union councils in individual plants) of the powerful steel-workers' union, the IG Metall *(Industriegewerkschaft Metall)*, called a strike of all its members. But in fact, a solution was already on the way. Adenauer and Böckler were no ideologues; they had, moreover, known each other since the 1920s and each respected the other as a man deeply concerned with what was best for Germany as a whole. Adenauer could point to the fact that Germany was not yet the master of its own policies; universal co-determination might well founder on Allied High Commission objections. Böckler, for his part, was not interested in a bitter confrontation; he also knew that the best guarantee of peace in industrial relations was economic growth, and he was enough of a realist to know that universal co-determination was not likely to engender enthusiasm for investment in German industry. He did insist, however, that co-determination in the steel industry, which the British military government and Böckler himself had introduced in 1947, be maintained and extended to include the coal industry. In addition, the question of German rearmament also played a part. Adenauer genuinely wanted to win the support of the DGB and, if possible, of the SPD, for a German contribution to Western Europe's defense. An anecdote has it that Adenauer asked Böckler during their talks: "Will the DGB support the creation of a new army?", to which Böckler replied at once: "Will the government pass the Metalworkers' co-determination bill?"[10] The result was a compromise. Adenauer proposed parity of representation on the boards of the relevant companies to be limited, however, by reserving the power of final decision in case of disagreement to the owners. Böckler gave in on this point. Adenauer was thus able to announce an

[10] Cited in Cioc, *Pax Atomica*, 17–18.

agreement on January 25, 1951. It affected 800,000 workers in the two vital heavy industries of West Germany, coal and steel, and provided a climate of industrial peace that proved permanent.

The Bundestag passed the required Law on Co-determination in the Iron and Steel-Producing Industries on April 10, 1951. Just over a week later another chapter in the early history of West Germany ended. While West Germany battled its way through the payment crisis, the struggle over co-determination, and the first stages of the economic boom, the Six completed their talks on the form and substance of the Schuman Plan. They established the ECSC on April 18, 1951, without Britain, whose government declined an invitation to join; and Adenauer paid his first visit abroad as chancellor to Paris to sign the treaty for Germany. For France and West Germany this agreement fulfilled many of the functions of a peace treaty. It was successful because it was not an over-ambitious design for a political union that no one really wanted, but was "firmly based, as much as any previous European peace treaty, on the real interests of the nation states which signed it."[11] It was a courageous decision, and in retrospect a momentous one. But it was not greeted throughout West Germany with the same hopes and enthusiasm that Adenauer held:

The Franco-German association which it created was in many respects a shotgun wedding. The German bride, although her other choices were not very enticing, had nevertheless to be dragged protesting by her aged father [Adenauer] to the altar while numerous members of her family staged noisy protests on the way and an equally large number of the bridegroom's friends and relations prophesied disaster. Yet the knot once tied, this surprising union soon settled into a safe bourgeois marriage in which the couple, rapidly becoming wealthy and comfortable as passions cooled, were held together, as such couples are, by the strong links of managing their complex joint economic affairs. To all those associated with the marriage and brought into the house the same bourgeois prosperity was vouchsafed. The United Kingdom was left in the position of a prim spinster who, having earlier rejected the bridegroom because of the lack of promise of his stormy adolescence, was later allowed into the household on not very flattering terms as a rather acidulous baby-sitter. If she leaves it will not make much difference, except to her. But if the marriage breaks up it will be the end of the peace settlement and perhaps of us all.[12]

Among the "noisy protests" were Kurt Schumacher's attacks on the ECSC as a capitalist conspiracy, a "Europe Inc.," to consolidate employer and government power against the rights of organized workers. But in fact, since all of continental Europe had an insatiable

[11]  Milward, *Reconstruction of Western Europe*, 420.
[12]  Ibid.

appetite for coal and steel for the next several years, the ECSC presided over fast growing production and productivity and, therefore, over considerable real increases in the workers' well-being.

The ECSC agreement gradually abolished all duties, limitations of quantity, and double pricing, which restricted export of (mostly German) coal and steel to the other member countries. These trade barriers were the expressions of political and economic fears and rivalries, chiefly French fears of Germany. The ECSC was a major breakthrough in ending those rivalries and turning the productive power of a revived German heavy industry to the benefit of a majority of West Europeans. It was the first step of any genuine significance toward integration, and it gave scope to Adenauer's policies which had been based on hopes and concern, but which now had actual basis in fact. This action removed "one of the greatest psychological barriers" to the eventual rapprochement between France and Germany.[13]

By 1953 economic recovery was clearly visible and assured the virtually uncontested dominance of Erhard's economic ideas in practice until the mid-1960s. The basic operating principles of those ideas were: (1) a conservative fiscal policy rather than artificial stimulation of demand in the interest of full employment; (2) the greatest possible liberalization of export and domestic trade instead of economic planning; and (3) a rejection of short-term relief in favor of long-term construction of the basic means of industrial production. The fact that the German mark was healthy and the government was committed to currency stability, provided the indispensable assurance – *Kalkulierbarkeit* – that German industry could depend without question on the stability of the currency, and therefore, unlike the period from 1945 to 1949, could pursue long-term planning and set long-term economic goals.

---

[13] Office of US High Commissioner, *3rd Quarterly Report* (1950), 18.

# 5

# First Steps towards Armed Forces

One of the prerogatives of a sovereign state is the right to defend its territory and to raise armed forces for that purpose, as it sees fit. West Germany clearly did not enjoy that prerogative in 1949, and for some years thereafter there were many people, both within Germany and abroad, who believed that it never should enjoy it; that the demilitarization of Germany was required formally by the Potsdam Protocol and morally by Germany's abuse of military power to attack its neighbors in two world wars. However, events in the wider world outside West Germany gradually convinced the Allied governments and, eventually, the majority of citizens of both West Germany and of the occupying powers, that it would be in the interest of all the democracies if West Germany were to be permitted to contribute, in some form, to the defense of Western Europe. These events included the final end, following the Moscow foreign ministers' conference of March 1947, of illusions that the East–West wartime alliance could continue; the communist coup in Czechoslovakia in 1948 that consolidated Soviet power in East Central Europe; the Berlin blockade; and most decisively, the Korean War. These developments led the American and European governments to regard Stalin's Soviet Union as a direct military and political threat to peace, freedom, and recovery in Western Europe. In addition, however, the Bonn republic faced a special problem, namely, the growing military power of the communist German regime in the Soviet zone, which since October 1949 called itself the "German Democratic Republic" – though, as many people pointed out, it was neither democratic nor a republic, whereas its claim to being German was at best loaded with irony.

From 1946 to the Berlin blockade, the US did not expect to defend any part of the European continent against Soviet attack. American planners assumed that the Soviet Union was engaged in expanding its influence politically and diplomatically and would not risk open war. If the Soviets did attack, however, the US did not have the resources to hold any position on the continent following its demobilization. In the event of war, American planning initially foresaw withdrawal to Britain and bases outside Europe.[1]

The Berlin crisis spurred a fundamental revision in American strategic thought. For the first time, the US government declared its official belief that "Soviet domination of the potential power of Eurasia, whether achieved by armed aggression or by political subversive means, would be strategically and politically unacceptable to the United States."[2] This meant that the US was now determined to enter actively, rather than passively, into the diplomatic and military struggle for Europe. The US would seek to hinder Soviet political and ideological encroachment by any means available, and would deploy its resources, in particular military forces, in Europe to deter and, if necessary, defeat a Soviet attack.

In the spring of 1949, Dwight D. Eisenhower, as chairman of the Joint Chiefs of Staff and special adviser to the president, ordered his aides to prepare plans for the defense of Europe. Since the resources and troops available were no greater than they were the year before, when the only existing war plan called for evacuation, the conceptual revolution in strategic thought remained an idea that only slowly took concrete form and substance. American occupation forces therefore were committed initially to fight a delaying action on the Rhine before being evacuated to Britain and the Mediterranean. There was one big difference between this concept of 1949 and its predecessor. Under the new policy, a new war would not end with American retreat and Soviet control of Europe. Rather, the Americans accepted an obligation to continue the war and to return to help win it in Europe, as they had done in 1917 and 1944.

While these plans were being made, the West Europeans had attempted to establish their own deterrent in the hope that this would encourage the US to take a more active role in the defense of Europe. The Brussels Pact governments proposed in 1948 to mount a defense on the Rhine in case of Soviet attack, but at first did not receive great encouragement from the US.

When NATO came into being in April 1949 as an alliance between the US and Western Europe, it inherited both the Brussels Pact plan for a Rhine defense and the emerging American plan for a temporary stand on the Rhine to be followed by retreat to bridgeheads on the Atlantic.

---

[1] Greiner, "The Defence of Western Europe," in *Western Security*, ed. Riste, 150–1.

[2] Cited ibid., 151.

The two schemes were incompatible. The Brussels Pact plan required more divisions than anyone expected NATO to have for many years, if ever, but on the other hand no European continental government could be expected to accept what the American plans implied, namely that its territory could be quickly abandoned to the Soviet Union.

The only alternatives that could satisfy both the Europeans and the Americans were to reinforce the existing forces of the West European NATO members; to increase the number of US troops in Europe; and to find new sources of strength.[3] The last point meant – and could only mean – to draw on German resources and to include West Germany in the Western defense system. In early 1950, few political leaders dared mention this possibility publicly. The Korean War and the perceived threat of imminent Soviet attack in Europe from the summer of 1950 on radically changed public perception and opinion.

As for the Germans themselves, the lingering effects of the Berlin blockade and the threat of armed forces in the Soviet zone generated a climate, in 1950, in which consideration of an eventual role for West Germany in Western Europe's defense alliance was, at least, conceivable, if not enthusiastic. The starting signal for this consideration in NATO circles was Acheson's remark to Bevin and Schuman at the Paris conference in November 1949, that the US regarded West Germany as an ally against the Soviet Union. The Schuman Plan of May 1950, while it did not deal with security matters, implied a sovereign Federal Republic as a partner. Finally, the Korean War, that began in June, soon convinced virtually all Western leaders that West Germany must cease being an occupied territory relying exclusively on foreign troops for its security, and become an ally.

Within West Germany Adenauer had, confidentially, discussed defense and rearmament for some time. He had no personal brief for a West German army: he was an anti-militarist to the bone and would certainly have preferred to avoid the expense and political consternation that German rearmament would surely generate. On the other hand, he believed not only that West Germany would be defenseless unless it made its own contribution, but also that a West German army was essential to Western Allied security in Europe and would, thus, provide leverage that West Germany could use in obtaining sovereignty. West Germany had something its neigbors needed: manpower and resources. The question was how to make use of this advantage to earn West Germany the recognition and the sovereignty that Adenauer, and with him most Germans, sought.

His approach was simple. The first step was to persuade the Western

---

[3] Ibid., 157.

Allies that their security interests required them to defend West Germany. The second step was to convince them that, like it or not, they needed the participation of German defense forces. The third step, and in many ways the most taxing, was to gain support for a West German defense contribution within the Federal Republic, and then to offer it on any reasonable terms that would tend to promote the integration and political unification of Western Europe.

Adenauer prepared the first step by carefully and quietly seeking expert advice, provided by respected political and military experts, concerning threats to West German security, and concerning West Germany's potential defense resources. Obtaining such evaluations was not a problem. As Hans-Peter Schwarz pointed out, "There was, after all, a good deal of military expertise about in the land" after 1945 in the shape of numerous former Wehrmacht generals. Adenauer merely needed to be certain that he called on the advice of respected military officers – men who were loyal to the new democracy, who did not have a nationalistic agenda, who were pro-Western, whose motives in recommending West German defense were not suspect, and who had conducted themselves with honor and dignity during the Third Reich.

One such general was Dr Hans Speidel (1897–1982), a rare combination of professional soldier and philosopher. Speidel had been German military attaché in Paris in the 1930s and spoke perfect French. During the war he became chief of staff to Field Marshal Erwin Rommel, in Army Group B in France in 1943–4, and was involved in the attempt to assassinate Hitler in July 1944. His hopes for the future of Germany and Europe coincided exactly with Adenauer's: he wanted to make reconciliation and alliance with France the cornerstone of West German integration into the democratic community of Europe. At the same time, he saw a dangerous threat in the Soviet Union and its policies in Central Europe, and considered defense against it essential, in cooperation with the Western powers.

From June 1948 to early 1949, Speidel, in collaboration with another former Wehrmacht general, Adolf Heusinger, wrote a series of papers arguing that the new German government must think seriously about its own and Europe's military security. The first paper was entitled "The Security of Western Europe." In it, Speidel argued that West German security was a concern for all of Europe. To abandon German territory at the outset of war was a bad idea not just for the Germans, but especially for the rest of Europe and for America. West Germany was a "bastion" that the Europeans should be willing to defend in their own interest. In other words, Speidel equated German security with that of Europe. In the interests of that security, he concluded, "the German authorities should make the appropriate demands on the Power which had not only the greatest interest in but also the sole means of fulfilling them, namely the United States."[4]

In a later memorandum of December 1948, which he addressed specifically to Adenauer as the president of the Parliamentary Council and thus the likely head of the future German government, Speidel concluded that without a German defense effort the East – the Soviet Union and the East German communist regime – enjoyed a vast superiority of 36 Soviet divisions plus the 70,000 "barracked People's Police" (*Kasernierte Volkspolizei*, KVP) in the Soviet zone. Shortly thereafter, in January 1949, Adenauer for the first time mentioned the idea of a German defense contribution in public. He was speaking in general terms about European security and said that he thought a common European army would promote European political unification, and that such an army might benefit from German contingents.

Thus, by the end of 1948, Speidel and his associates had sketched the outlines of a German security concept. The basic axiom of that concept was that to protect Western Europe one must protect West Germany. The Europeans alone were not strong enough to protect Germany. Therefore, the concept required an American security guarantee. More daringly, in the December memorandum Speidel raised the question of a German contribution. He did this indirectly, by writing that German representatives in any security talks which might take place with the Americans or the Brussels Pact states must "put forward proposals . . . for self-defense or a contribution to the defense of the heart of Europe."[5]

In Speidel's mind at least, events now moved quickly. In the December memorandum, he had recommended creating 15 German army divisions at once, to be equipped with American weapons. In a further memorandum of April 1949, the same month the Atlantic Treaty was signed in Washington, Speidel and Heusinger criticized other German experts who feared Soviet reactions, especially in the Soviet zone, if West Germany was associated closely with NATO. He repeated his point that West German security was inseparable from European security and went on to point out that this logically meant that the West Germans could impose "conditions" on their defense cooperation. The two most important such conditions were complete political and military equality with the other European states, and full membership in NATO.

Adenauer received Speidel's papers favorably and incorporated them both in his own emerging foreign policy strategy and in the official position of the CDU/CSU. He looked beyond the strategic and tactical

---

[4] Ibid., 162.
[5] Cited ibid., 164.

debates about troop strength and defensive lines to the political core of the problem. Accepting fully Speidel's point that German and European security interests were the same, Adenauer envisioned a NATO including Germany as the best and only deterrent to war.

Until mid-1950 few German public figures apart from Adenauer and Speidel and their immediate associates thought intensely about security matters. The Basic Law, the first elections, the hectic legislative agenda, and the economic problems of 1949–50 overshadowed the issues of defense. Following the Petersberg Agreement, however, Adenauer began to speak more freely about the defense of Europe. In an interview with the *Cleveland Plain Dealer*, an American newspaper in Ohio, well-known in the US but not in Europe, he made his first unambiguous offer to provide German contingents as part of a common European army. This approach – that the West German contribution should be part of a common European defense and not an independent national force – became Adenauer's basic public position which he held until events finally overtook it in 1954. He believed, probably rightly, that it was the only way to open discussion on German rearmament that would be even minimally palatable to the French, or to the other powerful constituencies inside and outside West Germany that were hostile to any German military effort.

The Allied powers began to address the same concerns in the winter of 1949–50. In November of 1949, Clay, the former US military governor, and Bernard Montgomery, the British field marshal and victor of Alamein, wrote a joint article arguing that a German contribution was essential to Western security. On December 16, the *New York Times* reported that the US Joint Chiefs of Staff (JCS) had discussed a proposal to call up five German divisions (about 60,000 men) to help defend West German territory under NATO command. On March 16, 1950, Winston Churchill, who was one of the first and most convincing proponents of West German political and military integration into Western Europe, called in the House of Commons for a West German contribution to European defense. At the same time, Adenauer remained concerned with Soviet military strength in Central Europe. He considered it possible that Stalin would announce that, with the establishment of the GDR, the war was officially over, that the Soviet Union would sign an official peace treaty with the GDR, and then ostentatiously propose to the Western powers that all four powers withdraw from Germany. Adenauer was also concerned with isolationist sentiment in the US. He knew that the British and French governments did not have the means to defend Germany without American support, and that therefore a Soviet proposal to withdraw all Allied forces from Germany might be attractive in the West. If this possibility became reality, West Germany, free of Western Allied troops, would face 70,000 East German soldiers, the KVP, which he called a "civil war army." Although described officially as a police force designed to protect the socialist GDR state from attack, the KVP was in fact a fully armed military force, divided into three services. As the extent of rearmament in the GDR became clear in West Germany, leading figures in Bonn no longer viewed the GDR as merely a territory to be liberated, but began instead to regard it as a possible threat.

The first six months of 1950, just prior to the Korean War, were full of ambiguous signals. Officially, the Allied High Commission opposed a resurgence of militarism in Germany, as well as German rearmament, the latter as late as June 1, 1950. But privately the US and British governments, although emphatically not the French, had already agreed that some form of West German defense contribution was necessary if West Germany were to be secure against the threat of a Soviet attack. In May, both governments suggested to Adenauer that he establish a confidential working group of military experts to advise him on the issue. The British proposed that he name former General Schwerin, like Speidel a military officer who had opposed Hitler, to be his main advisor on military issues.

The American government recommended Reinhard Gehlen (1902–1979), who had been in charge of military intelligence on the Eastern front and who had, in that capacity, built up a vast network of informants behind the Soviet lines who provided him with information about Soviet troop movements, but also about Soviet behavior and policies generally in the territories they occupied. In late 1946, when the Cold War with the Soviet Union seemed inevitable, the Americans asked Gehlen to begin supplying them with intelligence from Soviet-held areas. Now, in the spring of 1950, the Americans hoped that they could attach Gehlen to Adenauer, thereby providing Adenauer with a fully functioning foreign intelligence agency, while at the same time maintaining their own links to Gehlen and thus also to the top of the West German government.[6] Adenauer decided that choosing Gehlen to be his military advisor was too risky, given Gehlen's past. He therefore chose Schwerin. Gehlen continued to run his semi-official "Gehlen Organization" for the US until, in 1956, it was transferred to the Bonn government.

The Korean War caused a veritable explosion of discussion concerning German rearmament and European security, in Germany and Europe as well as in the United States. On July 11, 1950, Charles de Gaulle stated that German rearmament was inevitable. On July 28, the Allied High Commission approved the formation of a 12,000–man

[6]  See Gehlen, *Der Dienst* and *Verschlusssache*.

barracked police force in the Federal Republic. On August 11, an advisory assembly of all the members of the Council of Europe called for a European army to include German forces.

The following weeks marked the crucial turning-point on the issue of principle: German soldiers or no German soldiers. In mid-August analysts at the US State Department issued a position paper entitled "Establishment of a European Defense Force," in which they recommended a European army including West German contingents.[7] The State Department's policy planners had hitherto been opposed to West German armament and remained committed to German demilitarization for longer than any other Allied agency. Their turnabout in the August paper, spurred no doubt by the Korean War, marked the final end of the official Potsdam policy of demilitarization and the opening of a new era – that of the German contribution to Western security vis-à-vis the Soviet Union.

In Germany, however, discussion of rearmament was understandably highly emotional; indeed, there were still German soldiers held as prisoners of war in the Soviet Union. An opinion poll showed over two-thirds of the population opposed. But many German leaders recognized that the Federal Republic could not enjoy the luxury of remaining defenseless in Central Europe. One who helped Adenauer immeasurably in convincing a vital segment of public opinion that morality might require, not forbid, the West Germans to defend themselves was Cardinal Frings of Cologne. In July 1950, shortly after the outbreak of the Korean War, he gave a sermon in Bonn that turned out to be a crucial step toward gaining sufficient public support for a policy of military defense. Frings deliberately countered the arguments for pacifism propagated by left-wing Catholics. The pacifists argued that war or planning for war neither could nor should play a role in the peaceful socialist society of the future. Germany should reject both Soviet socialism and American capitalism and should not succumb to American anti-communism by joining NATO, which the pacifists regarded as an aggressive force directed against the East. In particular, Germans should not undertake planning for war, for that would lead, not to security against attack from without, but to dictatorship at home. This would, so they asserted, occur because remilitarization would strengthen anti-democratic forces that might easily overwhelm the fragile German democracy.

In his sermon, Frings boldly stated the traditional Catholic tenets of the theory of a just war, as recently revised by the pope in the light of the

[7] Wiggershaus, "The Decision for a West German Defence Contribution," in *Western Security*, ed. Riste, 202–3.

experience of total war and of the atomic bomb. "States or alliances of states," he declared, had both the right and the duty to restore peaceful order if that order were threatened or attacked. "Self-seeking neutrality" in the face of such attack on oneself or others was "irresponsible." Neither states nor people should use the catastrophic effects of modern war as an excuse to tolerate injustice. Rather, states had the duty to wage war against threats to the divinely sanctioned order. Therefore, also, conscientious objection was immoral and incompatible with Christian thinking.[8]

The Korean War provided Adenauer the opportunity to take the initiative toward regaining sovereignty, if he made a bold move to offer a German contribution to European defense while demanding an end to the occupation regime as a quid pro quo. He felt confident that, despite criticism and opposition, the SPD would support him: Schumacher was anything but a pacifist, and he despised and feared communism.

The Korean War and the State Department paper prepared the ground for the critical turning point on the road to the *Bundeswehr* and German inclusion in the Western defense system. Again it was Adenauer who seized the initiative. He knew that McCloy, the US High Commissioner, was leaving on August 30 for a very important meeting: a conference of the three Western foreign ministers in New York, at which the future of Germany was to be one of the main topics. Adenauer decided to make a dramatic offer. The US liaison officer to the federal German government, Charles W. Thayer, later described how that offer was conveyed in a passage that parenthetically illustrates how small and rural the Bonn of 1950 still was:

It was a warm summer afternoon in 1950. A shepherd was driving his flock past the windows of the Liaison Office in Bonn, cracking his whip noisily but harmlessly at the stragglers. It was all beautifully bucolic. Except for the shepherd Bonn was asleep. I was about to close up shop and go partridge shooting in the beetfields across the Rhine when the telephone rang. It was the Chancellor's alter ego, Herbert Blankenhorn. The Old Man was drafting a letter for McCloy to take to the Foreign Ministers' Conference in New York, he told me. It was an offer to raise twelve German divisions as a contribution to Europe's joint defense.

"But McCloy's flying from Frankfurt at dawn," I said.

"That's the hitch," Blankenhorn answered. "We've got to have the letter ready before he takes off."

Ordinarily governments don't ask foreign diplomats to help them with their letter writing but by then I knew Bonn was no ordinary government. Besides, at that critical moment in the Korean War an offer of twelve divisions was not to be brushed lightly aside. I hung up and with a wistful look at my shotgun

---

[8] Paraphrased in Doering-Manteuffel, *Katholizismus und Wiederbewaffnung*, 85.

hurried over to the Chancellery. With a crew of stenographers and translators Blankenhorn and I went over the letter, redrafting, editing, translating and checking. Occasionally the Old Man himself came in to lend a hand. In the early hours of the morning a special courier raced down the Autobahn to the airport whence McCloy was taking off.

That night, only five years after the most dangerous German Army in all history had been laid low, another German Army was born.

"We'll have the divisions ready in six months," Blankenhorn told me. He reckoned without his compatriots. It was in fact six years before the first German put on a uniform.[9]

Adenauer's package to McCloy consisted of two memoranda prepared secretly in the *Bundeskanzleramt*, without the knowledge of the cabinet or the Bundestag. The first dealt with "Securing the Federal Territory Against Domestic and Foreign Threats." It cited the formation of the KVP and argued that the Soviet forces in Germany were militarily prepared for war, whereas the Americans and the British each had only four divisions in West Germany. He repeated his earlier request to the Allied High Commission that the Allies reinforce their own forces and requested permission to form a federal police force to provide protection against possible domestic subversion. Concerning Europe, the critical passage read as follows: "The federal chancellor has furthermore repeatedly stated that he is ready to provide a contribution in the form of a German contingent, in case an international West European army is established. In doing so the federal chancellor has also made it clear that he rejects a remilitarization of Germany in the shape of a national military force."[10] This conclusion reflected Adenauer's earlier statements as well as Churchill's views, and rejected the alternative of establishing a German military force under NATO. The exact contents of the memorandum remained secret until 1977, although the general tenor became known quickly and caused an uproar in West Germany. Schumacher's reaction was that promising German soldiers was serious enough, but at least Adenauer could have insisted that they be under German command and not subject to the command and policies of the Americans or the French!

The second memorandum, on "Reordering Relations between the Federal Republic and the Occupying Powers," called for a revision of the Occupation Statute, for full sovereignty for West Germany in foreign and domestic policy apart from defense, for an official end to the state of war existing between the Western powers and Germany, and for the occupation forces to become protective forces defending

---

[9] Thayer, *Unquiet Germans,* 223–4.
[10] Schwarz, *Die Ära Adenauer, 1949—1957,* 116.

West Germany. He pointed to the "reintegration of Germany into the European community," as illustrated by discussions on the Schuman Plan and on membership in the Council of Europe, and continued:

In addition, the participation of the Federal Republic in the common defense of Western Europe has recently been the subject of an increasing measure of discussion in the Allied countries. If the German population is to fulfill, within the framework of the European community, the duties it may encounter as a result of the present situation and its particular dangers, it must be psychologically prepared for such a task. The German people must be given such freedom of action and responsibility so that fulfilling these duties will make sense. If Germans are to make sacrifices of every kind, then the road to freedom must be open to them just as it is to all other Western European peoples.[11]

Three days before the foreign ministers' conference was due to begin, on September 9, President Truman responded to Adenauer's offer by approving immediate preparations for West German armed forces within the NATO framework. At the same time, the president publicly confirmed that the revolution in American strategic thinking about Europe that began during the Berlin crisis was a completed fact, by declaring that the US would reinforce its troops in Europe. Truman's decision also helped to nudge France in the direction of supporting creation of a German contribution to European defense. Without a strong US presence in Europe the French were absolutely opposed to German rearmament in any form. The announcement therefore served as the best possible preparation for a meeting of the British, French and American foreign ministers, and representatives of the Atlantic Council (NATO's chief deliberative body) in New York in September.

The conference did not give Adenauer the breakthrough he sought, but it represented a considerable step forward, especially since the Federal Republic was only one year old. The foreign ministers recognized West Germany's claim to be the only legitimate German government. They enlarged on the Petersberg Agreement, as it concerned consular representation, by permitting Germany to reestablish a foreign ministry and diplomatic service. They lifted the remaining quotas on steel and ship production, which gave German heavy industry just the boost it needed to take full advantage of the situation caused by the Korean War. In return, they insisted – and Adenauer was not in a position to object – that West Germany accept liability for the Reich's foreign debts. In addition, the US promised a permanent presence of US military forces in Europe and a military aid program to America's

[11] Ibid.

NATO allies. The ministers were not yet prepared to countenance, officially, a West German defense contribution. They therefore authorized, instead, creation of a 30,000–man federal police force, which later became the *Bundesgrenzschutz* or Federal Border Patrol, and stated that they would regard any attack on the Federal Republic or on Berlin as an attack on themselves.

As advisor to the chancellor on security matters, Schwerin had suggested arming the *Bundesgendarmerie*, or federal constabulary, rather than forming a new army proper. This was what the SED government in the Soviet zone had done when it created the KVP. Schwerin's influence did not prevail, and in October 1950 Speidel persuaded Adenauer to dismiss him.

Shortly before, the chancellor had appointed a panel of former officers to develop further concrete proposals for a West German armed force. Apart from Speidel, the panel included two other generals, Adolf Heusinger and Hermann Foertsch. The two former had both opposed Hitler's government, whereas Foertsch (not to be confused with another Foertsch who was anti-Hitler) had been associated with ideological training in the Wehrmacht. Heusinger (1897–1985) was present at Hitler's headquarters at Rastenburg in East Prussia when the attempt on Hitler's life led by Colonel von Stauffenberg took place in July 1944, and he was severely wounded. He had known of the plot and shared the views of the plotters, yet probably the fact that he himself was a victim of the attempted coup saved him from Hitler's vengeance.

Adenauer considered the meeting of foreign ministers in New York very encouraging, and thought it possible that a German defense force could develop by the end of 1951. In October Adenauer asked his three advisors, who meanwhile had established a much larger working group of 15–20 former officers, to design a coherent defensive strategy for West Germany. During a confidential seminar at the Himmerod monastery in the Eifel near Bonn on October 6–9, the working group hammered out the basic principles and means of securing West German territory and defending it if attacked. The resulting document, known as the Himmerod Memorandum, reflected the experience of Wehrmacht officers on the Eastern front. They designed an offensive defense based on strong armored forces to be used outside the narrow territory of the Federal Republic, and as far to the East as possible. West Germany, they correctly pointed out, "was long and narrow; Soviet tanks were 80 miles from Frankfurt, a few 'tank hours' from the industrialized Ruhr region."[12] They wrote:

[12] Cioc, *Pax Atomica*, 4.

German territory must not be viewed as a forefield with the intent of utilizing the Rhine river as the primary line of defense. ... Wherever possible, the defense must be led offensively. This means that, at the outset, we must counterattack everywhere that is feasible. This method will impress the Soviets tremendously, and warn them to be cautious. There is no natural boundary east of the Rhine, no line that is suitable for a defense (except for the Thuringian forest, which lies in Soviet hands). Even with 50 divisions it would be impossible to achieve a stationary defense of the 800–kilometer border from Passau to Lübeck. Only a mobile fighting command can successfully hold the region from Elbe to Rhine. ... We must strive with all our means so that the battle gets pushed back onto East German territory as soon as possible.[13]

The force structure envisioned a German army of twelve armored (Panzer) divisions of about 250,000 men, an air force of 825 planes and ground staff, and a navy of 202 ships and 204 aircraft. The estimated total of this combined force approximated 500,000 men. The core of the Himmerod force structure, notably the twelve divisions, survived the politics of the years to come; the operational plans did not.

Even before Himmerod, Adenauer had lost the support of his interior minister, Gustav Heinemann, who resigned in October 1950 in protest at the modest measures for internal security which the Allies then had authorized Adenauer to take. In 1952 he also left the CDU and founded his own party, the All-German People's Party (Gesamtdeutsche Volkspartei, GVP), which campaigned on the single issue of opposition to West German rearmament, on the grounds that rearmament was both immoral and likely to make reunification with East Germany impossible. Heinemann's decision greatly stimulated the public campaign against rearmament, under the slogan "Ohne mich" – "Without Me." The campaign relied heavily on leading figures from the liberal Protestant establishment, including Heinemann himself, and Martin Niemöller and Helmut Gollwitzer. Some, like Heinemann, genuinely believed that rearmament would deepen the political division of the country. Others, especially in the SPD, believed that since the Allies had taken away German arms and had, as late as 1950, publicly condemned militarization and rearmament, they, and not the Germans, should bear the burden of German defense. A third group, consisting mainly of arch-conservatives and former Wehrmacht officers who denounced the Speidel group as collaborators, saw demilitarization as a national insult and considered it a provocation that they might be asked to serve under foreign commanders. Heinemann also shared the view of

---

[13] "Denkschrift des militärischen Expertenausschusses," *Militärgeschichtliche Mitteilungen* 21 (1977): 172. This was the first publication of the Himmerod Memorandum.

a fourth group which argued that the Soviet Union might feel threatened by German rearmament, or would choose to interpret rearmament as a threat. War would thus become more likely. Finally, a number of people in all groups pointed out that their fathers and brothers had died in World War II, that their surviving wives, sisters, and children received inadequate pensions, that there was still no peace treaty, and that Germans therefore should reject the idea of a new military force. Polls taken between 1951 and 1955 indicated that less than 20 per cent of men aged 16–30 "would like to join the army."[14]

The federal president, Heuss, shared Adenauer's belief that the Federal Republic must have the ability to defend itself. He was particularly concerned with the "Ohne mich" movement, because he believed that a healthy democracy could not survive with a "Without Me" attitude. On the contrary he felt strongly that an attitude of "With Me" was absolutely necessary, and indeed, that soldiers as a part of a viable democratic state, should not be looked upon as though they were opposed or external to it.[15] This notion that the future German army must be an army of "citizens in uniform," committed to defense of democracy and with respect for the primacy of politics, became the basic doctrine of the new German military. Although it did not come into being until 1955, the planners, like Adenauer and Speidel, were convinced from the very outset that the new army must be, in one particular respect, entirely different from the Wehrmacht of the Third Reich, namely, that the new German soldier should henceforth, above all, be a loyal member of the democratic society.

No matter how one judges the arguments of the German government and its critics, the Korean War had convinced the Allies, especially the United States, that the defense of Western Europe, facing a Soviet threat, was impossible without being able to rely on the expertise and the experience of the Germans. It was thus Korea that provided a decisive impetus for the efforts to create a credible defensive community among Western nations, including Germany. It also showed Adenauer that he had the means of gaining new respect for democratic Germany:

Sensitive to the burdensome legacy of international hatred and suspicion that Germany has inherited from Hitler ... [Adenauer] saw the Korean War as opening the door to Germany's return to the family of nations. He rejected any nationalistic feelings or sentiments he may have felt in favor of transforming himself and his image as a father figure to his people into becoming "a better European than a German." In that self-appointed role, Adenauer was to lead his truncated country in successive stages into the Schuman plan, the European

---

[14] Chaussy, "Jugend," in *Die BRD*, ed. Benz, 2: 49–50.
[15] Schmückle, *Ohne Pauken und Trompeten*, 129–31.

Coal and Steel Community, the Council for Europe, NATO, and the European Economic Community (EEC).[16]

Following preparation of the Himmerod Memorandum, Adenauer judged that the time had come to make defense planning an official part of the government, since it had become public knowledge. On October 26, he established the special office that became the nucleus of the future ministry of defense. Its chief was the CDU member of parliament and former Catholic trade union leader, Theodor Blank (1905–1972), who was given the peculiar title of "Special Assistant to the Federal Chancellor for Matters Related to the Increase of Allied Forces." By 1953, the Blank Office, as it was known, had a staff of 700. Speidel and Heusinger, however, served as independent consultants; the time had not yet arrived for former Wehrmacht generals, no matter how opposed to Hitler they had been, to be employed as bona fide members of the new German government.

Adenauer's official statement to the Bundestag in which he explained why West Germany should make a defense contribution clearly reflected his concern with Germany's integration into the European community:

The Western world finds itself in a truly great danger. West Germany is a part of the Western world, and due to its geographic situation, it is more exposed to that danger than other lands. At the present time, negotiations with the Soviets for the purpose of normalizing relations can only promise success if the Soviets know that their negotiating partner is strong enough to make aggression risky. This strength can only be maintained if the *Western world* organizes its *defense together*. The Western powers are agreed that this strength will only suffice if Germany also contributes. The German people cannot refuse, not only because it guards us against a lethal danger but also because we have duties to fulfill to Europe and the people of Western civilization.[17]

This was vintage Adenauer, combining the thesis that became known later as the "policy of strength" with an assertion of fact – that the Western powers had agreed to a German contribution – which was still only a hope. Indeed, in the latter part of 1950, the journalist and editor of the *Frankfurter Allgemeine Zeitung*, Paul Sethe, wrote: "The thought of rearming Germany is spreading like a drop of oil. . . . Germans will be allowed to wear the Stahlhelm again, although they never asked to."[18]

[16] Hartrich, *Fourth and Richest Reich*, 164.
[17] Cited in Cioc, *Pax Atomica*, 13, emphasis there; see also Bell, *Negotiation from Strength*.
[18] Cited ibid., 12.

This was exactly the impression Adenauer sought to create: the German defense contribution was necessary, the West wanted it, and the Germans owed it to civilization to produce it.

The French government was worried by the ramifications of arming the Federal Republic. It reacted to the recommendations of the New York conference, and therefore indirectly to Adenauer, with a proposal that derailed German rearmament for almost two years. This was the so-called "Pleven Plan" of October 24, 1950, named after René Pleven, the French prime minister, though its real author was none other than Jean Monnet. The Pleven Plan addressed an insoluble problem, which represented the French dilemma as they saw it. This dilemma was: how to make German forces stronger than Soviet forces while keeping them weaker than the French? The Pleven Plan's solution was to scatter German soldiers among units under non-German command, in such small numbers that there would be no such thing, in effect, as a German armed force, only groups of Germans in European uniform. The Plan also foresaw the size of a battalion, about 1,000 men, as the largest German unit France could accept. German officers would consequently be denied a role in formulating common policy, because there would be no German officers of any rank higher than battalion commander. This proposal did not correspond at all with the vision of Churchill and Adenauer for German contingents in a European army: Churchill envisaged fairly large units, either divisions or corps, under German officers and with German officers participating in the planning and execution of policy.

During the winter of 1950–1 Adenauer, the Americans, and the British designed a response to the Pleven Plan. The French government carried on a major diplomatic campaign to demonstrate that the Plan, or a similar concept, was an absolute precondition for French approval of German rearmament. Adenauer publicly welcomed the Plan as a recognition that the Allies wanted a German contribution, but insisted that West Germany must be accorded political parity with its future allies before it would make any contribution. The American response was basically to ignore the Plan and to proceed with talks between US officers and the Speidel-Heusinger group, talks that understandably annoyed the French when they learned of them. On December 18–19, 1950, the foreign and defense ministers of NATO met in Brussels and, over French objections, decided to initiate formal talks with the Bonn government on a German contribution to defense. The atmosphere was tense: only a few weeks earlier the Chinese communist government had intervened in the Korean War and was driving the American forces and their allies southward in retreat. Throughout the West, fears of attack on West Germany or indeed of world war with the Soviet Union, grew.

Adenauer welcomed the NATO decision, but also recognized that he must control his enthusiasm in order to avoid creating so much French resistance that the whole process would be stalled.

The Soviet Union attempted, not for the first or the last time, to complicate the process by introducing proposals aimed at delaying or preventing German rearmament. In October 1950 the Soviet government proposed a four-power conference of foreign ministers to discuss the withdrawal of occupation forces from Germany. The French and the British displayed interest, and a preparatory meeting on Germany was held between representatives of the four powers in the Marbre Rose palace in Paris from March to June 1951. The meeting produced no agreement, however, and was not followed by a four-power conference. But these months were nerve-wracking for Adenauer, who perceived the specter of German neutralization, American withdrawal, and Soviet advance as more menacing every day. Further, those opposed to armament in West Germany were rapidly growing in numbers and intensifying their campaign against a German defense contribution. It was during this same period – the Marbre Rose days – that Adenauer acquired the permanent fear that the Allies might, conceivably, agree to a neutralization of Germany, a concern that never left him. Some observers found it surprising that Kurt Schumacher gave Adenauer his full support and contributed his own efforts to prevent the Marbre Rose talks from damaging West Germany's interests.

Two highly visible, symbolic steps toward re-establishing a German army occurred in early 1951. First General Eisenhower, who at the time was the first designated Supreme Allied Commander of NATO's European Forces (SACEUR), and later Adenauer, made public statements rehabilitating the German soldier and distinguishing honorable service in the Wehrmacht from complicity in Nazi crimes. Ever since his first papers on the subject of West German security in 1948, Speidel had argued that it made no sense for the Allies on the one hand to denounce all German military traditions as tainted, while at the same time welcoming new military efforts from the Germans. In the months following the Himmerod Memorandum Speidel and Heusinger repeatedly told Allied High Commission representatives that it was "politically and psychologically essential" for leading Western public figures to reject the notion that all who had served in the Wehrmacht were guilty by association, and to distinguish between individual crimes committed by military officers and the German Wehrmacht as a whole.

A visit by Eisenhower to Europe in January 1951 gave Speidel and Heusinger the opportunity they sought. In his book on the war in Europe, Eisenhower had called the Wehrmacht "a completely evil conspiracy with which no compromise could be tolerated," and at the surrender ceremony in Reims in May 1945 he had refused to shake hands with his defeated enemies. Now, in 1951, the US national interest in a German defense contribution demanded what amounted to a retraction. Charles Thayer described what happened on the evening of January 22, 1951:

Boarding a plane, he [Eisenhower] flew to Germany to face his critics and, if his country's interest required, to eat a little crow.

The confrontation was arranged at McCloy's residence outside Frankfurt. I was instructed to bring a special trainful of officials concerned with re-armament, including Adenauer's military advisors, ex-Generals Heusinger and Speidel.

Although he was suffering from grippe and running a high fever, Eisenhower was standing erect and cheerful in the reception room when we entered. As I brought forward the two German ex-generals, the big Ike smile wreathed his round face and a large hand shot out to greet them. With that gesture at least two of his former adversaries were thoroughly cleansed of their resentment of the general who had refused to receive them.[19]

Together with Speidel and Heusinger, Eisenhower prepared a statement which, in its published English version, declared that he accepted the distinction between German soldiers and officers on the one hand and Hitler and his criminal henchmen on the other. The German soldier had not lost his honor. The German version, unpublished at the time, was much stronger: it included an outright apology for Eisenhower's earlier views and the statement that "the German soldier fought courageously and decently for his homeland."[20]

In the fall of 1951 the Conservatives under Churchill returned to government in Britain, while in France national elections produced a shift to the right, weakening the socialists and communists who were more amenable to Soviet attempts to divide West Germany and its allies. The result was new leadership in France and Britain that was distinctly more skeptical of Soviet proposals and more determined to bring about a German military force.

During the summer and fall of 1951, the western Allies discussed the Pleven Plan among themselves and with a German delegation led by Theodor Blank. During these talks Jean Monnet succeeded in convincing McCloy and Eisenhower in the US that a combination of the Pleven Plan and a common European security system based on the Brussels Pact, to be called the European Defense Community (EDC), was the proper solution. The EDC plan foresaw a West German

---

[19] Thayer, *Unquiet Germans*, 232–3.
[20] Cited in Wettig, *Entmilitarisierung und Wiederbewaffnung*, 401.

contribution of 12 army divisions, six armored and six mechanized infantry, with a total of about 310,000 men. The EDC plan envisaged divisions somewhat larger than those proposed in the Himmerod Memorandum. In addition, the plan projected an air force of 1,326 aircraft and a navy of 186 combat vessels and 54 aircraft. The total German manpower of all three services in the EDC would have been about 500,000 men. From that point onward until the summer of 1954, the EDC was the official policy of all the powers involved; the option of a German national force, under its own command within NATO, was not considered for three years, until negotiations on the EDC finally failed and left the NATO option as the only possibility.

This changing context encouraged Adenauer, again, to seek a breakthrough as he had done in the fall of 1950. He was reconciled to the EDC solution, albeit against the strong recommendations of Speidel, Heusinger, and Blank; and he hoped to combine establishment of the EDC with an end of the Occupation Statute, and conclusion of a "General Treaty" with France, Great Britain and the United States, thus bringing real, if limited, sovereignty to his country in 1952. On September 24, 1951, negotiations to revise the Occupation Statute were begun and lasted until May 1952, when the Federal Republic and the three Western powers signed the General Treaty and the agreement setting up the EDC. A brief phase of swift action followed: on December 27–30, 1951, the foreign ministers of Benelux, France, Italy, and West Germany met to discuss the Pleven Plan and agreed to establish a European armed force by June 30, 1954. On February 8, 1952, a majority of the Bundestag, against the votes of the SPD, formally voted in favor of a German defense contribution. One of the most impressive speakers on behalf of rearmament was a 36–year-old Bavarian CSU deputy, named Franz Josef Strauss. His speech on February 8 marked his recognition as a serious politician; he thus began a controversial and influential career in West German politics that continued to the 1980s.

One week prior to the vote, the SPD had attempted a new method to stop the movement toward rearmament: it called on the Federal Constitutional Court in Karlsruhe to judge whether the proposed EDC treaty violated the Basic Law. If the Court found this to be true, it would mean that West Germany could not ratify the EDC treaty without amending the Basic Law. This in turn required a two-thirds majority vote, which the government did not have. Accordingly the SPD hoped, via the Court, to obtain a German veto of the treaties. Adenauer's government argued that the treaties did not violate the Basic Law and therefore required only a simple majority in the Bundestag for ratification.

This action opened a legal and political drama that involved all the main actors on the political stage – the chancellor, the federal president, the government, the Constitutional Court, and even some *Land* governments. It continued until the CDU coalition's decisive electoral victory in September 1953. It also concluded the first act in the drama of German rearmament; the second opened in March 1952 when Stalin attempted, for the last time, to prevent the EDC and German rearmament.

# 6

# The Federal Constitutional Court

The Parliamentary Council of 1948–9 had decided that the new German republic should have a judicial authority, independent of the legislative and executive branches of government, with the specific right to rule on the constitutionality of laws and other government actions. Clearly, the Council was looking to the US Supreme Court as an example, since it considered that the absence of such a final constitutional arbiter was one of the reasons that Hitler was able to take power in 1933. Hitler had abolished the powers of the Reichstag and given the Reich government – in practice, himself – the power to issue and enforce laws on its own authority. His legal basis for doing so was a clause in the Weimar constitution that gave the Reich president emergency authority to maintain public order, subject to subsequent approval by the Reichstag. Accordingly, Hitler prevailed on the aging president, Paul von Hindenburg, to invoke this clause. Thereafter the Nazis coerced the Reichstag into passing another law, the Enabling Act, which made the emergency powers permanent and abolished the Reichstag's own right to approve them. This was a violation of the Weimar constitution, but there was no authority to so rule. Ironically, the authors of the Weimar constitution had refused to establish a method of judicial review because of what they considered the "stultifying actions" of the US Supreme Court.[1]

The fathers of the Federal Republic were determined that Germany would be governed according to law, and, in fact, the concept of the rule of law was interpreted so seriously that the West German Basic Law, dating from 1949, was amended more often in its history than virtually any other national constitution anywhere in the world. But, nonetheless,

[1] Abraham, *The Judicial Process*, 314–16; see also Kommers, *Judicial Politics in West Germany*, and "Bundesverfassungsgericht," in *Staatslexikon*, vol. 1, cols 1006–12.

above and beyond the authority of the Basic Law, there would be a supreme arbiter, a Constitutional Court.

Although the Court had been foreseen in the Basic Law, it took almost two years to establish, mainly because West Germany's political parties could not agree on how to appoint its members and on the procedure to obtain decisions from the Court. The final compromise was heavily political: there would be two chambers, or senates, on the court consisting of eight judges each. Half of the judges in each chamber would be appointed from a list proposed by the minister of justice, prepared by a special committee of twelve Bundestag members of all parties selected in accordance with their respective party's representation in the Bundestag; the other half of the judges would be appointed by the Bundesrat. The list would include all appellate court judges from the federal court system as well as a group of nominees of the government, the *Länder*, and the political parties. A judge of the Constitutional Court did not necessarily need to be a judge by training, but might be a university professor of law or even a political figure. In practice, after the first few years very few non-judges were ever appointed. The first selection of 16 judges reflected the distribution of power in West Germany: the chairmen of the two senates were well-known political figures; one had been an FDP member of the Bundestag and the other, from the SPD, had been minister of justice in the *Land* Schleswig-Holstein.

More burdensome for the Court's initial reputation and involvement in political battles of the day, such as the battle over the EDC and the defense contribution, was the fact that the two chambers reflected the differing political tendencies of their chairmen. Most of the judges of the first senate, which ruled on all cases dealing with civil and constitutional rights, were SPD members; most of the judges of the second, which handled all other cases, leaned toward the CDU. Accordingly the public dubbed the first senate the "Red Senate" and the second the "Black Senate" – black being the color of Catholicism and reaction. Later appointments modified this distinction, although critics continued to accuse the court of engaging in politics under the guise of judicial impartiality. Like the US Supreme Court, the German Constitutional Court could not avoid such accusations since its judgements primarily concerned the authority of political institutions. Between 1951 and 1986, however, the Court issued over 40,000 decisions and found 370 pieces of federal or *Land* legislation or administrative action to be unconstitutional. In view of this amount of work one should perhaps be surprised at how few of these decisions were or seemed to be overtly political.

The law establishing the Constitutional Court foresaw two principal means of access to it: (1) an appeal by a constitutional organ, either

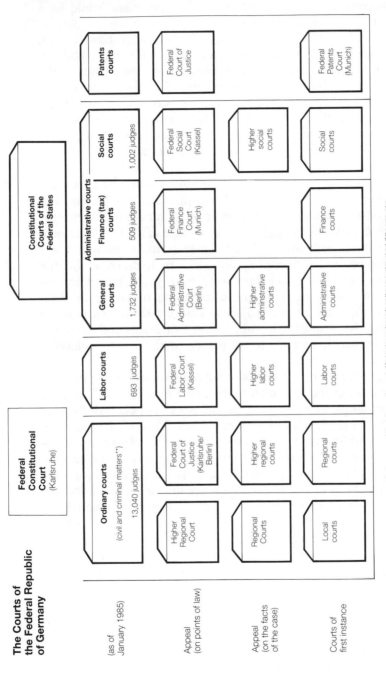

**Figure 1.4   The courts of the Federal Republic of Germany.**
*Source:*  Press and Information Office, *Law and Administration of Justice*

federal or state, that is, by an agency of government or a political party; (2) the "constitutional complaint" in cases concerning the alleged violation of individual rights involving any law or act of federal, *Land*, or local government. A third method, involving a request by a lower court to have the Constitutional Court render a judgement on a constitutional question in a pending case, was exactly parallel to the "certification" process of reaching the Supreme Court in the US, and, as in the US, was a method seldom used. In all cases it was the Court's prerogative to decide if the case merited consideration; there was no automatic right of appeal. Though clearly modeled on the judicial and constitutional review function of the US Supreme Court, there was a vital difference: unlike the American tribunal, the Federal Constitutional Court had only one function, that of judging whether actions of public authority violated the Basic Law, and were therefore unconstitutional. This was a very wide field, since it also included such matters as deciding problems of competence between levels of authority – federal and *Land* – but it was in no sense an ordinary appellate jurisdiction; that function belonged to the *Bundesgerichtshof*, or Federal Court of Justice, established in 1949.

One of the Court's first tasks, which arose before the issue of the constitutionality of rearmament, was to decide on the fate of the radical right-wing Socialist Reich Party (SRP, *Sozialistische Reichspartei)*, based mainly in Lower Saxony. The party leadership consisted primarily of former Nazis and its position was one of opposition to the Bonn government, of demands for regional autonomy, and of hostility to the occupying powers. In 1950 the SRP sent shock waves throughout Europe by winning 11 per cent of the vote in the Lower Saxony *Land* election, and this caused Adenauer's government great concern. The problem for the government was to prove that the SRP was a successor organization to the NSDAP or pursued aims incompatible with the Basic Law. The Basic Law did not allow the government simply to forbid organizations; it had to apply to the Constitutional Court for a judgement that the organization in question was hostile to the constitution, in which case the Court would order its dissolution.

As soon as the Court began its first session in the fall of 1951 the government applied for the appropriate judgment, which was rendered one year later. Foreseeing the verdict, the SRP dissolved itself voluntarily. At the same time, in order to appear consistently opposed to radical movements of all stripes, the government applied for a similar judgement on the KPD, the Communist Party. There was considerable debate in Germany concerning whether the KPD did endorse policies contrary to the Basic Law, and the Court's proceedings continued until 1956, when it in fact found the KPD to be unconstitutional.

During its first session the Court also made a preliminary decision on the status of former Reich civil servants, whom it defined as "civilian soldiers," that is, subject to rigid discipline and therefore not collectively responsible for the criminal decisions of their government. This decision complemented the federal law "regulating the status of persons falling under clause 131 of the Basic Law," civil servants who were expelled or fled from the Eastern territories or the Soviet zone, or who had been suspended from government service by the Allies or by a denazification court. In July 1953 the Bundestag passed the Civil Service Law which finally reinstated all civil servants who had not been sentenced for actual crimes, with seniority, in their rights and duties. The Constitutional Court took this occasion to emphasize the legal identity and continuity of the Federal Republic with the Reich, which entailed the Federal Republic's obligation to continue to provide for all former and present civil servants. A civil servant, the court ruled, owed a duty of obedience to the state and had undertaken to support its constitution; the state had a reciprocal obligation to care for him and his family by providing an adequate wage as well as pension, health insurance, and other benefits.

# 7

# The Note Controversy and the EDC Treaty

The Soviet government continued in 1952 to play, with some skill, on the differences within the West. Stalin's concern remained that of preventing West German rearmament and, presumably, in the long term, neutralizing of West Germany within the Soviet sphere of control. The first result of the Soviet diplomatic offensive against German rearmament, which was conducted indirectly and with subtlety, was the Marbre Rose meeting held between March and June 1951 in Paris, at which the Soviets failed to divide the West. The Soviet government probably made a basic mistake at this time by failing to offer free elections throughout Germany, if their aim was to prevent creation of a West German army. If the Soviets had miscalculated in 1951, however, Stalin sought to correct it the following year.

The Soviet diplomatic offensive of early 1952 became known as the "Note Campaign," because it turned on the wording and meaning of two notes that Stalin sent to the Western governments. The background to the notes of 1952 was that the Western European countries and the US had finally, so it seemed, agreed to go ahead with the EDC and with a General Treaty with West Germany that would effectively include West Germany as a partner in a common European security system. In a preliminary move, the East German *Volkskammer* (or parliament, controlled completely by the SED) had proposed free elections in all four zones in September 1951. This was an effective gesture in terms of West German public opinion; it particularly excited those, like Jakob Kaiser (CDU), who feared that rearmament would aggravate national division, and it set the stage for the Soviet offensive.

In February, two significant conferences took place. The first was a meeting of the foreign ministers of the member states of the future EDC, that is the Brussels Pact states plus West Germany. At this meeting Adenauer (who served as foreign minister since the re-establishment of the foreign ministry in March 1951, as well as chancellor) made a promise which was a condition for acceptance of German membership in the EDC by the other countries: he declared solemnly that West Germany would never produce or seek to produce nuclear or bacteriological weapons or missiles of any kind. He did not at this time promise that West Germany would never seek to obtain such weapons, only that it would never produce its own.

The second important meeting of February 1952 was the meeting of the NATO Council in Lisbon. It was the first general strategic planning session of all NATO members since the Soviet Union acquired nuclear weapons in 1949. The previous NATO strategy for defense against Soviet attack in Europe, predicated on US nuclear monopoly or near-monopoly, foresaw abandonment of German territory and protection of France and Italy for as long as it took to build up sufficient US forces for a counter-attack on Central Europe. Once the Soviet Union acquired nuclear weapons, however, this strategy, which anticipated a war of several years' duration, was obsolete. NATO, therefore, considered two options in Lisbon. The first was based on the force structure recommendations contained in the American document known as NSC-68 (issued by the National Security Council in April 1950), which provided the rationale for US defense policy for over a generation; to build up European conventional forces to the maximum extent possible, using the resources of a rearmed Germany, so that defense could be conducted at the East–West border, or even offensively (as proposed in the Himmerod Memorandum). The other, which partially replaced the Lisbon plan in 1954, required a somewhat smaller conventionally-armed force with the addition of tactical nuclear weapons. NATO hoped that tactical nuclear weapons would outweigh the Soviet superiority in manpower. The shift to nuclear weapons for defense in the European theater reflected the broader shift of US strategy that endorsed the concept of "massive retaliation:" the US would respond to Soviet attack on West Germany with an immediate nuclear strike on the Soviet homeland. The Lisbon conference recommended establishment of a conventional defense of Central Europe of 96 divisions by the end of 1952, including German units as well as German officers in senior command positions.

The Soviet response to the EDC talks and the NATO decision came quickly. On March 10, 1952, the Soviet government sent a note to the Western powers offering to "urgently discuss the question of a peace treaty with Germany," and included a draft of such a treaty. The draft proposed to reunify Germany (west of the Oder–Neisse line), to withdraw all foreign forces, to permit "free activity of democratic parties and organizations", to grant amnesty to "all former Nazis," to keep united Germany neutral, and, most surprisingly, to permit Germany "to have its own national armed forces (land, air, and sea) which are necessary for the defense of the country."[1]

The Soviet note puzzled historians ever after. Genuinely free political activity (the March 10 note did not specifically mention elections) would have meant the end of the communist regime in the GDR. Some historians argued that Stalin was indeed willing to sacrifice East Germany in order to prevent West German rearmament within the Western European context.[2] Others doubted that Stalin intended to go that far, but that it was morally incumbent on Adenauer and the West to take the note seriously, since it represented the "last chance" for reunification; by not taking that chance, it became a "lost opportunity."[3] Yet still other analysts, probably the majority, regarded the note as purely and simply an attempt, albeit shrewd, to prevent German rearmament, to sow dissension between West Germany and its new allies, and within West Germany between Adenauer and the opponents of rearmament. In that, it certainly succeeded. Jakob Kaiser, already disappointed that Adenauer had not been more eager to discuss free elections on the basis of the Volkskammer's proposal of September 1951, insisted that the note should be taken seriously. Adenauer's position was more ambiguous. He saw the note as a delaying tactic but also believed that even if it were meant seriously, reunification in the existing circumstances was not in Germany's interest, because it would inevitably lead to a complete US withdrawal from Europe and hence, indirectly, to Soviet hegemony. Once the US was gone, the democratic forces in reunited Germany would be defenseless against any future Soviet attempt to revise the status quo of 1945 in their favor, i.e. by annexing West Germany to the Soviet bloc.[4] Adenauer made this argument to Schuman and the British foreign secretary, Anthony Eden, on March 20–21, when they were preparing their response.

There is no doubt, as the former German ambassador to Washington, Wilhelm Grewe, pointed out in 1986, that, in the 1950s, Adenauer did not believe reunification was possible on acceptable terms in the foreseeable future, that he therefore concentrated on building respect for and commitment to freedom in the Federal Republic, and on binding the Federal Republic firmly with the West. Grewe also emphasized that there was no doubt that Adenauer rejected the idea of reunification if it was to be obtained at the price of a neutralized, reunified Germany that

---

[1] Dept of State, *Documents on Germany*, 361, 363–4.
[2] Ulam, *Expansion and Coexistence*, 535–7.
[3] See Steininger, *Eine Chance zur Wiedervereinigung?*
[4] Schwarz, *Adenauer: Der Aufstieg*, 881.

would be a perfect target for attempts to subvert freedom and democratic order, as had been so effectively demonstrated in Berlin and in the Soviet zone of occupation.[5]

The West declined to enter into talks on the basis of the March 10 note. In a second note, dated April 9, the Soviet Union repeated its offer of a peace treaty and added a proposal to permit free elections in a united Germany. This note further exacerbated the internal German controversy. In one of his last political gestures, Schumacher, who had carried the SPD with him in basic support of the idea of rearmament (although not of the EDC), attacked the government's position and demanded that Adenauer request four-power talks on Germany. Adenauer's reply repeated what became known as the "argument of the policy of strength;" namely, the view that a reordering of Europe, that might bring about German reunification in peace and freedom, would only come about if the West became strong enough to impose its will diplomatically and politically on the Soviet Union. Only if faced with a strong and united West, would the Soviet government genuinely accede to peaceful coexistence. German reunification, in this view, was inextricably tied to the introduction of freedom in Eastern Europe: there could be no lasting German reunification in a democratic state unless the communist regimes in Eastern Europe simultaneously changed.

The debate on the intent of Stalin's notes was still raging several weeks later when the foreign ministers of the Western powers held their first conference that included the Federal Republic, represented by the chancellor and foreign minister, Adenauer. On May 26, 1952, West Germany signed with the US, Britain, and France the "Convention on Relations with the Federal Republic of Germany" (the General Treaty) which had been ready in draft form since November 1951, along with related protocols concerning Allied troop presence, German financial obligations, and rules for the transfer of authority. The treaty terminated the occupation regime, recognized West German sovereignty in international affairs, and acknowledged it as an ally within the EDC. The Western Allies undertook not to take an official position on the issue of Germany's borders until they and the Soviets signed a peace treaty with a united German government. They also promised to work with the Federal Republic to bring about their "common goal," a reunited Germany which would have a free and democratic constitution similar to that of West Germany and would be integrated in the European community. In return for this grant of admission to the Western

---

[5] *Die Welt*, April 7, 1986; see also Graml, "Die Legende von der verpassten Gelegenheit." *Vierteljahrshefte für Zeitgeschichte* 29 (1981): 307–41.

The Kaiser Wilhelm Memorial Church, on the Kurfürstendamm in Berlin, was built in the 1890s and was substantially destroyed during the war. The first photograph was taken in 1946; the second, 40 years later in 1986. The church ruin was left standing as a testament to the devastation of war. Next to it the Berliners have built two new churches with stained glass windows, which when lighted at night are strikingly beautiful. [*Source*: Landesbildstelle Berlin]

From left to right: Anthony Eden, the British foreign secretary, Adenauer, Dean Acheson, the US secretary of state, and Robert Schuman, the French foreign minister, in Bonn at the signing of the treaty defining West Germany's relations with the Western powers (the General Treaty) in May 1952. Though never ratified, the treaty was the basis of the Paris Treaties of 1954 that finally ended occupation and admitted West Germany to NATO. [*Source*: GIC]

During his second visit to the US in late 1954, Adenauer met at the Waldorf Astoria Hotel in New York City with Herbert Hoover, the former US president who helped organize aid to Germany after World War I and during the 1945–9 occupation. [*Source*: GIC]

Carlo Schmid, of Franco-German descent, deputy speaker of the Bundestag and minister of federal affairs in the grand coalition, was the leading constitutional expert and political philosopher of the SPD. He embodied the unity of *Geist* (spirit or intellect) and *Macht* (power) often desired but rarely seen in German history. [*Source*: GIC]

Adenauer first visited the US in 1953, an event that few would have dared to foresee four years earlier. The picture shows him being warmly welcomed at the airport in Washington, DC, by Secretary of State John Foster Dulles and Vice President Richard M. Nixon. Between Dulles and Nixon is Heinrich von Brentano, the head of the CDU Bundestag group and later foreign minister. [*Source*: GIC]

*Below* A relaxed moment at the White House during the same trip with (from left to right) President Dwight D. Eisenhower, Secretary of State Dulles, and Heinrich von Brentano. [*Source*: Süddeutscher Verlag]

On June 17–18, 1953, workers in the Soviet sector of Berlin and throughout East Germany rose in revolt against their Soviet and German communist masters. This picture of two Berliners throwing rocks at Soviet tanks graphically illustrates the futility of the revolt, which was suppressed without intervention or protest from the West. [*Source*: GIC]

On the day the Allied occupation formally ended, May 5, 1955, West Berlin's daily, the *Berliner Morgenpost*, carried the headline: "Federal Republic sovereign today — at 12 noon the Treaty of Germany comes into force." [*Source*: Ullstein Bilderdienst]

Hausexemplar

# BERLINER

Die größte Zeitung des freien Berlin

**15 Pf.** AUSWÄRTS 20 PFENNIG

# MORGENPOST

**DONNERSTAG, 5. MAI 1955**

**58. Jahrgang — Nummer 104**

## Anderthalb Millionen Amerikaner wollen Europa besuchen / S. 8

# Bundesrepublik heute souverän

## Um 12 Uhr mittags tritt der Deutschlandvertrag in Kraft
## Feierliche Regierungserklärung des Bundeskanzlers

Von unserer Bonner Redaktion

Die Bundesrepublik wird heute souverän. Mittags um 12 Uhr wird nach der Hinterlegung der britischen und der französischen Ratifikationsurkunden der Deutschlandvertrag in Kraft treten. Damit endet nach zehnjähriger Dauer das Besatzungsregime in Westdeutschland. Die Bundesrepublik erhält „die volle Macht eines souveränen Staates über ihre inneren und äußeren Angelegenheiten". In einer Proklamation an alle Deutschen wird Bundeskanzler Adenauer die politische Bedeutung dieses Tages würdigen. Wie gestern abend nach einer Sitzung des Bundeskabinetts verlautete, wird der Kanzler die Proklamation in Form einer Regierungserklärung vor dem Bundestag bekanntgeben.

Für Berlin bringt das Deutschland-Abkommen, das heute in Kraft tritt, eine umfassende Garantieerklärung der USA, Großbritanniens und Frankreichs, die auch von den übrigen NATO-Staaten als verbindlich übernommen werden ist. Gleichzeitig geben die drei Westmächte ihrer Entschlossenheit Ausdruck, unserer Stadt das höchstmögliche Maß von Selbstregierung zu gewähren. In einer ergänzen-

### Saarlage wurde abgewiesen

Karlsruhe: Das Saarabkommen ist nicht verfassungswidrig

### Gespräch Kanzler–Ollenhauer

Einstündige Unterredung über aktuelle außenpolitische Fragen

### Wilder Streik in Bremen

### Neuer Vorstoß von PMF

Paris, 5. Mai

### SSD-Oberst droht

Berlin, 5. Mai

### Arbeiter im Ausstand

London, 5. Mai

DIE POLITIK KONRAD ADENAUERS gab der Bundesrepublik zehn Jahre nach dem Kriege die Souveränität wieder.  Foto: Schirner

### Differenzen um Wiener Öl

Österreichs Außenminister vermittelt zwischen den Großmächten

Wien, 5. Mai

### Mit 9 Mann abgestürzt

Reykjavik, 5. Mai

Adenauer and the first federal president, Theodor Heuss (FDP), both of whom enjoyed enormous popularity. [*Source*: GIC]

An image of the 1950s: policemen receiving Christmas gifts — mostly wine and tobacco — from local inhabitants thanking them for their work. This custom still continues. [*Source*: GIC]

In Moscow in September 1955, Adenauer secured the release of 10 000 German POWs from Soviet camps, but was unable to gain any concession from the Soviets on the matter of divided Germany. The photograph shows the German delegation welcoming the Soviet leadership to dinner. From left to right: Nikolai A. Bulganin, chairman of the USSR Council of Ministers; Vyacheslav Molotov, the Soviet foreign minister; Adenauer; Georgii M. Malenkov, the former Soviet minister-president; Nikita S. Khrushchev, general secretary of the Communist Party of the Soviet Union; Walter Hallstein of the German foreign ministry; Pervukhin, Bulganin's deputy. [*Source*: Süddeutscher Verlag]

Adenauer had to fight both Jewish opponents of direct negotiations with Germans and financial worries in his own party in forcing through the legislation that provided restitution to Jews, a policy that became a resounding success. In 1960, following an outbreak of apparent neo-Nazism in West Germany, the Israeli prime minister, David Ben Gurion (left) met Adenauer in New York and issued a statement in support of the Federal Republic. [*Source*: GIC]

Adenauer addressing the first volunteers in the new German army, in January 1956. He believed that a state which cannot defend its borders is not a secure state, and that German participation in the western defense alliance was vital. Adenauer overcame considerable resistance to the idea that West Germany should have a military force. [*Source*: Bundesbildstelle Bonn]

*Below* Franz Josef Strauss (left) stirred up more animosity, and more unswerving support, than any other politician of democratic Germany. Here, as minister of defense, he is seen with US Colonel Mark H. Vinzant, Jr (center) and the head of the newly established West German Luftwaffe (air force), Josef Kammhuber. [*Source*: GIC]

Herbert Wehner, "Uncle Herbert," the chief strategist of the SPD. A former communist, Wehner devoted his life to fulfilling the dream of Kurt Schumacher, that socialists should govern Germany and shape its future. At first, like Schumacher, he regarded the communists of the GDR as his main enemies, because they had discredited the idea of German socialism. Later, he became a supporter of the concept of Ostpolitik under Chancellor Willy Brandt. [*Source*: GIC]

Two leaders of the CDU in Adenauer's shadow: Eugen Gerstenmaier (left), president of the Bundestag 1954−68, had been active in the resistance to Hitler. Kai-Uwe von Hassel (right), served as minister-president of Schleswig-Holstein from 1954 to 1963, as minister of defense from 1963 to 1966, and succeeded Gerstenmaier as president from 1969 to 1972. Both were leaders of the CDU's Protestant wing. [*Source*: GIC]

Josef Cardinal Frings, archbishop of Cologne from 1942 to 1969, here shown at the 76th German Catholic Assembly in Fulda in 1954, was one of a powerful group of bishops that found new opportunities after 1945 to provide spiritual leadership and to shape a broad role for Catholicism in German politics and culture. In this task they could rely on the Church's traditional role in public education and on the fact that in postwar West Germany Catholics were no longer outnumbered by Protestants. [*Source*: GIC]

*Below* Karl Jaspers, the philosopher, shaped the moral and political debate of a generation on three occasions in postwar Germany: in 1946, when he denounced all Germans as collectively guilty of Nazi crimes; in 1958, when he explored the moral implications of nuclear weapons in defending freedom against totalitarianism; and in 1966, when he warned of anti-democratic tendencies in the Federal Republic and the absence of a sense of guilt for the past. [*Source*: GIC]

Gerd Bucerius, the Hamburg lawyer who became one of postwar Germany's most successful publishers. In 1946, he took over the paper *Die Zeit* which later became one of the three leading organs of progressive opinion (along with *Der Spiegel* and *Stern*). [*Source*: GIC]

A different solution to the divorce of *Geist* and *Macht* from that of Carlo Schmid was offered by Hans-Werner Richter and his associates in "Gruppe 47", the most influential institution of postwar German culture through the 1960s. The poets, novelists, and critics of "Gruppe 47" defined the agenda of intellectual and, increasingly, of political debate on the left, and shaped a climate of bitter opposition to Adenauer and his "CDU state." [*Source*: GIC]

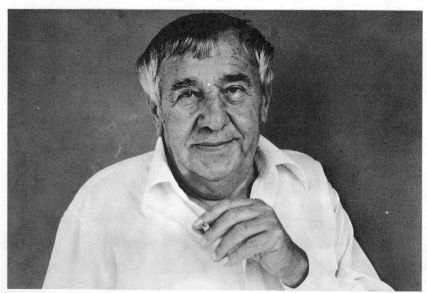

Günter Grass, West Germany's best-known novelist, interpreted the modern history of Germany, in particular of the Third Reich, in his "Danzig Trilogy" of novels. As a supporter of Willy Brandt and, later, of the Greens, Grass became an emotional spokesman for unilateral disarmament and against what he saw as US militarism. [*Source*: GIC]

Along with Grass, Heinrich Böll was the most famous writer to emerge from
"Gruppe 47". Born (like Adenauer) a Rhineland Catholic, Böll turned from religion
to political moralism. His earlier writings are monuments of postwar German literature, his later novels little more than anti-CDU and anti-capitalist tracts. He is
shown here at an anti-nuclear rally in the early 1980s. [*Source*: GIC]

community and alliance, the Germans promised to establish military forces within the EDC without delay.

The most controversial part of the treaty was clause 7.3, the transference clause. Under the terms of the first version of this clause, a future reunited Germany would be subject to the Federal Republic's Western ties as defined in the treaty as a whole and in other engagements like the EDC and the ECSC. Parts of the FDP and the CDU objected that this was an illegitimate constraint on the freedom of a future government of united Germany. They did not doubt that such a future government ought to remain integrated with the West, they merely doubted that the Federal Republic and its partners in 1952 had the authority to bind a non-existent third party. The Allies agreed to modify the clause. In the revised version, they undertook to grant to a reunited Germany the same rights as they were now granting to the Federal Republic, if the reunited German government in turn took on the Federal Republic's obligations. This satisfied the critics, though it still left some uncertainty about the preconditions for reunification. Accordingly, the entire clause was dropped when the treaties were revised in 1954, after the failure of the EDC.

The next day, May 27, the EDC members – the Brussels Pact states plus West Germany – signed the EDC treaty. At that moment the EDC seemed within reach; all that remained was for the member governments to ratify the treaty. But the ratification debates, primarily in France, continued for over two years. Since the two treaties were mutually dependent, the collapse of the EDC more than two years after the treaty was signed invalidated the General Treaty as well, necessitating the complete renegotiation in 1954–5 of Germany's contribution to Western European security on the basis of the formerly rejected NATO option.

Schumacher attacked the EDC treaty in the Bundestag, not because he was against rearmament, but because he thought the way it was designed asked too much of Germany and promised too little in return. Adenauer's view was that West Germany was the *demandeur*; the Germans had to earn the trust of their allies by accepting the terms of the EDC treaty as proposed. Schumacher, on the contrary, from his nationalist perspective argued that in reality the Western powers were the *demandeurs*: did they not want West German territory and resources for European reconstruction and defense? If that was true, and they needed the Germans at least as much as the Germans needed them, the Germans should ask a price for their defense contribution; at least they should insist that it be a national military force, not subject to foreign control. Above all, Schumacher did not see in the treaties any promise that the West was offering to share Germany's risks; after all, it was

Germans who lived on the front line, not Frenchmen, Britons, or Americans. In his view, Adenauer had not received a fair price for putting the Germans at risk.

Adenauer responded that the Western Allies had obligated themselves in clause 7.3 of the General Treaty to work toward reunifying the country, and were obligating themselves to defend West Germany. But the SPD persisted and called the German contingent, foreseen in the EDC, a "foreign legion," and asserted that the purpose was to place German soldiers under foreign control and to deny the German people an equal voice within both the EDC and NATO.[6] Schumacher called the act of signing a "clumsy victory celebration of the clerical coalition with the Allies;" a reference to what he perceived as a conspiracy of conservative, Catholic forces opposed to socialism and German independence.[7]

The result of the treaty's conclusion in 1952, though it did not finally take effect until 1955 in its revised form, was that the High Commission no longer acted in the arbitrary manner of the immediate post-1949 years. Prior to 1952 the Federal Republic enjoyed no status in the international system. It was a government which existed at the pleasure of the Allies, with no independent power outside of its own borders. But in 1952 it completed the transition that began with the Petersberg Agreement in November 1949: it became a treaty partner, rather than a subject. It was still without complete sovereignty vis-à-vis the outside world, but the difference was significant.

Meanwhile, despite Schumacher's objections, all seemed set for an end to occupation and for an improvement in German security through participation in the EDC. Adenauer was triumphant. For him, the EDC was the necessary second step after the ECSC of 1951; the third step, which depended on the first two, was political union of Western Europe.

[6] Wettig, *Entmilitarisierung und Wiederbewaffnung*, 523–6.
[7] Schwarz, *Die Ära Adenauer, 1949–1957*, 165.

# 8

# The SPD and the Death of Schumacher

For Schumacher the development of postwar Germany had brought seven years of frustration and crisis between 1945 and 1952. Nevertheless, the opinions that he had so forcefully, and sometimes virulently expressed between 1945 and 1952 were losing their popularity. Even though the EDC treaty of May 1952 was not yet ratified, and ultimately destined for defeat, Adenauer had successfully nurtured the impression that Germany was once again a respected member of international society. One direct result was a surge in the popularity of his government, and another was, regretfully, increasing isolation and embitterment on behalf of Schumacher. Yet when he died in August he was mourned across the land.

Many, not merely social democrats, rightfully regarded him as a national figure deeply committed to German national interests, and his death as the passing of an era. Schumacher had already, during his first serious illness, requested to be buried in Hannover. Therefore, the SPD decided to have his coffin transported, in a slow procession, to Hannover, with the hearse driving on the federal highway that connects the city with Bonn:

No witness will ever be able to forget the hundreds of thousands who lined the streets as the hearse carrying the remains of Schumacher passed by. ... Men, women and children gathered along the Heerstrasse, which leads through the Ruhr district, to honor the man who had fought and suffered for them, throwing flowers and freshly picked boughs for his last journey. ... In the streets of Hannover, hundreds of thousands more stood tightly packed and waited from seven o'clock in the evening till midnight to wave a last good-bye to Kurt Schumacher.

It's a good thing to remember this, and it's good to awaken this memory in others, because in our country one tends to forget too easily. The rare day, on which a nation does not shy away from showing its pain over the loss of a great human being in an impressive gesture of gratefulness, should be imprinted on the consciousness of the nation.[1]

Following his death the rise in the SPD of a strong neutralist and pacifist wing, partly inspired by the "Without Me" movement, led the SPD to pursue a course of increasingly vehement agitation for negotiations with Eastern Europe and the Soviet Union. This policy did not end until Herbert Wehner, in a famous speech in the Bundestag in 1960, announced that the SPD would henceforth recognize, and was in agreement with, the basic principles of West German foreign policy. His speech was marked by the conclusion that a divided Germany could not afford an incurable rift between Christian democrats and social democrats. But this attitude evolved, it did not suddenly appear. And it emerged largely as a consequence of Adenauer's leadership in the Federal Republic, and as a result of leadership within the Social Democratic Party by Carlo Schmid, by Schumacher's successor as chairman of the SPD, Erich Ollenhauer, and by a new generation of social democrats led by Willy Brandt, Fritz Erler and Helmut Schmidt.[2]

[1] Schmid, Carlo, *Erinnerungen*, 529–30.
[2] See Flechtheim, ed., *Dokumente zur parteipolitischen Entwicklung*, 226–45.

# 9

# Refugees and Expellees

B y 1950 about 12 million expellees, as they were called, were living in various degrees of poverty in the Federal Republic. It was as though all the people from Scotland, Wales, and Northern England had been expelled and accommodated into a Southern English rump state, itself badly damaged during the war. The analogy is fairly precise because, like Scotland and the north of England, the expellees' homelands were mostly rural and thinly populated, whereas most of West Germany, like the south of England, was densely populated, with many large cities and an economic and social structure based on industry and services.

The expellees fell into two general groups according to origin. About nine million were inhabitants of the former eastern parts of Germany itself – Silesia, Pomerania, and East Prussia. The remainder were ethnic Germans who had lived outside the borders of prewar Germany, in Czechoslovakia, Poland, the Baltic States, Hungary, Romania, or the Soviet Union. The government of the new Federal Republic took the view that because both groups consisted of Germans, they had an equal right to live in West Germany, since the new rulers of their homelands had expelled them and taken all their property. Morally this decision was absolutely correct, but in 1950, it was enormously difficult to house and feed such tremendous numbers of people. The expellees included all sorts of people, but with a preponderance of farmers and small businessmen, most of whom had little hope of continuing in their former lines of work.

Nevertheless the West Germans and the expellees together succeeded by the late 1950s in integrating the newcomers into West German society and the West German economy. This was perhaps the single most difficult and impressive feat of reconstruction not only in the material, but in the human and psychological sense. It was possible because large majorities in both groups stressed that the expellees

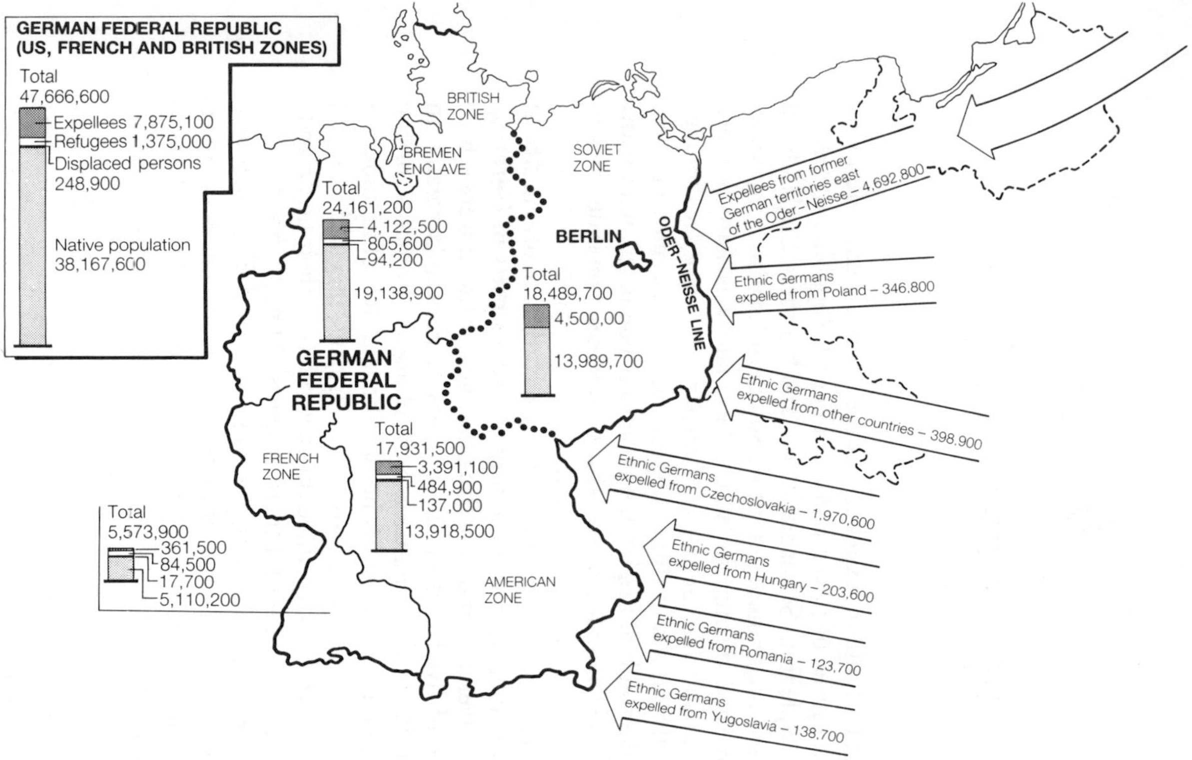
GERMAN FEDERAL REPUBLIC
(US, FRENCH AND BRITISH ZONES)
Total
47,666,600
Expellees 7,875,100
Refugees 1,375,000
Displaced persons
248,900
Native population
38,167,600
BRITISH
ZONE
BREMEN
ENCLAVE
SOVIET
ZONE
BERLIN
Total
24,161,200
4,122,500
805,600
94,200
19,138,900
Total
18,489,700
4,500,00
13,989,700
ODER–NEISSE LINE
GERMAN
FEDERAL
REPUBLIC
FRENCH
ZONE
Total
17,931,500
3,391,100
484,900
137,000
13,918,500
AMERICAN
ZONE
Total
5,573,900
361,500
84,500
17,700
5,110,200
Expellees from former
German territories east
of the Oder–Neisse – 4,692,800
Ethnic Germans
expelled from Poland – 346,800
Ethnic Germans
expelled from other countries – 398,900
Ethnic Germans
expelled from Czechoslovakia – 1,970,600
Ethnic Germans
expelled from Hungary – 203,600
Ethnic Germans
expelled from Romania – 123,700
Ethnic Germans
expelled from Yugoslavia – 138,700

Map 1.8 Population movements, 1945–1950. This map and statistics were published by HICOG in 1950. It was described by that office as follows: "The above map shows areas of origin of the expellee groups and the proportion of total population they represent in the zones of occupation where they have resettled. Also shown are the number of displaced persons remaining in the Federal Republic (in camps and out of camps), and the number of refugees who have entered the Federal Republic from the Soviet zone and Berlin."
*Source*: Office of the US High Commissioner, *5th Quarterly Report*, 1950

would only survive if they overcame their bitterness and despair and actively sought to build new lives for themselves. While a few farmers managed to find land to cultivate in the West, most became manual or white-collar workers, and many former businessmen and professionals from the East found themselves living through years of lower-paid work. As a whole, the expellees became a hardworking and ambitious group, in part because of the brutal stimulus provided by losing their homes and livelihoods, and in part because many of them, especially those from outside the old borders, had been among the leaders of society in their homelands. In the 1960s and 1970s, the Easterners comprised a large number of prominent public figures in politics, the media, and intellectual life in West Germany.

While adjusting themselves to new and at first harsh rules of survival, the expellees managed the feat of giving up the hope of return while retaining much of their regional and cultural identity. In 1950, their leaders published a fundamental statement, known as the Charter of the Expellees, in which they declared that the right to live safely in one's homeland was a basic human right and condemned violent conquest followed by massacres and theft of the inhabitants' property. Equally strongly, they rejected war and confrontation as a means to recover their former lands and hoped for a future peaceful reconciliation in which their rights would be restored. Thus, the Charter was an important symbolic statement, because it rejected hatred and resentment and, in effect, gave up a claim for restoration in favor of a hope for peace. Unfortunately, the communist rulers of the states that were then in control of the expellees' lands and property did not respond in kind. They continued to suppress what remained of German life and culture in the territories under their control and refused steadfastly to admit any guilt or acknowledge any responsibility for injustice or suffering in the expulsions.

When the expellees published the Charter, they were still at the beginning of their long road to security and prosperity in West Germany. They were a dispossessed group, with no money, very little property, living in poor housing. In addition, employment was hard to find. The majority of them lived in rural areas, since so much prewar housing had been destroyed in the cities. They made up almost one-fifth of the population of West Germany in 1950, and their rate of unemployment was more than double that of the so-called "native" population. At the end of 1950, the US High Commissioner, McCloy, concluded:

inadequately housed, homesick, and feeling themselves strangers in a sometimes hostile environment, they form a group which might readily be swayed by political extremists who offer a plausible solution to their problems.

In Germany's external relations they exert constant irredentist pressure through their determination to return to their former homes if political changes should make it possible.[1]

Initially the military government did not allow them to form political parties in the hope that they would take an active role in the parties already in existence. Thus, they formed "Regional Associations" (*Landsmannschaften*) in which refugees from the same area came together, e.g. from Silesia, Pomerania or East Prussia. They were bound not only by emotional ties, but also by the heartfelt conviction that they must keep alive the cultural customs and traditions of their home provinces.

It was not until the state elections in Schleswig-Holstein in July 1950 that their electoral power was dramatically felt. The "Bloc of Expellees and Disenfranchised" (*Bund der Heimatvertriebenen und Entrechteten*, BHE) formed earlier in the year received 23.4 per cent of the vote, ranking second to the SPD with 27.5 per cent. The party's three principal leaders had all been members of the Nazi party. The new minister-president, Dr Walter Bartram of the CDU, was also a former Nazi party member, elected by the legislature with BHE support. "Refugee parties do not fit readily into the normal pattern of political life. Should such a party arise on the national plane, it would not be likely to contribute to the stability of the German Federal Republic," concluded the US High Commissioner's Fourth Quarterly Report on Germany. However, the BHE did become a national party in January 1951 and was led by Waldemar Kraft (1898–1977). For the most part it was eventually, in the late 1950s, absorbed by the Christian democratic party.

The ministry for refugee affairs was founded when Adenauer's government took office in 1949, to focus greater attention on their problems, working together with the governments of Germany's eleven states. Overcrowding was a major problem, since no refugees were sent to the French zone initially. France had not been a party to the Potsdam Agreement which obligated Great Britain and the United States to accept refugees in their zones from Poland, Czechoslovakia, and Hungary. At the end of 1950 the McCloy report concluded:

> The tempo of housing construction must be increased. The Agricultural Resettlement Program, satisfactory on paper, must be given more vigorous support. Little has been done to carry out this program which seeks to place expellee farmers on land being reclaimed or land where there are no heirs to take charge of the property. Credit procedures must be simplified so that

[1] Office of US High Commissioner, *4th Quarterly Report* (July–September 1950), 30.

expellee businessmen can obtain loans quickly to save the export orders they are now losing. Local credit institutions must overcome their prejudice against the new businessmen among the displaced populations. And finally, social assimilation, which has been spurred on by international voluntary agencies, must be accomplished by the wholehearted cooperation of both the native Germans and the displaced populations.[2]

There was every reason to fear that the large number of uprooted and homeless people could form the nucleus of a subversive force and contribute to a renewal of right-wing extremism. This did not occur, thanks to the joint efforts of the leaders of the refugees and to the positive effects of the economic recovery which began in 1951. Although the BHE initially created an authoritarian impression that some feared would not contribute to the political stability of the new republic, it was led by practical men who were determined not to let emotional analysis undermine the strength and credibility of the new state.

The refugees had, in most cases, been forcibly expelled from their own homes and their land, and everything they could not carry or hide – their family heirlooms and their personal belongings – had been taken away from them by the Soviet-controlled governments of East Germany, Poland, Czechoslovakia or other Eastern European countries. The refugees had fled to the West to save their lives, and that was all they had been able to save. The BHE, therefore, was formed by people who represented the refugees' views concerning their legitimate wishes and efforts to have their property restored to them. Their views on this subject were clear and straightforward. Many saw them as ultra-conservative, because their demands did not waver. Those who judged their wishes to return to their homes and farms were often highly critical; but of those passing judgement, few had lost their own homes and possessions. For many of the refugees all they had left were memories, or if they were lucky, a map or a photograph of their former homes and farmlands now occupied by people they had never met. Or, if they were still more fortunate, they would later, much later in the 1970s, be able to visit their former homes and stare at them from across the road; homes, some of which had been in their families for generations.

There is little doubt that without the economic upswing, their demands and frustrations would have created major problems. As it was, the skills and experience of many refugees played a major and extremely productive role in both the economic and intellectual recovery of West Germany. In fact, without their expertise and their commitment to building a new life, reconstruction would, undoubtedly, have taken much longer. But this too, was done at great sacrifice. Central and

[2] Ibid., 63.

Eastern Europe were primarily agrarian societies, and many of the refugees had worked on farms all their lives. When they arrived in West Germany there was little land available for them, which meant that many had to learn new professions and be retrained. Farmers became locksmiths and estate owners became accountants. Psychologically it killed some of them.

One of the last of the great early pieces of social legislation of the Federal Republic, which affected millions of refugees and many other Germans directly, was the Equalization of Burdens Act of May 1952, passed by the Bundestag in the same month that Adenauer signed the treaties with the Western powers. The Parliamentary Commission charged with this responsibility realized the need to compensate those who had lost property, businesses or other assets. This affected mainly expellees from the Oder–Neisse territories. The law prescribed a special levy of half the value of real assets on June 21, 1948 – land, buildings, capital goods – on West German territory, the proceeds to be paid out of interest income or profits over 30 years and allotted to expellees and certain other victims according to claims, which would be carefully weighed by special committees. Minor losses were compensated fully; major financial losses in the old currency were compensated partially, generally in a ratio of 1 to 10. In the first 20 years of operation the equalization fund took in almost 83 billion marks, of which 67 per cent was paid to expellees and the rest to others who had lost real assets in the war.

The process of sifting and verifying claims was so cumbersome that many did not receive any compensation until the late 1950s; payments in fact continued to 1979. Also, because there were so many claims, and the value of the original 50 per cent levy of 1952 declined as time went by and the value of money declined, most claimants received at best some compensation for household goods. That is, they recovered a sum that would have bought back some of their household furniture or valuables, but in few cases enough to represent the whole value of a farm, a workshop, or a business. There was no humanly possible way to restore the effort of someone who had spent part of a lifetime building up a business in Breslau or Königsberg or Leipzig or Chemnitz (renamed Karl-Marx City by the SED), or the value of the lost assets. The mere attempt, however, contributed much to social peace in the Federal Republic, by conveying to the expellees and their leaders that they had more to gain by parliamentary methods and participation in democracy than by other means which could have produced disastrous results.

# 10

# Restitution and the Debt Problem

The London Debt Conference estimated the Reich debt to foreign countries at about 13 billion marks. Taking over this debt and declaring its liability to repay it did much to legitimize the West German republic abroad. Although the amounts payable – 567 million marks annually in debt service until 1958, thereafter 765 million[1] – seemed very high at first, the West German economy was soon running such a surplus and taking in so much foreign currency that the Bonn government was able to make payment without excessive hardship.

Another more morally frustrating and politically difficult kind of restitution was that to victims of Nazi persecution, above all to the survivors of the Holocaust and the heirs of those who perished. The government of the Federal Republic regarded itself as responsible for the obligations of the Reich, and considered itself liable for that government's debt and the consequences of the crimes committed. The two problems, restitution to victims of Nazi crimes and clearing the Reich debt, were inextricably connected. In dealing with both, the Federal Republic was cleaning up what it could of the debris of the past and restoring its international credit in both the moral and the financial sense. Adenauer broached the problem of restitution as soon as he became chancellor in 1949. He found a confused situation in which OMGUS had already taken some money and property out of Germany to give to victims of Nazi rule and had caused the *Land* governments to pass *Land* indemnification laws to regulate these proceedings. During his first period as chancellor, he put the entire issue on a more organized footing and combined these measures with the opening to Israel, which was as morally and politically difficult as it was important for the young republic.

---

[1] Schwarz, *Die Ära Adenauer, 1949–1957,* 183.

There was no question among West German leaders, across the political spectrum, that some kind of restitution should be made to the survivors and heirs of those who had lost property and their lives under Nazi rule.[2] In 1945, Jewish leaders claimed material compensation of eight billion dollars. Between 1947 and 1951, the Allied military governments obtained about 730 million dollars from Germany, which they turned over to Jewish organizations for initial satisfaction of some individual claims. After its creation in 1948 the Israeli government prepared a new claim of 1.5 billion dollars, a figure reached by multiplying the number of Jews entering Palestine as a consequence of German actions by 3,000 dollars. The Israelis asked the wartime Allies to support this claim, and the Western Allies did so; but the Soviet government did not even respond to the request, nor did the communist German regime in the GDR respond to Jewish claims for compensation until in 1988 it indicated willingness to discuss the issue. The GDR did not regard itself as having any moral or legal link to the past; it considered itself a new state altogether, representing the inevitable, socialist future of all Germany.

One of Adenauer's major concerns was support of restitution, and he announced in 1949 that his government was committed to provide assistance to Israel. But the amount he mentioned, ten million dollars, was so small that it contributed to Jewish indignation rather than eliciting a positive response. Adenauer let it be known that he was prepared to discuss restitution with any qualified Jewish representative, but at first few Jews even wanted to talk to the Germans. Nevertheless the Israeli government made contact with Adenauer via the Chancellor's Office in early 1950. Dr Nahum Goldmann, himself German by origin, but living in New York, was Adenauer's counterpart in the discussions. As head of the World Jewish Congress, and since October 1951 as president of the newly founded Conference on Jewish Material Claims against Germany, he was in touch with Jews in almost all countries of the world. The Claims Conference represented Jews worldwide and Adenauer agreed to meet their claims along with those of the Israelis.[3]

Adenauer's first and decisive meeting with Goldmann took place in December 1951, in London, at Claridge's Hotel. Goldmann was accompanied by the Israeli ambassador, who, because of Jewish resent-

[2] The following discussion of compensation to Jews is based largely on Schwarz, *Die Ära Adenauer, 1949–1957*, 184–6, and Hilberg, *Destruction of the European Jews*, 3: 1154–84.

[3] See Yeshayahu A. Jelinek, "Israel und die Anfänge der Shilumim," in Ludolf Herbst and Constantin Goschler, eds, *Wiedergutmachung in der Bundesrepublik Deutschland*, 119–38, concerning the earlier history of the Jewish negotiations with Germany and Jewish attitudes to restitution. The articles contained in this book explain, for the first time, an extremely complex and complicated subject.

ment of Jews meeting with Germans, appeared under an assumed name. Following this meeting, Adenauer wrote Goldmann that he accepted the Israeli claim of 1.5 billion dollars as the basis for talks, which started March 20, 1952, in Wassenaar, a small town near The Hague (Netherlands). It was chosen because its location would attract less publicity than a famous city, in view of the strong feelings of Jews toward the German as well as the Israeli delegations who took part in the talks. "In fact, the danger of an attack on someone's life was very real. In connection with these negotiations someone tried to assassinate me on March 27, 1952, by mailing a package with explosives, and one life was lost."[4]

The result of the negotiations was an agreement in June 1952 that the West German government would deliver to the state of Israel capital goods in the amount of three billion marks over the next twelve years. These amounts covered about 15 per cent of the value of Israeli imports and were of inestimable value to that country which, especially in the early 1950s, was close to bankruptcy. The amount would have by no means been as large, had Adenauer not insisted on the full amount with the support of the SPD members of the Bundestag, since he did not have unanimous support on the terms of restitution within his own party. In addition, Adenauer signed an agreement with the Jewish Claims Conference. In it, the Federal Republic undertook to provide 450 million marks at once to help victims and survivors not living in Israel. Of the 402 members of the Bundestag only 360 were present for the vote on March 18, 1953, to approve the two agreements committing payment of 3.45 billion marks. 239 voted for it, among them all social democrats, but only 106 delegates of the CDU/CSU, FDP and DP; 35 voted against (members of the CDU/CSU and the KPD), and 86 members abstained, including Franz Josef Strauss (who became deputy chairman of the CSU in 1952) and Fritz Schäffer, the minister of finance. Those who abstained or voted against believed the amount of restitution was too high, but they were also concerned with alienating the Arab states, as well as with the legitimate belief that all refugees, and not just Jews, had a right to full restitution. What prevailed, however, was the conviction that "in the case of Israel moral right takes precedence over formal right."[5]

The two Hague accords with Israel and the Jewish Claims Conference together constituted one of the two main aspects of the policy of indemnification. The other aspect consisted of the general measures taken to indemnify all persons, not only Jews, who had been persecuted

---

[4] Adenauer, *Erinnerungen 1953–1955*, 139. See also Rudolf Huhn, "Die Wiedergutmachungsverhandlungen in Wassenaar," in Herbst and Goschler, *Wiedergutmachung in der Bundesrepublik Deutschland*, 139–60.

[5] Schmid, Carlo, *Erinnerungen*, 512.

for national, political, ideological, or religious reasons. We mentioned above that, starting in 1947, the occupation authorities, OMGUS in particular, had caused the *Land* governments to take concrete steps to indemnify victims and to give back expropriated or stolen property. In 1953, the federal government followed up these early laws with the first federal law on the subject. This law soon turned out to be inadequate, since it covered only a small part of the total number of victims, and its criteria for determining the amounts of indemnification or restitution were vague. Therefore, in 1956, after more thorough preparation, the government passed the Federal Indemnification Law (*Bundesentschädigungsgesetz*). This law foresaw payments continuing well into the twenty-first century and constituted henceforth the foundation of all indemnification of, or restitution to, victims or to the survivors of victims of National Socialist presecution. In 1965, the Bundestag passed a revision of the law which further broadened the categories of claimants.

The laws of 1953 and 1956 were national German laws and as such valid only in and for the territory of the Federal Republic. They were administered by the *Länder* under procedures that were often slow, painful, and enervating for the former victims. Nevertheless, most claims were dealt with rather quickly. Though many were rejected, leading to accusations that the laws were inadequate or that the administrators were covering up Nazi crimes, the general practice was to decide claims as favorably as possible consistent with the laws. By 1957, the federal and *Land* governments, who shared the financial burden imposed by the laws, were paying out over two billion marks a year. From 1964 to 1983, the annual amounts varied between 2 and 2.2 billion marks, falling to 1.74 billion in 1987. In 1986, the government estimated that the total amounts paid in compensation would reach 102.6 billion marks by the year 2000. An expert further calculated in 1989 that the grand total, including pensions paid to the survivors of victims whose deaths were attributable to the actions of Nazi authorities, would be about 118 billion. The last of these descendants would live into the 2030s.

In the 1990s, Germans faced the question of whether to compensate innocent victims of communist rule in the GDR. In 1959, the Bonn government had declared that indemnification laws aimed at compensating victims of the Third Reich could not apply to victims of communism. The Federal Republic, the government said, was the legal representative of the Reich, and therefore responsible for its actions. It was not, however, responsible in the same way for the actions of the SED regime in East Germany. Therefore, victims of communism had to seek help under other laws, for example laws against wrongful imprisonment. In 1990, however, the Federal Republic, by the State Treaty of Unification, became the legal successor of the GDR, and some argued, therefore, that the Indemnification Laws should indeed be the model to follow in compensating victims from the GDR.[6]

Years later, Goldmann wrote that he found Adenauer to be one of the most impressive men he had ever met, "like a force of nature." From their first meeting at Claridge's, in December 1951, they formed a strong mutual bond that was unexpected for both of them and became decisive for the success of the negotiations. Goldmann could reassure the Israeli government and the parties of the Claims Conference that Adenauer was trustworthy, and Adenauer for his part knew that Goldmann was the best possible negotiator that he, as German chancellor, could hope for.

Goldmann's trust in and respect for Adenauer was not misplaced. The German chancellor had to overcome determined opposition in his own government to the reparations, both to the amounts involved and to the deadlines for payment. Yet he insisted that the government support him in honoring his promise to Goldmann and probably went further than any other German leader would have done. Why was he so determined? A historian later wrote: "In the depths of the great man's heart, on a level deeper than all his foxy tricks and Odysseus-like notions for the political struggle of the day, there was, very surprisingly, an almost childlike simplicity and grace – grace in the original sense of *gratia* – meaning mercy, thankfulness, and dignity."[7]

There was an additional motivation in his commitment to helping the Jews. He not only wanted to recognize responsibility for the past crimes of Germans, he wanted to repay a personal debt of honor. In his memoirs, he wrote that when he went to Luxembourg in September 1952 to sign the agreement with Israel, he recalled the day in 1933 when the Nazis dismissed him from his post as mayor of Cologne. They had immediately blocked his bank account and docked his pay. Within weeks, he and his family would be destitute. Two people came to him to offer help: one, Dannie Heinemann, was a friend who had emigrated to America and who gave Adenauer a substantial sum of money. Another was a retired professor from Frankfurt named Kraus, whose daughter Adenauer had appointed to a post in the Cologne city government. The professor, who was leaving Germany, offered Adenauer his life savings. Adenauer refused, but in his memoirs, he noted with bitterness: "As lord mayor of Cologne I had many friends. Heinemann and Professor Kraus were the only ones who offered me any help after I was dismissed."[8] Both were Jews.

[6] Hannes Kaschkat and Harry Schip, "Zur Entschädigung der Opfer des SED-Unrechtsregimes," *Deutschland Archiv* 24 (1991): 238–46.

[7] Gillessen, "Konrad Adenauer und der Israel-Vertrag," in *Politik, Philosophie, Praxis*, ed. Maier et al., 568.          [8] Adenauer, *Erinnerungen 1953–1955*, 158.

# 11

# The Ratification Debate Continues

In defending the General Treaty and the EDC Treaty in the Bundestag, Adenauer argued that they, along with the London Debt Agreement, represented the "liquidation of a lost war." There is no doubt he was anxious to move ahead rapidly; unfortunately, he was not in control of the international arena. The entire history of German rearmament and return to sovereignty, from 1949 to 1955, can be compared to a river rushing rapidly in parts and flowing slowly in others. The period from March to May 1952, from the first Stalin note to the signing ceremony, resembled the rapid part; from then until late summer 1954, everything moved slowly.

Adenauer's task after signing the treaties was to have them ratified, to obtain the approval of the Bundestag of the necessary laws authorizing military forces, and to have the Blank Office draw up the precise plans for raising, instructing, and organizing those troops. The first obstacle on the domestic German road to ratification was the SPD's complaint, which they had lodged in the Constitutional Court in January 1952. The resulting saga of legal maneuvers and countermaneuvers was probably the most dramatic in the history of the Court.

The competent chamber to decide the SPD complaint was the first, so-called "Red Senate", so Adenauer had some reason to fear a ruling declaring the treaties in violation of the Basic Law, thus requiring a two-thirds majority in the Bundestag for the necessary change in the constitution. At this juncture the federal president, Heuss, whom Adenauer had convinced that the policy of Western integration and contribution to European security was right, intervened. On June 10, 1952, Heuss asked the Court as a whole to issue an opinion whether the EDC, as such, was compatible with the Basic Law. The Court decided that responding to this request, which was intended to help the president decide whether the laws he would be asked to sign were constitutional, was more urgent than dealing with the SPD's case.

Months passed while the judges at Karlsruhe considered the terms of the EDC treaty and the Bundestag desultorily debated both treaties. In November Adenauer heard rumors that the Court, in its non-binding opinion to Heuss, was going to rule that the EDC was not compatible with the Basic Law in its present form, and that the EDC treaty was therefore equivalent to a change of the constitution which required a two-thirds majority in the Bundestag – which the government did not have.

Adenauer's solution was to have 201 coalition members of the Bundestag make a joint complaint to the Constitutional Court against the 128 SPD members. The ground for the complaint was that the SPD members, by claiming that the treaties required a constitutional change to be ratified, were infringing on the rights of the coalition members. The latter accordingly asked the Court to find that ratification required only a simple majority. This request was a procedural gambit. Because the Court's responsibilities were divided between two chambers, the CDU-led complaint, which took the official form of an *Organklage* or "complaint against an organ of the constitution" – in this case a political party – would come before the second, or CDU-dominated "Black Senate," whereas the SPD complaint was pending in the first, or "Red Senate." Furthermore, since the CDU complaint concerned the ratification procedure directly, the rules governing the Court required that it be dealt with before the SPD complaint, which took the form of a *Feststellungsklage* or "complaint on a point of fact."

At this point the judges' resentment at being the objects of political manipulation by the parties in Bonn boiled over. On December 8, 1952, they issued a joint declaration that the opinion for Heuss would be binding for both chambers. In other words, if the Court, in its opinion to Heuss, should state that the EDC was not compatible with the Basic Law as it stood – i.e., that the treaty required a two-thirds majority of the Bundestag for ratification – then neither the first nor the second chamber would admit the CDU claim that ratification required only a simple majority.

Adenauer, now worried that the court would find against the EDC treaty and provoke a genuine constitutional conflict, asked Heuss to withdraw his request for an opinion. Heuss did so willingly because he, too, was annoyed by the joint declaration of the judges, which he considered an unwarranted usurpation of constitutional authority. When Heuss' decision to withdraw his request became known, the public uproar was tremendous. Thomas Dehler, the minister of justice, further infuriated the SPD and, presumably, the judges sympathetic to the SPD, when he stated "The Federal Constitutional Court has departed shockingly from the path of law and has thereby created a serious crisis."[1] Unfortunately he also infuriated Heuss with some ill-tempered remarks, and when the time came for Adenauer to form his second government after the national elections of 1953, he decided to dispense with Dehler's services. This was undoubtedly one reason that Dehler later became a disappointed and bitter enemy of Adenauer and his foreign policy.

On March 19, 1953, the Bundestag finally ratified the treaties, by a simple majority. The next hurdle was ratification by the Bundesrat, composed of representatives of the *Land* governments. The key to a government majority in the Bundesrat was the delegation from the newest, and in some ways, most interesting *Land* of West Germany: Baden-Württemberg. This "south-western state" was established in 1952 by a referendum of the inhabitants of Württemberg-Baden, Württemberg-Hohenzollern, and Baden. These were three *Länder* created artificially in 1945, whereas the new south-western *Land* had specific, historical roots. Its proponents saw it as a counterweight to Bavaria in the south of Germany and were anxious that the region's many ties to France and the West, the traditional industrial and commercial skills of the people, and the region's cultural and religious heritage, should play their full part in the new German society.

The first minister-president of Baden-Württemberg was Reinhold Maier (1889–1971), who had been minister-president of Württemberg-Baden since 1945. Maier was a leader of the FDP, which enjoyed exceptional strength – up to 20 per cent – in the region. He also enjoyed the reputation of being the only other "sly fox" in the entire country who was a match for Adenauer. Although by no means a neutralist or opposed to German integration with western Europe, he was nevertheless skeptical about the treaties and thought that perhaps the Federal Republic should think more carefully before joining the EDC and binding itself so firmly to a Western policy. He began his political life in the National Liberal party, which until 1893 was the largest political party in the Wilhelmine Reich and remained powerful until World War I. In the Weimar Republic, the national liberal tradition continued in the German People's Party, the party of the republic's most successful chancellor, Gustav Stresemann. Like the progressive liberals, the national liberals supported business interests, material progress, and free enterprise. However, they did not share the progressives' distrust of military institutions and supported both a large army and strong central government. Both these tendencies continued in the national wing of the FDP. Baden, Maier's home region, had been a bastion of the national liberals since the mid-nineteenth century.

---

[1] Schwarz, *Die Ära Adenauer, 1949–1957*, 177.

As perhaps the most powerful *Landesfürst* and leader of the FDP's national wing, Maier was an indispensable ally for Adenauer. Maier disapproved of the way Adenauer handled Stalin's notes, and believed that it was worth waiting to see what price the Soviet government would really ask in return for permitting German reunification and a liberalization in Eastern Europe. On this point he agreed with his fellow-south-westerner, Karl Georg Pfleiderer, who in June 1952 produced his own concept of *Ostpolitik* (Eastern policy) for the reunification of a neutral Germany with a small army – the dream of the nationalists in the FDP – that suggested demilitarizing the area between the Rhine and the Oder–Neisse without prejudice to the territorial question in a peace treaty. This stance was based on the conviction that the Federal Republic should accept the USSR as the dominant power in Central Europe. These concerns of Maier and the ideas of Pfleiderer closely resembled the proposals of the British foreign minister, Eden, in 1954, and those of many Eastern bloc spokesmen since. In the 1980s, they were taken up with renewed vigor, in a very different context, by the SPD.

Maier may have been skeptical of the EDC and he may have enjoyed political fencing with Adenauer, but he decided not to let the treaties fail in the Bundesrat. His fellow minister-president, Hans Ehard of Bavaria, who also resisted the approval of the treaties as a demonstration of *Land* prerogatives, finally gave in and permitted the Bundesrat to ratify them on May 15, 1953. Thus, the German parliament had done its part; unfortunately, the delay only exacerbated the debate in France, where a powerful coalition of Gaullists on the right, and socialists and communists on the left, outnumbered the pro-EDC Europeanist liberals in the center. By summer of 1953 it was clear that the German defense contribution would begin, at the earliest, in 1954, and that was assuming that the EDC became a reality.

In April 1953 Adenauer paid his first visit to the United States, where he was received almost as a hero and certainly as a trusted ally. A poignant moment came at Arlington national cemetery in Virginia when the US Marine Corps band played both *The Star-Spangled Banner* and the *Deutschlandlied*. Adenauer might well have reflected that no one would have imagined in his wildest dreams in May 1945, that less than eight years later, a German chancellor would visit Washington in triumph and be greeted with the German national anthem. Adenauer was able to tell the new president, Eisenhower, and his secretary of state, John Foster Dulles, that ratification of the treaties was certain and a German military contribution likely by the end of the year. For Germany, he was right; unfortunately the drift was now strongly against the EDC in a very important country, France.

# 12
## Berlin 1949–1953

At the same time as Adenauer was serving his first term as chancellor, leadership in the American, British and French sectors of Berlin was provided by the city's governing mayor, since Berlin was not legally a *Land* of the Federal Republic, but was, and remained until 1990, legally subject to quadripartite administration. The Soviet Union did not recognize four-power control in Greater Berlin, and in 1950 transferred executive power in its sector to the government of the GDR.

The situation in Berlin following the end of the blockade in May 1949 was superficially stable, but by no means clear. Berlin, described by Bertold Brecht as "a city of nets," was divided politically, but travel throughout it was still possible. Since East German control of the entrances to West Berlin was not complete, refugees continued to enter the Western sectors of the city as they fled communism in the Soviet zone. The Allied powers held supreme authority in the Western sectors and, in fact, never relinquished that authority. The reason for this special status for Berlin, agreed upon in 1944 by the four powers, was that the Allies assumed, as did the Germans, that when a sovereign government was formed for all of Germany, by the Germans, such a government would formally sign a peace treaty with Germany's former enemies and take its seat in the old German capital.

The German government of West Berlin was a coalition under Ernst Reuter and the SPD, with the CDU and the FDP. While the parties and population shared political differences, they also shared the commitment to defend the freedom of their city that they saw being destroyed in East Berlin and in the Soviet zone of occupation. Because Berlin was surrounded geographically by the Soviet zone, its population and its government experienced daily contact with the suppression being carried out in the Soviet zone and in the Soviet sector of Berlin, and they learned from it. Indeed, the East German communist party paper, *Neues Deutschland*, made the reasons for the concerns of free Berliners clear following the Berlin blockade, by uttering a threat that became famous: "He who lives on an island should not make an enemy of the sea." As a consequence of the successful efforts made by the East German government in 1948 to split the city's government and subsequently to sever most physical connections, such as telephone lines, between East and West Berlin between 1949 and 1955, the SPD government in Berlin was composed of very realistic men and women. The party endorsed a foreign policy vis-à-vis the Soviet Union which was much more realistic than that of the main body of the party in West Germany.

Ernst Reuter had become governing mayor of Berlin (of the Western sectors of the city) in 1948 at the time the Soviet government blockaded the city's land, rail and water routes to West Germany. He had been born in 1889 in northern Silesia and as a young man became committed to the socialist movement. As a prisoner of war, he experienced the Russian Revolution, joined the Bolsheviks thereafter and was appointed by Lenin as commissioner of the German Volga territory. After becoming secretary general of the new German Communist Party in the 1920s, he eventually broke with communism and joined the SDP. He emigrated from Germany to Turkey in 1935, where he spent the next eleven years in exile, and returned to Berlin in 1946. He was, without question, one of the most ardent and articulate supporters of freedom, liberty and democracy following the war and remained so until his death in 1953.

A committed social democrat, Reuter strongly supported Adenauer's efforts to build democracy in Germany, as well as to preserve freedom in at least one part of the divided country. He was more tolerant of Adenauer's Western foreign policy than the leader of his own party, Kurt Schumacher, probably because he was the mayor of the beleaguered and divided city of Berlin, and he knew that caustic criticism of Adenauer was not as important as keeping Allied support and drawing the world's attention to his city. During his tenure as mayor, he repeatedly called on the "people of the world [to] look at this city." Reuter believed that "the fate of our people" would be decided in Berlin, and extolled the efforts of the Berliners to defend themselves and to survive the blockade. He correctly believed that free Berlin would survive only as long as West Germany, and the Western Allies, remained firmly committed to protecting the freedom of the city. In his speech at the dedication ceremonies of the Free University of Berlin in December 1948, at the height of the blockade, he emphasized his conviction with the following words: "Truth and freedom are inextricably bound together. Only in freedom can one find truth, and only those dedicated to the search of truth can be truly free men."[1]

---

[1] Brandt and Lowenthal, *Ernst Reuter*, 467.

Together with Kurt Schumacher and Theodor Heuss, Reuter rejected the idea of German collective guilt for the war and its horrors, but stressed the imperative of re-establishing the German people as respected citizens of the world. He also felt equally strongly about German prisoners of war still in captivity, and thus at Christmas 1952 he appealed to the Berliners to place a candle in their windows to symbolize their unity with those who had not yet returned home. When the Berliners learned of his death in 1953, they spontaneously placed lighted candles in their windows in honor of a strong and beloved political leader of postwar Germany.

Reuter's governance of Berlin faced formidable obstacles. The East German communists and the Soviets had formed the GDR government in October 1949 under Walter Ulbricht and Wilhelm Pieck, both members of the former KPD, and Otto Grotewohl, formerly of the SPD, who had been Schumacher's competitor for SPD leadership immed-iately after the war. The GDR was a true communist state, and in the early years carried out collectivization of the land which largely ruined agricultural productivity in these formerly very productive central German provinces of Mecklenburg and Saxony. The SED also carried out gradual politicization of all aspects of normal life, eliminating all remaining vestiges of personal independence.

The condition of the workers in the GDR quickly fell far behind that of their West German counterparts. Dismantling was much more extensive and the economy was used as a source for rebuilding the Soviet state and not the Soviet zone of Germany. The consequence of German communist repression was an uprising of German workers in East Berlin and in major cities in East Germany on June 17, 1953, as a result of a law reducing wages but requiring greater production. For a brief period of two days these Germans were able to reveal their true feelings, and it was clear that in free elections the SPD would have won an overwhelming victory. The uprising, however, was put down by Soviet forces without any attempt by the Western powers to stop them.

The day of June 17 illustrated more dramatically than any other event since the creation of two separate German governments within Germany in 1949, the difference between East and West Germany. On that day, workers throughout East Germany threw stones at Soviet tanks. They were defeated, arrested by the thousands, and jailed. Many were killed. Nevertheless, the revolt achieved for one day the collapse of SED control throughout the GDR. As Rolf Lahr, a diplomat in the foreign ministry, wrote to his sister on June 19, the workers "*did* revolt and they *did* achieve a victory! If the world had not known it before, now it knows that the Germans behind the Iron Curtain did not want this system. . . . The 17th of June was a revolt of the people, the scream of a tormented soul. . . ."[2]

The revolt became "a wave of bitterness, of despair, encompassing the whole of the Soviet occupied zone," wrote Adenauer in his memoirs.[3] It was also a graphic and painful example of why Adenauer was so concerned with preserving West Germany's security by alignment with the West. It was also the first time the Western Allies made clear that they would not cross the demarcation lines of 1945 to support an uprising of the victims of Soviet dictatorship. The refusal of France, Britain, and the United States to take strong measures, or even to condemn Soviet oppression by means of sanctions, had long-term effects in West Germany. It probably convinced Adenauer, if he was not already convinced, that reunification would not occur soon, and that a strong defense was an absolute necessity in West Germany.

The day of the uprising was declared a national holiday by the West German Bundestag in 1955, as the "Day of German Unity." In memory of the uprising and its victims, the Berlin government renamed the Western part of the main east-west avenue in the city, the avenue that ran through the Brandenburg Gate from the Soviet sector to the British sector, and which, in East Berlin, was *Unter den Linden.* The new name was "Avenue of June 17."

[2] Lahr, *Zeuge von Fall und Aufstieg,* 199.
[3] Adenauer, *Erinnerungen 1953–1955,* 220.

# 13

# From the 1953 Election to Sovereignty

While Adenauer was battling for ratification of the Western treaties in Germany, two momentous events changed the constellation of power on the international level. Both the superpowers, as the media were beginning to call them, changed leaders. On January 20, Dwight D. Eisenhower, who had served as Supreme Allied Commander Europe (SACEUR), NATO's top military officer, between 1950 and 1952, became president of the United States, succeeding Harry S. Truman. The result was no great surprise, but the possibility that William Howard Taft, a Democrat and an isolationist, might be elected had given Adenauer – and many other Europeans – sleepless nights during the spring of 1952. With Ike in the White House there was every reason to expect a firm commitment of the US to the peace and security of democratic Europe for a long time to come. What few in Germany yet realized was that Eisenhower, as the commanding general of NATO, had come to agree with those in the US who supported greater reliance on nuclear weapons in NATO and were hence less concerned with the EDC.

On March 5, a bare two weeks before the Bundestag finally ratified the EDC and the General Treaty, Joseph Stalin died in Moscow, ending a reign unparalleled in Russian history for bloodshed and violence. The "little son of a bitch" whom Truman "liked" at Potsdam had deliberately ordered actions that led to the death, by starvation or imprisonment in concentration camps (the gulags), of somewhere between 20 and 30 million Russians out of a total population in 1930, when the terror began, of about 156 million.[1] In addition, the war with Germany in 1941–5, which Stalin and his generals prosecuted with a disregard for human life that appalled Germans and Westerners alike, had cost the Soviet Union another 20 million dead.

[1] Conquest, *Harvest of Sorrow*, 299–301; see also Antonov-Ovseenko, *Time of Stalin.*

Although few in the West knew or cared to know the price in human blood that Stalin extracted in order to make his own rule as complete as possible and to make Soviet power an instrument of his will, his shadow nevertheless loomed menacingly over the deliberations and thoughts of Western politicians. His death caused general relief: his replacement, whomever he might be, must, most Westerners thought, be someone more civilized, easier to deal with and less likely to unleash a world war. However justified or unjustified these expectations may have been, they influenced Western actions vis-à-vis Stalin's successors.

The power struggle in the Kremlin following Stalin's death lasted almost three years, but by late 1953 the former head of the Ukrainian communist party, Nikita S. Khrushchev, was emerging as Stalin's likely successor. He became first secretary of the Party in September 1953, although it was not until early 1957 that he finally removed from power his chief rivals Malenkov, Kaganovich, and the foreign minister, Molotov. In 1953, however, Molotov was still in charge of Soviet foreign policy; his familiar stone face and arrogant rudeness reappeared at the four-power foreign ministers' conferences on the German question held in Berlin in early 1954 and in Geneva in late 1955.

One month after the Berlin uprising, the foreign ministers of the three Western powers met in Washington to discuss the German question. They agreed to propose to the Soviet Union a four-power conference on Germany. That conference raised the curtain on the final act of the drama of sovereignty and rearmament. But before it took place West Germany held its second national and free election.

By 1953 Adenauer's leadership had earned him increasing popularity, and this was clearly evident in the second elections for the Bundestag held in September 1953. An overwhelming voter turnout of almost 86 per cent resulted in a stunning election victory for the CDU/ CSU which obtained 45.2 per cent of the vote (1949: 31 per cent). The SPD did not fare well with 28.8 per cent (1949: 29.2 per cent) and was further from national power than it had been in 1949. The big losers were the small parties, most of whose supporters were moving toward support for the CDU. The BHE, which had not yet existed in 1949, obtained its first and only representation in the Bundestag (6 per cent and 27 seats). The remaining parties were the DP and the Center, both of which supported the CDU. The KPD lost its seats. Adenauer's government, therefore, continued, vastly strengthened. He retained the offices of chancellor and foreign minister; Gerhard Schröder, a rising young star of the Protestant wing of the CDU, became minister of the interior, and Franz Josef Strauss of the CSU, who had established his reputation in the rearmament debate in early 1952, entered the cabinet as minister without portfolio.

By this time Adenauer realized that the EDC was likely to fail because of French opposition. In the fall of 1953 he told the editor of the *New York Times*, Cyrus L. Sulzberger, what he was considering doing in the event that the EDC was not ratified by the French. He knew that France was capable not only of rejecting the EDC, but also even of vetoing German NATO membership. Therefore he envisioned a European security system including the US, West Germany, Britain, Spain, and Turkey – but not necessarily France. More than twelve years before France left NATO in 1966, Adenauer foresaw that the military element of the Western Alliance might eventually have to make do without the difficult partner in Paris.

For Adenauer, the EDC, efforts to recover the Saar province on the border with France, which the French still intended to keep, and a political community of Europe were interdependent, and all three were necessary to accomplish what Adenauer regarded as the two over-whelmingly important political tasks of democratic Europe: unity for prosperity and progress, and unity to be able to deter and, if necessary, defeat a Soviet attack.

He was nevertheless realistic enough to recognize that the EDC was likely to fail. His response was to move toward German participation in NATO, and toward a solution of the Saar question by concluding a bilateral agreement with France. In 1953, however, he could not make this move publicly. He considered it essential to act as though the EDC would be approved, in order to combat his domestic neutralist opponents of rearmament. During the spring of 1954, in fact, in order to preserve focus on German unity, Jakob Kaiser, Thomas Dehler, and the SPD chairman, Ollenhauer, together founded a bipartisan "All-German Movement," which the federal president Heuss approved as an official organization in the public interest under the name *Kuratorium Unteilbares Deutschland*. It was not stridently anti-Adenauer, but its members were concerned that western integration not obscure the goal of reunification. Headquartered in Bonn, the organization continued to be active in the late 1980s, under the chairmanship of Johann Baptist Gradl, a member of the CDU from the Soviet zone and in 1965–6 minister for all-German affairs. In 1990, following unification, the government pro-posed to abolish the *Kuratorium*, as it had already abolished the ministry of all-German affairs (or inner-German relations, as it was called from 1969). Its members and well-wishers were to devote their energies henceforth to integrating the former GDR territories into the united democratic Germany.

On November 11, 1953, Adenauer declared to the Bundestag that he favored the continued presence of US troops in West Germany after the EDC came into existence. His position did not come as a great surprise, since few political leaders in West Germany believed that the EDC would mean Europe could dispense with the support of US troops in Europe; in fact, from Adenauer's viewpoint the EDC was a way of making it worthwhile for the Americans to remain. Far more significant in the long run, given that the EDC failed, was another announcement of Adenauer's; namely, that he regarded the deployment of nuclear weapons in West Germany as essential for defense. In fact, he had already indicated his support to the American government; several days after the election, the first US nuclear weapons arrived at American bases in West Germany. They were 280–mm nuclear-capable artillery cannon, which were followed during 1954–5 by nuclear-capable tactical fighter aircraft. The 280–mm cannon "made their journey down the Rhine River amidst a fanfare of publicity. A curious sight, massive and cumbersome, they attracted press speculation as to their purpose and capabilities, which the US army only vaguely revealed."[2]

The American decision to supply their forces in Germany with nuclear weapons was, in part, a response to Adenauer's encouragement, and, in part, a reflection of a general shift in US strategy for the European theatre under the Eisenhower administration. The administration set forth the "New Look" and the overall US strategy of which it was a part in a document known as NSC-162/2 of October 1953, which partially superseded NSC-68 of April 1950.[3]

The concept behind the "New Look" was to contain Soviet expansion without harming the American economy: "To achieve these ends it [NSC-162/2] recommended a greater emphasis on alliances and on the deterrent utility of strategic and tactical nuclear (as compared to conventional) forces."[4] Accordingly, the "New Look" did not envision a massive conventional deterrent against Soviet attack. Rather, the conventional forces of the EDC would serve as a "shield" to defend Europe temporarily, until the US unleashed NATO's nuclear "sword;" namely, the American bomber force of the Strategic Air Command.[5] On December 14, the chairman of the JCS, Admiral Radford, spelled out the implications of the "New Look" for Europe: the continent would be defended in the first instance by air power and tactical or intermediate-range nuclear weapons, that is, artillery, bombs, or missiles. The American "sword" would follow. Secretary of State Dulles, in January 1954, publicized the strategic concept of "massive and instant retaliation"

---

[2] Cioc, *Pax Atomica*, 21.

[3] Ibid., 4–6.

[4] Friedberg, "Making of American National Strategy." *National Interest* 11 (Spring 1988): 68.

[5] Cioc, *Pax Atomica*, 7.

with nuclear weapons on the Soviet homeland in response to a Soviet attack (the "New Look" was not formally adopted by the NATO ministers until their meeting in Paris in December 1954). Although the Soviet Union had already developed the atomic bomb, it did not, in early 1954, have the hydrogen bomb; nor did it have a nuclear stockpile or means of delivering weapons.

The SPD objected vigorously to the presence of American atomic cannon on West German soil and the implied NATO strategy that Western Europe would be defended by means of a tactical nuclear battle on German territory. Fritz Erler, who was becoming the SPD's leading defense and security expert, asked the Bundestag on November 19 to "imagine concretely what it would mean if, with a few shots, a city such as Frankfurt or a part of the Ruhr were destroyed. These weapons are not just directed at the enemy. Their use would also entail massive destruction of the surrounding area where the enemy might happen to be, in this case a part of the Federal Republic."[6] Thus, following the death of Schumacher more than one year earlier, the SPD was developing a very specific theme – that integrating West Germany with the US-led security system in any manner, whether by EDC or by NATO, meant transferring risks to Germans that ought to be borne by Americans, Frenchmen, or Britons. This theme was to continue until 1960, and was to emerge again in the 1980s.

On December 14–16, 1953, the NATO Council, at its meeting in Paris, expanded on Radford's statement and officially buried the Lisbon decision of February 1952 to base European defense on a massive conventional deterrent. Secretary of State Dulles later summarized the "New Look" for NATO with the following explanation: "The United States considers that the ability to use atomic weapons as conventional weapons is essential for the defense of the NATO area in the face of the present threat."[7]

At that same NATO meeting in December 1953 Dulles, fearing, with justification, that the EDC was lurching toward defeat in France, announced unequivocally that if the EDC failed the US would have to conduct an "agonizing reappraisal" of its foreign and security policies vis-à-vis Europe. What he meant was that without the EDC the US – assuming it remained committed to the defense of Europe – would support full West German membership in the Atlantic Alliance, with its own autonomous military forces.

The conference of foreign ministers in Berlin in January-February of 1954 ended without a conclusion. The main point of interest was a

---

[6] Cited ibid., 25.
[7] Cited ibid., 6.

British proposal, the Eden Plan, indirectly drawing on Stalin's two diplomatic notes of 1952, recommending German reunification through free elections guaranteed by the four powers. The Soviets responded with a draft peace treaty of their own.[8] This manner of waging the Cold War by means of written proposals became a fixture of East–West relations in the 1950s, as did Soviet proposals, also made in Berlin in 1954, for a treaty on "collective security" in Europe. In effect this was a demand that the West recognize the legitimacy and inviolability of the communist regimes in Central Europe, including the GDR. The Soviet government was thus playing simultaneously with the idea of a reunited Germany with which to make peace, and with the idea of securing the GDR and the rest of its empire by persuading the West to promise never to threaten it or to demand liberalization and democracy. In the 1950s most Western leaders firmly rejected the "collective security" idea as a Soviet trick to secure its illegitimate gains, but by the late 1960s they had come to accept it, and in the 1970s it became the basis of East–West policy in Europe.

Following what proved to be a fruitless meeting, the Western foreign ministers issued a statement which accurately pointed out that the Soviet proposals "would have involved the dissolution of the Western security system" – NATO and the EDC – "while the military power of the Soviet bloc in Europe remained intact." They were, the statement said, "forced to the conclusion that the Soviet Government is not now ready to permit free, all-German elections or to abandon its control over Eastern Germany."[9] One month later, in March, the Soviet Union ended its official occupation of East Germany and formally granted the GDR full sovereignty; the Western Allies responded with a declaration denying that the East German regime was, in fact, a legitimate and sovereign state.

In April 1954 Adenauer made a last attempt to win wavering French support for the EDC, but without success. Accordingly he began to try to separate the issue of sovereignty from the issue of security; the General Treaty from the EDC Treaty. On June 24 he obtained official assurance from the US and Britain that they would recognize the full sovereignty of West Germany irrespective of the fate of the EDC treaty. In West Germany, Adenauer's party colleague, Eugen Gerstenmaier, the president of the Bundestag, spelled out Adenauer's priorities, in the same month, in a speech on foreign policy in unambiguous terms. West Germany's first goal, Gerstenmaier said, must be freedom; second, peace; and only in third place came reunification.[10]

---

[8] See Dept of State, *Documents on Germany*, 408–13.
[9] Ibid., 417.
[10] Schwarz, *Die Ära Adenauer, 1949–1957,* 226.

On August 30, 1954, the French National Assembly finally rejected – by refusing to consider – the EDC treaty, which the French government had already encumbered with amendments so numerous that all the other Western governments would have had to reconsider the treaty if France had in fact ratified it. The French action, which came after a long summer of delay and confusion, was the final nail in the coffin of the EDC. The alternative was to return to the option that had been rejected when France proposed the Pleven Plan in 1950; namely, West German membership in NATO according to the plan adopted at the Lisbon conference in 1952 and a German national defense contribution under the command of German officers.

The shift in speed and decisiveness of Western policy in the weeks following the French decision, was certainly "one of the most astonishing episodes in postwar German history."[11] It had taken the Western governments four years to debate, sign, and finally reject the EDC. It took less than two months for the same governments to agree to end the occupation regime in West Germany, to admit West Germany to the Brussels Pact and NATO, to permit German rearmament, and to return the Saar to Germany.

In 1952, West Germany had signed two treaties: one with the three occupying powers ending occupation and providing a framework for their mutual relations (the General Treaty), and one with the Brussels Pact countries setting up the EDC. The former was revised in the clauses on reunification and sovereignty, though its basic purpose, of making the new Germany an equal partner in Western security, remained unchanged, the latter was superseded by protocols admitting West Germany to the Brussels Pact and NATO.

The agreements recast the relationships of the Western European nations more decisively than any other event since the war. They produced a system of stable peace, while keeping open the question of German unity, that, as a later writer put it, compared favorably with the reordering of Europe at the Congress of Vienna in 1814–15.[12] The final agreements were reached at two conferences held in London and Paris in September and October of 1954. The London conference included the foreign ministers of the former EDC states (West Germany, France, Italy, the Benelux), the US, Britain, and Canada. According to the Final Act, the foreign ministers

dealt with the most important issues facing the Western world, security and European integration within the framework of a developing Atlantic community dedicated to peace and freedom. In this connexion the Conference considered

[11] Ibid., 246.
[12] Ibid., 247.

how to assure the full association of the German Federal Republic with the West and the German defense contribution. . . .

All the decisions of the Conference formed part of one general settlement which is, directly or indirectly, of concern to all the NATO powers and which will therefore be submitted to the North Atlantic Council for information or decision.[13]

The Final Act included five distinct undertakings. In the first, the three occupying powers agreed to end occupation as soon as possible, "recognising that a great country can no longer be deprived of the rights properly belonging to a free and democratic people; and desiring to associate the Federal Republic of Germany on a footing of equality with their efforts for peace and security." In the second, the nine governments undertook to invite West Germany and Italy to join the Brussels Pact. In the third, Adenauer expanded on his 1952 commitment that West Germany would not "manufacture in its territory any atomic weapons, chemical weapons or biological weapons" as well as long-range missiles, large warships, or bombers. Dulles took the occasion to specify that this assurance was, of course, only binding in international law *rebus sic stantibus* – as long as conditions remained as they were. In other words, a dramatic change in international relations would implicitly release West Germany from its obligation.

The fourth part of the Final Act was a declaration by West Germany and the three Western powers that the Federal Republic would conduct a peaceful foreign policy and in particular would never "have recourse to force to achieve the reunification of Germany." The fifth summarized the Western powers' recognition that the West German government was

the only German Government freely and legitimately constituted and therefore entitled to speak for Germany . . .

A peace settlement for the whole of Germany, freely negotiated between Germany and her former enemies . . . remains an essential aim of their policy. The final determination of the boundaries of Germany must await such a settlement.

The achievement through peaceful means of a fully free and unified Germany remains a fundamental goal of their policy.

The security and welfare of Berlin and the maintenance of the position of the Three Powers there are regarded by the Three Powers as essential elements of the peace of the free world in the present international situation. . . . They therefore reaffirm that they will treat any attack against Berlin from any quarter as an attack upon their forces and themselves.[14]

[13] Dept of State, *Documents on Germany*, 419–20.
[14] Ibid., 420–24.

On October 21–3, the nine foreign ministers met again in Paris where they signed the agreements set forth in London. These agreements, notably the revised version of the General Treaty, known henceforth in German as the *Deutschlandvertrag*, were known in the West as the Paris Treaties, which Erich Ollenhauer described as sealing the "eternal division of Germany."[15] The *Deutschlandvertrag* was in large part a straight copy of the General Treaty. It contained a few changes, particularly in the clauses concerning reunification and sovereignty. The transference clause (7.3) of the General Treaty was gone, though its substance remained: the Allies undertook to work peacefully with West Germany for the common goal of a reunited democratic Germany. Missing from the new treaty was the condition that the united German government would enter into West Germany's rights and duties under its international engagements.

The Paris Treaties, unlike the General Treaty, included protocols on the Allied reserve powers in relation to Germany and Berlin as a whole. The Allies proposed to retain their forces in Germany on the basis of separate deployment agreements with Bonn, similar to those entered into with other NATO members, known as Status of Forces Agreements (SOFA). In 1965, France unilaterally withdrew from its SOFA: by this precedent, any NATO member could cancel its deployment agreement. On the other hand, the Allies explicitly tied their troop presence in Germany to their reserve powers. If the SOFA was linked to what were in essence occupation rights, no German government could unilaterally abolish them. With unification in 1990, the western Allies renounced their last remaining reserve powers, thereby in principle putting Germany on a par with other NATO members as far as concluding or abolishing the SOFA was concerned.

In 1954 the Allies retained all emergency powers necessary to ensure the safety of their troops in Germany. This represented a significant restraint on German domestic sovereignty, to which the German negotiators agreed in order to achieve the treaty's main purpose, which was West Germany's equal status and the right to join NATO. Domestic political opponents of Adenauer used the emergency powers clause to argue that Germany remained occupied, since under cover of an emergency the Allies could override German police authority and do virtually anything they wanted in the name of ensuring the safety of their troops. What would happen if the Allies claimed that German subversives were planning to disrupt troop movements? Could the Allies suspend civil rights, invade privacy, mobilize German civilian resources? The answer was formally "yes." Few Germans felt much fear on that score, however. They were well satisfied to have the Allies

[15] Cited in Berlin Senat, *Berlin Chronik der Jahre 1951–1954*, 27.

remain in their country as allies and protectors, even at the cost of some formal lack of sovereignty. In 1968, after years of intense and divisive debate, the Bundestag passed amendments to the Basic Law that turned responsibility for ensuring the safety of Allied troops over to German authorities.

In another separate protocol, West Germany undertook to assure the economic survival of the western sectors of Berlin by, among other things, subsidizing business, industry, and communications. A separate meeting of representatives of all NATO countries issued a protocol to the North Atlantic Treaty authorizing the US to invite West Germany to become a member of the Atlantic Alliance. In addition, the members of the Brussels Pact, in admitting Germany and Italy, transformed the Western Union into the Western European Union (WEU). At Paris the creation of the WEU was viewed by some as a vehicle that could carry forward efforts toward further Western European integration. In fact, the WEU remained without significant influence until the 1980s, when a number of European politicians revived it as a means to develop European policies on East–West relations and security that differed from US preferences.

By the end of 1954 the Western countries had maneuvered their common interest past some potentially very dangerous shoals, and the Soviet Union had failed to exploit differences of opinion. Many were astonished that the French accepted German NATO membership, when in 1950 they had launched the Pleven Plan and given lip service to the EDC for almost four years to prevent just such a development. In the interim, however, the French had recognized that NATO might be an effective instrument for controlling German power. They believed that the WEU would be an effective and useful way of restraining the Germans and proposed that the WEU control the production and distribution of armaments among its members. When the US and Britain refused to participate in this system, Adenauer expanded upon his assurance concerning nuclear weapons, which finally satisfied the French. Adenauer's position appalled Speidel and the other officers in the Blank Office, who were conversant with the "New Look" and the concept of massive retaliation, and who assumed that West German military forces would need nuclear weapons if they were to play a serious part in the Western defense strategy. In fact, Adenauer's government never ceased to insist on West Germany's right to have nuclear weapons; it only promised never to build its own.

A separate but, for Adenauer domestically, highly significant agreement concerned the Saar province, which he signed with the French government in January 1955. Talks had taken place intermittently since 1949. The French vehemently insisted that the Saar had been part of

France since the collapse of Hitler's Reich in 1945, and demanded a Saar Statute that would confirm the region's semi-autonomous status in economic union with France. By mid-1954 Adenauer had conceded as much as he could on the matter: France and Germany would settle the problem bilaterally, the Saar could remain autonomous, and it could even remain economically united with France. In a decisive night meeting during the Paris Conference, Adenauer and Pierre Mendès-France, the French premier, agreed on a Saar Statute that would keep the Saar province tied to France, but which the citizens of the Saar province *(Saarländer)* themselves would have to ratify in a referendum. At that time the French hoped and expected that the *Saarländer* would prefer to remain French. When the referendum finally took place a year later, in October 1955, the political atmosphere had changed. The population rejected the Statute and, to the surprise of many, the French government did not object strenuously to the return of the Saar province to Germany. The reason was that the French government, now dominated by Europeanists, was more interested in obtaining West German support for the eventual creation of the European Common Market (EEC), that was to take place in Rome in 1957.

# 14

# Society, Education, and Religion

The period of the first Adenauer government until 1953 was not only a period of major decisions about West Germany's place in Western Europe and in the West as a whole, but also the years of the first consolidation of West German society, as distinct from life under occupation between 1945 and 1949. The strength of the economy was becoming increasingly apparent, and provided the self-confidence which allowed the country's image to change its shape. The picture of shabby clothing and little personal wealth was slowly altering too, and, as it did so, it gave greater hope for the future.

West German democracy, in 1953, four years after the first election, was still fragile and uncertain. But the electorate gave Konrad Adenauer an overwhelming vote of confidence as the re-elected chancellor began his second term with almost 50 per cent more voters expressing their support for the CDU/CSU than in 1949. Self-esteem is essential to regaining one's pride, and Adenauer's leadership had contributed a large measure to the country's health. The SPD's failure to attract the German voters was disappointing and frustrating as Carlo Schmid's memoirs so poignantly display: "Had we not voiced the Germans' innermost thoughts? ... Didn't we receive an unbelievable amount of evidence of their rejection of any kind of military service? ... Why didn't the voters notice that we are the better fighters for the re-establishment of Germany's unity? ... Had it escaped the voters that the government's economic policy in the first instance served those who already owned property?"[1]

Schmid's answers to his own questions were, in most cases right on the mark. The SPD had not developed sufficient "talent" among its members, nor had it "sold" its ideas and policies well. And there was another reason that is part of human nature in a free society:

[1] Schmid, *Erinnerungen*, 545.

The behavior of the voters ... made clear that in times of uncertainty no slogan is more powerful than the call "No Experiments." The voter preferred representatives who helped him keep what he had. ... Even the only moderately wealthy is afraid of interference in the wealth of the "Big Fish:" "Today it's the turn of the millionaires, but tomorrow it's my turn." How often did I hear that. ...[2]

His conclusions were supported by what had transpired since the currency reform just five years before. The gross national product had risen by 56 per cent. Industrial production had tripled. Real weekly earnings of industrial workers were up 80 per cent. Agricultural production had climbed 40 per cent. What people had to eat – average caloric intake – had grown by 25 per cent. And the unemployment rate had been cut to 6 per cent.

These figures, dry when you read them on paper, meant something very tangible to the Germans. Their currency was real, and the black market had gone. The West German government's gold and dollar reserves, non-existent in 1948, were approaching the billion-dollar level. This fact alone was of enormous significance. In 1948 there had been no gold or dollar reserves to give the new German mark real value. Had confidence in the mark been absent or eroded in Germany, it would have left the populace destitute. But seven years after the currency reform of 1948, the value of the mark in 1955 was firmly tied to real assets. It reflected tremendous growth in the country's financial health and, in turn, was a major source of stability for the currency. The economic changes had brought food, income, places to live, clothing to wear, and maybe even some extra money for a glass of beer. The country's exports had risen by 600 per cent. In 1953 the trade *surplus* totaled more than 200 million dollars; in 1949 the trade *deficit* had been more than one billion dollars. There were still large numbers of Germans – about 6.5 million – who were mainly dependent on unemployment, social insurance or public welfare. But the point was that the ruins of Hitler's Reich were being replaced by something positive. It was not perfect, but it was far better than the chaos and despair of 1945; the changes must have seemed to many like a miracle. And the Germans coined a famous name for it, the "Economic Miracle."[3]

According to the Basic Law, and indeed to German tradition, education and cultural and religious policy was a matter for each *Land*, and not the province of federal law. Each *Land* had its own ministers of culture and education, which meant that each *Land* differed from the

---

[2]  Ibid., 546.
[3]  See Office of US High Commissioner, *Report on Germany* (September 21, 1949–July 31, 1952).

others in education policy. The Northern *Länder*, where the SPD was strong, favored the secular schools, while the Catholic-controlled states continued to favor the confessional school which, the political Catholics said, respected the family's rights. The period from 1948, when Alois Hundhammer in Bavaria successfully defied OMGUS demands that he declericalize the Bavarian public schools, to late 1954 were the glory days of postwar political Catholicism in Germany. Almost half the population of the Federal Republic was Catholic, and until the later 1950s this still meant, for most people, a serious commitment and not just a nominal affiliation for statistical purposes. The church directly, in the parishes, and through its organizations like the Katholikentag, wielded great influence and, in education, made the primary policy determinations where it held the majority. Lutheran churches too were strong. Frederic Spotts in his book *The Churches and Politics in Germany*, pointed out that guidelines in the Basic Law

set the minimum standards; the *Länder* may endow the churches with greater privileges and a higher status; many *Länder* have, in fact, done so. In the guidelines alone the churches enjoy a favored position in the state that is probably unique in the world, while admitting no political authority over themselves in return. The churches regard this arrangement, moreover, not as a *concession,* but as a *recognition* of their rightful status in society....

By the terms of the Basic Law the churches have an unrestricted right to regulate and administer their affairs independently of the state. This means that the churches alone determine who may hold office even when this involves political factors (such as a Nazi past). The Reichskonkordat further expressly gives the Holy See complete freedom in its relations with the German hierarchy. Churches – in practice, Protestant provincial churches – have an unqualified right to unite or confederate without the approval of the state and may establish new ecclesiastical jurisdiction at will....

What makes the German ecclesiastical scene unusual and probably unique in the world is the constitutional guarantee of annual cash grants and the authority of the churches to levy taxes. The state grants, in a few cases traceable to customs and agreements of the immediate post-Reformation situation, are principally a consequence of the secularization of 1803. In that year the Imperial Reichstag ... gave monasteries, church treasures, and church lands to the states but in compensation ordered the state ... to cover the churches' expenses with annual payments. ... The 1803 arrangement was guaranteed in the Weimar constitution, was honored by the National Socialists as well as by the four occupation powers, and is maintained in the Basic Law. Some of the original donations in kind – firewood and agricultural produce, for instance – are still made to parishes by many South German towns. The financial payments have gradually increased over the past 50 years; in 1965 they amounted to 241 million marks.[4]

---

[4] Spotts, *Churches and Politics,* 190, 191, 193–94 (Spotts' italics).

338     THE ESTABLISHMENT OF THE FEDERAL REPUBLIC

The West German government always permitted the church to collect taxes. Whereas before the war the church tax was about 3–4 per cent of the individual income tax, the rate was increased to 10 per cent at the time of the establishment of the FRG. These high taxes, automatically deducted from one's earnings and collected by state authorities on behalf of the churches, brought complaints from some otherwise faithful and church-going citizens, who, as a result, officially resigned from the church to avoid payment.

The sweeping authority of the churches to raise taxes as they wish has always been fully upheld by the courts. Astonishingly enough, only since 1965 have the churches even been restricted to taxing their own members. Prior to that time, by a strange but deliberate provision of the "church articles" of the Weimar constitution, they were permitted to tax juridical persons. As late as 1958, for example, the federal administrative court upheld a tax imposed by Catholic parishes in Heidelberg upon the German Shell Oil Company to cover the costs of a church construction program. Two textile manufacturers similarly assessed by another Catholic parish, however, managed in 1965 to bring their case to the federal constitutional court, which found that while such taxation was clearly permitted by the "church articles," it is inconsistent with the ideological neutrality of the state as guaranteed by the Basic Law.[5]

Statistics show that the tax income of the churches increased tremendously over the years. Within seven years, from 1961 to 1968, Catholic church tax income rose from 700 million to 1,300 million DM. From 1953 to 1968 Protestant churches had a fivefold increase in tax income.[6] The *Statistisches Jahrbuch 1988* of the Statistisches Bundesamt registered the following figures for 1987 for total income from church tax and collection: Protestant church DM 6.2 billion; Catholic church DM 6.3 billion.[7]

Unlike the old German Reich, the Federal Republic was divided almost equally among Catholics and Protestants. Catholics were therefore able to fight for a greater say in public affairs in ways hitherto impossible. One of the problems between the FDP and the CDU/CSU was that the FDP as a liberal party, in the European sense, had strong anti-clerical traditions, whereas the CDU/CSU were split between Erhard's and Schröder's liberal and secular wing and a pro-clerical Catholic wing whose leaders were Heinrich von Brentano, Heinrich Krone, and Jakob Kaiser. Adenauer was obliged to tread a thin line between these factions which he did with great skill, but unavoidably became involved in deeply-felt disputes.

[5] Ibid., 195.
[6] Ibid., 196.
[7] Stat. Bundesamt, *Statistisches Jahrbuch 1988*, 93–4.

In many repects Adenauer's early years, and especially the mid-1950s, were a transitional period in which the last phase of an older Germany was giving way to a new and very different society, a society that was modern in the sense that France, Britain and the United States were modern. The values and attitudes of most Germans in 1955 were overwhelmingly those of the 1920s and the 1930s, and this at a time when social and economic processes were rapidly competing with dramatic changes of the early postwar years that were molding Germany into a largely middle-class society, divided not according to rank, but according to function and status.

In a modern industrial society in which one's acquired skills are more important than one's inherited position, education becomes a crucial factor. In the 1950s in West Germany higher education was still a preserve of the elite, whereas the next decade saw great expansion of the university and other systems of higher education, as well as academic administrative and structural reforms.

In 1953 the sociologist Helmut Schelsky wrote a famous study about what he described as the "skeptical generation." These were the people who were too young to have voted for Hitler, but who were old enough to have suffered and fought in the war and who were now responsible for reconstruction – those born between 1915 and 1928. Schelsky argued that Nazism, war, and defeat had made the members of this generation immune to ideological seduction. They had seen the gap between the promises of the Nazis and the disgrace and destruction that Hitler's regime brought about. Even before they knew that the Nazis had also killed millions of Jews and other innocents, they had been, as it were, inoculated against any political doctrine that promised power and glory. They wanted to rebuild their lives and their country and had derived from their experience a thoroughly practical, or in some cases anti-idealistic, view of politics. They rejected the Weimar political intrigue (*Parteiengezänk*) that had obscured a clear vision of the danger posed by Hitler, as well as the ideological politics of Hitler and the Nazis. They also despised the old officer class whose militarism, they felt, had given Hitler his chance to launch the war and thus destroy Germany. The skeptical generation included Franz Josef Strauss, Gerhard Schröder, Helmut Schmidt, and, among academics, Schelsky himself.

According to Schelsky it was perfectly natural that these people would react negatively to the ideological passions of their parents, many of whom had been Nazis, communists, or socialists, by focusing exclusively on immediate and material concerns, family values and respectability. He asserted that the outlook of this group would determine the basic political temper of the new German state for a long time, and he was right. On the other hand Schelsky predicted that the children of that

TABLE 1.3    CHURCH MEMBERSHIP BY GEOGRAPHICAL LOCATION AND/OR DIOCESE

(a)  Church membership 1970–1986: Catholic church

|  | Members (in thousands) | Average attendance (in thousands) |
|---|---|---|
| Totals (by year) | | |
| 1970 | 27,195 | 10,159 |
| 1980 | 26,713 | 7,769 |
| 1985 | 26,309 | 6,800 |
| 1986 | 26,284 | 6,373 |
| | | |
| Members by diocese[a] 1986 (in thousands) | | |
| Aachen | 1,303 | |
| Augsburg | 1,531 | |
| Bamberg | 830 (archdiocese) | |
| Berlin (West) | 270 | |
| Cologne | 2,438 (archdiocese) | |
| Eichstätt | 443 | |
| Essen | 1,145 | |
| Freiburg | 2,238 (archdiocese) | |
| Fulda[b] | 465 | |
| Hildesheim[b] | 709 | |
| Limburg | 801 | |
| Mainz | 864 | |
| Munich and Freising | 2,238 (archdiocese) | |
| Münster | 2,092 | |
| Osnabrück[b] | 890 | |
| Paderborn[b] | 1,825 (archdiocese) | |
| Passau | 522 | |
| Regensburg | 1,309 | |
| Rottenburg–Stuttgart | 2,024 | |
| Speyer | 677 | |
| Trier | 1,784 | |
| Würzburg[b] | 935 | |

[a] The 22 dioceses, including five archdioceses, of the Roman Catholic Church in West Germany do not correspond to the postwar *Länder* of the Federal Republic. They date from the fourth through eleventh centuries and were based in the most important towns of the era.
[b] Excluding portions in the GDR.

(b)  Church membership 1970–1986: Protestant church (EKD)

|  | Members (in thousands) | Average attendance (in thousands) |
|---|---|---|
| Totals (by year) | | |
| 1970 | 28,480 | (not available) |
| 1980 | 26,104 | 1,410 |
| 1985 | 25,106 | 1,343 |
| 1986 | 24,910 | 1,315 |

| Membership 1986, by member church (in thousands) | |
|---|---|
| Baden | 1,332 |
| Bavaria | 2,561 |
| Berlin–Brandenburg | 866 |
| Braunschweig | 505 |
| Bremen | 333 |
| Hannover | 3,453 |
| Hessen–Nassau | 2,045 |
| Kurhessen–Waldeck | 1,033 |
| Lippe | 230 |
| Nordelbien | 2,656 |
| Northwest Germany | 195 |
| Oldenburg | 502 |
| Palatinate | 633 |
| Rhineland | 3,194 |
| Schaumburg–Lippe | 69 |
| Westphalia | 2,914 |
| Württemberg | 2,392 |

*Note*:  The territories of the 17 member churches of the EKD bear little or no relation to the postwar *Länder* of the Federal Republic. Most of the regional Protestant churches in Germany were established by territorial rulers in the Reformation era, and their borders therefore represent the political divisions of the sixteenth century.

*Source*:  Stat. Bundesamt, *Statistisches Jahrbuch 1988*, tables 5.1.1 and 5.2.1

generation would become ideological in conviction, and this did indeed come to pass in the 1960s, when a new generation came to the fore that did not share the formative experiences of the skeptics and was therefore once again open to the claims of radical and absolutist political ideologies.

Education policy after the war remained a matter for the *Länder* and not for the federal government. However, the need at least for coordination of higher education and research was recognized, and accordingly the *Land* education ministers established in 1948 a Permanent Conference in which they or their representatives could meet to discuss policies and experiences and formulate guidelines that would combine the necessary coordination with the equally necessary local freedom and independence. In 1957 the federal government established the German Science Council to provide recommendations on higher education, thus for the first time intervening in the hitherto absolute prerogative of the *Länder* to determine educational policy and financing. In the 1970s, the government finally took the step of establishing a federal ministry; but *Land* autonomy in educational policy was never entirely surrendered and remained vital in the 1990s. Educational policy also remained the main area of political struggle between the clerical and pro-clerical forces and the forces of the new secularism, and it was in the educational policy arena that political Catholicism suffered its first major defeat, following which it rapidly lost influence as a front-line factor in West German politics.

The issue concerned the content of the *Land* school laws. In the south and west, the CDU/CSU had fought on behalf of the denominational public school and had won. In Lower Saxony a secular majority of SPD, FDP, and liberal CDU members passed a school law in 1954 that abolished the denominational public school and instituted a secular school system without religious instruction. Adenauer's government, spurred by the Catholic wing of the CDU/CSU, lodged a complaint in the Constitutional Court challenging the Lower Saxony law on the grounds that it violated the *Reichskonkordat* which guaranteed that the state would protect and sponsor Catholic denominational schools. In its verdict of March 26, 1957, the Court found that the *Land* parliaments were not obliged to respect church wishes in their educational policies. This verdict restored the autonomy of the *Länder* in cultural policy and invalidated the most important legal protection of Catholic interests.

In 1963 German educational policy and debate turned a corner when the theologian and educational philosopher, Georg Picht, proclaimed that West Germany faced an "educational disaster," and when the young liberal sociologist and thinker, Ralf Dahrendorf, declared education to be a "civil right." What had been a privilege and, in the case of the universities, a privilege for the few, became a right necessary to the exercise of citizenship as defined by the Basic Law. Picht and Dahrendorf, from their very different perspectives, focused public attention on the issue and helped establish the political and cultural basis for the expansion of higher education and for the student movement of the later 1960s. The resulting policies and sometimes violent arguments led to serious problems, as well as undeniable success, with which the Germans struggled intensively in the 1970s and 1980s. Higher education could not both be available to all and provide all with the privileges, standards, and prestige enjoyed by the small elite who had attended universities in the 1950s and earlier. The best that an honestly conceived policy of educational expansion could do was, in the words of the British conservative politician Iain Macleod, to give young people "more equal opportunities of proving themselves unequal."[8] Picht and Dahrendorf, however, appeared to believe that talent was fairly equally spread throughout the population, and that the only problem was to open higher education to all by leveling the real or imagined barriers to universal access. Yet the result turned out to be both falling standards of scholarship and research and continued inequality of results. Hellmut Becker, the Director of the Max Planck Institute for Educational Research in Berlin from 1963 to 1981, wrote in 1983: "The fact that more freedom can mean less equality and more equality can lead often to less freedom, had also become a basic problem for educational policy decision in the Federal Republic." Becker also addressed another point, equally as important, that would continue to pose problems. As he defined the issue, "it will be a long time before the individual understands that a good education does not necessarily mean that one will be immediately employed in the profession for which one has been educated. . . . To live in freedom and to learn in freedom must be learned."[9]

The changes of the 1960s, which were widely described as the process of "democratization" of the universities, provided the catalyst and the fuel for the student unrest of the later 1960s and 1970s. The student movements and protests, directed against the established moral and social standards of West German society, were inconceivable in the early 1950s; they were only possible thanks to the success of the reconstruction of West Germany from social, economic, and political ruins, into social, economic, and political freedom and stability.

[8] Cited in *The Economist*, December 15, 1990, 36.
[9] Cited in Becker, "Bildungspolitik," in *Die BRD*, ed. Benz, 2:345.

# 15

# Ten Years On

From November 1954 to April 1955 Adenauer and the occupying powers prepared for the return of sovereignty to the Federal Republic. West Germany's future allies all had to ratify the Paris Treaties. In Germany the government faced a bitter opposition from the SPD and the DGB (German Trade Union Federation), which rejected rearmament at its third regular congress in October 1954. In the late fall, NATO conducted a field exercise in West Germany under the code-name "Battle Royal." The purpose was to determine what would occur if the Soviet Union launched an armored attack on West Germany and NATO defended itself, according to the "New Look," with tactical nuclear weapons. In the wargame, NATO won, but Carlo Schmid and many others were appalled at the implied civilian casualties. "Hasn't anyone done any thinking at all about civilian losses caused by the use of such atomic weapons?" he questioned, echoing the social democratic argument that the Germans were being asked to assume extra and unjustifiable risks. Fritz Erler, the SPD's security expert, argued against the Paris Treaties as follows: "Nowhere is there a binding clause in which one can say in good conscience: here it is unambiguously agreed upon and planned that the Federal Republic will be defended with the goal of maintaining its human existence in the event of a conflict."[1]

The government had, following the Himmerod recommendations as elaborated by the Blank Office, offered twelve divisions in a total force of approximately half a million men to NATO, which the Western Allies had accepted at Paris. Erler objected: "One cannot defend Germany *without* twelve German divisions; but that doesn't mean one can actually defend Germany *with* those twelve divisions."[2] He did not understand why West Germany should accept the "New Look," which appeared

---

[1] Cited in Cioc, *Pax Atomica*, 25, 28.
[2] Cited ibid., 28, Erler's emphasis.

increasingly as a device to save the US money by relying on tactical nuclear weapons in Europe and massive retaliation on the strategic level, while reducing the only forces which would be really useful in Europe, the conventional. The twelve German divisions could not fill the vacuum that was being created by the withdrawal of other NATO conventional forces. In response, Adenauer asserted that while it might be true that NATO could only defend Europe on the Rhine, the German forces – the Bundeswehr – would in fact make feasible a defense on or across the interzonal border. "As long as we do not belong to NATO we are the European battlefield in any hot war between Soviet Russia and the United States. Once we are in the Atlantic organization our land won't be the battlefield any longer."[3] Adenauer was here repeating the strategic theory held by Adolf Heusinger, the former general who was one of the two key figures in the early stages of planning German security. Heusinger believed in conventional deterrence at a modest level; that is to say, he was convinced that the mere existence of twelve German divisions and of a coherent strategy of mobile defense, as outlined in the Himmerod Memorandum of October 1950, would deter Soviet attack.

Despite Erler's best efforts the Bundestag ratified the Paris Treaties in February 1955 over the opposition of the SPD. On May 5, 1955, the Allied High Commission issued its last proclamation revoking the Occupation Statute and abolishing itself. It had lasted longer than the military governments – six years versus four – but had been a far less prominent and intrusive part of German political and social life. The American, British, and French flags on the Petersberg came down for the last time; the black-red-gold German colors went up. Despite their misgivings on the defense issue, even the SPD shared fully in the government's pride at achieving sovereignty, earning recognition as a legitimate and honored partner in the affairs of democratic states. An era had ended, an era that took Germans from misery and degradation, through doubt and fear, to a modicum of hope, albeit a hope somewhat tempered by the fact that national division seemed to be the price to be paid for freedom and security. One perspective on that era was offered by a diary entry in Berlin of May 8, 1945, but published in the *Frankfurter Allgemeine Zeitung* ten years later, on May 5, 1955:

*Ten Years Ago*
From a Diary by Brigitte Beer

Berlin, May 5, 1945
On this day I walked from Wilmersdorf to the North of the city in order to check out the fate of my close relatives. When I returned home in the evening, I had

---

[3] Cited ibid., 29.

walked for hours the scene of the battle for the capital, which had ended three days ago. Burning streets, detonated bridges, and Russians who stopped every German they saw, to put him to work, had forced me to take long detours. On this sunny day in May I looked at this city, filled with the smell of burning fires and decay, yet there was the tender green emerging from trees, riddled with bullets, and birds were building their nests in the branches.

Kaiserplatz, Hindenburgpark, Prager Platz – everywhere new graves – for one, for many. A wooden cross, a helmet, a Russian fur hat, a red flag, a piece of wood with the inscription: "unknown woman," "a soldier" – these are their gravestones.

Russian soldiers, foreign and German civilians are streaming through the wide open doors of the Wilhelmshallen at the railroad station "Zoo," empty-handed when they go in, loaded with bags and bottles when they come out. They push their way past the dead woman in the black riding costume, who, shoved close to the doorframe, is lying across the threshold; and whose short hair is mixed with the dust of the street by the wind. Men and women are cutting big chunks of bloody meat from the carcasses of horses, and fill the bowls they brought along with food for the next few days. . . .

# PART IV

# Consolidation and Division, 1955–1961

*We can only pay our debt to the past by putting the future in debt to ourselves.*

John Buchan, Lord Tweedsmuir (1875–1940)
Address to the people of Canada on the coronation of George VI, May 12, 1937

*In looking back over the ten years that have passed since then, the change that has come over Germany appears almost impossible to grasp. Through the perseverance and diligence of the whole German people, through the efforts of the communes, the counties and the* Länder, *and through the careful planning and daring policy of the federal government, reconstruction in all sectors has been achieved to an extent which nobody would have believed possible in 1945.*

Konrad Adenauer, 1955

# Introduction

A different world began taking shape during the second half of the
1950s. The period began with confidence and hope. It ended,
however, in renewed East–West confrontation over the fate of Berlin
and, a decade and a half after the end of the war, with renewed uncertainty about the place of West Germany in the West European and
Atlantic economic and security systems. Nonetheless, the atmosphere of
crisis of the later years of Adenauer's chancellorship concealed the true
extent to which West Germany had not only arrived as a sovereign and
independent European power, but had also become an essential and
desired partner and coveted ally. This advance towards acceptance and
respect abroad, and the growing strength of the West German economy
and social structure, explain why the end of the second Berlin crisis of
1958–61 had such a dramatic effect. The year 1955, however, was a year
of diplomatic and political triumph for Konrad Adenauer and his
strategy of Western integration and security.

On May 5, the Paris Treaties, signed in October 1954, took effect,
granting the Federal Republic sovereignty, with conditions, and
membership in NATO. The Allied High Commission was dissolved
and its representatives were replaced by ambassadors of the former
occupying powers. West Germany's new allies – France, Great Britain
and the United States – undertook commitments to seek reunification,
to support the Bonn government's "claim to sole representation" of the
German people, to refuse recognition of the 1945 frontiers until a peace
treaty could be signed by a reunited Germany, and to guarantee the
freedom of Berlin – in principle, of all of Berlin, not just the Western
sectors. If these safeguards appeared as victories for Adenauer, they
were in reality much more than victories, and more than pieces of paper.
They meant something of enormous psychological and political
importance. It is difficult to explain the meaning of sovereignty as it
must have felt at that time. But if one imagines that the president of the

United States suddenly, from one day to the next, had the power to make decisions without approval from occupying German troops, it is easier to visualize. All at once, after waiting from one year to the next – for ten years – the German government was free. For the first time since 1945 the West Germans were mainly dependent on their own abilities, creativity, and wisdom.

The years after 1955 showed that the Western powers were prepared to give their commitments substance to the extent that it coincided with their own interests; and to the extent that it was possible at all. But there was a built-in conflict between German interests, as seen both by Adenauer and the SPD, and Western Allied willingness to risk conflict with the Soviet Union. The second Berlin crisis brought this into the open.

# 1

# The Geneva Summit and the "Rélance de l'Europe"

In the spring of 1955, political observers perceived a "thaw" of East–West relations in Europe. The clearest indication was seen in Austria, that had remained under four-power occupation since 1945. On May 15 the four former Allies – France, Great Britain, the Soviet Union and the United States – concluded the Austrian Treaty that ended the four-power occupation of Austria and restored sovereignty to that country. That the Soviet Union and the Western powers were able to agree on how to end their joint occupation of a former enemy state, albeit a less important one than Germany, and on a framework for that state's future neutrality, gave many in Germany, especially in the SPD, hopes that a similar agreement might be possible for their country. Adenauer's critics argued that, since Austria was genuinely neutralized in 1955, why not Germany as well? But there was a difference; the Soviet government had never set up a communist state in a separate part of Austria. It had done so in East Germany. Indeed, it could hardly have abandoned the East German communist regime without endangering every other communist regime in Eastern Europe. Moreover, as far as Austria itself was concerned, the Soviet Union gained from the neutralization by driving a geographic wedge between the northern and southern components of NATO.

The SPD continued to envision an arrangement that would remove the risk of nuclear war, which it regarded as the likely consequence of NATO membership, while avoiding the risk of Soviet domination; namely, the creation of a unified and neutral German state. Adenauer, however, continued to believe that this was an unacceptable concept: the choice, in his view, was not between NATO membership and an opportunity for reunification and neutrality, but rather between security and a lower risk of war as a member of NATO on the one hand, and the certainty of eventual Soviet domination and the permanent end of German democracy on the other.

Adenauer's logic was compelling if one accepted, as most Western leaders certainly did, that the Soviet government sought to extend its hegemony in Central Europe to include a neutralized Germany – if not to Western Europe itself – and that what prevented it from doing so were NATO and the other institutions of Western integration, of which West Germany was clearly a part. As Adenauer himself recognized, however, democratic societies and, in particular, democratic political leaders, find it very difficult to sustain prolonged confrontations; inevitably, the wish for peace engenders the belief that peace can be made more permanent via a process of negotiation and compromise and the belief that one can turn one's opponent into a partner by friendly persuasion. He had observed this tendency on more than one occasion in the past, especially among his British friends; during the early summer of 1955 he found it emerging again, not merely in Britain, but also in the United States, where he least expected it.

On May 18, three days after the Austrian State Treaty and obviously inspired by it, President Eisenhower, in an interview with the Paris daily, *Le Monde*, expressed his personal sympathy for the concept of neutral zones in Central Europe. Adenauer suspected that if Eisenhower's view was representative of changing Western attitudes, in the wake of the Austrian State Treaty, West Germany's precious sovereignty, and especially its military defense, might become the subject of a Western compromise with the Soviet Union. Adenauer's concern was heightened in early June when the Western Allies proposed to the Soviet government a meeting of their respective four heads of government in Geneva to discuss primarily issues of European security.

The summit conference began July 18 and was attended by the French prime minister, Edgar Faure, the chairman of the Soviet council of ministers, Nikolai Bulganin, the British prime minister, Anthony Eden, and the US president, Eisenhower. The Western heads of government, their foreign ministers and advisors arrived in Geneva two days before the summit conference and met in the library of Eisenhower's villa on Sunday, July 17, for a general discussion of the Western position. The British foreign secretary, Harold Macmillan, who participated, described the first luncheon meeting: "We all lunched with the President – a disgusting meal, of large meat slices, hacked out . . . and served . . . with marmalade and jam. The French were appalled."[1]

The actual conference took place in the old League of Nations building. Adenauer, in an effort to preempt any Western inclination to compromise West German security, had forwarded to the US and British governments a secret plan, prepared by General Heusinger and

[1] Macmillan, *Tides of Fortune*, 616.

Herbert Blankenhorn, West Germany's ambassador to NATO, that proposed to demilitarize a zone on both sides of the Oder–Neisse rivers and to remove nuclear weapons from West Germany. The British government, however, had prepared its own plan for "thinning out" military forces in Central Europe, as well as for creating an all-German government and a European security pact, and so informed Adenauer. Indeed, at Geneva, Prime Minister Anthony Eden presented the British proposal for a solution of the German problem, arguing that there could be no winners in a nuclear war, and that the Eastern and Western powers therefore were obligated to come to an agreement on the future of Germany, and on security in Central Europe. An agreement, however, was not reached, and the tenor of the exchanges among them may suggest why. Macmillan summarized the dialogue in his memoirs:

19 July 1955
FIRST ROUND

*Anthony Eden:* What about safeguards?

*Bulganin:* We are strong; we do not want safeguards. Abolish NATO.

*President:* I assure you NATO is for peace.

*Faure:* We must unite Germany.

SECOND ROUND

*Anthony Eden:* You say you do not want safeguards. Why do you propose a European pact?

*Bulganin:* Abolish NATO. No more to say about Germany.

*President:* I have said my piece.

*Anthony Eden (interrupting):* The question of Germany is not exhausted. We must think about it.

*Bulganin:* Let's get on to the question of European security.

*Faure:* All right. But the two questions are interlocked.

Then we all went away.
All this took about three hours.[2]

Macmillan's words belied the serious issues at stake in the discussion. In the view of Anthony Eden, the issues were of fundamental importance for the future of democracy and freedom in Germany. As he interpreted the Soviet objective, it was unambiguous:

either an indefinite continuation of the division of Germany, or possibly some German reunion which extracted West Germany out of its association

[2] Ibid., 618.

with the West. Even the latter would hardly have satisfied them, except in conditions which would have given a Communist Government in East Germany virtual control. The dilemma in which the Soviets found themselves, and still do, on this issue is inescapable. They know that the great majority of Germans, in whatever part of Germany they now live, are antagonistic to communism and all that it stands for.[3]

The summit concluded after five days. On July 23, the four heads of government issued a "directive" to their foreign ministers to meet subsequently to discuss the terms of a general German and European peace settlement. Thus, for the last time, the Soviet Union accepted a joint responsibility with the West for resolving the German problem. But the Geneva summit marked the final end of the era that began in 1941 when Hitler's attack on his erstwhile ally, Stalin, brought about the great wartime alliance between the Soviet Union, France, Great Britain and the United States. The directive stated:

The Heads of Government, recognizing their common responsibility for the settlement of the German question and the reunification of Germany, have agreed that the settlement of the German question and the reunification of Germany by means of free elections shall be carried out in conformity with the national interests of the German people and the interests of European security.[4]

The foreign ministers' meeting called for in the directive took place from October 27 to November 15, 1955. In the meantime, on September 20, 1955, the Soviet Union concluded a treaty on mutual relations with the GDR. Thus, when the Western foreign ministers presented their old agenda of free elections, then reunification, as proposed in the Eden Plan at the previous foreign ministers' conference in Berlin in January 1954, it was rejected by the Soviet government. The Soviet foreign minister insisted at the conference that "cooperation between the GDR and the G[erman] F[ederal] R[epublic]" was a precondition for any "settlement of the problem of Germany's national reunification."[5] From that moment on, the Soviet Union unilaterally dissociated itself from four-power responsibility for Germany and maintained that reunification and conclusion of a peace treaty could only be achieved through negotiations between the two German states themselves. Henceforth, the Western Allies were obliged to acknowledge that even the elements of a common platform with the Soviets were now gone, and

[3] Eden, *Full Circle,* 335–6.
[4] Dept of State, *Documents on Germany,* 455.
[5] Ibid., 470.

did so at the conclusion of the foreign ministers' meeting in a joint statement on Germany and European security:

Marshal Bulganin [the Soviet head of government] in July had agreed that the Reunification of Germany was the common responsibility of the Four Powers and should be carried out by means of Free Elections. The Soviet Foreign Minister, however, despite the Directive of the Heads of Government, made it plain that the Soviet Government refused to agree to the Reunification of Germany since that would lead to the liquidation of the East German regime. He made counterproposals which would have involved the continued division of Germany as well as the eventual dissolution of the Western security system.[6]

The conclusion of the foreign ministers' meeting marked the transformation of East–West division on Germany's future to a struggle of rhetoric aimed at public opinion, in an effort to determine which side could impose its version of reality on the other. The Western powers committed "their efforts to end the injustice and wrong now being done by dividing the German people." The Soviet government, in turn, pursued a tactic of insisting that "life itself will force those who are responsible for the policy of the Federal Republic to renounce their hostility to the German Democratic Republic." The two German states, it claimed, were facts of life, and eventually the West would have to agree.

The Geneva summit, and the prospect it offered of possible momentous decisions on Germany, overshadowed the significance of another event that took place prior to Geneva, and which turned out in the long term, to be more important for Germany's place in the West. The failure of the EDC in 1954 marked the collapse of Adenauer's original strategy of European integration. When France defeated the EDC, it destroyed the premise of Adenauer's entire national policy and of his Ostpolitik, which depended on a politically and militarily integrated Western Europe. That strategy foresaw a gradual move from the functional integration of the coal and steel industries of the Six (West Germany, France, Italy, and the Benelux) in the ECSC, via the integration of military forces of the Six plus Britain, to the political confederation of those states in a European Political Community. He viewed this West European political and military union as the necessary basis for the deterrence and, if possible, the rollback of Soviet power in Central Europe, according to a "policy of strength" – the view that only a strong, credible, and united Western Europe could force the Soviet Union to

[6] Ibid., 472.

permit German reunification and to modify its domination of Central Europe.

What remained after the EDC failed was to continue the functional integration of the economies of the Six while abandoning the high hopes of the political community. The broader purpose of West European unity, namely the weakening of Soviet power in Central Europe, could not be attained via European institutions because it was no longer possible to move beyond functional economic integration. Yet, that integration, though modest by comparison with the original design and, therefore, doubtless frustrating for Adenauer, was also worthwhile. Within its framework, at least, Adenauer could, and did, achieve one great step of enormous political and not merely of economic importance: the reconciliation of France and Germany.

In the aftermath of the failure of the EDC, narrow nationalism and perceived differences of national interest, particularly between those French leaders who wanted to preserve their African colonies and maintain the French population of Algeria and the West Germans who sought reunification, threatened the very idea of economic integration. Despite that failure, prospects for movement toward European economic integration were not bad in the mid-1950s. There were two reasons for this. First, Adenauer had the support of a skilled and experienced staff of committed Europeanists, led by Walter Hallstein and Herbert Blankenhorn. Second, other European leaders, above all Jean Monnet of France, fully understood Adenauer's concern and accepted the argument that stability in and around Germany demanded progress on Europe. As in the case of the German defense contribution, therefore, Adenauer had a strong hand of cards to play. The other Europeans needed German economic strength and productivity; in order to keep Germany stable, therefore, they had to take account of German interests.

Within Germany there were two schools of thought about how to proceed. One school, which had Erhard's personal sympathy, was led by the free-market liberal Wilhelm Röpke and supported by the respected and influential *Frankfurter Allgemeine Zeitung*. These "functionalists" saw a European common market as merely a stepping-stone to global free trade, and were opposed to any European measures that would tend to hinder wider economic freedom. They also feared that a common market restricted to Europe and dictated by governments would inevitably become bureaucratized and would in fact lead to more, not less, state control of the economy. Thus, they proposed to continue integrating areas of the economy, as was done for coal and steel in the ECSC, but without establishing a bureaucratically controlled common market.

Members of the other school, the "institutionalists," were found mainly in government itself, particularly in the council of ministers of the ECSC. They argued that it was important to develop European institutions for political as well as economic reasons. They also pointed out that integrating particular areas of the economy, as the ECSC had done, created unnecessary friction with other areas. The functionalists' plan to work for global free trade in particular areas therefore struck them as likely to cause nothing but trouble.

By 1955 the two groups had come to a compromise that foresaw a regional common market open to the outside world. This was the basis of a memorandum presented by the German delegation to a conference of foreign ministers of the Six in Messina in June. The memorandum recommended that the Six establish an expert committee to design a common market resting on common institutions. The chairman of this committee was the Belgian foreign minister Paul-Henri Spaak, who put his finger on the political importance of establishing new European institutions when he said that the common market was "the best way to solve the German problem." Adenauer, he noted, saw in an active European policy the most effective means to

> protect Germany from itself. ... A Germany integrated in European associations and in the North Atlantic Treaty will defend itself not only against an individualism that only too easily takes on the trappings of nationalism ... but also against the temptation to turn to the Russians in order to solve disputed problems directly with them without respecting the interests of the West. European integration gives Germany a framework that limits its expansion, and creates a community of interests that gives it security while protecting us from certain attempts and adventures.[7]

At the Messina conference the Six decided to follow the logic of the Schuman Plan of 1950, to broaden the scope of the economic integration that had already occurred in the coal and steel industry, and to begin dismantling tariff and other barriers to trade and exchange among them. Jean Monnet named this new effort at European integration the "rélance de l'Europe." The rélance led, after less than two years, to the Rome Treaties that established the Common Market.

---

[7] Cited in Schwarz, *Die Ära Adenauer, 1949–1957*, 341. See also Marjolin, *Architect of European Unity: Memoirs 1911–1986*.

# 2
# Adenauer in Moscow

O ne issue of sovereign importance and integrity was the fate of the
Germans still held captive in the Soviet Union. Adenauer was able
to crown his achievements of 1955 with his trip to Moscow and the
release of the last surviving German POWs. Some observers later argued
that Adenauer paid a heavy price for saving the prisoners, because to do so
he had to abandon hope for speedy reunification. By opening diplomatic
relations with Moscow, he deprived himself and the Allies of their best
remaining chance to bargain with the Soviet leaders for reunification.

The atmosphere in which he made the trip was highly charged with
emotion that had built up over the past ten years. The ostensible
purpose was to discuss establishment of diplomatic relations between
Bonn and Moscow. But there were other issues involved, including
diplomatic, economic and cultural relationships, and "the unity of
Germany as a state, on the solution of which depends the creation of a
system to guarantee European security." There was no question, however, that the most immediate problem was how to persuade the Soviet
government to release the approximately 10,000 surviving German
prisoners held in the USSR.[1]

Adenauer and his delegation arrived at Vnukovo Airport near
Moscow in the afternoon of September 8:

The Chancellor was received with much ceremony: Prime Minister
Bulganin, Foreign Secretary Molotov, Deputy Foreign Ministers Gromyko and
Semyonov, as well as the chief ideologue Suslov, were all lined up in a row. . . .
The guard of honor was specially chosen and made up of very young,
splendid-looking lads who were wearing the colorful parade uniform for the
first time it had been worn since 1917. They produced the intended effect of
determination, concentration, precision on all of us. In the evening there was a
great gala banquet with high-sounding toasts, expansive hospitality, and

[1] See *Facts on File*, August 11–17, 1955.

general fraternization. The next day the two declarations of intent were read out. The German declaration was a masterpiece of restrained remorse and spontaneous warmth combined with a call for a new beginning. The next day the practical talks began, and a deep rift immediately became apparent.[2]

Adenauer was accompanied by Heinrich von Brentano, his foreign minister, Kurt Georg Kiesinger (CDU), the chairman of the foreign relations committee of the Bundestag, Carlo Schmid (SPD), the committee's vice chairman, and Karl Arnold, who was minister-president of North Rhine-Westphalia and chairman of the foreign relations committee of the Bundesrat, as well as by his close advisors Hallstein, Blankenhorn, and Grewe. Altogether the German delegation was 15 strong. They were housed in the Hotel Sovietskaia, which Wilhelm Grewe described as "seen from the Russian point of view a big-city luxury hotel, for us a middle-class hotel with old-fashioned comfort and the taste of the petty bourgeoisie. . . ."[3]

Part of Adenauer's delegation travelled to Moscow by train. On arrival the train was parked in a siding of the Moscow railway station, and became the work room of the German visitors. It contained a "special bug-proof wagon, Mitropa dining car, radio and telephone equipment, typing facilities etc. – in short a kind of itinerant embassy whose installation we had demanded during preliminary procedural talks, to make up for the lack of a not yet existing embassy."[4]

The negotiations lasted six days and began with a luxurious breakfast buffet, including large bowls of caviar, in the hotel. As Adenauer reports in his memoirs, a great deal of alcohol was consumed, and, prior to every reception, Adenauer's assistant Hans Globke gave each member of the delegation a large drink of olive oil to prevent intoxication. The final result, an agreement to exchange ambassadors, followed discussion of a wide spectrum of issues, including Khrushchev's request that the Germans aid Moscow in its efforts to deal with the Chinese and with the United States, to which Adenauer did not respond. The flavor of the discussions included anger:

Khrushchev boasted, "The wind is not blowing in *our* face." Adenauer too gave vent to his anger, "Foreign Secretary Molotov said the Germans were incapable of throwing off Hitler's yoke. Permit me to ask a question: who was it who signed an agreement with Hitler: you or I?" Adenauer says in his memoirs: "Khrushchev became very agitated, and not everything could be translated,

[2] Dönhoff, *Foe into Friend*, 59.
[3] Grewe, *Rückblenden*, 235.
[4] Ibid., 236.

because he spoke too fast. From time to time he made threatening gestures with his fists. So then I got up and shook my fist back at him."[5]

The talks, however, also contained assertions about the future of Germany:

"I do not ask you to agree with my point of view," he [Khrushchev] continued, "indeed while I am telling you this, I know that you do not agree with me. But" – and now he made a decisive statement that was, and still is, of utmost importance in assessing Russian conduct – "the GDR and its foundation, that is the future. It is not only the future of the German people, but the future of all mankind, and it was not I who said it but Karl Marx and Engels!" Triumphantly Khrushchev looked at me, but then he added: "Excuse me if I told you something unpleasant!"[6]

The US ambassador to Moscow in 1955, Charles Bohlen, who had participated in the conferences at Yalta and at Potsdam, considered Adenauer's trip a failure, for, in his view, the initiation of diplomatic relations constituted the formal recognition of the division of Germany. But Bohlen miscalculated, according to Wilhelm Grewe, in his assumption that Adenauer fell into a trap by only extracting the release of the prisoners at the expense of reunification. Adenauer and his government had made it clear since 1949 that they viewed reunification only in the context of the four-power responsibility for Germany as a whole; it was not merely a matter over which the Soviet government had to rule. On the contrary, Grewe emphasizes, diplomatic relations with Moscow were a necessary precondition for future discussion of reunification which could only be achieved by consensus among Germany's four former enemies.[7] What Adenauer did achieve was something concrete and something which only the Soviet government could give: release of the remaining prisoners of war in Russia.

It is ironic that Adenauer's principal achievement – gaining Soviet agreement that the German prisoners of war could go home – was not agreed upon at all during the five days of negotiations. In fact, the Soviet government denied that there were still any German prisoners in Russia, but Bulganin's answer to Adenauer's question acknowledged that, indeed, "9,628 persons remain in our country ... [but] these are violent criminals, arsonists, murderers of women, children and old people. They have been sentenced accordingly by the Soviet courts and

[5] Dönhoff, *Foe into Friend*, 61.
[6] Adenauer, *Erinnerungen 1953–1955*, 520.
[7] Grewe, *Rückblenden*, 251.

cannot be considered prisoners of war." It was only on the last day, during the gala reception in the Kremlin, that Bulganin "without forewarning and very impulsively" declared: "Let us come to an agreement: write me a letter [he meant the note establishing diplomatic relations] and we'll give them all to you – all! One week thereafter! We are giving you our word of honor!"[8]

When the joint communique was issued at the conclusion of the meeting, the release of prisoners of war was not formally addressed. In his press conference, however, held before he departed for Bonn, Adenauer announced that Bulganin had assured him the necessary steps would be set in motion for their release.

In order to understand the significance of this result, as it was measured in West Germany, it is necessary to recall that the issue of release of the prisoners was one with which more than 40 per cent of West Germans were either directly or indirectly very closely connected. During the war almost one-third of the German army, 3,155,000 men, had been captured or killed by the Red Army. By 1950 about 1,959,000 had returned to Germany. An unknown number, however, remained in the Soviet Union, and thus when the Soviet government announced in May 1950, that the repatriation of German war prisoners was closed, the reaction in West Germany was one of outrage. Accurate or complete lists of who remained in captivity did not exist, and thus the hope that one's relative might still return remained very much alive. In a poll in West Germany taken in September 1955, 27 per cent responded that they had one or more family members who were either captive or missing in the Soviet Union, and 15 per cent declared that they had one or more friends suffering the same fate.

Thus, in 1955 the resolution of this issue was a national problem, even if it did not attract the attention on an international level that it had during the first years after the war. Frustrations with the lack of progress had been intensified because the Soviet government had discussed the issue with East Germany and had concluded an agreement with the GDR in August 1953, in which the release of 18,000 prisoners would take place by the summer of 1955. The GDR government took this opportunity to declare that the FRG would enjoy the same results "if the West German population voted against Adenauer" in the second Bundestag election held in September 1953.[9]

The issue of prisoners of war, therefore, taken together with the larger question of a future reunification of Germany, generated domestic

[8] Adenauer, *Erinnerungen 1953–1955,* 506, 545.
[9] See Foschepoth, "Adenauers Moskaureise 1955." *Aus Politik und Zeitgeschichte,* B22/86 (May 31, 1986).

debate that Adenauer's government could not ignore. Early in the year, in January 1955, the Soviet government invited members of the SPD and FDP to come, on their own, to Moscow to discuss both questions, but did not offer to invite members of the CDU or CSU. Fortunately, from both the viewpoint of Adenauer and of the FDP and SPD, the invitation was refused; had the SPD and FDP accepted it, it would have placed Adenauer's government in the embarrassing position of apparent recalcitrance, and it would have placed the SPD and the FDP in the position of conducting foreign policy when, in fact, neither party was empowered to do so. Indeed, the invitation was an attempt to divide the political parties within West Germany on the emotionally charged issue of how to help fellow Germans in captivity.

When the Soviet invitation to Adenauer arrived in June 1955, interest in both issues was extremely keen; especially because the treaty resulting in the withdrawal of Soviet troops from Austria had recently been signed. Therefore, the hope existed that the Soviet government might follow the same policy in Germany, and eventually agree to German reunification on German terms. Thus, the vision of Adenauer's trip to Moscow raised hopes as well as questions. From the viewpoint of West Germany's principal allies, the invitation to discuss diplomatic relations was interpreted as Moscow's wish to codify, as it were, the existence of two separate German states. While this was not necessarily the case from the standpoint of the Germans in the Federal Republic, it was nonetheless the view of some. For example, the journalist Marion Dönhoff wrote in the weekly *Die Zeit* (September 22, 1955) that the establishment of diplomatic relations meant "for the moment at least, the acceptance of the division of Germany," and, she continued, "diplomatic relations in exchange for the return of prisoners of war means, therefore ... to weigh living human beings on a scale (not dead souls), so that the freedom of those ten thousand seals the slavery of seventeen million" [people living in East Germany]. What she meant, more directly put, was that Adenauer had bought the freedom of 10,000 prisoners of war for West Germany at the price of 17 million who remained living in East Germany. Her analysis, however, neglected the fact that Adenauer had no leverage or power to bargain. In establishing diplomatic relations with the Soviet Union ten years after the war, he did only what he considered a reasonable alternative. In exchange for the recognition, he achieved the release of the German prisoners; that was no small accomplishment. He did not have the means, albeit the desire, to affect the fate of Germans living in East Germany in a positive way.

In a sense Dönhoff was right, but her conclusion, phrased the way she wrote it, implies that there was another choice. In fact, there was no other choice, unless one was willing to discuss with the Soviet government the possibility of a reunified but neutral German state. This would have required the support of the governments of France, Great Britain and the United States; for even though West Germany had been sovereign since May 5, 1955, no West German government could have pursued such a negotiation with the Soviet Union unless it had the full confidence of its former enemies. The fact of the matter was, in 1955, that no one in Western Europe or the United States wished to see Germany reunified under a government that was not completely loyal to the Western alliance, and some did not wish to see Germany reunified at all. Moreover, if Germany were to be reunited and a new government formed as a result of free elections, the communist government in East Berlin, would have been voted out of power. In 1955, that was an unacceptable price for Moscow. Not until the changed circumstances of 1990 did a Soviet government see any virtue in permitting unification and using what was, in some respects, a major geopolitical defeat to present itself as a paragon of peace in Europe.

Wilhelm Grewe, who had accompanied Adenauer to Moscow, drew the following conclusion more than a decade later:

If Adenauer made a false calculation in his visit to Moscow, it was this: he thought his visit could be a mere starting-point for other negotiations which would not have to be carried out under pressure of time, in the glaring light of world publicity. . . . Adenauer had got himself into a tight corner: he was forced to agree to a settlement and to accept the minimum conditions which he had previously thought of as a last resort.[10]

From Adenauer's perspective, the question of whether Germany should be reunified was never at issue. The only question was under what terms and conditions. His thoughts and concerns on this matter were put best, at his request, by the German ambassador to London, Hans Herwarth von Bittenfeld, to the permanent undersecretary of state in the British Foreign Office, Sir Ivone Kirkpatrick, just ten days before Christmas in 1955. At that time Adenauer did not believe that reunification was a practical possibility, and given the history of Germany from 1933 to 1945 he would have found little support among West Germany's allies for reunification as a neutral country. According to Kirkpatrick, "the bald reason was that Dr Adenauer had no confidence in the German people. He was terrified that when he disappeared from the scene a future German Government might do a deal with Russia at the German expense. Consequently he felt that the integration of

---

[10] Cited in Dönhoff, *Foe into Friend,* 60.

Western Germany with the West was more important than the unification of Germany."[11] The British foreign minister, Harold Macmillan, agreed with Adenauer and noted his agreement in the margin of Kirkpatrick's memorandum.

In early October 1955 the first trainloads of German prisoners of war began to arrive in the transition camp of Friedland (near Kassel in West Germany). "A strange mixture of people . . . climbed out of the busses," among them generals who had been loyal to Hitler until the last day of the war, former regular soldiers, but also men and women who had been arrested or disappeared from the Soviet occupied zone as late as 1947 or 1948. They included top communist functionaries, such as Kurt Müller, an East German parliamentarian, and Leo Bauer, who had served as editor-in-chief of the East Berlin radio (*Deutschlandsender*) and who were now "presented to Germany as returnees." Furthermore, the group included West German civilians, like the journalist Dieter Friede, who had been kidnapped in the Soviet zone, and a reporter of the West Berlin newspaper, *Der Tagesspiegel,* who had disappeared in the Soviet sector of Berlin in 1948.[12]

By the end of October the prisoner transports stopped coming. Under the headline "Word of Honor," *Die Zeit* accused the Soviet government:

> The Kremlin is maliciously holding back the German prisoners. A train with returning prisoners consisting of 25 wagons with 600 men has been sent back from Brest-Litovsk to Moscow. For ten years most of them suffered the cynical inhumanity of the Bolshevik prison camps – hunger, dirt, and the cold, humiliation and torture. . . . Millions perished, only a small group miraculously survived. Now they were on their way home, already very close, when Moscow forced them to return. The disappointment, the despair, for the victims as well as their families . . . can hardly be imagined. . . .
>
> The Kremlin gave its word of honor to release the prisoners of war. . . . One can forcefully suppress the accusations of people who have been violated – but no earthly power can silence them.[13]

Not until December did Moscow explain the delay of further prison transports. And even then there was no official statement. Through an article published in the official government newspaper, *Izvestia,* it emerged, however, that Moscow attempted to use blackmail techniques: "Return those people who have fled to your country out of our sphere of influence and the prisoner trains will roll again." Moscow "linked the POWs with the repatriation of Soviet citizens allegedly detained by

---

[11] Cited in Foschepoth, "Adenauers Moskaureise 1955." *Aus Politik und Zeitgeschichte,* B22/86 (May 31, 1986): 39n.

[12] *Die Zeit,* November 3, 1955.

[13] Ibid., November 24, 1955.

West Germany."[14] Indeed, there were approximately 100,000 Soviet nationals in West Germany. Some of them had been in Germany since the early days of the war, as slave laborers from Soviet territories occupied by the Germans, or as refugees who had fled west with the retreating German troops, and who had since opted to remain in the West (among them people from the former Baltic states and Eastern Poland, which the Soviet Union seized in 1944–5). As a goodwill gesture Bonn offered to release 31 Russians who were serving prison sentences in West Germany, but pointed out that all the others were under the protection of the UN High Commissioner for Refugees and were free to stay or go as they chose. During the second half of December 1955 and January 1956 the Soviet government released the remaining German POWs (approximately 4,150).[15]

[14] Cited in *Die Zeit*, December 8, 1955.
[15] *Keesing's Contemporary Archives*, May 12–19, 1956; *Facts on File*, December 1–7, 1955.

# 3

# The Bundeswehr

The original Himmerod proposals for the German force structure as refined and revised by Blank's office since late 1950 called for twelve divisions within a total force of almost 500,000 men, based on conscription. The Western powers accepted this structure in the Paris Treaties. To raise a German army, however, Adenauer and the government would somehow have to persuade the opposition to support the vital legislation.

Adenauer was convinced that he needed to show the world Germans in uniform quickly. He was especially worried, in the summer of 1955, that the Western powers might reach agreements with the Soviet Union inimical to Germany's interests. The army would therefore give him leverage in dealing with Germany's new NATO allies. Moreover, those same allies had defense plans that depended on a German contribution. The longer it took for that contribution to materialize, the more fragile NATO's deterrent would be.

The planners in the Blank Office had optimistically assumed that it would take only 18 months after the necessary laws were in place to make the first units operational. At Adenauer's urging, Blank in May 1955 offered the NATO allies approximately 500,000 men under arms within three years, including twelve army divisions by 1959 and an air force of 80,000 and a navy of 20,000 by 1960. This offer was not only ambitious, but it also aggravated the political opposition within West Germany and disrupted an orderly planning process. The Bundeswehr, indeed, did not reach its planned complement until the early 1970s.

On June 6, 1955, Adenauer transformed the Blank Office into the federal ministry of defense, with Blank as the first minister. That was the first step in a debate between the chancellor, the Bundestag, and the public over the formulation and passage of the required constitutional legislation establishing and organizing the West German armed forces. Initially Adenauer asked the Bundestag to authorize the government to ask for volunteers to serve as officers and instructors in the new army. The appropriate law was passed in July 1955. After the summer, the SPD and groups in Adenauer's own party became concerned that the government did not have sufficient authority to reject former Nazis and other undesirable volunteers. To solve this problem the Bundestag established a personnel screening committee with extensive powers to examine personal histories. Excluded applicants had no right of appeal against the committee's decisions.

The SPD's support for the legislation was essential because the laws involved changes in the constitution and thus required a two-thirds majority. Moreover, no political figures, least of all Adenauer, advocated passage of such important measures without bipartisan approval. In the fall of 1955, the SPD demanded that the minister of defense, unlike all other members of the cabinet, should be subject to the direct supervision and control of the Bundestag. This demand was incompatible with the principles of executive authority laid down in the Basic Law, and after much debate Adenauer persuaded the SPD to withdraw its demand. As a quid pro quo the Bundestag established the office of special commissioner for the armed forces. The holder of this office would have authority equivalent to that of an investigative committee of the Bundestag. Thus, all political parties had at their disposal an effective instrument of oversight and control of the internal structure of the armed forces.

In late June 1955 the debate on the volunteer bill, called the "28–line law" because of its extreme brevity, began on the very day that NATO was concluding a massive exercise, "Carte Blanche," which portrayed the use of nuclear-armed tactical air power against a Soviet attack also using atomic bombs. It was by far the largest exercise yet held in Germany and the first to simulate massive nuclear strikes. As far as NATO was concerned, the exercise was a success: the "Western" forces beat off the "Red" forces without having to call on the Strategic Air Command. Franz Josef Strauss, the CSU's rising younger member, who would replace Blank at the defense ministry in October 1956, was a firm believer in the New Look, massive retaliation, and the deterrent value of nuclear weapons. He concluded:

The political meaning of the NATO air maneuver was to demonstrate to the Soviets NATO's capacity to slice off their outstretched atomic arm. The possible consequences ought not to be minimized. It should not be claimed that the aggressor would not cause horrible carnage. But according to the maneuver's results, the enemy could not win the war any longer, even in its first phase. The Soviets must reckon that the strategic retaliatory power of the Americans would force them within a brief period to halt an attack on Central Europe. . . . Making this observation does not mean we are pursuing American policy. . . . But we are thankful to be anchored in an integrated security system in which we all sit in the same boat. . . . For us it is only important that our defense readiness render the first battle hopeless to the aggressor.[1]

Others were less happy at this demonstration of the value of NATO's strategy. *Der Spiegel* published confidential estimates that an attack, as portrayed in Carte Blanche, would cost 1.7 million civilian dead and twice that number of wounded. In his criticism of the volunteer bill, SPD chairman Ollenhauer repeated the common SPD argument: "Everyone knows that in the age of atomic warfare, neither the six thousand volunteers nor the twelve divisions which the Paris Treaties oblige us to recruit, can or will represent any contribution to the security of the Federal Republic's citizens."[2] Nevertheless, Adenauer succeeded in obtaining the authorization to raise 6,000 volunteers for the three services of the Bundeswehr. The price he had to pay was to accept the first of a number of laws imposing strict parliamentary control of the armed forces. Thus, in March 1956 the Bundestag passed, with the requisite two-thirds majority including the support of most of the SPD members, a revision of the Basic Law to permit the draft of armed forces. Curiously, when the question of the name of the new military establishment arose, the FDP's leading defense spokesman, Erich Mende, proposed to resurrect the name *Wehrmacht* (defense force), which had been its name in the Weimar republic and in the Third Reich. It was probably a good thing for the peace of mind of West Germany's new allies, particularly the French, that the SPD vetoed the idea and insisted on the name *Bundeswehr* (federal defense).

In the second half of 1955 and the first months of 1956, the first volunteer soldiers, sailors and airmen were called together at Andernach, Wilhelmshaven, and Nörvenich. The first staffs and cadres of West German military units began to be integrated into European defense posture under German officers, just as were the forces of the other members of the alliance.

The supporters of the Bundeswehr argued that the new army should be integrated into West German society to prevent the revival of a militaristic state within a state, that had plagued German politics between 1871 and 1933. The founders of the new army also wanted to abandon the spit and polish and barracks-square drill popularly associated with the old armies. The crucial phrase which should set the tone for the role of the new German soldier in West German society was "citizen in uniform," an ideal made popular by one of the best known

---

[1] Cited in Cioc, *Pax Atomica*, 31–2.
[2] Cited ibid., 31.

advocates of military reform, Wolf Graf von Baudissin (1907–). Together with a handful of other officers, Baudissin had been charged by Blank in 1951 with formulating the concept underlying the army's position in society and its political and legal relationships inside and outside the ranks. His vision, reminiscent of the Prussian social and military reformers of the early nineteenth century, was that of a mature, ethically conscious soldier, who, in the service, would enjoy the same democratic freedoms he had sworn to defend.

This new soldier, in Baudissin's view, should be freed of needless barracks-square formalism and blind obedience, in order to fulfill his mission in a spirit of teamwork and technical professionalism as found in the crews of armored vehicles, aircraft, and submarines. The new soldier was also to be psychologically equipped to withstand the siren call of communist propaganda through a system of political education, but not the propagandistic indoctrination of the Nazi past. These reforms, the subject of intense controversy for years after in West Germany, became known as *Innere Führung,* an untranslatable phrase that emphasizes the "leadership and participation" of the German soldier in the army and society.

When the decision to rearm West Germany was taken, it was clear that Adenauer's government, and therefore the army, navy and the air force, needed the services of sophisticated military officers who could explain the concept to the public from a position of knowledge and respect, although the concept of *Innere Führung* was the responsibility of all officers. One of the individuals asked to come to Andernach, where the Bundeswehr was being formed, was Gerd Schmückle, who was born in 1917, and had served as a major in the German army during the war. Between 1945 and 1955 he had operated a family farm and in 1955 moved to Munich to become a journalist on economic affairs; when the position was offered to him he recognized the unusual opportunity it presented to participate in the rearmament of Germany. Schmückle reported to Andernach in January 1956, shortly before Adenauer visited there for the first time to participate in the ceremony of the newly formed companies of the Bundeswehr, approximately 1,000 strong, on January 20.

Schmückle found a situation which was chaotic. The government hoped, subject to the SPD's approval of the constitutional change, to achieve the twelve-division, 500,000 man army in three years: 90,000 men in the first year, 250,000 men in the second, and 500,000 in the third. But there was only one French tank with which to teach the soldiers. In addition, Schmückle found that any soldier could be summarily dismissed within the first three months without cause. Clothing was of poor quality, and the pay was low; indeed, Schmückle himself received 800 marks per month. (Schmückle retired in 1980 as the deputy commander-in-chief of NATO).

The ceremony was held in the morning, under a grey and drizzling sky on the Rhine. In the dead of winter it was a somber occasion. The scene, as Schmückle described it in his memoirs, was made darker by the dirt-grey uniforms, and the guests reacted as though they were attending a funeral, rather than a "baptism." When Adenauer arrived for the ceremony the sound of the pipe and drums was heard for the first time since the end of the war. His speech emphasized the basic concerns with which he had been occupied since 1949; namely, that a state which cannot defend its borders is not a secure state, that the army's ability to defend would strengthen Germany's position in Europe, and that its inclusion in the western defense alliance was more important than a peace treaty. It appeared clear to Schmückle – as it did to West Germany's allies – that the rapid development of the army was the means to a political end, integration with the West.[3]

As Adenauer departed the ceremonies, the assembled soldiers sang a song, and the reaction to it, given by a French reporter, illustrated why feelings about the creation of a new German army were so intense and so mixed, both within and without Germany:

The singing suffices to evoke old ghosts in me: the memory of the days in June 1940, when the sweat-covered German infantry, with fur-covered knapsacks on their backs, surrounded by the smells of leather and rancid fat, entered our villages, accompanied by the rattling of the motorcycles and the noisy motors of the tanks with their *Balkenkreuz* [German cross]. I am not certain whether the Germans understand that even a song with its "Halli and Hallo" awakens anxiety.[4]

Schmückle thought that Blank would soon be replaced. He had, indeed, done a formidable job of organization, but Adenauer needed a strong defense minister to deal not only with the development of the Bundeswehr, but also with the reputation that was associated with the German military in general. In addition, there were major internal problems. Exorbitant prices were charged the soldiers for housing, food was insufficient, health care was uneven, and equipment was poor. To make matters worse, when the soldiers went home on weekends, they were insulted, spat upon, and in Hamburg, beaten up. In Schmückle's words, "Seeds of hate sprouted."[5]

These circumstances resulted in the proposal, of which Schmückle

[3] Schmückle, *Ohne Pauken und Trompeten*, 103–9.
[4] Ibid., 108.
[5] Ibid., 109.

was a strong advocate, to form an "Association for the Protection of German Soldiers," which should be unpolitical in nature, and which should focus, in the immediate term, on pay, housing costs, health care, and the legal rights of the soldiers. In addition to these internal organizational problems Blank and Adenauer faced the challenge from the public opponents of military service, led by Erler in the SPD. Erler argued, as he had done before, that the twelve German divisions were little more than atomic cannon fodder in NATO strategy, an argument that NATO did little to refute. In May 1956 the Bundestag debated conscription to replace the interim volunteer system. In that debate, Erler failed to stop conscription but he did manage to get the draft period reduced from 18 to twelve months.

These battles tired Blank, who was already ill, and in October 1956 Strauss took over the ministry of defense. Strauss was not always an easy collaborator for his colleagues in the government, Adenauer, his assistant Hans Globke, and the foreign minister Heinrich von Brentano. He had his own specific ideas not only about military strategy and policy, but on broader foreign policy issues as well. In the 1950s, he was often more inclined to support American defense plans and to ignore the concerns of Germany's European allies than they were; in the 1960s, it was the other way around. More important, as minister of defense Strauss believed that the indispensable foundation of West German security was a credible and efficient Bundeswehr, whereas Brentano and Globke, as political men who recalled the ambiguous record of strong military institutions in Germany, were inclined always to search for political solutions to strategic problems. Strauss was often very impatient with this sort of thinking.

To help him get his message across to the public and to rally public support for the concept and the role of the Bundeswehr, Strauss in 1957 appointed Schmückle, the soft-spoken and quick-witted former Wehr-macht officer, as his press spokesman. By the time Strauss was appointed the early constitutional and political problems concerning rearmament, which had spurred acrimonious debate in West Germany, were largely overcome. Strauss was not unhappy that conscription had been eased; he even revised the schedule from a goal of 500,000 men in uniform within three years, to 350,000 in six years. His reason was that if the army was built up too rapidly it would only have outdated equipment at a time when defensive technology was rapidly changing. What he meant was that to be efficient, the Bundeswehr should have nuclear weapons or at least nuclear delivery systems. He held fast to this position throughout the tremendous battles over the morality of nuclear weapons and their utility in achieving security for West Germany, that were about to begin.

Between 1957 and 1963 the Germans gradually took a more positive view of the Bundeswehr. This proved true not only because the passage of time solved some of the problems, but also because politics in Germany were continuing to change. But the development of US and allied concerns in Europe also affected the stature of the German military, as did advances in technology, the political constellation of forces within the Federal Republic, and Khrushchev's ultimatum on Berlin. As events unfolded the original goal of a Bundeswehr of 500,000 (army, navy and air force) was not lost sight of, but it was not attained for almost two decades.

# 4

# Dissent over Ostpolitik

R earmament was only one source of contention in West Germany in
1955–7, albeit one that brought together virtually all of the main
themes of German political life ten years after the war. Historically and
morally, the existence of a German army raised the question of German
guilt for the war and for mass murder. In strictly contemporary terms,
the debate on rearmament was linked inextricably with the debate on
West Germany's foreign policy, which in turn was influenced by
American and NATO strategic developments and by what Germans
saw, or thought they saw, in Eastern Europe. The argument over what
was happening in Eastern Europe influenced the defense debate
directly: those who did not perceive a Soviet threat and believed that
liberalization of the East European communist regimes was on the way,
or at least possible, also thought that a West German army, and in
particular nuclear arms in West Germany, were likely to eliminate that
possibility by forcing the Soviet Union to crack down on Eastern
Europe in order to secure its own defense perimeter. Others, like
Adenauer and Dulles, argued on the contrary that an undefended West
Germany, or a West Germany outside the protective reach of the New
Look NATO strategy, was a temptation for East German or Soviet
subversion. German weakness, moreover, would tend to make the
Soviets more aggressive abroad and more, not less, repressive at home.
Two world-views, two ways of understanding the forces at work in
European politics and the implications of defense strategy were in
opposition, and remained so for the rest of the decade.

The year of 1956 was one of crisis in Eastern Europe. The uprisings
in Poland and Hungary, although they were suppressed, led to the
replacement of Stalinist governments by somewhat more liberal regimes
that were interested in receiving aid from the West in building up their
economies, but not in Western influence that might strengthen the
forces of opposition to communist rule. Ever since that time, West

Germany faced the question of how to deal effectively with these East European regimes, and the nature of relations with Eastern Europe became a steadily more important element in West German foreign policy.

In 1956 the options were restricted by the Hallstein Doctrine, a policy conceived by Adenauer's government following the establishment of diplomatic relations with Moscow, and formulated by Wilhelm Grewe, a colleague of West Germany's deputy foreign minister, Walter Hallstein, and later West German ambassador to the United States. Its purpose was to discourage other countries from establishing diplomatic relations with the GDR. Thus, the West German government would, in accordance with this doctrine, regard such diplomatic recognition as an unfriendly act since it would aggravate the division of Germany. It was designed, (1) to prevent diplomatic legitimacy being accorded the East German dictatorship to whatever extent possible, (2) to emphasize that the GDR was not a sovereign state in the normal sense of the term, and (3) to support the West German government's claim that it was the only German government freely elected by the German people, and therefore entitled to represent them.

In Eastern Europe Yugoslavia was the only country that did not yet recognize the GDR diplomatically, and, therefore, was a potential point of entry for West Germany to Eastern Europe. Adenauer recognized that contact with Yugoslavia could be useful, even though it was unlikely that any immediate tangible result would develop. In 1956 Bonn offered Yugoslavia 240 million marks for economic development in the hope that this support would assure Yugoslav goodwill on the German question. It was a positive step, but at the same time Yugoslavia's leader, Marshal Tito, made it clear that his government considered Germany to be divided into two separate states. Although West Germany's foreign minister, Brentano, declared that relations with Yugoslavia could not move forward from such a position, the loan was nonetheless approved by the Bundestag. It was a decision of major symbolic and practical importance; it marked the first step toward what became the new Ostpolitik of the late 1960s.

Interest in developing relations with the countries of Eastern Europe was held not only by Adenauer. During these years, 1956–7, the idea was put forward within the FDP and the SPD, and by many political writers, that it might be possible to achieve momentum in the German question via Eastern Europe. In this connection many leftists and liberals argued that the loss of the Eastern provinces, with several hundred years of German culture, was a justifiable penalty for Nazi aggression under the Third Reich; and that it was, therefore, necessary to recognize reality and deal with the governments of Eastern Europe. Carlo Schmid of the SPD and Thomas Dehler (1897–1967), chairman of the FDP from 1954 to 1957, supported especially a German-Polish dialogue. Many observers inside and outside Germany encouraged such a dialogue as well. One such influential observer was the Swiss journalist Fritz René Allemann, who in a famous book of 1955 explained why "Bonn was not Weimar," and why the Bonn republic was not going to succumb to the same dangers as its predecessor. He also argued that in order to promote peace, West Germany should open a dialogue with Poland and the other communist regimes. These regimes, Allemann believed, feared German revanchism and so bound themselves closely to the Soviet Union. The Polish regime, for its part, actively sought diplomatic relations with West Germany in an effort to gain West German recognition that the territory taken from Germany and given to Poland, legitimately belonged to Poland. In 1957 these Polish initiatives coincided with the internal West German discussion, to produce a concerted effort on the part of several leading figures to produce a new Ostpolitik.

The origins of this concept were found, in part, in a speech given in the south German city of Waiblingen in June 1952 by Karl Georg Pfleiderer, a FDP Bundestag member who maintained that the establishment of relations with Eastern Europe could not be avoided. Since the early 1950s, Pfleiderer had argued that a new Ostpolitik vis-à-vis Eastern Europe was necessary, an Ostpolitik that would recognize legitimate Soviet security interests. What this phrase, which later became much more common, really meant, was that one should no longer seek to restore a unified Germany as a major European power. Instead one should accept the Soviet Union as the dominant power in Central Europe, and West Germany should, therefore, attempt to improve its relations with the Soviet government. Pfleiderer was ahead of his time. He recognized that Germany had a legal claim to re-establish its unity as it existed before the war (namely, its territorial borders of 1937), and to sign a peace treaty with its former enemies. But he also argued that these goals were steadily becoming unrealistic and that the value of relations with East Europe was becoming greater in comparison to the value of insisting on unenforceable legal claims. His hope was that it would be possible by improving relations with the East to avoid recognition of the GDR by West Germany's Western allies, and at the same time to obtain some leverage over the GDR by an active policy vis-à-vis Eastern Europe. However, he also realized that the chances of any sort of reunification were slim, and that the immediate effects of his proposals would very likely weaken West Germany's formal position as the sole representative of the German people.[1]

---

[1] Schwarz, *Die Ära Adenauer, 1949–1957*, 159, 178, 191, 211, 225.

Pfleiderer's ideas, which coincided closely with those put into practice by the SPD/FDP government of 1969–82, did not become policy under Adenauer, although Pfleiderer did become West Germany's ambassador to Yugoslavia in 1955. Adenauer consistently maintained his government's position concerning the sovereignty of the Federal Republic vis-à-vis the illegitimacy of the GDR. One year after the loan to Yugoslavia, however, Poland's leader Wladyslaw Gomulka and Yugoslavia's Tito issued a joint statement – on the very day of the third election to the Bundestag in September 1957 – in which they recognized the Oder–Neisse line as the eastern border of the GDR and recognized the GDR as a second and legitimate German state. Following this Adenauer saw no option but to to break diplomatic relations with Yugoslavia and to cease discussions relating to diplomatic relations with Poland. The Yugoslavs and the Poles were indignant, but it is unclear whether their governments had hoped realistically for diplomatic recognition by West Germany, or whether they were primarily concerned with causing division, debate, and uncertainty in West German government circles, and among the population as a whole, concerning the merits of how to deal with the GDR and with the issue of what constituted the legitimate border dividing Poland and East Germany.

The Soviet government followed these developments with considerable interest, and undoubtedly actively encouraged them. It is likely that the spectacle of disagreement between and within West Germany's parties, and primarily between the SPD and the CDU/CSU, led Khrushchev to believe that further gains for the Soviet Union in the German question were possible. This belief was supported by political developments in the United States, Britain, and France. On the one hand the American policy of "rollback," declared by Secretary of State John Foster Dulles, had failed to change communist governments in Europe, and it was clear from events in 1956 in Hungary that US policy did not include military assistance to anti-communist movements in Eastern Europe. In addition, the Soviet Union, which had exploded its first nuclear weapons in 1949, was now in a military position in Europe that made the the New Look, and the US strategic policy of massive retaliation, gradually seem less credible. In Britain and France, moreover, the Suez crisis in Egypt had led to tensions with the United States, and leading political forces in all parties, in all three countries, were talking increasingly of the need for detente in Europe.

The increase in Soviet power, but also the popularity of concepts such as Pfleiderer's or the defunct Eden Plan for free elections or the "thinning-out" of military forces, as well as continued hopes for reunification, were factors driving the FDP away from the CDU/CSU, which the FDP regarded as obsessed with military security, ties to the West, and nuclear arms. The first result of this disaffection was the end of the coalition in early 1956; the second, and indirect result, was the great nuclear arms debate of 1957–8, which spanned the CDU's election triumph of September 1957 and the argument over the proposals for disarmament made by George Kennan and the Polish foreign minister Adam Rapacki. By 1960, these developments, and their aftershocks, would permanently change the West German political landscape by bringing about the first broad SPD-CDU consensus on defense and foreign policy since 1949.

# 5

# The Coalition Breaks Down

Bipartisan cooperation within the second Adenauer government broke down in the winter of 1955–6, following a crisis in the FDP, which left the coalition in February 1956. The collapse of the CDU/CSU and FDP coalition was a function of long-term interests on both sides of the political spectrum. Younger liberal leaders, especially in North Rhine-Westphalia, resented the domination of the CDU in the coalition. They also had particular policy differences with the Christian democrats. The North Rhine FDP was the industrial party par excellence of the early Federal Republic, committed to the interests of free trade and industry. Its supporters advocated policies that favored business and economic growth without the religious and ideological ballast of the CDU. They saw themselves as liberals for pragmatic reasons – liberal policies produced prosperity – rather than for ideological reasons such as fear of communism. They further resented what they saw as Adenauer's domineering influence, even though Adenauer had in fact turned the CDU into a pro-capitalist and liberal (in the European sense) party. Finally, they believed that the SPD had become sufficiently integrated with bourgeois society so that cooperation with it would not threaten the basic social structure of the Federal Republic. These new leaders launched the FDP on its subsequent career as the swing party between the two major parties of the right and left.

Dehler, as FDP party chairman, disagreed with Adenauer primarily on issues of foreign policy, and Adenauer preferred a new leader of the FDP in the hope that the party would be more amenable to his policies. In turn, the FDP feared Adenauer's plans, announced in December 1955, for electoral reform, which would have greatly strengthened the electoral position of the CDU, CSU and the SPD at the expense of the FDP and other small parties. Had they succeeded, it would have meant the virtual disappearance from the Bundestag of the FDP and all other smaller parties, by eliminating the double vote system that allowed the voter to vote for a party *and* a candidate – who might belong to another party. The electoral reform was supported especially by the CSU and by the conservative wing of the CDU. For Adenauer, however, it was largely a tool to effect change in the leadership of the FDP, and not an attempt to destroy the party. Adenauer hoped the prospect of electoral reform would force the FDP to replace Dehler with a leader more sympathetic to Adenauer's foreign policy.[1] But his efforts had the opposite effect, and when he realized this, he withdrew the proposal.

Adenauer's concerns were neither fully understood nor appreciated in the FDP, and the resulting debate within the party produced the internal crisis. In February 1956, a group of younger members of the FDP, known as "young Turks" *(Jungtürken)* engineered the "Düsseldorf Coup" in the government of North Rhine-Westphalia: the FDP left the coalition with the CDU and formed a coalition with the SPD which took over the *Land* government through a constructive vote of no confidence. This had immediate repercussions on the federal level: 36 of the 52 Free Democrats in the Bundestag left the government coalition. The remainder, along with the four FDP ministers in the government, formed their own new party which the CDU absorbed within the next two years. Since the CDU/CSU, however, was only one member short of an absolute majority in the Bundestag, the government was not put at risk by these defections. When the debate ended in 1956, the FDP's left wing emerged greatly strengthened, as did those forces that looked for detente with the East and hoped for a "disengagement" of both the US and the USSR from Central Europe. Dehler emerged as the leader of this faction alongside Mende, Pfleiderer, Wolfgang Döring, and Walter Scheel. Their victory, however, was short-lived.

In 1956–7, the argument over Ostpolitik affected mainly the FDP, since the SPD had already made up its mind in 1952–3, following Schumacher's death, and influenced by the rise of neutralist tendencies provoked in part by the New Look and by the fear of nuclear war. Dehler, and the party's nationalist wing, suspected US-German collusion in the failure of the Geneva summit and the foreign ministers' conference to make progress on reunification. During the following months and years, Dehler's resentment of Adenauer, which came to the fore after the chancellor refused to reappoint him as minister of justice in 1953, turned into a dislike verging on hatred; this produced a division within the FDP between followers of Dehler and those who supported continued collaboration with the CDU. This split reflected, ultimately, the uneasy marriage within the liberal party of two tendencies which

[1] Adenauer, *Erinnerungen 1955–1959*, 88; Schwarz, *Die Ära Adenauer, 1949–1957*, 307.

were often antagonistic: the national-liberals, like Dehler, who hoped for reunification in a neutral state with its own small armed force, as in the Pfleiderer Plan, and the economic liberals who supported reunification, but who were mainly concerned with economic growth, individual rights, and the protection of small and middle-size business as the economic backbone of the country.

During 1956 the FDP moved rapidly in the direction of neutralism in its Ostpolitik. Erich Mende was the rising star of the FDP's "young Turks." Born in Silesia in 1916, he was a highly decorated war veteran who had joined the new liberal party immediately after the war and by late 1946 was chairman of the party in North Rhine-Westphalia. In 1949 he was elected to the Bundestag and became a member of the party executive. He spoke of reunification and neutrality in terms that reflected Pfleiderer's ideas of 1952, and which were now dominant in the FDP. On the question of nuclear weapons the party took more time to reach a position. In mid-1956 Mende, like Strauss, advocated nuclear weapons for the Bundeswehr: "In the Paris Treaties, we renounced only the production of atomic weapons, but not the equipping of our armed forces with them. It is imperative to equip the Bundeswehr with tactical atomic weapons." But by April 1957 the party had decided to oppose "the production and stockpiling of atomic weapons on German soil."[2] This position was no different from SPD policy. It made the FDP ineligible as a coalition partner with the CDU until Mende, in 1961, persuaded the party once again to shift 180 degrees.

The leaders of the smallest of the three major parties of West Germany were not the only ones who were uncertain about how to achieve peace, security, and, if possible, reunification. In 1957–60, the ambiguities concerning West Germany's place in Europe, its relations with East and West, and the argument over nuclear weapons combined to produce outbreaks of confusion, fear, outrage, and anger that did not subside until all three parties found a common ground for their security policies.

[2] Cioc, *Pax Atomica*, 41.

# 6

# The Founding of the European Economic Community

In April 1956, the expert committee established by the Six at Messina recommended that the Six begin direct negotiations between their governments on the establishment of a common market and a common policy on nuclear energy. The decision to proceed caused uproar in France, where the government had great difficulty in getting the National Assembly's approval. In Bonn almost no one was present in the Bundestag when, after a debate of two hours, it gave Adenauer the authority to go ahead. The SPD, which had been so fiercely critical of the EDC and of the German defense contribution, accepted the common market almost without a single complaint. One reason was that leading social democrats had come to accept Jean Monnet's arguments that European integration was essential for international stability and security. This bipartisan agreement lasted through the signing of the Treaty of Rome itself in March 1957, which established the European Economic Community (EEC) and the European Atomic Energy Community (EURATOM). The Rome Treaty was thus the first major international agreement that had the unequivocal support of both the major parties.

In the final agreement, reached in late 1956, the Six agreed on what procedures and institutions to establish for the future community. The planners at that time foresaw a set of genuinely federal institutions with real policy-making powers vis-à-vis member governments. The core of the system was the Commission of the EEC (since 1967, of the European Community), which at the outset consisted of eleven members "pledged by treaty (and under oath) not to act as national representatives, nor to seek or accept national instructions. Their collective task is to identify, represent, and promote the common interest of the Community as a whole, rather than the member states' national interests."[1]

---

[1] "Commission (European Community)," in *Blackwell Encyclopaedia of Political Institutions*, 118–19.

Walter Hallstein was the first president of the Commission and made it the driving force of integration in the community.[2] After his time, the influence of the Commission declined until the later 1980s.

The central decision-making authority of the EEC was the Council of Ministers, in which France, Germany, and Italy each had four votes, Belgium and the Netherlands two, and Luxembourg one. The Commission provided policy proposals for the Council to decide and took part as well in executing the Council's decisions. The treaty also established a European Parliament, with members appointed by the parliaments of member states (since 1979, by direct election). The parliament was not a truly federal legislature, however, since it could only advise, not compel, the Council. Nor did it have control over the community's budget, which was negotiated by the member states in the Council.

The treaty would come into force in all member countries on January 1, 1958. The signatories obliged themselves to remove all tariffs and unfair hindrances to trade within twelve years from that date, to co-ordinate their domestic industrial, agricultural, and fiscal policies, and to establish free movement of labor, capital, and other factors of production.

In the original Treaty, the Council of Ministers had the power to make binding decisions by majority vote, except that any member government could veto the admission of new candidate governments, as France did on two occasions vis-à-vis Britain in the 1960s. The principle of majority decision was a victory for Europeanists like Walter Hallstein, who wanted the common market to be an "incipient federal state." Over time, the emerging federation would start to deal with political issues not included in the original Treaty and would thus ultimately become the European union that the founders of the original European movement in 1946–8 had hoped for. Hallstein foresaw that this process of federation would occur naturally, as member states fulfilled their Treaty obligation to harmonize their laws, regulations, and administrative practices. The majority rule was indeed an extremely important principle, since it meant that each member state bound itself to obey decisions and carry out policies decided by the Council, even if its own government was opposed to them. This was a genuine surrender of sovereignty which implied that the Council and the other institutions of the EEC were in truth federal institutions.

Unfortunately for the Europeanists, France under Charles de Gaulle nullified this essential aspect of federalism when, by threatening to bring all EEC functions to a complete halt, it obtained the agreement of the other members to a revision of the Treaty in the compromise of Luxem-

---

[2] See Hallstein, *United Europe: Challenge and Opportunity*.

bourg of January 30, 1966. Henceforth Council decisions had to be unanimous if any member state regarded the issue in question as being of "fundamental importance." The Luxembourg compromise reduced the community to a forum where fully sovereign states coordinated their economic and trade policies. It was not until the 1980s that a new generation of Europeanist politicians began, in modest ways, to move back toward the original conception of the community as a federation.[3]

In the longer view, the most important institution established by the treaty was the European Court of Justice, sitting in Luxembourg and consisting of (at first) seven judges and four advocates-general appointed by the member governments. The court's jurisdiction covered complaints by the Commission or any member against any other member for not fulfilling the treaty obligations as well as references from national courts on questions of community law. Reflecting on the history of the community in the 1980s, an observer commented:

Because the nature and scope of its jurisdiction are defined in the treaties, the Court is not a "supreme court" and has no general or overriding power. . . . But that may be a measure of its success because, in spite of the weakness of the European Parliament, the inertia of the Council of Ministers and the shackling of the Commission, it is through the Court that the momentum of integration has been maintained. The Court has therefore had a profound (if largely unnoticed) political influence in post-war Europe . . . the Court has insisted . . . that the law deriving from the treaties must be applied uniformly throughout the Community. Consequently member states cannot be allowed to derogate unilaterally from Community law and national courts must apply it in preference to national law (including subsequent parliamentary legislation) which is inconsistent with it.[4]

The court also insisted that the member states in the Rome Treaty and later treaties had conferred rights not only on community institutions, but on persons, both legal and physical. Based on this doctrine, called the doctrine of direct effect, the Court was able to "give immediate and binding effect to the key provisions of the EEC treaty on freedom of movement of goods, persons, services and, to a limited extent, capital."[5] The court and the growing corpus of EEC law showed that the community was not merely a forum where six otherwise independent governments met to coordinate their industrial and trade policies, but an actual supranational institution with the authority to make and

[3] Theodor Schieder et al., "Europa," in *Staatslexikon*, vol. 2, cols 414–32.

[4] "European Court of Justice," in *Blackwell Encyclopaedia of Political Institutions*, 215–17.

[5] Ibid.

enforce decisions. Although the road to full European integration was far longer and rockier than either Adenauer, Monnet, or Hallstein foresaw in 1957, the Rome Treaty nevertheless was an indispensable foundation for economic growth and political stability in the 1960s, and for the renewed initiative toward the single European market of twelve member states that was due to come into being in 1992.

One of the more curious aspects of the Rome Treaty, which reflected the German situation, was the clause that guaranteed the continuation of interzonal trade, that is, trade with the GDR. The Germans insisted that interzonal trade must remain free of tariffs, since to put tariffs on GDR goods would be, in effect, to declare the GDR to be foreign territory, which violated every principle of national policy held by all parties in West Germany. On the other hand, the community members undertook to treat all goods coming from outside the community equally in terms of tariffs and preferences. At Adenauer's request, the community agreed to treat imports from the GDR to West Germany as though they were produced in West Germany.

The purpose of EURATOM was to promote and supervise the development of civilian nuclear power in Europe. The Germans were eager supporters because they foresaw problems with oil supplies from the Middle East. Franz Josef Strauss, who was minister for atomic affairs from 1955 to 1956 and retained a lively interest in nuclear matters, wanted a nuclear industry that would not only provide power but help to produce a generation of trained nuclear engineers. The French, for their part, did not want a strong central authority in EURATOM that might delay or hinder France's own atomic bomb program. In the final agreement, the French side kept their arms program safe while instituting heavy controls on the German civilian nuclear industry.

Without French support, the Rome Treaty and the EEC would never have come into existence. As in 1954, the future of the Federal Republic was decided in Paris, when the French government and National Assembly decided whether to ratify the Treaty. Fortunately, the French government was in the hands of committed Europeanists, and the majority in favor was more than 100. As a historian later noted, French ratification came in the nick of time. Within a few months, France was wholly absorbed in the Algerian crisis, which produced political stagnation and economic recession and led directly to the fall of the Fourth Republic. It is hard to imagine that the French government under those conditions would have engaged in an adventure as risky and uncertain as the EEC.[6]

In Bonn, the Rome Treaties were ratified by all parties except the

[6] See also Marjolin, *Architect of European Unity: Memoirs 1911–1986*, 284–307.

FDP and the BHE, and came into force on January 1, 1958. Both the FDP and the BHE regarded the Rome Treaties as an obstacle to re-unification, since they did represent another step in the process of West German integration with the West. For the SPD, however, this latter attitude was not a compelling argument; indeed, the SPD saw the EEC as a mechanism with which to more easily achieve a Socialist Europe. SPD support was guaranteed by the leadership of Ollenhauer and Wehner, both of whom were influenced by an initiative of Jean Monnet in 1955, the "Comité d'Action pour les États-Unis d'Europe" (Action Committee for the United States of Europe), which brought together leading politicians and non-communist union leaders in the Six to work for European confederation. Erhard was presciently skeptical, warning that the French could well turn the EEC into a protectionist bloc against outside countries and that a simple free-trade zone would prove more constructive.

# 7

# The European Power Balance: Strategy and Nuclear Arms

The SPD and, after April 1957, the FDP, regarded the introduction of nuclear weapons to the NATO arsenal in Germany and elsewhere in Western Europe, as simply a further consolidation of the military blocs dividing Europe, and therefore an additional impediment to any future possibility of reunification. The CDU/CSU, whose undisputed leader in the defense debate was the defense minister, Strauss, disagreed: they considered nuclear weapons in Allied or German hands as essential deterrents to attack. NATO, moreover, in December 1956, adopted new guidelines in the Military Committee directive known as MC-14/2. It called for 26 divisions on the front to Eastern Europe, including twelve German divisions, all equipped for nuclear warfare. Thus, the line of defense in Central Europe was drawn down the middle of Germany, when Adenauer inadvertently set alight a powder-keg of emotions and arguments on the nuclear issue with a few casual remarks he made in April 1957, that came to be known as the "artillery statement."

Adenauer had never focused on concrete issues of strategy or technology. He was primarily interested in and feared the political effects of Soviet power on the democracies – intimidation, appeasement, disunity, mutual suspicion – and welcomed any method, policy, or technical implement that in his view might make that power seem less threatening and make Western Europeans feel more secure. In early 1957 Adenauer considered this an urgent concern, for three reasons. First, in October 1956, democratic forces in Hungary had risen in revolt against the Soviet Union and the local communist regime. By November 2, Soviet tanks had crushed the Hungarian revolution, thus demonstrating that the Soviet government would not tolerate pluralism in their sphere of interest and that the West could or would do nothing to help anti-communist revolutions east of the Iron Curtain. Second, just prior to the Hungarian revolution the West German and Soviet governments exchanged acrimonious notes on the German question. The West

German government demanded free elections and reunification, but the Soviet government refused even to acknowledge the issue, and referred the Bonn government to the GDR to discuss the question of re-unification. Third, the Western powers had agreed to conduct arms control talks with the Soviet Union throughout the spring and summer of 1957 – talks that became known as the London Disarmament Conference.

These matters, as well as the forthcoming elections in the fall, were on Adenauer's mind, so he was not prepared for a technical discussion when, on April 5, journalists asked him the three principal questions concerning German defense plans: Did he plan to equip the Bundeswehr with nuclear weapons? Did he plan to do so regardless of whether the East German army had nuclear weapons? Did he think that tactical nuclear weapons in West Germany increased the danger of Soviet nuclear strikes that would lay waste Central Europe?

On the first point, Adenauer said that his government did indeed approve equipping the Bundeswehr with American tactical nuclear weapons: "Tactical atomic weapons are basically nothing but the further development of artillery." He continued, "It goes without saying that, due to such a powerful development in weapons technique (which we unfortunately now have), we cannot dispense with having them for our troops. We must follow suit and have these new types – they are after all practically normal weapons."[1]

Adenauer did not specify if, by "we," he meant NATO or the Federal Republic. It did not matter; the damage was done both at home and abroad. The Soviet government seized the opportunity to denounce Adenauer for turning West Germany "into a NATO atomic base." In a sharply worded note of April 27, the Soviet Union stated that "the preparations for the equipment of the West German Army with atomic weapons lead to the conversion of the Federal Republic of Germany into the main European springboard and chief NATO shock force for atomic warfare in Europe." With bluntness unusual even for them, the Soviet government threatened the Germans with nuclear attack if they did not cease and desist from their alleged plans to obtain nuclear weapons:

The conversion of the territory of the Federal Republic of Germany into a NATO atomic base is bound to make Western Germany in case of war the immediate object of retaliation with the use of all types of modern weapons, including rocket weapons.

There is no need to dwell in detail on the consequences this would have for the population and the economy of the Federal Republic of Germany, which

[1] Cited in Cioc, *Pax Atomica*, 42–3.

has such a density of population and concentration of industry that the vital centers of the country can be paralyzed by the action of a single modern hydrogen bomb. . . .

One can easily see that Western Germany, whose territory would become the object of the most powerful and concentrated blows of these weapons, would be destroyed, would become one big cemetery.[2]

It was typical of Soviet tactics that, having made this crude and obvious threat, the note immediately added that "Nothing can be more alien to the policy of the Soviet Goverment than the use of threats and intimidation."

In Germany itself, the "artillery statement" catalyzed, inside and outside the political arena, the diffuse opposition to nuclear weapons in general and to a nuclear Bundeswehr in particular. It provoked Gustav Heinemann to dissolve his own anti-rearmament party and join the SPD, on the grounds that the chances of defeating the introduction of nuclear weapons and neutralizing Germany were vastly improved by the opposition of a big party than of a small one, that was not even represented in parliament. However, the response to Adenauer's interview that made headlines came from a group of 18 eminent physicists, many of whom worked for the ministry of atomic affairs, which Strauss had headed in 1955–6. A week after the "artillery statement" the press carried reports about a document that became known as the Göttingen Manifesto, because most of its signatories worked at the Max Planck Institute for Theoretical Physics in Göttingen, and because Göttingen University had been associated, since the 1830s, with liberal and democratic causes and with resistance to authority. Its chief author was Carl Friedrich von Weizsäcker, a nuclear physicist, Lutheran, and philosopher. His father, Ernst von Weizsäcker, had been an assistant foreign minister during the Third Reich. Though anti-Nazi, he had served the regime and thus given his children an example of the moral dilemmas of power that they never forgot. Weizsäcker devoted most of his life, following the Manifesto, to NATO defense strategy and its moral implications, which he tried to interpret and improve in accordance with his religious and humanistic view of man and morality.

The 18 physicists who signed it, along with the majority of West German scientists, opposed nuclear weapons for or in Germany, partly because they regarded preparation for nuclear war in general as immoral, and partly because they considered that Germany, of all countries, should eschew such weapons, given Hitler's abuse of power in 1933–45. Indeed, Strauss, as defense minister, had already aroused the ire of the opposition by a statement in January, in which he "rejected

[2] Dept of State, *Documents on Germany*, 497–8.

a German atomic armament under national sovereignty" but "considered a massive atomic armament of the European NATO forces a necessity . . . a large supranational Western European atomic defense, in case the Americans withdraw someday from Europe."[3] Some of the physicists, including Weizsäcker, were not convinced they opposed a *European* nuclear force, only a *German* one. Therefore, Adenauer's "artillery statement" and the US deployment in the same month of additional tactical nuclear weapons in Germany caused a major furor. The Manifesto stated in part:

We profess our allegiance to the freedom that is today safeguarded by the Western world against Communism. We do not deny that the mutual fear of thermonuclear bombs makes an essential contribution both to the maintenance of peace in the whole world and to freedom in a part of the world. But we view this mode of protecting peace and freedom as unreliable in the long run, and we consider the danger in the case of its breakdown to be lethal. . . .

We believe that a small country like the Federal Republic best guarantees its own safety and contributes to world peace by expressly and voluntarily renouncing the possession of nuclear weapons of any sort. Under no circumstances would the undersigned be willing to participate in the production, testing or use of atomic weapons in any way.[4]

Among the signatories were many whose work had earned worldwide respect for German physicists prior to the Third Reich, and who were doing their best to restore a part of that respect: Max Born, Otto Hahn, Werner Heisenberg, Max von Laue, as well as Weizsäcker himself.

Although the Manifesto did not call for neutralization or the withdrawal of US troops or of American nuclear weapons, the public was quickly given the impression that the physicists were saying that pacifism was the best defense. The East German government was ecstatic, the Soviet government used the Manifesto to best effect in its accusations that West Germany was arming for world war against the East, and Adenauer was angry. Karl Jaspers, the eminent philosopher, offered a more cogent critique of nuclear weapons in a book entitled *Die Atombombe und die Zunkunft der Menschen,* published one year later. He began by equating two threats to mankind's existence: the bomb and totalitarian rule, "with its terroristic structure that obliterates all liberty and human dignity. By one, we lose life; by the other a life worth living."[5] But he also believed that deterrence would not last forever. As a later commentator summarized it:

[3] Cited in Cioc, *Pax Atomica,* 75.
[4] Cited ibid., 79.
[5] Cited ibid., 82.

Jaspers felt a one-sided renunciation would simply weaken NATO, without bringing the Russians a step closer to the negotiating table. . . . A renunciation would not promote a new political ethos based on the principle of freedom, nor permit West Germany to escape the consequences of nuclear war. Further-more, Jaspers saw in the manifesto an unhealthy dose of the "count me out" nostrum, and a "tendency toward neutralism." . . . [T]he scientists had appealed to the public, thereby turning a personal ethical decision into a political decision affecting the lives of millions of fellow citizens. The political direction they chose, Jaspers concluded, promoted neither Germany's security nor world peace.[6]

Weizsäcker himself also followed the Manifesto with the publication of a treatise in 1958, entitled *Mit der Bombe leben* (Living with the bomb). He argued for a nuclear test ban, a freeze on weapons production and deployment, and eventual world government. He had learned from American strategists and physicists, including Edward Teller, that technology was making the doctrine of massive retaliation obsolete. He now argued that NATO should raise the nuclear threshold by increas-ing its conventional forces, acquire new, low-yield tactical nuclear weapons for limited strikes in the event that conventional forces failed to stop an attack, and adopt an overall political and diplomatic strategy of binding the Soviet Union into a peaceful international order by means of trade and economic incentives.[7] Weizsäcker introduced the phrase "graduated deterrence" to the German debate, to describe a strategy offering options other than massive retaliation. Thanks in large part to Weizsäcker's influence, the SPD eventually, in late 1958, began moving away from its hostility to NATO and nuclear weapons, and toward a position of consensus with the CDU.

As a Lutheran, Weizsäcker was also deeply concerned by how the nuclear controversy was dividing his church. In 1958–9, German Protestantism came close to open schism, between those who would permit defense with nuclear weapons and those who rejected any strategy involving nuclear use as a greater moral evil than communist occupation.

German Protestants had been divided on the issue of defense ever since rearmament first became an issue in 1950. In 1955, the leftist pastor Helmut Gollwitzer had tried to start a movement against ratifica-tion of the Paris Treaties which failed for lack of public support. In 1957 the situation was different: the "artillery statement" and Strauss' overt agitation for some kind of German involvement in nuclear production worried many people. In addition, many on the left also hoped to use the

---

[6] Ibid., 83–4.
[7] Ibid., 88–90.

nuclear and defense issue against the CDU in the upcoming elections. Since February 1956, the CDU had been governing alone, and the SPD and FDP hoped that the prospect of continued single-party government would frighten enough people to bring about a change of power at the elections in September. This did not happen; instead, Adenauer won his greatest electoral victory ever, primarily because of his government's achievements in social and economic policy.

# 8

# The Economic Miracle

The Korean War was, in the 1950s, "the father of all things."[1] The spectre of communist aggression it called forth served to push West Germany toward sovereignty and toward rearmament. But the war also gave strong impetus to Germany's recovery between 1949 and 1953; and the effects continued to be felt throughout the decade. The war created an unusual constellation of economic priorities and forces. In the United States and in Western Europe, especially in France and in Great Britain, production of armaments and war-related goods was close to capacity. But the West Germans, who were not allowed to produce such goods as a consequence of the occupation, concentrated on producing industrial goods such as chemicals, machine tools, steel, optics, construction equipment, and electrical goods. In so doing, they were able to take significant steps towards recapturing their leadership in many of their traditional markets.

Initially, however, the Federal Republic experienced the same difficulties as many other Western nations concerning the purchase of raw materials whose prices skyrocketed in 1950 and 1951. In 1950, the Federal Republic ran a trade deficit of 3.02 billion marks and received 2.07 billion marks in transfers under the Marshall Plan. In 1955, West Germany ran a surplus on goods and services of 3.07 billion marks, while transferring 834 million marks abroad – primarily in the form of financial restitution *(Wiedergutmachung)* to Israel, and to Jews and other victims of Nazi persecution living elsewhere. The economy grew by an average of 8.8 per cent per year in 1950–4, albeit at a declining rate. The boom was driven by exports, because the Korean War and conditions in Europe spurred worldwide public and private demand for German products. In addition, the war in Asia opened the floodgates of rearmament in all the major countries of the Western Alliance. By 1953,

[1] Schwarz, *Die Ära Adenauer, 1949–1957*, 105.

German heavy industry was feeling the demands of this rearmament boom. West Germany's own rearmament and membership in the Atlantic Alliance from 1955 onward placed new and heavy burdens on the productive sector which had the combined effect of pushing capacity utilization to a new maximum and indirectly stimulating domestic demand.

Between 1955 and 1959, the average growth rate was 7.2 per cent per year, still extraordinary by the standards of any period since the outbreak of World War I in 1914. The forces of growth and success, however, were also changing character and attitudes, and this transformation was of fundamental importance for the subsequent history of the Federal Republic.

From the first beginnings of sustained recovery in 1947 to the mid-1950s, the most common way in which German enterprises increased their production was to develop their extensive spare capacity. The primary problem in 1945–7 had not been the destruction of plant and capital goods, but the collapse of communications and, reinforcing this problem, the zonal division of Germany. The solution to this dilemma, under the guidelines of Erhard's social market economy, provided the basis for the first great wave of the Economic Miracle. By the mid-1950s, however, capacity utilization was at its limit in many industries, particularly iron and coal. The extensive phase of recovery, characterized by rapidly increasing production from existing plants and by insatiable domestic and foreign demand, gave way to an intensive phase in which the decisive factors were new capital investments, new plants, and, perhaps most important, the efficient use of the "non-material capital,"[2] represented by the still unemployed or underemployed workforce.

This labor force consisted, in the first instance, of people native to West Germany, but it was continually increased throughout the 1950s by immigration from or through the GDR. By January 1951, there were already 9.4 million more people living in the territory of the Federal Republic than there had been in 1939. This figure represented the refugees from the Eastern provinces who came between 1944 and 1950.[3] During the 1950s, another 3.6 million arrived via the GDR. Particularly prominent in the latter group were the young, the skilled, and the highly educated. This fact was of tremendous importance. The GDR educated, on average, twice as many engineers as the Federal Republic, yet the number of engineering graduates working in the GDR

[2] Abelshauser, *Wirtschaftsgeschichte der BRD*, 95.
[3] Office of US High Commissioner, *7th Quarterly Report on Germany* (April–June 1951), 102.

was only 0.07 per cent of the workforce in 1955, much less than the average for industrial countries. The reason was that most of the graduates had fled to West Germany, where their share of a much larger workforce was 0.3 per cent, or almost 15 times as high in absolute terms. The situation was similar for other skilled occupations such as doctors or science teachers. If one assumes that the cost of training one such person was 15,000 marks, the Federal Republic "saved" over 30 billion marks in education costs in the 1950s alone, thanks to the attraction it exercised on East Germans as a place to live and work. These funds were thus available for investments, housing construction, and other uses, although in the 1960s, when the stream of immigration dried up following the construction of the Berlin Wall, the "education gap" came to be a serious and contentious issue.

The availability and efficient use of this human capital was what set the Economic Miracle apart from booms or periods of growth in other countries. The virtually free supply of highly qualified workers – who wanted to work – gave the West German economy great elasticity and provided an enormous market in both directions, first as a source of supply of labor, and second as a source of new consumer demand. West German industry, and the West German people as a whole, made the best of this extraordinary situation. The result of their efforts was the stable economic and political system of the early 1960s. That this system was to be shaken by the cultural and political transformations of that decade was a consequence of changing expectations and opportunities available as a result of the work of those who managed and carried out the process of the economic recovery itself. Primary responsibility for the success rested with Ludwig Erhard, the minister of economics, but also with the minister of finance, Fritz Schäffer, who had served in this capacity since 1949.

The period of strong economic growth, and the Economic Miracle resulting from it, continued until 1966. The importance of this achievement was not only material, but also psychological, since the Germans were able to emerge from the ashes of ruin in a constructive fashion, and to thus earn respect for their positive abilities to create, rather than destroy. At the same time increasing wealth made it possible to consider increased state expenditure, and such groups as farmers, and spokesmen for war victims and pensioners, increasingly insisted that the government use the accumulated surpluses to help these groups. The most important consequence of these debates was the pension reform in 1957, by which the level of all pensions was tied to the cost of living index. Even before the pension reform, however, the social services portion of the federal budget had become by far the greatest single item (in 1957 it was 43 per cent, and 66.35 million DM). The effects of war and disruption had made this necessary, and even a decade after the war, in 1955, every second household was dependent, to a varying degree, on some form of transfer payments from the state.

In 1955 several million people were still living in humble or miserable conditions and were unemployable, and no one disputed the fact that they needed assistance. The problem was that they needed help from a country that was still recovering. Since 1949 the Bundestag had been particularly concerned about housing, and Adenauer's government included a special ministry for this purpose, the ministry for housing construction. Throughout the 1950s, but especially after 1953, the housing sector was a primary locomotive of domestic demand.

Shelter was an absolute necessity, and its absence caused serious problems. Looking back it is difficult to imagine how people lived in a country filled with rubble. Housing construction did not really begin until after the currency reform of 1948 and by 1950 the housing shortage had assumed catastrophic proportions. A three-member family, for example, living in a flat of three rooms and one kitchen, was required to rent at least one room to at least one and preferably two people. The kitchen and toilet, if there was one within the flat, were shared, and showers were normally taken once a week in a public bath.

The first post-war census, taken in 1950, indicated that approximately five million apartments were needed for the close to 16 million households. In that year 3.8 billion German marks were devoted to housing construction, and by 1953 that number had doubled. By 1959 that number had doubled once again. Between 1950 and 1959 about 91 billion marks was spent on housing, with the federal government subsidizing approximately one-third of the total amount through a variety of means, including special savings accounts for building purposes (Bausparkassen). The average apartment size in 1950 was about 540 square feet (by comparison: a tennis court is almost 2,800 square feet, so that the floor space of more than five apartments could fit onto one court). By 1959 the size of an apartment had grown to about 730 square feet. In 1953 only six per cent of apartments had central heat and every fourth apartment had a toilet, but no bathroom. Following 1953 one new apartment was being built every minute of every day and night, which equalled 1,440 per day or 525,600 per year. By 1959, 14 years after the war, the housing shortage had been reduced by more than 80 per cent to approximately 1.2 million.

By 1963 the shortage was officially declared to be over. But thousands of Germans in West Germany and Berlin continued to live in old buildings severely damaged during the war. Many of these were rent-controlled so that there existed little incentive to repair them. Beginning in the mid 1960s, and into the next two decades, construction in West

Germany and in Berlin continued apace, but with emphasis on filling housing needs according to competing demands. By the 1980s many had forgotten the privation and sacrifice necessary for almost two decades after the end of the war. But it had taken 18 years to solve the housing shortage, and the achievement was remarkable. It had been accomplished by the Germans themselves who, with their own savings, provided almost two-thirds of the funds for construction.[4]

At the beginning of his second term in 1953 Adenauer announced major social reforms. He faced the reality that, thus far, primarily active members of the workforce had benefited from economic growth, and that the government could now begin to improve the conditions of life for the unemployed, for old-age pensioners, for invalids, for orphans, and for the survivors of war dead. There were two means of doing this, both of which went hand in hand. One was to continue the policies of economic growth, and the other was by means of a major reform of social policy.

For Adenauer, social policy was the defensive, domestic aspect of his overall strategy of Western survival. By creating a state and society with which the majority of the people could identify, he and his government would make West Germany a "magnetic pole of attraction" to Germans in the East. A successful foreign policy of strength aiming at reunification in freedom thus depended, in Adenauer's view, on a solid foundation of social welfare and individual freedom at home.

The years 1953–6 were taken up with discussions about the contents of the planned reforms. The all-encompassing idea of a complete overhaul of social security, including youth and old-age programs and state-covered protection against sickness, disability, unemployment, and loss of the breadwinner, was revised, and what remained by 1955 was simply a proposal for improving old-age pensions. Nevertheless, the resulting Law on Pension Insurance of 1957 was one of the two most important pieces of social legislation of the 1950s, the other being the Equalization of Burdens Act of 1952. The effect of both laws was to give a powerful boost to the Germans' efforts to regain their self confidence and to become legitimate members of postwar society.

The SPD and the German Trade Union Federation (DGB) had, in the Schreiber proposal of 1955, demanded a centralized, unitary system of pensions and insurance encompassing all groups. (Wilfrid Schreiber, 1904–1975, was a professor of economics at the University of Bonn and executive director of the Federation of Catholic Employers from 1949

---

[4] See Bundesministerium für Wohnungsbau, *Grundsätze, Leistungen, und Aufgaben der Wohnungsbaupolitik der Bundesregierung;* and Bundesministerium für Vertriebene, *Bundesgesetze und Leistungen für die durch Krieg und Kriegsfolgen Geschädigten.*

to 1960.) It foresaw that all those in the active workforce would pay a certain percentage of their income into a pension fund each year, which would be distributed *in toto* to pensioners. This idea guaranteed that the amount of benefits would correspond to the actual price level and cost of living at the time they were received. In the existing system, the amount of benefits depended on what each recipient had paid in. Since wages and prices were rising, this meant that the existing system provided unrealistic and inadequate annuities.

The CDU accepted the argument that pensions must be indexed, that is, made to correspond in each given year to actual changes in the real cost of living. Many, however, were afraid that abandoning the insurance principle by which the pensions had hitherto been funded, in favor of what was essentially a government guarantee that pensions would keep pace with inflation, using tax revenues if pension contributions were insufficient, was the thin end of the wedge of a welfare state antithetical to the vision of a social market economy. Wilhelm Röpke (1899–1966), the renowned neo-liberal and professor of economics in Geneva, feared that "mass welfare organized by the state will become a crutch for a society crippled by proletarianization."[5] Nevertheless, the concept of benefits linked to gross income enjoyed almost universal support – with the exception of the unanimous opposition of the FDP – and was passed into law with the combined votes of the CDU/CSU and the SPD in the spring of 1957, with the new system effective retroactively from January 1 of that year. The procedure was a portent; it gave both the main parties a foretaste of a grand coalition and boosted those elements in both that welcomed the prospect of such a coalition.

This reform was not without effect on the third Bundestag elections, scheduled for September 1957. Hans-Peter Schwarz wrote of the indexation of pensions: "Never before nor since in the history of the Federal Republic has there been a better timed or better targeted election gift, nor one with such far-reaching socio-political consequences".[6] At the time, the entitlement to state-subsidized pensions tied to the cost of living seemed a small matter in the overall federal budget. Thirty years later, in 1987, with an aging population and an everdecreasing number of young people entering the workforce, it seemed more like a ticking time bomb under the welfare state.

The CDU fought the election campaign on its achievements, notably the pension reform, and with the slogan, "No Experiments!" Adenauer firmly insisted that the question of nuclear weapons was not an issue at the moment: "The nuclearization of the Bundeswehr is not a matter for

[5] Doering-Manteuffel, *Die BRD in der Ära Adenauer*, 204.
[6] Cited ibid., 205.

decision at this point." He referred to the ongoing London Disarmament Conference, and spoke instead of the risk of Soviet domination inherent in an SPD victory. The elections, he said, "revolve around the question as to whether Germany and Europe remain Christian or become Communist."[7] Adenauer's analysis, which sounded exaggerated in the political context of the late 1980s, was not at all out of place in the political atmosphere of 1957. Indeed, the CDU/CSU jumped an extraordinary seven percentage points and won an absolute majority of the vote (50.2 per cent). It was the first time in German electoral history that a single party had won an outright majority of the popular vote. The SPD did well too, gaining three points to 31.8 per cent, and breaking the magic 30 per cent barrier for the first time. The SPD increased its vote in all successive elections from 1957 to 1972, but in 1957 any feelings of triumph were tempered by the overwhelming victory of the Christian democrats who could continue to govern alone. As the Germans said, *Alles bleibt beim Alten* (a common phrase, literally meaning "everything remains the same," but which, as a play of words in the German language, could also mean "everything remains with the Old One," that is, with Adenauer, who was 81).

In all, the two major parties won 10 per cent more of the total vote (83 per cent versus 73 per cent) than in 1953. Of the four other parties in parliament after the 1953 elections, only the FDP survived; the liberals won 7.7 per cent, a loss of almost two points. The FDP had started with 12 per cent in 1949; were they doomed to fall below 5 per cent and disappear from the national parliament like all the other small parties? This was the grim prospect facing them after 1957. Breaking with Adenauer and playing with nationalism and anti-nuclear politics was clearly not a winning strategy; it seemed that opponents of nuclear weapons, and of Adenauer's foreign policy, found the SPD a more credible defender of their interests.

[7]  Cited in Cioc, *Pax Atomica*, 45.

# 9

# The Defense Debate Continues

The intensity of the nuclear debate inside West Germany undoubtedly encouraged the Soviet Union in its efforts to drive wedges between West Germany and its allies, and to prevent formation of a common platform on foreign and security policy of all democratic parties in the Federal Republic. This debate, in various forms, continued until Strauss was forced from government in 1962, partly because of the sustained and virulent campaign waged against him by forces on the left in West Germany – forces awakened and stimulated by the anti-nuclear issue – and partly because of his reaction to it. The Bundeswehr, in the meantime, did not receive US nuclear arms.

Concurrent with the rearmament of the Federal Republic occurred major political changes in the Soviet Union. In 1957, Khrushchev finally defeated his rivals in the succession struggle in the Soviet Union following Stalin's death in 1953. At the twentieth congress of the Soviet communist party, in February 1956, he already demonstrated control by launching the denunciation of Stalin's terror regime in what became known as the famous "Secret Speech." The contents of the speech were made known in the Soviet Union and Eastern Europe, where it had a tremendous impact, particularly on young people who had been educated to regard Stalin as little less than a god. By the spring of 1956, the speech was known in Western Europe as well. It had been obtained by the Central Intelligence Agency via a tapped telephone line in Eastern Europe. As the US ambassador to Moscow in 1956, Charles E. Bohlen, wrote, "later Khrushchev joked that the CIA had not paid enough for its copy of the speech – only 500 zlotys – or about $100."[1] Its content led to widespread speculation, and renewed hopes, that the new Soviet leader might be less hostile to the West than Stalin and therefore more willing to minimize the effects of Europe's division, via a policy of

[1] Bohlen, *Witness to History,* 398–401.

detente. The Soviet government, as might be expected, took an extremely dim view of NATO nuclear weapons in Germany and especially of the prospect that West Germany might at some point have or share in control of such weapons.

One who feared this was George F. Kennan, the American diplomat and historian who, as head of the State Department's Policy Planning staff in 1947–50, had conceived the policy of containment of the Soviet Union. Kennan understood Soviet postwar behavior from firsthand experience. In September 1952, after having been in Moscow for five months as the new American ambassador, Kennan, while visiting Berlin, responded to a journalist's question on life in the Soviet capital: "Well, I was interned here in Germany for several months during the last war. The treatment we receive in Moscow is just about like the treatment we internees received then, except that in Moscow we are at liberty to go out and walk the streets under guard." The Soviets were so furious that Kennan was recalled in October 1952, following accusations that his statement was "completely false and hostile to the Soviet Union."[2]

At the time Khrushchev's speech became public, Kennan was a historian at Princeton University and still a figure whose opinions commanded great respect in Western Europe as well as in Washington. Thus, during 1956 and 1957 Kennan's views on the significance of changes in Soviet political leadership were given wide attention. While lecturing at the University of Oxford in 1957, he was invited by the BBC (British Broadcasting Corporation) to deliver the "Reith Lectures" over the Home Service of the BBC in November and December of that year. The Reith Lectures consisted of six talks, presented live on six successive Sunday evenings. In these lectures, he argued that a united but neutralized Germany would satisfy Soviet security needs and might encourage the Soviet Union to withdraw militarily from Eastern Europe. As a countermeasure he proposed that the US should withdraw its troops from Western Europe and Great Britain.

Kennan's proposals caused a sensation in West Germany. The North German Radio commented: "Scarcely ever before has any political lecture series in the world aroused such interest. . . . Even the man in the street, so often charged with being politically uninterested, is pricking up his ears. . . . And this without any propaganda and certainly without any official support." President Heuss praised him as well, which infuriated Adenauer, who insisted again that "unification could not be obtained by the neutralization of Germany."[3] Adenauer's response to Heuss was a sharply worded note, which concluded that "Mr Kennan is

[2] Kennan, *Memoirs*, 159, 163.
[3] Ibid., 236, 249.

at this point the one man who, thanks to his unrealistic viewpoint, contributes most embarrassingly to soft-mindedness here in Germany."[4] Criticism of Kennan's views as unrealistic was not limited to Adenauer. The former secretary of state, Dean Acheson, for whom Kennan had worked in the Department of State, attacked him vigorously in *Foreign Affairs*, but from Adenauer's viewpoint the damage was done.

The SPD, just emerging from its fearful defeat at the polls in September 1957, was delighted to find a respected American former policy-maker supporting its policy of unification through neutralization. While the West resumed its debate over the strength of its military and technological position vis-à-vis the Soviet Union, the Soviet government simultaneously pushed forward its campaign against US deployments of nuclear weapons in Western Europe to counter the Soviet increase of conventional and nuclear arms. It was in this setting, before the United Nations in October 1957 and prior to a meeting of the NATO heads of government in December 1957, that the Polish foreign minister Rapacki proposed a nuclear-free zone in Central Europe, to be followed by mutual arms reductions and disengagement of Soviet and US troops: "Poland declares that if the two German States should consent to enforce the prohibition of the production and stockpiling of nuclear weapons in their respective territories, the People's Republic of Poland is prepared simultaneously to institute the same prohibition in its territory."[5]

Two days after Rapacki announced his proposal, the Soviet Union launched Sputnik, the first artificial satellite. Western scientists were not only impressed with Sputnik – it weighed nine times as much as the planned US Vanguard satellite – but they were also nervous, as were US policy-makers, because the technological ability required to build and launch Sputnik suggested the capability to build new weapons systems as well. The event was overwhelming to Western officials who feared a rapid buildup of a Soviet force of intercontinental ballistic missiles (ICBMs). The event signified a revolutionary change in military technology and caused concern, not only in Western Europe, but also in the United States. Stewart Symington, a Democratic senator from Missouri, remarked that "if Russia's now known superiority over the US develops into a supremacy, the position of the free world will be critical."[6]

Sputnik and the implied threat of ICBMs made the West even less likely than it might otherwise have been to consider the Rapacki Plan,

[4] Schwarz, *Die Ära Adenauer, 1957–1963*, 45.
[5] Dept of State, *Documents on Germany*, 513.
[6] *Facts on File*, October 3–9, 1957.

which resembled others that the Soviet Union would propose in the years to come. The denuclearized buffer zone meant nothing, since the Soviets would be next door to it, while the US would be 3,000 miles away. "The West's geostrategic disadvantage was so obvious that Western leaders felt the implementation of the Rapacki Plan would make Europe the political hostage of the Soviet Union."[7]

Although Adenauer endorsed the idea of East–West talks at the December NATO meeting, he was worried that President Eisenhower wished to be known in American history as a president of disarmament and peace, and thought Eisenhower might endorse the Rapacki Plan. Adenauer rejected both Kennan's and Rapacki's proposals in early 1958: "In my opinion a nuclear-free zone had no purpose given the current status of weapons technology, and in view of the experience which had been gathered in the last two wars concerning respect for neutrality. It offered no protection to the countries involved. ... The creation of such a zone would mean the end of NATO and, therefore, the end of freedom of Western Europe, and also the end of our freedom."[8]

Throughout the winter Poland and the Soviet Union elaborated on the Plan in notes to the US and West Germany, who in turn rejected it and repeated their demand for free elections in all of Germany, to be followed by reunification and a peace treaty. Adenauer's obvious skepticism concerning the East bloc proposals infuriated the opposition, who wanted to combine Rapacki's nuclear-free zone with the "thinning-out" concept of the old Eden Plan of 1954 and the FDP's own Pfleiderer Plan of 1952.

During early 1958, CDU leaders discussed at great and agonizing length the question of nuclear deployments in Germany, either by the US or the Bundeswehr. In January 1958, the SPD, in the Bundestag, demanded official government assurance that the Bundeswehr would receive no nuclear weapons, and that West German territory would not be used for the deployment of nuclear missiles or for the construction of launching pads. Later that month, as the Bundestag was debating the Rapacki Plan, the SPD and FDP scored a public-relations coup when they succeeded in giving Dehler and Heinemann speaking-time at the end of the debate, which was broadcast over national radio.

This meant that two of the government's bitterest foes ... monopolized nearly three hours of prime-time radio to indulge in a massive attack on the chancellor. Dehler accused Adenauer of doing "everything humanly possible to hinder reunification." The government, he charged, had pursued

[7] Cioc, *Pax Atomica*, 47.
[8] Adenauer, *Erinnerungen 1955–1959*, 363.

only the twin goals of US friendship and nonrecognition of East Germany, while neglecting the goal of reunification. He drew a parallel between the Stalin note (March 1952) and the Rapacki Plan. "The chancellor explained to us at that time: it is a diversionary tactic! That is exactly what he is saying today. I trusted him then ... I stayed in the government. I am ashamed of myself!"[9]

Heinemann, as befitted a former president of the synod of the Protestant Church, blended religious and political arguments in an outline of the position he was to pursue much later, as federal president in 1969–74:

Our political task since the last war has been and continues to be a twofold one, and that means, in other words, that it is a good deal more difficult than the CDU presents it to us. It is a twofold task, namely to combine a hard, unshakeable "no" to the totalitarian system with a "yes" to being the neighbor of Eastern peoples ruled by totalitarianism. We must manage to combine them, this "no" and this "yes" at one and the same time. I have never criticized the chancellor for seeking a settlement with our Western neighbors. That was imperative. But I have always criticized him – and do so again today – for having combined a Western reconciliation with a new hatred for the East.[10]

Whatever the merits of their cause – and certainly Heinemann's accusation that Adenauer was responsible for sowing "hatred for the East" was a gross misrepresentation – the two opposition leaders won the rhetorical battle on that occasion. In response, the government introduced a resolution – the March Resolution of 1958 – which advocated solution of the nuclear issue by arms control talks, while reserving Bonn's right to acquire nuclear weapons if such talks were to fail: "We want peace and controlled arms reductions, we want these efforts to succeed. Should they be unsuccessful, then the armament of our troops with nuclear weapons is unavoidable. ... The parliamentary group has decided this without opposition."[11]

By an unfortunate coincidence, the debate on the resolution started 25 years to the day after the Reichstag abolished its own authority, and so put an end to the first German democracy by passing the Enabling Act that gave Hitler and the Nazis total power in Germany. This gave the opposition a rhetorical device that it used to the full in painting the government's intentions in the blackest colors. Control of the debate broke down; by the second day deputies were yelling insults at each other from their seats. The spectacle lasted four days, and illustrated the

[9] Cioc, *Pax Atomica*, 48.
[10] Cited ibid.
[11] Schwarz, *Die Ära Adenauer, 1957–1963*, 50.

depth of feeling on both sides, as well as the absolute incompatibility of views. This was not merely a disagreement on means to an end – that is, peace and security; it was a fundamental opposition of world-views and moral priorities.

As minister of defense, Strauss emphasized that West Germany did not want nuclear weapons simply for the sake of having them. However: "We are not willing to weaken the West's defense potential through our 'no,' so that an aggressor can hope one day to capture all of Europe without risking a third world war." He distinguished between the morality of nuclear weapons and the morality of those who have them: "Nuclear weapons are not immoral. A gun in the hand of a murderer is immoral. Effective defense weapons are not immoral. A totalitarian state – which considers the use of force a permissible principle, when its goals can be achieved with little risk – is immoral." Erler, speaking for the SPD, considered this statement as the moral equivalent of Hitler calling on the Germans to face "total war." Reinhold Maier, the old chieftain of the south-west, who chaired the FDP from 1957 to 1960, summarized the emotions of those who feared Strauss and nuclear arms:

I would never trust the defense minister with a field gun. A man who speaks like our defense minister does, such a man will also shoot. That was no longer the speech of a statesman, that was a speech about war. It was nothing but a war-whoop. . . . Today we did not hear the defense minister discussing the arms buildup of the Federal Republic; rather we heard a Reich's war minister. It was a megalomaniacal speech. It was no longer the language of a friendly minded state, it was the language of a highly armed military state.

Helmut Schmidt, a rising figure in the SPD who was soon to rival Erler in the role of defense specialist, denounced Strauss as power-mad and dangerous:

When you speak of NATO unity, you mean nuclear bombs for the Bundeswehr. When you speak of atomic bombs for your Bundeswehr, you really mean military power, nothing but power and power for its own sake. . . . We say to the German people, in complete and earnest conviction that the decision to equip both parts of our fatherland with atomic weapons directed against each other will be seen by history as a decision as important and ominous as previously the Enabling Act was for Hitler.[12]

The March Resolution was the last in a long series of parliamentary victories for Adenauer that began with the EDC treaty and included the Conscription Law of July 1956. One reason that the March Resolution

[12] All cited in Cioc, *Pax Atomica*, 50, 62, 63.

debate was so unrestrained and bitter was that everyone knew before-hand that the CDU/CSU, with their absolute majority, could pass whatever resolution or bill Adenauer sought. The irony was, as a later writer put it, that Strauss' delayed program for the buildup of the Bundeswehr had given NATO a good argument to fill West Germany with US-held nuclear weapons. If the SPD wanted fewer nuclear weapons, it could either try to convince the people to vote for their policy of neutralization or, more realistically, to support conscription in order to get a bigger conventional army that would make nuclear weapons less necessary. Until 1960, however, the SPD opposed increased conscription as well as nuclear defense. As a result, the party won very few elections. One of the few pro-Bundeswehr social demo-crats of the 1950s was Fritz Beermann, who pointed out just before the March debate that "no party with pacifist tendencies has a prayer to win Bundestag elections."[13] It took two years for him to convince his party that he was right.

In the meantime various factions within the SPD tried to fight the battle against nuclear arms in other ways. Heinemann, concerned less with power than with conscience (as he perceived it), continued his religious agitation against rearmament and nuclear arms in the Protes-tant group known as the Church Brethren. He and others on the SPD left also attempted to overturn the Bundestag's will by their one and only excursion into extraparliamentary activity: the *Kampf dem Atomtod*.

[13] Cited ibid., 153.

# 10

# Fight Atomic Death!

In early 1958, the SPD approved the German Campaign against Nuclear Death (GCND, *Kampf dem Atomtod*) modeled on the British Campaign for Nuclear Disarmament (CND), which staged its famous "Aldermaston Marches" in the late 1950s and early 1960s against the British nuclear program. The German Trade Union Federation (DGB) provided organizational support. Eventually the committee managed to gather a number of well-known public figures, including Heinemann, Maier, and two younger liberals, Erich Mende and Wolfgang Mischnick. Other members had been active in the first round of the campaign opposing German rearmament. This group included the theologians Helmut Gollwitzer and Martin Niemöller, the writers Heinrich Böll and Erich Kästner, and the left-wing Catholic intellectuals Eugen Kogon and Walter Dirks of the *Frankfurter Hefte*.

Dirks and Kogon were lonely voices in their church; the official Catholic position on rearmament was as Cardinal Frings declared it in 1950: bearing arms against totalitarianism was a moral duty. In 1959 the Jesuit theologian and social thinker Gustav Gundlach even went so far as to declare that totalitarian rule was so evil, and would be the direct cause of so much sin, that even the destruction of the world in a nuclear war was preferable to dictatorship. This statement went further than even the conservative Catholic mainstream wanted to carry the argument: in 1960, two young lay Catholic theologians, Ernst-Wolfgang Böckenförde, later a well-known constitutional lawyer, and Robert Spaemann, a philosopher, wrote a pamphlet denouncing Gundlach's position as heretical, and lending cautious support to disarmament proposals. Compared to the turmoil in the Protestant Church, however, these arguments were insignificant. It was not until the 1970s that left-wing Catholicism became a serious factor in German political and social debate.

The GCND began its operations by issuing a manifesto which

declared: "In the event of war between East and West, the German people on both sides of the border zones will be the certain victims of nuclear death. There is no protection against it." This was a new approach: hitherto the SPD had insisted that if the government became involved in nuclear defense, at least it should provide as much civilian protection as necessary. After 1958, the opponents of NATO strategy rarely reverted to this position. The peace movement of the 1980s, for example, insisted that there was no such thing as protection against nuclear attack; therefore, it was immoral even to consider civil defense because considering it implied that it might work, thereby making nuclear war more thinkable, hence more likely. The GCND manifesto concluded: "We demand of the Bundestag and federal government not to participate in the nuclear arms race, and instead to support an atomic-weapon-free zone in Europe as a contribution to the relaxation of tensions."[1]

The strategy of the GCND was to try to raise popular feeling against nuclear arms for the Bundeswehr and for removal of Allied nuclear forces from West Germany. Ultimately the GCND hoped to bring about a referendum on the issue. In fact the SPD-controlled governments of Hamburg, Bremen, and Frankfurt passed laws permitting referenda on nuclear weapons. At that point Adenauer lodged a complaint in the Constitutional Court, arguing that foreign policy was a federal prerogative and that the plan for a national referendum "signifies an attempt to exert influence on the Bundestag and federal government in an unauthorized manner." In the end only three small SPD-ruled villages near Frankfurt actually held referenda declaring themselves nuclear-free. The Court found in favor of the government.

The DGB employed both strikes and demonstrations against the government's defense policy. In Hamburg, in April, good organization by the DGB brought out 150,000 people in an anti-nuclear rally, a figure not exceeded until the great peace movement demonstrations of 1981–3. The real test of the GCND, however, came in July 1958 in the *Land* elections in North Rhine-Westphalia, where the FDP had switched partners from the CDU to the SPD in 1956. Observers nationwide regarded the Rhineland election as an unofficial test of popularity of the anti-nuclear movement. Unfortunately for the SPD and FDP, economic issues tended to predominate in *Land* elections, and here the two parties were miles apart. Adenauer also waged a skilful campaign on behalf of his party. The result was a disaster for the FDP, which slid to 7 per cent, and a triumph for the CDU, which captured an absolute majority of votes in the most heavily industrialized *Land* in Germany. Just as in the national election of 1957,

---

[1] Cited in Cioc, *Pax Atomica*, 119.

the SPD did better in the Rhineland than in any other election since the war. This success sent the SPD leaders the clear signal that they should fight the next few *Land* elections on the anti-nuclear issue.

They soon changed their minds, partly because Khrushchev's political offensive that began in November 1958 reminded many people that if there were potential risks to a nuclear defense policy, there were real and immediate risks to a policy of disarmament. Shortly thereafter, in January 1959, the communist peace movement, which served the East German regime, took over the Berlin branch of the GCND. The Berlin communists were led by Klaus Rainer Röhl, a Marxist writer and editor, and his wife, Ulrike Meinhof, who became a notorious terrorist in the 1960s and 1970s. The Berlin events were the beginning of the end of the GCND. By mid-1959 it had virtually ceased to operate. A conglomeration of communists and sympathizers formed the short-lived German Peace Union, which was in reality nothing more than a front for the communist party, forbidden since 1956. Other members of the GCND returned to the SPD and FDP.

The GCND represented a political attempt to stop what its members perceived as Adenauer's and Strauss' dangerous policies. At the same time, leaders of the Protestant church and public figures of German Protestantism were trying to come to moral terms with the issues of nuclear defense, pacifism, and the dictates of foreign policy.

Since the early 1950s, mainstream Protestants in the EKD had debated the morality of defense. Gollwitzer, on the left, argued that pacifism was the only moral response to the existence of nuclear weapons. "It is a sin before God and a crime against humanity to continue threatening with these weapons; and the temporary retention of nuclear weapons cannot be justified (as was the case with previous weaponry) for use in the event of an emergency." Helmut Thielicke, a well-known Hamburg pastor and theologian, argued to the contrary that some form of defense using nuclear weapons might still be morally justifiable. "Would not a renunciation of one's defense readiness give unrestricted scope to the arbitrariness of a nuclear-equipped opponent, thereby making the right of the stronger the guiding world principle? Would it not entail surrendering to the means of mass destruction and to a cynic willing to use these means?" asked Thielicke, in terms identical to those put forward by the American Jesuit and theologian of peace, John Courtney Murray, in 1960. Gollwitzer and the pacifists, Thielicke said, believed that the only choice was nuclear war or communist domination. What if there were a third choice, nuclear deterrence, that could prevent either eventuality?[2]

[2] Ibid., 96–8.

Thielicke's realistic position was taken up by a group within the EKD that called itself the Rhine Convent. It spent the next several years in furious argument with Heinemann's even more rigidly pacifist group, the Church Brethren. He and other leading Brethren had been members of the Confessing Church during the Third Reich and drew heavily on the neo-orthodox theology of the Swiss thinker Karl Barth. He believed that the suffering of Germany since the war, and national division, were God's punishments for the evil of Nazism. He also believed that communism, unlike Nazism, was not wholly or ultimately evil; much more evil was the desire to resist communism in the interests of a secular, capitalist society.

The Brethren rejected the traditional Protestant argument of the "two swords:" that the morality of the secular, political authority, the state, was not the same as the morality of the church and of religious life. In Lutheran teaching, the state was permitted measures to protect its citizens and guarantee order that would be forbidden to any private individual. Arguing that the "two swords" argument had prevented Protestants from acknowledging that Hitler's regime was criminal, the Brethren insisted that the teaching was, at best, obsolete: in the nuclear age no moral person could afford to grant the state the presumption that what it did was right. They wanted belief and behavior to coincide completely. "The church and the individual Christian must say 'no' in advance to a war that will be fought as a nuclear war," they argued in their "Ten Theses." "The preparation for such a war is under all conditions a sin against God and your neighbor, for which no church and no Christian ought to make himself culpable. We demand in the name of the gospel that the preparations for this war in the realm of our land end immediately, without taking into account any other considerations. ... An opposing position or neutrality on this question is indefensible."[3]

The Brethren did not succeed in persuading the Synod of the EKD to say no to nuclear defense, nor were they able to stop the Synod from approving the Military Chaplain Treaty in 1957. This was an agreement between the federal government and the EKD to appoint chaplains for Protestant members of the Bundeswehr. It was a "treaty" because it presumed that the state and the EKD were equivalent authorities for its purposes; German states had signed such treaties with Lutheran churches since the seventeenth century.

In 1958 the Synod of the EKD debated the "Ten Theses." Weizsäcker intervened to argue that the new, low-yield nuclear weapons then being produced were not "means of mass destruction." All nuclear

[3] Cited ibid., 108.

bombs were not city-busting H-bombs; the smaller weapons might well have a morally defensible role to play as deterrents. He was supported by the Bundestag president, Eugen Gerstenmaier, another fervent Lutheran deeply troubled by the radical division in his church between the two incompatible positions. The Synod passed a resolution that simply stated: "The antagonism among us over our judgement of nuclear weapons is very deep. . . . We remain together under the roof of the gospel and strive to overcome the opposing views."[4] Advised by Weizsäcker, a study group in the EKD then prepared an amended document that they hoped could command general assent: the Heidelberg Theses of 1959. They, and the Synod's resolution of 1958, became the foundation of German Protestant thinking on defense and nuclear issues and were so durable that not even the peace movement of the 1980s was able to compel a revision.

The Heidelberg Theses stated in part:

1   The nuclear era has made peace a prerequisite for living. . . .

5   In the past, the "just war" doctrine has guided Christians. But this prin-
    ciple cannot be applied to nuclear war. It destroys what it claims to
    preserve. . . .

7   Pacifism is a Christian way of behaving. The church must recognize the
    right of conscientious objecting. . . .

8   A Christian can believe that nuclear weapons safeguard peace and
    freedom. Any realistic political proposal must foresee the provisional
    retention of these armaments. . . .

11  . . . Nuclear weapons preserve a realm of freedom in which conscientious
    objectors enjoy civic liberties. And objectors help keep a spiritual realm
    open within which new decisions may become possible.[5]

Everyone gave a bit to achieve this compromise. Thielicke and Weiz-säcker acknowledged that the "just war" doctrine was no longer valid – something that Catholics still had not decided 30 years later. The Brethren had received formal EKD approval of conscientious objection. But they were not satisfied. The Heidelberg Theses remained as one opinion among several within the EKD. Brethren sympathizers founded activist groups – the Action Committee for Reconciliation/Peace Service and the Action Committee in the Service of Peace – that were destined to play major parts in organizing and indoctrinating the peace movement of the 1980s.

[4] Ibid., 109.
[5] Ibid., 112.

# 11

# The Spirit of the Fifties

The important political developments of this half-decade – years six to twelve in the history of the Federal Republic – were not in relations with East Germany (there were no such relations) but with the West. Economic integration with her Western neighbors had begun with the formation of the Bizone Economic Council in 1947. It was followed by the constitution of the Federal Republic with its capital in Bonn on the Rhine, the Petersberg Agreement to end the dismantling of industries, the European Coal and Steel Community, the long road to rearmament, and the Paris Treaties. The decision for the West, taken by Adenauer and the Bundestag, and supported by the majority of West Germany's voters, all served to make the West German Republic a part of the emerging West European political and economic system. For the first time in history the major German state was fully Western. But Europe, Germany and Berlin remained divided. While the Western part of Germany was free, the Eastern parts of Europe were not; but there was no acceptable alternative. This consequence of the war – an incontrovertible fact – had been determined while Germany was still at war. The decision to administer postwar Germany in occupation zones meant the partitioning of the country by the Allies. The three Western Allies did not intend it to be permanent, but it lasted until 1990. The price – if that is a fair way to express it – for freedom in the West was paid by the East Europeans and the Germans in the Soviet occupied zone of Germany.

The economic miracle and the developing integration of West Germany with Western Europe absorbed most of the energies of the German people in these years. Critics noted that, with the establishment of the Bonn government and the beginning of serious reconstruction, the cultural, political, and intellectual vitality of the occupation period died down. The will to deal with complex philosophical and ideological issues was diminished by a competitor: attention to material and personal concerns, not a surprising result after years of deprivation. The Germans, the people of "poets and thinkers," became, in the eyes of German critics, a people of operators and profiteers. This alarmed even Wilhelm Röpke, who had helped to lay the intellectual basis of the social market economy. The human communities which, for him, were the necessary foundation of the fully rounded human personality capable of functioning in the free market, were, in his view, being neglected and undermined as corporations grew in size and the welfare state expanded. "The center of gravity of our society is being pushed upward, away from the genuine, easily comprehensible communities of human warmth and toward an impersonal state administration and other spirit-less mass organizations."[1]

The Germans, by losing the war, seemed to have lost their chance, and their aspirations, for a dominant position in Europe, a position based on political wisdom, economic power, and cultural vigor. A majority reacted to this loss, and to the horror of Nazi tyranny, by withdrawing as soon as possible from the competitive pressures of political life, and concentrated on solving the daily problems of surviving in a land decimated morally and physically. The withdrawal was dominated by the demoralizing political experience of the Nazi regime, the physical destruction of war, and the foreign elements of occupation. In some ways it was analogous to the feelings an individual suffers after a heart attack. The desire to be left alone, to be rid of exterior pressures, is enormous. The need and effort to analyze what is really important in one's life is overwhelming, and necessary. Initially it produces withdrawal, but later it may yield renewed energy. In postwar Germany some of the restraints and habits of old Germany were gone, and few had the will to replace them. The initial result was not only the materialistic mentality of which Röpke warned, but also a provincialization of spirit.

This reaction to the war, and to occupation of one's own land, had two sides. Before Hitler, Germany had been, despite the loss of World War I, a cultural center of Europe. German arts and sciences competed for world respect and recognition with those of Britain and France. The German language had been the primary language of communication and commerce in Central and Eastern Europe, and German economic power stretched far beyond Germany's borders. The Nazi regime discredited German culture, the war had destroyed German economic strength and political prowess. Much of what could be restored in the 1950s was economic power, and that only in part, because the road to Eastern Germany was closed. But with economic recovery there also occurred a recovery of spirit, of confidence in the value of one's own

[1] Glaser, ed., *Bundesrepublikanisches Lesebuch*, 358.

ideas, and of the willingness to make firm commitments to supporting, creating, and defending the kind of government and society in which one wished to live. This aspect of recovery took longer, much longer, but it did proceed hand in hand with getting well again.

The importance of introspection in the occupation years, and of the later prominence of a new generation of writers, was significant. The writers were almost exclusively politically left, and many were associated with the "Gruppe 47." But this development should not conceal the fact that the flowering of German literature, that had begun before World War I with the rise of Thomas Mann (1875–1955) and Gerhard Hauptmann, and that had continued in the Weimar years with Bertolt Brecht, Gottfried Benn, Alfred Döblin, and Werner Bergengruen, to name only a few, continued to the mid-1950s.

Thomas Mann, who had originally refused to return to Germany from emigration after the war and who had commented "that all books published in Germany between 1933 and 1945 carried the stench of blood and shame,"[2] played a part in the change to a new era when he gave the last lectures of his life in Stuttgart and in Weimar (now in East Germany) in 1955. Here he attempted to bridge the division of Europe with allegiance to pure good will, and called for divided Germany to "feel united" in the name of the great eighteenth-century poet and novelist, Friedrich Schiller.[3] Admired in both parts of Germany, Thomas Mann, at the time of his eightieth birthday in 1955, had received honors from West Germany as well as from the University of Jena in the Soviet occupied zone. But his pleas for unity were not as powerful as the reasons for political division. Following his death the same year, Mann's books continued to be enormously popular, much more so than the writings of the new generation (during the decade of the 1950s Mann's *Buddenbrooks*, published in 1901, sold 1.2 million copies and *Confessions of Felix Krull*, published in 1922, sold 720,000 copies). But the disappearance of the uncontested leader of German literature nevertheless was a turning point.

From 1956 onward, the literary business of the Federal Republic fell increasingly into the hands of a different generation, antagonistic if not hostile to what they saw as the narrow-minded provincialism and the self-satisfied neglect in the Adenauer republic of the moral duty of repentance for past German evils and injustices. These younger writers and publicists felt keenly that the West Germany of the economic miracle had become a cultural desert, remote from the centers where world culture was being defined – primarily in New York and Paris.

---

[2] Parkes, *Writers and Politics in West Germany*, 15.
[3] See Mann, *Last Essays*.

They tended to blame their countrymen for this, however, and so marked out a position that became typical of the West German left-wing intelligentsia – that of extreme antagonism to the political, social, and cultural nation of which they, nevertheless, were a part. A graphic expression of this instinctive antagonism, this sense that what is, is flawed and wrong, came from the playwright Günter Eich in 1960:

> I profess to a literary art that is opposition. . . . However, in confessing this, I must mention that I have a few allies. . . . They are all part of the brotherhood of the tragic countenance, they are powerless and adversaries of power by instinct. Yet I think that the dignity of man has been given into their hands. By their rebellion and their suffering they fulfill our best possibilities.
>
> I include all those who will not let themselves be classified and regimented, the loners, the outsiders, the heretics in politics and religion, the dissatisfied, the unwise, the fighters of lost battles, the fools, the incompetent, the luckless dreamers, the sentimentalists, the disturbers of peace, all those who cannot forget the misery of the world when they are happy.[4]

Hermann Glaser (born 1928), author and editor of numerous books, who quoted this passage, described the intelligentsia of the Adenauer Era as "cosmopolitan and urbane," and therefore "in opposition to the dominant provincialism." He had a point; apart from these writers, German culture was not noted for creative spirit during the 1950s outside of certain – very important – academic fields. However, the posture of pretended weakness and the sense of constantly being offended, which Eich expressed so well, and which was described very powerfully by Heinrich Böll, concealed a reality which these writers did not often or willingly accept. It was that they, in fact, had tremendous power. They largely created the image of the West German 1950s as an era of political reaction and authoritarian repression which was passed on in schools and universities to new generations of Germans in the 1960s, 1970s, and 1980s. Their power over the minds and souls of their younger fellow-citizens was, one could argue, as great as the political power of Konrad Adenauer, Theodor Heuss, Kurt Schumacher, Erich Ollenhauer, and the other senior political figures of the same era.

Refusing to admit the reality of this power was part of its force. This point was well illustrated in an anthology of literary essays on life in West Germany, published in 1960. The first chapter was entitled "The Impotence of Literature." It argued that to be a good writer one had to be to the left, especially in Germany, where by definition, elementary political morality presented any other view as unacceptable.[5] The left,

---

[4]  Glaser, ed., *Bundesrepublikanisches Lesebuch*, 490.
[5]  Ibid., 489.

however, was "homeless:" even the SPD was no longer a seriously leftist party; it was coming to accept the market economy, the EEC, and NATO, all examples of entities and policies abhorrent to the literary purists.

The combination of power with pretended powerlessness only worked, however, if no one pointed it out. So important was membership in the correct circles that few journalists or other public figures with aspirations to influence in the literary world had any incentive to reveal what was evident to any objective observer. One of the few who did notice how the West German cultural scene operated was Wolf Jobst Siedler, cultural editor of the West Berlin newspaper *Der Tagesspiegel*. He described the intellectuals as:

> people who look at themselves with such emotion that they gave themselves the sentimental label "Homeless Left." This expression means that they feel neglected in our state, that they constitute a small, spread-out group that does not belong, that they feel like outsiders in our society. When you meet them, they will tell you how they are persecuted, and how hard the life of the spirit is in this society of the economic miracle. . . . It is a pathetic picture that they paint, which almost makes you forget that the German left intellectuals are the most powerful and, as it were, market-controlling group in German literature and cultural activity today.
>
> The "Homeless Left" has conquered almost all positions from which art is controlled and administered. The drama departments of German theaters – with few exceptions – are controlled by left-leaning intellectuals. The arts sections of our major newspapers are in the hands of publishers who prefer Heinrich Mann to Reinhold Schneider. The editorial policies of almost all important publishing houses are controlled by editors who have signed almost every authors' manifesto of recent years. . . . Those who proclaim their weakness are in fact the powers in the land. If a young writer wants to make a career, he had best make his arrangements with the German left. . . . It is surprising that they still see themselves as the stepchildren of Germany. It is amusing how they hunger for governmental approval and public praise. They want to provoke the state and yet be rewarded by it; they want to be critics with medals. . . .
>
> In solemn proclamations whose elevated tone resembles that of papal encyclicals, writers, editors, and radio directors announce that interest groups and associations are trying to exercise unconstitutional influence on culture. They have not noticed that it is precisely the conflict between various interest groups, institutionalized associations, and political parties that constitutes the nature of a pluralist society. What they really want is a society in which the bishops read Enzensberger and directors of ministries are friends of Arno Schmidt.[6]

---

[6] Ross, *Mit der linken Hand geschrieben*, 45–7.

Hans-Magnus Enzensberger and Arno Schmidt were prominent and widely recognized writers whose careers began in the 1950s. The former was a member of the "Gruppe 47," the loosely-knit association of writers, editors, and publicists maintained by Hans Werner Richter from 1947 to 1968. Almost all the writers who personified West German culture at home and abroad were invited by Richter to one or more of the annual meetings of the group, which had no formal roster or organization, but which was given form by Richter's personal mailing list. By the late 1950s, he had brought in Heinrich Böll, the playwright Günter Eich, the writers Uwe Johnson, Wolfdietrich Schnurre, Martin Walser, and Enzensberger, the literary critics Walter Jens and Hans Mayer, as well as Wolfgang Hildesheimer and Joachim Kaiser, two writers who represented a combination of intellectual music criticism with literary interests that had a long tradition in Germany.

Contrary to the common impression, the 1950s were not a time of stagnation in German culture. True, the literary giants of the first half of the century, Gerhart Hauptmann and Thomas Mann, were gone, but their spirit and style lived on to inspire the next generation. This was the split generation of writers, poets, playwrights, and literary scholars who came of age during or after World War I and all of whom had to deal, in one way or another, with Nazism. Some, like Carl Zuckmayer or Bertolt Brecht, emigrated. Others, like Erich Kästner or Werner Bergengruen, went into "inner emigration," keeping silent or saying only what they could justify in their conscience. A few, like Ernst Jünger or Gottfried Benn, continued to write and publish during the Third Reich without being in any way loyal servants of the regime. After the war, some of the emigrés returned. A few decided that they preferred the communist regime in the east, whether out of genuine conviction that it promised a better future, or out of hope of reward. Even they, like Brecht, the literary critic Hans Mayer, or the Marxist philosopher Ernst Bloch, came to exercise a growing influence on West German students of the 1950s and later.

By the late 1950s the influence of the Gruppe 47 dominated the literary landscape. Its outlook was a mixture of deep suspicion and distrust of Adenauer and the political system he represented. To the members of Gruppe 47, the West Germany of the late 1950s was a restoration of many bad tendencies of the old Germany – authoritarian, rigidly hierarchical, a society dominated by the interests of business and industry, with a population lacking in true democratic values. In its critique of the German present the Gruppe 47 was an influential precursor of the New Left of the 1960s; indeed one might say that the Gruppe 47 *was* the archetypal West German version of the intellectual and literary New Left.

Almost without exception the Gruppe 47 authors published their books with Peter Suhrkamp in Frankfurt. Two of them wrote books in the 1950s that, 30 years later, represented their best work. Heinrich Böll (1917–1987), a disaffected Rhineland Catholic, described the moral and psychological problems of Germany after the war as he saw them in *Billard um halbzehn* (*Billiards at Half-Past Nine*) and *Ansichten eines Clowns* (*The Clown*). Although he may never have re-attained the literary force of his early writing, Böll went on to become a moral spokesman of the German intellectual establishment. His opinions during the 1960s, the 1970s, and the 1980s were sought and freely given on all political and moral matters, especially concerning the problem of the past and relations with the communist east. On both issues Böll represented a rigorous moralism. At times he insisted that the West German state was little better than the Third Reich and that West Germans as a whole had failed to deal personally and psychologically with the consequences of Nazism and the Holocaust. Anti-communism, he argued, was misplaced, since there was no threat of subversion from the east. The Soviet bloc countries, rather, had cause to fear Adenauer's aggressive policies; West Germans were anti-communist because they had been indoctrinated by Hitler.

The other new writer of the 1950s whose influence continued to grow was Günter Grass, born in Danzig in 1927. For most of his career, Grass was a less emotionally moralistic writer than Böll. It was characteristic of the difference between them that Böll considered even the SPD far too conservative for his taste, whereas Grass – to the anger of many of his radical colleagues – openly supported the SPD in the 1960s and 1970s and rejected the demands of Marxist revolutionaries as undemocratic. In his best works, he showed a keen eye for surrealistic absurdities in everyday human life in general and in recent German history in particular. The hero of *The Tin Drum* (1959), Oskar Mazerath, is a boy from Danzig who remains a boy in size but becomes an adult in mind, a condition that permits him to observe the Nazi period and the war in the guise of a child. *The Tin Drum* was the only Gruppe 47 work to reach a genuinely wide audience; by the 1980s it had sold well over a million copies. Not since Thomas Mann had a work of serious literature achieved such popularity in Germany.

Grass went on to publish two further volumes of what he called his "Danzig Trilogy," *Cat and Mouse* in 1961, and *Dog Years* in 1963. Grass, like other members of the group, sought "to supply the postwar generation with spectacles that would enable them to see the true past," as they defined it. And while they demonstrated "the banality and shoddiness of the Nazi movement by deliberately demythologizing it,"[7]

---

[7] Craig, *The Germans*, 145, 216.

they also sought to pass judgement on contemporary postwar German society – almost as though, somehow, they were in possession of the truth.

On the one hand, in the case of Enzensberger, Grass and Böll, "the desire of all three was a society of free people determining their own destinies, and all of them found that this ideal was threatened in the world that emerged in the second half of the twentieth century." On the other hand, their approach to dealing with this perceived problem differed. Enzensberger openly opposed the capitalist system of free enterprise. Grass condemned West German society and its leaders for an effort "to seek a refuge from the past in material pleasure . . . and of the manipulations of its press lords and industrial tycoons," although he apparently did not consider Rudolf Augstein or Henri Nannen to be among lords of the media. And Böll condemned a country that he asserted "believed only in power, influence and money."[8] The words that these writers chose to express their views, however, were not universally praised, and it is questionable, too, how many Germans agreed with them, or how many of Germany's friends abroad shared these opinions. When *The Tin Drum* appeared in English translation in the United States in 1963, Orville Prescott reviewed it for *The New York Times* and wrote, "Reading *The Tin Drum* is rather like experiencing a Teutonic nightmare. There are crowds of people, all of them a little larger than life, all of them stupid, malevolent, lustful or eccentric. . . . How much more eccentric *The Tin Drum* would have been if written with a modicum of restraint, selectivity and taste!"[9]

The "spirit of the 1950s" was not made up merely of the sayings and doings of the literary left. Political journalism, political science, economics, history, philosophy, theology, and some natural sciences, were areas where Germans made impressive contributions. Political satire experienced a sophisticated revival, in large part because the first political cabaret had opened almost immediately after the war and captured the Germans' imagination (the first to open was *Die Schaubude* in Munich in August 1945). They became an "important forum of political opinion," and "if all plans of those weeks could have been realized, there would soon be more cabarets than undamaged houses."[10] Since Germany was no longer the center of Europe, however, these achievements, although valuable in themselves, became subsumed in an asserted, feigned and, in part, real provincialism and were not given the wide recognition they deserved.

[8]  Ibid., 219, 221, 222.
[9]  *New York Times,* February 8, 1963.
[10]  Glaser, *Kulturgeschichte der BRD,* 1: 266.

Two journals, both founded in the late 1940s, represented levels of excellence in political journalism of the 1950s that contrasted remarkably with the grim picture of a narrow, rather boring, cultural landscape drawn by the Left. The editors of *Merkur* styled it a "journal of European thought." Until the late 1960s it remained a forum for liberal and humanistic thought with articles, essays, and reviews on political and cultural issues. By 1970 the New Left controlled the editorial board and transformed the journal largely into a vehicle for the views of the left wing of the SPD and its allies in academe and the media. *Der Monat*, the other of the two, was founded in 1948 by Melvin J. Lasky, an American who had remained in Germany after the war. In 1953, Lasky moved to London to found another journal, *Encounter*, and *Der Monat* was carried on by his associates, Fritz René Allemann and Helmut Jaesrich, until 1971. Its heyday was the 1950s. It was one of the most important forums of transatlantic dialogue, an exponent of an "American liberalism that still believed in itself." The editorial positions reflected those of ex-communists and democratic socialists – called neo-conservatives in the 1980s – for whom articles were skirmishes in the Cold War.

There was no new standard for political science or sociology in the 1950s. The strong German tradition in these fields, personified by Max Weber (1864–1920), who exercised a broad influence on culture and politics, was broken by the Third Reich, and the most influential postwar ideas in methodology and subject-matter came from America, often with returning emigrés like Arnold Bergstraesser. Along with a much younger man, Karl Dietrich Bracher, whose first important work, on the collapse of the Weimar Republic, was published in 1955, Bergstraesser introduced "democracy theory" to West Germany. This was an American blend of normative and empirical analysis which, on the one hand, described the institutions and procedures of modern liberal democracy, and on the other, attempted to demonstrate that democracy was both the best and the inevitable result of political modernization, of the change from traditional and hierarchical to contemporary and pluralist societies.

The writing and teaching of history was, from the very beginning, a vital issue in the Federal Republic. The respect for history and historians was a legacy of the nineteenth century, when great historians such as Leopold von Ranke, Johann Gustav Droysen, Heinrich von Treitschke, Theodor Mommsen, and Jacob Burckhardt were leading public figures, whose opinions and judgements on current affairs carried great weight in society. But after 1945 two other motives contributed to the interest in history. One was the need to understand the causes of the Third Reich. The other was the need for a history that would illustrate Germany's other traditions, better than those that culminated in National Socialism, such as the democratic revolutionary tradition of 1848 or the tradition of federalism and regional autonomy. Historians who could supply these needs in ways that were imaginative and positive were therefore much in demand in the 1950s.

Most historians who were not Jewish or left-wing – and most were neither – had survived the Nazi years in reasonable safety. Obviously, certain fields of study were more popular than others, the riskiest being modern political and diplomatic history, and the safest being medieval studies. Only a few historians, such as the medievalist K. A. von Müller or the modern historian Walter Frank, had been active Nazis. Frank committed suicide in 1945, but Müller continued to teach and publish until his death in the 1970s. The most important dissident historian was Friedrich Meinecke, who respected the Prussian traditions of devotion to the state, but despised what he regarded as the Nazi barbarization of those traditions. When the Nazis took over he was already retired from teaching, but was still editor of the distinguished journal, the *Historische Zeitschrift*, from which he was dismissed in 1935. In 1949, when the journal appeared again for the first time since 1944, it bore again the name of the then 87–year-old Meinecke as honorary editor.

In the 1950s, the leaders of the profession were men who had begun teaching and writing in the Weimar years or before – Franz Schnabel, Hans Herzfeld, Gerhard Ritter, and Percy Ernst Schramm. Friedrich Meinecke, the dean of German historians, died, at age 92, in 1954. He was the last representative of a cosmopolitan, anti-nationalistic view of German and European history, and had been during his active career from the 1890s to the 1930s strongly opposed to the nationalistic Prussian school, which saw the unification of Germany under Prussian leadership in 1866–71 as the logically and morally desirable culmination of German history. He lived long enough to witness the collapse of National Socialism in 1945 and the vindication of his own position within the discipline of history itself.

Franz Schnabel (1887–1966), a south-westerner, was a skillful and popular teacher who wore his immense learning modestly. He was the author of a brilliant and unconventional history of Germany in the nineteenth century, in which he emphasized developments in science, technology, and industry, changes in religious habits and beliefs, and social conditions rather than politics. All his life he maintained close ties to France and French culture and tried, in his work, to draw Germans closer to the West and to show that western and southern Germany were no less authentically "German" than Prussia or the east. He was one of the very few German historians who could say proudly after 1945 that he had no cause to change a single word of what he had written during the

Third Reich, since nothing he had written bore the least taint of Nazism or chauvinism of any kind. In 1945, the American military government entrusted him with the chief responsibility for reconstructing the school system in Württemberg-Baden. In 1947, he took up a chair in the university of Munich, where he influenced another generation of students. His views on Franco-German relations and the need for Germany to turn to the West were exactly those of Adenauer, Blankenhorn, and the other designers of postwar West German foreign policy. His interest in what later came to be called social history anticipated developments in the field by 20 years or more, though none of the later social historians came near to matching his learning or his literary skills. Yet despite these qualities he remained curiously obscure, though a republication of his main work in the 1980s signaled a possible renaissance.

One reason for Schnabel's lack of fame may have been that he was too forthright in rejecting the national school of historiography, whose leader after the war was Hans Herzfeld (1892–1982). Despite what critics argued, it was untrue that the nationalist historians as a whole supported Hitler or promoted Nazi ideas. Furthermore, they believed strongly that their focus on the political sphere and especially on foreign relations and international politics was quite simply a logical way to study history. The best historians of the national school, such as Herzfeld, achieved a grasp and a presentation of world politics, of grand strategy, of the thoughts and beliefs of statesmen, and of the logic of their actions, that no other method could rival. Herzfeld, a World War I veteran, was the author of many exhaustive studies of German and European political history of the nineteenth and twentieth centuries. He continued to write with vigor into his eighties, his last work being a comprehensive and eloquently written history of Berlin from 1945 to 1973. One of the present authors had the privilege of being his last doctoral student.

Gerhard Ritter (1888–1967) and Percy Schramm were, in different ways, historians of the ideas and concepts behind political action rather than of politics as such. Both represented a conservative bourgeois humanism – in Ritter's case colored by Lutheran piety of the "two swords" variety – untainted by Nazism, but increasingly rejected by a younger generation of students and professors who, like the Left intellectuals, wanted to carry through the promises of the new beginning of Zero Hour. Ritter had published a powerful study of the moral dangers of power exercised during the Third Reich (*Die Dämonie der Macht*, 1940), and in 1951 produced a broad panorama of the sixteenth century, setting Germany firmly in the European context and thereby contributing to the Europeanization of postwar West German culture. Ritter argued that this Europeanized German culture should not forget its origins or national heritage, but this hope did not attract a broad audience. By the early 1960s, this kind of humanistic history was being replaced by social history and by studies implicitly critical of the very bourgeois culture that, for Ritter, was the foundation of civilization. Even as younger scholars were rejecting the tradition he represented, Ritter produced his final, massive masterpiece, an uncompleted four-volume work on statecraft and militarism in Prussian and German history (*Staatskunst und Kriegshandwerk*). Ritter's main purpose was to examine the causes of World War I and to explain, if not justify, Germany's part in those causes and German politics and strategy during the war.

Percy Schramm (1894–1970), a noted historian of medieval kingship, had taught at the University of Heidelberg, and, from 1929 onwards, at the University of Göttingen. To the younger generation he was best known as the diarist of the High Command of the Wehrmacht after he was ordered to report to the Führer's headquarters in 1943, where, replacing Helmut Greiner, he was charged with recording all events, decisions and conversations in minute detail. Defying Hitler's order to destroy all the material in the final days of the war, he was able to publish the 6600–page *Kriegstagebuch des Oberkommandos der Wehrmacht*. These precise and, at the time, classified written recordings of all events and decisions made at Hitler's headquarters are of inestimable historical value. Donald Detwiler, in a tribute to Percy Schramm, wrote very accurately that Schramm "himself was never an active supporter of Hitler," and, in addition, described the positive as well as the negative reactions after the publication of the *Kriegstagebuch* "with an extensive introductory essay" by Schramm:

> The harsh criticism Schramm received for his controversial "humanization" of Hitler, ... was more than counterbalanced by the response of younger readers whom he had helped come to terms with the older generation. Everyone, a young Berliner observed in a letter to the editor of the *Spiegel,* had long since known Hitler was evil, but it was high time that someone had finally come along and explained to his generation what had finally been "brought out by Professor Schramm. If our fathers had simply been taken in by someone who obviously was a beast, a proletarian, and perhaps also a stupid boor, I would have lost all respect for them. . . . Professor Schramm has done a splendid job of making it clear to us what it was that could delude so many."[11]

Oddly enough, the opening salvo in the progressive campaign against old-fashioned bourgeois humanism in West German historiography

---

[11] Detwiler, "A Tribute to Percy Schramm." *Central European History* 4 (1971): 90–4.

came not from any early new leftist or unreconstructed Weimar radicals, but from a conventional political and diplomatic historian, Fritz Fischer. His cultural background was a Protestant ethical liberalism and moralism close to the traditions of the Confessing Church of Martin Niemöller and Gustav Heinemann. In the 1950s, Fischer began study- ing the causes of World War I. While not as sensitive an issue as the Third Reich in the postwar period, it was nevertheless an emotional one for many Germans, especially older ones, because they felt that the victorious Allies in 1918 had blamed the war on Germany, when in fact all parties were guilty of the conflagration. This argument, that the 1914 war was largely the unplanned result of accidents and miscalculations, had won great favor in Germany, because it absolved the nation of guilt, but it was also gaining ground in the countries of the victors of that war.

Fischer concluded from careful studies in the surviving archives and elsewhere, that this view, that more or less everyone was guilty, was wrong, and that the original Allied view, that the Germans deliberately provoked the war, was correct. In 1961 he published his results in a book which he called *Griff nach der Weltmacht*. In this and other works, he argued that World War I was the result of a deliberate German bid for continental hegemony, for control of Europe and for the status of a world power, comparable to that of Britain or Russia: "Germany under- took in full awareness of the implications and with all her energy to advance from the position of a great power which it had reached, under Bismarck, among the five European states, to that of a world power."[12] While inspired to some extent by an ethically motivated need to argue against apologists for the Wilhelmine state, Fischer had not intended to cause a sensation or to undermine public trust in the Federal Republic. Nevertheless his book was a sensation, particularly among younger historians such as Hans-Ulrich Wehler, at the University of Bielefeld, who devoted much of his career to developing Fischer's analysis and extending it to the Third Reich as well as to other periods in German history.

In its effects on West German culture and society and on the image West Germans had of their own past, Fischer's book was far more significant than a mere contribution to the study of World War I. In fact, many of his conclusions were eventually even accepted by more pragmatic and conservative historians – who understood the real power of ideas – such as Herzfeld, who wrote in 1968 that the position argued by German historians in the 1920s was incorrect; that the idea that the war was primarily caused by Germany's defensive reactions to hostile encirclement was untenable, and that German public opinion was

---

[12] Cited in Herzfeld, *Der Erste Weltkrieg*, 28.

prepared for and welcomed war. On the other hand, Herzfeld found no deliberate long-prepared plot. Nor did Ritter, who was working on his multi-volume study on militarism in German history. Unlike Herzfeld, however, Ritter believed that Fischer's thesis was simply wrong, a propagandistic exercise in placing blame rather than an example of scholarship. What the public remembered from the Fischer controversy was that a professional historian of impeccable scholarly credentials had exploded the myth of relative German innocence in 1914. In conjunction with the other events of the nascent cultural revolution of the 1960s – the *Spiegel* affair, the Auschwitz trial of 1963–5, and Karl Jaspers' attack on the West German political system in 1966–7 – the Fischer controversy was a symptom of the rise of a new, more critical, even radical attitude on the part of many West Germans toward their own history and, in this case, toward bourgeois humanist attempts to give West Germany a positive history to set against the negative history of Nazism.

Thanks, above all, to the unparalleled intellectual and moral authority of Karl Jaspers, philosophy enjoyed a respect and interest in the 1950s which it has not since attained. Jaspers came closest of all in the older generation of public figures to the stature of Max Weber in the Wilhelmine Reich – a politically concerned professor who took the obligation of concern for national and international events and their impact on his country seriously. Jaspers spoke from an untainted vantage point of the moral responsibility and duties of Germans that arose from the crimes of the Third Reich. His ideas generated controversy at Germany's universities, where comparisons between the Bonn and the Weimar republics were of great interest; a good illustration was Berlin professor Kurt Sontheimer's *Antidemokratisches Denken in der Weimarer Republik* (Anti-democratic thinking during the Weimar Republic), published in 1962. But Jaspers did not stimulate the younger generations, to whom his ideas were addressed, to think in a positive way about the accomplishments of the Federal Republic. For many of them, his book *Wohin Treibt die Bundesrepublik?* (*The Future of Germany*), published in 1966, confirmed their own conclusion that the Federal Republic was a continuance of the Reich, while the views of responsible German historians, like Ritter and Herzfeld, were largely ignored by the younger generation in the 1960s.

He was, however, despite the tremendous publicity he attracted abroad to the contrary, far and away not the only spokesman qualified to pass judgement on moral questions or issues of responsibility. Carl Zuckmayer's *The Devil's General*, written in Vermont toward the end of the war and premiered in Zürich in December of 1946, is without question one of the most powerful and dramatic expressions of the efforts on behalf of Germans, not only to repudiate the dictatorship of Hitler Germany, but also to take responsibility for their actions. It drew overflow crowds to German theaters more than two decades later in the 1960s, and exerted unforgettable impact on the audiences that witnessed actors dressed as Nazi Gestapo officers on West German theater stages. No one who has seen this play can forget the power of opposition which so many Germans, in their varied and different ways, brought to bear against Nazism.

German scholarship in the traditional humanistic disciplines reached a final flowering before the activists of the 1960s changed completely the understanding of what scholarship was or should be. All the scholars and writers, moreover, had to deal in one way or another with the overarching problems facing German society and culture in that decade: how to preserve freedom from a totalitarian threat in the present and regain dignity from a totalitarian burden of history?

Adenauer's choice was to seek integration in the West while giving the Western powers reason to help Germany defend itself against the East. In late 1958 the Soviet Union began a political and diplomatic offensive against West Germany and NATO in order to drive a wedge between Bonn and its allies. Not for the first time, Adenauer feared that the US and Britain would give in, and make an agreement with the Soviet government at German expense. That was why he was particularly happy that he was making progress in relations with the third Western power: France.

# 12

# The Franco-German
# Rapprochement Begins

From 1945 to 1955 French governments remained suspicious and fearful of Germany. Their occupation policy was the harshest of any in the Western zones; they were opposed to returning the Ruhr industries to German control; they intended to annex the Saar to France; they agreed to establish the Federal Republic only because the alternative of continued occupation was too costly and might possibly invite Soviet interference; they were especially opposed to German rearmament, as the history of the five years from the Himmerod Memorandum to the formation of the Bundeswehr illustrated. But the French could point to World War II, as well as centuries of earlier history, to justify their suspicions. Given this background it was the more astonishing that a genuine change of climate in Franco-German relations took place in the late 1950s and early 1960s. For the first time, the two countries appeared not as grudging allies who only stood together because of the Soviet threat, but as actual friends.

There were negative as well as positive reasons for this new alignment. Negatively, both Adenauer and the new French government of Charles de Gaulle (1890–1970, president of France 1958–69) suspected that the US might leave Europe, which meant that the European powers would be forced to organize their own defense. Positively, both favored close economic and political cooperation of the continental Western European states in the EEC; both came to oppose, for different reasons, British membership; both believed that France and the new Germany had more in common with each other than either had with Britain or the US.

The successful creation of the ECSC of 1951 marked the end of the first period of tentative reconciliation and cooperation between France and Germany, masterminded on the French side by Jean Monnet and by the German-speaking Robert Schuman from Lorraine. The next stage of the process, however, creation of the European Defense Community

(EDC), never took place. Adenauer was very disappointed that the EDC was defeated by the French, possibly as part of an undefined Franco-Soviet understanding directed against Germany and, indirectly, as opposition to the broader interests of uniting Western Europe. The collapse of the EDC resulted in distinctly cooler relations between West Germany and France between 1954 and 1958. During this time the Saar, a major center of the coal and steel industry, was released from French control and reverted to German sovereignty (in 1956). Some Frenchmen continued to resent what they regarded as the loss of the Saar, which the French government had hoped to incorporate fully into France.

Adenauer for his part was never very concerned about the Saar. He was even prepared, if necessary, to let it remain with France if the population wanted it and if that was the price to pay for French goodwill. In the Europe of the 1950s, faced with the Soviet threat on one side and with doubts about the American commitment on the other, Adenauer was far more concerned to restore the momentum toward European integration that was lost when the EDC failed. He also believed that progress in European integration was necessary as a counterweight to the SPD's appeal on the German question. If the Germans were not bound to the West by strong ties of interest and commitment, he thought, they would inevitably begin to look toward Moscow for a solution to their problems. And that would be fatal, not merely for German democracy, but for Europe. Accordingly he fully supported the plans for the common market and the resulting Treaty of Rome of March 25, 1957, establishing the EEC and EURATOM with their important new institutions, the Commission, the Council of Ministers, the European Court of Justice, and the European Parliament.

The EEC was only one aspect of Adenauer's Western strategy in the later 1950s. Intimately connected with it, but nevertheless quite distinct in conception and execution, was his policy of reconciliation with France. The Rome Treaty gave further momentum to this policy, which reached its culmination in 1959–63. And while French obstruction gradually undermined the federal purpose of the institutions of the common market, especially the Commission, Franco-German cooperation grew and flourished, until by the 1980s it had become the foundation of European stability.

In 1958, the series of weak and short-lived governments known as the Fourth Republic came to an end, when the president, René Coty, and the National Assembly recalled de Gaulle, leader of the Free French during the war, to power. The main reason for the Fourth Republic's fall was the war in Algeria between Arab nationalists and the French colonial government. The Algerian War cost several hundred thousand casualties during 1954–8, and split French political society into hostile camps that respectively defended and attacked the effort to preserve French rule and protect the interests of the native supporters of France, the *pieds noirs*. In April 1958, the French government, weakened by four years of war and terrorism in Algeria, and by the international repercussions of the Suez crisis of 1956, decided to move toward granting independence to Algeria. The *pieds noirs*, supported by important elements of the French armed forces in Algeria, promptly rebelled and this rebellion brought down the Fourth Republic. De Gaulle, in retirement since 1946, returned to power under a new constitution establishing the Fifth Republic. Many people expected that de Gaulle would continue the war to victory; in fact, he moved almost immediately to disengage from Algeria and grant full independence to the Arabs. This made him bitterly hated by the *pieds noirs*, who formed about one-tenth of the Algerian population, and all of whom had to leave or be killed. From 1958 to 1962 terrorist groups of *pieds noirs* tried on several occasions to assassinate de Gaulle.

The new constitution prescribed a strong presidency, virtually an elected monarchy. De Gaulle, who was elected the first president under the new constitution in 1958, used these powers to the fullest in his ten-year effort to "make France less ridiculous." He was profoundly convinced that France was a country destined for greatness or *grandeur*. The weakness of the Fourth Republic, the inability of governments to conduct firm or consistent foreign or economic policies, pained him deeply, since he regarded such an inability as a betrayal of French character. He was determined to return France to its true fate, which was one of performing great deeds on the world stage.

"The sword is the axis of the world and greatness is indivisible," he had written in an essay on military strategy in 1934, meaning that military power and the will to acquire military power was the mark of any sovereign state with claims to be taken seriously, and that each nation must pursue its own greatness without relying on others to protect its power or independence. Accordingly, he refused to accept that France should play a subordinate role in NATO or the EEC. He did not reject alliances as such, but simply believed, as a matter of profound conviction, that a people can and must rely only on itself for survival; and that to rely on alliances, instead of one's own policies and efforts, was to admit that one was incapable and unworthy of independence. His policy in Europe and toward the US and the Soviet Union during his presidency from 1958 to 1969 was consistent with this view. He broke away from NATO and vetoed the admission of Britain to the EEC in order to make France the dominant

European power. In this strategy West Germany played an important role.

De Gaulle deliberately sought to bind West Germany closer to France economically, diplomatically and militarily, in order to counteract what he considered excessive US influence in Western Europe. He was the only European leader in the late 1950s who possessed the personal strength and determination to undertake such a venture vis-à-vis Germany, and within France his stature was unparalleled. "De Gaulle in his lifetime dominated his nation with a personal ascendancy unknown to the French since the age of Napoleon a century and a half before."[1] A long-time observer of European politics since 1945, Don Cook, wrote of de Gaulle in 1981:

> In the French spectrum, his greatness and place in history will be secure. But on the wider scale of Europe and his role in world affairs, de Gaulle's true stature will long be debated. . . .
> Often it seemed that he was born to oppose rather than create. He thrived on battering at obstructions and surmounting opposition, which he would often invent for himself. For de Gaulle, the Atlantic Alliance was not a guaranty of French security but a threat to French independence. The European Common Market was a roadblock. The United Nations was an obstruction. . . .
> He restored France as a dynamic and stable European power, and that was his great, undying achievement. But he weakened the Atlantic Alliance, played games with the European security, and kept Europe divided and uncertain of its future. Only history will balance out how right General de Gaulle was and how wrong he was.[2]

Throughout his career, all who met him testified to his impressive personal presence, the outward manifestation of his unbending will, immensely strong character and self-discipline, and titanic ego. De Gaulle seemed never to have been young or unserious. From his earliest days he saw himself, and made others see him, as a man of special destiny. He fulfilled that destiny both from 1940 to 1944, when he single-handedly declared himself to be the embodiment of France, and as president from 1958 to 1969. Of his presence, Don Cook wrote:

> No one who ever saw General de Gaulle in person was likely to forget – not merely his great height, but the powerful sense of authority and presence that he generated simply walking down the street, or when he stood up before a crowd with his arms stretched out and his fists clenched, or merely sitting behind a table passively and imperiously answering questions at a news conference.[3]

[1] Cook, *Ten Men and History*, 199.
[2] Ibid., 199–200.
[3] Cook, *Charles de Gaulle*, 18.

His priorities in 1958 were to end the Algerian war that was absorbing so much blood and energy and paralyzing French foreign policy. To obtain greater leverage vis-à-vis the United States de Gaulle also wanted a modern French army deployed on the European continent. This could be done in various ways, and de Gaulle tried all of them. One way was to propose a restoration of the wartime alliance of the three Western powers, the US, Britain, and France. This tripartite coalition would, in de Gaulle's plan, replace NATO and grant France permanent dominance on the European continent, keep Britain out of the EEC and encourage a continuation, in modified form, of Britain's global imperial responsibilities in conjunction with the United States. This concept was outlined in a memorandum, the text of which remained secret for a long time, that de Gaulle sent to President Eisenhower and Prime Minister Macmillan in September 1958:

It is therefore not the view of France that NATO in its present form can do justice either to the security requirements of the free world, or to its own. It therefore seems to France that an organization comprising the United States, Great Britain and France should be created and function on a world-wide political and strategic level. This organization would make joint decisions in all political questions affecting global security and would also draw up and, if necessary, implement strategic action plans, especially as regards the use of nuclear weapons. . . .

The French Government considers such an organization of security indispensable. As of now, it will make all further development of its present participation in NATO contingent on it and intends, should that become necessary, to invoke the revision procedures of the North Atlantic Treaty as set down in Article 12 for this purpose.[4]

Some observers have wondered how seriously de Gaulle intended his implied threat. For example, "was he really ready to submit to the same veto power over France's emerging *force de frappe* that he was asking over the American strategic nuclear deterrent?"[5] In any event, this "grand design" did not elicit the support of the United States government, and the strategy that de Gaulle finally did follow was one more harmful to Western solidarity and strength. It was still based on the belief that Britain had no role on the European continent and that France should be the dominant power there. But since neither the Eisenhower nor the Kennedy administration believed in a global co-dominium with France and Britain, France was, in de Gaulle's view, obliged to take a more independent, and by definition, anti-American stance internationally

4 Cited in Grosser, *The Western Alliance*, 186–7.
5 Cook, *Charles de Gaulle*, 346.

simply to emphasize and maintain its responsibility for leadership. One aspect of that independence was the nuclear *force de frappe* (strike force), which turned from a dream into a promise when France detonated its first nuclear device in 1960. Once the *force de frappe* was underway, de Gaulle could contemplate the further step of removing France from NATO's military organization, which he did in 1966. At his request NATO's military headquarters were moved from Paris to Brussels, but the Alliance's administrative headquarters remained in Versailles.

To exercise the influence and leadership in Europe that he sought, de Gaulle designed a strategy of three elements: (1) increasing French independence from the US and Britain, and, therefore, more room for maneuver for France vis-à-vis both Anglo-Saxon powers – this element followed directly from de Gaulle's conviction that "greatness is indivisible;" (2) detente with the Soviet Union based not on any sympathy for Marxism-Leninism, but on what de Gaulle considered joint French and Soviet interests in restraining American and German economic and political power and influence in Europe; (3) drawing Germany away from close alignment with the US in order to use German economic power to bolster French political power in Europe.

De Gaulle recognized the moral and political obligations and burdens of the Third Reich and of Nazism that would prevent West Germany from assuming political power and aspirations commensurate with its size. His attitude to Germany was sometimes sympathetic and sometimes suspicious. On the one hand, he believed that the maxim "greatness is indivisible" applied to all nations, including Germany; he believed therefore that Germany had every right to try to recapture some of its traditional international status by overcoming the moral and material burden of Nazism and war. On the other hand, he also believed that the new Germany was in a way not German enough, it was America's puppet, and as such an obstacle to French designs. De Gaulle therefore sought to maintain West Germany in a position of moral and political subordination, so that France, economically and demographically the weaker partner, nonetheless could become superior to its eastern neighbor and ancient rival. The defeat of Germany in 1945 had, in de Gaulle's view, finally decided the outcome of a thousand years of struggle between the powers to the west and to the east of the Rhine for predominance in Western Europe. History had awarded victory to France, albeit at the broader price of European subservience to the policies and strategies of the new superpowers, the United States and the Soviet Union. Within the constraints of this two-power nuclear co-dominium, however, de Gaulle intended to carve out a fairly broad niche for French power and policy. He did so with consummate skill, regardless of the broader costs to European security interests his policies entailed. But he could only do so with West Germany's cooperation.

Thus, de Gaulle appeased the Soviet government by emphasizing that France was not an imperialist puppet of US design, and by repeating what Soviet leaders very much wanted to hear: that they and he (de Gaulle) had a common interest in controlling the economic and political influence of a reviving West Germany. France would be the guardian of security in Western Europe, just as the Soviet Union was the guardian of security in Central Europe. France would take it upon herself to control the West Germans and make sure they concentrated on economic development, rather than political ambitions; legitimate German concern about how to reunify Germany was anathema to the USSR, and Soviet control of Central Europe depended on the division of Germany. In turn, de Gaulle would use West German economic strength as a locomotive to pull France's lagging economy forward, while keeping French interests firmly in control. The Germans, de Gaulle judged, were bound into a position of permanent inferiority by the burden of history, enshrined in the Paris Treaties that established the permanent limits beyond which West German military and political ambitions could not go.

To implement this three-pronged strategy of promoting French power independent of the US and Britain, placating the Soviet Union and holding down the Western part of divided Germany, de Gaulle needed to convince the West Germans that their own interests would be better served by alignment with France than with the US. He never completely succeeded in doing this, but he did help generate a split in the West German political community between the Atlanticists, who supported close alignment with the US, especially in seeking detente, and the German "Gaullists," who sought alignment with France and a more generally European, rather than American, focus of German foreign policy. This split compounded the disarray in which West German foreign policy interests found themselves, caused by the Berlin crisis of 1958–61, and also by an apparent stagnation in Ostpolitik since Adenauer's visit to Moscow in 1955. While de Gaulle did not get the complete subservience he desired, he did partially paralyze West German foreign policy until, in 1969, a new West German government was prepared to compromise with the Soviets in the battle over reunification, accept the status quo, and enter wholeheartedly on the road to detente. This was completely in de Gaulle's spirit. The French, as it were, had helped to "deliver" the West Germans to the Soviets; henceforth, the Germans neither could, nor would undertake any foreign policy in Europe antagonistic to the interests of the Soviet Union, such as actively seeking to subvert the regime of the GDR.

The Atlanticists, despite de Gaulle's efforts, remained in overall control of German foreign and security policy until 1966. Very few Germans seriously thought that relying on France for defense against the Soviet threat was sensible. There was, in the early 1960s, no reason to think that the US would withdraw its troops or otherwise reduce its security guarantee for the Federal Republic. There were also West German political thinkers who considered that the Bonn-Washington axis, bypassing France, was a way of preventing that French predominance for which de Gaulle was aiming. But the burdens of history made it impossible for the Germans to present their policy in such straightforward power-political terms.

Adenauer himself took an intermediate position, one that, in the end, satisfied neither de Gaulle nor the Americans, but which admirably demonstrated his agility. He did not think it wise, even if it were possible, to look to France for security guarantees, and he was certainly not interested in playing France against the US, or acting himself as a pawn in a French campaign for greater independence and leverage in Europe. On the other hand, he believed, as he always had, that future stability and security of the free part of Germany must rest both on the transatlantic security guarantee provided by the United States and NATO, and on West European integration. Close and formalized ties between West Germany and France in particular, would help stabilize West German society and political opinion, and make it difficult for any future government of the Federal Republic to wander too far either in the direction of neutralist appeasement of the Soviet Union and the GDR, or in the direction of nationalist agitation against NATO and the West. Thus, closer ties to France were, for Adenauer, an addition to and not a replacement of the US connection.

Adenauer and de Gaulle met for the first time in September 1958, two months before Khrushchev began the Berlin crisis with his ultimatum, in de Gaulle's country house in Colombey-les-deux-Églises. In this house, built at the beginning of the nineteenth century and surrounded by a large garden, de Gaulle worked in his study "from a straight-backed arm chair with a red leather seat and a red-topped table-desk," where he "wrote by hand to the heads of government."[6]

Adenauer, accompanied by Heinrich von Brentano, his foreign minister, and the latter's assistant, Karl Carstens, met with de Gaulle and the French foreign minister, Maurice Couve de Murville, and several other high French officials. Couve de Murville had been ambassador to Bonn from 1956 to 1958 and had established a close relationship with the chancellor. In de Gaulle Adenauer found "a

[6] Ibid., 382.

completely different man" from his expectations, and received "quite a different impression from that which one could gain from the German and foreign press of recent months."[7]

Adenauer had come prepared to be suspicious of the French president, but the meeting was a phenomenal success, a perfect example of successful personal diplomacy, in the words of de Gaulle's biographer Jean Lacouture.[8] Both had come of age before World War I and shared the memory of the old European world of open frontiers and faith in the progress of civilization; both, also, had shared the experience of watching Europe lose that faith through 30 years of struggle between democracy and totalitarianism and the breakdown of the European state system. Both wanted, in different ways, to defend what was left of European culture; the difference was that de Gaulle conceived of that defense purely in nationalistic terms ("greatness is indivisible"), whereas Adenauer knew that Germany could no longer be nationalistic, but must be European. This latter difference was fortunately alleviated at their first meeting by what they had in common. Most important, they shared a Catholicism deeply imbued with historical consciousness and awareness of the symbolic significance of public acts. Lacouture recalled that, for a Catholic, the word "reconciliation" has a special meaning, namely the return of an errant sinner, a prodigal son, to the bosom of the Mother Church, and, he adds, de Gaulle saw himself, vis-à-vis Adenauer and the Germans, as one in a position and with the authority to grant such absolution.[9]

Adenauer took considerable comfort from this reconciliation in the tough days ahead that began in November 1958. Throughout the Berlin crisis of 1958–61 Adenauer continued to improve on the relationship with de Gaulle, which ripened so quickly that the Berlin crisis had hardly ended when the two elderly statesmen launched a year of visits and counter-visits, culminating in the treaty of friendship of 1963.

[7]  Willis, *France, Germany, and the New Europe*, 279.
[8]  Lacouture, *De Gaulle*, 3:293.
[9]  Ibid., 292.

# 13

# The Soviet Offensive Begins:
# The Berlin Ultimatum

On November 10, 1958, Khrushchev delivered a speech in Moscow, indirectly addressed to the three Western powers of France, Britain, and the United States, which opened a new and challenging era in German history:

> The imperialists have turned the German question into an abiding source of international tension. The ruling circles of Western Germany are doing everything to whip up military passions against the German Democratic Republic, against the Polish People's Republic, against all the socialist countries. Speeches by Chancellor Adenauer and Defense Minister Strauss, the atomic arming of the Bundeswehr and various military exercises all speak of a definite trend in the policy of the ruling circles of West Germany. . . .
>
> The time has obviously arrived for the signatories of the Potsdam Agreement to give up the remnants of the occupation regime in Berlin and thereby make it possible to create a normal situation in the capital of the German Democratic Republic. The Soviet Union, for its part, would hand over to the sovereign German Democratic Republic the functions in Berlin that are still exercised by Soviet agencies.[1]

It is impossible to know exactly what Khrushchev hoped to gain when he decided in 1958 to launch his general offensive against the West, but it is possible to make an educated guess, based on Soviet behavior in Central Europe and pronouncements on Germany since 1949. The aims were probably designed to achieve, or might well have achieved, the following three objectives in different combinations. First, the abandonment by NATO of proposed nuclear deployments in West Germany and a combined Soviet-East German seizure of all of Berlin. This result would have discredited US guarantees to defend the security of Western Europe and given powerful impetus to neutralist and

---

[1] Dept of State, *Documents on Germany*, 542, 545.

accommodationist forces in West Germany, as well as to similar groups, albeit indirectly, in France and Britain. Such developments, and the associated political wrangles, would also have contributed powerfully to sowing distrust among the Germans, the French, and the British, and between each of the three and the United States. The ultimate consequence might have been the collapse of NATO, the withdrawal of US forces from Europe, and the recognition by the West Europeans of de facto Soviet political hegemony on the continent.

Second, the abandonment of West Berlin by the Western Allies and its transformation into a "free city," subject to subversion by the East German government, in view of its position as an "island in a red sea." In West Germany and elsewhere in Western Europe, the result would have been Soviet hegemony, but more gradual: the rise of neutralist feeling and, in time, the effective dissolution of NATO.

Third, the final division of Berlin and the takeover of the Soviet sector by the East German regime (which, de facto, had already occurred); the fall of Strauss and the abandonment of the idea of supplying the Bundeswehr nuclear arms; the clear demonstration that the US would not risk open confrontation with the Soviet Union to honor its commitment to the defense of Berlin and to German reunification; as a consequence, a gradual erosion of US leadership in Western Europe and a growing tendency for the West Europeans to seek detente and accommodation with the Soviet Union.

The Soviet offensive was a combined arms operation, including dramatic diplomatic gestures, subtle political pressures, military sabre-rattling, judicious use of the carrot and the stick, assertion of outrageous claims that should provide the basis of negotiations, followed by seemingly magnanimous concessions leaving the West both grateful and worse off, and, last but not least, the ubiquitous Soviet instruments of disinformation and active measures.

Three examples well illustrate the varied instruments. First, espionage in the Federal Republic was widespread. The German government dealt with approximately 12,500 such cases in 1958, of which more than 400 resulted in convictions for spying for the Soviet Union during the same year.[2] The second example concerned the swastikas and Nazi slogans smeared on gravestones in Jewish cemeteries in West Germany at Christmas time in 1959, acts that seemed to indicate the presence of violent neo-Nazis, who objected to the series of trials of Nazi murderers that began in German courts in 1958. The defamation embarrassed and distressed West German leaders at a critical moment of the Berlin crisis and reawakened anti-German feelings, particularly

---

[2] Adenauer, *Erinnerungen 1955–1959*, 460–1.

in France and the US. In fact, Soviet agents had painted the Nazi symbols to embarrass the Bonn government and alarm Germany's allies.[3] The third was the successful attempt, heavily supported by Soviet disinformation agents,[4] to interrupt and permanently damage the career of Franz Josef Strauss, that culminated in the "*Spiegel* affair" of October–November 1962. The *Spiegel* affair, in fact, did more than remove Strauss from the ministry of defense and discredit his support for a nuclear-armed Bundeswehr. It encouraged public distrust of the government and seemed to confirm the left's argument that the "CDU state" was dangerously authoritarian and obsessively anticommunist at precisely the moment that the social and cultural forces of radical change were growing rapidly in strength, and the communist government of the Soviet Union was seeking to isolate Berlin.

Khrushchev escalated the offensive when he issued an ultimatum on Berlin on November 27, 1958, which began a three-year period of heightened tension which constituted the most serious crisis in Germany since the blockade of Berlin in 1948–9. The ultimatum took the form of a note from the Soviet Union to the governments of France, Great Britain, the United States and the Federal Republic. In it Khrushchev argued, as he had done on previous occasions, that the Western Allies had violated the Potsdam Protocol by establishing the Federal Republic, and insisted that the German question be solved by the conclusion of a peace treaty with both German states. Khrushchev also demanded the "demilitarization" of Berlin and its transformation into an "independent political unit" as a "free city." Should the Western Allies refuse to conclude a peace treaty with the two German states, the Soviet Union would transfer all their rights in Berlin and in the GDR to the East German government. This would mean "the question would arise of some kind of arrangement with the German Democratic Republic concerning guarantees of unhindered communications between the free city and the outside world. . . . In its turn West Berlin would undertake not to permit on its territory any hostile subversive activity directed against the GDR or any other state." Khrushchev proposed "to make no changes in the present procedure for military traffic of the USA, Great Britain, and France from West Berlin to the FRG for half a year," and concluded that the Soviet government "regards such a period as fully sufficient to provide a sound basis for the solution of the questions connected with the change in Berlin's situation. . . ."[5]

This ultimatum was a clear threat to the security of West Berlin, but it

---

[3] Schwarz, *Die Ära Adenauer, 1957–1963,* 209–10; Pincher, *Secret Offensive,* 38.
[4] Pincher, *Secret Offensive,* 32–45.
[5] Dept of State, *Documents on Germany,* 557–9.

was also a threat to Adenauer's entire foreign policy vis-à-vis the GDR and to his position concerning reunification, to which Germany's allies committed themselves in the Paris Treaties of 1954. Adenauer expressed his concern in a letter to Secretary of State Dulles on December 11, in which he wrote that to combine the questions of Berlin and the future of Germany in negotiations with the Soviet Union would either put the freedom of Berlin in question or risk surrender to Soviet demands on the question of Germany's future.[6]

In West Berlin the sense of threat to the city – and it was shared by the majority of Berliners to varying degrees – undoubtedly contributed to the victory of the SPD and of Willy Brandt as governing mayor in the municipal elections of December 1958. The SPD received an absolute majority (53 per cent of the vote), and the coalition between the SPD and the CDU in the city was dissolved.

Willy Brandt, at this time, was regarded, and considered himself, as the leader of the anti-Soviet and anti-communist right wing of the SPD, committed to close ties with the United States and to the defense of Western Europe. During the Berlin crisis Brandt ardently opposed making any concessions to the Soviet Union, and, therefore, indirectly to the GDR. On the contrary, he took the initiative, and in his first public declaration as governing mayor of Berlin called for a referendum on the status of Berlin to be held in all four sectors of the city, a proposal which the Soviet government and the SED ignored. SPD leaders in West Germany – Ollenhauer, Wehner and Erler – also rejected the Soviet demands, but they did endorse negotiations with the Soviet Union and repeated their calls for the demilitarization of Germany and for the rejection of NATO's nuclear defense strategy. At the end of 1958, therefore, Brandt was the only SPD figure of major influence who supported, unequivocally, close ties with the West. This was understandable in view of the fact that Berlin, as during the blockade ten years earlier, was once again being threatened by the Soviet Union. Thus, Brandt maintained close ties with figures across the political spectrum in Germany and in the West in general, who felt committed to the defense of democracy and to reunification in peace and freedom. One of these figures was Axel Springer, the conservative publisher of one of West Germany's most important newspapers, *Die Welt,* who supported Brandt's efforts to build bridges to the West in an effort to support the foreign policy of Adenauer's government.[7]

The initial Western reaction to the ultimatum was a meeting of the NATO Council in Paris in December 1958, at which Brandt made his

[6] Schwarz, *Die Ära Adenauer, 1957–1963,* 83.
[7] Ibid., 82.

first major international appearance. The NATO allies rejected the Soviet assertions contained in the ultimatum, and declared that "no state has the right to withdraw unilaterally from its international engagements. It [the NATO Council] considers that the denunciation by the Soviet Union of the interallied agreements on Berlin can in no way deprive the other parties of their rights or relieve the Soviet Union of its obligations."[8] Despite this strong declaration, particularly the British government expressed concern with the tone and character of the Soviet note, as well as with the dangers inherent in a possible confrontation with the Soviet Union, and therefore argued for the "pabulum" stance (negotiations).

Following the position taken by the NATO Council, the United States government and that of the Federal Republic, on December 31 and January 5 respectively, responded to Khrushchev's ultimatum in lengthy notes to the Soviet government, in which they set forth the Western position on Berlin. The purpose of these notes was not only to keep the record straight, but also to reject the contention that the Soviet position could serve as a basis for negotiation.

Whether or not the Soviet government sought to modify its position in view of the Western response, or because it perceived a willingness, at least on behalf of the British government, to negotiate, on January 10, 1959, the Soviet government sent a new note to the Western Allies and to all other states that had fought against Germany. It contained a draft peace treaty with the two existing German states, to be followed by unification of Germany as a neutral country. The proposals, as such, repeated those of the Eden Plan submitted unsuccessfully to the Berlin conference of 1954, and the purpose was clearly to combine the issue of Berlin with the German question as a whole, and thereby to break up the unity of the Western powers.

A break of unity occurred when the British prime minister, Harold Macmillan, and his foreign minister, Selwyn Lloyd, reacted to the Soviet offensive by announcing a trip to Moscow for February 20, without consulting in advance the governments of France or West Germany. There were several motivations for Macmillan's decision. He was not fond of Germany or the Germans, and could not readily accept the premise that Britain should risk war for a nation which had been her enemy during two world wars. He had little understanding of or sympathy for the West German government's moral and legal arguments opposing the ultimatum, and was prepared to recognize the GDR. He was also concerned by the growing economic momentum of the EEC, and especially with the specter of a Franco-German axis dominating

---

[8] Dept of State, *Documents on Germany*, 560.

Western Europe. He saw his trip to Moscow as part of an effort to restore British influence on the continent and to restrict and limit West Germany's growing influence in Europe.

Others in Great Britain, however, saw his trip differently, and he and his wife received an enormous number of letters before their departure, which probably echoed, to some extent, similar feelings held in West Germany: "Please, don't allow our Prime Minister to go out shooting bears in Russia, it may be very dangerous – and what would we in Britain and America do if he had [an] accident."[9]

The trip to Moscow had no immediate diplomatic result, but it obviously served Soviet interests, since it signaled a clear division of opinion and policy within the West. In Adenauer's words: "With its disengagement plan the British government seemed to break out of the Western united front, and this meant that the Western world would be extraordinarily damaged. Heaven only knew what might result from that."[10]

[9] Macmillan, *Riding the Storm*, 592.
[10] Adenauer, *Erinnerungen 1955–1959*, 481.

# 14

# The SPD: The German Plan and the Godesberg Program

After the nuclear debate and the failure of the GCND in 1958–9, as well as the Berlin crisis, a growing number of SPD leaders began to question whether their defense conceptions were based on illusions about the nature of East–West relations. "As long as there were global tensions between the Soviet Union and the United States, as long as regional tensions plagued the European nations, the West Germans would have to seek security within the Western alliance. SPD and FDP leaders only gradually came to realize that the chancellor's foreign and defense policies were based on a more realistic evaluation of world affairs than their own." Both parties were undergoing a generational shift that brought to the fore younger men willing to consider the wisdom of the presuppositions, methods, and understandings of Adenauer's foreign policy; they have been called by one historian "the young Adenauerians."[1] In the FDP, Erich Mende swung the party's defense and nuclear policy through a full 180–degree turn, starting in March 1959, with the backing of the old party chief, Reinhold Maier, and ably assisted by a group of young activists including a 36–year-old Saxon named Hans-Dietrich Genscher, who had escaped from the GDR in 1953. On a larger scale the same thing occurred in the SPD during 1959–60. The new men did not share the Ollenhauer group's instinctive emotional commitment to reunification and neutrality, nor its equally instinctive rejection of what they considered Adenauer's brand of comfortable democratic capitalism. Their names were Fritz Erler, Willy Brandt, and Helmut Schmidt. They were supported by two older men, Carlo Schmid, the party's chief political philosopher and a man of wide European horizons and interests, and Herbert Wehner. Ironically, Wehner, who was somewhat older than the others, never did abandon his emotional hopes for reunification in some form or his

---

[1] Cioc, *Pax Atomica*, 142, 151.

socialist beliefs. Other party intellectuals celebrated or supported the change in various ways, such as the political scientist, Richard Löwenthal of the Free University of Berlin, who provided much of the party's new understanding of American foreign policy and of possible changes in the Soviet Union.

Before the reorientation could truly begin, the Berlin crisis elicited one last attempt by the SPD to replay its old game of asking for re-unification. The proposal was the German Plan (*Deutschlandplan*) of March 1959. It foresaw a European-wide security pact and nuclear- free zone, in a kind of combination of the Eden Plan and the Rapacki Plan, as well as of aspects of other proposals. Khrushchev replied with the expected Soviet position that any and all discussion of reunification must start with talks between the two Germanies, adding, in accordance with his latest demands, that West Berlin must become a free city. The German Plan "marked the high and final point of social democratic efforts for a foreign policy alternative."[2] It remained as party policy until June of 1960, but it was effectively defunct as soon as it was written. Nevertheless, one of its authors, Helmut Schmidt, used the opportunity to present it to the Bundestag to again debate defense issues. Since March 1958 the arguments on defense and nuclear arms in Germany had taken place outside the parliament. When Schmidt raised the issue in November 1959, observers noted a radical and significant departure from earlier SPD arguments. Schmidt spoke of *West* Germany's defense needs, and downplayed the reunification question. There was no doubt that change was occurring within the party.

One of the German Plan's strongest proponents was Wehner. Among his motives may have been the wish to appeal to the nationally-minded communists he believed existed in the SED, in East Germany. Wehner averred that "national" communists might, by appropriate inducements, be encouraged to work for reunification of a socialist and neutral Germany. One major obstacle in Wehner's way, however, was the *Ostbüro* (Eastern Office) of the SPD, located in West Berlin. The *Ostbüro* was responsible for contacts and assistance to the clandestine SPD, which continued to exist in the Soviet zone and the GDR after the communist party absorbed and suppressed the official SPD in the zone in 1946. Needless to say, the *Ostbüro* was anathema to the SED, and any SED leaders who might collaborate with Wehner would have to demand that it be closed. Wehner, therefore, actively attempted to take over the *Ostbüro* from its chief, Stephan Thomas, and close it down, and Thomas was correspondingly opposed to what he, with some justification, regarded as the dangerous illusions represented by the German Plan.

[2] Schwarz, *Die Ära Adenauer, 1957–1963,* 42.

THE SPD: GERMAN PLAN AND GODESBERG PROGRAM

If anyone doubted that seismic shifts were indeed taking place in Germany's oldest still-functioning political party, it was only necessary to turn from defense to the broader issues of social and economic policy and fundamental party doctrine. In these areas, the party's existing policy positions had little in common with the concerns of the people the SPD sought to represent. In both the short and the long term the political fortunes of the SPD were affected by the social transformation of West German society in the 1950s. For the SPD, it meant that their old voter base of blue collar workers was, on the one hand, shrinking, and on the other hand the country's social structure was changing, so that many workers no longer saw their interests as best expressed by the SPD, as had been the case historically. The turn within the party, under Ollenhauer's leadership, to a revision of its programs was, therefore, also a search for new voters among public employees, teachers, and even to some extent small businessmen. This decision did not generate its full momentum until the 1960s and the 1970s, but it was already clear by the late 1950s that the old revolutionary party of the working class was no more.

The mounting frustration in the SPD was the result of a paradox. The party was gaining ground at almost every election: federal, *Land*, or local. Yet actual power, except in isolated cases, such as Hamburg, Bremen, and Berlin, seemed ever farther away, for the awkward, if simple, reason that the CDU was *also* gaining votes constantly. The losers were the small parties, and the SPD's great task from 1959 onward – a task the party accomplished to perfection – was to make inroads in those marginal voting blocs, so as to halt and, if possible, reverse the CDU's progress while maintaining its own momentum toward the chancellery. But if the SPD was to win marginal votes outside its historical bastions, it had to change its image of a party bound to emotion, history, and traditional working-class interests. The analysis of the 1957 election results by Carlo Schmid (SPD), vice president of the Bundestag, reflected the party's frustration, and was also the harbinger of a dramatic change in how the SPD would view its future role in German politics:

As to the causes of the election defeat of the Social Democrats there existed contradictory opinions within the party. Many saw the reasons solely in the unscrupulous demagoguery, with which Adenauer, contrary to his opponents, had led the campaign. . . .

My opinion was that the campaign slogan of the CDU, "No Experiments," expressed exactly what most voters wanted: whatever they had managed to gain in material goods and modest prosperity, they knew; what progressive reforms might bring, they didn't know. This security complex was the deepest reason for the mandate that the majority of the voters had given Konrad Adenauer. He protected them from experiments, and with his "policy of strength," supported by the Americans, from the red danger in the East.[3]

After the election defeat one might have expected Ollenhauer to have been replaced as party chairman. But social democrats have consistently maintained solidarity with their leaders, and party leadership remained in his hands. The nuclear debate was another reason for the party's younger and more flexible leaders – Erler, Brandt, Schmidt – to rally round the chairman. Henceforth, however, these and other advisors exercised their influence to an increasing degree and gave the party new direction.

The decisive moment in the effort to define its role came swiftly and emerged in the form of the Godesberg Program, so named because it was the result of a SPD party meeting in 1959 in Bad Godesberg, next to Bonn on the Rhine river.

Of Ollenhauer's advisors who were among the architects of the party's new direction, the most controversial was Herbert Wehner. Born in 1906, he started his political career as a member of the KPD in 1927. In the early 1930s he participated in anti-Hitler movements, was imprisoned several times, and emigrated to Prague in 1935, where he was arrested and deported to the Soviet Union. From 1935 to 1941 he served as an assistant to the head of the Comintern, Dimitrov, and was sent by the Soviet communist party to Stockholm in 1942, where he was arrested for espionage. He returned to Germany in 1946 with the help of the British, became a member of the SPD, and was elected to the Bundestag in 1949. He later served as chairman of the Bundestag's committee on all-German questions, and as minister for all-German affairs from 1966 to 1969. In 1969 he was elected SPD party whip, and continued to serve as the principal party strategist and ideologue. His abilities and loyalties were regarded with mixed emotions by both his friends and enemies, and he was seen by many as a guarantee that the Marxist-leftist tradition of the SPD would continue. He was an ambiguous figure, with what many conservatives regarded as a very questionable political past, who was capable of broad flexibility. But his influence was considerable, and he was called by the *Frankfurter Allgemeine Zeitung* "after Adenauer the most important politician since World War II." Indeed, journalists labeled him a "dyed in the wool politician, disciplinarian, old coachman," and the social democrats called him "Onkel Herbert," just as Adenauer was called the "Old Man" ("der Alte"). And Wehner was known by his more vehement critics as "communist pig," "Bolshevik," or "traitor."[4]

[3] Schmid, *Erinnerungen*, 619–20.
[4] See Terjung, *Der Onkel*.

The party was fortunate in commanding the loyalty of several skilled economists who understood something of the complex nature of modern mixed economies, and who could recommend policies that satisfied both the basic social democratic urge for equality and what the SPD considered "social justice," and reasonable criteria of efficiency. One was Karl Schiller, a professor of economics at Kiel in the late 1950s. In 1953, speaking about the social market economy, he had coined a phrase to describe how social democrats might wish to change it: "Competition as far as possible, planning as far as necessary."[5] Schiller clearly aspired to become his party's answer to Ludwig Erhard, an ambition he fulfilled to some extent as minister of economics from 1966 to 1972. The second was Heinrich Deist (1902–1964), a SPD member of the Bundestag since 1953 whose major expertise was economics. The SPD had, in fact, committed itself to the idea of competition in the economy in recommendations approved in Dortmund in 1952, but it was Deist who formulated the crucial economic passages of the Godesberg Program, which as a formal document, superseded the policy guidelines designed in Dortmund.

These two figures, together with others in the party, produced a document that was the first basic program of the party since the promulgation of the "Heidelberg Program" of 1925, a time which saw the principal SPD youth organization use as its motto: "Democracy does not mean much, socialism is the goal" ("Demokratie ist nicht viel – Sozialismus ist das Ziel"). The program represented a fundamental shift in philosophical direction for the party, from primary emphasis on Marxism and Marxist solutions for problems of social and economic life, to primary emphasis on recognizing the achievements of liberal capitalism. In so doing, the program reflected the conclusion that socialist concepts of society did not appeal to a majority of the population. It therefore rejected the goal of state ownership of the means of production and the Marxist ideology of which that aim was a part. It meant that the past world of revolutionary class struggle was officially given up, and while many of the party members and the party leadership remained rigidly committed to socialism, the SPD now appeared, at least on the surface, to have become a democratic party like all the others.

The Godesberg Program was characterized by vague formulations and, in some cases, contradictory philosophical positions, which indicated that the struggle between liberals, Marxists and other factions in the SPD was by no means over:

[5] Körner et al., eds, *Wirtschaftspolitik, Wissenschaft und politische Aufgabe*, 86.

The socialist movement fulfills a historical mission. It began as a natural and moral protest of wage earners against the capitalistic system. The enormous development of productivity through science and technology brought wealth and power to a small stratum, but only poverty and misery to the wage earners. To eliminate the prerogatives of the ruling classes and to bring freedom, justice and prosperity to all men – this was and is the aim of socialism.[6]

Some of the party's younger leaders, like Willy Brandt, thought the program did not go far enough in its rejection of Marxism, and he called for a stronger anti-communist line as well. Indeed, part of the program squarely addressed this issue:

The communists radically suppress freedom. They violate human rights and the right to self-determination of the individual and the people. Increasingly, even the people of communist-governed countries now oppose their power apparatus. There too, changes are occurring. There too, the desire for freedom is growing which, in the long run, no regime can suppress. But the communist dictators are fighting for their self-assertion. On the backs of their people they are building an economic and military power, which is becoming a growing threat to freedom.[7]

The Godesberg Program was overwhelmingly approved at a special party meeting in November 1959. The strategic meaning of the program for the party was well expressed by Herbert Wehner, who argued that, as a former communist, he knew well that Marxism was not a good doctrine for practical policy, although its tenets should be retained as a method underlying the tactical approach to political issues. Wehner claimed that the SPD must now seek to democratize as much of society as possible. Furthermore the party program must be such that it could, and would be supported by the greatest possible number of people. After all, he stressed, the point was to gain power, and the SPD must have a program to allow it to do so. Once in power it could then do what it thought right. With this argument Wehner appealed both to the center right of the party, by arguing that the program was proper, since it was no longer couched in Marxist rhetoric, and to the left, because it could claim that, after all, once in power, the party's concepts could be transformed into socialist reality. In this speech, as well as in his speech the following year on security policy, Wehner established himself as the leading strategic thinker of the SPD, a position he retained until he retired from political life in 1983.

On the other hand, the party's remaining Marxists, such as the

[6] Flechtheim, ed., *Dokumente zur parteipolitischen Entwicklung*, 3: 224.
[7] Ibid., 225, 226.

political scientist Wolfgang Abendroth (1906–) and a few younger members of the left wing such as political scientist Peter von Oertzen (1924–) from Lower Saxony, objected to the program, because it no longer interpreted the world in Marxist terms and did not call for nationalization and confiscation of capital and property. In the 1970s, when Oertzen served as minister of culture in Lower Saxony at a time when the SPD was experiencing a revival of Marxism within the party, he was able to enforce Marxist ideas of "democratization" in higher education.

The Godesberg Program passed the convention with few objections. It was far easier for the party to agree on the need for a modern economic and social philosophy than on a reorientation of defense policy. Here the old attachments, indeed, died hard. The program's authors repeated the many statements of the 1950s calling for a united Germany that would be neutral, largely disarmed, and free of nuclear weapons:

The Social Democratic Party is striving for the inclusion of the whole of Germany in a European zone of reduced tensions and of a controlled limitation of arms, a zone to be cleared of foreign troops in the process of German re-unification in freedom and in which atomic weapons and other means of mass destruction are neither produced nor stored nor used.[8]

But change was on the way. Even before the German Plan or the Godes-berg Program, Fritz Erler had decided that a rapprochement on the issue of defense was necessary. The Godesberg convention approved his work in the words: "The Social Democratic Party declares its allegiance to the defense of a free and democratic order. It approves the home defense."[9] This, along with Schmidt's comments on the German Plan in the Bundestag the same month – comments that implicitly ridiculed the wisdom of the plan itself – signaled the shift.

Erler and Schmidt understood that the party had to define policies consistent both with the instincts and wishes of its leaders, and with the currents of public opinion and thinking on domestic and foreign policy issues that Carlo Schmid had analysed following the 1957 Bundestag elections. Schumacher had accepted Adenauer's option for the West, putting freedom ahead of reunification, while nonetheless asserting that there had been a choice. And he had recognized that reunification under Soviet control, or even reunification at the price of neutralization, entailed grave risks for the survival of German democracy. His

[8] Basic Programme of the Social Democratic Party of Germany, adopted by an Extraordinary Conference of the SPD held November 13–15, 1959. Bonn: SPD (printed by Bonn-Druck, Storbeck & Co.), 9.
[9] Cited in Cioc, *Pax Atomica*, 154.

successors – Ollenhauer, Wehner, Schmid, Erler, and Willi Eichler – were more optimistic in this respect and tended, at least during 1953–8, to give greater credence to the proposition that the Soviet Union was a lesser threat to European security than nuclear arms in the West, or at least that the Soviet Union would be a lesser threat if there were no NATO and no nuclear weapons. They felt that Adenauer had gone too far, and that he was not trying hard enough to achieve reunification on conditions which the Soviet Union would accept. Most party leaders concluded that reunification would have to mean neutralization, preferably as part of a general process of troop withdrawals and arms reductions in Central Europe, if the Soviet government were to agree.

Seldom did the SPD concentrate on how the Western powers would react to neutralism in Germany under any kind of circumstances. Fritz Beermann had told his party comrades in 1958: "Our Western allies would regard a Social Democratic government as an uncertain factor with pro-Communist tendencies. By contrast, the chancellor enjoys the support of world opinion."[10] His argument fell on deaf ears, because the party was still conducting politics by emotion: reunification would be a good thing, so it ought to be possible. In reality there was no chance that the Soviet government would accept reunification on any terms except its own; its stated position, since 1955, was that reunification must come about through direct talks between the Federal Republic and the GDR. The Western powers still insisted on free elections first, then reunification, but few viewed that rhetoric as a proposal that would be given serious consideration by the Soviets.

While the SPD was floundering like a beached whale on the shoals of the social market economy and Adenauer's triumphant *Westpolitik*, Khrushchev was providing "the young Adenauerians" in the party with more good reasons to look West, and not East, for security.

[10] Cited ibid., 153.

# 15

# Geneva, Again

The Soviet ultimatum on Berlin did not achieve its stated goal of a peace treaty, signed by all four powers with both German states, which would have meant West German recognition of the GDR. Soviet pressure did, however, lead to a conference of the foreign ministers of the four powers in May and June 1959 in Geneva. It began at the time of Dulles' death, and was the last time the foreign ministers of the four former Allies were to meet together to discuss the question of Germany. The Western goal at this meeting was to gain time. Elections were scheduled in Britain for the fall, and, in November 1960, presidential elections in the United States were to be held. This short-term objective was reached. But the West made conciliatory proposals at Geneva which, if the Soviets had accepted them, would have jeopardized the freedom of Berlin in exchange for the withdrawal of Khrushchev's ultimatum.

Almost as though they were following a precise script, both sides submitted draft peace treaties as they had done so many times before – but were not to do again. The US secretary of state who succeeded Dulles, Christian Herter, denounced the Soviet draft treaty as a "treaty for the permanent partition of Germany;" Andrei Gromyko, who became Soviet foreign minister in 1957, responded in kind. Nevertheless, there was a change in the script: it dealt now primarily with Berlin, not with Germany as a whole. This occurred primarily because Khrushchev had chosen to launch his offensive on Berlin, but that in itself was symptomatic. In effect, since 1954–5, the inner-German situation was stabilized: East and West each had its Germany. The question was which side would impose its version of reality on the other, in regard to the status of Germany as a whole. Berlin was another matter: it was still legally under four-power control, and the problem was that the Soviet government unilaterally contended that it had to give control of its sector to the GDR, and was now trying to gain control over the Western sectors as well.

In the diplomatic shadows some voices in the West were prepared to concede East German control of the access routes to Berlin and to eliminate activities in the city that might be construed as constituting interference in the internal affairs of the GDR, such as radio and press coverage critical of conditions in East Germany. What that might include was spelled out by Gromyko:

> When we [the USSR] speak about the Berlin question, we mean primarily the ending of the occupation regime in West Berlin. . . . It is necessary to get rid of the essentially abnormal situation in which West Berlin, as a result of the artificial support of the occupation regime, is being used by the NATO Powers, including the Federal Republic of Germany, and by certain extremist groups in Western Germany, for the purpose of carrying on subversive activity and hostile propaganda against the USSR, the German Democratic Republic and other socialist countries. . . .
>
> And what are we to say about the activity of RIAS . . . ? The dissemination of lying rumours, slanders, incitements to sabotage and disorders – this is the weapon which this notorious broadcasting station is using day by day.[1]

RIAS (Radio in the American Sector) was a US-sponsored station that broadcast in German, and continues to do so to this day. It irritated the Soviet Union and the German communists in the GDR because of its honest coverage of terror and oppression in East Germany, and its frank and critical reportage on West German affairs. The attack on RIAS was a serious matter, because it was a clear indication that the Soviet government and the GDR regarded any democratic political activity and any free expression of opinion in West Berlin as potentially equivalent to interference in their affairs. At the end of July, Herter implied that the West was ready to sign an interim agreement on Berlin that would include a ceiling on Western force levels and "measures . . . to avoid activities in or with respect to Berlin which might either disturb public order or seriously affect the rights and interests, or amount to interference in the internal affairs, of others." Adding that "we insist that both parts of the city be treated evenhandedly" was cold comfort to Adenauer and Brandt, who saw the thin end of the wedge of Soviet and East German control of free democratic activity in the Western sectors.[2] In retrospect Gromyko would have been wise to accept these proposals, which were never repeated, but he did not. Why was not clear, but scholars have presumed that Khrushchev hoped to gain agreement to his demands, without conditions, on his trip to the US planned for September. He may have calculated that the death of Dulles in May

[1] Dept of State, *Documents on Germany*, 642–3.
[2] Ibid. 679; see also Schwarz, *Die Ära Adenauer, 1957–1963*, 92.

1959, Macmillan's distrust of Germany and increasingly pronounced tendencies to appeasement, and Eisenhower's desire to complete his term as a builder of peace and understanding, had weakened the solidarity of a unified Western position. Gromyko's position, for whatever reason, reflected the assumption that the West's foremost priority was reaching agreement with the Soviet Union over Germany. When the Western leaders finally decided, following the Geneva conference, that despite 14 years of effort since 1945, no such agreement on Germany was possible, the Soviet position perceptibly hardened. It appeared that Khrushchev's chance of total victory had passed, but that did not mean that the crisis of Berlin was over.

Adenauer was greatly relieved that the Soviet government did not accept the Western proposals, which he believed would have fatally undermined the strength of the Allied position in Berlin, and ultimately the freedom and security of West Germany itself. The death of Dulles at a critical time may have contributed to the accommodating position of the Western Allies at the Geneva conference, and it also represented a personal loss of importance to Adenauer. During his last visit to Bonn in February 1959, Dulles, already appearing weak and pale, declined, for health reasons, to attend a dinner party in his honor. However, Adenauer promised to have his cook prepare a special kind of porridge, which Dulles proceeded to eat with great relish. Christian Herter, representing the hospitalized Dulles at the next meeting in Bonn, had received a message minutes before leaving Washington to ask Adenauer for the recipe for the porridge that Dulles had so much enjoyed during his last visit. Herter first believed this to be a special code word, but Adenauer reassured him and immediately sent the recipe and special oats, not available in the US, to Dulles. Adenauer was told, attending the funeral of Dulles at the end of May, that this porridge was the last meal Dulles ate before dying.

By 1959 Adenauer himself was 83 years old. He had led the Federal Republic for ten full years, and had provided it with unusually firm and clear leadership. He was, in many ways, an extremely tough man, who, when he called a spade a spade, often did so in a way that antagonized his critics far more than was necessary. Adenauer's wavering popularity in the late 1950s was partially explained by his political views, but also by how he expressed them. An illustration concerned Adenauer's announcement in April 1959 that he would be the candidate for the office of federal president, which was to be vacated after a decade of distinguished service by Theodor Heuss.

Two months later, however, in June, Adenauer announced that in view of the current difficult foreign policy situation – the Berlin crisis and the Geneva conference – he wished to remain chancellor. Moreover, he added that the office of the federal president was endowed with so few political and constitutional powers that he preferred to continue to determine the political course of the republic in his current office. This amounted to, and was so interpreted by Heuss and others, as a public denigration of the importance of the highest office of the land, and it produced a seven-page letter from Heuss to Adenauer, in which Heuss sought to educate the chancellor on constitutional law.

The letter, by mutual agreement, was never made public during the lifetime of either man. Several days after he read it, however, Adenauer took the opportunity to explain his decision to remain as chancellor to the chairman of the FDP Bundestag caucus, Erich Mende. The occasion was a dinner given by Adenauer in honor of Robert Schuman at the chancellor's residence, Palais Schaumburg, in Bonn. During dessert Adenauer ventured that the chancellor's office had an especially good wine cellar containing the best white wines grown in the hills along the Rhine and Moselle rivers, but that the president's office did not have a similar cellar. Adenauer knew this, he explained, because he had sent his assistant, Hans Globke, to inspect the president's cellar, and Globke discovered that it contained primarily Dr Heuss' favorite red wines which came from his home *Land* of Baden-Württemberg in south-west Germany, but none of Germany's fine white wines. Thereupon Adenauer told Globke that when he became president he would take his cellar of white wines with him, but Globke responded that it was against the law to move a wine cellar from one office to another. Adenauer's response was simple and to the point: "Then I am going to remain here and I will not be a candidate [for president]."[3] Indeed, Adenauer remained chancellor, and Heinrich Lübke, a CDU member of the Bundestag, and minister of agriculture from 1953 to 1959, was elected by the federal assembly to succeed the Federal Republic's first president.

[3] Mende, *Die neue Freiheit*, 428–9.

# 16

# Foreign Policy East and West: Franco-German "Pas de Deux"

F ollowing Geneva, confidence in Western commitment to Berlin's defense remained high, although healthy skepticism also prevailed; Krushchev's visit to the United States in September 1959 had produced no results. The number of persons crossing from the Soviet sector to West Berlin and continuing on to West Germany was exceeding 10,000 a month, so that the GDR was suffering significant losses of skilled workers and citizens in professional occupations such as medicine and engineering. It was these groups who found life most unsupportable in the GDR, but whom the GDR desperately needed to continue construction of its communist system. The GDR, therefore, had a very strong interest in blocking access to West Berlin, and at best, isolating it completely, if it proved impossible to absorb it.

In April 1960 Khrushchev visited de Gaulle in Rambouillet near Paris and renewed the crisis by threatening to conclude a peace treaty with the GDR which would, he asserted, cancel all Western rights in West Berlin. Shortly after his return to the Soviet Union, Khrushchev opened the second phase of the Berlin crisis by declaring that the Western presence in Berlin must end, and that the four powers must sign a peace treaty with both German states. If they would not do so, the Soviet Union would sign a peace treaty with the GDR alone, an act that Khrushchev insisted would automatically terminate the Western right to be in Berlin. He justified this conclusion by repeating his argument from 1958 that all of Berlin was on GDR territory; therefore, if the Soviet Union signed a peace treaty with the GDR, all occupation rights on GDR territory, including all of Berlin, would end. If the West did not withdraw at that point, "this force will be countered with the force of the other side." To underline his point, he stated: "Comrades, at the present time, the Soviet Union is stronger than ever before. Our might is indomitable."[1]

---

[1] Dept of State, *Documents on Germany*, 704–5.

In May 1960, Khrushchev again visited Paris, as preparations were being made for a summit later that month between the four powers. When it began, also in Paris, Khrushchev leveled a blistering attack against the US and the West German government and then left the meeting, using as an excuse the announcement that the Soviet Union had shot down an American U-2 reconnaissance plane over Soviet territory on May 1. Adenauer was relieved, justifiably concerned that the meeting might have led to major Western concessions. Adenauer confessed that he had found the preliminary negotiations he had held with Eisenhower, Macmillan, and de Gaulle to prepare the Western position to be the most depressing experience he had ever endured.[2]

Khrushchev's drum-beating was somber background music to the rapidly flowering Franco-German relationship. Doubts about the steadfastness of the US and British position in defense of German interests and against Soviet encroachments on Berlin, and the apparent firmness of de Gaulle, had encouraged Adenauer to respond warmly to the French rapprochement that began in the winter of 1958–9. France had by no means accepted Adenauer's vision of Europe, which included a free trade zone for all of Western Europe and not only for the Common Market. De Gaulle actually had vetoed this very suggestion in November 1958. However, stimulated by positive developments in the EEC, specifically the efficient operation of the European Commission as the executive body of the community, many Germans and Frenchmen hoped for movement toward stage two of European economic integration as foreseen in the Rome Treaty.

Adenauer and de Gaulle also met in May 1960 to discuss the East–West summit. Since the West Germans were not invited to participate, de Gaulle undertook to defend their interests at the summit. The summit failed, and immediately afterward de Gaulle declared on French television that the community of Western Europe was "a condition of world stability," and that it must and could only be based on Franco-West German agreement.[3] He and Adenauer next met at Rambouillet, outside Paris, in late July 1960, when de Gaulle presented his vision of a united Western Europe in greater detail. This meeting, second in importance only to the first encounter at Colombey, was the beginning of an extraordinary 30–month *pas de deux* – combining periods of harmony with minor quarrels and irritations – between these two statesmen, last heirs of a nineteenth-century European political culture which sharply distinguished the secular from the religious, and thus was able to be both profoundly democratic and traditionally Catholic at the same

---

[2]  Schwarz, *Die Ära Adenauer, 1957–1963*, 104–7.
[3]  Lacouture, *De Gaulle*, 3:298.

time. Rambouillet was a magnificent example of de Gaulle's use of historical settings. He himself wrote in his autobiography:

I had developed a liking for the latter [Rambouillet] as a site for such meetings, Versailles, Compiegne and Fontainebleau, by reason of their size, being unsuitable for restricted gatherings. Housed in the medieval tower, where so many of our kings had stayed, passing through the apartments once occupied by our Valois, our Bourbons, our emperors, our presidents, deliberating in the ancient hall of marble with the French Head of State and his ministers, admiring the grandeur of the ornamental lakes stretched out before their eyes, strolling through the park and the forest in which for ten centuries the rites of official shooting and hunting parties had been performed, our guests were made to feel the nobility behind the geniality, the permanence beyond the vicissitudes, of the nation which was their host.[4]

De Gaulle used the atmosphere of tradition and the ambiance of power to surprise Adenauer with a much more far-reaching proposal for West European integration than the German leader expected. De Gaulle proposed an organized cooperation of the two states in the areas of diplomatic, defense and economic affairs – in effect, he resurrected the plans for a European political community of 1952–3, but restricted them to France and West Germany only. The French president combined this proposal with a reform of NATO which would put an end to what he referred to as American integration, by which he meant European dependence on American security guarantees. Instead he proposed Europe for the Europeans, with a Franco-West German political union with a common defense and foreign policy as its mainstay. The members of the EEC would be restricted to economic cooperation, whereas their political activity would be conducted by their national governments, with the Franco-German union as the overwhelmingly dominant player. De Gaulle coupled this proposal with the resurrection of the idea of a directorate of three – France, Germany and Great Britain – to replace either NATO as a whole or, at least, American predominance in the making of strategy and political decisions within the Alliance. Each member of this directorate would have equal influence on the military strategy and defense policies that affected all.

Adenauer was initially skeptical. Then, as de Gaulle continued to expand and press the case for a restructuring and revitalization of West European security and unity, the West German leader became more enthusiastic. On the last day of the meeting, July 30, 1960, de Gaulle presented Adenauer with a nine-point memorandum. Here, for the first

[4] De Gaulle, *Memoirs of Hope*, 210–11.

time since 1954, Adenauer found his hopes for a European defense community restated in a new form, and by the ruler of the country that had rejected the earlier version. In this memorandum de Gaulle abandoned the idea of a directorate of the three Western allies, and suggested instead a European defense union based on the combined political and economic strength of France and West Germany. When Adenauer responded that the Americans remained indispensable because no coalition or union of West European states could resist Soviet expansionism, de Gaulle replied that if NATO were not immediately reformed, France would leave in three months.[5]

It was an astonishing proposal. Taking de Gaulle's ideas as a serious basis for discussion on European security was to reject all that NATO and three US administrations had built in Europe. Adenauer was vulnerable to the French blandishments because, since late 1958, he suspected that the US would ultimately prove unreliable and be willing to compromise West German interests in order to appease Khrushchev. So he left Rambouillet believing that something could be made of the French plan. Yet, back in Bonn, he soon realized that de Gaulle's plan was impossible for Germany. Unreliable or not, the Americans had to remain the mainstay of German security; France was simply not strong enough. Also, though de Gaulle played with ideas of a Franco-West German union, he believed in a *Europe des patries* (Europe of nations), that was incompatible with Adenauer's conception of full political integration and rejection of the sovereignty of the old national states in economic and political matters. France would never submit to the only kind of union Adenauer and the Germans could seriously consider, namely one that overrode national interests. In the sober and heavy atmosphere of the Rhine river in August, and surrounded, in Bonn, by the advice of Brentano, Blankenhorn, the German ambassador to Paris, and others, Adenauer, to de Gaulle's annoyance, returned to the American fold. Thus, Rambouillet had produced incomparable atmosphere, but nothing tangible, either on NATO or on Western European integration. Yet symbols and atmosphere are always important in politics, as no one knew better than de Gaulle. He did not persuade the Germans to join his union, and perhaps he never intended them to, but he had shown them a way forward that was not the American way. That path became a permanent temptation for some West German politicians.

In 1960–1 the US also faced the challenge of the new French nuclear capability and of the broader French attempt to lure the Germans onto new paths of European security. In October 1960, less than a month

[5] Schwarz, *Die Ära Adenauer, 1957–1963*, 114–18.

before John F. Kennedy won the election for president, General Lauris Norstad, the NATO supreme commander, proposed a nuclear force made up of contingents from various NATO countries and based on US-supplied ballistic-missile submarines. In May 1961, President Kennedy elaborated on this proposal for a multilateral force (MLF), composed of US nuclear-armed submarines manned by NATO contingents.

From then on until late 1964 the MLF was at the center of arguments over how to preserve European security. The purpose of the MLF was political as well as military. Politically, it was designed to satisfy growing French and West German ambitions and, in particular, the wishes of some West Germans, including Adenauer and Strauss, for some access to the control of nuclear weapons and nuclear decisions. The Americans hoped that the MLF, by giving the French direct influence on NATO nuclear planning, would discourage their development of the *force de frappe*. As far as the Germans were concerned, they hoped to satisfy both the Straussians, who wanted a direct German role in nuclear deterrence, and the up-and-coming SPD strategists like Erler and Schmidt who were advocating that all NATO nuclear weapons be sea-based. Militarily, the sea-based MLF was designed to help fill the gap that had resulted since the mid-1950s from Soviet deployment of IRBMs in Central Europe and the USSR; deployment that, just as the SS-20 deployment did much later, in the 1970s, threatened to drive a wedge between NATO's tactical nuclear and conventional deterrent on the one hand, and the US strategic umbrella and the threat of massive retaliation on the other. In fact, the Soviet IRBMs, coupled with the Soviet ICBMs that began to appear in the early 1960s, and the concomitant abandonment by the United States of active air defense of its own territory against Soviet bombers, were undermining the concept of massive retaliation. The result was a process of adjustment in the United States, and within NATO, from a situation of undeniable Western nuclear supremacy to one of at least potential strategic balance and Soviet conventional superiority. It presaged the strategy of flexible response first proposed by the US in 1961, but not adopted by European NATO members until 1967.

During 1960–1 the French and German governments continued to discuss closer cooperation, albeit not to the extent contemplated in de Gaulle's Rambouillet plan. De Gaulle faced a referendum in France in early January 1961 on his policy of granting Algeria independence. In fact the referendum was more than that; it was a general verdict on the first three years of de Gaulle's presidency. The result was a splendid victory for him. Adenauer then rediscovered his earlier confidence in the wisdom and reliability of the French president. He was the more tempted to lean to de Gaulle, given his doubts about the experience and reliability of the new US administration of John Kennedy, which took power almost simultaneously.

In 1961, de Gaulle continued to argue to the Germans that a move away from the United States and NATO by France, and, hopefully by others, could very well lead to detente with the Soviet Union. De Gaulle viewed the Soviet Union as a Russian national state with reasonable security aspirations that could be fulfilled if NATO were weakened. Thus, his policy was to fragment NATO to show the Soviet government that Western Europe did not intend to be part of any threat to Soviet security in Eastern Europe, to win Soviet confidence, and then to move toward some sort of general European state system – detente, entente, cooperation – which would embrace West Germany's interests in Central Europe.

De Gaulle was anything but anti-German, and his European vision was, in some respects, close to that of Egon Bahr and other proponents of social democratic Ostpolitik in the 1970s and 1980s. In 1959 de Gaulle had spoken on the German problem:

The reunification of the two parts into a single Germany, which would be entirely free, seems to us the normal destiny of the German people, provided they do not reopen the question of their present frontiers to the West, the East, the North and the South, and that they move toward integrating themselves one day in a contractual organization of all Europe for cooperation, liberty, and peace. But, pending the time when this ideal can be achieved, we believe that the two separated sections of the German people should be able to multiply the ties and relations between themselves in all practical fields. Transport, communications, economic activity, literature, science, the arts, the goings and comings of people, etc., would be the subject of arrangements which would bring together the Germans within and for the benefit of that which I would call "Germanness" and which, after all, is common to them, in spite of differences in regimes and conditions.[6]

Although de Gaulle probably did not know it, his vision corresponded, virtually word for word, with that of the leading strategist of the SPD, Herbert Wehner. During the summer and fall of 1960, Wehner, Erler, and Brandt completed the reorientation of the SPD's foreign and defense policy by accepting NATO, the Common Market, and the Federal Republic's existing foreign commitments and orientation as beneficial and desirable in themselves, and as the foundation of their own foreign policy. Though Wehner did not state it clearly, that vision

[6] Republic of France, *Major Addresses of Charles de Gaulle*, Press Conference, March 25, 1959.

behind that foreign policy would increasingly emerge, in the 1960s, as a close analogue to de Gaulle's vision of closer contact between East and West based on acceptance of the existing facts. In what turned out to be an important address to the Bundestag on June 30, Wehner, speaking for the SPD, accepted NATO and the Paris Treaties as the starting-point of any discussion of Germany's international relations, and when the SPD held its annual convention in Hannover thereafter, it issued a statement supporting the Bundeswehr.

As late as July 1959, Fritz Erler had written in a memorandum that "the SPD will continue the battle against a nuclearized Bundeswehr." However, he also reminded his comrades that if the SPD wanted to change defense policy, it first had to recognize realities, including the Bundeswehr: "The army must not become a power factor in political controversies." In 1959–60 he and Schmidt had continued their search for a viable defense policy. The first fruit of that search was Wehner's speech. "The SPD, Wehner asserted, recognized NATO as the guarantor of peace in Europe . . . the socialists would accept the government's position that free elections were the first (rather than the last) step toward reunification."[7]

This speech was a milestone in West German history. Even though Strauss immediately objected that the SPD had not yet accepted conscription, the turning-point was clearly reached. Erler responded to the debate on Wehner's speech with a memorandum of his own, setting forth the new SPD view that the West needed both "deterrence *and* and effective defense. . . . A defense against local aggression . . . must be constructed so that even without nuclear weapons it presents unacceptable risks to an aggressor. . . . NATO units must be equipped so they are not dependent on nuclear weapons." He pointed out that the Bundeswehr had obtained American dual-purpose rockets, but without the nuclear warheads. This was a serious mistake, he said: "They are too inaccurate to have military value at the conventional level; they therefore invite an early resort to nuclear warheads in a conflict. If the Bundeswehr is equipped with weapon systems that are militarily useless without atomic warheads, then it can only be concluded that these atomic warheads are going to be used in a conflict. Otherwise, you have given troops a revolver with no ammunition."[8]

Schmidt elaborated on these points in a book he was writing at the time, published in English as *Defense or Retaliation: a German View*, that summarized what he had learned over the previous four to five years. "The SPD, he argued, must push for a conventional buildup of the

[7] Cited in Cioc, *Pax Atomica*, 155, 158.
[8] Ibid., 160.

Bundeswehr in order to eliminate the rationale for tactical nuclear warheads."[9] Schmidt and Erler were *au courant* with the American strategists who rejected the, by now, rather old New Look, in favor of a new concept they called "flexible response." Like Weizsäcker, whom he respected, Schmidt advocated a Bundeswehr of highly mobile, conventional forces, supported by preferably sea-based intermediate-range nuclear missiles. The existing land-based IRBMs should be removed. Such missiles in densely populated regions like Germany were a mistake. This was exactly Weizsäcker's and the left's position 20 years later, during the second missile debate between 1979 and 1983. But in the intervening two decades, Schmidt changed his mind.

At the party convention in Hannover in November 1960, the SPD chose the governing mayor of Berlin, Willy Brandt, to be its candidate for chancellor in the federal elections of 1961. Brandt stated at the time that he would abide by the Bundestag's March 1958 resolution, interpreting it to mean that the Bundeswehr should not have nuclear weapons. He also said he planned to reject the GCND approach completely and operate within the parameters of Adenauer's foreign policy, which he praised. At the convention, he introduced a defense resolution that was the final stage on the SPD's road to accepting reality, in order to change it. "West Germany needs the protection of NATO, to which it will loyally fulfill its obligations," the mayor of Berlin stated; adding that West Germany should "not push for the nuclearization of the Bundeswehr."[10]

The SPD left-wing was very angry at what it regarded as a betrayal, but Brandt, Erler, and Schmidt remained firm and even Ollenhauer did not give the left any encouragement. The anti-nuclear, neutralist left had dominated the party from 1953 to 1959; it had every chance to put its policies into practice, but it had failed to win the support of the German electorate and bring the party to power. Throughout 1958, Schmidt and Brandt had loyally supported the GCND. It was Erler who had persistently and stubbornly worked to change the foundations of party policy, and he had succeeded. It was Germany's, and the party's, great loss that he never lived to serve his country in government; he died in 1967.

By late 1960, the "young Adenauerians" had overcome their comrades' inveterate tendency to back political positions long after they had been proved unacceptable to the voters: "As in the Weimar era, socialist leaders celebrated every parliamentary defeat as a moral triumph, interpreted every election loss as proof that their policies were

[9] Ibid., 162.
[10] Cited ibid., 165.

correct, wrung their hands over Germany's predicament without taking charge of affairs themselves."[11] That 80–year-old tradition was about to end.

Looking back on those days, symbolic of so much of the struggle for freedom and democracy in Germany, the journalist, editor, historian, and transatlantic public figure, Melvin Lasky, wrote in 1977, following a visit to Berlin:

Since the dramatic days of the Blockade and the Wall (August 1961), the moves in the East–West struggle for the Spree [the river running through Berlin] have been small, simple, but nonetheless systematic. I remember talking in the early 1950s with Mayor Ernst Reuter, and I expressed my doubts whether the Western Allies, always changing commanding generals and general-consuls, surrounded by foreign correspondents whose political education dates back to last week, would remember in 20 or 30 years time what the basic issues were all about. Would they know what the struggle for Steinstücken was (in which the Western Allies "almost went to war" for a handkerchief-sized enclave of West Berlin along the Havel River)? or the battle for the Masuren-Allee (in which they finally reclaimed the Soviet-held radio-broadcasting building in the British sector)? or the dozens of conflicts at Dreilinden (in order to keep the flow of traffic moving between Western Germany and Free Berlin some hundred miles behind what used to be known as – although it still is – the Iron Curtain)? Ernst Reuter was an optimist. As a former general-secretary of the German Communist Party, and with first-hand experience of Lenin in Moscow, he knew that the wheels of revolution turn slowly. "They never forget," he used to insist, "and they never give up. . . ." Each tiny issue was important. Every absurd technicality had to be watched like a hawk. "Oh, it will be hard for us – we who believe in prudence and moderation and compromise – to wear stony faces and feign implacability. But we will and we must. I do not believe Berlin will be betrayed, or abandoned. But then no piece of it, and no paragraph of its rights, no matter how ambiguous or dubious, has to be given up. For a Bolshevik chess-master each pawn is involved in the ultimate checkmate. . . ."[12]

---

[11] Ibid., 175.
[12] Lasky, "Journey among the 'Ugly Germans'" (first published 1977). *Encounter*, Pamphlet no. 17 (1987): 56.

# 17

# The Berlin Wall

The election of a new US president, John F. Kennedy, who took office
in January 1961, posed new problems for Adenauer. He did not
respect what he considered to be inconsistencies in Kennedy's declared
foreign policy positions. The great age difference between the two men
made him uneasy, and it appeared that the leader of the United States
would be susceptible to pressure and therefore inclined to make concessions to the Soviet government.

The "young Adenauerians" in the SPD and FDP, on the other hand,
were pleased with the new government in Washington, and Brandt in
particular admired the American leader whose politics were closer to his
own. There were direct ties between Brandt's wing of the SPD and
President Kennedy's supporters in the Democratic Party in the United
States, and of a kind that had not been politically possible during Eisenhower's administration. At the same time, Brandt's views on Berlin and
the division of Germany were rapidly becoming the position of the SPD
in general, and this strengthened his credibility as a leading spokesman
for the SPD in West Germany and abroad. Brandt's views were also,
however, the reflection of the new orientation given the SPD by the
Godesberg Program, and by Herbert Wehner's Bundestag speech in
June 1960, accepting NATO and the EEC as the foundation of West
German foreign policy – thus implicitly rejecting the strategy of reunification through neutralization and East–West troop withdrawals,
that had been predominant since the death of Schumacher.

Only one month following Kennedy's inauguration in January 1961,
Khrushchev declared that the Berlin problem must finally be solved.
During the spring Soviet pressure on West Germany and the United
States increased. In early June Khrushchev and Kennedy met in Vienna,
and the communist leader once again addressed the German question:
"The USSR deems it necessary in the interests of consolidating peace
formally to recognize the situation which has developed in Europe after

the war, to legalize and to consolidate the inviolability of the existing German borders, to normalize the situation in West Berlin on the basis of reasonable consideration for the interests of all parties concerned."[1] If the West refused to enter into such an agreement, and to demilitarize West Berlin as an independent "free city" within six months, Khrushchev threatened once again, as he had in 1958 and 1960, to sign a peace treaty with the GDR, which, he insisted, would unilaterally abolish Western rights in Berlin.

Kennedy's response was outwardly firm. In February, he had called Dean Acheson from retirement to direct military and political planning of US policy on Berlin and instructed him to prepare plans to use force, if necessary, to defend the Western positions. Acheson, who had played a leading role in assuring the US commitment to the security of Western Europe in 1950–2, and who symbolized Western realism and the Western will to resist Soviet encroachments, coordinated his strategy in close consultation with Adenauer and Strauss. Ultimately, however, the Germans and their allies found themselves in an exceedingly difficult, if not untenable position. If they elected force to defend their rights in Berlin, they faced virtually insurmountable logistical obstacles, as the blockade of Berlin during 1948–9 had so well illustrated. At the same time, while evacuation of the city was always a possibility, it too was an unacceptable solution. Although this easy way out was suggested by the extreme left in West Germany during the crisis, the West German government and the Western Allies remained committed to the defense of Berlin. The unanswered questions in this regard were: what should be defended, under what circumstances, and with what means?

There were differences of opinion in the American camp too, and this resulted in compromise. Acheson, who, probably rightly, saw Khrushchev's Berlin thrust as part of a general offensive designed to humiliate the West and inflict a global political defeat on the United States,[2] recommended strong measures in the spring of 1961: the proclamation of a state of national emergency in the US (in July the US Senate gave President Kennedy the authority to call up 250,000 reservists), transfer of three divisions to Germany, and, if the access routes to Berlin were closed, a thrust of military troops into East Germany. Others, who included the secretary of state, Dean Rusk, the former ambassador to Moscow and special envoy, W. Averell Harriman, and yet another figure from the Roosevelt-Truman era, Charles Bohlen, counseled negotiations. Kennedy's public statements, while seeming unambiguous,

---

[1] Dept of State, *Documents on Germany*, 730.
[2] Cf. Ulam, *The Rivals*, 294–312.

CONSOLIDATION AND DIVISION, 1955–1961

actually reflected the dovish view that the stakes in Berlin were not all that high and that Khrushchev's main concern was to consolidate his hold in East Germany and not to defeat and discredit the US globally. Kennedy carefully spoke of West Berlin and declined to assert any Western interest in Berlin as a whole, clearly implying that Khrushchev could behave as he pleased in the Soviet sector.

In early August, the NATO Council asserted the "three essentials" in Berlin which the West would, presumably, defend: (1) the presence of Western troops in (the Western sectors of) the city, (2) freedom of transit between Berlin and the Federal Republic, and (3) the survival of West Berlin via maintenance of its economic, cultural and political ties to West Germany. In his "Report To The Nation" in July 1961 President Kennedy outlined these three essentials:

> We are there [in Berlin] as a result of our victory over Nazi Germany, and our basic rights to be there deriving from that victory include both our presence in West Berlin and the enjoyment of access across East Germany. These rights have been repeatedly confirmed. . . . But in addition to those rights is our commitment to sustain – and defend, if need be – the opportunity for more than two million people to determine their own future and choose their own way of life.
>
> Thus our presence in West Berlin, and our access thereto, cannot be ended by any act of the Soviet Government. . . . an attack in that city will be regarded as an attack upon us all. . . .
>
> We cannot and will not permit the Communists to drive us out of Berlin, either gradually or by force.[3]

Undoubtedly the Soviet government and Ulbricht, the head of the SED, noted that Kennedy spoke carefully of *West* Berlin, and of an attack "in that city," that is, across the sector borders, rather than "on that city," which would have implied that the US was serious about objecting to the GDR presence in East Berlin – a presence that clearly violated the four-power agreements on Germany which the Soviets declared to be defunct. The president defined the Western interest as security of the Western sectors and their two million people – not as maintaining the four-power fiction for all of Berlin subject to quadripartite authority, or as ejecting Ulbricht from East Berlin. Ulbricht concluded correctly that the West was not concerned with the fate of East Berlin and would do nothing to oppose any measures taken by the Soviets or the German communists outside the Western sectors. He had first proposed a barbed-wire ring around West Berlin to a meeting of the Warsaw Pact states in March. By summer the mounting number of refugees from the GDR crossing the open sector borders in Berlin forced Ulbricht to a

[3] Dept of State, *Documents on Germany*, 763–4.

decision. On August 5, the Soviet government approved building a wall around all of West Berlin.[4]

Amid the diplomatic exchanges and public clarification, that the Western Allies would defend Berlin if necessary, rumors spread in the West that the Soviets and the GDR were planning something dramatic in Berlin. In June, Ulbricht had publicly stated: "Nobody intends to put up a wall." On the same occasion he repeated Khrushchev's claim that "West Berlin forms part of the territory of the GDR." When a reporter asked him why Germans from the East could not travel freely to the West, Ulbricht put the blame on Adenauer and accused him of raising an "iron curtain."[5] During the first half of August alone, over 16,000 persons crossed the Soviet sector border to the Western sectors. In the early hours of Sunday, August 13, 1961, the counterstroke began. East German workers under the guard of East German police sealed off the border between the Soviet sector of Berlin and the three Western sectors, and West Berlin's border with the GDR.

The Western powers did not react for almost 24 hours. President Kennedy was at his country home in Hyannisport, Massachusetts. Harold Macmillan was also on vacation. In the Pentagon, officials held plans for counterattack in readiness, but received no orders to act. During the morning, Brandt tried to get a promise of action from the Western commandants in Berlin. In the afternoon he called a special session of the Berlin house of representatives where he stated that he had received a promise of action from Dean Rusk, the American secretary of state:

The measures ordered and begun by the Ulbricht regime at the suggestion of the Warsaw Pact states to cut off the Soviet zone and the Soviet sector from West Berlin are an outrageous injustice. They mean that right through Berlin there runs not only a sort of state border, but the barrier of a concentration camp. With the approval of the Eastern bloc states the Ulbricht regime is aggravating the situation around Berlin, transgressing yet again all legal bonds and commands of humanity. The Senate [government] of Berlin denounces before all the world the illegal and inhuman measures taken by those who divide Germany, oppress East Berlin, and threaten West Berlin. . . .

I have requested the commandants to take action in the territory for which they are responsible and to propose to their governments to undertake energetic steps vis-à-vis the government of the Soviet Union. . . .

I surely speak for the honorable assembly and in the name of the entire population of Berlin when I express the opinion that mere protests will not be enough.[6]

[4] Weber, *Die DDR 1945–1986*, 54–5.
[5] Dept of State, *Documents on Germany*, 737.
[6] Cited in Brandt and Ammon, *Die Linke und die nationale Frage*, 199.

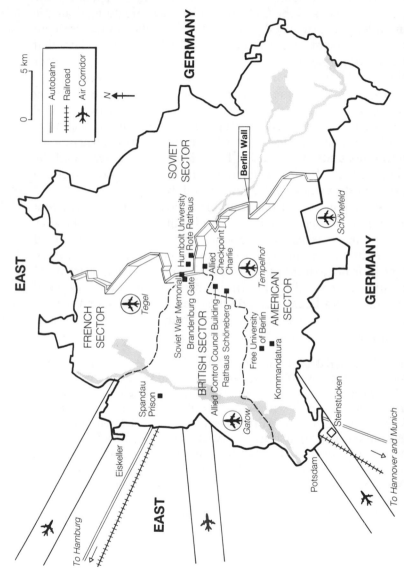

Map 1.9    Berlin after the Wall. This map illustrates the division of Berlin into an eastern and western part following the Soviet decision to build the Berlin Wall in 1961.
*Source:* Bark, *Agreement on Berlin,* frontispiece

The next day Brandt sent a letter by special messenger to President Kennedy, reminding him of solemn US obligations to protect its own legal rights in Germany and the interests of democratic Germans. Kennedy responded on August 17 in a letter to Brandt, which was not made public until 1985. The president declared that, while the US clearly sympathized with the Berliners and agreed that the wall was an outrage, he could not recommend military action to tear it down. In his memoirs Brandt describes his feelings on reading this message, and his resulting conviction, that the primary goal of Western policy must henceforth not be to try to uphold claims, but to recognize that the communist regimes were not going to disappear and that the cause of peace therefore demanded negotiations with the Soviet Union and the GDR.

I said later that in August 1961 a curtain was drawn aside to reveal an empty stage. To put it more bluntly, we lost certain illusions that had outlived the hopes underlying them – illusions that clung to something that no longer existed in fact. Ulbricht had been allowed to take a swipe at the Western super-power, and the United States merely winced with annoyance. My political deliberations in the years that followed were substantially influenced by this day's experience, and it was against this background that my so-called Ostpolitik – the beginning of detente – took shape. . . . My new and inescapable realization was that traditional patterns of Western policy had proved in-effective, if not downright unrealistic.[7]

The GDR regime also changed its policies after the Wall, and this was not without eventual significance for the actions and attitudes of West Germans. Until the Wall, the primary purpose of the regime in the East had been the establishment of a Stalinist political system based on ideological conformity, mass indoctrination supported by political repression and imprisonment, and control of individual thought and behavior. Immediately after the Wall the SED intensified these measures – which amounted to terror – persecuting those it defined as "enemies of the state and shirkers," people who, before August 13, would have been able to escape, but now could not. The regime maintained this policy of the "hard fist" until Khrushchev, at the twenty-second congress of the Soviet communist party of October 1961, initiated a new phase of de-Stalinization. The Soviet party secretary denounced Stalin's use of constant terror or threats of terror as a means of keeping order, and Ulbricht followed suit. In 1956, after the twentieth party congress when Khrushchev had first denounced Stalin, Ulbricht had pointedly refused to go along. On November 28, 1961, by contrast,

[7] Brandt, *People and Politics*, 20.

*Neues Deutschland*, the organ of the SED, even wrote of "crimes" committed "under Stalin's leadership."[8]

From then on the SED began restricting its use of force against those it regarded as enemies, preferring ideological indoctrination to neutralize the ability of dissidents to spread discontent. "The people, who could no longer simply depart, had to come to terms with the regime . . . there was no alternative for the inhabitants of the GDR after the wall went up, they had to make do. That made it easier for the GDR leadership to reach its goal: many people now tried to make the best of their situation; by making greater efforts they tried both to raise their standard of living and to get promotions . . . the material improvements reduced the force of dissident feelings, the relations between the leadership and the population gradually took on a more normal character."[9]

The regime began to experiment with new ways of modernizing the economy, while not abandoning the ideological tenets of Marxism-Leninism and, in the German context, the claim that the GDR represented the future and the Federal Republic the imperialist, reactionary past. Having made the point that it was permanent, the GDR now prepared for a long period of peaceful coexistence in Germany. For some years it made a "German confederation" its goal, as proposed by the Soviet Union since 1958. As long as Bonn maintained the Hallstein Doctrine and the claim to sole representation (*Alleinvertretungsanspruch*) and refused to recognize the GDR, this SED line was mainly effective as a means of keeping domestic order. While advocating a confederation, the SED continued to proclaim in public that the division of Germany was caused by the imperialist machinations of the United States and its West German puppets.

In reality the Wall protected the GDR government from itself:

As Ulbricht reasoned, the Wall would act like a kind of protective womb, isolating citizens and restricting their options while creating the ideal situation under which they might become convinced believers in the GDR's cause. In a remarkably revealing speech he explained: "With the measures of 13 August, we have created a kind of 'Cordon sanitaire,' a convalescent girdle which surrounds the frontline swamp of West Berlin."[10]

In the words of Ernst Lemmer, however, the minister for all-German affairs in 1961, the Wall accomplished something else:

[T]he sealing-off measures . . . have now converted the barrier between the communist-ruled and the free part of Germany into a prison wall. A wall which

---

[8]  Weber, *Die DDR 1945–1986*, 57.
[9]  Ibid.
[10]  McAdams, *East Germany and Detente*, 31.

separates married couples, which prevents children who are minors from reaching their parents. . . .

Defenceless refugees, who can no longer stand the Communist reign of terror and who in desparation try to break out of their huge prison, are shot down. Before the eyes of all the murderers cruelly leave their wounded victims to their fate, until they have died a painful death. . . .[11]

From January 1, 1961, to the building of the Wall almost 160,000 people fled to West Berlin. Within 24 hours, before the Wall was erected on August 12, some 2,400 refugees from the Soviet sector and the Soviet zone of occupation arrived at the emergency reception center in West Berlin. From August 13 to December 31, 1961, however, that number was dramatically reduced, to practically zero. The trickle continued to be reduced as the Wall became more and more difficult to climb. It represented, indeed, a formidable obstacle: the actual Wall at that time was 9.4 miles in length and consisted of about 85 miles of barbed wire entanglements (almost 7000 miles of barbed wire were used) and about 600,000 square yards of aisles through forests, death strips and guarded zones; 163 watch towers were also built in and around Berlin.

With the improvements to the Wall, as the barbed wire was replaced with concrete, came more deaths. In fact, the most appalling murder occurred in August 1962, just one year later:

On 17 August, 1962, towards 14.12 hours [2:12 p. m.], two 18-year-old youths attempted to reach West Berlin by climbing over the Wall in Zimmer-strasse (Soviet Sector), between Charlotten- and Markgrafenstrasse. They were discovered and fired upon by Soviet zonal border guards. While one of them succeeded in reaching West Berlin unhurt, the 18-year-old Peter Fechter, last resident in Berlin-Weissensee, Beheimstrasse 11, was hit and lay severely wounded between the barbed wire and the Wall.

West Berlin police threw bandage material across to him, but owing to weakness he was unable to make any use of it. . . .

The wounded boy was left lying on the Soviet sector side of the Wall for over an hour without any help being brought to him. He was then carried away by border guards without a stretcher. It is presumed that he was already dead.[12]

The building of the Berlin Wall, so quick and so final, drew a curtain across divided Berlin that was of barbed wire, stone, and death. It also demonstrated that the human capacity for evil in Germany – done unto Germans by Germans – had not died with the Third Reich. There seemed to be nothing that would, or could, be done about it, and,

[11] Federal Ministry for All-German Questions, *Violations of Human Rights*, 5–6 and *Flights from the Soviet Zone* 13, 15.
[12] Ibid., 21, 38.

therefore, its finality was all the more effective and grotesque. The inability, or decision, to do nothing about it, produced frustration, and born of that, a reassessment of what was possible. More and more people, both in Western Europe and America, began to see negotiations as the solution where the policy of strength had failed. This was the origin of the belief in detente, and condemnation of the Cold War. Indeed, as time passed, judgement of the Wall altered too. For some it became a macabre monument to the failure of socialism, and a real prison gate guarding its prisoners who attempted to pass. For others, such as American economist John Kenneth Galbraith, it represented a pillar of detente. In a famous interview with *Die Zeit*, in 1968, Galbraith was asked the question:

Professor, we are holding this conversation here in view of the Berlin Wall, which has been built by a state that has socialism written on its flag. Don't you believe that in this case an essential difference between the two systems is expressed?

Galbraith: "I think the Wall is a good thing. At any rate, it has preserved peace."[13]

The second Berlin crisis was the high point of the Soviet diplomatic and political offensive, and was truly the last step to division of the country. It also defined anew the German question as it was set in 1945; namely, the problem of how to persuade the Soviet Union to permit German reunification. This crisis showed everyone, including Adenauer himself, that the Soviet government opposed reunification unless it was to be achieved on its own terms. The final step of the crisis, of actually building a wall to separate people, was reviled throughout the world. But it also created a new reality of European affairs. A real wall physically divided Berlin, and real minefields physically divided Germany.[14] If the West was not prepared to remove the Wall, the only alternative was to redefine the terms guiding relations between East and West Germany, and between Eastern and Western Europe. And this is exactly what happened. In 1961 it was too late for Adenauer himself to draw the consequences. He was retiring, but there were others who could, notably the new SPD leader Willy Brandt. How they changed the terms of the German question and found what they regarded as a practical approach, is the subject of the 1960s.

[13] *Die Zeit*, July 5, 1968.
[14] The total length of the inner-German border was 1,393 km.

# 18

# The 1961 Elections

In 1960, Erich Mende replaced Reinhold Maier as FDP party chairman. When Mende became a member of the Bundestag in 1949, the FDP was a curious amalgam of free-market liberals who did not like the sectarian, Catholic orientation of the early CDU and national liberals. The latter group rejected both the CDU's mix of religion and politics, and the SPD's socialism, but was nevertheless strongly nationalistic and, to some extent, neutralist. Initially, Mende did not belong to this group, and from 1949 to 1957 his reputation was that of a leader of the liberal faction critical of the coalition with the CDU. He changed his position somewhat following the rearmament debate of 1952–4, and the debates of 1956–7 over the Rapacki Plan and Pfleiderer's suggestions for a new Ostpolitik, both of which found wide support among the younger members of the FDP, those who came to exert increasing influence on the party after 1967. He began to worry about the possible neutralist and pacifist tendencies of the party's left wing and began moving back toward the idea of a coalition with the CDU – but one without Adenauer, who increasingly became anathema to the FDP.

Opposition to Adenauer's leadership within the party contributed to the development of the career of one of Germany's most influential figures, Rudolf Augstein, the editor and publisher of *Der Spiegel*, and also to the changing nature of German politics in the 1950s. He joined the FDP in 1955, after having opposed rearmament in 1952–4, and quickly identified with its left wing under Dehler, who was a close friend. After Dehler's loss of influence in 1957, Augstein began a campaign in his journal on behalf of Dehler's strategy for a coalition with the SPD, a new Ostpolitik, and neutralism. By 1961 it became clear that the pro-SPD forces in the party were still too weak to bring about a coalition, should the SPD and the FDP produce a strong showing in the fourth Bundestag elections, scheduled for October 1961. Augstein, therefore, began to attack and vilify Mende as a traitor to the true aim of the FDP, which, in Augstein's view was to support the SPD, and lead the way to a new Ostpolitik of accepting the status quo asserted by the Soviet Union. When the election campaign began Mende was hoping for a coalition with the CDU, but also expected the CDU to pay a price for his support. That price was to be Adenauer's resignation and Erhard's appointment as chancellor.

The SPD went into the elections on a rising tide of popular confidence. Wehner, Erler, and Brandt had declared the SPD's support of NATO, Western integration, and Allied security policies, while refusing nuclear weapons for the Bundeswehr. Brandt's government of Berlin, and especially his denunciations of the Wall, further helped spread the impression that the SPD was finally and firmly on the side of the West. At the same time, Adenauer's inability to force Allied action against the Wall led many to question the efficiency of the CDU strategy for dealing with the German question. After twelve years of CDU/CSU government, many also felt a vague, but real need for change. As a result, the SPD made its greatest single gain thus far in a national election: 4.4 percentage points, for a 36.2 per cent share of the total vote. The CDU remained the largest party, but slipped almost five percentage points to 45.4 per cent, losing the absolute majority and making a coalition necessary for the first time since the election of 1953. The FDP experienced its best result since 1949 with 12.8 per cent, a gain of slightly more than five percentage points.

For the first time since 1949 the steady underswell of change in the views of the electorate manifested itself. The CDU was on a downward slide; twelve years of power had produced signs of wear and exhaustion. The party seemed short of ideas on foreign and German policy. Equally obvious was the fact that West Germany under CDU government had more than doubled its real gross national product between 1949 and 1961, and that the real income of virtually all West Germans was more than twice what it had been when Adenauer took office.

The election result created a new situation. An SPD/FDP coalition was possible, and the FDP left wanted it. On the other hand, the precedents were not good; the FDP had suffered a disastrous defeat in North Rhine-Westphalia after two years of coalition with the SPD, and the SPD had profited as a result. It seemed as though the FDP suffered whenever it was in a coalition, but perhaps less with the CDU than with the SPD.

After the election, therefore, Mende abandoned his demand that Adenauer resign at once and accepted the 85–year-old chancellor's promise that he would step down after two years. Thomas Dehler, who had hoped for a coalition with the SPD, was sarcastic. The FDP, he said, had only one of three bad choices: "To capitulate, to be excluded, or to be bamboozled."[1] After hearing of this betrayal, as he saw it, Rudolf Augstein's attacks on Mende reached new heights. *Spiegel* journalists were not noted for moderate or soft-spoken commentary, and aggressively attacked Mende. They derisively referred to him as "the FDP Major," using his former military rank to imply that he had an authoritarian or unsavory character. The German word *umfallen* can mean either "fall down" or "give in," and the *Spiegel* journalists made endless fun of Mende's surrender to Adenauer using this double meaning. According to a joke which they reported with relish, Mende's wife, Margot, used to wake her husband up by calling, "Time to get up and advance your career, Erich!", but now she called, "Time to get up and fall down [or give in], Erich!" The opening passage of the article reporting on, but actually denouncing, Mende's first appearance before the newly elected Bundestag is a good example of the inimitable *Spiegel* style:

Derisive laughter echoed through the fully occupied plenary hall of the Upper House [Bundestag] in Bonn. FDP Major Erich Mende, summoned by Bundestag Speaker Dr Eugen Gerstenmaier, marched with wooden steps from his deputy's seat to the podium, his curly head held stubbornly high and his thin lips compressed. Mende pressed both clenched fists against the podium. His well-trained pastor's voice vibrated nervously as he ... voluntarily put into the record how willingly he can fall down and give in.[2]

Thus, in 1961, the FDP returned to a coalition with the CDU under Adenauer, which in 1956 they had never expected to do again. Mende and his allies since 1956, the national liberal faction, had won, but it was their last victory. The internal struggles of 1957–61 and the divisive arguments of 1961, fueled by Augstein's constant drumfire in the background, left a bad feeling in the party and permanently weakened its right wing. In fact, however, the FDP and, by extension, the SPD, did well in the coalition talks in 1961. Mende and his "young Turks" succeeded in breaking the CDU's hold on foreign and defense policy. Thereafter, the FDP participated in every federal government except the grand coalition of 1966–9. From 1961 onward, the party gained a growing measure of influence on foreign and defense policy until, in 1969, one of its members became foreign minister, a post of vital importance it still held 20 years later.

[1] Cited in Cioc, *Pax Atomica*, 182.
[2] *Der Spiegel*, no. 44, October 25, 1961.

# PART V

# The End of the Adenauer Era, 1961–1963

*History has given our generation the task of uniting Europe. . . . Europe will not become poorer but richer by uniting.*

Foreign Minister Gerhard Schröder, July 4, 1962

# Introduction

L eading Christian democrats and social democrats read the election result of September 1961 as a suggestion, from the German people, for change: the CDU majority was gone, the SPD continued its ascent in the polls that began after the 1953 election. Following the election, Herbert Wehner, the SPD's leading strategist, proposed a grand coalition with the CDU as a means of introducing the SPD to power. Strauss, Freiherr von und zu Guttenberg (1921–1972), Heinrich Krone, and others from the Catholic and south German wings of the CDU/CSU agreed. In fact, they were unable to bring about the coalition at this time, over the opposition of the north German Protestants in the CDU gathered around Gerhard Schröder. Nevertheless, the idea was on the agenda for later use.

Historians have judged that the decline in popularity of Adenauer's party was the manifestation of a political change which finally resulted in the election of the SPD as the largest party in the Bundestag in 1972. Though the governments of 1961–9 were still dominated by the Union parties, a growing number of Germans, particularly of the political and intellectual elite, began to sense that there would be an eventual transfer of power – a *Machtwechsel* – from the right to the left side of the spectrum. During the 1960s the German electorate was seeking alternatives to the Adenauer model of power, while at the same time developing and enjoying what they had accomplished under the social market economy of the 1950s.

For the CDU/CSU, the problem was one of adjusting to an international climate of detente, without rejecting anti-communism and the moral imperative of seeking reunification in peace and freedom; that is to say, bringing about the end of the totalitarian system of the GDR. This task finally proved impossible, and the shift of power to the SPD was as much a result of dissension in the CDU/CSU as of the SPD's own efforts. For the SPD, the dominant question was how to convince a sufficient number of voters that it was not going to renounce the Federal Republic's integration in Western Europe and US protection, in order to obtain some kind of unspecified rapprochement with the Soviet Union and the GDR. The task, in other words, was to convince voters that Herbert Wehner meant what he said in his epochal Bundestag speech of June 30, 1960, in which he announced that Western integration and, specifically, membership in the Atlantic Alliance, were the essential preconditions of any Ostpolitik involving acceptance of the Soviet-imposed status quo in Europe.

Wehner's position was not, in fact, so very different from the beliefs of the new foreign minister appointed by Adenauer after the 1961 elections, Gerhard Schröder. The choice of Schröder as foreign minister represented a concession to the FDP, since Adenauer had favored Walter Hallstein. Hallstein (1901–1982) was a professor of law, had served as state secretary in the foreign ministry, and from 1958 to 1967 was president of the EEC Commission. But he was considered too conservative for the FDP, who sought a foreign minister who would actively undertake an initiative of detente with Eastern Europe.

Schröder, born in 1910 in Saarbrücken and the son of a state railway official, served in the German army during the war. He was elected to the Bundestag in 1949 at the age of 39 and served as minister of the interior from 1953 until his appointment to the foreign ministry in 1961. He was a prominent member of the Protestant wing of the CDU and was a firm advocate of the Western alliance. If Schröder and Wehner had been in the same party, the Ostpolitik of later years might have developed earlier and might have been executed with more care and less haste, and therefore less compromise with the Soviet government and the GDR. Since they were on opposing sides, however, the struggle continued between the SPD and a CDU-controlled government precariously hanging on to a commitment to reunification whose achievement seemed increasingly remote; realistic hopes for German unity under conditions of freedom had long since been overtaken by events. The entire question of a new Ostpolitik remained a matter for intense debate, but little movement, until 1969. It is possible, indeed likely, that this long delay meant that the change, when it finally came, was somewhat more rapid, and characterized by more optimism and good faith in the peaceful intentions and benevolence of the Soviet Union and the GDR regime, than was in fact justified.

# 1

# The Berlin Crisis Abates:
# Reappraisal and Realignment

The immediate effect of the Berlin Wall was to destroy even the symbolic hope that the old German capital would be revived, and it created a barrier which served as a zone of death whenever Germans from the East tried to climb over it to get to West Berlin. But the Wall was also the primary catalyst for changes that slowly transformed the domestic political landscape of the Federal Republic and, eventually, the West Germans' sense of their place and role in Europe, vis-à-vis both East and West. The development of a basis for a new West German approach to the conduct of its foreign policy in Central Europe took almost the entire decade of the 1960s. The public stance, the emotional fervor, and moral positions of both major parties could not be quickly changed. Moreover, the republic, while rebuilt, had not yet earned the full respect of its allies that Adenauer knew it must achieve.

At first sight it might seem surprising that the Berlin Wall should have strengthened the SPD and the FDP, rather than the Union parties, who were identified with strong anti-Soviet views and with a commitment to the unification of Germany as a democratic state with a freely elected government. The SPD did not, in fact, gain as much in the 1961 election as its leaders had hoped; the new party line and profile represented by Brandt, Erler, and Wehner had not achieved the hoped-for breakthrough to popular parity with the CDU/CSU. But the Berlin Wall crystallized the latent doubts that many West Germans held concerning the wisdom of the Hallstein Doctrine, the *Alleinvertretungsanspruch* (claim to sole representation), and the general CDU/CSU policy of rejection of the Soviet-imposed status quo in Germany and Central Europe. It became increasingly apparent after August 13, 1961, that reunification was unlikely to come about as a result of Western action. The only way to bring about any sort of change in the German situation was with the approval of the Soviet Union. This had, one might argue, been tacitly admitted by the federal government as early as 1955, when it established diplomatic relations with the Soviet Union in the absence of reunification. Nevertheless, the Wall brought these doubts to the fore. Continual emphasis on reunification, abstractly demanded and now seen to be impossible of achievement, gradually, like a balloon, faded into the distance, despite and because of the Berlin Wall.

What might come in its place? Acceptable alternatives appeared impossible, and the Union parties found it difficult to explain clearly what options were available. This position of frustration was the main reason for the shift of foreign policy dynamism to the SPD and its ideas throughout the 1960s. The SPD, moreover, had become a legitimate actor on West Germany's political stage, since shedding its neutralism and support for reunification via disarmament and withdrawal of American and Soviet troops. This did not mean, however, that the SPD now supported the CDU/CSU line of principled commitment to "re-unification in peace and freedom," which lacked any concrete strategy of execution. Rather, the Brandt wing of the SPD, representing primarily those who had come to political maturity since 1945, combined – at least initially – a strong anti-communism and resistance to GDR and Soviet demands for recognition and respect, with a fine understanding of the likely direction of US foreign policy in the coming years. Since the US was, and remained, the guarantor of West German security and, particularly, of the freedom of West Berlin (if not of Berlin as a whole), any party that was not in tune with US priorities was in the position of losing international influence and, eventually, domestic support. This was, in part, what happened to the Union parties in the 1960s and, indeed, until the early 1980s, when the leftward slide of the SPD and the conservative turn of the US, once again made the Union parties the preferred interlocutors of America in West Germany.

The Americans, for their part, and even more so the British and French, were relieved that the Berlin Wall was having the effect, not of driving West Germany into stubborn opposition to detente, but of gradually aligning it with the general thrust of Western policy toward the Soviet Union, Eastern Europe, and arms control. The purpose of Western policy now began to change, and to focus on obtaining agreements with the Soviets on the basis of the status quo in Europe. In this general picture the role of the Federal Republic would be to recognize facts – namely, the Wall, the subjection of 17 million Germans to communist rule in the GDR, and the loss of the Eastern territories – that neither could nor would be changed in the foreseeable future; and then, on this basis, to negotiate agreements with the holders of power in East Berlin and Moscow that might, over time, appease their inveterate hostility to West Germany and alleviate the social, economic and political burdens borne by the Germans living in the GDR.[1] It took the better part of a decade to complete the political and strategic realignment of the Federal Republic from a strategy of reunification through strength, to one of diplomatic progress toward increased contacts and humanitarian aid on the basis of acceptance of the status quo.

The Berlin Wall heralded a change in the cultural, social, and educational environment of the Federal Republic, over which the West Germans could exercise little control. The closing of the loophole by which Germans from the East had been able to escape, and the Wall as one of the most important tangible reminders of the unfinished business of reunification, produced a certain turning inward in West Germany. In the words of Caspar von Schrenck-Notzing:

> Bonn gradually abandoned the goal of reunification, and Germany ceased being one of the international crisis centers of the world. For the population of the Federal Republic, the construction of the Wall had shifted the point of crisis. Instead of occurring in the foreign policy-military field, it now moved to the sphere of domestic policy, culture, and morality. The construction of the Wall dammed the flow of national energies of the people and turned them inward. Within a few months the cultural revolution began on a broad front. Its themes and strategies were indistinguishable from those of the re-education period.[2]

This "cultural revolution" took the form of a general and gradual change of temperament and attitudes throughout West German society, and emphasized the moral issue of *Vergangenheitsbewältigung* (overcoming the past). The first stage of this change, which was largely complete by 1969, was to draw consequences from the existence of the Wall. Its construction not only isolated the Western sectors of Berlin from their hinterland, and from the Soviet sector, but it was the symbol for and the final step in Germany's division. The efforts of the West German government to achieve reunification, in peace and in freedom, had failed. A time of reappraisal followed.

Following Adenauer's re-election in September the Berlin crisis abated, but only gradually. Both the US and the West German governments were in the process of transition in terms of what policies to adopt on the Berlin question and on the issue of reunification. The common problem was that there was really very little that either the Western powers or West Germany could do given the intransigent position of the GDR and the Soviet Union. The Soviet government had recognized, in 1945, a unique opportunity to install, in a part of Germany, a communist

---

[1] See Besson, *Aussenpolitik*, 287–364.
[2] Schrenck-Notzing, "Die Umerziehung der Deutschen," in *Handbuch*, ed. Willms, 381.

government, and did so. In 1961, neither the Soviet Union nor the communists controlling the East German government, were prepared to give up their control, and did not do so. During the early 1960s the Western powers were not prepared to jeopardize the freedom of West Berlin, but at the same time they sought ways to mitigate the extent of family tragedy caused by Germany's division, and appeared ready to accord the GDR greater legitimacy, including diplomatic recognition, if such a concession would positively influence how the East German government treated its German population.

Several weeks after the GDR built the Wall, President Kennedy named General Lucius D. Clay, the former US military governor, as his personal representative in Berlin. This was Clay's first public service position since he was head of OMGUS; he had been a successful businessman in the intervening years. Shortly after his appointment, Clay said in an interview that the existence of two German states was a fact, and that perhaps the Western Allies and West Germany should grant the GDR more rights of control of the access routes to Berlin.[3] At almost the same time, on September 25, 1961, President Kennedy addressed the UN General Assembly in firm tones, stating: "If there is a dangerous crisis in Berlin – and there is – it is because of threats against the vital interests and the deep commitments of the Western Powers, and the freedom of West Berlin. We cannot yield these interests. We cannot fail these commitments. We cannot surrender the freedom of these people for whom we are responsible." Even in this tough speech, however, the president held out an olive branch to the Soviets: "But we believe a peaceful agreement is possible which protects the freedom of West Berlin and Allied presence and access while recognizing the historic and legitimate interests of others in assuring European security."[4] Those "others," of course, were the Soviets, whose "legitimate interests" no American president had so respectfully acknowledged before. On the contrary: since 1946, the Americans had held that the Soviet Union was a threat to European security; now all of a sudden it was a possible guarantor of it. The age of detente was close at that moment.

Adenauer worried that the US was prepared to give up positions held since the Berlin blockade. In November 1961 he visited Washington, reminded President Kennedy of the Western guarantees to Germany in the Paris Treaties, persuaded him to promise not to give away any claims on Berlin in the US–Soviet talks that were just then beginning between the US secretary of state, Dean Rusk, and the Soviet foreign

[3] Koerfer, *Kampf ums Kanzleramt*, 611.
[4] Dept of State, *Documents on Germany*, 795–6.

minister, Gromyko, and insisted on West German access to nuclear weapons in a crisis. No sooner had Adenauer returned to Germany, ill with influenza, than Kennedy in an interview with Khrushchev's son-in-law, Aleksei Adzhubei, editor of *Izvestia*, stated on November 25: "Now we recognize that today the Soviet Union does not intend to permit reunification."[5] He also said that he did not like the idea of a German finger on the nuclear trigger, and that peace in Central Europe would be possible if the West and the Soviet Union could reach an agreement on Berlin.[6] Those were the most conciliatory words spoken by an American president since World War II.

The Berlin crisis and its aftermath, and the apparent changes in the strategic relationship between the US and the Soviet Union, also affected the political background of the movement toward West European integration, and closer ties between West Germany and her neighbors. One important indirect result was rapid development and deepening of the Franco-West German relationship.

For Adenauer, the Soviet Union was an aggressive ideological state – demonstrated in Berlin on August 13, 1961, by the Wall – whose security interests could not be appeased at any price; to try to do so would mean the self-destruction of the Western democracies. Therefore, he could not support French plans directed overtly against the United States' role in Europe. Unlike de Gaulle, he thought that a return to national sovereignty by the West European states would not lead to more peaceful relations with the Soviet Union, but to an increased danger of Soviet political and diplomatic aggression. On the other hand, given his disappointment with the United States after the Wall, from 1961 to 1963 Adenauer was very interested in a close French connection. He also believed that West Germany could help persuade France to remain in NATO by being a mediator between France and the US. Unfortunately, both de Gaulle and Adenauer's colleagues in Germany refused to support him. De Gaulle wanted the direct opposite of Adenauer's concept; he wanted to wean Bonn away from loyalty to the US. In Bonn, both Erhard, the economics minister, and Schröder, the foreign minister, were opposed to a close rapprochement with France for a different reason: they wanted to remain close to the US and to bring Britain into the Common Market as a counterweight to France.

In July 1961, with tension and uncertainty rising over Berlin, the heads of government of the EEC – the Six – had met in Bad Godesberg without reaching any agreement on how to proceed toward political union. They released a declaration stating that "only a united Europe

[5] Ibid., 802.
[6] Koerfer, *Kampf ums Kanzleramt*, 613–14.

that would be allied with the United States and other free nations would be in a position to counter the dangers which threatened the existence of Europe." This rhetoric was not a binding agreement of any kind. But to demonstrate their desire for action, the governments of the Six set up a committee of experts to work out a plan for political union under the chairmanship of the French ambassador to Copenhagen, Christian Fouchet.

In October 1961, the Fouchet committee produced a first version of a treaty of unification for the Six. This version, which became known as "Fouchet Plan I," was a draft treaty of union between the Six which envisioned a joint foreign and defense policy, but which also allowed for and required the unanimity of all member governments in all major decisions. In the debate that followed presentation of the plan, the Belgians and the Dutch demanded that Britain, and other smaller European states, be included in the proposed union. These smaller members of the EEC had always favored a political union or, at least, a supranational organization restricting national sovereignty, because such a solution would counterbalance the influence of the larger members. By contrast, de Gaulle – and, he hoped, Adenauer – favored a confederation "respectful of national sovereignties,"[7] which would give what de Gaulle considered proper weight to the larger members. In response to these objections, de Gaulle had the Fouchet commission prepare a more modest version, known as "Fouchet Plan II," which was presented in January 1962.

In December 1961, Adenauer discussed US policies with de Gaulle in Paris. Kennedy, Adenauer made clear, thought that France was not playing its part in resolving the East–West conflict in Europe. De Gaulle reacted with irritation: had he not restrained the Americans and the British from negotiating with the Soviet government over Berlin when such negotiations would have harmed the West, in 1959–60? But if the US, Britain, and West Germany wanted to give up Berlin, then France obviously would not stand in the way. This remark, in its turn, infuriated Adenauer, who broke off the discussion. Yet, the final communique spoke of "a total unity of views" between the French and German leaders on questions of common security and West European integration.[8]

The US and British governments in 1961–2 consistently took a more conciliatory line than the French concerning Soviet demands on Berlin. The tension between Bonn and Washington came to a head in early 1962. On April 9, the German ambassador in Washington, Wilhelm

---

[7] Lacouture, *De Gaulle*, 3: 301.
[8] Ibid, 301–2.

Grewe, received from Dean Rusk a series of proposals that the US intended to make to the Soviets on Berlin and Germany. The US offered to accept existing borders in Europe and international control of the access routes to West Berlin, which would involve GDR participation. When Adenauer's cabinet saw this memorandum it nearly split apart. It appeared that the division between the "hard liners" and the "soft liners" divided both the CDU/CSU as well as the FDP in half. Schröder and the FDP leader, Mende, argued that the offer should be supported in the interest of Western unity; it was important that West Germany not be seen to be dragging its feet. On the other hand, conservatives like Guttenberg (CSU), and to some extent Adenauer himself, feared what they saw as the slippery slope of negotiation leading to concession.

The Germans were given 48 hours to make their views known. Adenauer called an emergency meeting of the heads of the party groups in the Bundestag. One of his closest advisors, Heinrich Krone, noted in his diary that Adenauer and Heinrich von Brentano, head of the CDU group, whom Adenauer had replaced with Gerhard Schröder at the foreign ministry, "regarded this step as dangerous and as a shift of American policy. If there were to be an agreement with the Soviets on this basis the moving vans of Berlin would not be enough; Berlin would be a dead city. . . . The Americans are no longer the Americans they were years ago. They want an understanding, and the only way to get that is at the expense of the Germans."[9] On April 14, Adenauer himself wrote to Kennedy stating firmly that there was no chance of an agreement on Berlin that would not be against the West's interests. Even before the letter arrived at the White House, details of the American offer surfaced in the German press. This led Rusk to speak of a "serious breach of confidence" on the part of the Germans. Adenauer was furious. If anyone was breaking any confidence, in his opinion, it was the Americans; he was simply doing his duty as head of the German government in letting his citizens know what the Americans had in store for them.

On April 24, Adenauer summarized his objections to US foreign policy in a memorandum he wrote while on Easter vacation in his favorite spot of Cadenabbia near Como in northern Italy. "I am worried by both the method and the content of American foreign policy," he wrote. The Americans had broadened the Berlin talks to encompass the entire German question without consulting the Germans; Kennedy had even refused to answer Adenauer's letter. Concerning the views in Washington, Adenauer continued: "We have no idea at all of what is being negotiated," and insisted that the West had

---

[9] Cited in Koerfer, *Kampf ums Kanzleramt*, 636.

already made needless concessions to the Soviets. He also criticized Schröder for not standing up to Rusk and Kennedy: "I am afraid that Schröder, right from the beginning of the talks with Rusk, has always played the faithful captive."[10]

On May 7 Adenauer gave a public speech in Berlin which included what Grewe, looking back in 1979, called the sharpest criticism ever heard from any German head of government of American policy.[11] Adenauer insisted strenuously that no agreement was possible and that the US would never recognize the sovereignty of the GDR. He showed his uncertainty and fear of possible US concessions, however, in an almost despairing comment, that, "I think it would be much better if things remained as they are than to continue this line [of negotiation]."[12] Kennedy responded on May 9 by criticizing the chancellor in equally unprecedented terms, and emphasized that the talks with the Soviets would continue.

Not everyone agreed with Adenauer that the Americans were on a dangerous path. Within his own party Schröder took the line that the American proposals were not that original, and that West Germany, in any event, could not afford to be seen as opposing detente. Brandt and Erler of the SPD, and Mende of the FDP, agreed with Schröder, who repeatedly, over the next five years, took positions in support of the US, even against powerful figures in his own party. The most powerful such figure, of course, was Adenauer, who became even more intent on finding a successor who would not betray what he considered the German interest to the Soviets or to the Americans.

In view of such trends it was not surprising that Adenauer's last two years in office were overshadowed by his fears for the future. These fears were not only for Berlin and for the consequences of a Western abandonment of long-held legal claims, but were also of a moral nature. He had a sense that the Germans were losing their moral commitment to the principles of integrity and individual responsibility, and the rectification of injustice committed during the Third Reich. Increasingly, Adenauer worried that his successors would embark on dangerous paths unless he tied West Germany as tightly as possible to its Western allies. Until 1961, that meant to the United States. What he perceived as dangerous vacillation by both Eisenhower and Kennedy during the Berlin crisis, convinced him to place more hope in de Gaulle's fifth French Republic. Schröder did not share these fears and remained opposed to a European policy focused exclusively on France. The

---

[10]  Cited ibid., 640-1.
[11]  Grewe, *Rückblenden*, 555.
[12]  Dept of State, *Documents on Germany*, 815.

foreign minister was an Anglophile, genuinely fond of English life. He also believed that it was very much in the German interest that Britain join the Common Market so Germany would not be forced to rely on France alone as its partner in Europe.

Adenauer's most likely successor, Ludwig Erhard, the economics minister, agreed with Schröder. He believed that West Germany would not be well served by closer alignment with France and remained committed to the transatlantic connection to the US. This disagreement did nothing to reduce Adenauer's already considerable mistrust of Erhard. The chancellor was unable to choose another successor, however, since both the FDP, necessary as a coalition partner since the 1961 elections, and the vast majority of the CDU leadership, stood behind the economics minister. One way out of this dilemma was to reject the FDP and form a grand coalition with the SPD, and a number of Adenauer's close allies in the CDU/CSU wanted to pursue this option in 1961–2. They were frustrated and exasperated with what they saw as the FDP's insistence on being in government, and regarded the liberals as having an inflated sense of their own importance.

The distrust of possible US concessions, felt by Adenauer and those of the CDU/CSU right wing, was the mirror image of the distrust felt by many in the US two decades later, in the 1980s, at what concessions the West Germans might make concerning East–West relations. In the early 1960s the foreign policy of the Kennedy administration was groping for an all-encompassing detente with the Soviet Union in the belief that a stable world order was possible, one that included the Soviet Union as a partner. In this design of hope, the particular meaning and value of maintaining claims and preserving positions on the German question received less attention than it had between 1945 and 1961.

From long experience Adenauer knew that, even if it should prove necessary to make concessions to the Soviet Union on the shape of Germany's future, it should not be done until the final minute, because any other position could be interpreted as weakness and lead to further pressure. For Adenauer, the basic point remained that the division of Germany was a source of tension and a great burden, especially for the Germans in the East, and that acceptance of the status quo by the West would not serve peace or help German needs. On the other hand, the view underlying US foreign policy, and increasingly prevalant in the SPD, was that the only way to alleviate the hardships of division was to accept the facts, and seek to negotiate humanitarian agreements with the Soviet and East German regimes. Rusk expressed this view at a news conference on April 26, 1962, in which he reported on his talks with Gromyko. While stating that reunification of Germany and a single peace treaty with a reunited, democratic German state was the ideal, he acknowledged that "the factual situation" might continue for a long time, and that perhaps both sides should recognize the status quo on that basis.[13] This view was gradually adopted by leading SPD figures, and enunciated clearly by Willy Brandt in a speech delivered at Harvard University in October 1962, entitled "The Ordeal of Coexistence."

In October 1962, however, the Berlin question became secondary in importance to the confrontation between the United States and the Soviet Union over the installation of Soviet missiles in Cuba. When this crisis had ended, discussions on Berlin continued in 1963, but not with the same intensity, since the Soviet government began a reassessment of its position on the world stage following the outcome of the Cuban crisis. In the interim the Wall had apparently, from the Soviet viewpoint, solved the problem of instability in the GDR, and had removed for the time being the necessity to continue pressure on West Berlin. The next step, however, remained. It was to persuade the West to accept GDR control of the access routes to Berlin, and ultimately GDR sovereignty in East Berlin, as well as the legitimacy of all the Central European borders imposed by the Soviet Union in 1944–5. Soviet and GDR leaders methodically pursued these goals as the decade of the 1960s developed.

The waning of the Berlin crisis was not complete victory or defeat for either side. The Soviet Union had not succeeded in moderating the status of Berlin; so West Berlin remained free. This was primarily due to the Western commitment to West Berlin, uncertain though it appeared to Adenauer, and to the commitment of the West German government to preserve freedom in the city. One could have expected that the prospect of war over Berlin could have led the West German government to abandon the city, and to cast the blame on the Allies. Given the pressure so consistently applied on the Western sectors, it is remarkable that proposals of this kind were never heard, except from the left. West Germany remained committed to the defense of West Berlin, with the full knowledge that the city would also remain a constant source of potential tension and blackmail, as well as a serious financial burden, since the city's budget was subsidized significantly from the federal budget in Bonn.

The existence of West Berlin meant that West Germany would always be exposed to the uncertainty of whether the United States, Great Britain and France would be able to counteract Eastern pressure successfully. West Germany, as a consequence, would never be an independent West European power, like France or Britain, and could not hope to negotiate on an equal footing with the Soviet Union. This

[13]  Ibid., 810–12.

exposure to pressure gave West German foreign policy a peculiar style characterized by a certain "fearfulness and a lack of natural self-confidence which is normally more typical of small dependent states than of a state with the potential of the Federal Republic."[14] But it should also be kept in mind that self-confidence requires a long period of time to develop.

In 1961, the Federal Republic was only twelve years old. It had started from nothing but chaos and hope. West German foreign policy, before it could take shape, began with the burden of the Third Reich, and the need to be perceived at all times to be the opposite. This consideration, as well as the problem of Berlin, meant that it was virtually impossible for West Germany to define "normal" foreign policy interests. West Germany needed American support for its independence and security, but feared that the Americans might make agreements with the Soviets in what they saw as their own higher interests, at the expense of the Federal Republic. On the other hand, Adenauer's recipe for firm integration of West Germany into Western Europe as a counterweight both to German tendencies to neutralism and appeasement, and to potential American weakness, was not a guarantee of firmness either. France, Adenauer's main hope toward the end of his chancellorship, had its own agenda in East–West relations and in Western Europe which by no means coincided with that of any conceivable West German government, whether conservative or social democratic. Full security and satisfaction for Bonn was a case of squaring the circle.

Despite a certain resentment at a perceived failure of the US to prevent the Wall, the Berlin crisis led to an enormous strengthening of US-German relations on both psychological and political levels. It was the American president, John F. Kennedy, who was able to dramatize the depth and emotion of the bonds felt between Berlin, Germany and the United States during his visit to Berlin in June 1963. Accompanied by Adenauer, Brandt and Lucius Clay, the father of the airlift and the president's special representative in Berlin, Kennedy delivered one of his most famous speeches to several hundred thousand West Berliners gathered before the Schöneberg Rathaus (city hall) in the American sector of the city. He emphasized that the defense of freedom in Berlin was analogous to the defense of freedom in Paris and New York, and that "we will never permit that city [Berlin] to fall under communist influence." He appealed to both reason and emotion, coining, in the process a phrase that became a symbol of German-American relations:

---

[14] Schwarz, *Die Ära Adenauer, 1957–1963*, 251.

There are many people in the world who really don't understand, or say they don't, what is the great issue between the free world and the Communist world. Let them come to Berlin. There are some who say that communism is the wave of the future. Let them come to Berlin. And there are some who say in Europe and elsewhere we can work with the Communists. Let them come to Berlin. . . .

What is true of this city is true of Germany – real, lasting peace in Europe can never be assured as long as one German out of four is denied the elementary right of free men, and that is to make a free choice. . . . When all are free, then we can look forward to that day when this city will be joined as one and this country, and this great Continent of Europe in a peaceful and hopeful glow. When that day finally comes, as it will, the people of West Berlin can take sober satisfaction in the fact that they were in the front lines for almost two decades.

All free men, wherever they may live, are citizens of Berlin, and, therefore, as a free man, I take pride in the words "Ich bin ein Berliner."[15]

The remarks made by Adenauer and Brandt on the same occasion were equally memorable, because they illustrated two basic concerns central to the growing discussion regarding the direction of West German foreign policy. Brandt stressed that "we must hold our strong position in Berlin if Western statesmen are to negotiate in earnest about European security," while Adenauer pointed to one of the most agonizing costs of the war:

We are distressed that the Soviet zone has been sliced away from the rest of Germany, that 17 million Germans live today in bondage, with no rights, no freedom. The Russians say we must pay for the lost war. I agree. Indeed we must pay. But we must not be asked to pay with the liberty of 17 million.[16]

The leading figures of the German side of this trans-Atlantic relationship, that emerged from the Berlin crisis, were Willy Brandt and Gerhard Schröder. To the West German public they symbolized the hope for more peaceful conditions, through close alignment with a new and forward looking US foreign policy. It was precisely these progressive circles in West Germany, who professed themselves to be the most important partners of the US in Europe, that became frustrated by US involvement in Vietnam. The resulting disappointment of a formerly very pro-American German left in the wisdom of US foreign policy in Asia, explains much of the peculiar mixture of anti-Americanism and accommodation with the Soviet Union that was to characterize parts of SPD foreign policy from the 1970s onward.

[15] Dept of State, *Documents on Germany*, 849–50.
[16] Both in *Berliner Illustrirte* [sic], special issue, 1963.

# 2

# The Succession Problem and Continued Rapprochement with France

During the spring and summer of 1962 many observers saw signs that Adenauer was losing control of the CDU and that the party leaders were openly fighting over the succession. He was unable to convince Schröder to support his own strategy of developing closer relations with France; on the contrary, the foreign minister, in 1962–3, worked assiduously to keep relations with the US as cordial as possible, while also lobbying in Western capitals for British membership in the EEC, even though both he and Adenauer knew that de Gaulle was against it. On May 15, 1962, Adenauer was outvoted in the CDU Bundestag group for the first time in his life. The issue was a trivial one: Erhard wanted to lower customs duties on automobiles, partly in order to put pressure on the Volkswagen company to cancel a proposed price increase for its most popular product, the "Beetle." Adenauer opposed the motion in the group, and to his own amazement, he was defeated. The CDU/CSU subsequently passed the motion into law in the Bundestag, with the support of the SPD and against its own coalition partner, the FDP. For some this was another early indication that among the CDU, support for cooperation with the SPD was developing.

Even many of those who were politically closest to Adenauer began to wish for his retirement. In their view, and in that of the West German press, Adenauer was losing his grip, unable to control his government, his coalition, or his relations with Germany's allies and neighbors. Their impatience came to a head at the 1962 annual party conference, held in Dortmund in July. Adenauer took the opportunity to announce that he intended to fulfil his side of the agreement with the FDP from 1961; namely, to retire in time for a successor to campaign for the next election. However, he added, foreign and domestic policy considerations might make it necessary for him to stay a while longer, perhaps past 1963. Other CDU leaders were alarmed. Gerstenmaier replied, by saying what no one had yet dared to say, but many had thought: that Adenauer should resign sooner rather than later.

We know that we are faced with the task of carrying out the change of leadership, that is coming upon us, as precisely and as smoothly as possible, so that our ability to act, our solidarity, and our political efficacy at home and abroad are not seriously affected. We should be under no illusion that this will be all the more difficult, the greater the authority, yes, ladies and gentlemen, the greater the historical rank of the first German federal chancellor. . . . The more powerful a man is, the greater his historical effect and significance, the more difficult it is for his faithful followers . . . to solve the question of succession halfway satisfactorily. . . .[1]

A younger delegate to the conference stated the problem even more bluntly: "We want to make it absolutely clear . . . that the retirement of our honored chancellor should take place while he remains at the peak of his powers. . . . Rather two years earlier than necessary, than one day too late."[2] The majority at the conference made two things clear: they wanted Adenauer to promise to resign by a specific date, and they wanted him to designate Erhard as his successor.

Despite having promised to do so, Adenauer, in reality, did not want to resign at all, and he certainly did not want Erhard to succeed him. He now began toying with other names, but because the confidence in his own leadership had kept him from facing the question of retirement for so long, he had waited until it was too late to stop the momentum for Erhard. One other name that came up as a possible choice was that of Eugen Gerstenmaier (1906–1986). He was president of the Bundestag from 1954 to 1969 and deputy chairman of the CDU during the same period. During the war he had been part of the resistance group of Graf von Stauffenberg and the mayor of Leipzig, Carl Goerdeler. After the war he joined the CDU and quickly became an unofficial leader of the party's Protestant faction. Throughout the 1950s and 1960s he worked hard to turn the CDU into a genuinely interdenominational party. By 1963 this task was largely complete. Gerstenmaier supported Erhard in the succession, although he still hoped that he might have a chance himself at becoming chancellor if Erhard should fail.

Erhard enjoyed the support of most of the CDU and the FDP. Adenauer could not force selection of another candidate without endangering party unity. What particularly worried Adenauer, however,

---

[1] Cited in Koerfer, *Kampf ums Kanzleramt*, 650–1.
[2] Ibid., 652.

## IMAGES OF THE BERLIN WALL

No single event symbolized the Cold War and communist tyranny better than the barrier that the German communist regime of the GDR, in collaboration with its Russian occupiers, erected around the western sectors of Berlin, starting on August 13, 1961. For the SED, the Wall was a resounding success: it stopped unauthorized flight to the West and led to West German recognition of the GDR in 1972.

The first barrier was merely barbed wire strung along the boundary of the western sectors and protected by armed GDR police, here shown using water cannon to stop people from approaching the barrier from the east through the Brandenburg Gate. The sector boundary runs just west of the Gate. Through the Gate, looking east, lies Pariser Platz and Unter den Linden, the main avenue of the old city center. [*Source*: GIC]

At first, escape was still possible from houses facing one of the many streets divided lengthwise by the sector boundary, if one was prepared to leap from the windows and cross the street to safety. The doors had been bricked up from the inside. [*Source*: GIC]

Another famous image of the Cold War. A GDR policeman chooses an unguarded moment to leap across the barbed wire to freedom. [*Source*: GIC]

The next stage was to cover the windows with barbed wire. This picture, taken from the western side, shows a man looking to freedom from the window of a house in the Soviet sector. [Source: GIC]

Even barbed wire can be cut. After a few weeks the SED authorites removed all inhabitants from houses facing the boundary and walled up the windows. Later, most of these houses were razed and replaced by a mined death zone up to 100 yards wide and, in the 1980s, a secondary wall some 50 yards behind the boundary itself. [*Source*: GIC]

The Potsdamer Platz, once the busiest crossroads in Europe. At this early stage the Wall was still a single line of concrete blocks topped with barbed wire. The secondary wall, and innumerable guard towers came later. In left background, the Brandenburg Gate. In right background, former government buildings of the Reich along the Wilhelmstrasse. [*Source*: GIC]

The Wall separated thousands of families who were totally unable to communicate, since all telephone wires were cut and there was no mail service. Here a woman and her child look into the east, hoping perhaps to catch a glimpse of relatives. [*Source*: GIC]

On August 17, 1962, GDR border troops fatally shot Peter Fechter, a construction worker, as he was trying to climb the Wall a few yards east of Checkpoint Charlie. They carried off the body after leaving him for over an hour to bleed to death. [*Source*: GIC]

The sign reads, "Whoever attacks us will be destroyed," as soldiers of the East German People's Army fortify the Wall and death strip in 1962. The East German government officially described the Wall as the "anti-fascist protective wall" (*Antifaschistischer Schutzwall*). [*Source*: Bundesbildstelle Bonn]

The most famous visitor to Berlin in the aftermath of the Wall was the American president, John F. Kennedy. Never again would an American president be greeted with such unanimous adulation and support. A few years after the visit, the Vietnam War and the cultural revolution within West Germany challenged the faith of young Germans in America.

*Main picture* Kennedy giving his famous "Ich bin ein Berliner" speech to an enthusiastic crowd in front of the West Berlin city hall in the American sector. Today the square is called John F. Kennedy-Platz. [*Source*: GIC]

*Inset* Kennedy with Brandt and an interpreter, arriving at Tegel airport in Berlin. [*Source*: GIC]

Though the Western powers did nothing to stop the Wall, they sent many of their leading figures to West Berlin in the following months to demonstrate that they were not going to abandon the western sectors. In February 1962, the US attorney-general, Robert F. Kennedy, visited Berlin and is seen here (center left) with the governing mayor, Willy Brandt (center right), and German trade union leaders in a Berlin beer house. [*Source*: GIC]

The *Spiegel* affair rallied students, intellectuals, and journalists against the government in a pattern that became familiar during the 1960s. Here students at the University of Munich are holding up a poster with a picture of Strauss on the cover of *Der Spiegel* and the exclamation "My God, what will become of Germany?" The students were turning this phrase, used by Adenauer, into a weapon against Adenauer's government. [*Source*: Süddeutscher Verlag].

Rudolf Augstein, the enormously successful publisher (since 1947) of the left-leaning newsmagazine *Der Spiegel*, being arrested on the order of Franz Josef Strauss in October 1962. His arrest provoked the fall of Strauss and rallied the political and intellectual forces that bore the cultural revolution in the years ahead. Augstein, a strong opponent of Adenauer and Strauss, joined the FDP in the 1950s and contributed decisively to its leftward swing in the later 1960s. [*Source*: Süddeutscher Verlag]

Franco-German reconciliation after centuries of strife was a hope of Adenauer's since the 1920s. In his last years as chancellor he turned to France to seek security and cooperation. Since 1958, France was reviving under the strong rule of General Charles de Gaulle (left), here shown visiting Bonn in May 1961. [*Source*: GIC]

The Franco-German Friendship Treaty of January 1963 crowned Adenauer's efforts at reconciliation with France. Though initially opposed by many Germans who saw it as an obstacle to good relations with the US, the Treaty later became a cornerstone of European integration. The picture shows the signature page of the German original of the Treaty. [*Source*: GIC]

Geschehen zu Paris am 22. Januar 1963
in zwei Urschriften, jede in deutscher
und französischer Sprache, wobei jeder
Wortlaut gleichermassen verbindlich ist.


Der Bundeskanzler                    Der Präsident
der Bundesrepublik          der Französischen Republik
Deutschland


Der Bundesminister              Der französische
des Auswärtigen der              Premierminister
Bundesrepublik Deutschland


Der französische
Aussenminister

# ELECTION POSTERS FROM 1949 AND 1957.

1949. From left to right, top row: The CDU poster states, "We cannot make magic, but we can work." The SPD poster calls for "Work for everyone − Co-determination for the workers − The best schools for our children." The FDP reminds the voters to "Make the center strong!" Bottom row: The CSU poster proclaims that "It must get better still!" The Bavarian party poster points to "the straight road" to the sun. The Communist poster promises "unity, freedom, independence." [*Sources*: CDU − Bundesgeschäftstelle der CDU; SPD − Archiv der sozialen Demokratie; FDP − Bundesgeschäftstelle der FDP; CSU − Hans-Seidel-Stiftung; BP and KPD − Bundesarchiv Koblenz]

1957. These posters call the voter to the polls for the third federal election. The Federal Republic is eight years old, and the tone of the election campaign is changing. Top row: The CDU poster speaks for itself. The SPD poster promises "Security with Ollenhauer." The FDP poster reminds the voter that "Everything depends on the FDP." Bottom row: The CSU promises further progress, using a design not in vogue in 1949. The poster of the Bloc of Expellees and Disenfranchised (BHE) depicts Germany in three parts and insists that "Everything is at stake." Note the three parts of Germany: the Federal Republic, the GDR, and the eastern territories annexed by Poland and the USSR. The poster of the German Party, depicting a roll of the dice, suggests that the choice "lies in your hand." [*Sources*: CDU, SPD, FDP, CSU – as above; DP and BHE – Bundesarchiv Koblenz]

Three ages of German history in Aachen. In the foreground, the remains of a Roman gate from the second century AD. In the background, the medieval cathedral where Germany's kings and emperors were crowned. In between, typical nineteenth-century houses. [*Source*: GIC]

was that Erhard would not be able to conduct as firm and consistent a policy as Adenauer himself, and in general he doubted his political skills. As an economist, Erhard's decision to institute the currency reform and to lift rationing was an extraordinary example of both foresight and courage. But as a chancellor Adenauer feared he would find it difficult to make independent decisions. Nonetheless, he was a man of independence, both of thought and mind, as described by the journalist Hermann Schreiber in 1965:

He joined the party as if he had joined a company, which promises to make the most successful use of his invention – the social market economy. He became an official member of the CDU, retroactively, when he was chancellor. Deep in his heart he will never belong to it.[3]

Erhard's personality and sense of style was very different from Adenauer's. He presented, for many, the picture drawn by Hermann Schreiber:

Erhard's image is apolitical, but strongly emotional and sensitive. ... Basically we are dealing here with a mother image. The "fatherly" nicknames [grandfather, father, uncle] present a false father image. In this case, the father has primarily a maternal function, he provides first and foremost warmth and protection instead of embodying the principles of firmness and order.[4]

The only realistic choice for chancellor was that between Erhard and Schröder. Schröder had wide support from those outside the government who supported detente, but he had little support in the south of Germany, where he was regarded with suspicion as a liberal Protestant. Erhard remained. He had few enemies and great prestige. If Adenauer was considered the "father" of Germany, Erhard became the father of Germany's prosperity during his 14 years as economics minister (1949–63). His weaknesses were not as apparent, even though his lack of firmness eventually earned him the nickname the "Rubber Lion." But his round face, which resembled that of a lion, and the ever-present cigar, which reminded people of Winston Churchill, were somehow reassuring. Erhard's reputation provided the self-confidence that West Germany still needed in a world which was changing rapidly almost two decades after the end of the war.

Yet, Adenauer did not give up easily. Few gave Gerstenmaier much of

---

[3] *Der Spiegel* no. 37 (1965), 28.
[4] Ibid.

a chance, and Schröder actively discouraged those who tried to draft him for a candidacy. In view of this situation, and of the chancellor's apparent intransigence, some party leaders began looking at yet another possible candidate, Josef Hermann Dufhues. Like Adenauer, he was a Catholic Rhinelander, but had his own power base in the party and his own convictions that permitted him a degree of independence vis-à-vis the old chancellor that encouraged many people. He was party secretary, a new post created by the Dortmund conference as part of a seven-member presidium. This new leadership body consisted of members chosen to give the two religious denominations and the different regions of Germany roughly equal weight at the party's senior level. Apart from the chairman, Adenauer, the first presidium included Dufhues, the Protestants Erhard and Gerstenmaier (from the south and south-west respectively), the Catholics Krone and Blank, and the deputy chairman Kai-Uwe von Hassel (a northern Protestant).

If the party thought the presidium would help in urging Adenauer toward a decision for either Erhard or Dufhues, it was wrong. Despite appearing weak and old to some, Adenauer was in fact regaining his strength and optimism in the summer of 1962, and the reason was France.

In April 1962, the Fouchet II plan for European political union, like its predecessor, failed. At a meeting on April 17, the foreign ministers of the Six abandoned plans for a political union. But only a month later de Gaulle cheered Adenauer tremendously when he turned this failure into a promise of Franco-German rapprochement during a press conference on May 15:

[T]here is a solidarity between Germany and France. On this solidarity depends the immediate security of the two peoples. . . . On this solidarity depend all hopes of uniting Europe on the political and defense levels, as on the economic level.

On this solidarity depends, in consequence, the destiny of the whole of Europe, from the Atlantic to the Ural Mountains; for if a structure, a firm, prosperous and attractive organization, can be created in Western Europe – then there reappear the possibilities of a European balance with the Eastern States and the prospect of a truly European cooperation . . . if this solidarity, about which I am speaking did not exist or ceased to exist, Europe as a whole would be exposed to being the arena of the demons of misfortune.[5]

Adenauer and de Gaulle now agreed to move toward a Franco-German rapprochement. Officials in Bonn and Paris started planning

---

[5] Republic of France, *Major Addresses of de Gaulle*, 179.

the framework of a bilateral relationship within (and, in Adenauer's view, below) the overarching EEC and NATO relationships. Adenauer proceeded from two convictions; first, that France and West Germany together were the foundation of European security, particularly given the apparent weakening of the US; and second, that any move by Bonn away from Washington was a free gift to the Soviet Union. De Gaulle, for his part, sought precisely to draw the Federal Republic away from the US and Britain. These divergencies, however, became temporarily less important during 1962 and 1963, as both countries fell under a spell of excitement concerning Franco-German relations. In July 1962, Adenauer visited France and was received with overwhelming cordiality. De Gaulle addressed Adenauer at Orly, July 2, 1962, upon his arrival:

[E]veryone here recognizes you as the historic personality who stood tall in the midst of misery and ruins into which Germany had been thrown by a tyrannical regime, a personality who has led Germany decisively in the opposite direction, along the path of reason and respect of other countries, a personality who has ensured that Germany, in this way, has found its freedom, its prosperity and the respect of other nations.[6]

The visit culminated in the city of Reims in north-eastern France, not far from the German frontier and in the heart of the territory over which forces of the French kingdom and the German empire had fought for centuries in scores of wars. It was a city full of historic memories of the French monarchy and of French "greatness," as de Gaulle called it, since it was the archbishops of Reims who had the traditional prerogative of crowning and anointing the kings of France from the tenth century onward. For de Gaulle, as for millions of his countrymen, Reims symbolized French political power. The city's twelfth-century cathedral also symbolized the continuity of French history, going back far beyond the revolution of 1789. De Gaulle exploited the historical resonance of this beautiful French city to the fullest, particularly in the high mass which Adenauer, as a Catholic, attended with him. This joint demonstration of a common religious and cultural heritage had a great effect on observers and on public opinion in both countries. De Gaulle greeted the chancellor in the vestry of the cathedral on July 8, 1962:

A wave of deference and admiration of your extraordinary personality powerfully embraced you – be that in the streets and squares of Paris or in Versailles, Rouen, Bordeaux and Reims. But you could also feel the understanding, the well-meaning, in short, the warmth that poured out of the depth of

[6] Stercken, ed., *De Gaulle hat gesagt*, 182–3.

the French soul which through you we send to the Germany of today and tomorrow.[7]

While Adenauer and de Gaulle were continuing their honeymoon in France, the succession and coalition struggles continued at home in Bonn. Mende, the FDP chairman, went so far as to call the climate within the coalition "unbearable." On July 8, both the CDU and the FDP lost ground in the election in North Rhine-Westphalia. The CDU lost the same proportion of votes as in the national election of September 1961, that is, five percentage points; and, as in the national election, they lost the absolute majority, retaining 46.4 per cent. The FDP loss was modest, from 7.1 to 6.9 per cent. The SPD had reason to celebrate, jumping from 39.2 to 43.3 per cent. Observers read the results as yet another sign that the tectonic plates of postwar German politics were shifting, and that the future belonged, at least in part, to the SPD.

After his return from France Adenauer was faced with the continued resistance of his party to the French connection, and with its insistence that Britain must be included in the EEC. It was a sign of Adenauer's waning authority that he was now completely unable to keep the quarrels at the top of the CDU out of the press. On August 22 the pro-CDU paper, *Die Welt*, headlined "CDU supports London's accession to EEC." In a letter to Brentano, the chairman of the Bundestag caucus, Adenauer deplored what he saw as a tendency for members of the party leadership to leak their own opinions to the press in order to put pressure on him. "Our party is literally destroying itself. . . . An important cause for these conditions is the disgusting struggle for my succession."[8] The next day was even worse. A journalist, Georg Schröder, published an article in *Die Welt*, entitled "England must join – Adenauer's defeat – no longer King of the Hill?"[9] in which he openly attacked the chancellor and indicated that the latter stood alone in his opposition to British EEC membership and in his pro-French orientation. It was not a good background to de Gaulle's return visit to Germany, which took place in September. Surprisingly – or not so surprisingly for those who knew him – Adenauer seized the opportunity of hosting de Gaulle to set in motion one final publicity campaign for his policies and leadership.

One of de Gaulle's many stops was the free city of Hamburg, where the future chancellor of Germany, the young Helmut Schmidt, as Hamburg's senator for internal administration, was responsible for his

[7] Ibid., 186.
[8] Cited in Koerfer, *Kampf ums Kanzleramt*, 664.
[9] Ibid., 665.

safety. De Gaulle delivered one of his most successful speeches, without notes, and in German. He completed it, as he did his other speeches during the visit, by raising his arms to the sky and declaring (in German), "Es lebe Deutschland! Es lebe die deutsch-französische Freundschaft!" (Long live Germany! Long live German-French friendship!). He even repeated a phrase he had used in the difficult year of 1945: "Sie sind ein grosses Volk!" (You are a great people!). But at the same time he told his entourage: "If they really were still a great people they wouldn't be cheering me so!"[10]

At the start of his visit, in Bonn, he introduced its theme, which was an emotional appeal for Franco-German collaboration and cooperation. De Gaulle never defined precisely what he meant by it, but it was an offer the public received with great enthusiasm:

> For the first time both of our nations and our peoples are acting together. This is an enormous task, a reason to be modest, but also to be decisive. . . .
> Is there any one subject, be that the economy, defense, or culture . . . where something that would be good for Germany would damage France? Or vice versa, where something that makes France happy could hurt Germany?[11]

The public high point of his trip was his speech to the officers of the Bundeswehr college in Hamburg, where he said things few German politicians dared to say, after 1945,[12] and no foreigner had wanted to say:

> The French and the Germans have in common that they have never done anything great in history, either from a national or from an international point of view, in which the military did not play an eminent role, and this applies to both countries. Therefore, by reason of our very nature and because of the common danger, the organic cooperation of our armies for the purpose of a single, common defense is essential to the union of our two countries. As your writer Zuckmayer has said: "Yesterday it was our duty to be enemies, today it is our right to become brothers."[13]

Later in the same speech he added: "If we want to create a Europe, then not for the sake of Europe, but for the world in general."[14]

Adenauer had kept the Americans fully informed of the progress on concluding a treaty with France. Secretary of State Dean Rusk had

[10] Lacouture, *De Gaulle*, 3: 305.
[11] Stercken, ed., *De Gaulle hat gesagt*, 190–1.
[12] A notable exception was former Federal President Theodor Heuss: see Grosser, *French Foreign Policy under de Gaulle*, 70.
[13] Lacouture, *De Gaulle*, 3: 305.
[14] Stercken, ed., *De Gaulle hat gesagt*, 196.

assured him that the US had no objection and, in fact, would regard a Franco-West German treaty as a positive step. The US administration believed that the effect of a treaty might be what Adenauer hoped; namely, to restrain de Gaulle from anti-American adventurism and to bolster West German self-assurance. The plans for a treaty were, in the first instance, discussed in diplomatic channels, where they were over-shadowed in the months to come by the *Spiegel* affair and its aftermath.

# 3

# The Spiegel Affair

In late 1962 West Germany was shaken by domestic turmoil as a result of a scandal involving the weekly magazine *Der Spiegel* and the minister of defense, Franz Josef Strauss. Strauss was strongly pro-American, ardently anti-communist, and committed to a nuclear defense of West Germany. He was also a possible future candidate for chancellor. The FDP, and most of the CDU, wanted Erhard to succeed Adenauer, but Strauss had hopes of succeeding Erhard, whom he did not expect to last long. In this conclusion he was right, although his conduct during the affair permanently laid to rest his own aspirations.

The new vitality Adenauer demonstrated during de Gaulle's visit was soon overshadowed by the continued bickering over his succession. The reason was straightforward: all the leading figures in the CDU and the FDP wanted him to retire, and soon. Many of them wanted him to choose Erhard. Some held out for Dufhues or Schröder. But the main point was that they wanted "der Alte" to resign gracefully, or at least make definite preparations to do so. Adenauer would not; not merely because he loved power, which he certainly did, but because he was genuinely terrified of what his weak successor would, or could, do. And in his view all his potential successors were weak, Erhard more than most.

The *Spiegel* affair abruptly, if temporarily, put an end to pressure on Adenauer. The affair involved two issues: freedom of the press, and the substantive issue of nuclear strategy and defense policy. The SPD had accepted NATO and integration in Western Europe as the foundation of West German foreign policy since 1960, but they continued to resist the idea of nuclear arms for the Bundeswehr and regarded Strauss as the single greatest obstacle to their own defense policies. The SPD, and also others, regarded him as a right-wing extremist on other issues as well. His rhetorical skill and abrasive personal manner had made him many enemies since he first became prominent in the early 1950s. The editor of *Der Spiegel*, Rudolf Augstein, was one of his most implacable enemies, and his magazine had spearheaded many vitriolic attacks on Strauss over the years. Augstein hoped by his incessant attacks on Strauss to achieve two things: to make the minister an embarrassment to the government and so force him out of the cabinet, and to drive a wedge between the FDP and the CDU. This would serve Augstein's broader ambition, which was to help end the reign of the Christian democrats in Bonn and to bring about a liberal or left-liberal government.

Augstein's role was important given the increasing influence of his magazine in forming public opinion in West Germany. In an unusually long and extremely polemical article in April 1961, *Der Spiegel* asserted that Strauss was a threat to democracy and a risk to peace, that he was planning nuclear war, and that he was mad for power.[1] The *Spiegel* writer implied that, if Strauss ever became chancellor, he would introduce a new dictatorship in Germany. Strauss responded to these attacks by suing *Der Spiegel* for libel. The magazine's chief defense lawyer was none other than Gustav Heinemann, who sympathized with Augstein's attacks on the government's defense policy. The lawsuit gave Augstein even more publicity, including the opportunity to repeat his polemical attacks. The verdict of the court of appeal in March 1962 was only a partial vindication of Strauss. Augstein continued his campaign.

The next stage occurred in the spring of 1962 when *Der Spiegel* accused Strauss of having profited personally from a contract given by the Seventh US Army to a German construction company. Again Strauss sued, and obtained a judgement that the magazine could not claim that he had profited from the contract. Again it was a hollow victory: Augstein had succeeded in raising doubts about the minister's integrity, and although convicted of no wrong-doing, Strauss nevertheless began to appear as a liability. Augstein followed the classic tactics of the political journalist who wants to destroy an enemy: he alluded to possible scandals about Strauss which, on investigation, proved groundless, yet the mere publicity was enough to damage the minister's reputation. No court verdict could restore that.

By mid-1962 Augstein had achieved one of his aims. He had succeeded in inciting enough hostility to Strauss in the FDP that the party's Bundestag members voted with the SPD opposition in rejecting an official government report exonerating Strauss. The minister had enjoyed excellent relations with the liberals since Erich Mende and the other "young Turks" dropped their anti-NATO attitudes in the late 1950s. But because of the *Spiegel* affair, those days were now over. Strauss and the FDP became irreconcilable enemies; as late as 1980 the

[1] *Der Spiegel*, April 4, 1961.

FDP campaigned successfully in the general election under the slogan "stop Strauss."

Elections were due in Strauss' home *Land* of Bavaria in late 1962, where he had been chairman of the CSU since 1961. Augstein's constant attacks and the hostility of the FDP undoubtedly made the prospect of campaigning for minister-president of Bavaria very appealing. At 46 he was still young for a leading politician. A period of time in Munich would remove him from Bonn politics and from the direct sight of the media. It would also provide him the opportunity to build up his power base, from which to campaign for nomination as the CDU/CSU candidate for chancellor in the future. Unfortunately for Strauss, the CSU right wing under Alois Hundhammer, supported by the Catholic clergy, opposed him since he belonged to the liberal wing of the CSU. Not only was he unacceptable to the left in Germany as a whole, he was considered a closet liberal by the right in his own state. His decision not to enter the electoral race in Bavaria was therefore made for him, and he remained in Bonn.

In doing so, he also followed Adenauer's wish. The chancellor did not want to lose his defense minister at a time when the US was revising its defense strategy for NATO, and when the SPD, led by its defense expert Fritz Erler, was assiduously cultivating its own image as a better partner for American security policy and strategy in Germany than the CDU/CSU. Erler was wholly in sympathy with the new strategic thinking of the Kennedy administration, which corresponded more closely with the SPD's defense posture as he had developed it since 1958, than with the concepts of the CDU. The US secretary of defense, Robert McNamara, was revising the doctrine of massive retaliation in favor of what was to become known later as "flexible response" – the idea that NATO should be able to respond to a Soviet attack either by conventional or nuclear means, or a combination thereof, without stating in advance how it would react in any given case. Massive retaliation was becoming less credible because the Soviet Union was now capable of delivering nuclear warheads to continental US targets by bomber or missile. The US government and NATO thus argued that massive retaliation was losing its credibility as a useful deterrent, and, in fact, might incite an attack because the Soviet government no longer considered the deterrent realistic. This was the position that pro-defense social democrats, such as Erler and Schmidt, had been arguing since the late 1950s, when they rejected the location of nuclear weapons on German territory and any form of automatic response that restricted flexibility.

Strauss, on the other hand, had been familiar with the ins and outs of American military thinking since the early 1950s and was indispensable, so Adenauer believed, as the German representative in any changes the

US or NATO might want to make. A less experienced man, or one presumably less trusted by the Americans, might not be able to defend German interests effectively during the process of strategic revision that was taking place in NATO.

In the fall of 1962 the controversy surrounding Strauss reached a crescendo. The opening phases of the affair coincided with the Cuban missile crisis. Since the summer, the Soviet Union had been installing long-range nuclear missiles on Cuba capable of hitting targets over most of the United States. On October 22, President Kennedy revealed the existence of these missiles to the world and demanded that they be removed. After four weeks of tension Khrushchev on November 27 agreed to remove them. In return, the US in 1963 removed its intermediate-range nuclear missiles from Europe.

The Cuban missile crisis in October-November 1962 raised the threat of imminent war and formed the background to the further course of the *Spiegel* affair. The events in Cuba had another bearing on Germany. Khrushchev had failed to force the West out of Berlin in 1958-9 and in 1960-1. He had repeatedly demanded that the West join him in signing a peace treaty with both Germanies to be followed by Western withdrawal from Berlin and, as a logical consequence, eventual subjection of West Berlin to the GDR. Such a peace treaty would have included a provision that West Germany never obtain nuclear arms. In fact, some observers argued that it was the fear that Germany might acquire nuclear weapons, as Strauss advocated, that was the main motivation behind Khrushchev's Berlin ultimatum:

> Careful weighing of the evidence leads to the conclusion that by keeping up the harassment of Berlin, the Soviet Union in 1962 could have gotten from Washington a pledge against nuclear arms for West Germany and some sort of international authority for control of access to Berlin from the West, which in due time would have enabled them to interfere with Western presence in the city even more effectively.[2]

Khrushchev may very well have expected that the threat posed by Soviet missiles in Cuba would force the American government to conclude a general agreement with him that would include, among other things, a prohibition of nuclear arms for West Germany. If Khrushchev was genuinely worried by the prospect of nuclear arms in German hands, it helps to explain why he might have been especially eager to see Strauss resign, the leading figure in the German government still committed to

---

[2] Ulam, *The Rivals*, 327.

obtaining nuclear weapons for the Bundeswehr. The *Spiegel* affair produced this result.

The affair was highlighted by the publication of an article in *Der Spiegel* on October 10, 1962, entitled "Bedingt abwehrbereit" (Conditionally prepared for defense). The article, based on research by the magazine's deputy editor, Conrad Ahlers (1922-1981), a close ally of Augstein, analyzed NATO maneuvers which had taken place in September under the codename Fallex 62. These maneuvers were the last in a series of exercises that began with Battle Royal in 1954, and which played through a defense of West Germany using tactical and intermediate-range nuclear weapons in accordance with the New Look strategy for Europe.

The article alleged, drawing on classified NATO documents – according to Cioc, "obtained from a disgruntled member of Strauss' defense ministry"[3] – that NATO planners envisioned a scenario involving a simulated Soviet nuclear attack on NATO installations and retaliation by the West, resulting in heavy destruction in England and West Germany, leaving an estimated ten to 15 million dead. It also claimed that civil defense and communications were entirely inadequate, and that the Bundeswehr itself could not be properly mobilized; in fact, it was "conditionally prepared for defense." This was embarrassing because Strauss had insisted consistently that West Germany's rearmament program was on schedule and fully sufficient; indeed, in late 1961, the Bundestag took the final step when it extended the draft from twelve to 18 months, as originally proposed but defeated by the SPD.

The article also asserted that Strauss and the Americans could not agree on strategy. While Strauss sought tactical nuclear weapons for the Bundeswehr, McNamara wanted to centralize control over nuclear weapons and therefore recommended fewer nuclear weapons in Europe and more conventional forces. Finally, repeating earlier allegations, Ahlers insisted that German military officers, sympathetic to Strauss, foresaw a pre-emptive nuclear strike with West German Lockheed F-104 fighter-bombers (Starfighters) in case of a threat of imminent attack by the East.

The magazine did not reveal its source for this material, which *Der Spiegel* considered highly confidential. Augstein used the familiar press argument that the public deserved to know the truth, no matter what reasons there might be for preserving state secrets, nor how questionable the source. Adenauer and Strauss responded by calling for an investigation to determine from whom *Der Spiegel* had received its infor-

---

[3] Cioc, *Pax Atomica*, 183.

mation. There was no question that the publication of secret material was a violation of German law. The problem was to find evidence, which presumably was in *Der Spiegel*'s possession.

Adenauer and Strauss ordered a search of the magazine's offices. In order to avoid warning Augstein and Ahlers, the official in the ministry of justice who was handling the case chose not to inform the justice minister, Wolfgang Stammberger of the FDP, who had close ties to Dehler and so indirectly to Augstein. There was no evidence, then or later, that either Strauss or Adenauer had told the official not to inform his minister about the search. Augstein was arrested on suspicion of treason on Saturday, October 27, 1962. At this time, Ahlers was vacationing in Spain. Strauss personally called the German military attaché in Madrid to insist that the German embassy find Ahlers and have him arrested by the Spanish police. Later, Strauss was to deny his personal role in bringing about Ahlers' arrest, and it was this denial, more than any other single incident, that forced his later resignation. According to Cioc, Strauss did not come under fire for mishandling West Germany's defenses. Rather, he was dismissed from Government service for sidestepping the constitution: he had ordered an illegal search of the magazine's main offices and arrested editor Rudolf Augstein on charges of treason. When political activists took to the streets, they protested the anti-democratic nature of Strauss' actions, not the defense issues raised by the Fallex 62.[4]

A storm of protest followed Augstein's arrest in West Germany. The SPD, and much of the media, compared Strauss to Nazi censors and alleged that the government was violating freedom of the press. The SPD accused the government of creating a "crisis of the rule of law." At first the FDP leaders, who were coalition partners of Strauss, had no comment, but they could not stifle a rising sense of unease which *Der Spiegel* and other media eagerly fueled. On October 31, Stammberger resigned from the cabinet, arguing that he had not been informed ahead of time about the proposed arrests and the search of the *Spiegel* offices, which were carried out by the Federal Criminal Police (*Bundeskriminal-amt*), for which he was responsible. On November 7 and 8, Strauss presented his side of the affair to the Bundestag, but minimized his own role in the proceedings against Augstein, and in particular his role in bringing about the arrest of Ahlers in Spain.

One of the primary reasons the affair received so much publicity was the apparently arbitrary way the police handled the arrests, as well as the search of *Der Spiegel*'s offices. It seemed to many to represent not only a violation of freedom of the press, but to recall arbitrary actions of a

---

[4] Ibid.

similar type which had occurred during the Third Reich. Indeed, the entire West German press condemned the action. As the prestigious *Frankfurter Allgemeine Zeitung* wrote, "what stinks here, embarrasses not only *Der Spiegel*, not only the press, it embarrasses democracy in our country, which cannot live without a free press, without indivisible freedom of the press."[5]

Commentators of all political persuasions agreed that what Strauss had done was unacceptable. The conservative columnist of *Die Welt*, Sebastian Hafner, addressed the issue in a column published in the *Süddeutsche Zeitung* in early November:

What is usually referred to as "the accompanying circumstances of the Spiegel affair" is in reality the affair itself. The fateful question for Germany which is being raised at this time is not whether the *Spiegel* has – in some articles that may be weeks or months old – crossed the uncertain and flexible limit that distinguishes legitimate public information on defense matters from treason. Let the lawyers calmly decide that point for themselves. The question is whether the Federal Republic of Germany is still a free and constitutional democracy, or whether it has become possible to transform it overnight by some sort of coup d'état based on fear and arbitrary power.[6]

In solidarity with Stammberger the FDP withdrew its ministers from the cabinet on November 19. Adenauer and the foreign minister, Schröder, had just returned from Washington, where they had spent two days discussing the Cuban missile crisis and defense strategy in Germany. The CDU/CSU could not govern alone, and the FDP refused to rejoin the coalition unless Strauss left. Strauss, who also had powerful enemies in the CDU, was, therefore, obliged to resign on November 30, although unwillingly. Ironically, given Strauss' previous interest in campaigning for minister-president of Bavaria, the CSU had won a resounding victory in Bavaria just five days earlier. For the Bavarians, Strauss had become, by election day, the victim of left-wing Prussian (i.e. North German) intellectuals and journalists. Indeed, two CSU campaign slogans were "Treason or Security: CSU," and "Khrushchev, Ulbricht, Wehner, and Mende reach out to each other in spirit."

On November 21, Brentano, the CDU caucus chairman, drew a depressing picture of the government's situation: "The coalition crisis that reached its temporary high point with the FDP decision of November 19 is in reality a permanent crisis which began with the formation of the government." He saw two reasons for this crisis. One

[5] Cited in *Der Spiegel*, November 7, 1962.
[6] Cited in *Der Spiegel*, November 14, 1962.

was Adenauer's written promise to the FDP, and to his own party, in 1961, to resign in good time before the next elections. This promise was "a decisive and irretrievable weakening" of the government, because it sacrificed "the idea of stability anchored in the Basic Law. . . . A head of government who signs a draft, payable on demand, on his own resignation is no longer free in his decisions." The other reason was that the actual leaders of the FDP, Mende and Wolfgang Döring (1919–63), who were not members of the cabinet "necessarily . . . became the organizers of opposition within the coalition."

In Brentano's view the *Spiegel* affair was simply an occasion that demonstrated this weakness. "The government has completely surrendered its initiative to the opposition in the parliament, in the press, in the radio, and on television. . . . Government spokesmen, who clearly were ill informed, made contradictory statements." He concluded: "The crisis is in reality a crisis of the chancellor. The chancellor must not fall because of Augstein." Therefore, according to Brentano, if Adenauer was to form a new government without Strauss, he had do so with Erhard's collaboration, he had to fix a date for his resignation, and the members of the new government would have to promise to continue under Erhard.[7]

Politicians on both sides of the spectrum wanted to exploit the opportunity offered by the breakdown of the CDU/CSU-FDP coalition, to form a grand coalition with the SPD. Since 1961 Herbert Wehner had been discussing such a coalition with the CSU politician Guttenberg, who was no friend of Strauss', and with several leading CDU politicians, including the minister of housing, Paul Lücke, and the secretary of the party, Dufhues. One of the premises on which the rationale for the coalition was based was that it would offer the opportunity to exclude the FDP from playing a role in German politics. Such a coalition would have a majority of votes in the Bundestag, and could therefore pass any legislation it wished. A grand coalition, therefore, would introduce an electoral reform, prescribing majority, or single constituency, elections on the British or American model, where the majority of votes in each constituency elects the representative and all other votes are lost. Such a system would destroy all smaller parties which thereafter could not win a single seat, and would give the CDU/CSU and SPD a permanent monopoly of power. To propose majority elections was therefore tantamount to destruction of the FDP as a political factor. In addition, some of those interested in a grand coalition also saw it as a way to avoid having Erhard succeed Adenauer. Erhard's support was in the CDU and the FDP; the SPD had not liked him ever

---

[7] Quotes from Koerfer, *Kampf ums Kanzleramt*, 688–9.

since the currency reform of 1948. A grand coalition would not have chosen Erhard to succeed Adenauer.

In meetings of the CDU/CSU leadership on December 3 Adenauer succeeded, over Erhard's objections, but with the tacit support of Gerstenmaier, Strauss, and Rainer Barzel, a younger man of rising reputation in the Catholic wing of the CDU, in obtaining authorization to negotiate with the SPD. The next day Ollenhauer, Wehner, and Erler came to the chancellery for talks with the CDU/CSU on a coalition at the federal level. Adenauer, who would be 89 by the time of the next elections in 1965, insisted that he would make no promises about resignation. He and Wehner further agreed that a grand coalition should propose to the Bundestag, as law, a project for majority elections; at that moment, both were determined that the FDP should be destroyed as a political factor. Erler, more sympathetic to the FDP and opposed to a grand coalition, insisted that no decision on majority elections should be made before the next national elections in 1965. The FDP leaders were justifiably terrified, and were very much aware of who had proposed destruction of their party on this occasion, notably Wehner and some of Adenauer's close allies in the CDU. On December 5 the FDP continued its own talks with the CDU but also began negotiating with the SPD.

The decisive event of that day was the caucus meeting of the SPD to discuss the state of negotiations with the CDU/CSU. The caucus decided that Wehner had gone too far, especially in agreeing to permit Adenauer to continue as chancellor. Both the SPD and the public at large, seemed impatient for a change at the top. "The old gentleman simply no longer seemed in touch with the times as a chancellor. People found his autocratic leadership style and his bipolar view of the world outmoded, antiquated, uninteresting. And on top of it all the social democrats were supposed to forgive this man for his merciless attacks on them for more than a decade and give him permission to extend his period in office? Yes, they wanted to get off the hard opposition benches – they wanted to become members of the government – but not at this price."[8] The SPD caucus refused to discuss a grand coalition further, unless Adenauer promised to resign. Later that day the talks came to an end. In the CDU the "Erhard brigade," and Strauss himself, successfully blocked any further efforts to probe the issue.

According to Krone's diary, the next day Adenauer seemed defeated. The FDP and CDU succeeded in obtaining a statement from him to the effect that he intended to step down after the parliamentary holidays of 1963. The entire party leadership breathed a sigh of relief; but a few

[8] Ibid., 701.

days later he had once more regained his will to continue. In an interview with an American broadcasting company, CBS, he replied to a question about what lay in store for the Federal Republic after his resignation: "That question cannot be answered at all. First, no date has been set for my retirement. Second, the political situation – both the domestic situation here in our country and especially the international situation – is unclear, and we don't know what the year 1963 will bring."[9] By mid-December the old coalition of FDP and CDU/CSU was restored, without Strauss.

On December 11, 1962, Adenauer presented a new cabinet in Bonn. The new defense minister was Kai-Uwe von Hassel (born 1913, minister of defense 1963–6, president of the Bundestag 1969–72, member of the European Parliament 1979–84), and Strauss' potential as a candidate for chancellor disappeared. He served once more in the federal government, as minister of finance from 1966 to 1969, but his main arena of political activity was henceforth his native region of Bavaria.

In the 1980s evidence came to light that suggested that the information published by Der Spiegel came from Soviet sources, and that the affair was, in large part, the result of a Soviet campaign aimed at ruining Strauss. Whether this allegation is true or not, it illustrates the complexity of West German politics at a time when the Federal Republic was only 13 years old. The whole affair challenged the credibility and stability of the German state severely, and perhaps more than any previous domestic dispute. The state survived well. But the question remains whether Augstein was aware of the possible source of his material, and if he was aware, whether he considered its use a contribution to freedom of the press, or a weapon, albeit illegitimate, to attain a political goal by circumventing the legitimate, democratic, electoral process.[10]

The Spiegel affair, and in its aftermath, the complicated negotiations among the parties, symbolized a transition in the character of postwar German politics. The transition had two aspects which were closely connected. First, the change from sharp confrontation between the parties to a period of maneuvering, flexibility, and dissent within the parties, was a sign of a healthy political process. The second change was generational. The old-style conservatism of Adenauer, in which the reason of state was all important, and the personal fortunes of those affected by it secondary, was giving way to a liberalism which often put individual designs and purposes before principles of state.

[9] Cited ibid., 705–6.
[10] Pincher, The Secret Offensive, 32–67 and Schwarz, Die Ära Adenauer, 1957–1963, 268, 272.

In the *Spiegel* affair the new liberalism appeared in the almost universal public condemnation of Strauss and the vast increase of power and prestige of the three North German journals, *Der Spiegel, Stern* and *Die Zeit*. As a result of the affair, the editors and journalists of these three media saw their power to form opinion and influence politics increase rapidly. No public figure could afford to ignore a magazine that had overthrown Strauss. The affair also reflected other changing political fortunes. It was characteristic that, among the leading figures of the SPD in the 1960s were Gustav Heinemann and Horst Ehmke, a professor of law, who strongly supported *Der Spiegel* in the affair. Ehmke, born in 1927 in Danzig, was elected to parliament in 1969 and later became chief of staff of the chancellor's office under Willy Brandt and federal minister without portfolio. The power of the emerging new liberalism of the 1960s was also demonstrated by the academic intelligentsia and its students, who were vocal critics of Strauss. But Strauss' actions themselves had equally important consequences: they discredited the idea that the state was above the law.

# 4

# Change through Rapprochement

The wide-reaching change in the style of West German politics, in the role of the press, and in the political beliefs of academics and students, corresponded to a much broader change in world politics which found its expression in the new US policy of detente which was announced by President Kennedy in June 1963. The transition from confrontation, as it had taken place since the Cuban missile crisis in October 1962 – at the time of the *Spiegel* affair – to a new belief in the power of contact and communication to overcome the tensions of the East–West conflict, occurred with surprising speed. It affected Soviet-American relations in a major way; namely, the decision taken by the Soviet government that it would never allow itself again to be in a military position inferior to that of the United States, so that it would be forced to back down, as it had during the Cuban missile crisis. But this change in approach – the new emphasis on detente – also affected Germany and probably to a greater degree than any other country.

Within the SPD the debate concerning how best to deal with the realities of the country's division intensified. Herbert Wehner, the party's chief strategist, had long believed that the way forward in Ostpolitik went through Moscow – that is, via agreements entailing West German recognition of the status quo and rejection of the Hallstein Doctrine. It was Wehner who, in 1960, had declared that the SPD was prepared to accept the status quo in the West – NATO, the EEC, and the Western integration of the Federal Republic in general – as the foundation of West German foreign policy. For Wehner, the other side of the coin was to begin an effort for better relations with the communist regimes in Eastern Europe, based on that Western integration. Most Christian democrats were not yet prepared to go this far: for them, Western integration meant that West Germany could not, and should not, recognize the status quo, but should insist on the moral obligation to change it and to bring democracy to East Germany.

Wehner took the opposite view: it was precisely Western integration and the resulting stability of the Bonn republic that made a new Ostpolitik possible.

The first leading social democrat to indicate publicly that the SPD was reappraising its policy vis-à-vis East Germany and Eastern Europe was Egon Bahr, who did so in a speech in July to the Evangelical Academy in Tutzing on Lake Starnberg in Bavaria. Bahr, who was born 1922 in Treffurt, in the former GDR served as a commentator for RIAS (Radio in the American Sector) in Berlin from 1950 to 1960. At the time he made his speech he had been director of the press and information office in the city of Berlin since 1960 and was thus a close collaborator of the governing mayor and SPD candidate for chancellor in 1961, Willy Brandt. Observers accurately guessed that the speech reflected Brandt's views and those of the rising pro-detente wing of the party. Since the Kennedy administration was also in favor of detente, Brandt's position on this matter, as on others, was close to the American one; so close, in fact, that he and his supporters were called "Atlanticists" – in favor of close transatlantic ties to the US.

In his speech Bahr anticipated the dramatic alteration in the course of West German foreign policy that took place in the late 1960s. He doubted that "we can change the totally negative result of the policy of reunification if we continue our present policy" and stated that he was convinced "that the time has come, and that it is our obligation, to rethink it anew as objectively as possible." He concluded that the government, and all those who played a role in shaping Bonn's *Deutschlandpolitik* – its policy in regard to national division – should consider "whether there are no possibilities of gradually reducing the justifiable worries of the [East German] regime so that a relaxation at the border and the Wall would be practicable, because the risk becomes bearable. This is a policy which could be formulated as 'change through rapprochement.'" Along with a growing number of other younger social democrats and liberals, Bahr believed "that we can have enough self-confidence to pursue such a policy without illusion, a policy which, furthermore, fits smoothly into the Western concept of peace strategy, because otherwise we may have to wait for a miracle, and that is no policy."[1]

Bahr's critics feared that change through rapprochement would eventually result in diplomatic recognition of the GDR and that the East German government would come to be looked upon by other foreign governments, and eventually by the public, as a legitimate government

---

[1] Bundesministerium für innerdeutsche Beziehungen, *Dokumente zur Deutschlandpolitik*, IV/1963, 9: 572, 575.

representing the hopes and aspirations of its citizens. If this happened, they argued, it would prove even more difficult to reunify the country in the future and, in fact, the obligation felt by Germans and Germany's friends to unify the country would become weaker and weaker. In addition, Bahr's critics believed that diplomatic recognition would mean recognizing the GDR as a sovereign state, and its border with Poland; and that the refugees from the Oder–Neisse territories would no longer have a legal, if unenforceable, claim to return to what had been stolen from them.

Bahr's supporters accepted that change through rapprochement might mean accepting that there were two German states, but they argued that this recognition was becoming inevitable in any case. Denying the GDR's right to exist, they believed, was to deny reality and to cut oneself off from any influence in shaping a future of less tension for all Europeans. Since 1945, they pointed out, the two parts of Germany had in fact grown apart. The Ulbricht regime in East Germany, as well as the Soviet Union, had first insisted that West Germany remain outside the Western alliance system in order to be reunited with the East, and since 1954 they had insisted that the GDR was now a sovereign state and that any reunification must start from that recognition. Since neither Ulbricht nor the Soviet government was likely to change his position, Bahr argued, an offer of rapprochment would cost nothing, and might conceivably improve relations among the Germans in both countries.

Adenauer's policies had never been designed to reunify the country as a sine qua non. As Eugen Gerstenmaier remarked in 1954: first came freedom, then peace, and then reunification. Moreover, Adenauer believed that his main task as chancellor was to make absolutely sure that the West German republic was tied irrevocably to its Western neighbors and allies politically, militarily, and economically. Only such ties would prevent a future government, advocating reunification of Germany as a neutral country, from abandoning democracy in favor of national unity. Adenauer considered that such a development would be a disaster for both Germany and all of Europe, and devoted all of his energies to making it impossible. Unlike many of the party leaders of the 1950s, Bahr and the younger social democrats accepted Bonn's ties to the West, but they wanted to maintain their traditional commitment to peace and social democracy via detente with the East. They believed, rightly or wrongly, that the only way to alleviate conditions for Germans in the East was to accept that Moscow would never permit reunification in freedom and to start from that proposition. This is essentially what Bahr proposed in 1963. How to translate the idea into policy, however, was a matter of fierce debate. This debate, which, in a sense, began publicly with Bahr's Tutzing speech, continued throughout that decade and after.

Bahr could also point to the American interest in detente as an argument that West Germany must endorse it as well, if it was to continue to be respected within NATO. This was Brandt's view, and Bahr was a friend and associate of Brandt's; yet Bahr's idea had distinct nationalist overtones. Bahr considered himself a socialist-nationalist, which meant that the hope for national unity and socialism demanded that the GDR be officially recognized and its regime drawn into a relationship with West Germany in the hope that it would lead to some kind of confederation. Bahr's concept of the German national interest was that this interest could be preserved through negotiations with the GDR. This was the exact opposite of the concept held by Adenauer, that German national interests could not be served by recognizing the GDR, because its government was a dictatorship whose very existence was a contradiction of the German national interest. Bahr also distrusted the United States government and was inclined to belittle the importance of NATO. Certainly by 1963 he no longer believed that a Soviet threat to the security of Germany and Europe existed, and seemed, almost casually, to give the impression from time to time that the Soviet government was more reliable than that of the United States.

Nonetheless, the policy of reappraisal was welcomed by Brandt and the SPD, and it was so reflected in parts of the German press. *Der Spiegel* called for a new Eastern policy and declared that anti-communism was a relic of the past to be discarded. In *Die Zeit* the editors Marion Dönhoff and Theo Sommer had long argued for accommodation with the East, and their position now found a much wider echo. A year earlier, in the spring of 1962, a group of leading Protestants, including the physicists Werner Heisenberg and Carl Friedrich von Weizsäcker, who had played such an important part in the public opposition against nuclear armament and in reforming the SPD's defense conceptions in the late 1950s, published a manifesto in *Die Zeit,* calling for recognition of the two Germanies and of the Oder–Neisse line. Adenauer found these developments much too rapid, and therefore alarming, but he had promised to resign in October of 1963 and was not in a position to exert great influence on this development. His best hope was to try and ensure that the government to follow him would be less inclined to concessions and less optimistic about the possible outcome of detente than the US president.

# 5

# Adenauer's Last Success: The Franco-German Friendship Treaty

B y December 1962, while the *Spiegel* affair was still reverberating throughout German public life, French and West German negotiators had completed their discussions on the future relations of the two countries. In accordance with the provisional agreements reached during de Gaulle's visit in September, the two governments would henceforth consult closely on all matters of mutual interest. The negotiators proposed a regular schedule of meetings of the heads of the two governments and of their foreign and defense ministers. Adenauer was delighted, the Atlanticists (led, in this instance, by Erhard and Schröder) much less so. On January 14, de Gaulle confirmed their worst fears about what close alignment with France might mean.

At a dramatically stage-managed press conference in Paris on that day, de Gaulle declared that Britain was too different from the continental countries to fit easily within the EEC; the negotiations for membership had therefore no point and should be broken off. He mentioned economic structure, international trade links, and agriculture as areas where Britain differed too much from the interests of the original Six. But these were specious arguments. The real reason de Gaulle was angry with the British was that Prime Minister Harold Macmillan in December 1962 had concluded an agreement with President Kennedy at a meeting in Nassau in the Bahamas. Under this agreement the US would supply Polaris nuclear-armed missiles to British submarines which might later form part of the proposed NATO multilateral force (MLF). Though the British would obtain full control of the missiles, de Gaulle read the Nassau agreement as a British capitulation to the Americans. He refused even to discuss a similar arrangement for France. The Americans were not going to be the sole suppliers – and, by implication, the sole controllers – of European nuclear forces. On January 16, he took the logical next step and formally announced the *force de frappe*: France would establish its own nuclear strike force, independent of NATO.

Both these moves were directly opposed to West German interests as the Atlanticists saw them. On the nuclear issue, Bonn and in particular the new defense minister, Hassel, no longer hoped for German nuclear weapons and, precisely for that reason, strongly desired an arrangement like the MLF: an integrated, sea-based, NATO nuclear force not subject to national control, either American or otherwise. On the issue of British accession, the Atlanticists saw this as an essential element of European integration. Even Adenauer's closest associates, like Gerstenmaier and Blankenhorn, insisted that the chancellor try to change de Gaulle's mind. When Adenauer arrived in Paris to sign the treaty resulting from the negotiations on Franco-German cooperation, Jean Monnet himself asked the chancellor to insist that he would only sign if de Gaulle changed his mind. To accomplish that, however, was beyond even Adenauer's legendary powers of persuasion. On January 22, he and de Gaulle signed the treaty that Adenauer thought would prevent de Gaulle from dealing with the Soviet Union at Germany's expense, and that de Gaulle thought would wean Bonn from alignment with Washington. Given such opposed expectations it was not surprising that the treaty, at least during its early years, often seemed more of a disappointment than a new beginning.

Nevertheless, the treaty marked the symbolic end of decades, if not centuries, of hostility and mistrust. In a joint statement issued at the signing of the treaty, de Gaulle and Adenauer declared that they were "convinced that the reconciliation of the German people and the French people, ending a centuries-old rivalry, constitutes a historic event which profoundly transforms the relations between the two peoples." The treaty itself, on "organization and principles of cooperation," stated:

1  The Heads of State and Government shall give the necessary directives as required and shall follow regularly the execution of the program. .... For this purpose, they shall meet as often as necessary and, in principle, at least twice a year.

2  The Foreign Ministers shall supervise the execution of the program as a whole. They shall meet at least every three months. .... [H]igh officials of the two Foreign Ministries – charged respectively with political, economic, and cultural affairs – shall meet every month.

3  Regular meetings shall take place between the appropriate authorities of the two countries in the fields of defense, education, and youth.[1]

---

[1] Dept of State, *Documents on Germany*, 833–5.

After setting forth the organization of cooperation, the treaty stated its extent, which was broad:

The Two Governments [*sic*] shall consult before any decision on all important questions of foreign policy and primarily on questions of common interest with a view to reaching as far as possible parallel positions. This consultation shall apply, among others, to the following subjects:
Problems relating to the European Communities and European political cooperation;
East–West relations both in the political and economic fields;
Matters dealt with in the North Atlantic Treaty Organization;
In the field of strategy and tactics, the competent authorities of the two countries shall endeavor to bring their doctrines closer together;
Exchanges of personnel between the armed forces shall be increased.[2]

The defense provisions were possibly the most important, because they implicitly involved the planned French nuclear force and because they were unaffected by France's later withdrawal from NATO in 1966. At this moment they provoked an immediate Soviet response that recalled the occasions in 1957–8, when the Soviet Union had threatened West Germany with nuclear war for daring to want to defend itself with nuclear weapons if attacked: "The Soviet Union has more than once warned the Federal Government of what a fatal danger it is inviting to its country. ... It is not difficult to imagine that, should it come to a thermo-nuclear war, powerful and concentrated blows of nuclear rocket weapons would inevitably fall upon Western Germany. She would not survive a third world war."[3]

The 1963 treaty had a symbolic importance that far outstripped its – at first sight – meager results in terms of concrete policies. For the first time, many Frenchmen and West Germans, and many Europeans outside those two countries, saw tangible evidence of the complete and irreversible reconciliation between the modern successors of the two regional powers which had, since the ninth century, contested the mastery of Europe between them. The fact that both had abandoned the struggle and that the master of European destiny was, arguably, the Soviet Union (restrained from Western Europe by the United States), was temporarily overshadowed by the moving spectacle of the two senior statesmen meeting to celebrate the treaty at another pontifical high mass in the cathedral at Reims. This was their second visit to the city in less than seven months. Celebrating the treaty there, had, for de Gaulle and many other Frenchmen, an emotional power that is

[2] Ibid.
[3] Ibid., 838–9.

impossible to put into words. Some observers referred to the ceremony as "the marriage of the two old men," because Adenauer and de Gaulle knelt at the front of the congregation, side by side, on a *prie-dieu* before the altar, as would a bride and bridegroom.

For Adenauer, a Catholic and a West German in the regional as well as the political, postwar sense, traveling to mass at Reims with the president of France was no less a gesture of deep significance, and also a vital step in the reconciliation that Adenauer recognized was absolutely essential to the stable future of the Federal Republic. On this visit, Adenauer discussed specific points with de Gaulle, which astonished everyone familiar with the German chancellor's commitment to the Atlantic Alliance and his belief that any deviation from it could only be harmful to the Western interest. Instead of begging de Gaulle to return to the Atlantic fold, Adenauer urged him to lead it:

I remarked that de Gaulle underestimated the influence of France as well as his own. . . . General de Gaulle enjoyed great popularity in the United States where France was loved and esteemed . . . even more, perhaps, than Britain. I believed that the Americans needed Europe. Kennedy wanted the benefit of European counsel. . . . I begged de Gaulle insistently to make use of any occasion that might arise. Personal influence might not be able to change everything, but it could influence the course of events.[4]

Adenauer implored de Gaulle "to influence the Americans by his personality and by the wisdom of his policies." Sentimental worship by an old Rhinelander of a great Frenchman, or a last, Machiavellian attempt to flatter de Gaulle into moving in a direction he would never choose freely? No one knows. In any case, for Adenauer, who was to resign just eight months later, the treaty was a crowning achievement. Upon his return to Germany on January 23, 1963, Adenauer addressed the nation:

It has taken the Foreign Ministry of France and the Foreign Ministry of the Federal Republic many months and careful study to prepare this treaty. I believe that the treaty, as it stands now, is unique in history, because it provides for friendly relations between both our peoples over an unlimited period of time. . . .

The French president, de Gaulle, called the signing of the treaty a unique event in history, and in my opinion rightly so. If we look at this treaty, we must clearly remember what preceded it. For more than four centuries tensions and stress, often leading to bloody wars, existed between Germany and France. I may remind you that the last war with France, a war in which we were the losers, lies not that far in the past. . . .

[4] Cited in Lacouture, *De Gaulle*, 3: 307.

There would be no Europe, if this true reconciliation between France and Germany had not taken place. . . .

I am absolutely convinced that this treaty will be considered one of the most important and most valuable treaties in the annals of the postwar era, and I am absolutely convinced that it will benefit both our peoples and benefit Europe and world peace.[5]

With the treaty de Gaulle hoped to rescue as much as possible of his strategic initiative toward West Germany and to present Adenauer's successors with a unique and permanent bond to France of a nature very different from Germany's relationship with the United States. De Gaulle was disappointed in this hope, for a close working relationship between the leaders of both countries was not developed until Helmut Schmidt and Valéry Giscard d'Estaing gave it real substance between 1974 and 1981. Adenauer and the majority of the members of the West German Bundestag remained wary of alienating the United States and believed that such a development would jeopardize the American commitment to the defense of the Federal Republic.

The treaty came at a critical moment of the succession struggle. From the *Spiegel* affair onward Erhard clearly recognized that politely waiting in the wings was not sufficient to secure the chancellorship and that Adenauer was adamantly opposed to him. More forceful action was needed. Though Erhard never felt comfortable engaging in the rough-and-tumble of power politics – that indeed was the reason his government fell in 1966 – he did conduct enough of a campaign within the CDU, and in the German public at large, that Adenauer was finally obliged to concede defeat. Erhard was motivated to do so by his worry that the Franco-German treaty was likely to hurt Germany's real security interest, which lay in close alignment with the US and in British membership of the Common Market.

On January 29, 1963, the Council of Ministers of the EEC definitively adjourned the negotiations for British membership. Erhard considered the decision "a black hour for Europe." The next day he compared de Gaulle to Hitler in a cabinet meeting, remarking that 30 years earlier, Hitler had forced Germany under his yoke, now de Gaulle was doing the same to Europe. A few days later the *Süddeutsche Zeitung* in Munich published an explosive interview with Erhard entitled "We do not want to bear the burden on two shoulders." The interviewer, Hans Ulrich Kempski, asked if Erhard intended to remain true to his "clear line in favor of the Atlantic community and against attempts to cobble together mini-European, special alliances," even at the risk of widening the

[5] Adenauer, *Erinnerungen 1959–1963*, 211–12.

differences of opinion between himself and Adenauer. Erhard responded with an unequivocal "yes." But Kempski continued:

*Kempski*:   The majority of the CDU is convinced that you will take up the heritage of Adenauer. The chancellor for his part has dropped many hints that he would like to prevent such an inheritance from taking place. You have so far avoided making any public statement on the matter. . . . [S]ince Adenauer presumably intends to retire in the fall, the time seems to have come to ask you if you are prepared to respond to your party's call to take up the office of chancellor?

*Erhard*:   Yes, I am. I would be ready to follow a call to the chancellorship if my party and the Bundestag so decide.[6]

Observers sensed that at last Erhard was being decisive; but he still could not declare, "I want to be chancellor" but had to say, "I will serve if asked." His friend Gerd Bucerius, publisher of *Die Zeit* and owner of *Stern*, wrote him a scathing letter on February 23 saying that he had only himself to blame if he was still not sure of the succession. "You become a statesman in your own right, not by permission of a failed predecessor. . . . Your interview was good, except for the end: you must never say that others will make you chancellor. You will become it on your own or not at all."[7] The war of nerves between Adenauer and the Erhard brigade was bringing disaster to the party. On February 17, in elections in West Berlin, the CDU fell to 29 per cent, a loss of ten percentage points, its biggest loss in any election, while the SPD, led by Brandt, increased its absolute majority from 52 to 62 per cent of the vote, an almost incredible achievement. In the Rhineland-Palatinate on March 31 the CDU lost about five points, but remained, at 44 per cent, slightly ahead of the SPD, which received 41 per cent.

In the late winter of 1962-3 it seemed, for a moment, as though Schröder might be the only candidate of the Atlanticist-Protestant wing not only to have the party's, but also Adenauer's confidence. But in reality it was too late to stop the momentum for Erhard. Adenauer had promised to resign; he could not now refuse to fulfil his pledge without destroying the party completely. Most observers regarded Erhard not only as the most competent and experienced statesman in the CDU, but as the one most likely to restore the party's electoral fortunes. Since 1953 Erhard had been known as "the electoral locomotive" of the CDU, and many were anxious to see him in sole command.

Adenauer delayed making a final commitment, on resigning and on Erhard, as long as possible. Perhaps, like the poet Goethe, he believed

[6]   Cited in Koerfer, *Kampf ums Kanzleramt*, 718–19.
[7]   Cited ibid., 729–30.

that he could not die as long as he was in office, that his almost super-natural vitality – how many 87–year-olds have seriously considered fighting a national election two years in the future? – was somehow a function of power. On April 22 the party leaders finally insisted on a decision. At a meeting of the CDU/CSU caucus leadership Adenauer acknowledged that Erhard was the only choice acceptable to the party. Even so, when the full party caucus voted on the candidates the next day, Adenauer could not resist giving expression once more to his basic worry about Erhard: "A man can be the best possible economics minister without having the same understanding of political questions. ... It gives me no pleasure to say that the man, with whom I have collaborated for 14 years, and who has accomplished extraordinary deeds, from my point of view, is not suitable for another position, which he would like to have."[8] While supporting Erhard, Strauss echoed this fear, telling Erhard that politics was more important than the economy, and that he, Erhard, had not always understood the importance of power.

Though Adenauer had given in at last, it was very hard for him to accept what had happened. A Swiss historian has put it as follows:

For him, in whom the *libido dominandi* was truly distinctive, for whom ruling, governing was a genuine pleasure, the events of April 22 and 23 must at first have seemed almost inconceivable. ... His own party had turned against him and ambushed him.

Only gradually the events of April 1963 set in motion [in Adenauer] a comprehensive, emotionally painful and turbulent labor of grief. In the course of it Adenauer's face changed. It became even narrower, the contours became sharper and more clearly defined, the furrows deeper. Although on the outside his physiognomy remained that of an aged, stoical Indian, it nevertheless revealed something of the inner struggles, the tremendous tension of those weeks and months, revealed what only his closest confidants knew. The rapidly changing moods; bitterness, anger, rage. ... "It feels as though my arms and legs have been cut off," he said during those days. The forced resignation – the hardest step of his life. He felt cut to the bone. The third dismissal was the worst; not being deposed by the National Socialists in 1933, not the arrogant treatment by the British twelve years later – no, the enforced resignation in 1963 had shaken him the most violently, he confided to Eugen Gerstenmaier.[9]

The CDU greeted the change with relief. Erhard appeared to prove his reputation as an electoral locomotive in Lower Saxony, where the CDU improved its standing by seven points in June, an achievement that broke the party's losing streak since 1960. During the summer

[8] Cited ibid., 743.
[9] Ibid., 745.

Adenauer threw himself into a hectic round of traveling throughout Germany, Europe, and to the US. Everywhere the departing patriarch was greeted with respect, accorded both himself and the achievements of Germany since 1945. Gradually the "old man" came to terms with his resignation, with the fact that his very love of power and his skill in exercising it would have made any departure painful. More serious was his concern that his successors would carelessly destroy what he had so carefully built.

When the CDU finally chose Erhard to succeed Adenauer it lifted a millstone from its own neck. One could go back to business. The main item was the ratification of the Franco-German treaty. When the Bundestag ratified the treaty on May 16, 1963, it added a preamble that declared that all of Germany's multilateral treaty obligations remained valid, and emphasized the will to maintain a close transatlantic partnership and the integration of NATO forces, as well as the desire to include Britain in the Common Market. As Jean Lacouture wrote: "One could hardly find a more complete contradiction of the entire principle of the treaty itself. Preamble? No, a declaration that all that followed was null and void. It was as if Ronald Reagan had written a preface to the *Capital* of Karl Marx."[10] A month before the preamble was made public de Gaulle had learned of it from his ambassador in Bonn, who added his opinion that the SPD – which meant Brandt and Erler – was largely responsible for it. In fact, it was the product of consultations among Atlanticists in several countries, including France: Jean Monnet, who believed in European integration with, not against, the American alliance, and who disapproved of de Gaulle's vision of a Europe of national states, was one of its principal authors, as Couve de Murville reported in his memoirs. De Gaulle's vision of greatness was not one shared by all French patriots by any means.

By early summer 1963 the opposed purposes of de Gaulle and Erhard – but with the exception of Adenauer – in entering into the bilateral treaty were dominating the common concerns shared by both leaders. This development was apparent in the enthusiastic reception of President Kennedy in West Germany in June. Kennedy's visit provoked even more enthusiasm than de Gaulle's a year earlier, and convinced the French president that there was little hope of drawing Bonn out of Washington's orbit:

At the end of the summer de Gaulle was scheduled to visit Adenauer in Bonn for the first of the twice-yearly Franco-German summit conferences called for under the new friendship treaty. But his irritation with the Germans over their

[10] Lacouture, *De Gaulle*, 3: 308.

loyalty to NATO was by now so great that he was already running his own treaty down. To a group of French parliamentarians on the eve of his trip, he remarked: "Treaties are like young ladies and roses. They last while they last." And he went on to quote a line of poetry from Victor Hugo: "Alas how many young ladies I have seen die."

But when this was relayed to Adenauer in Bonn, the old chancellor adroitly turned the metaphor back around: "I know quite a lot about roses, for I have raised them all my life," he said. "And the plants which have lots of thorns are the most resistant ones."[11]

De Gaulle remained critical of what he regarded as Bonn's subservience to Washington and its attempts to bring Britain into the EEC. He vetoed British entry for the second time in 1967. Meanwhile, West Germany had changed chancellors twice. Both Adenauer's successors, Erhard and Kiesinger, endorsed Franco-German collaboration, but remained committed to the Atlantic Alliance. On a secondary level, the two bureaucracies faithfully fulfilled the more modest elements of the treaty: increased economic cooperation, avoidance of mutually harmful trade policies, normalization of trade practices. But it was not until de Gaulle was gone from the scene that a new, more pragmatic form of Franco-West German cooperation could emerge.

Even the elderly ruler himself, three days before his resignation in April 1969, told Maurice Schumann, his minister for social policy and old comrade-in-arms, that there could be no French foreign policy in the future that was not "founded on the irreversibility of the Franco-German reconciliation."[12] And, bearing in mind the traditional Catholic significance of the term "reconciliation," that is how it remained.

[11] Cook, *Charles de Gaulle*, 365–6. See also Lacouture, *De Gaulle*, 3: 308–9.
[12] Lacouture, *De Gaulle*, 3: 312.

# 6

# The Succession Completed

The Bundestag's preamble to the Franco-German treaty was a victory for Schröder and the Atlanticists. In the summer of 1963 Schröder's mainly north German and Protestant wing of the CDU leadership fought again with the conservatives around Adenauer, Heinrich von Brentano und Heinrich Krone, over the direction of German foreign policy. (Krone, born in 1895, was a member of the Reichstag from 1925 to 1933, and was elected to the Bundestag from 1949 to 1969; he kept one of the most detailed and fascinating diaries of postwar Germany.) It was the last time the chancellor tried to lay down the law for his successors, and he did not succeed. From this time onward the influence of liberal northern Protestants in the CDU grew and gave the party a very different profile from that of the early years, when it was guided primarily by conservative Catholics, including those of the CSU.

Erhard became chancellor in October 1963, at the age of 66. Adenauer resigned full of doubts and with the bitterness that had always been one of his characteristics, but, as Gerstenmaier noted in his hour-long speech on October 15 honoring "der Alte:" "In a hundred years of storm-tossed German history you are the only one to depart undefeated and in peace after long service of government from a seat like this one and to return calmly to the seat from which you rose on September 15, 1949." Adenauer did not, indeed, leave undefeated and in peace; he had been forced out. But Gerstenmaier compared the great Otto von Bismarck unfavorably to Adenauer. Bismarck had served longer as chancellor (from 1862 to 1890), and he achieved the unity of the German Reich, but he was dismissed against his will. Adenauer, who at that moment must have felt very much like Bismarck, responded in-directly to Gerstenmaier's praise by, typically, praising the German people: "I am proud of the German people ... proud of what the German people have accomplished in this relatively short span of time. We Germans can carry our heads high again, for we have entered the alliance of free nations and have become a welcome member of the alliance of free nations."[1]

A few days earlier, Adenauer had given an interview to a paper that always loyally supported him, the *Rheinischer Merkur*, a Catholic weekly. In it he looked back once again at the challenges he had overcome:

> One starts to forget the chaos that Hitler left behind: Germany destroyed, half of Central and Eastern Europe left to the Soviets. Millions of dead soldiers, expellees, and victims of concentration camps, and millions of prisoners of war; hunger and misery, hatred against Germany, dismantling in East and West. . . .
>
> It was necessary, therefore, to raise the morale of the German people beaten down by . . . the effects of occupation, to fight the physical and moral destitution, and, above all, to convince the Western powers that an annihilated Germany, incapable of survival, could only play into the hands of Stalin and his goals of world revolution. This most important preparatory task was necessary for the reconstruction of Germany and had to be achieved before the Federal Republic could be founded. In the immediate postwar years I worked, together with all the positive forces of our people, to convince particularly our present Western partners that a renewal of Europe will be impossible without a strong and free Germany.[2]

Rolf Lahr, state secretary in the foreign ministry, described one of Adenauer's last official acts, a state breakfast in honor of the Belgian prime minister, Lefèvre, in the chancellor's official residence, the Palais Schaumburg. Noticing the curiosity of his guests as to why every place setting had three wine glasses, instead of the usual two, Adenauer, the wine connoisseur, explained:

> Before I move out of here, I asked Mr Globke to find out what still remains in the wine cellar. And he told me that there are still eight bottles of *Trocken-beerenauslese*. Well, they would be wasted on Mr Erhard, who understands nothing about wines – we'll finish them now.[3]

Only a month after Adenauer resigned, President Kennedy was assassinated in Dallas by Lee Harvey Oswald. Kennedy's death shocked the world. Unlike Adenauer, who never learned to trust him completely, most Germans felt that Kennedy genuinely wanted peace with freedom in Europe, and that he understood that Europe was now strong enough to pursue its own policies in partnership with the United States. Helmut Schmidt wrote in his memoirs:

[1] Cited in Koerfer, *Kampf ums Kanzleramt*, 749.
[2] *Adenauer: Briefe über Deutschland*, 12.
[3] Lahr, *Zeuge von Fall und Aufstieg*, 384.

The president corresponded to the ideal vision that many Germans had of a political leader: an idealist with a great vision and a little bit of romanticism, but also a man of practical, visible success. ... Given this impression, many Germans were prepared to place themselves unconditionally under American leadership. We would even have been prepared to make sacrifices to German-American friendship if Kennedy had asked us to do so. His speech on July 4, 1962, in Philadelphia seemed to demonstrate: this American president understood Europe, he offered us Europeans partnership on equal terms with his own nation – an impression I have had only once again thereafter, namely with Gerald Ford. We loved Kennedy and with him America. When he was murdered, the shock and grief were felt no less in Germany than in his own country. But at the same time we perceived the first inkling of that fear of the political future, that has often plagued the Germans since, to a lesser or a greater degree.

On the evening of November 22, 1963, I was making a speech at a social democratic party meeting in Hamburg-Winterhude. As I was speaking someone reached up to the podium and handed me a note with the news of Kennedy's assassination. I interrupted my speech and read the news. It was impossible to go on talking or listening. I said: "This death shocks us all. It changes the world. Let us go home quietly." The people acted as though someone had struck them with a club: mute confusion, uncomprehending horror and grief. They rose and silently left the hall. A star had been extinguished. Never were we as close to the American nation as on that evening.[4]

[4] Schmidt, *Menschen und Mächte*, 173–4.

# Bibliographic Essay

The following essay is intended to help the non-specialist reader or student who wishes to pursue the study of one or more aspects of the postwar history of West Germany. In compiling it, the authors at once faced the problem of language. German ranks eighth in number of native speakers among the languages of the world, and the output of works on our subject in German is enormous. Despite the growing interest of American and British scholars and writers in the society, politics, and history of the Federal Republic, it remains true that most important writings are and will continue to be in German. We therefore direct the reader to a range of useful, informative, and authoritative works on each aspect of the subject regardless of language, although we have included English-language works when available.

Full citation of the works mentioned will be found in the bibliography.

## Bibliographies, general works, and works of reference

A fairly full bibliography of works on West German history and politics through 1969 can be found in Morsey's *Bundesrepublik*, which also includes a concise narrative overview and a survey of important controversial issues. The best general bibliography on contemporary Germany is the *Bibliographie zur Zeitgeschichte*, which until 1989 appeared as a supplement in every issue of *Vierteljahrshefte für Zeitgeschichte* (1953–). Starting in 1989, the *Bibliographie* appears as a separate annual special issue of the journal rather than as a section in each regular issue. The *Bibliographie* provides a comprehensive listing by subject of books and articles on twentieth-century world history and politics with special reference to Germany. Before 1989 titles dealing with the post-1945 period were listed in even-numbered years. The Institut für Zeitgeschichte, which publishes the journal, issued the cumulative listings through 1980 (over 40,000 items) as *Bibliographie zur Zeitgeschichte 1953–1980* (1982), and will update this with a new cumulative list (through 1990) in 1991.

The starting-point for all serious study of our subject is the *Geschichte der Bundesrepublik Deutschland*, published in the 1980s in six large tomes of close to 500 pages each, covering the period 1945–82. This is the definitive history of West Germany for the next generation. There is nothing like it in any other language or for any other country. Each volume covers politics, foreign affairs, economy, society, culture, and attitudes. The authors went to great lengths to write both clearly and accurately. In many cases, they had access to unpublished diaries or other hitherto confidential sources, so that the account is often not merely informative but original.

A short introduction, emphasizing social structures rather than individuals, is Berghahn's *Modern Germany*, which begins in 1871 but emphasizes the period since 1933. The author takes a more critical view of many aspects of the Federal Republic than do the authors of the *Geschichte*. Michael Balfour, the author of several outstanding works on German subjects, published a revised version of his *West Germany* in 1982, a lively, detailed, and well-written account of the period from occupation through the chancellorship of Schmidt. Turner's useful overview *Two Germanies*, covers two decades more than Balfour, but is intended as an introduction rather than as a comprehensive account. As the title indicates, Turner includes the GDR, which leaves even less space for West German affairs. The best account of the GDR, one of the best books on Germany altogether, is Childs' *The GDR*.

Most other German works pale into insignificance beside the *Geschichte*. Hillgruber's *Deutsche Geschichte* is a well-written, concise account, periodically updated, focusing on the national issue and Germany's place in East–West relations. It is particularly useful for the reader who wants to understand the main themes and stages of West German history. Thränhardt's book is the view of a leftist opposed at most points to Hillgruber and to the moderate world-view presented in the *Geschichte*. A leading historian of the older generation, Hans Herzfeld, left as his last work a history of *Berlin in der Weltpolitik 1945–1970*. This is more than merely a history of Berlin politics, rather, it is an attempt to understand the course of world history since the surrender as it affected and was affected by what happened in the divided German capital.

Besson's *Aussenpolitik*, although published in 1970, remains an indispensable as well as beautifully written interpretation of the course and the rationale of West Germany's foreign policy in the first 25 years since 1945. It is one of the two or three books that anyone who really wants to know what the Federal Republic "is all about," as the phrase goes, simply *must* read. After almost two decades, Besson found a worthy successor in Hacke, whose *Weltmacht wider Willen* covers the whole story from 1945 to 1987. Hacke himself points out that he is supplementing and not replacing Besson; both works are equally important for understanding the geostrategic situation and foreign policy choices of Europe's pivotal state. Wolfram Hanrieder provided the first serious overview in English of West German foreign policy from the Basic Law to 1989 in his excellent *Germany, America, Europe*. For the history of security policy in the narrower sense, see Haftendorn's *Security and Detente*. All important government documents and treaties, as well as a selection of official statements and communiques concerning Germany are in *Documents on Germany*, published by the US Government Printing Office. Münch's *Dokumente* is a comprehensive collection of all official documents and statements dealing with the problem of divided Germany.

The student of the West German political system has a choice between introductory surveys in English and in-depth analyses, all of which are in German. The surveys are Conradt's *German Polity*, Dalton's *Politics in West Germany*, and Katzenstein's *Policy and Politics*. All three of these reliable handbooks were revised in the mid-1980s. The standard German text is Ellwein's *Regierungssystem*, first published in 1963 and known to tens of thousands of German undergraduates as "der Ellwein." It is periodically revised and updated; for the sixth edition (1987) Ellwein took a co-author and announced that he intended gradually to retire from the project. Anyone seriously interested in German constitutional law and the system of government will want to refer to Stern's *Staatsrecht*. Two of the planned five volumes were available at the time of writing.

Germany has always been a land of multivolume histories and dictionaries. One of the most outstanding is the *Staatslexikon* of the Görres society, first published in the 1890s. A seventh, entirely recast, five-volume edition of this institution of German scholarship and political culture appeared in 1985–9. In it, the reader will find detailed, concisely written, and highly informative entries (with bibliographies) on every conceivable aspect of West German politics, society, culture, and public life, as well as on political theory, constitutional law, theology, and other general subjects.

An often lively and occasionally provocative series of articles and essays on West German politics, society, and culture are found in the three volumes of *Die Bundesrepublik Deutschland*, edited by Wolfgang Benz, one of the leading historians of the postwar period of the younger generation. The reader who knows German may find these pieces a good place to start before picking up Ellwein. Burdick's *Contemporary Germany* is a similar, if less comprehensive, anthology of essays in English. The volume *Sozialgeschichte*, edited by Conze, contains articles on many aspects of social change and social policies. For culture and the politics of culture in West Germany, see Glaser's *Kulturgeschichte*, of which two volumes, covering the years 1945–67, were available at this writing and a third was promised. Glaser, himself an active journalist and politician, likes to tell stories rather than analyze structures, which makes his work fascinating and valuable as an informal introduction to postwar West Germany. A somewhat acerbic view of what the author sees as the political agenda of postwar German writers is Ross' *Mit der linken Hand geschrieben*, worth reading for its unusual and courageous, if all too brief, attempt to provide an alternative interpretation. Religion and the churches were the subject of Spotts' *Churches and Politics*, which is not only outdated (1973), but has been severely criticized in Germany. In view of the important developments in the political role and theology of both the major denominations since the early 1970s, this is clearly a subject that needs new treatment.

There is no good survey of West German education and educational policy in any language, even though these issues were highly prominent throughout our period. The relevant sections of the *Geschichte* are useful. Tent's volume on the *Free University of Berlin* is a real boon to the field and provides elements of a general history of higher education in the Federal Republic.

Abelshauser's *Wirtschaftsgeschichte* and Berghahn's *Americanisation of West German Industry* are surveys of the economy, but both emphasize the 1940s and 1950s and provide almost no in-depth information for the period after 1969. Emminger's *D-Mark, Dollar, Währungskrisen* deals with the 1970s and early 1980s, but Emminger was a banker, not a writer: his account is anecdotal, spotty, and occasionally he contradicts himself. Lampert's *Wirtschafts- und Sozialordnung* is a concise handbook full of interesting information on a broad range of issues, written from the standpoint of the defenders of the social market economy. Like Ellwein, it is frequently updated. For continuing data on the economy and competent evaluations of current and future trends, see the annual *OECD Economic Surveys: Germany*.

After the war, many people both in and outside Germany asked two questions: why did democracy fail in Germany in 1933, and what should be done to make it more secure the second time round? Conservatives blamed the problem on Germany's geopolitical position "in the middle," surrounded by enemies. Such a country could not afford democracy and was easy prey for demagogues. The American David Calleo rehabilitated this argument in *The German Problem Reconsidered*. Liberals tended to blame domestic forces for the fragility of democracy. The basic statement of this position remains Dahrendorf's *Society and Democracy*. In that book, written in the mid-1960s, he blamed the failure of democracy on the failure of political liberalism and wondered whether the new democracy was stable. Both before and after Dahrendorf, other observers tried other means of interpretation. One was to monitor public opinion intensively. As a result, West Germans answered more opinion polls on more subjects than any other people in the world, and the science and technology of public opinion surveys became one of the staples of postwar German political science and policy analysis. The leader of this movement in Germany was Elisabeth Noelle-Neumann, who founded the Allensbach Institute. The Institute's two volumes of opinion polls from 1967 and 1981, *The Germans*, provide a mass of evidence on beliefs, opinions, attitudes, and sentiments. The other method was to develop a science of "political culture" to measure and monitor underlying trends in belief and attitudes to life because, as one of the advocates of political cultural studies put it, "the evolution and persistence of mass-based democracy requires the emergence of certain supportive habits and attitudes among the general public."[1] Almond and Verba's *Civic Culture* found that Germans were democratic on the outside but authoritarian on the inside in 1960; by the 1980s, this had changed. The reasons, the course, and the significance of this change is the subject of Inglehart's *Culture Change*, which summarizes his work over the previous two decades. Taken together, these books provide important background to political and social history and give essential information for evaluating the strength of democratic sentiment in Germany.

*Volume II*

Wilharm's *Deutsche Geschichte* picks up where Steininger leaves off and provides interpretative essays and documents for the period 1962–83. Otherwise, the period after 1963 is not by any means as well served as the first ten to fifteen years since 1949, partly because the relevant archives were not yet open by the late 1980s. Useful memoirs by leading figures include those of Brandt, *People and Politics*, and Schmidt, *Menschen und Mächte*. The latter describes Germany's dealings with the Soviet Union, the USA, and China under Schmidt's leadership. He has promised a further volume on Europe. The American ambassador to Germany in 1963–8, George McGhee, published his recollections of

[1] Inglehart, "Renaissance of Political Culture," *American Political Science Review* 82 (1988): 1204.

that period, which was troubled by disputes over offset payments and the nuclear non-proliferation Treaty, under the title *At the Creation of a New Germany*.

The cultural revolution of the 1960s had many participants, but so far few historians. Source material for the New Left's world-view can be found in the anthology by Karsunke and Michel, taken from the main journal of the cultural revolution, *Kursbuch*. Nolte's *Deutschland und der Kalte Krieg* is, in part, a conservative professor's response to the political and methodological radicalism of his own students and contains useful documentation as well as provocative interpretations of what happened at the West German universities in 1965–70. Bieling's *Tränen der Revolution* is, on one level, a useful chronicle of the successive states of mind and political strategies of the student left in the later 1960s; on another level, it is the apologia of a participant who denigrates the conservative opposition. Langguth's *Protestbewegung* is a detailed and essential account of radical extremism of all types from the mid-1960s to the early 1980s; a task the same author extended to the Greens in his study *The Green Factor*.

On terrorism there are two useful works. J. Becker's *Hitler's Children*, last revised in 1979, remains the best English-language survey of the Baader-Meinhof gang and its associates, who they were, and why they chose the actions they did. Horchem's *Verlorene Revolution* describes the international and ideological context of both right- and left-wing terrorism and continues the story to the mid-1980s. A third book, Lübbe's *Endstation Terror*, links terrorism and its sympathizers to the anti-authoritarianism of the New Left and the failure of the constituted authorities to protect law and order.

The background and course of the new Ostpolitik are the subject of two good English-language studies: Stent's *Embargo to Ostpolitik* which focuses on economic relationships, and Griffith's *Ostpolitik*, which is more general. Bender's *Neue Ostpolitik* is an optimistic chronicle of the road from the Berlin Wall to the Eastern treaties. Zündorf's *Ostverträge* is an authoritative account of what the Brandt government thought it was getting in the treaties, as well as a useful analysis of the international context of Ostpolitik. Wolffsohn's *West Germany's Foreign Policy* is a sympathetic account of the years 1969–82, but is not as useful as Hacke's *Weltmacht*. An extraordinary chronicle of the Brandt years is Baring's *Machtwechsel*. Some have compared it to Kissinger's *White House Years*. Actually, it is more comprehensive, since Baring is telling the story of *all* the government's policies as well as the story of the internal struggle between radicals and moderates in the SPD.

West Germany's international position and its foreign economic and security policy in the Schmidt period are sympathetically described and interpreted in Haftendorn's *Sicherheit und Stabilität*. More detail, and somewhat more criticism, can be found in the final volume of the *Geschichte*, which also includes an important essay on the cultural revolution and its effects by Karl Dietrich Bracher. Joffe's *Limited Partnership* surveys US-European relations in the 1980s with special emphasis on Germany.

Domestic politics under Brandt and Schmidt are extensively treated in the relevant volumes of the *Geschichte*. In public debate, literature, scholarship, and intellectual life the cultural revolution sharpened the contrast between a moderate to conservative and a leftist to radical mentality, each with its own journals of opinion, publishing houses, and media apparatus. In the later Schmidt years and, *a fortiori*, under Kohl, leftists argued that West Germany was undergoing a conservative restoration, a *Tendenzwende*. Conservatives disputed this and pointed to the continuing influence of New Left ideas among students and journalists and the growing acceptance in public opinion of the moderate left's social and international political agenda as carried out by Schmidt and Genscher. The leftist arguments for where Germany stood and where it should be going in the later Schmidt years are found in Habermas' anthology *Stichworte*, which is a broad panorama of progressive opinion. For conservative criticism of progressive assumptions, see Lübbe's *Politischer Moralismus* and Stürmer's *Dissonanzen*. Lübbe, a professor of philosophy at Zürich, was a former social democrat who left the SPD in the mid-1970s.

The *Stichworte* anthology signaled, among other things, a renewed interest on the left in questions of national identity and history. This rediscovery led to intense, and sometimes emotional, debates. First in time came the concern with history, which blended into a concern with national division, documented in Venohr's *Deutsche Einheit* and Brandt and Ammon's anthology of the German left's attitude to reunification, *Die Linke und die nationale Frage*. Second came the debate over how to deal with National Socialism, an argument ostensibly provoked by Ernst Nolte, but which had in fact been simmering ever since the mid-1960s. Maier's *Unmasterable Past*, one of the more valuable English-language books on postwar Germany, is an analysis both of the arguments over national identity and of the historians' debate, by an American historian sympathetic to the left-liberal position. The main German contributions to the debate are assembled in *"Historikerstreit."* On German-Jewish relations see the useful and optimistic overview by Wolffsohn, *Ewige Schuld?* In the late 1980s, German enthusiasm for Gorbachev and for disarmament threatened to cause serious disputes in the Western camp. Arnulf Baring cogently criticized the German ambition to play a leading role in East–West relations in *Unser neuer Grössenwahn*. Harold James skilfully analyzed the long history of argument over what it meant to be a German in his *German Identity*.

Periodically, foreigners living in or dealing with Germany put their discoveries and their amazed or gratified comments into words, more or less successfully. The *New York Times* reports of James Markham in the early 1980s were a high point not only of American journalism, but of all writing on Germany; unfortunately, they had not been assembled into a book at the time of writing. Ardagh's *Germany* is a mine of useful information on most aspects of German politics, society, and culture in the 1980s, but is a less satisfying and complete work than the same author's justly renowned books on France. Two other British journalists, David Marsh of the *Financial Times* and Daniel Johnson of the *Daily Telegraph*, reportedly were preparing books on Germany for publication in 1989 or 1990.

## Supplement 1992

The unification of Germany 1989–90 stimulated an avalanche of research and writing, as scholars, journalists, and other observers sought to understand what was taking place before their eyes. By mid-1992, a number of these efforts had made their way into print. They focused on three themes: the unification process itself, its causes and consequences for Germany and Europe; the history of the GDR and of German communism, seen for the first time without ideological blinkers and with the benefit of hitherto unavailable evidence; and, last but not least, the history of Germany and of the Federal Republic before 1989, many of whose aspects appeared in a new light when seen from the vantage point of united Germany.

An excellent starting-point for getting a handle on the manifold issues and problems of unification – social, economic, ideological, cultural, and political – is the *Handwörterbuch zur deutschen Einheit*, edited by Weidenfeld and Korte. Most of the articles, all by recognized experts, are gems of concise, authoritative information about a surprisingly wide range of topics, from the history of the GDR and the positions of the various German political parties and groupings on the national question to the psychological and financial costs and effects of unification.

The monthly journal *Deutschland Archiv* covers all aspects of unification, just as it formerly covered the GDR and inner-German relations exhaustively.

The statements and documents leading to unification are edited by von Münch, *Dokumente*, a companion volume to his *Dokumente des geteilten Deutschland*.

As the East German reformers uncovered the structure of corruption and intimidation that formed the essence of the communist regime, they overturned two decades of – deliberate or misguided – disinformation purveyed as "GDR scholarship" in West Germany and elsewhere. On these errors see Hacker, *Deutsche Irrtümer*. Weber and Fricke were among the few GDR scholars in the West whose work stood the test of reality. Fricke, in particular, found his interpretation of the GDR as, in essence, a secret police state, confirmed; see his *MfS intern*.

Many East Germans made heroic efforts to understand their own history and their own individual fates as victims and/or collaborators of an insidious regime. Among the victims' tales, Kunze, *Deckname "Lyrik"*, stands out as a classic account of a *Stasi* operation designed to intimidate an "enemy of the state." Maaz described the results of such policies for East German social and personal relations in *Der Gefühls-stau*. Not all East Germans were victims; many were both victims and collaborators. Gerlach's memoirs *Mitverantwortlich* are an exemplary account by a man who was not a communist, yet found himself serving the communist regime.

In a remarkable parallel to 1945, few, if any, communist leaders and *apparatchiks* were prepared to defend their record; most of their published accounts were either self-serving or evasive, such as Mittag, *Um jeden Preis*. Honecker's personal character and political role were mercilessly unveiled by a former close collaborator in Przybylski, *Tatort Politbüro*, which chronicles how the regime, with the connivance of foolish or venal westerners, swindled its way to substantial hard currency revenues.

Gauck, *Die Stasi-Akten*, is a first attempt to talk about the future of the millions of surviving secret police files and how they should be handled. A vivid chronicle of how East German citizens' committees tried, often succeeded, but sometimes failed, to secure these files is Worst, *Ende eines Geheimdienstes*, to be read in conjunction with Fricke's work, cited above. Blaschke, "Geschichtswissenschaft", is a bleak chronicle of how the SED destroyed intellectual and scholarly life in the GDR, which indirectly helps to explain why protest and dissidence were so rare before 1989. Blaschke kept his integrity as a historian at a high cost, which included being deprived of virtually all contact with Western colleagues for over two decades. For a contrast, see Elm, *Nach Hitler, nach Honecker* an evasive account by a former servant of the regime who tries to show that the GDR started out well and was, in many ways, superior to the old Federal Republic.

Few reappraisals of West German history and society in the light of unification had reached book form by mid-1992. That year, the Hamburg historian Wolf Gruner published a new edition of his broad and readable survey of *Die deutsche Frage*, in which he described how

Germans and others had understood Germany's role and position in Europe since the early nineteenth century. In 1991, Weidenfeld and Korte published a study of German beliefs and opinions: *Die Deutschen*.

*Aus Politik und Zeitgeschichte*, published as a supplement to the weekly newspaper *Das Parlament*, is a current-affairs forum, which regularly includes contributions concerning unification, the history of the two German states, and German foreign policy. Along with *Deutschland Archiv*, it remains the best place to look for analysis of the changing German scene and its international context. The history of the old Federal Republic temporarily fell out of view, as many historians turned their attention to the immediate present. One important contribution, published shortly before the first edition of this work appeared, is Klessmann, *Zwei Staaten — eine Nation*, which continues his history of postwar Germany to 1970. It is worth noting that Klessmann, writing in the 1980s before unification, chose to put the words "one nation" in his title. Not all his colleagues would have done so. Another is the concluding volume of Schwarz' authoritative biography of Adenauer, entitled *Der Staatsmann* and covering the years 1952–67. This exhaustive and well-written account is the culmination of three decades of work on the early history of the Federal Republic.

# Documents and Sources

*Archiv der Gegenwart* (1980–7) St Augustin (Cologne): Siegler and Co., Verlag für Zeitarchive.

Ausschuss der deutschen Statistiker für die Volks- und Berufszählung, 1946. *Volks- und Berufszählung vom 29. Oktober 1946.* Berlin: Duncker und Humblot, 1949.

Berlin Senat. *Berlin — Chronik der Jahre 1951—1954.* Vol. 5 of *Schriftenreihe zur Berliner Zeitgeschichte.* Berlin: Heinz Spitzing, 1968.

Bundeskriminalamt, "Sonderkommission Bonn," und Bundesamt für Verfassungschutz (Aus den Akten des). *Der Baader Meinhof Report.* Mainz: v. Hase und Köhler, 1972.

Bundesministerium für Arbeit und Sozialordnung (Federal Ministry for Work and Social Order). *Der Lastenausgleich.* By Peter Paul Nahm. *Sozialpolitik in Deutschland,* no. 50. Stuttgart: Kohlhammer, 1962.

Bundesministerium für innerdeutsche Beziehungen (Federal Ministry for Inner-German Relations). *DDR Handbuch.* Cologne: Verlag Wissenschaft und Politik, 1979.

—— *Dokumente zur Deutschlandpolitik.* IV/1963, vols 9–12; and V/1966–7, vol. 1. Frankfurt: 1978–84.

Bundesministerium für Vertriebene, Flüchtlinge und Kriegsgeschädigte (Federal Ministry for Expellees, Refugees and War Victims). *Bundesgesetze und Leistungen für die durch Krieg und Kriegsfolgen Geschädigten.* Edited by Friedrich Panse and Edgar von Wietersheim. Mainz: Deutscher Fachschriften-Verlag, 1959.

—— *Die Vertreibung der Deutschen Bevölkerung aus den Gebieten östlich der Oder—Neisse.* Edited by Theodor Schieder. Vol. 1 of *Dokumentation der Vertreibung der Deutschen aus Ost-Mitteleuropa* [1954], reprint. Munich: Deutscher Taschenbuch Verlag, 1984. A selection and translation was published as *The Expulsion of the German Population from the Territories East of the Oder—Neisse-Line.*

Bundesministerium für Wohnungsbau (Federal Ministry for Housing). *Grundsätze, Leistungen und Aufgaben der Wohnungsbaupolitik der Bundesregierung.* Bonn: 1959.

Bundeszentrale für politische Bildung. Böhme, Irene, in Michael Richter et al., eds. *Geschichte der DDR.* Bonn: Bundeszentrale für politische Bildung, 1991.

"Denkschrift des militärischen Expertenausschusses über die Aufstellung eines Deutschen Kontingents im Rahmen einer übernationalen Streitmacht zur Verteidigung Westeuropas vom 9. Oktober 1950." *Militärgeschichtliche Mitteilungen* 21 (1977): 168–90.

Department of State. "European Unity: United States will Cooperate, not Initiate." By George C. Marshall, United States Secretary of State. Delivered at meeting of Harvard University Alumni, Cambridge, MA, June 5, 1947.

—— *Documents on American Foreign Relations.* Vol. 5, 1942–1943; vol. 6, 1943–1944; vol. 7, 1944–45; vol. 8, 1945–46. Princeton, NJ: Princeton University Press, 1947.

—— *Documents on Germany 1944–1985.* Department of State Publication no. 9446. Office of the Historian, Bureau of Public Affairs [1986].

—— "Restatement of US Policy on Germany." By James F. Byrnes. Publication 2616. GPO, 1946.

Deutsche Presse Agentur report, September 15, 1985.

Deutscher Bundestag. *Verhandlungen des Deutschen Bundestages.* Stenographische Berichte. Vol 16. Bonn: 1952.

*Europa-Archiv.* Bonn: Verlag für Internationale Politik.

*Facts on File* (1955–1988). New York: Facts on File.

Federal Ministry for All-German Questions. *The Flights from the Soviet Zone and the Sealing-off Measures of the Communist Regime of 13th August 1961 in Berlin.* Bonn and Berlin: Federal Printing Works, 1961.

—— *Violations of Human Rights, Illegal Acts and Incidents at the Sector Border in Berlin since the Building of the Wall (13 August 1961–15 August 1962).* Bonn and Berlin: Federal Printing Works, 1962.

Federal Republic of Germany. *Elections, Parliament and Political Parties.* New York: German Information Center, 1986.

Federal Statistical Office. *Statistical Compass 1987.* Wiesbaden, 1987.

—— *Statistical Pocket-book on Expellees.* Wiesbaden, 1953.

Foreign Broadcast Information Service, West Europe, 1989–92. Washington, D.C.: National Technical Information Service.

*Freiheit der Wissenschaft,* no. 6 (July 1985).

Hauptamt für Statistik von Gross-Berlin. *Berlin in Zahlen 1947.* Berlin: Berliner Kulturbuch-Verlag, 1949.

Haute Commissariat de la Republique Francaise en Allemagne. "Naissance de la Republique Federale d'Allemagne." *Realités Allemandes* 9–10 (September/October 1949): 25–38.

Institut der deutschen Wirtschaft. *Wirtschaftstruktur der Bundesländer.* Cologne, 1986.

Institut für Zukunftsforschung. *Ausländer oder Deutsche.* Cologne: Bund-Verlag, 1981.

*Interview der Woche.* Archiv für Christlich-Demokratische Politik. St Augustin (Cologne): Pressedokumentation der Konrad-Adenauer-Stiftung.

*Jahresbericht des Koordinators für die deutsch-amerikanische zwischengesellschaftliche kultur- und informationspolitische Zusammenarbeit 1989* (Bonn: Auswärtiges Amt, 1990).

John F. Kennedy. *Public Papers of the President of the United States: John F. Kennedy, 1960–1963.* GPO, 1964.

*Keesing's Contemporary Archives — Record of World Events* (1956–1987). Vols 25–33. England: Longman Group.

Office of the Federal Register. *Weekly Compilations of Presidential Documents.* vol. 23, no. 24 (June 22, 1987), 658–9.

Office of the Military Government, US Sector, Berlin. *A Four Year Report* (July 1, 1945 – September 1, 1949). Civil Affairs Division (Army Dept).

Office of the Military Governor for Germany, US. *The German Press in the US Occupied Area 1945–1948.* Special Report of the Military Governor, November 1948. Prepared by the Information Services Division.

— *Monthly Report of the Military Governor.* Nos 36–50. (June 1948–September 1949).

Office of the US High Commissioner for Germany. *Elections and Political Parties in Germany, 1945–1952.* Office of Executive Secretary, 1952.

— *History of the Allied High Commission for Germany.* Office of the Executive Secretary, Historical Division, 1951.

— *Postwar Changes in German Education (US Zone and US Sector Berlin).* Office of Public Affairs, 1951.

— *Press, Radio and Film in West Germany.* By Henry P. Pilgert. Office of the Executive Secretary, Historical Division, 1953.

— *The West German Educational System.* By Henry P. Pilgert. Office of the Executive Secretary, Historical Division, 1953.

— *Quarterly Report on Germany.* (September 21, 1949–July 31, 1952).

Press and Information Office of the Federal Republic of Germany. *The Development of the Relations between the Federal Republic of Germany and the German Democratic Republic.* Bonn, 1973.

— *Employers and Unions.* (Information 16.) Bonn, 1986.

— *Erfurt, March 19, 1970: A Documentation.* Bonn, 1970.

— *Germany Reports.* 2nd rev. edn. Wiesbaden: Wiesbadener Graphische Betriebe, 1955.

— *Housing and Town Planning.* (Information 22.) Bonn, 1986.

— *Kassel, May 21, 1970: A Documentation.* Bonn, 1970.

— *Law and the Administration of Justice.* (Information 24.) Bonn, 1986.

— Typewritten communication. July, 1986.

Presse- und Informationsamt der Bundesregierung. *Bulletin.* Bonn.

Regierung der Bundesrepublik Deutschland (Government of the Federal Republic of Germany). *Gesellschaftliche Daten.* Presse und Informationsamt, 1982.

*Relay from Bonn.* Vols 1–15 New York: German Information Center.

Republic of France. *Major Addresses, Statements and Press Conferences of General Charles de Gaulle.* (May 19, 1958–January 31, 1964). Press and Information Division, New York.

Senate Committee on Foreign Relations. *Hearings on United States Policy toward Europe.* Statement of Dr Henry A. Kissinger, June 27, 1966.

*Statements and Speeches.* New York: German Information Center.

540 DOCUMENTS AND SOURCES

Statistisches Bundesamt. *Lange Reihen zur Wirtschaftsentwicklung, 1986.* Cologne: Institut der deutschen Wirtschaft, 1986.

—— *Statistisches Jahrbuch für die Bundesrepublik Deutschland, 1962, 1966, 1986, 1987* and *1988.* Stuttgart and Mainz: Kohlhammer, 1962, 1966, 1986, 1987, 1988.

Statistisches Bundesamt. *Volkswirtschaftliche Gesamtrechnungen,* Fachserie 18, Reihe 1.3, Konten und Standardtabellen. Wiesbaden, 1988.

Statistisches Reichsamt. *Statistisches Jahrbuch für das Deutsche Reich 1921/1922.* Berlin: Verlag für Politik und Wirtschaft, 1922.

*The Week in Germany.* New York: German Information Center.

# Bibliography

Note: Accented letters are alphabetized along with the unaccented letter.

Abelshauser, Werner. *Wirtschaftsgeschichte der Bundesrepublik Deutschland 1945– 1980.* Frankfurt am Main: Suhrkamp, 1983.

Abenheim, Donald. *Reforging the Iron Cross: The Search for Tradition in the West German Armed Forces.* Princeton, NJ: Princeton University Press, 1989. In German: *Bundeswehr und Tradition: Die Suche nach dem gültigen Erbe des deutschen Soldaten.* Munich: Oldenbourg, 1989.

Abraham, Henry J. *The Judicial Process.* 5th edn. New York: Oxford University Press, 1986.

Adenauer, Konrad. *Erinnerungen 1953–1955.* Stuttgart: Deutsche Verlags-Anstalt, 1966.

—— *Erinnerungen 1955–1959.* Stuttgart: Deutsche Verlags-Anstalt, 1967.

—— *Erinnerungen 1959–1963: Fragmente.* Stuttgart: Deutsche Verlags-Anstalt, 1968.

—— *Konrad Adenauer: Briefe über Deutschland, 1945–1951.* Hans Peter Mensing (ed.). Berlin: Siedler, 1986.

—— *Memoirs 1945–1953.* Chicago: Henry Regnery, 1966.

—— *Nachdenken über die Werte: Weihnachtsansprachen.* Walter Berger (ed.). Buxheim, Allgäu: Martin Verlag/Walter Berger, 1976.

Agnoli, Johannes, and Brückner, Peter. *Die Transformation der Demokratie.* Berlin: Voltaire, 1967.

Albert, Michel. *Capitalisme contre capitalisme.* Paris: Seuil, 1991.

Alexiev, Alexander R. *The Soviet Campaign Against INF: Strategy, Tactics, Means.* Rand Note N-2280-AF. Santa Monica, CA: RAND Corporation, 1985.

Allemann, Fritz René. *Bonn ist nicht Weimar.* Cologne: Kiepenheuer und Witsch, 1956.

Almond, Gabriel A., and Verba, Sidney. *The Civic Culture: Political Attitudes and Democracy in Five Nations.* Princeton, NJ: Princeton University Press, 1963.

Alt, Franz. *Frieden ist möglich: Die Politik der Bergpredigt.* Munich: Piper, 1983.

Ammer, Thomas. "Es ist nicht alles Recht, was Gesetz ist." *Deutschland Archiv* 25 (1992), 118–20.

—— "Rehabilitierung der Justizopfer des SED-Regimes." *Deutschland Archiv* 24 (1991), 900–4.

Anderson, Martin. *Revolution*. San Diego: Harcourt Brace Jovanovich, 1988.

Andreas-Friedrich, Ruth. *Schauplatz Berlin: Tagebuchaufzeichnungen 1945 bis 1948*. Frankfurt am Main: Suhrkamp, 1984.

*Anfänge westdeutscher Sicherheitspolitik, 1945–1956*. Publ. by Militärgeschichtlichen Forschungsamt. Vol. 1, *Von der Kapitulation bis zum Pleven-Plan*, by Roland G. Foerster, C. Greiner, G. Meyer, H.-J. Rautenberg, and N. Wiggershaus. Vol. 2, *Die Europäische Verteidigungsgemeinschaft*. Munich: Oldenbourg, 1982–9. Vols 3 and 4 in preparation.

Antonov-Ovseenko, Anton. *The Time of Stalin: Portrait of a Tyranny*. New York: Harper and Row, 1981.

Ardagh, John. *Germany and the Germans: An Anatomy of Society Today*. New York: Harper and Row, 1987.

Aron, Raymond, and Lerner, Daniel, eds. *La querelle de la C.E.D*. Paris: Armand Colin, 1956.

Asmus, Ron. "The GDR and Martin Luther." *Survey* (Autumn 1984), 124–56.

—— "*Pravda* Attacks East–West German Ties." RFE-RL Background Report/ 145, (August 8, 1984).

Augstein, Rudolf. "Die neue Auschwitz-Lüge" in *"Historikerstreit."* Munich: Piper, 1987.

Bahr, Egon. *Zum europäischen Frieden. Eine Antwort an Gorbatschow*. Berlin: Siedler, 1988.

Baker, Kendall; Dalton, Russel J.; and Hildebrandt, Kai. *Germany Transformed: Political Culture and the New Politics*. Cambridge, MA: Harvard University Press, 1981.

Balfour, Michael. *West Germany*. London, Croom Helm, 1982.

Baring, Arnulf. *Machtwechsel: Die Ära Brandt–Scheel*. Stuttgart: Deutsche Verlags-Anstalt, 1982.

—— *Unser neuer Grössenwahn: Deutschland zwischen Ost und West*. 2nd edn. Stuttgart: Deutsche Verlags-Anstalt, 1989.

—— *Deutschland was nun?* Berlin: Siedler, 1991.

Bark, Dennis L. *Agreement on Berlin*. Washington: American Enterprise Institute for Public Policy Research; Stanford, CA: Hoover Institution on War, Revolution and Peace, 1974.

—— *Congressional Record*, Vol. 117, No. 1 (Jan. 21, 1971), reprinted from a speech delivered to the Commonwealth Club of California in San Francisco, Dec. 18, 1970.

Bark, Dennis L., and Rowen, Henry S. "The German Question." Unpublished paper, 1986.

Barnett, Correlli. *The Pride and the Fall*. New York: Free Press, 1986.

Bartel, Heinrich. *A. N. Jakowlew und die USA: Leitgedanken und Feindbilder eines Gorbatschow-Beraters*. Berichte des Bundesinstituts für ostwissenschaftliche und internationale Studien no. 47/1988. Cologne, 1988.

Barzel, Rainer. *Im Streit und umstritten: Anmerkungen zu Konrad Adenauer, Ludwig Erhard und den Ostverträgen*. Frankfurt am Main: Ullstein, 1986.

Becker, Hellmut. "Bildungspolitik" in *Die Bundesrepublik Deutschland*, vol. 2, Wolfgang Benz (ed.). Frankfurt am Main: Fischer Taschenbuch Verlag, 1983.

Becker, Jillian. *Hitler's Children: The Story of the Baader-Meinhof Terrorist Gang.* Philadelphia: J. B. Lippincott, 1977.

Bell, Coral. *Negotiation from Strength: A Study in the Politics of Power.* New York: Knopf, 1963.

Bender, Peter. *Neue Ostpolitik: Vom Mauerbau bis zum Moskauer Vertrag.* Munich: Deutscher Taschenbuch Verlag, 1986.

— "Zwei neurotische Riesen." *Merkur* 34 (1980), 529–41.

— *Das Ende des ideologischen Zeitalters.* Berlin: Siedler, 1981.

— "Die sieben Gesichter der DDR." *Merkur* 45 (1991), 292–304.

Benz, Wolfgang. *Die Gründung der Bundesrepublik: Von der Bizone zum souveränen Staat.* Munich: Deutscher Taschenbuch Verlag, 1984.

— *Potsdam 1945: Besatzungsherrschaft und Neuaufbau im Vier-Zonen-Deutschland.* Munich: Deutscher Taschenbuch Verlag, 1986.

— *Von der Besatzungsherrschaft zur Bundesrepublik.* Frankfurt am Main: Fischer Taschenbuch Verlag, 1984.

Benz, Wolfgang, ed. *Die Bundesrepublik Deutschland.* 3 vols. Frankfurt am Main: Fischer Taschenbuch Verlag, 1983.

Berghahn, Volker R. *The Americanisation of West German Industry, 1945–1973.* Leamington Spa, England: Berg, 1986. Originally published as *Unternehmer und Politik in der Bundesrepublik.* Frankfurt am Main: Suhrkamp, 1985.

— *Modern Germany: Society, Economy and Politics in the Twentieth Century.* 2nd edn. Cambridge: Cambridge University Press, 1987.

Bergmann, Uwe; Dutschke, Rudi; Lefevre, Wolfgang; and Rabehl, Bernd. *Die Rebellion der Studenten oder die neue Opposition.* Reinbek: Rowohlt, 1968.

Berkhahn, Karl Wilhelm; Dönhoff, Marion Gräfin; Klasen, Karl; Koerber, Kurt; Sommer, Theo; Stoedter, Helga and Rolf; and Trebitsch, Gyula, eds. *Hart am Wind: Helmut Schmidts politische Laufbahn.* Hamburg: Albrecht Knaus, 1978.

Bernstein, Barton J., ed. *Politics and Policies of the Truman Administration.* Chicago: University of Chicago Press, 1970.

Bertelsmann Lexikon-Institut. *Facts about Germany.* 1st edn; 6th rev. edn. Gütersloh: Bertelsmann Lexikon Verlag, 1979, 1988.

Besson, Waldemar. *Die Aussenpolitik der Bundesrepublik.* Munich: Piper, 1970.

Beyme, Klaus von. *The Political System of the Federal Republic of Germany.* New York: St. Martin's Press, 1982.

— "Intrigiert wird in diesem Hause nicht!" in Hermann Rudolph, ed. *Den Staat denken. Theodor Eschenburg zum Fünfundachzigsten.* Berlin: Siedler, 1990.

— *Hauptstadtsuche. Hauptstadtfunktionen im Interessenkonflikt zwischen Bonn und Berlin.* Frankfurt am Main: Suhrkamp, 1991.

Beyme, Klaus von, ed. *Die grossen Regierungserklärungen der deutschen Bundeskanzler von Adenauer bis Schmidt.* Munich: Carl Hanser, 1979.

*Bibliographie zur Zeitgeschichte 1953–1980.* 3 vols. Publ. by Institut für Zeitgeschichte. Munich: Saur, 1982–3.

*Bibliographie zur Zeitgeschichte*, 1981–. Supplement to *Vierteljahrshefte für Zeitgeschichte.* Publ. by Institut für Zeitgeschichte. Munich: Oldenbourg.

Bieling, Rainer. *Die Tränen der Revolution: Die 68er zwanzig Jahre danach.* Berlin: Siedler, 1988.

Binder, David. *The Other German: Willy Brandt's Life and Times.* Washington, DC: New Republic, 1975.

Binder, Gerhart. *Deutschland seit 1945.* Stuttgart: Seewald, 1969.

Birke, Adolf M. *Nation ohne Haus: Deutschland 1945—1961.* Deutsche Geschichte, vol. 6. Berlin: Siedler, 1989.

*Blackwell Encyclopaedia of Political Institutions.* Vernon Bogdanor (ed.). Oxford: Blackwell, 1987.

Blaschke, Karlheinz. "Geschichtswissenschaft im SED-Staat." *Aus Politik und Zeitgeschichte* B17-18/92 (April 17, 1992), 14–27.

Blumenwitz, Dieter; Gotto, Klaus; Maier, Hans; Repgen, Konrad; and Schwarz, Hans-Peter, eds. *Konrad Adenauer und seine Zeit.* 2 vols. Stuttgart: Deutsche Verlags-Anstalt, 1976.

Blumenwitz, Dieter. "Wie offen ist die Verfassungsfrage nach der Herstellung der staatlichen Einheit Deutschlands?" *Aus Politik und Zeitgeschichte* B49/91 (November 29, 1991), 3–11.

Bohlen, Charles E. *Witness to History, 1929—1969.* New York: W. W. Norton and Co., 1973.

Bolesch, Hermann Otto. *Typisch Mischnick.* Munich: C. Bertelsmann, 1974.

Bölling, Klaus. *Bonn von aussen betrachtet.* Stuttgart: Deutsche Verlags-Anstalt, 1986.

Bonhoeffer, Emmi. *Auschwitz Trials: Letters from an Eyewitness.* Richmond, Virginia: John Knox, 1967.

Borkowski, Dieter. *Für jeden kommt der Tag.* Frankfurt am Main: Fischer Taschenbuch Verlag, 1983.

Borst, Arno. *Reden über die Staufer.* Frankfurt am Main: Ullstein, 1978.

Botting, Douglas. *From the Ruins of the Reich: Germany 1945—1949.* New York: Crown, 1985.

Bracher, Karl Dietrich; Jäger, Wolfgang; and Link, Werner. *Republik im Wandel, 1969—1974, Die Ära Brandt.* Vol. 5/I of *Geschichte des Bundesrepublik Deutschland.* Stuttgart: Deutsche Verlags-Anstalt; Wiesbaden: Brockhaus, 1986.

Brandt, Peter, and Ammon, Herbert. *Die Linke und die nationale Frage.* Reinbek: Rowohlt, 1981.

Brandt, Peter; Schumacher, Jörg; Schwarzrock, Goetz; and Suehl, Klaus. *Karrieren eines Aussenseiters: Leo Bauer zwischen Kommunismus und Sozialdemokratie, 1912 bis 1972.* Berlin: Dietz, 1983.

Brandt, Willy. *Die Abschiedsrede.* Berlin: Siedler, 1987.

—— *The Ordeal of Coexistence.* Cambridge, MA: Harvard University Press, 1963.

—— *People and Politics: The Years 1960—1975.* Boston: Little, Brown and Co., 1978. Originally published as *Begegnungen und Einsichten.* Hamburg: Hoffmann und Campe, 1976.

—— *Willy Brandt Bundestagsreden.* Helmut Schmidt (ed.). Bonn: az studio, 1972.

—— *Zum sozialen Rechtsstaat: Reden und Dokumente.* Arnold Harttung (ed.). Berlin: Berlin-Verlag, 1983.

Brandt, Willy, and Lowenthal, Richard. *Ernst Reuter: Ein Leben für die Freiheit.* Munich: Kindler, 1957.

Bredow, Wilfried von. "Perzeptions-Probleme." *Deutschland Archiv* 24 (1991), 147–54.

Bredow, Wilfried von, and Jäger, Thomas. "Die Außenpolitik Deutschlands." *Aus Politik und Zeitgeschichte* B1-2/91 (January 4, 1991), 27–38.

*Brockhaus Enzyklopädie*. Vol. 6. 17th edn. Wiesbaden: F. A. Brockhaus, 1968.

Broder, Henryk M. *Der Ewige Antisemit: Über Sinn und Funktion eines beständigen Gefühls*. Frankfurt am Main: Fischer Taschenbuch Verlag, 1986.

Broszat, Martin; Henke, Klaus-Dietmar; and Woller, Hans, eds. *Von Stalingrad zur Währungsreform*. Munich: Oldenbourg, 1988.

Brown, Anthony Cave. *The Last Hero: Wild Bill Donovan*. New York: Times Books, 1982.

Bruns, Wilhelm. "Deutsch-Deutsche Beziehungen: Vom Sonderkonflikt zum Sonderkonsens?" *Politische Bildung* 20: 1 (1987), 38–52.

—— "Deutschlands Suche nach einer neuen außenpolitischen Rolle." *Deutschland Archiv* 24 (1991), 715–24.

Brzezinski, Zbigniew. *Power and Principle: Memoirs of the National Security Advisor, 1977–1981*. New York: Farrar, Strauss, Giroux, 1983.

Buber-Neumann, Margarete. *Von Potsdam nach Moskau*. Stuttgart: Deutsche Verlags-Anstalt, 1957.

—— *Als Gefangene bei Stalin und Hitler*. Stuttgart: Deutsche Verlags-Anstalt, 1958.

Bülow, Andreas von. *Das Bülow-Papier*. Frankfurt am Main: Eichborn, 1985.

Bundy, McGeorge; Kennan, George F.; McNamara, Robert; and Smith, Gerard. "Nuclear Weapons and the Atlantic Alliance." *Foreign Affairs* 60 (1981–2), 753–68.

Burdick, Charles; Jacobsen, Hans-Adolf; and Kudszus, Winfried, eds. *Contemporary Germany: Politics and Culture*. Boulder, CO: Westview, 1984.

Calleo, David. *The German Problem Reconsidered: Germany and the World Order, 1870 to the Present*. Cambridge: Cambridge University Press, 1978.

Caro, Michael K. *Der Volkskanzler, Ludwig Erhard*. Cologne: Kiepenheuer und Witsch, 1965.

Carr, Jonathan. *Helmut Schmidt: Helmsman of Germany*. London: Weidenfeld and Nicolson, 1985.

Catudal, Honore M. *The Diplomacy of the Quadripartite Agreement on Berlin: A New Era in East—West Politics*. Berlin: Berlin-Verlag, 1978.

Charlton, Michael. *The Eagle and the Small Birds*. Chicago: University of Chicago Press, 1984.

Chaussy, Ulrich. "Jugend" in *Die Bundesrepublik Deutschland*, vol. 2, Wolfgang Benz (ed.). Frankfurt am Main: Fischer Taschenbuch Verlag, 1983.

Childs, David. *The GDR: Moscow's German Ally*. 2nd edn. London: Unwin Hyman, 1988.

Childs, David, and Johnson, Jeffrey. *West Germany: Politics and Society*. New York: St. Martin's Press, 1981.

Churchill, Winston S. *The Second World War*. Vol. 6, *Triumph and Tragedy*. Boston: Houghton Mifflin Co., 1953.

Cioc, Mark. *Pax Atomica: the Nuclear Defense Debate in West Germany during the Adenauer Era*. New York: Columbia University Press, 1988.

Clay, Lucius D. *Decision in Germany*. New York: Doubleday and Company, 1950.

—— *The Papers of General Lucius D. Clay*, vol. 1. Jean Edward Smith (ed.). Bloomington, Indiana: University of Indiana Press, 1974.

—— "Proconsul of a People, by Another People, for Both Peoples" in *Americans as Proconsuls*, Robert Wolfe (ed.). Carbondale, IL: Southern Illinois University Press, 1984.

Clemens, Clay. *Reluctant Realist.* Durham, NC: Duke University Press, 1989.

Codevilla, Angelo. *While Others Build.* New York: Free Press, 1988.

Collier, Richard. *The Freedom Road, 1944–1945.* New York: Atheneum, 1984.

Conquest, Robert. *The Harvest of Sorrow: Soviet Collectivization and the Terror Famine.* New York: Oxford University Press, 1986.

Conradt, David P. *The German Polity.* 4th edn. New York: Longman, 1989.

Conze, Werner; and Lepsius, M. Rainer, eds. *Sozialgeschichte der Bundesrepublik Deutschland: Beiträge zum Kontinuitätsproblem.* Industrielle Welt. Schriftenreihe des Arbeitskreises für moderne Sozialgeschichte, no. 34. Stuttgart: Klett-Cotta, 1983.

Cook, Don. *Charles de Gaulle.* New York: G. P. Putnam's Sons, 1983.

—— *Ten Men and History.* New York: Doubleday and Company, 1981.

Cornelsen, Doris. "DDR-Wirtschaft: Ende oder Wende?" *Aus Politik und Zeitgeschichte*, B1/1990 (January 5, 1990), 33–8.

—— *Betrachtungen über die Revolution in Europe.* Stuttgart: Deutsche Verlags-Anstalt, 1990.

Craig, Gordon A. *The Germans.* New York: G. P. Putnam's Sons, 1982.

—— *Germany 1866–1945.* Oxford: Clarendon Press, 1978.

Dahrendorf, Ralf. *Bildung ist Bürgerrecht: Plädoyer für eine aktive Bildungspolitik.* Hamburg: C. Wegner, 1968.

—— *Law and Order.* The Hamlyn Lectures. London: Stevens and Sons, 1985.

—— *A New World Order?* [Legon]: University of Ghana, 1979.

—— *Society and Democracy in Germany.* New York: Doubleday, 1967.

—— *Betrachtungen über die Revolution in Europa.* Stuttgart: Deutsche Verlags-Anstalt, 1990. Published in English as *Reflections on the Revolution in Europe.* New York: Times Books, 1990.

Dalton, Russell M. *Politics in West Germany.* Boston: Scott, Foresman, 1989.

Davis, Kingsley; Bernstam, Mikhail; and Ricardo-Campbell, Rita, eds. *Below-Replacement Fertility in Industrial Societies.* New York: Cambridge University Press, 1987.

Davison, W. Phillips. *The Berlin Blockade: A Study in Cold War Politics.* Princeton, NJ: Princeton University Press, 1958.

de Gaulle, Charles. *Memoirs of Hope: Renewal and Endeavor.* New York: Simon and Schuster, 1971.

de Zayas, Alfred M. *Nemesis at Potsdam: The Anglo-Americans and the Expulsion of the Germans.* Rev. edn. London: Routledge and Kegan Paul, 1979.

Detwiler, Donald. "A Tribute to Percy Schramm." *Central European History* 4: 1 (March 1971), 90–4.

Deuerlein, Ernst. *CDU/CSU 1945–57.* Cologne: J. P. Bachem, 1957.

—— *Deutschland 1963–1970.* Hannover: Verlag für Literatur und Zeitgeschehen, 1972.

Deutsch, Karl Wolfgang, and Edinger, Lewis J. *Germany Rejoins the Powers.* Stanford, CA: Stanford University Press, 1959.

Dieckmann, Friedrich. *Glockenläuten und offene Fragen.* Frankfurt am Main: Suhrkamp, 1991.

Diwald, Hellmut. "Deutschland – was ist es?" in *Die Deutsche Einheit kommt bestimmt,* Wolfgang Venohr (ed.). Bergisch Gladbach: Gustav Lübbe, 1982.

— *Geschichte der Deutschen.* Berlin: Ullstein, 1978.

Doeker, Günther, and Brückner, Jens A., eds. *The Federal Republic of Germany and the German Democratic Republic in International Relations.* Vol. 1, *Confrontation and Co-operation.* Dobbs Ferry, NY: Oceana Publications, 1979.

Doering-Manteuffel, Anselm. *Die Bundesrepublik Deutschland in der Ära Adenauer.* Darmstadt: Wissenschaftliche Buchgesellschaft, 1983.

— *Katholizismus und Wiederbewaffnung.* Veröffentlichungen der Kommission für Zeitgeschichte, ser. B, vol. 32. Mainz: Grünewald, 1981.

Dönhoff, Marion. *Foe into Friend.* London: Weidenfeld and Nicolson, 1982.

Dorn, Walter L. *Inspektionsreisen in der US-Zone.* Lutz Niethammer (ed.). Stuttgart: Deutsche Verlags-Anstalt, 1973.

Drummond, Gordon D. *The German Social Democrats in Opposition, 1949–1960: The Case against Rearmament.* Norman, Oklahoma: University of Oklahoma Press, 1982.

Dyson, Kenneth H. F. *Party, State and Bureaucracy in Western Germany.* Beverly Hills, CA: Sage, 1978.

Eden, Anthony. *Full Circle.* London: Cassell, 1960.

Edinger, Lewis J. *Kurt Schumacher.* Stanford, CA: Stanford University Press, 1965.

— *West German Politics.* New York: Columbia University Press, 1986.

Ehmke, Horst. *Das Porträt: Reden und Beiträge.* Dieter Dettke (ed.). Bonn: GHM-Verlag, [1980].

— "What is the German Fatherland?" in *Observations on "The Spiritual Situation of the Age,"* Jürgen Habermas (ed.). Cambridge, MA: MIT Press, 1984.

Eiche, Hans. *Heinrich Lübke: Der zweite Präsident der Bundesrepublik Deutschland.* Bonn: Beinhauer, [1961].

Ellwein, Thomas. *Das Regierungssystem der Bundesrepublik Deutschland.* 5th edn. Opladen: Westdeutscher Verlag, 1983.

Ellwein, Thomas, and Bruder, Wolfgang, eds. *Ploetz — Die Bundesrepublik Deutschland: Daten, Fakten, Analysen.* Freiburg/Würzburg: Ploetz, 1984.

Elm, Ludwig. *Nach Hitler, nach Honecker. Zum streit der Deutschen um die eigene Vergangenheit.* Berlin: Dietz, 1991.

Emminger, Otmar. *D-Mark, Dollar, Währungskrisen: Erinnerungen eines ehemaligen Bundesbankpräsidenten.* Stuttgart: Deutsche Verlags-Anstalt, 1986.

Eppler, Erhard. *Ende oder Wende: Von der Machbarkeit des Notwendigen.* Stuttgart: Kohlhammer, 1975.

Erhard, Ludwig. *Prosperity through Competition.* London: Thames and Hudson, 1958.

Eschenburg, Theodor. *Jahre der Besatzung, 1945–1949.* Vol. 1 of *Geschichte der*

*Bundesrepublik Deutschland*. Stuttgart: Deutsche Verlags-Anstalt; Wiesbaden: Brockhaus, 1983.

Evans, Richard J. *In Hitler's Shadow: West German Historians and the Attempt to Escape from the Nazi Past*. New York: Pantheon Books, 1989.

Feher, Ferenc, Heller, Agnes, and Markus, György. *Dictatorship over Needs*. Oxford: Blackwell, 1983.

Ferrell, Robert H., ed. "Truman at Potsdam." *American Heritage* 31: 4 (June/July 1980), 36–47.

Filbinger, Hans. *Die geschmähte Generation*. Munich: Universitas, 1987.

Filmer, Werner, and Schwan, Heribert. *Helmut Kohl*. Düsseldorf: Econ, 1985.

Fischer, Arthur, et al., eds. *Jugend '81*. Published by Jugendwerk der Deutschen Shell. Leverkusen: Leske und Budrich, 1985.

Fischer, Erika J., and Fischer, Heinz D., eds. *John J. McCloy und die Frühgeschichte der Bundesrepublik Deutschland*. Cologne: Verlag Wissenschaft und Politik, 1985.

Fischer, Fritz. *Griff nach der Weltmacht*. 3rd edn. Düsseldorf: Droste, 1964. Published in English as *Germany's Aim in the First World War*. London: Chatto and Windus, 1967.

Flechtheim, Ossip K., ed. *Dokumente zur parteipolitischen Entwicklung in Deutschland seit 1945*. 3 vols. Berlin: Dokumenten-Verlag Dr Herbert Wendler und Co., 1962.

Forster, Karl. "Der deutsche Katholizismus in der Bundesrepublik Deutschland" in *Der soziale und politische Katholizismus*, vol. 1, Anton Rauscher (ed.). Munich: Olzog, 1981.

Foschepoth, Josef. "Adenauers Moskaureise 1955." *Aus Politik und Zeitgeschichte* B 22/86 (May 31, 1986), 30–46.

Frei, Norbert. "Presse" and "Hörfunk und Fernsehen" in *Die Bundesrepublik Deutschland*, vol. 3, Wolfgang Benz (ed.). Frankfurt am Main: Fischer Taschenbuch Verlag, 1983.

Frenzel, Paul. *Die rote Mark: Perestroika für die DDR*. Fritz Schenk, ed. Herford: Busse & Seewald, 1989.

Fricke, Karl Wilhelm. *Die DDR-Staatssicherheit*. 3rd edn. Cologne: Verlag Wissenschaft und Politik, 1989.

—— "Die Akten lagen dem ZK vor." *Deutschland Archiv* 23 (1990), 1484–7.

—— "Entmachtung und Erblast des MfS." *Deutschland Archiv* 23 (1990), 1881–90.

—— *MfS intern. Macht, Strukturen, Auflösung der DDR-Staatssicherheit*. Cologne: Verlag Wissenschaft und Politik, 1991.

—— "Kaderpolitik und Staatssicherheit in der DDR," in *Die Gesellschaft der DDR. Untersuchungen zu ausgewählten Bereichen*. Dieter Voigt, ed. Schriftenreihe der Gesellschaft für Deutschlandforschung, 10, Jahrbuch 1984.

—— "Ein Federzug von Ulbrichts Hand: Todesstrafe." *Deutschland Archiv* 24 (1991), 840–46.

—— *Opposition und Widerstand in der DDR*. Cologne: Verlag Wissenschaft und Politik. 1984.

—— "Zur Abschaffung des Amtes für nationale Sicherheit." *Deutschland Archiv* 23 (1990), 62.

—— "Urteil gegen K. W. Fricke durch Kassation aufgehoben." *Deutschland Archiv* 24 (1991), 907–8.

Friedrich, Wolfgang-Uwe. *DDR: Deutschland zwischen Elbe und Oder.* 2nd edn. Stuttgart: Kohlhammer, 1989.

Friedberg, Aaron L. "The Making of American National Strategy, 1948–1988." *National Interest* 11 (Spring 1988), 68–75.

Frielinghaus-Heuss, Hanna. *Heuss-Anekdoten.* Munich and Esslingen: Bechtle, 1964.

Friend, Julius W. *The Linchpin: French—German Relations, 1950—1990.* New York: Praeger, 1991.

Fuchs, Dieter; Klingemann, Hans-Dieter, and Schöbel, Caroline. "Perspektiven der politischen Kultur im vereinigten Deutschland." *Aus Politik und Zeitgeschichte* B32/91 (August 2, 1991), 35–46.

Gaddis, John Lewis. *Strategies of Containment.* New York: Oxford University Press, 1982.

—— *The United States and the Origins of the Cold War, 1941—1947.* New York: Columbia University Press, 1972.

Garton Ash, Timothy. *The Polish Revolution: Solidarity.* New York: Scribner's, 1984.

Garton Ash, Timothy, et al. *Reden über Deutschland.* Munich: Bertelsmann, 1990.

Gatz, Erwin. "Caritas und soziale Dienste" in *Der soziale und politische Katholizismus,* vol. 2, Anton Rauscher (ed.). Munich: Olzog, 1981.

Gauck, Joachim. *Die Stasi-Akten: Das unheimliche Erbe der DDR.* Reinbek: Rowohlt, 1991.

Gaus, Günter. *Wo Deutschland liegt: Eine Ortsbestimmung.* Hamburg: Hoffmann und Campe, 1983.

Gehlen, Reinhard. *Der Dienst.* Munich: Kindler, 1970.

—— *Verschlusssache.* Munich: Kindler, 1976.

Gelb, Norman. *The Berlin Wall.* London: Michael Joseph, 1986.

Genscher, Hans-Dietrich. *Deutsche Aussenpolitik.* Stuttgart: Verlag Bonn Aktuell, 1977.

Gerlach, Manfred. *Mitverantwortlich. Als Liberaler im SED-Staat.* Berlin: Morgenbuch, 1991.

*Geschichte der Bundesrepublik Deutschland.* 5 vols. Stuttgart: Deutsche Verlags-Anstalt; Wiesbaden: Brockhaus, 1981–7.

Gibowski, Wolfgang G., and Kaase, Max. "Auf dem Weg zum politischen Alltag." *Aus Politik und Zeitgeschichte* B11-12/91 (March 8, 1991), 3–20.

Gillessen, Günther. "Konrad Adenauer und der Israel-Vertrag" in *Politik, Philosophie, Praxis,* Hans Maier , Ulrich Matz, Kurt Sontheimer, and Paul-Ludwig Weinacht (eds). Stuttgart: Klett-Cotta, 1988.

Gimbel, John. *The American Occupation of Germany: Politics and the Military, 1945— 1949.* Stanford, CA: Stanford University Press, 1968.

—— "Governing the American Zone of Germany" in *Americans as Proconsuls,* Robert Wolfe (ed.). Carbondale, IL: Southern Illinois University Press, 1984.

Glaser, Hermann. *Kulturgeschichte der Bundesrepublik Deutschland.* 2 vols. Munich: Carl Hanser, 1985–6.

Glaser, Hermann, ed. *Bundesrepublikanisches Lesebuch*. Frankfurt am Main: Fischer Taschenbuch Verlag, 1980.

Golay, John Ford. *The Founding of the Federal Republic of Germany*. Chicago: University of Chicago Press, 1958.

Goldman, Guido. *The German Political System*. New York: Random House, 1974.

Gollancz, Victor. *In Darkest Germany*. Hinsdale, IL: Henry Regnery Company, 1947.

—— *Our Threatened Values*. Hinsdale, IL: Henry Regnery Company, 1948.

Gottlieb, Manuel. *The German Peace Settlement and the Berlin Crisis*. New York: Paine-Whitman, 1960.

Gotto, Klaus. "Adenauers Deutschland- und Ostpolitik 1954–1963" in *Adenauer-Studien*, vol. 3, Rudolf Morsey and Konrad Repgen (eds). Mainz: Mathias Grünewald, 1976.

Gotto, Klaus, ed. *Der Staatssekretär Adenauers: Persönlichkeit und politisches Wirken Hans Globkes*. Stuttgart: Klett-Cotta, 1980.

Gradl, Johann B. *Anfang unter dem Sowjetstern: Die CDU 1945–1948 in der sowjetischen Besatzungszone Deutschlands*. Cologne: Verlag Wissenschaft und Politik, 1981.

Graml, Hermann. *Die Alliierten und die Teilung Deutschlands: Konflikte und Entscheidungen 1941–1948*. Frankfurt am Main: Fischer Taschenbuch Verlag, 1985.

—— "Die Legende von der verpassten Gelegenheit." *Vierteljahrshefte für Zeitgeschichte* 29 (1981), 307–41.

Grass, Günter. *Aus dem Tagebuch einer Schnecke*. Neuwied: Luchterhand, 1972.

—— *On Writing and Politics 1967–1983*. Orlando, FL: Harcourt Brace Jovanovich, 1985.

—— *Widerstand lernen*. Darmstadt: Luchterhand, 1984.

Grebing, Helga; Pozorski, Peter; and Schulze, Rainer. *Die Nachkriegsentwicklung in Westdeutschland 1945–1949*. 2 vols. Stuttgart: J. B. Metzler, 1980.

Greiner, Christian. "The Defence of Western Europe and the Rearmament of West Germany, 1947–1950" in *Western Security: The Formative Years*, Olav Riste (ed.). Oslo: Norwegian University Press, 1985.

Gress, David. *Peace and Survival: West Germany, the Peace Movement, and European Security*. Stanford, CA: Hoover Institution Press, 1985.

Grewe, Wilhelm G. *Rückblenden 1976–1951*. Frankfurt am Main: Propyläen, 1979.

Griffith, William E. *The Ostpolitik of the Federal Republic of Germany*. Cambridge, MA: MIT Press, 1978.

Groll, Klaus Michael. *Wie lange haften wir für Hitler*. Düsseldorf: Droste Verlag, 1990.

Grosser, Alfred. *French Foreign Policy under de Gaulle*. Boston: Little, Brown, 1967.

—— *La IVe république et sa politique extérieure*. 3rd edn. Paris: Armand Colin, 1972.

—— *L'Allemagne de notre temps*. 2nd edn. Paris: Pluriel, 1978.

—— *Germany in Our Time*. New York: Praeger, 1971.

—— *L'Allemagne en Occident*. Paris: Fayard, 1985.

—— *The Western Alliance*. Rev. edn. New York: Viking, 1982.

—— *Le Crime et la Mémoire*. Paris: Flammarion, 1989.

Grosser, Alfred, and Seifert, Jürgen. *Die Staatsmacht und ihre Kontrolle*. Vol. 1 of *Die Spiegel-Affäre*, Jürgen Seifert (ed.). Olten: Walter- Verlag, 1966.

Grossmann, Thomas. *Zwischen Kirche und Gesellschaft. Die Zentralkomitee der deutschen Katholiken 1945—1970*. Veröffentlichungen der Kommission für Zeitgeschichte, no. 56. Mainz: Matthias-Grunewald-Verlag, 1991.

Gruner, Wolf D. *Deutschland mitten in Europa*. Hamburg: Hoffmann & Campe, 1992.

—— *Die deutsche Frage. Ein Problem der europäischen Geschichte seit 1800*. 2nd ed. Munich: Beck, 1992.

Günther, Horst. *Versuche, europäisch zu denken: Deutschland und Frankreich*. Frankfurt am Main: Suhrkamp, 1990.

Günther, Klaus. *Der Kanzlerwechsel in der Bundesrepublik: Adenauer-Erhard-Kiesinger*. Hannover: Verlag für Literatur und Zeitgeschehen, 1970.

Guttenberg, Karl Theodor Freiherr von und zu. *Fussnoten*. Stuttgart: Seewald, 1971.

Habermas, Jürgen. "Eine Art Schadensabwicklung" in *"Historikerstreit."* Munich: Piper, 1987.

—— *The New Conservatism: Cultural Criticism and the Historian's Debate*. Shierry Weber Nicholsen ed. and trans. Cambridge: MIT Press, 1990.

Habermas, Jürgen, ed. *Observations on "The Spiritual Situation of the Age": Contemporary German Perspectives*. Cambridge, MA: MIT Press, 1984. Partial translation of *Stichworte zur "Geistigen Situation der Zeit."* Frankfurt am Main: Suhrkamp, 1979.

Hacke, Christian. *Weltmacht wider Willen: Die Aussenpolitik der Bundesrepublik Deutschland*. Stuttgart: Klett-Cotta, 1988.

Hacker, Jens. *Deutsche Irrtümer. Schönfärber und Helfershelfer der SED-Diktatur im Westen*. Berlin: Ullstein, 1992.

Haffner, Sebastian. *Von Bismarck zu Hitler*. 2nd edn. Munich: Knaur.

Haftendorn, Helga. *Security and Detente*. New York: Praeger, 1985.

—— *Sicherheit und Stabilität: Aussenbeziehungen der Bundesrepublik zwischen Ölkrise und NATO-Doppelbeschluss*. Munich: Deutscher Taschenbuch Verlag, 1986.

Hahn, Reinhardt O. *Ausgedient. Ein Stasi-Major erzählt*. Halle & Leipzig: Mitteldeutscher Verlag, 1990.

Hahn, Walter F. "West Germany's Ostpolitik." *Orbis* 16 (1973), 859–80.

Hallett, Graham. *The Social Economy of West Germany*. London: Macmillan, 1973.

Hallstein, Walter. *United Europe: Challenge and Opportunity*. Cambridge, MA: Harvard University Press, 1962.

Hamburger, Michael. *From Prophecy to Exorcism*. London: Longman, 1965.

Hanrieder, Wolfram F. *Germany, America, Europe: Forty Years of German Foreign Policy*. New Haven, CT: Yale University Press, 1989.

Hartrich, Edwin. *The Fourth and Richest Reich*. New York: Macmillan, 1980.

Hattenhauer, Hans. *Geschichte des Beamtentums*. Cologne: Carl Heymanns Verlag, 1980.

Hättich, Manfred. *Weltfrieden durch Friedfertigkeit?: Eine Antwort an Franz Alt*. Munich: Olzog, 1983.

—— *Fragen an Richard von Weizsäcker*. Mainz: von Hase und Koehler, 1990.

Heidenheimer, Arnold J. *The Governments of Germany.* 4th edn. New York: T. Y. Crowell, [1975].

Heinrich, Gerd. *Geschichte Preussens.* Frankfurt am Main: Propyläen, 1981.

Heller, Michel, and Nekrich, Aleksandr. *L'utopie au pouvoir: Histoire de l'URSS de 1917 a nos jours.* Paris: Calmann-Levy, 1982.

Herbst, Ludolf, and Goschler, Constantin, eds. *Wiedergutmachung in der Bundesrepublik Deutschland.* Schriftenreihe der Vierteljahrshefte für Zeitgeschichte, special issue. Munich: Oldenbourg, 1989.

Herf, Jeffrey. *War by Other Means: Soviet Power, West German Resistance, and the Battle of the Euromissiles.* New York: Free Press, 1991.

Herles, Helmut, ed. *Die Haupstadtdebatte.* Bonn, Berlin: Bouvier, 1991.

Herzfeld, Hans. *Berlin in der Weltpolitik 1945–1970.* Berlin: Walter de Gruyter, 1973.

—— *Der Erste Weltkrieg.* Munich: Deutscher Taschenbuch Verlag, 1968.

Hettlage, Robert, ed. *Die Bundesrepublik: Eine historische Bilanz.* Munich: Beck, 1990.

Hilberg, Raul. *The Destruction of the European Jews.* Rev. edn. New York: Holmes and Meier, 1985.

Hildebrand, Klaus. *Von Erhard zur Grossen Koalition, 1963–1969.* Vol. 4 of *Geschichte der Bundesrepublik Deutschland.* Stuttgart: Deutsche Verlags-Anstalt; Wiesbaden: Brockhaus, 1984.

Hildebrandt, Horst, ed. *Die deutschen Verfassungen des 19. und 20. Jahrhunderts.* Paderborn: Ferdinand Schöningh, 1983.

Hilgemann, Werner. *Atlas zur Deutschen Zeitgeschichte, 1918–1968.* Munich: Piper, 1984.

Hillgruber, Andreas. *Deutsche Geschichte 1945–1982: Die "deutsche Frage" in der Weltpolitik.* 5th edn. Stuttgart: Kohlhammer, 1984.

—— *Zweierlei Untergang: Die Zerschlagung des deutschen Reiches und das Ende des europäischen Judentums.* Berlin: Siedler, 1986.

*"Historikerstreit": Die Dokumentation der Kontroverse um die Einzigartigkeit der nationalsozialistischen Judenvernichtung.* Munich: Piper, 1987.

Hollander, Paul. "The Survival of the Adversary Culture." *Orbis* 33 (Fall 1990), 566–77.

Homann, Fritz. "Treuhandanstalt: Zwischenbilanz, Perspektiven." *Deutschland Archiv* 24 (1991), 1277–87.

Horchem, Hans Josef. "Der Verfall der Roten Armee Fraktion." *Aus Politik und Zeitgeschichte* B46-47/90 (November 9, 1990), 54–61.

—— *Die verlorene Revolution: Terrorismus in Deutschland.* Herford: Busse Seewald, 1988.

Horn, Gyula. *Freiheit, die ich meine.* Hamburg: Hoffmann und Campe, 1991.

Howard, Michael. *The Causes of Wars and other Essays.* 2nd edn. Cambridge, MA: Harvard University Press, 1984.

Hübner, Emil, and Rohlfs, Horst-H., eds. *Jahrbuch der Bundesrepublik Deutschland 1986/87.* Munich: Beck/dtv, 1987.

Independent Commission on International Development Issues. *North–South: A Programme for Survival.* Cambridge, MA: MIT Press, 1981. Published in German as *Die Zukunft Sichern.* Bericht der Nord–Süd Kommission.

Inglehart, Ronald. *Culture Change in Advanced Industrial Societies.* Princeton, NJ: Princeton University Press, 1989.

—— "The Renaissance of Political Culture." *American Political Science Review* 82 (1988), 1204.

—— *The Silent Revolution.* Princeton, NJ: Princeton University Press, 1977.

Isby, David C., and Kamps, Charles, Jr. *Armies of NATO's Central Front.* London: Jane's, 1985.

Jäckel, Hartmut. "Unser schiefes DDR-Bild. Anmerkungen zu einem noch nicht verjährten publizistischen Sündenfall." *Deutschland Archiv* 23 (1990), 1557–65.

Jäger, Manfred. "Verdeckte Gemeinsamkeiten." *Deutschland Archiv* 24 (1991), 1287–94.

Jäger, Wolfgang, and Link, Werner. *Republik im Wandel, 1974—1982, Die Ära Schmidt.* Vol. 5/II of *Geschichte der Bundesrepublik Deutschland.* Stuttgart: Deutsche Verlags-Anstalt; Wiesbaden: Brockhaus, 1987.

Jakobs, Hans-Jürgen, and Müller, Uwe. *Augstein, Springer & Co. Deutsche Mediendynastien.* Zürich: Orell Füssli Verlag, 1990.

James, Harold. *A German Identity: 1770—1990.* London: Weidenfeld and Nicolson, 1989.

Jaspers, Karl. *Antwort: Zur Kritik meiner Schrift "Wohin treibt die Bundesrepublik?"* Munich: Piper, 1967.

—— *Die Atombombe und die Zukunft der Menschen.* Munich: Piper, 1958. Published in English as *The Atom Bomb and the Future of Man.* Chicago: Chicago University Press, 1961.

—— *Die geistige Situation der Zeit.* Berlin, Leipzig: Walter de Gruyter, 1931.

—— *Hoffnung und Sorge: Schriften zur deutschen Politik, 1945—1965.* Munich: Piper, 1965.

—— *Wohin treibt die Bundesrepublik?* Munich: Piper, 1966. An English translation, *The Future of Germany*, contains parts of *Wohin treibt die Bundesrepublik?* as well as parts of *Antwort: Zur Kritik meiner Schrift "Wohin treibt die Bundesrepublik?"* Chicago: University of Chicago Press, 1967.

Jenkins, Peter. *Mrs Thatcher's Revolution: The Ending of the Socialist Era.* London: Jonathan Cape, 1987.

Jesse, Eckhard. "Linksextremismus in der Bundesrepublik Deutschland." *Aus Politik und Zeitgeschichte* B3-4/92 (January 10, 1992), 31–9.

Joffe, Josef. "The Battle of the Historians." *Encounter* (June 1987), 72–7.

—— *The Limited Partnership: Europe, the United States, and the Burdens of Alliance.* Cambridge, MA: Ballinger, 1987.

—— "Is there a German-American Question? Defense, Detente, Neutrality, Reunification." Paper presented at the International Security Council Roundtable on "The Future of German-American Relations," Berlin, FRG, (June 8–10, 1987).

Junker, Detlef. "Die 'revisionistische Schule' in der US-Historiographie" in *Die Deutschlandfrage und die Anfänge des Ost-Westkonflikts 1945—1949.* Studien zur Deutschlandfrage, vol. 7. Publ. by Gottinger Arbeitskreis. Berlin: Duncker und Humblot, 1984.

Kaiser, Bruno. *Notstandsgesetzgebung in der Grossen Koalition.* Unpublished manuscript in Archiv K. G. Kiesinger, Bonn.

Kaltefleiter, Werner. *Parteien im Umbruch.* Düsseldorf: Econ, 1984.

Karsunke, Ingrid, and Michel, Karl Markus, eds. *Bewegung in der Republik 1965 bis 1984: Eine Kursbuch-Chronik.* 2 vols. Berlin: Rotbuch, 1985.

Katzenstein, Peter J. *Policy and Politics in West Germany.* Philadelphia: Temple University Press, 1987.

Kelleher, Catherine McArdle. *Germany and the Politics of Nuclear Weapons.* New York: Columbia University Press, 1975.

Kempf, Udo. "Die Deutsch-Französischen Beziehungen seit October 1982: Versuch einer Bilanz." *Zeitschrift für Politik* 34 (March 1987), 31–55.

Kennan, George F. *Memoirs 1925–1950.* Boston: Little, Brown and Company, 1967.

—— *Russia and the West under Lenin and Stalin.* Boston: Little, Brown and Company, 1961.

—— *Russia, the Atom and the West.* New York: Harper and Brothers, 1958.

—— "The Sources of Soviet Conduct." *Foreign Affairs* 65 (1986–7), 852–68.

Kennan, George F.; Urban, George; Seton-Watson, Hugh; Pipes, Richard; Novak, M.; Weiss, S.; Luttwak, E. N.; Rostow, E. V.; Gaddis, J. L.; and Mark, E. *Decline of the West?* Washington, DC: Ethics and Public Policy Center, Georgetown University, 1978.

Kershaw, Ian. *The Hitler Myth.* Oxford: Oxford University Press, 1989.

—— *Popular Opinion and Political Dissent in the Third Reich: Bavaria, 1933–1945.* Oxford: Clarendon Press, 1983.

Kissinger, Henry. *The Troubled Partnership.* New York: McGraw-Hill, 1965.

—— *White House Years.* Boston: Little, Brown and Company, 1979.

—— *Years of Upheaval.* Boston: Little, Brown and Company, 1982.

Kistler, Helmut. *Bundesdeutsche Geschichte.* Stuttgart: Bonn Aktuell, 1986.

Klarsfeld, Beate. *Wherever They May Be.* New York: Vanguard Press, 1975.

Klemm, Volker. *Korruption und Amtsmißbrauch in der DDR.* Stuttgart: Deutsche Verlags-Anstalt, 1991.

Klessmann, Christoph. *Die doppelte Staatsgründung: Deutsche Geschichte 1945–1955.* Göttingen: Vandenhoeck und Ruprecht, 1982.

—— *Zwei Staaten, eine Nation: Deutsche Geschichte 1955–1970.* Göttingen: Vandenhoeck & Ruprecht, 1988.

—— "Opposition und Dissidenz in der Geschichte der DDR." *Aus Politik und Zeitgeschichte* B5/91 (January 25, 1991), 52–62.

Klimow, Gregory. *Berliner Kreml.* Cologne: Kiepenheuer, Witsch and Co., 1952.

Knabe, Hubertus. "Vergangenheitsbewältigung per Gesetz?" *Deutschland Archiv* 24 (1991), 1011–15.

Koch, H. W. *A Constitutional History of Germany in the Nineteenth and Twentieth Centuries.* London: Longman, 1984.

Koch, Thomas. "Kein Ende der Kollusion in Deutschland?" *Deutschland Archiv* 24 (1991), 285–8.

Kocka, Jürgen. *Die Angestellten in der deutschen Geschichte, 1850–1980.* Göttingen: Vandenhoeck und Ruprecht, 1981.

—— "Überraschung und Erklärung. Was die Umbrüche von 1989/90 für die Gesellschaftsgeschichte bedeuten können." In Manfred Hettling et al., eds, *Was ist Gesellschaftsgeschichte?* Munich: Beck, 1991.

Koerfer, Daniel. *Kampf ums Kanzleramt: Erhard und Adenauer.* Stuttgart: Deutsche Verlags-Anstalt, 1987.

Kohl, Helmut. *Helmut Kohl: Bundestagsreden und Zeitdokumente.* Horst Teltschik (ed.). Bonn: az studio, 1978.

Köhler, Anne, and Hilmer, Richard. "Ein Jahr Wirtschafts-, Währungs- und Sozialunion." *Deutschland Archiv* 24 (1991), 931–6.

Kolko, Gabriel. *The Politics of War.* New York: Random House, 1968.

Kommers, Donald P. *Judicial Politics in West Germany: A Study of the Federal Constitutional Court.* Beverly Hills: Sage Publications, 1976.

Kopelev, Lev. *To Be Preserved Forever.* Philadelphia: Lippincott, 1977.

Körner, Heiko; Meyer-Dohm, Peter; Tuchtfeldt, Egon; and Uhlig, Christian, eds. *Wirtschaftspolitik — Wissenschaft und politische Aufgabe: Festschrift zum 65. Geburtstag von Karl Schiller.* Bern: Paul Haupt, 1976.

Kortmann, Erhard, and Wolf, Fritz, eds. *Die Lage war noch nie so ernst!: Doctor Adenauers geflügelte Worte.* Bergisch Gladbach: Gustav Lübbe, 1966.

Krauss, Melvyn. *How NATO Weakens the West.* New York: Simon and Schuster, 1986.

Krisch, Henry. *German Politics under Soviet Occupation.* New York: Columbia University Press 1974.

Krockow, Christian Graf von. *Die Stunde der Frauen: Bericht aus Pommern 1944–1947.* Stuttgart: Deutsche Verlags-Anstalt, 1988.

—— *Les Allemands du XXe siècle (1890–1990): Histoire d'une identité.* Paris: Hachette, 1990. In German: *Die Deutschen in ihrem Jahrhundert.* Reinbek: Rowohlt, 1990.

Kuklick, Bruce. *American Policy and the Division of Germany.* Ithaca: Cornell University Press, 1972.

Kunze, Reiner. *Deckname "Lyrik."* Frankfurt am Main: Fischer Taschenbuch Verlag, 1990.

Lacouture, Jean. *De Gaulle.* Vol. 3, *Le Souverain 1959–1970.* Paris: Seuil, 1986.

Lafontaine, Oskar. *Angst vor den Freunden.* Reinbek: Rowohlt, 1983.

—— *Das Lied vom Teilen.* Hamburg: Hoffmann und Campe, 1989.

Lahr, Rolf. *Zeuge von Fall und Aufstieg.* Hamburg: Albrecht Knaus, 1981.

Lampert, Heinz. *Die Wirtschafts- und Sozialordnung der Bundesrepublik Deutschland.* 10th edn. Munich: Olzog, 1990.

—— "Sozialpolitische Aufgaben der Umgestaltung der Wirtschafts- und Sozialordnung der DDR." *Aus Politik und Zeitgeschichte* B33/90 (August 10, 1990).

Lampugnani, Vittorio. "Architektur und Stadtplanung" in *Die Bundesrepublik Deutschland*, vol. 1, Wolfgang Benz (ed.). Frankfurt am Main: Fischer Taschenbuch Verlag, 1983.

Langguth, Gerd. *Protestbewegung: Entwicklung, Niedergang, Renaissance.* Cologne: Verlag Wissenschaft und Politik, 1983.

—— *The Green Factor in German Politics: From Protest Movement to Political Party.* Boulder, Colorado: Westview, 1986. Originally published as *Der Grüne Faktor: Von der Bewegung zur Partei?* Osnabrück: Fromm, 1984.

Lapp, Peter-Joachim. "Die neuen Bundesländer I. Mecklenburg-Vorpommern." *Deutschland Archiv* 24 (1991), 680–5.

—— "Die neuen Bundesländer II. Brandenburg." *Deutschland Archiv* 24 (1991), 913–19.

Larrabee, Stephen, ed. *The Two German States and European Security*. New York: St Martin's Press, 1989.

Lasky, Melvin. "Journey among the 'Ugly Germans.'" *Encounter* Pamphlet No. 17 (1987), 56–63.

Lehmann, Hans Georg. *Öffnung nach Osten*. Bonn: Neue Gesellschaft, 1984.

Leonhard, Wolfgang. *Child of the Revolution*. Chicago: Henry Regnery Company, 1958. Originally published as *Die Revolution entlässt ihre Kinder*. Cologne: Kiepenheuer und Witsch, 1955.

Leyendecker, Hans, and Rickelmann, Richard. *Exporteure des Todes*. Göttingen: Steidl, 1990.

Lippmann, Walter. "The Cold War." *Foreign Affairs* 65 (1986–7), 869–84.

—— "Rough-hew Them How We Will." *Foreign Affairs* 15 (1936–7), 587–94.

Lobkowicz, Nikolaus. *Was brachte uns das Konzil?* Würzburg: Naumann, 1986.

Loewenberg, Gerhard. *Parliament in the German Political System*. Ithaca: Cornell University Press, 1967.

Löwenthal, Richard. "Vom kalten Krieg zur Ostpolitik" in *Die zweite Republik*, Richard Löwenthal and Hans-Peter Schwarz (eds). Stuttgart: Seewald, 1974.

Löwenthal, Richard, and Schwarz, Hans-Peter, eds. *Die zweite Republik: 25 Jahre Bundesrepublik Deutschland — eine Bilanz*. Stuttgart: Seewald, 1974.

Lübbe, Hermann. *Endstation Terror: Rückblick auf lange Märsche*. Stuttgart: Seewald, 1978.

—— *Politischer Moralismus*. Berlin: Siedler, 1987.

Luft, Hans. "Die Treuhandanstalt." *Deutschland Archiv* 24 (1991), 1270–6.

Lukacs, John. "The Soviet State at 65." *Foreign Affairs* 65 (1986–7), 21–36.

—— *A New History of the Cold War*. New York: Doubleday, 1966.

Maaz, Hans-Joachim. *Der Gefühlsstau. Ein Psychogramm der DDR*. Berlin: Argon, 1990.

—— "Psychosoziale Aspekte im deutschen Einigungsprozeß." *Aus Politik und Zeitgeschichte* B19/91 (May 3, 1991), 3–10.

McAdams, A. James. *East Germany and Detente*. Cambridge: Cambridge University Press, 1985.

McCloy, John J. "From Military Government to Self-Government" in *Americans as Proconsuls*, Robert Wolfe (ed.). Carbondale, IL: Southern Illinois University Press, 1984.

McGhee, George. *At the Creation of a New Germany*. New Haven: Yale University Press, 1989.

Macmillan, Harold. *Riding the Storm*. New York: Harper and Row, 1971.

—— *Tides of Fortune: 1945–1955*. New York: Harper and Row, 1969.

Maier, Charles S. "The Two Post-War Eras and the Conditions for Stability in 20th Century Western Europe." *American Historical Review* 86 (1981), 327–52.

—— *The Unmasterable Past: History, Holocaust, and German National Identity.* Cambridge, MA: Harvard University Press, 1988.

Malia, Martin. *Comprendre la revolution russe.* Paris: Seuil, 1980.

Mampel, Siegfried. "Föderalismus in Deutschland." *Deutschland Archiv* 24 (1991), 804–14 & 919–30.

Mann, Golo. *History of Germany since 1789.* New York: Praeger, 1968. Reprinted London: Penguin Books, 1988.

Mann, Thomas. *Thomas Mann's Addresses Delivered at the Library of Congress, 1942–1949.* Washington: Library of Congress, 1963.

Marcuse, Herbert. *An Essay on Liberation.* Boston: Beacon Press, 1969.

—— *One-Dimensional Man.* Boston: Beacon Press, 1964.

Marjolin, Robert. *Le travail d'une vie: Memoirs 1911–1986.* Paris: Laffont, 1986.

Marsh, David. *The Germans: A People at the Crossroads.* New York: St Martin's Press, 1990.

Massing, Peter. "Die Bildungspolitik" in *Die Bundesrepublik in den siebziger Jahren,* Gert-Joachim Glaessner, Jürgen Holz, and Thomas Schlüter (eds). Opladen: Leske und Budrich, 1984.

Mastny, Vojtech. *Russia's Road to the Cold War.* New York: Columbia University Press, 1979.

Mayne, Richard. *Postwar: The Dawn of Today's Europe.* London: Thames and Hudson, 1983.

Mearsheimer, John J. "Back to the Future: Instability in Europe after the Cold War." *International Security* 15/1 (Summer 1990), 3–54.

Mehnert, Klaus, and Schulte, Heinrich, eds. *Deutschland-Jahrbuch 1949.* Essen: West, 1949.

Meier, Christian. "Kein Schlusswort" in *"Historikerstreit."* Munich: Piper, 1987.

—— *Die Nation die keine sein will.* Munich: Hanser, 1991.

Meinecke, Friedrich. *The German Catastrophe.* Cambridge, MA: Harvard University Press, 1950.

Meissner, Boris. *Russland, die Westmächte und Deutschland: Die sowjetische Deutschlandpolitik 1943–1953.* Hamburg: H. H. Noelke, 1953.

Mende, Erich. *Die neue Freiheit, 1945–1961.* Munich: Herbig, 1984.

Merkl, Peter H. *German Foreign Policies, West and East.* Santa Barbara: ABC Clio, 1974.

—— *The Origin of the West German Republic.* New York: Oxford University Press, 1963.

Merritt, Anna J., and Merritt, Richard L., eds. *Public Opinion in Occupied Germany: The OMGUS Surveys, 1945–1949.* Urbana, IL: University of Illinois Press, 1970.

—— *Public Opinion in Semisovereign Germany: The HICOG Surveys, 1949–1955.* Urbana, IL: University of Illinois Press, 1980.

Mertz, Peter. *Und das wurde nicht ihr Staat: Erfahrungen emigrierter Schriftsteller mit Westdeutschland.* Munich: Beck, 1985.

Milward, Alan S. *The Reconstruction of Western Europe, 1945–1951.* Berkeley: University of California Press, 1984.

Mitchell, B. R., ed. *European Historical Statistics 1750–1975.* 2nd rev. edn. New York: Facts on File, 1981.

Mitscherlich, Alexander. *Society Without the Father.* New York: Schocken, 1970. Originally published as *Auf dem Weg zur vaterlosen Gesellschaft.* Munich: Piper, 1963.

Mitscherlich, Alexander, and Mitscherlich, Margarete. *The Inability to Mourn: Principles of Collective Behavior.* New York: Grove Press, 1975. Originally published as *Die Unfähigkeit zu trauern, Grundlagen kollektiven Verhaltens.* Munich: Piper, 1967.

Mittag, Günter. *Um jeden Preis.* Berlin: Aufbau, 1991.

Mitter, Armin. "Die Ereignisse im Juni und Juli 1953 in der DDR." *Aus Politik und Zeitgeschichte* B5/91 (January 25, 1991), 31–41.

Mont Pelerin Society Records, 1945–1981. Hoover Institution Archives, Stanford, California.

Morgan, Roger P. *The United States and West Germany, 1945–1973.* London: published for the Royal Institute of International Affairs and the Harvard Center for International Affairs by Oxford University Press, 1974.

Morgenthau, Henry, Jr. *Germany Is Our Problem.* New York: Harper and Brothers, 1945.

Morsey, Rudolf. *Die Bundesrepublik Deutschland: Entstehung und Entwicklung bis 1969.* Oldenbourg-Grundriss der Geschichte, vol. 19. Munich: Oldenbourg, 1987.

Mühlfenzl, Rudolf, ed. *Geflohen und vertrieben.* Königstein: Athenaeum, 1981.

Münch, Ingo von. "Deutschland: gestern – heute – morgen. Verfassungsrechtliche und völkerrechtliche Probleme der deutschen Teilung und Vereinigung." *Neue Juristische Wochenschrift* 44 (1991), 865–71.

—— ed. *Dokumente des geteilten Deutschland.* 2 vols. Stuttgart: Kröner, 1968–74.

—— ed. *Die Verträge zur Einheit Deutschlands.* Munich: dtv, 1990.

—— *Dokumente der Wiedervereinigung Deutschlands.* Stuttgart: Kröner, 1991.

Nagel, G., ed. *Berlin 91: Das Jahr im Rückspiegel.* Frankfurt am Main: Ullstein, 1991.

Naumann, Bernd. *Auschwitz.* New York: Frederic A. Praeger, 1966.

Negt, Oskar. "Studentischer Protest – Liberalismus – 'Linksfaschismus'" in *Bewegung in der Republik 1965 bis 1984: Eine Kursbuch-Chronik*, vol. 2, Ingrid Karsunke and Karl Markus Michel (eds). Berlin: Rotbuch, 1985.

Nelson, Daniel J. *Wartime Origins of the Berlin Dilemma.* University, AL: University of Alabama Press, 1978.

Nicholson, Frances, and East, Roger. *From the Six to the Twelve: The Enlargement of the European Communities.* Keesing's International Studies. Harlow: Longman, 1987.

Niethammer, Lutz. *Die Mitläuferfabrik: Die Entnazifizierung am Beispiel Bayerns.* Berlin: Dietz, 1982. Originally published as *Entnazifizierung in Bayern.* Frankfurt am Main: S. Fischer, 1972.

Niethammer, Lutz, and Plato, Alexander von, eds. *Lebensgeschichte und Sozialkultur im Ruhrgebiet 1930 bis 1960.* Vol. 3, *"Wir kriegen jetzt andere Zeiten."* Berlin: Dietz, 1985.

Noelle, Elisabeth, and Neumann, Erich Peter, eds. *Jahrbuch der Öffentlichen Meinung, 1947–1955.* Allensbach am Bodensee: Verlag für Demoskopie, 1956.

Noelle-Neumann, Elisabeth. "Who Needs a Flag?" *Encounter* 60, no. 1 (January 1983), 72–80.

Noelle-Neumann, Elisabeth, ed. *The Germans: Public Opinion Polls 1967–1980.* Allensbach Institut für Demoskopie. Westport, CT: Greenwood, 1981.

Noelle-Neumann, Elisabeth, and Köcher, Renate. *Die verletzte Nation.* Stuttgart: Deutsche Verlags-Anstalt, 1987.

Noelle-Neumann, Elisabeth, and Neumann, Erich Peter, eds. *The Germans: Public Opinion Polls 1947–1966.* Allensbach am Bodensee: Verlag für Demoskopie, 1967.

Noll, Hans. "Die unsichtbaren Schäden." *Deutschland Archiv* 24 (1991), 25–30.

Nolte, Ernst. *Das Vergehen der Vergangenheit.* Frankfurt am Main: Ullstein, 1987.

—— *Der europäische Bürgerkrieg, 1917–1945.* Berlin: Propyläen, 1987.

—— *Deutschland und der Kalte Krieg.* 2nd edn. Stuttgart: Klett-Cotta, 1985.

—— *The Three Faces of Fascism.* New York: Holt, Reinhart and Winston, 1963.

—— *Universitätsinstitut oder Parteihochschule?* Cologne: Markus-Verlagsgesellschaft, 1971.

—— "Zusammenbruch und Neubeginn." *Zeitschrift für Politik* 32 (1985), 296–303.

Oberndörfer, Dieter, ed. *Begegnungen mit Kurt Georg Kiesinger.* Stuttgart: Deutsche Verlags-Anstalt, 1984.

*OECD Economic Surveys: Germany*, 1969–. Paris, Organization for Economic Cooperation and Development.

Olson, Mancur. *The Logic of Collective Action.* Cambridge, MA: Harvard University Press, 1965.

Ostwald, Thomas. *Karl May: Leben und Werk.* 4th edn. Braunschweig: Graff, 1977.

Overesch, Manfred. *Das besetzte Deutschland 1948–1949.* Vol. 3/II of *Chronik deutscher Zeitgeschichte* (Droste-Geschichts-Kalendarium). Düsseldorf: Droste, 1986.

Parkes, K. Stuart. *Writers and Politics in West Germany.* London: Croom Helm, 1986.

Pfaff, William. *Barbarian Sentiments.* New York: Hill and Wang, 1989.

Pfahl-Traughber, Armin. "Rechtsextremismus in den neuen Bundesländern." *Aus Politik und Zeitgeschichte* B3-4/92 (January 10, 1992), 11–21.

Picht, Georg. *Die Deutsche Bildungskatastrophe.* Olten and Freiburg: Walter-Verlag, 1964.

Pincher, Chapman. *The Secret Offensive.* New York: St. Martin's Press, 1985.

Plischke, Elmer. "Denazification in Germany: A Policy Analysis" in *Americans as Proconsuls,* Robert Wolfe (ed.). Carbondale, IL: Southern Illinois University Press, 1984.

Pond, Elizabeth. *After the Wall: American Policy toward Germany.* A Twentieth Century Fund Paper, n.p. [New York]: Twentieth Century Fund, 1990.

Poppinga, Anneliese. *Meine Erinnerungen an Konrad Adenauer.* Stuttgart: Deutsche Verlags-Anstalt, 1970.

Pridham, Geoffrey. *Christian Democracy in Western Germany.* New York: St. Martin's Press, 1977.

Prittie, Terence. *Konrad Adenauer.* Stuttgart: Bonn Aktuell, 1983.

—— *Willy Brandt: Portrait of a Statesman.* New York: Schocken, 1974.

Przybylski, Peter. *Tatort Politbüro: Die Akte Honecker.* Berlin: Rowohlt, 1991.

Putnam, Robert G., and Bayne, Nicholas. *Hanging Together: The Seven-Power Summits.* London: Heinemann, 1984.

Raddatz, Werner. *Das abenteuerliche Leben Karl Mays.* Gütersloh: Sigbert Mohn, 1965.

Rehlinger, Ludwig A. *Freikauf: Die Geschäfte der DDR mit politisch Verfolgten 1963– 1989.* Berlin: Ullstein, 1991.

Reinfried, Hubert, and Schulte, Ludwig. *Die Sicherheit der Bundesrepublik Deutschland.* Vol. 1, *Die Bundeswehr.* Regensburg: Walhalla und Praetoria, 1985.

Revel, Jean-François. *La Connaissance inutile.* Paris: Laffont, 1988.

Richter, Horst Eberhard. *Die Chance des Gewissens: Erinnerungen und Assoziationen.* Hamburg: Hoffmann und Campe, 1986.

Richter, Michael, et al., eds. *Geschichte der DDR.* Informationen zur politischen Bildung, 231. Bonn: Bundeszentrale für politische Bildung, 1991.

Riste, Olav, ed. *Western Security: The Formative Years.* Oslo: Norwegian University Press, 1985.

Roellecke, Gerd. "Entwicklungslinien deutscher Universitätsgeschichte." *Aus Politik und Zeitgeschichte* B 3–4/84 (January 21, 1984), 3–10.

Ross, Werner. *Mit der linken Hand geschrieben . . .: Der deutsche Literaturbetrieb.* Zürich: Edition Interform, 1984.

Rothenberger, Karl Heinz. *Die Hungerjahre nach dem Zweiten Weltkrieg.* Boppard: Boldt, 1980.

Rovan, Joseph. *Geschichte der Deutschen Sozialdemokratie.* Frankfurt am Main: Fischer Taschenbuch Verlag, 1980.

Rückerl, Adalbert. *NS-Verbrechen vor Gericht.* Heidelberg: C. F. Müller, 1982.

Rudolf, Hermann. *Die Gesellschaft der DDR — eine deutsche Möglichkeit?* Munich: Piper, 1972.

Ruhl, Klaus-Jörg, ed. *"Mein Gott, was soll aus Deutschland werden?": Die Adenauer Ära 1949–1963.* Munich: Deutscher Taschenbuch Verlag, 1985.

Rumpf, Helmut. "Die deutschen Reparationen nach dem Zweiten Weltkrieg" in *Handbuch zur Deutschen Nation,* vol. 1, Bernard Willms (ed.). Tübingen: Hohenrain, 1986.

Rutschky, Michael. "Neues aus der Strauss-Forschung." *Merkur* 41 (January 1987), 78–82.

Rytlewski, Ralf, and Opp de Hipt, Manfred. *Die Bundesrepublik Deutschland in Zahlen, 1945/49–1980.* Munich: Beck, 1987.

Salomon, Ernst von. *Der Fragebogen.* Hamburg: Rowohlt, 1952.

Schafranek, Hans. *Zwischen NKWD und Gestapo. Die Auslieferung deutscher und österreichischer Antifaschisten aus der Sowjetunion an Nazideutschland 1937–1941.* Frankfurt am Main: ISP-Verlag, 1990.

Schäuble, Wolfgang. *Der Vertrag: Wie ich über die deutsche Einheit verhandelte.* Stuttgart: Deutsche Verlags-Anstalt, 1991.

Schick, Jack M. *The Berlin Crisis, 1958–1962.* Philadelphia: University of Pennsylvania Press, 1971.

Schickling, Willi. *Entscheidung in Frankfurt: Ludwig Erhards Durchbruch zur Freiheit, 30 Jahre Deutsche Mark, 30 Jahre Soziale Marktwirtschaft.* Stuttgart: Seewald, 1978.

Schillinger, Reinhold. *Der Entscheidungsprozess beim Lastenausgleich, 1945–1952.* Sankt Katharinen: Scripta Mercaturae, 1985.

Schlesinger, Arthur Meier. *A Thousand Days.* New York: Houghton Mifflin, 1965.

Schmid, Carlo. *Erinnerungen.* Bern: Scherz, 1979.

Schmid, Claudia. "Staatliche Hochschulpolitik in der Bundesrepublik: Daten, Strukturen und Tendenzen." *Aus Politik und Zeitgeschichte* B 3–4/84 (January 21, 1984), 11–23.

Schmid, Günther. *Sicherheitspolitik und Friedensbewegung.* Munich: Olzog, 1983.

Schmidt, Helmut. *The Balance of Power: Germany's Peace Policy and the Super Powers.* London: William Kimber, 1971. Originally published as *Strategie des Gleichgewichts.* Stuttgart: Seewald, 1969.

— *Defense or Retaliation: a German View.* New York: Praeger, 1962. Originally published as *Verteidigung oder Vergeltung.* Stuttgart: Seewald, 1961.

— *Der Kurs heisst Frieden.* Düsseldorf: Econ, 1979.

— *Helmut Schmidt: Perspectives on Politics.* Wolfram F. Hanrieder (ed.). Boulder, Colorado: Westview, 1982.

— *Menschen und Mächte.* Berlin: Siedler, 1987.

Schmückle, Gerd. *Ohne Pauken und Trompeten: Erinnerungen an Krieg und Frieden.* Stuttgart: Deutsche Verlags-Anstalt, 1982.

Schneider, Peter. "Der Sand an Baaders Schuhen" in *Bewegung in der Republik 1965 bis 1984: Eine Kursbuch-Chronik*, vol. 1, Ingrid Karsunke and Karl Markus Michel (eds). Berlin: Rotbuch, 1985.

— *The German Comedy: Scenes of Life after the Wall.* New York: Farrar, Straus & Giroux, 1991. In German: *Extreme Mittellage: Einge Reise durch das deutsche Nationalgefühl.* Reinbek: Rowohlt, 1990.

Schoenbaum, David. *The Spiegel Affair.* Garden City, New York: Doubleday, 1968.

Scholz, Günther. *Herbert Wehner.* Düsseldorf: Econ, 1986.

Schönhuber, Franz. *Ich war dabei.* Munich: Langen-Müller, 1983.

Schöpflin, George. "Post-communism: Constructing New Democracies in Central Europe." *International Affairs* 67 (1991), 235–50.

Schrenck-Notzing, Caspar. *Charakterwäsche: Die amerikanische Besatzung in Deutschland und ihre Folgen.* Stuttgart: Seewald, 1965.

Schrenck-Notzing, Caspar von. "Die Umerziehung der Deutschen" in *Handbuch zur Deutschen Nation*, vol. 1, Bernard Willms (ed.). Tübingen: Hohenrain, 1986.

Schröder, Christina, and Schröder, Harry. Review of Maaz, *Gefühlsstau, Merkur* 45 (1991), 161–7.

Schröder, Gerhard. *Decision for Europe.* London: Thames and Hudson, 1964.

Schulze, Hagen. *Weimar.* 2nd edn. Berlin: Siedler, 1983.

Schumpeter, Joseph A. *Capitalism, Socialism, and Democracy.* 3rd edn. New York: Harper, 1950.

Schwan, Gesine. "Die SPD und die westliche Freiheit" in *Wohin treibt die SPD?:*

*Wende oder Kontinuität sozialdemokratischer Sicherheitspolitik,* Jürgen Maruhn and Manfred Wilke (eds). Munich: Olzog, 1984.

Schwarz, Hans-Peter. *Adenauer: Der Aufstieg, 1876—1952.* Stuttgart: Deutsche Verlags-Anstalt, 1986.

—— *Die Ära Adenauer, 1949—1957.* Vol. 2 of *Geschichte der Bundesrepublik Deutschland.* Stuttgart: Deutsche Verlags-Anstalt; Wiesbaden: Brockhaus, 1981.

—— *Die Ära Adenauer, 1957—1963.* Vol. 3 of *Geschichte der Bundesrepublik Deutschland.* Stuttgart: Deutsche Verlags-Anstalt; Wiesbaden: Brockhaus, 1983.

—— *Die gezähmten Deutschen: Von der Machtbesessenheit zur Machtvergessenheit.* Stuttgart: Deutsche Verlags-Anstalt, 1985.

—— *Adenauer. Der Staatsmann: 1952—1967.* Stuttgart: Deutsche Verlags-Anstalt, 1991.

Seebacher-Brandt, Brigitte. *Die Linke und die Einheit.* Berlin: Siedler, 1991.

Seifert, Jürgen. "Die Verfassung" in *Die Bundesrepublik Deutschland,* vol. 1, Wolfgang Benz (ed.). Frankfurt am Main: Fischer Taschenbuch Verlag, 1983. Munich: Piper, 1986.

Seiffert, Wolfgang. *Das ganze Deutschland: Perspektiven der Wiedervereinigung.* Munich: Piper, 1986.

—— "Die DDR – Herrschaftsinstrument der SED und Produkt sowjetischer Deutschlandpolitik" in *Die DDR auf dem Weg in das Jahr 2000,* Hermann von Berg, Franz Loeser and Wolfgang Seiffert (eds). Cologne: Bund, 1987.

Seton-Watson, Hugh. *The East European Revolution.* London: Methuen, 1956.

Sharp, Tony. *The Wartime Alliance and the Zonal Division of Germany.* Oxford: Clarendon Press, 1975.

Shelton, Judy. *The Coming Soviet Crash.* New York: Free Press, 1989.

Sherwood, Robert E. *Roosevelt and Hopkins: An Intimate History.* New York: Harper and Brothers, 1950.

Shirer, William L. *20th Century Journey.* Vol. 2. Boston and Toronto: Little, Brown and Company, 1984.

Shlaes, Amity. *Germany: The Empire Within.* New York: Farrar, Straus & Giroux, 1991.

Slusser, Robert M. *The Berlin Crisis of 1961.* Baltimore: Johns Hopkins University Press, 1969.

Smith, Bradley F. *The Road to Nuremberg.* New York: Basic Books, 1981.

Smith, Gordon R. *Democracy in Western Germany.* 2nd edn. New York: Holmes and Meier, 1982.

Smith, Hedrick. *The Power Game: How Washington Works.* New York: Random House, 1988.

Solzhenitsyn, Aleksandr I. *The Gulag Archipelago, 1918—1956.* 2 vols. New York: Harper and Row, 1974.

Sommer, Theo, ed. *Reise ins andere Deutschland.* 2nd edn. Reinbek: Rowohlt, 1989.

Sonnenhol, Gustav Adolf. *Untergang oder Übergang? Wider die deutsche Angst.* Stuttgart: Seewald, 1983.

Sontheimer, Kurt. *Antidemokratisches Denken in der Weimarer Republik.* Munich: Nymphenburger Verlagshandlung, 1962.

—— *The Government and Politics of West Germany*. London: Hutchinson, 1972.

Sozialdemokratische Partei Deutschlands. *Bundesdelegierten-Konferenz und Ausserordentlicher Parteitag, 18.-19. November 1983*. Bonn: Vorstand der SPD, 1983.

—— *Wir informieren: Bilanz einer Wende*. Bonn: Vorstand der SPD, 1983.

Speer, Albert. *Spandau: The Secret Diaries*. New York: Macmillan, 1976.

Spotts, Frederic. *The Churches and Politics in Germany*. Middletown, Connecticut: Wesleyan University Press, 1973.

*Staatslexikon*. Publ. by Görres-Gesellschaft. 5 vols. 7th rev. edn. Freiburg: Herder, 1985–9.

Staden, Wendelgard von. *Nacht über dem Tal: Eine Jugend in Deutschland*. Düsseldorf: Diederichs, 1979.

Steinberg, Rudolf, ed. *Staat und Verbände zur Theorie der Interessenverbände in der Industriegesellschaft*. Wege der Forschung, vol. 298. Darmstadt: Wissentschaftliche Buchgesellschaft, 1985.

Steininger, Rolf. *Deutsche Geschichte 1945–1961*. 2 vols. Frankfurt am Main: Fischer Taschenbuch Verlag, 1983.

—— *Eine Chance zur Wiedervereinigung?: Die Stalin-Note vom 10. März 1952*. No. 12 of *Archiv für Sozialgeschichte.* Bonn: Neue Gesellschaft, 1985.

Stent, Angela. *From Embargo to Ostpolitik*. Cambridge: Cambridge University Press, 1981.

Stercken, Hans, ed. *De Gaulle hat gesagt . . .* Stuttgart: Seewald, 1967.

Stern, Carola. *Willy Brandt in Selbstzeugnissen und Bilddokumenten*. Reinbek: Rowohlt, 1975.

Stern, Fritz. *Dreams and Delusions*. New York: Alfred A. Knopf, 1987.

Stern, Klaus. *Das Staatsrecht der Bundesrepublik Deutschland*. Vol. 1, *Grundbegriffe und Grundlagen des Staatsrechts, Strukturprinzipien der Verfassung*. 2nd edn 1984. Vol. 2, *Staatsorgane, Staatsfunktionen, Finanz- und Haushaltsverfassung, Notstandsverfassung*. Munich: Beck, 1980. Vols 3–5 in preparation.

Stern, Klaus, and Schmidt-Bleibtreu, Bruno, eds. *Staatsvertrag*. Munich: Beck, 1990.

Sternberger, Dolf. "Die deutsche Frage" in *Bundesrepublikanisches Lesebuch*, Hermann Glaser (ed.). Frankfurt am Main: Fischer Taschenbuch Verlag, 1980.

Strauss, Franz Josef. *Die Erinnerungen*. 2nd edn. Berlin: Siedler, 1989.

Stürmer, Michael. *Dissonanzen des Fortschritts: Essays über Geschichte und Politik in Deutschland*. Munich: Piper, 1986.

Szabo, Stephen F. "The German Social Democrats after the 1987 Elections." *SAIS Review* (Summer/Fall 1987): 36–7.

Talbott, Strobe. *Deadly Gambits*. New York: Alfred A. Knopf, 1984.

Tatu, Michel. *Gorbatchev*. Paris: Le Centurion, 1987.

Teltschik, Horst. *329 Tage*. Berlin: Siedler, 1991.

Tenbruck, Friedrich. "Alltagsnormen und Lebensgefühle in der Bundesrepublik" in *Die zweite Republik*, Richard Löwenthal and Hans-Peter Schwarz (eds). Stuttgart: Seewald, 1974.

—— "Frieden durch Friedensforschung?" in *Friedensforschung: Entscheidungshilfe gegen Gewalt*, Manfred Funke (ed.). Munich: List, 1975.

Tent, James F. *The Free University of Berlin.* Bloomington, IN: Indiana University Press, 1988.

—— *Mission on the Rhine.* Chicago: University of Chicago Press, 1982.

Terjung, Knut, ed. *Der Onkel: Herbert Wehner in Gesprächen und Interviews.* Hamburg: Hoffmann und Campe, 1986.

Thayer, Charles W. *The Unquiet Germans.* New York: Harper and Brothers, 1957.

Thom, Françoise. *Le Moment Gorbatchev.* Paris: Hachette, 1989.

Thomas, Gina, ed. *The Unresolved Past.* London: Weidenfeld & Nicolson, 1991.

Thomas, Heinz. "Das Identitätsproblem der Deutschen im Mittelalter." *Geschichte in Wissenschaft und Unterricht* 43 (1992), 135–56.

Thomas, Hugh. *Armed Truce: The Beginnings of the Cold War, 1945–46.* New York: Atheneum, 1987.

Thomas, Michael. *Deutschland, England über alles.* Berlin: Siedler, 1984.

Thränhardt, Dietrich. *Geschichte der Bundesrepublik Deutschland.* Frankfurt am Main: Suhrkamp, 1986.

Tilford, Roger, ed. *The Ostpolitik and Political Change in Germany.* Westmead, England: Saxon House; Lexington, MA: Lexington Books, 1975.

Tindall, George Brown. *America: A Narrative History.* New York: W. W. Norton, 1984.

Topitsch, Ernst. *Stalin's Krieg.* Munich: Olzog, 1985.

Treverton, Gregory F. *The Dollar Drain and American Forces in Germany.* Athens: Ohio University Press, 1978.

Tüngel, Richard, and Berndorff, Hans Rudolf. *Auf dem Bauche sollst Du kriechen . . .: Deutschland unter den Besatzungsmächten.* Hamburg: Christian Wegner, 1958.

Turner, George. "Hochschulreformpolitik: Versuch einer Bilanz." *Aus Politik und Zeitgeschichte,* B 3–4/84 (January 21, 1984), 24–35.

Turner, Henry Ashby, Jr. *The Two Germanies since 1945.* New Haven: Yale University Press, 1987.

Ulam, Adam B. *Expansion and Coexistence: Soviet Foreign Policy, 1917–73.* 2nd edn. New York: Praeger, 1974.

—— *A History of Soviet Russia.* New York: Praeger, 1976.

—— *The Rivals: America and Russia Since World War II.* New York: Viking Press, 1971.

Vaizey, John. *The Squandered Peace.* London: Hodder and Stoughton, 1983.

Van Cleave, William R. *Fortress USSR: The Soviet Strategic Defense Initiative and the U.S. Strategic Defense Response.* Stanford, CA: Hoover Institution Press, 1986.

Vassiltchikov, Marie. *Berlin Diaries, 1940–1945.* New York: Alfred A. Knopf, 1987.

Vaubel, Ludwig. *Zusammenbruch und Wiederaufbau: Ein Tagebuch aus der Wirtschaft, 1945–1949.* Wolfgang Benz (ed.). Munich: Oldenbourg, 1984.

Venohr, Wolfgang, ed. *Die Deutsche Einheit kommt bestimmt.* Bergisch Gladbach: Gustav Lübbe, 1982.

Vogel, Angela. "Familie" in *Die Bundesrepublik Deutschland,* vol. 2, Wolfgang Benz (ed.). Frankfurt am Main: Fischer Taschenbuch Verlag, 1983.

Volze, Armin. "Die Devisengeschäfte der DDR." *Deutschland Archiv* 24 (1991), 1145–59.

Wallich, Henry C. *Mainsprings of the German Revival.* New Haven: Yale University Press, 1955.

Walser, Martin, *Über Deutschland reden.* Frankfurt am Main: Suhrkamp, 1988.

Watson, Alan. *The Germans — Who Are They Now?* London: Thames Methuen, 1992.

Weber, Hermann. *Aufbau und Fall einer Diktatur. Kritische Beiträge zur Geschichte der DDR.* Cologne: Bund, 1991.

— "Aufdeckung stalinistischen Terrors durch Gerichtsurteil bedroht?" *Deutschland Archiv* 24 (1991), 1015–18.

— "Aufstieg und Niedergang des deutschen Kommunismus." *Aus Politik und Zeigeschichte* B40/91 (September 27, 1991), 25–39.

Weber, Hermann. *Die DDR 1945–1986.* Munich: Oldenbourg, 1988.

— *Geschichte der DDR.* Munich: Deutscher Taschenbuch-Verlag, 1985.

Weber, Hermann, ed. *DDR: Dokumente zur Geschichte der Deutschen Demokratischen Republik 1945–1985.* Munich: Deutscher Taschenbuch Verlag, 1986.

— "Werden DDR-Geschichtswissenschaft and Marxismus plattgemacht und ausgemerzt?" *Deutschland Archiv* 24 (1991), 246–57.

Weber-Fas, Rudolf. *Das Grundgesetz.* Berlin: Duncker und Humblot, 1983.

Wehler, Hans-Ulrich. *Preussen ist wieder chic....* Frankfurt am Main: Suhrkamp, 1982.

Wehner, Herbert. *Wandel und Bewährung: Ausgewählte Reden und Schriften, 1930–1975.* Gerhard Jahn (ed.). Frankfurt am Main: Ullstein; Hannover: Dietz, 1976.

Weidenfeld, Werner, and Korte, Karl-Rudolf. *Die Deutschen — Profil einer Nation.* Stuttgart: Klett-Cotta, 1991.

— eds. *Handwörterbuch zur deutschen Einheit.* Frankfurt: Campus, 1992.

Weizsäcker, Carl Friedrich von. *Mit der Bombe leben.* Hamburg: Die Zeit, 1958.

Weizsäcker, Richard von. *Die deutsche Geschichte geht weiter.* 3rd edn. Berlin: Siedler, 1983.

Wesel, Uwe. *Juristische Weltkunde.* Frankfurt am Main: Suhrkamp, 1984.

Wettig, Gerhard. *Entmilitarisierung und Wiederbewaffnung in Deutschland, 1943–1955.* Munich: Oldenbourg, 1967.

— "Die Rolle der Sowjetunion beim Umsturz in der DDR und bei der Einleitung des deutschen Vereinigungsprozesses." In Jürgen Elvert and Michael Salewski, eds., *Der Umbruch in Osteuropa.* Historische Mitteilungen der Ranke-Gesellschaft, Beiheft 3. Stuttgart: Steiner, 1992.

Whetten, Lawrence L. *Germany East and West.* New York: New York University Press, 1980.

Wiggershaus, Norbert. "The Decision for a West German Defence Contribution" in *Western Security: The Formative Years,* Olav Riste (ed.). Oslo: Norwegian University Press, 1985.

Wilharm, Irmgard, ed. *Deutsche Geschichte 1962–1983.* 2 vols. Frankfurt am Main: Fischer Taschenbuch Verlag, 1985.

Willis, F. Roy. *France, Germany and the New Europe, 1945–1967*. Rev. and exp. edn. London: Oxford University Press, 1968.

Wilms, Dorothee. *The German Question and Inner-German Relations*. Occasional Paper Series, no. 8–87. St Augustin bei Bonn: Konrad Adenauer Stiftung, 1987.

Windsor, Philip. *Germany and the Western Alliance*. London: International Institute for Strategic Studies, 1981.

Winkler, Heinrich August. "Nationalismus, Nationalstaat und nationale Frage in Deutschland seit 1945." *Aus Politik und Zeigeschichte* B40/91 (September 27, 1991), 12–24.

Wolfe, Robert, ed. *Americans as Proconsuls: United States Military Government in Germany and Japan, 1944–1952*. Carbondale, IL: Southern Illinois University Press, 1984.

Wolffsohn, Michael. *Ewige Schuld? 40 Jahre deutsch-jüdisch-israelische Beziehungen*. Munich: Piper, 1988.

—— *West Germany's Foreign Policy in the Era of Brandt and Schmidt, 1969–1982*. Frankfurt am Main: Lang, 1986.

Worst, Anne. *Das Ende eines Geheimdienstes. Oder: Wie lebendig ist die Stasi?* Berlin: LinksDruck, 1991.

Wunder, Bernd. *Geschichte der Bürokratie in Deutschland*. Frankfurt am Main: Suhrkamp, 1986.

Yost, David M. *Soviet Ballistic Missile Defense and the Western Alliance*. Cambridge, MA: Harvard University Press, 1988.

Ziemke, Earl F. "Improvising Stability and Change in Postwar Germany" in *Americans as Proconsuls*, Robert Wolfe (ed.). Carbondale, IL: Southern Illinois University Press, 1984.

Zink, Harold. *The United States in Germany, 1944–1955*. Princeton, NJ: Van Nostrand, 1957.

Zöllner, Detlev. "Sozialpolitik" in *Die Bundesrepublik Deutschland*, vol. 2, Wolfgang Benz (ed.). Frankfurt am Main: Fischer Taschenbuch Verlag, 1983.

Zuckmayer, Carl. *Des Teufels General*. Stockholm: Bermann-Fischer Verlag, 1946.

Zündorf, Benno. *Die Ostverträge: Die Verträge von Moskau, Warschau, Prag, Das Berlin-Abkommen und die Verträge mit der DDR*. Munich: Beck, 1979.

# Index

257, 356–7; *formierte Gesellschaft*, 2:
38–40; free vs. social market, 1:
133–4, 192–7, 207–9; 2: 3, 49–50;
growth rates, 1: 336, 392–6; 2: 12–
13, 86–7, 227, 282–3, 372;
problems of reconstruction, 1:
261–4; stabilization, 2: 83–6, 284–
7
Eden Anthony, 1: 21, 50, 299, 352–4;
2: 113
Eden Plan, 1: 329, 439, 442
education, Allied reform of, 1: 165–
74; policy, 1: 220, 336–7, 342–3;
2: 31; reform of, 2: 5, 10, 238–43,
419; *see also* universities
Egypt, 2: 27, 111, 295, 296
Ehard, Hans, 1: 96, 101, 187, 242–4,
319
Ehmke, Horst, 1: 508; 2: 156, 226,
417–18
Eich, Günter, 1: 416; quoted, 1: 414
Eisenhower, Dwight D., and armed
forces, 1: 273, 288–9; and EDC, 1:
289, 430; at Geneva summit 1955,
1: 352–3; and occupation, 1: 28,
49, 104, 137; at Paris summit
1960, 1: 454
Eitel, Antonius *see* Zündorf, Benno
Elbe river, 1: 48; 2: 326, 328
elections, Berlin in 1948, 1: 217;
West Berlin, in 1958, 1: 438; in
1963, 1: 518; in 1981, 2: 370–1,
375; in 1987, 2: 399, 477; in 1989,
2: 555–6
elections, Bundestag, in 1949, 1:
236–44; in 1953, 1: 325, 33; in
1957, 1: 397–8; in 1961, 1: 472,
477; in 1965, 2: 37; in 1969, 2:
145–6, 151; in 1972, 2: 214–15,
252–3; in 1976, 2: 364–5; in 1980,
2: 368–9; in 1983, 2: 382–3, 387–
8; in 1987, 2: 399, 475; table, 2: 8–
9; first all-German elections in
1990, 2: 745–6
elections, of federal president, in
1949, 1: 244–5; in 1959, 1: 451–2;
in 1964, 2: 25; in 1969, 2: 139–41;

in 1974, 2: 255, 265; in 1979, 2:
366–7; in 1984, 2: 428; in 1989, 2:
565
elections, first local, 1: 93, 104–5
elections, *Land*, Bavaria 1966, 2: 57;
Hamburg 1982, 2: 374; Hamburg
1987, 2: 477, Hamburg 1991, 2:
751; Hesse 1987, 2: 476–7; Hesse
1989, 2: 560; Hesse 1991, 2: 751,
Lower Saxony 1990, 2: 734; North
Rhine-Westphalia 1950, 1: 264;
North Rhine-Westphalia 1958, 1:
407–8; North Rhine-Westphalia
1962, 1: 496; North Rhine-
Westphalia 1966, 2: 51; North
Rhine-Westphalia 1990, 2: 734;
Rhineland-Palatinate 1963, 1: 518;
Rhineland-Palatinate 1987, 2: 476;
Rhineland-Palatinate 1991, 2: 751;
Schleswig-Holstein 1950, 1: 308;
Schleswig-Holstein 1987, 2: 497,
499
elections, *Länder*, in 1966 and 1967,
2: 117; in 1970 and 1972, 2: 208;
new *Länder* elections in 1990, 2:
741
elections GDR 1989, 2: 621; March
1990, 2: 714, 719, 728–31; GDR
municipal elections 1990, 2: 732
elections, rules of, in 1990, 2: 745
electoral reform, 1: 235–6, 378–9; 2:
94, 114–18
Emminger, Otmar, 2: 287, 293–4
Engholm, Björn, 2: 254, 498–9, 552
Ensslin, Gudrun, 2: 133–5, 351–2
Enzensberger, Hans Magnus, 1: 164,
416, 418
Eppler, Erhard, 2: 233, 278, 306,
374, 450; SPD-SED contacts, 2:
393, 394, 491
Equalization of Burdens Act, 1: 203–
4, 310, 396
Erfurt, GDR, 2: 175–8, 752
Erhard, Ludwig, becomes chancellor,
1: 522; 2: 11–13; and Bizone
Economic Council, 1: 191–3; and
currency reform, 1: 198–200, 202,